A Highly Arbitrary Collection *of* Our Favorite Gardens

What makes a garden beautiful? Why do some quite humble gardens draw you in and under their spell, while others—filled with exotic species and spectacular vistas—somehow fall short of paradise?

The gardens we admire all share something invisible—call it a vision, or a guiding spirit. Each has been choreographed with the rigor applied to any cohesive, cogent work of art—not to mention a sympathy for both the predictable and fickle demands of nature. These gardens impress as much by what is missing as by what has been planted. Quirky, iconoclastic, classical, they invite, delight, and inspire us as gardeners.

KIFTSGATE COURT

GLOUCESTERSHIRE, ENGLAND

Overlooking the Vale of Evesham, Kiftsgate Court is a short walk down the road from Hidcote Manor. With Lawrence Johnston as her neighbor and adviser, Heather Muir embarked on her garden in 1918, creating an immensely personal statement that is every bit as remarkable as her friend's garden. As relaxed and adventuresome as Hidcote is formal and geometric, Kiftsgate plays off the honey-colored, porticoed house and its dramatic setting. Everywhere there are places to stroll, pause, and reflect—terraces, steps, and meandering paths. In the frothing double borders, shrubs spill out over perennials and old-fashioned roses, and the interplay of color is ubiquitous—pastel pinks and creams spiked with arches of carmine and crimson.

SISSINGHURST

KENT, ENGLAND

Laid out among the ruins of a Tudor house,
the garden at Sissinghurst Castle, begun in
1930 by Vita Sackville-West and her husband, Harold Nicolson, is a series of themed
garden "rooms"—a concept inspired by the
design at Hidcote. In the rose garden, and
throughout Sissinghurst, Vita's aim was for
"profusion, even extravagance . . . within the
confines of the utmost linear severity." The
vine-embraced brick walls and neatly clipped
box hedges barely contain the billowing forth
of old roses and companion plantings of
various shrubs, perennials, and bulbs. The
framework acts as a foil for the famed White
Garden as well as the massed colors and
cottage-style planting (what Eleanor Perenyi
calls "a studied air of untidiness"), expressing
the essence of Vita's gardening aesthetic—
soft colors, nostalgic plants, and botanical
excess kept in check by architecture.

WISLEY

SURREY, ENGLAND

To stroll through Wisley, the garden of the Royal Horticultural Society, is to experience many different gardens in a single afternoon—meadow, wildland, formal garden, walled garden, conifer lawn, canal, rose garden, fruit field, rock garden, greenhouses galore, and much more. G.F. Wilson, who purchased the land in the 1870s in order to make "difficult plants grow successfully," bequeathed it to the Society in 1903. Today it is a blend of the inspirational and the instructive, with extensive demonstration gardens, a laboratory, and trial grounds for vegetables and ornamentals. Because of its diversity, Wisley has something to offer at every time of year. In early April, the Alpine meadow is transformed into a sheet of sulfur yellow with thousands of naturalized hoop-petticoat daffodils; the lavender-pink erica glows in the midst of the new heather garden in August, and even in cold months the winter garden is alive with color and scent.

TINTINHULL HOUSE

SOMERSET, ENGLAND

Thirty years after her first visit to Tintinhull House, Penelope Hobhouse became a National Trust tenant with responsibility for this classic English garden designed by Phyllis Reiss in the 1930s. The balance of informal plantings within a more formal framework of yew hedges and stone walls, paths, and steps has been maintained and enhanced by Hobhouse, one of the world's most influential garden designers, writers, and keepers of the Jekyll tradition. Each of the many plants in the primarily (but not exclusively) herbaceous borders has been chosen with a keen regard for shape, foliage, and color. Here, the summer air is filled with the scent of roses and climbing honeysuckle amidst a drift of airy purple-rose verbena.

HIDCOTE MANOR

GLOUCESTERSHIRE, ENGLAND

In 1907, when expatriate American Lawrence Johnston began his garden at Hidcote Manor, he probably had little idea how profoundly it would influence garden design for the duration of the century. Called "a jungle of beauty" by Vita Sackville-West, Hidcote was revolutionary: it ushered in the practice of filling formally structured garden rooms with color- and variety-themed plant material. Rather than using stone or brick, Johnston created his rooms with living architecture—immaculate hedges and arches of yew, hornbeam, beech, and box—that has a softening effect while offering a tantalizing mixture of greens.

GIVERNY

EURE, FRANCE

An anarchy of color, the Clos Normand—Claude Monet's three-acre, overgrown farmhouse garden—is not for the horticulturally faint of heart. In this painter's garden, called "a never-ending feast for the eyes" by one of the artist's contemporaries, flowers are not so much planted as massed in rich clumps and streaks of pure color whose tones and depth evolve continuously according to the changing light and darkening shadows. To ensure a never-ending source of color and texture, annuals are everywhere tucked between the perennials. Here, old roses, opium and Flanders poppies, bearded iris, lychnis, and yarrow converge in a giddy pyrotechnic display.

VILLANDRY

INDRE-ET-LOIRE, FRANCE

A moated Renaissance château dating from 1536 and restored in 1906, Villandry is situated by the banks of the river Cher before it flows into the Loire. Its three tiered gardens include an elaborate ornamental garden, a soothing water garden, and the famous potager, or kitchen garden— a visually delicious tapestry of fruits, vegetables, and flowering annuals. Consisting of nine equal squares of different design, the plots are outlined by low box hedges and offer a lively contrast of shapes and colors disciplined by geometric rigor. While the plants are rotated every year, spring is likely to include radishes, peas, oak-leaf lettuce, strawberries, artichokes, and savory—all framed by rows of pansies and forget-me-nots. In summer, improbably huge ornamental cabbages stand out in sculptural relief against gourds, leeks, and tomatoes, chosen as much for the beauty of their leaf and fruit as for their taste, and edged with herbs such as verbena and blue sage.

DUMBARTON OAKS
WASHINGTON, D.C.

Referred to by some as the "last great American garden," Dumbarton Oaks is an outstanding example of landscape architect Beatrix Farrand's philosophy of making the plan fit the grounds rather than forcing the grounds to conform. Embarking in 1922, Farrand worked for 25 years to marry formal, European-inspired design elements to the Georgian estate's existing topography—which includes numerous native American oaks, silver maples, Japanese maples, paulownia, katsura, and beech trees. One discerns Italy in the sweeping carved stone balustrades and fountains, France in the numerous courtyard terraces, and England in the stone- and hedge-walled garden rooms. An extraordinary plantswoman, Farrand once wrote that gardeners "must notice the different lights and shadows and see how they change the effect; they must remember the plants whose scent begins at dusk and those whose fragrance stops with the light." At Dumbarton Oaks, this level of botanical detail is still very much in evidence.

SARAH HAMMOND'S GARDEN

BOLINAS, CALIFORNIA, U.S.A.

In Sarah Hammond's California coastal garden, the botanical choices are dictated by climate and geography (the garden designer and plant importer calls it "gardening by necessity"). Mounds of Mediterranean natives thrive in the dry summers and mild, wet winters, and there's enough water even during the cyclical droughts to support her astonishing collection of old roses—but even the most tenacious trees have been downed by the 80-mile-an-hour gusts. Wind-sheltering rooms are formed by hedges and by the walls of the house and two small cottages, the rustic wood creating a harmonious backdrop for the soft colors she favors. The large, rectangular spaces are broken up by transecting paths and circular plantings, which are echoed in the lovely mounded plants. Everywhere Hammond's choice of ornaments—antique pots planted up with herbs, water-smoothed stones placed on a weathered table—remind the viewer that every garden is a melding of artifice and nature.

MONTICELLO

VIRGINIA, U.S.A.

Hewn from the side of a mountain, Monticello's two-acre kitchen garden (here restored with early varieties of vegetables) flanks the rebuilt Garden Pavilion, Jefferson's retreat for reading and contemplation. The productive and decorative vegetable terrace was divided into 24 growing plots that contained as many as 40 types of beans and 17 different lettuces—all part of Jefferson's quest to "select one or two of the best species or variety of every garden vegetable." Fruit orchards approach the woodland beyond, and both blur into the blue Virginia haze, creating what Jefferson called his "sea view"—an aspect that embraces a harmonious balance of domestic landscape and untamed nature.

"The more
you garden,
the more
you grow."

THE BOOK of OUTDOOR GARDENING

BY THE EDITORS OF SMITH & HAWKEN

ILLUSTRATIONS BY JIM ANDERSON

WORKMAN PUBLISHING, NEW YORK

To all those who till the soil and reap its benefits.

We wish to express our heartfelt appreciation to all the contributors to this book
who generously shared their gardening wisdom and expertise. Their collective knowledge and years of hands-on experience
greatly enhanced the scope of this book and widened the Smith & Hawken community of gardeners.

We also wish to thank Jim Anderson for his attractive and lucid illustrations, as well as for his sunny disposition
and timely performance.

For her wisdom and creative energy, we are indebted to Bonnie Dahan, who sowed the first seeds of
The Book of Outdoor Gardening, and to those staff members and fellow gardeners at Smith & Hawken who helped in countless ways. Special
thanks go to Scott Appell for his garden plans, and to Karen Costanza and Jack Allen for their devotion to environmentally responsible gardening.

Without the confidence and support of Workman Publishing, *The Book of Outdoor Gardening* would never have
reached fruition. Its dedicated and talented staff saw the book through each stage of its growth and met
every obstacle with good humor. Our gratitude and thanks go to Sally Kovalchick for her impeccable stewardship
and commitment to excellence; to Lynn Strong, who made every word count; and to Mary Wilkinson,
for her scrupulous attention to our Plant Guide.

Paul Hanson's exquisite design brought order and beauty to every page.
A big thank-you goes to Lisa Hollander for her expert art direction and execution of the book's design,
and to Lori Malkin and Natsumi Uda for their design assistance.

Library of Congress Cataloging-in-Publication Data
The book of outdoor gardening / by the editors of Smith & Hawken.
p. cm.
Includes bibliographical references (p.   ).
ISBN 0-7611-0231-0 (hc.)
ISBN 0-7611-0110-1 (pbk.)
1. Organic gardening. I. Smith & Hawken.
SB453.5.B67 1996
635'.0484—dc20   ·   96-41374 CIP

WORKMAN PUBLISHING COMPANY, INC., 708 Broadway, New York, NY 10003-9555

Manufactured in the United States of America

First printing October 1996

10 9 8 7 6 5 4 3 2 1

CONTRIBUTORS

ELVIN MCDONALD is the author and photographer of more than 50 books on a wide variety of gardening topics. He was editor for *The American Horticultural Society Encyclopedia of Gardening.* Elvin has lived and gardened in many regions of the U.S.; currently he is garden editor of *Traditional Home* magazine, and resides in Des Moines, Iowa. He is a fellow of the Garden Writers Association of America (GWAA).

LIZ BALL is the author and photographer of eight garden books, including Rodale's Garden Problem Solver series. A regional director of GWAA, she lives and gardens outside Philadelphia, Pennsylvania. Liz writes a weekly garden column for *The Springfield Press.*

CATHY WILKINSON BARASH is the author and photographer of six garden books, including *Edible Flowers: From Garden to Palate* and *Evening Gardens.* A lifelong organic gardener, she lives and gardens in Cold Spring Harbor, New York, lectures and photographs throughout the U.S., and is a national director of GWAA.

DEBORAH BISHOP is Smith & Hawken's editorial director. Her urban garden in San Francisco includes a mass of perennials, an overzealous avocado tree, and cats of all stripes.

BRADY BRUNDRED is a freelance writer living in Northern California. Sharing space in Brady's small Berkeley garden are perennial borders, vegetable beds, water features, fruit trees, a patch of lawn, a flagstone patio, a pair of dogs, and a generous helping of ornament.

RUTH ROGERS CLAUSEN, a freelance writer, teacher, and lecturer, is horticultural consultant for *Country Living Gardener* magazine. She co-authored *Perennials for American Gardens* and wrote three books in the American Garden Guides series. She gardens in Westchester, New York, where she has a small design firm.

JUNE HUTSON, curator of the temperate house, rock garden, and dwarf conifer collections at the Missouri Botanical Gardens, wrote *American Garden Guide to Annuals.* She lectures nationally, and is restoring her naturalistic landscape in St. Louis.

JUDY LOWE has been a garden editor at the Chattanooga *Free Press* since 1979; her articles have won numerous national awards. The treasurer of GWAA, Judy lives and gardens in Soddy Daisy, Tennessee.

MIMI LUEBBERMANN, a freelance writer with a particular interest in organic gardening and farming, is the author of ten books, including *Terrific Tomatoes* and *Climbing Vines.* She farms and gardens in Petaluma, California, and is a member of GWAA.

CLAIR MARTIN III has been curator of the rose collection at the Huntington Botanical Gardens in San Marino, California, since 1983. He is an international lecturer and garden consultant who specializes in restoring old rose gardens.

CAROLE OTTESEN is a garden designer and photographer who writes about the cutting edge of garden design. Her latest book is *The Native Plant Primer*. She maintains a two-acre garden in Maryland.

LINDA JOAN SMITH, who has gardened in many regions of the U.S., is the author of *The Potting Shed*. She writes about American gardens and gardeners, and is a contributing editor for *Home Garden* and *Country Garden* magazines.

JOHN TRAGER has been curator of the Desert Collection at the Huntington Botanical Gardens in San Marino, California, since 1983. He photographs and writes about cacti and succulents for many publications.

BEN WATSON is a consulting editor for Chelsea Green Publishing and the author of *Taylor's Guide to Heirloom Vegetables*, as well as other books and articles. His abundant vegetable garden is in New Hampshire. Ben is a member of GWAA.

STEPHEN YAFA is a writer who has been gardening organically for 25 years in Marin County, California. He estimates that during that time his heirloom beans, corn, tomatoes, and numerous other crops have converted 10 tons of turkey manure and kitchen scraps into delicious edibles through a process that can be explained by logic but owes its true essence to magic.

PREFACE

SMITH & HAWKEN is a company of gardeners, founded some years ago as an environmentally responsible resource for tools, soil amendments, and other goods. And while our aesthetics and techniques might reach back across the Atlantic toward England, France, and Italy, we are a company of *American* gardeners who appreciate the fact that we have not only our own climates and microclimates, but also our own traditions, tools, architectural styles, and ways of being.

With this book we offer a distinctly American approach to the art, craft, and pastime of gardening. And a point of view that embraces British perennial beds, French intensive techniques, old roses, heirloom tomatoes, alternative lawns, and a native-grown preference for ease over formality. Everything—from how we choose our plants to how we keep them alive—is driven by our belief that gardening is a life-affirming act, to be practiced in cahoots with the ecosystem rather than behind its back.

The distillation of many years' experience and the wisdom of many gardeners from around the country, this book is intended as a companion for novice gardeners, master gardeners, gardeners with sprawling verdant acres, and those with 40 square feet to till—for anyone who shares our belief that *every garden counts.*

The Editors of SMITH & HAWKEN

CONTENTS

A HIGHLY ARBITRARY COLLECTION *of* OUR FAVORITE GARDENS

IT ALL BEGINS WITH *the* SOIL
2

PLANTS JUST WANT *to* LIVE
22

EVERY GARDEN COUNTS
72

The GARDENER'S TOOLS
102

DIGGING IN: *from* CLEARING *to* PLANTING
128

TENDING *the* GARDEN
170

START SMALL, THINK BIG: PROPAGATION
216

ADDING *the* FINISHING TOUCHES
246

A GUIDE *to* GARDEN PLANTS
275

INTRODUCTION

It is there in almost all gardeners: the urge to beautify and better our small corner of the world. To plant 'Old Blush' roses that will tumble over the backyard fence and season the breeze with scent. To harvest a fringe of 'Thumbelina' carrots that are sweet on the palate and tender as spring. To grow an arching buddleia to beckon the swallowtails, or a berried pyracantha to welcome the birds.

When faced with a plot of naked earth, gardeners imagine countless pleasures, then set about with spade and trowel to call them forth. No matter how practical our other leanings, we are hungry for the richness of life.

We long to feel the warmth of the thin spring sun as we kneel and pay homage to the daffodils. We welcome the fingers of the wind in our hair as we hoe the weeds between the string beans and the sweet corn. We thrill to each blossom that opens, from the silky-petaled poppy to the golden trumpets of daylilies. And as the frosty breath of fall withers the foliage of all but the hardiest plants, we savor the slow decline, the raking and tidying, the final harvest, and then the winter's rest.

As we work, thinning the lettuce or pruning apple trees, we are in good company—members de facto of an ancient fellowship devoted to beauty, sustenance, and the care of the land. "Cultivators of the earth are the most valuable citizens," wrote Thomas Jefferson, himself a consummate gardener. "They are the most vigorous, the most independent, the most virtuous, and they are tied to their country and wedded to its liberty and interests by the most lasting bonds."

It is this sense of stewardship that leads many gardeners to embrace the tenets of organic gardening: to learn to work in concert with the earth.

The temptations to do otherwise are great. Plastic jugs of herbicides, bottles of pesticides, and bags and boxes of chemical fertilizers promise an easy solution for every garden problem. Banish plagues of aphids, cabbageworms, scale, and leaf miners with simple insecticidal sprays. Vanquish snails by sprinkling bait pellets, like cornflakes, from a cardboard box. Promote luxuriant growth and a wealth of blooms by screwing a sprayer filled with fertilizer to the garden hose and gently showering the plants. Rid the roses of black spot and powdery mildew with potions doled out on a regular schedule, like aspirin or cough syrup. Who wouldn't want such helpmates?

But organic gardeners have a more powerful helpmate still. Nature is firmly on our side, enhancing each and every action. It is nature that sweetens the juice of plum and peach, and nature that scatters the welcome seed of Johnny-jump-up and linaria. It is nature that keeps the weeds at bay when we cover the ground with mulch, and nature that supplies a cure for nearly every insect plague. From nature we reap rich rewards and learn vital garden lessons: to cultivate plants that are well suited to our site, to rotate and diversify our crops, to prune hard and water deeply.

Most important, nature teaches us to feed our soil—a task at which chemical fertilizers fall short. Nurture the earth itself, and the plants will thrive; it is this simple and enduring premise that is at the heart of organic gardening.

The Good Earth

Fertile soil is a living thing, as bursting with vitality as any healthy plant or gardener. Thrust your hands into just-turned garden loam, warmed by the sun of spring, and you can feel the pulse of the earth itself. Sift it through your hands and you can see its essential elements: bits of decaying plant matter that provide food, hold moisture, and allow the soil and plants to breathe; the earthworms and insects that help break down the fallen leaf of oak or berry; the tiny particles of rock.

Such living soil is the precious legacy of countless plants, animals, and insects—along with minute bacteria, fungi, and algae—that have contributed to a cyclical alchemy as close to reincarnation as we may ever get. In this perpetual circle, life arises from the soil, expires and returns to the soil, and rises anew, time and time again.

In virgin forest or meadow, this ancient rhythm of renewal continues unceasingly. Fed by the bodies of their forebears, plants from ground-hugging mosses to towering redwoods spring from the rich earth to flower and drop their spores or seeds. They may survive for only a season; they may endure through centuries. But when their lives are through, their stems wither or their trunks topple, and they drop back to the earth from which they came.

During their lives, these plants nourish countless creatures, from field mice and grizzly bears to aphids and Steller's jays. When they drop their leaves or succumb to old age, they continue to do much the same, providing sustenance for grubs, 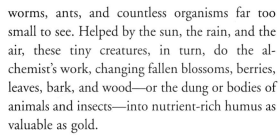 worms, ants, and countless organisms far too small to see. Helped by the sun, the rain, and the air, these tiny creatures, in turn, do the alchemist's work, changing fallen blossoms, berries, leaves, bark, and wood—or the dung or bodies of animals and insects—into nutrient-rich humus as valuable as gold.

With plant, insect, and animal life in perfect balance, nature's cycle perpetuates itself. And as the years go by, the good earth deepens.

The Gardener's Labors and Rewards

In the garden, nature can perform her soil-building sleight of hand only if we provide the needed raw materials. In the following chapters, you'll learn what these vital elements are and how to incorporate them into your gardening. You'll learn to work in partnership with nature through composting, deep digging, amending, cultivation, cover-cropping, mulching, and companion planting: techniques as benevolent as the rain and as logical as the Golden Rule. You'll learn practical, time-honored methods of caring for your plants, and master simple ways of discouraging pests with a taste for your tulips, carrots, or kale. In all these practices (unlike the use of chemicals), there is no danger to you; no risk to birds, bees, dogs, and children; no damage to soil or groundwater.

Instead, each passing season provides evidence that you are making the earth a little better than you found it. The spade enters the planting beds with less resistance. The soil you scoop up in your hands deepens in color, and your weeding and watering chores diminish. Steam rises from the compost pile, ladybugs police the roses, and mockingbirds nest safely in the holly. And as you wander in the morning light, among the fruit trees or along the beds of brilliant lettuce, you note the fragile pyramids of castings, left like presents by the earthworms, and know that underground your helpmates are at work.

With living soil around their roots, your tomatoes grow plump; in the warmth of the garden, their tangy juice runs in rivers down your chin. The apricots that cluster on your trees are nectar-sweet, the onions in the earth as full as harvest moons.

Yes, there is a bit of black spot on the 'Double Delight' rose, some sourgrass is camping briefly in the flower beds, and a renegade slug has been munching the 'Freckles' violas; but these, too, are part of life. In organic gardening, perfection is measured by a new yardstick: the vigor of the oak and the maple, the strength of the twining clematis and the brilliance of the larkspur, the heft of the cabbages and pumpkins. As their roots sink deep, your spirits soar.

In the Beginning

Though organic techniques are new to many gardeners, their source can be traced to the beginnings of life on earth. Nature was the first organic gardener, slowly scraping up a thin blanket of rock particles over much of the barren planet, then feeding it with the bodies of tiny, spore-bearing plants and gradually cloaking it in green.

In time, we too became gardeners, mimicking the masterful methods of nature as best we could. Over millennia, successful husbandmen observed the world around them and learned to plant fishes in their hills of corn, to interplant turnips with peas, to summon insect-eating birds, and to mix in the leavings of cow, horse, and bat to revive their tired dirt.

By the mid to late 19th century, however, chemists had come to the farmer's and gardener's aid, revolutionizing their ancient practices. The instruments of change included new inorganic fertilizers that promised both ease of application and the fast growth of plants, along with potent potions for combating insect and fungal plagues: miracle cures in a powder or spray. Like manna from heaven, such offerings seldom were refused; by the end of the century they were considered as essential as a gardener's fork and spade.

What was missing, for most farmers, gardeners, and even the chemists themselves, was the ability to see the future. To know that the sprays they were breathing might sicken themselves and their children. To know that the birds and fish and foxes that were disappearing would probably not return. To know that without replenishing the humus, the soil would grow barren as dust and eventually blow away. Without understanding the connections, they could not predict the consequences.

A handful of visionary gardeners and scientists, however, believed there was a better way.

In France, market gardeners outside Paris had long been coaxing enormous quantities of vegetables from just a few acres of land, using little more than horse manure—well composted and a foot and a half deep. So rich was this medium that gardeners could grow vegetables cheek to cheek, forming a living mulch that discouraged weeds and kept the soil moist. With the use of this intensive technique, no manufactured fertilizers were required.

In Switzerland, Austrian-born philosopher Rudolf Steiner attributed the lessening quantity and quality of Europe's crops to the use of chemical fertilizers and pesticides. He promoted a method called biodynamic farming, which included future tenets of organic gardening such as composting, crop rotation, and companion planting.

But it is Sir Albert Howard, an English agronomist, who is largely credited with doing the scientific spadework for the 20th-century organic gardening movement. Working on an agricultural research station in India in the 1920s, he came to understand that it was healthy, humus-rich soil—not chemical fertilizers—that most promoted nutritious, abundant, pest-free crops as well as the health of the animals and humans who ate them.

To help the native farmers replenish their land without using up scarce stores of animal dung, Sir Albert developed an efficient, layered form of composting that drew upon thousands of years of agricultural tradition. In his native England and other developed nations, where automobiles and tractors were fast replacing the horse, compost piles would make possible the organic amendment of soil—and the subsequent growth of soil fertility—even as sources of manure dwindled.

Other pioneers would follow, including J. I. Rodale, who founded *Organic Gardening* magazine in the 1940s; biologist Rachel Carson, whose book *The Silent Spring* (first published in 1962) awakened many to the dangers of potent postwar pesticides; and Alan Chadwick, whose West Coast teachings in the 1960s and '70s (a synthesis of French intensive and biodynamic techniques) inspired a new generation of gardeners.

Inevitably, reports of organic gardening's promise bubbled up in the news, alongside ever more frequent tales of ecological disasters. To the many who read or heard about it, the practice of organic gardening made immediate sense. It was logical. It was simple. It was healthful. And it was something people could *do*—right in their own backyards—that just might alter how the world would turn out.

Forward from the Past

Today, the legacy of these and other pioneers surrounds us. Garden sheds that once harbored arsenic or DDT on their shelves now keep insecticidal soaps or homemade pepper sprays close at hand. Compost piles, neatly corralled in bins, are as common—and welcome—in the garden as zinnias and petunias. Catalogs offer up untreated seeds and helpful insects from ladybugs to *Trichogramma* wasps, and cities give away mounds of wood chips for garden mulch. Slowly but surely, like morning glories on a latticework fence, the commonsense principles of organic gardening are weaving their way through the fabric of our thinking.

As you begin to implement these principles and practices, be prepared to spend more and more time in the garden. Not because there is work to do (though in any garden there almost always is), but because you won't want to miss a moment. From the first pale light of dawn on the spires of the foxgloves to the final rays that gild the sunflowers, the garden calls. Linger there, and you'll keep company with the unseen forces that send roots forth from seeds and push tiny new leaves up into the light. You'll experience, firsthand, the magic that transforms a translucent blossom into a succulent pear or the crispest of apples, or brings a mysterious hellebore into winter bloom. You'll feast on the best the earth can offer and know you had a hand in bringing forth that bounty.

In time, the garden will give you many gifts,

wrapped in light, air, and the beauty of fruit and flower. The patience to wait months for hardwood cuttings of currant or kerria to sprout or years for a cherry tree to bear fruit. The faith it takes to plant those bare brown bulbs and trust that tulips or towering lilies will arise in the spring, or to believe that the naked canes of the climbing rose will once again be cloaked in pink. The stillness to sit, like a statue, while the timid towhee scuffs up the dirt or the monarch sips from the heliotrope, and to reverently savor the garden's glory.

Tending to the vigorous honeysuckle or the delicate campanula, or nurturing the seedlings of pansy or sweet pea, you grow, too. And soon you will come to know—with the certainty that you know the ground is underfoot and the sky overhead—that your gardening makes a difference, whether confined to a window box or reaching across acres.

"The care of the earth is our most ancient and most worthy, and after all, our most pleasing responsibility," wrote Wendell Berry. When you garden organically, with every thrust of the spade, every pull of the hoe, every turning of the compost pile, you break the ground for a better world. A world of beauty and peace. A world of pure air and crystal waters. A world of fertility and abundance.

The Book

of Outdoor

Gardening

IT ALL BEGINS
WITH *the* SOIL

There is something deeply primal about the feel of sun-warmed earth. Indeed, one of the authentic delights of gardening is the tactile experience of handling soil, feeling the gritty texture of sand, the loose crumbliness of loam, the slick smoothness of clay. "Dirt under the nails" gardeners know that to be physically in touch with the soil is to reap its highest rewards. After all, if you can't feel the earth and sense its energy, you diminish the bond between you and your garden.

An awareness of the soil and its role in the health and beauty of growing things is the essence of gardening. If you nourish the soil, then the soil in turn will be able to nourish your plants. To this end, you need to know the properties of the particular soil in your garden; only then can you best serve the plants that grow there.

THE IMPORTANCE OF GOOD SOIL

The soil in your garden is a complex biological system consisting of air, water, inorganic matter (fine rock particles), and organic components including plant and animal matter in varying degrees of decay, insects, earthworms, fungi, and microorganisms. Picture your soil teeming with life, from the smallest microbes to the fattest earthworms, and you'll understand that the more life your soil supports, the more it will be able to support.

To properly sustain plant growth, soil must provide adequate support, a place for plants to put down roots, and a medium from which they can absorb the water and nutrients vital for their healthy development. How effectively soil does its job depends on its texture, its ability to absorb water, the availability of essential macro- and micronutrients as well as calcium, magnesium, and sulfur, and the presence of an active population of beneficial soil organisms.

The ideal garden soil is friable—light and crumbly—and rich enough in nutrients to yield strong, healthy flowers, fruits, and vegetables. This "good dirt" also makes gardening infinitely easier by producing plants that are substantially more resistant to pests and diseases than those raised in poor soil.

Basic Soil Types

All soil is arranged in three layers, or horizons: topsoil, subsoil, and the layer of rock from which the soil has eroded. Topsoil is the good dirt directly under your feet, the layer of soil that is enriched when fallen leaves and other organic material naturally decompose. Its color can range from deep brown (near black) to pale beige or yellowish tan. If you dig down a spade's depth (a spit) through the soil of an uncultivated area, you'll notice a clear delineation between the darker, crumbly topsoil and the lighter, compressed subsoil. The depth of this demarcation line may vary within the same garden; the nearer the demarcation line is to the surface, the shallower the layer of fertile topsoil. If there is no color variation between the topsoil and the subsoil, the topsoil probably lacks sufficient organic matter.

Soil is usually classified according to the size of its particles. Sand has the largest particles, clay the finest; silt (the stuff that makes water muddy) falls between the two. Loam is the ideal blend of sand, silt, clay, and organic matter and is what most gardeners strive for.

The size of soil particles affects the way they clump together, and the clumping determines the amount of space between particles. This spacing is crucial because it determines how well plant roots penetrate the soil and absorb air, water, and essential nutrients. It also affects the soil's tilth, or ability to retain air and moisture in the proper

THE FIST TEST

To perform your own quick soil analysis, take a handful of slightly moist (not wet) soil from your garden and close your fingers around it. Then open your fist and watch how the soil behaves. If it shatters immediately, it's sand. If it holds its shape briefly, then crumbles into small chunks, it's loam. If it maintains its shape, complete with impressions of your fingers, it's clay.

amounts. Good tilth is achieved by digging in plenty of organic matter; the process of turning and digging the soil provides the air. Bacteria and fungi in the soil break down the organic matter and form "cementing" materials that glue the soil into crumbs, or coarse grains. These crumbs absorb moisture effectively, improve drainage, and increase soil aeration.

CLAY SOIL

The heaviest of all soil types is clay, usually yellowish-tan in color, compacted when dry, and sticky to the touch when moist. Gardeners who deal with clay soil joke that they can only garden 15 minutes a year, during that brief interlude when the soil is neither sodden and slimy nor so dry and hard that it must be dug with a jackhammer. The microscopic particles in clay tend to cling tightly together, leaving little room for plant roots to penetrate or for essential oxygen and water to pass freely through them. Moreover, because of its density, clay soil takes so long to warm up that it's often late spring before seeds can be sown and the growing season is sharply curtailed, particularly in cool northern climates.

SOIL PROBLEMS

■ **Compaction** occurs when the spaces between soil particles are squeezed, resulting in badly aerated and slowly draining soil. You can easily compact the soil in a bed simply by stepping on it after the bed has been dug and prepared. Compaction can also be the result of heavier insult, such as the wheels of a car. On new properties, it is often caused by builders repeatedly driving heavy equipment over the ground.

■ **Hardpan** is severely compacted soil that has become nearly impenetrable. This condition is often discovered in the process of digging or when existing plants fail to grow, become stunted, or die, indicating a serious drainage problem. Hardpan usually occurs naturally, but it can be the result of repeated compaction over time—as in the case of soil in a driveway or dirt parking area. Water cannot drain through hardpan; instead, because the ground is so tightly compacted that roots cannot penetrate deep enough to anchor plants securely, it accumulates on the surface. Some hardpan layers are thin enough to punch through with a soil auger, or even a trowel or spade if wielded with sufficient force. It may be possible to break up hardpan by cultivating to a depth of 12"–18" and amending the soil heavily with organic matter. Creating raised beds or a planting soil are other possible solutions (see pages 135 and 139). If these options don't work, a landscape architect can suggest appropriate drainage systems.

■ **Blue mottling,** a condition in which the soil turns bluish-black with a slimy green surface and a bad smell, is found most often in north-facing areas that have minimal light and air circulation like those surrounded by high buildings or tall, closely spaced evergreen trees. The soil becomes waterlogged and stagnant in hot weather, possibly even turning into a breeding place for all sorts of unwelcome pests. To correct blue mottling, first remove the most offensive portions of the surface and let the soil dry out; then work in plenty of organic matter.

■ **Capping** is a troublesome condition that occurs in areas of hard-crusted soil, especially in hot weather, and is recognizable by cracks in the surface. This problem results when soil dries to a crust after torrential rains or after excessive watering has washed away or damaged much of the fine crumb on the surface. While there's little you can do to control heavy rains, you can control the amount of watering you do in the garden. Compacted soil is more likely to develop capping, so avoid walking, riding, or driving on your soil—especially if it's wet. If you find that capping is a fairly common problem in your garden, add organic amendments to the soil in order to improve its structure.

Nonetheless, if you have clay soil, don't despair. Clay does have advantages over other soil types. It's generally fertile, with plenty of the essential plant nutrients, and it holds moisture well (a plus because plants can absorb only those nutrients that are dissolved in water). In addition, the problems of gardening with clay soil can be solved by digging in organic soil amendments at every opportunity. When sufficient amounts of compost, humus, well-rotted manure and/or leaf mold are added each time a bed is dug or a planting hole is prepared, the soil becomes loose enough for roots to penetrate and water to drain—and also becomes progressively easier to work. Of course, soil improvement is a long-term process; there is no way to alter the character or texture of any given soil significantly in a single season or even two. Eventually, however, you'll

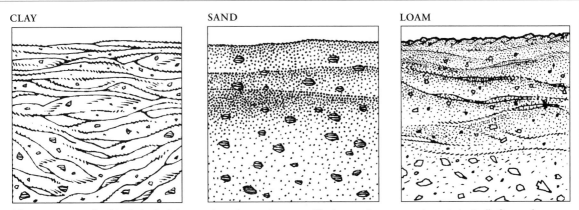

CLAY   SAND   LOAM

The composition of soil includes both inorganic and organic matter. The inorganic components are principally fine rock particles, whose density determines whether the soil is clay, sand, or loam.

be rewarded with good soil that will support a multitude of healthy plants.

SANDY SOIL

Generally grayish-tan in color and gritty to the touch, sand contains the largest particles of any soil type. Water can drain right through the loose, open spaces between these particles, carrying away most of the essential nutrients (a process called leaching). Sandy soil is often both dry and infertile; beach or desert winds can add to the problem by blowing sand around until plants are buried or stripped of their anchorage.

Like clay, however, sandy soil has some redeeming features. This soil type is a pleasure to work, since both digging and weeding are so easy, and the oxygen in the spaces between particles tends to keep plants from rotting out. Sandy soil warms up and dries out earlier in spring than other soils, so seeds can be sown sooner—a special boon for eager vegetable gardeners who look forward to the first fresh harvest. And since sand creates such a hospitable environment for roots to penetrate, plants establish themselves much faster than in heavier soils.

The prescription for sandy soil is precisely the same as for clay (indeed, for all types of soil). Dig in generous amounts of compost, humus,

well-rotted manure, and/or leaf mold every time the soil is worked. These amendments not only improve the texture of the soil but also increase its fertility. In addition, it's especially important to mulch sandy soil. A good organic mulch reduces moisture lost from the soil by evaporation and helps to maintain soil moisture. A 2"–6" layer of mulch also controls topsoil loss from wind and water erosion; heavier than the sand, the mulch is not so easily carried off by wind or rain. As it breaks down over time, organic mulch can be dug in to improve the soil even further or can simply be topped off with another layer of mulch. As with improving clay, improving sand is a long-term process. It's best to make peace with the fact that gardening requires patience.

LOAM

Neither as heavy as clay nor as light as sand, loam represents a compromise between the two extremes. In fact, as far as gardeners are concerned, loam is just right. Usually a rich, warm brown color with a smooth, silky feel, this soil type is a balanced combination of silt, sand, and clay plus organic matter. It retains moisture yet drains quickly enough to keep plant roots from drowning; well aerated, with plenty of oxygen, it's loose enough for roots to penetrate easily. Loam is

TESTING SOIL DRAINAGE

If you have any qualms about the drainage of your soil, especially in an area that has not been previously cultivated, it's a good idea to do a more sophisticated test than the simple "fist test." Dig a hole 1' across and 2' deep. If the soil is at all moist (from a recent rain or watering), cover the hole and a 1' area around it with plastic. After a week, or when the soil has dried completely, fill the hole with water. Monitor the time it takes for all the water to drain. If it takes less than 5 minutes, the soil is too loose or sandy; more than 10 minutes, the soil is too dense with too much clay. To remedy either problem, mix plenty of organic matter into the soil.

fertile, providing plants with all the nutrients they need to develop, bloom, and thrive. It's also easy to dig and weed. In short, loam is generally guaranteed to produce healthy, well-nourished plants.

Although it certainly needs far less improvement than clay or sand, loam still requires maintenance. Any soil that is not continuously improved and enriched will wear out eventually, becoming less fertile and less productive. This is an important consideration when growing annuals and vegetables, which, in their short lives in the garden, require more nutrients than longer-lived plants like perennials, trees, and shrubs. Compost, humus, well-rotted manure, or leaf mold should be dug in when preparing these beds each spring. In climates with high winds, heavy rains, or extreme heat, an organic mulch is particularly useful in preventing erosion, reducing excess evaporation, and moderating summer soil temperatures. Mulching and adding organic matter to loam is, in essence, preventive medicine. By adding organic matter, the gardener can, in a single stroke, enhance both tilth and fertility.

Making Sense of Soil pH

Once you know your basic soil type, you need to know whether your soil is acid or alkaline and to what degree. This information, derived by testing the soil pH (potential hydrogen factor), is crucial because the level of acidity or alkalinity determines whether or not your plants can easily absorb essential nutrients. Acid soil tends to tie up phosphorus, while very alkaline soil can tie up iron, boron, copper, manganese, and zinc. Testing your soil pH is especially important when developing a new bed or when investigating the causes of a plant's failure to thrive in existing beds (once you've eliminated such causes as over- or underwatering, pests, or disease).

The pH scale ranges from 1 to 14. Neutral is 7. Less than 7 is acid, and greater than 7 is alkaline. A difference of a point in one direction or another may seem negligible; however, the pH scale is logarithmic, so that soil with a pH of 5.0 is 10 times more acidic than soil with a pH of 6.0 and 100 times more acidic than soil with a pH of 7.0. Generally speaking, areas of the United States and Canada with normal to heavy rainfall (40" or more a year) have neutral to acid soil. The exceptions exist where the soil has developed from underlying limestone rock, in which case the soil is alkaline. In places where the rainfall is low, such as California, the Southwest, and the deserts, both clay and sandy soils tend to be alkaline.

To get a general sense of your soil pH, look at what plants have grown there naturally. Certain plants have a preference for either acid or alkaline soil. Plants that grow best in acid soil include rhododendrons and azaleas. Lilacs and delphiniums are examples of plants that prefer more alkaline soil. Vegetables and most garden perennials do best in a neutral or slightly acid soil with a pH between 6.0 and 7.0. Annuals generally prefer a pH range between 5.5 and 7.0. However, it's always helpful to know the pH requirements of individual plants.

Soil-test kits are available at garden centers and nurseries as well as from mail-order garden sources. The testing procedure is quite straightforward—always follow the directions to the letter. Most soil-test kits include a solution which, when mixed in a tube with a sample of the soil, will change color according to the pH of the soil. The pH can fluctuate greatly on a single piece of property, so take and test soil samples from each separate area you intend to develop. Often soil is more alkaline near the house, since calcium leached from a concrete foundation lowers pH. Many people needlessly lime their lawns every year without retesting the pH; in time, the result can be a pH that is too high and soil that is too alkaline. If you don't want to bother with testing the pH yourself, you can take samples of garden soil to your local Cooperative Extension service and have the samples tested for a small fee. (The report will include the levels of nutrients in the soil as well as recommendations for amending and fertilizing.) Some nurseries and garden centers also do soil testing, often as a courtesy to regular customers.

When you know the pH of the soil, you can modify it if necessary to make it amenable to the plants you want to grow. To make the soil less acidic, dig in bonemeal or the right amount of wood ash. For lawns and other large areas, use dolomitic limestone, following package instructions for the quantity necessary to change the pH to the desired level. The amount will vary with the basic soil type. To raise a soil pH from 5.0 to 6.5, for example, you'd have to apply 41 pounds of limestone per 1,000 square feet of soil; in sandy loam, 78 pounds; in loam, 106 pounds; and in clay, 152 pounds. To make the soil less alkaline, dig in organic soil amendments that are acidic, like peat moss, oak leaves, shredded bark, and well-rotted manure. For large areas and quick results, add sulfur, gypsum, or lime-sulfur, following package instructions. Again the amount varies with the soil type: 11 pounds of sulfur per 1,000 square feet will lower the pH from 7.5 to 6.5 in

PLANTS FOR ACID AND ALKALINE SOIL

Many plants are fussy about where they put down their roots, preferring either acid or alkaline soil. Eastern gardens, for example, are heralded for their luxurious stands of ericaceous (heath family) and other acid-loving plants. (Such plants are often described by catchphrases like "prefers a rich and peaty mixture.") Gardens west of Ohio (and in low rainfall regions), where soil is more often at the other end of the pH scale, can take advantage of the plethora of plants that prefer alkaline soil.

FOR ACID SOIL

Blueberries (*Vaccinium corymbosum*) *
Camellias (*Camellia* spp.) *
Fringed bleeding heart
     (*Dicentra eximia*) *
Heathers (*Erica* spp.)
Japanese andromeda (*Pieris japonica*) *
Mountain laurel (*Kalmia
     latifolia*) *
Rhododendrons and azaleas
     (*Rhododendron* spp.) *

Serviceberry (*Amelanchier
     canadensis*) *
Turtlehead (*Chelone obliqua*) *
Wild ginger (*Asarum caudatum*) *

FOR ALKALINE SOIL

Baby's breath (*Gypsophila
     paniculata*) *
Clematis (*Clematis* spp.) *
Delphiniums (*Delphinium elatum*) *

Lilacs (*Syringa* spp.) *
Pasque flower (*Pulsatilla
     vulgaris*)
Peonies (*Paoenia lactiflora*) *
Sweet peas (*Lathyrus odoratus*) *
Sweet William (*Dianthus
     barbatus*)
Wallflower (*Erysimum cheiri*) *

Included in the Plant Guide, pages 276-479.

A GARDEN LEGEND

ALAN CHADWICK'S INTENSIVE METHODS

I t seemed a feat of alchemy when Alan Chadwick transformed a barren, clayey hill in Santa Cruz, California, into a fertile garden filled with fragrant flowers and delicious, disease-resistant vegetables—without so much as a drop of chemical fertilizer.

> *"The gardener does not make the garden; the garden makes the gardener."*

The ancient Greeks were the first to notice that plant life thrives in landslides where the loose soil allows air, moisture, warmth, nutrients, and roots to freely penetrate. Two thousand years later Alan Chadwick, a true horticultural genius, introduced us to biointensive gardening techniques—and initiated a renaissance in the organic methods that produce not only higher yields but tastier and healthier crops.

Chadwick received his formal training at England's Wisley Gardens; practiced the intensive method favored by French farmers; studied with the Austrian philosopher Rudolph Steiner, an early proponent of the biodynamic and holistic approach to gardening; and incorporated the principles of Sir Albert Howard, considered the father of the organic movement. The result is a gardening method that embraces the interrelatedness of all things—including not only plant and animal life but the gardener as well.

In the 1960s, Chadwick established his student garden for the University of California at Santa Cruz on a site where even weeds were reluctant to grow. Within two years, the garden's yield was about four times greater than that obtained using commercial methods. Charismatic as well as horticulturally gifted, Chadwick attracted legions of devoted followers, and the phrase "intensive gardening" entered the lexicon for good.

sand; in loam, you need 18 pounds; in clay, 23 pounds.

Most plants will tolerate a variation in soil pH of a point or more from the ideal if the soil is rich in organic matter. In a healthy, well-aerated soil, alive with earthworms and beneficial microorganisms, the pH factor is much less important to the health of the plants.

Nutrients in the Soil

Thirteen of the 16 nutrients needed for a plant to grow must come from the soil. (The other three—carbon, hydrogen, and oxygen—are available from air and water.) Nitrogen, phosphorus, and potassium are primary nutrients; these need replenishing most often since plants use them in the greatest amounts. Magnesium, calcium, and sulfur, considered secondary nutrients, are present in most soils in adequate amounts for most plants. Trace elements, or micronutrients, are also available in most soils and are needed by plants only in small amounts.

The structure and pH of your soil will affect how well your plants can make use of essential nutrients, especially nitrogen, phosphorus, and potassium (often identified by their respective chemical symbols N, P, and K). Good soil contains all three of these nutrients in water-soluble form so they can be absorbed by plant roots.

Soil nitrogen, derived from organic matter, encourages stem and leaf growth, resulting in lush, full plants. (One reason plant leaves look greener after a rain is that the leaves have absorbed nitrogen from the raindrops.) Plants that lack nitrogen have leaves that turn pale green, then yellow from the base of the plant upward; the yellowing starts at the leaf tip and progresses toward the stem. In general, nitrogen deficiency is signaled by slow, spindly, and even stunted growth, dying branches, and small fruit.

Phosphorus (or phosphate) is essential for strong roots and sturdy growth as well as for intense flower colors. This nutrient brings plants into bloom faster (of critical importance in short-summer climates), increases the number of viable seeds produced (helpful if you're saving seeds or encouraging self-sowing annuals and biennials), encourages resistance to disease and winter cold, promotes fruiting, and increases the vitamin content of fruits and vegetables. Plants in need of phosphorus are often small and scrawny with purplish leaves. Insufficient phosphorus results in stunted growth and seeds that will not develop.

Potassium (or potash) is essential to plant cell division and growth. It functions as the jack-of-all-trades of plant nutrients and is credited with increasing drought tolerance in plants, helping them to utilize nitrogen and balancing the effects of excess nitrogen or calcium. Of special importance when growing fruits, nuts, and vegetables, potassium greatly contributes to improved flavor, color, and texture by aiding in the production of starches, sugars, and oils. Like phosphorus, it increases resistance to disease and winter cold, an important consideration when plants are grown in climates beyond their native range. Potassium deficiency is most likely to occur in soils that are sandy, low in organic matter, or acidic. Symptoms of potassium deficiency include lower

GARDEN SOIL IS NOT POTTING SOIL

One of the advantages of gardening in containers is that you can match each plant with its preferred growing medium. Garden soil is generally not recommended for containers because it is too dense and also may be host to pests or diseases. Potting soil is readily available at nurseries and garden centers and from mail-order sources. See pages 168 and 230 for information on container planting mediums.

NUTRIENT DEFICIENCIES

Plants let you know when they're not geting the proper nutrients. Yellow leaves, for example, can indicate a shortage of nitrogen, the most common nutrient deficiency. Yellowing and other symptoms, however, can also be signs of pests or disease. Always be sure to rule out those probelms before feeding plants.

ELEMENT (Chemical Symbol)	DEFICIENCY SYMPTOMS
PRIMARY NUTRIENTS	
Nitrogen (N)	Yellowing of leaves (starting with older leaves, eventually affecting entire plant). Oldest leaves drop. Stunted and retarded growth.
Phosphorus (P)	Stunted and retarded growth. Purpling of leaves (some plants only). Sparse flowering and fruiting.
Potassium (K)	Retarded growth; weakened stems. Browning of leaf edges and tips (especially older leaves). Small fruit or shriveled seeds.
SECONDARY NUTRIENTS	
Calcium (Ca)	Poor growth. Death of growing points.
Magnesium (Mg)	Yellowing between veins of young leaves (veins remain green). Black spots next to veins.
Sulfur (S)	Yellowing of leaves. Plant appears stiff.
TRACE NUTRIENTS	
Zinc (Zn)	Yellowing between veins of young leaves. Undersize new leaves.
Iron (Fe)	Yellowing between veins of young leaves; small veins also yellow.
Manganese (Mn)	Yellowing between veins of young leaves (veins remain green). Black spots next to veins.
Copper (Cu)	Stunted growth. Sunken dead spots on leaves (starting with youngest). Wilted leaf tips.
Boron (B)	Death of growing tips causes development of lateral buds and witches' brooms (fans of stiff shoots). Brittleness of stems, then rest of plant.
Molybdenum (Mo)	Yellowing (paleness) between veins (older leaves first, then rest of plant). Curling upward of leaf edges.
Chlorine (Cl)	Wilting, followed by loss of color.

leaves that become crisp at the edges before turning brown and dying, and shriveled, sterile seeds.

AMENDING THE SOIL

The structure and fertility of any garden soil can be improved by adding organic matter in the form of compost, manure, leaf mold, or similar materials. This organic matter is food for the microorganisms that transform soil into humus. The process is quite simple: without food, the microorganisms cannot thrive; without microorganisms, there is no production of humus. The higher the humus content, the more friable the soil, and friable (easily crumbled) soil is what you want for your plants.

As plants consume the soil's reserve of nutrients and other resources, they deplete the supply. Without restocking, the soil is bound to become weakened and unable to afford the necessary high-quality nourishment required for continued healthy plant growth. Therefore, every time you work the soil, it's important to amend it with organic matter. A particular benefit to the gardener who grows fruits and vegetables (and eats them) is that foods grown in organically amended soil have no poisonous chemical residues.

In addition to replenishing nutrients, amendments improve the soil's texture and drainage. A further benefit of organic amendments is that they break down within a season or two, adding to the soil's fertility. Inorganic amendments such as gypsum or vermiculite (see page 18), which break down at a much slower rate, do not affect soil fertility but can improve its texture immediately.

Compost: A Homegrown Garden Treasure

Commonly referred to as black or brown gold, compost is the substance that results from the partial decomposition of organic material. This valuable soil amendment can be dug in when preparing a bed, added to a planting hole or to an existing planting (as side-dressing in the top several inches of soil around the outer limits of the root zone), or even used as an organic mulch.

Homemade compost, consisting of kitchen vegetable scraps, uncontaminated grass clippings, and garden debris (perhaps with the addition of well-rotted manure), allows you to recycle what might otherwise be waste or garbage into the best possible amendment for your soil. Easy to do, good for the environment, and great for the garden, composting inspires a sense of having done the right thing by returning to the soil what the plants have taken from it. Compost provides the perfect amendment for any type of soil, improving aeration and drainage in heavy clay soil, increasing water retention and fertility in light,

sandy soil, and maintaining good soil structure, tilth, and fertility in loam soils.

Organic compost requires four basic elements: carbon, nitrogen, air, and water. The carbon comes from dried leaves, straw, and wood chips—what some people call "the dry brown stuff." Fresh or green materials such as vegetative kitchen waste, untreated grass clippings, hedge trimmings, and well-rotted manure provide the nitrogen. Fungi, bacteria, and other microorganisms secrete enzymes and acids that break down the cells of dead vegetation and animal matter. These enzymes form the "cementing" materials that glue soil particles into the desirable coarse grains. The grains or crumbs allow moisture to be absorbed most efficiently, improve drainage, and increase soil aeration. Microorganisms use the carbon from organic matter for energy and the nitrogen to grow and reproduce. The indigestible

WHAT IS HUMUS?

Humus, essential for friable soil, is the dark, sticky, nutrient-rich organic substance that results from the complete decomposition of plant and/or animal matter. Though often used interchangeably, the terms "humus" and "compost" are not quite synonymous. Compost is a stage of decay in which most of the matter has been broken down, but it may still be possible to identify individual parts such as leaves and twigs. Humus is the final phase of decay, in which the original materials can no longer be distinguished. Compost, while not totally decayed, is nonetheless rich in humus. Leaf mold, also rich in humus, is the dark, crumbly substance found at the bottom of a leaf pile after it has sat undisturbed for a year or more. Duff is the natural leaf mold found on the forest floor—nature's own compost.

portion of their diet—the partially decomposed organic matter—is what we call compost.

Temperature also plays a role in the decaying process. The microorganisms that break down the organic matter of the compost heap generate heat by releasing the energy locked in the debris. Called thermophilic (heat-loving) bacteria, these organisms remain at work as long as they have organic matter to feed on.

Turning the pile lets in the air that keeps the microorganisms active by giving them new materials to work on and sustains a high internal temperature to speed up the composting process. It also helps to aerate the pile, keeping leaves and other matter from matting and becoming odiferous. Generally, if a compost heap smells, it needs more air.

Compost and its hungry microbes need moisture as well as air. Ideally, the moisture content of the materials in the pile should be between 40% and 60%. During dry periods and in dry climates, it speeds things up considerably to sprinkle the pile with water at each turning or whenever a new layer of organic material is added. If the materials are already very wet (rain-soaked leaves, for example), it's a good idea to mix in some dry organic material at the same time to maintain a good air-moisture balance.

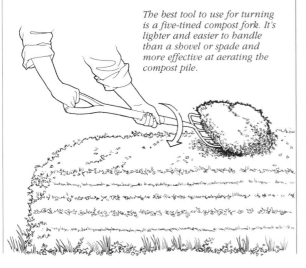

The best tool to use for turning is a five-tined compost fork. It's lighter and easier to handle than a shovel or spade and more effective at aerating the compost pile.

THE WORM TURNS

Earthworms feed on grass clippings and other organic matter in the compost pile and excrete the indigestible portions as castings, which beneficial soil microbes feed on and turn into humus. In this way, worms accelerate the decomposition of the compost pile.

Even if you don't have room for a compost pile, you can benefit from a worm bin. For vermiculture, use red worms or brandlings (*Eisenia foetida, Lumbricus rubellus*), which you can find at fishing shops or order by mail from many garden suppliers.

In mild climates, you can keep a worm bin outdoors (just don't allow them to freeze or overheat). Otherwise, bins should be kept inside: under the sink, in the basement, or even on a bookshelf. Just feed the worms your kitchen vegetable scraps (with no butter or oil on those vegetables), and they'll reward you with rich castings that serve the same function as compost. Apartment dwellers can use the castings to sidedress potted plants. In warm months, worms from the bin can also be added to a slow compost pile; they'll move throughout the compost and find the best temperature for themselves but only at the periphery; they won't survive the heat at the center of the pile.

Diseased plant materials or seedheads (especially those of noxious weeds) should never be added to the compost pile. Most disease pathogens are killed when exposed to temperatures of 131°F. for 25 minutes, and most weed seeds die at temperatures between 140°F. and 150°F.; however, it's better not to invite the problem than to deal with the consequences of amending your soil with compost that contains active plant pathogens or viable weed seeds.

GOOD COMPOST STUFF

Pine needles

Grass clippings (Use only unsprayed clippings; let dry and never add more than 1" at a time to pile.)

Weeds (It's best to let weeds dry before adding them to the pile; otherwise they compact and start to smell.)

Cleared brush, small branches, wood chips, pinecones (Even shredded, these take a long time to break down, but they make a good mulch.)*

Spoiled straw

Hay

Leaves*

Newspaper*

Sawdust (except from allelopathic trees such as black walnut, eucalyptus, and red cedar)

Wood ash (in small amounts)

Vegetable kitchen waste, including coffee grounds and tea bags (Omit meat, salad greens with oil-based dressings, and buttered vegetables.)

Dried corncobs*

Eggshells

Dried or rotted manure (from farm animals)

Dried seaweed or kelp

Soil

BAD COMPOST STUFF

Dog, cat, or human feces

Coal or charcoal ashes

Diseased garden plants

Glossy, slick, or colored magazines

Meat and meat products (including grease, gravy, bones)

Pesticide- or herbicide-sprayed plant material

Bermuda Grass

Noxious or invasive weeds (such as poison oak and poison ivy); weeds that resprout from cuttings (such as blackberry and spiderwort); weeds in seed (especially those with heat-tolerant seeds like buttercup, bindweed, burdock, cheeseweed, and quack grass)

Material must be shredded before being added to compost pile.

COMPOSTING METHODS

Early in the 20th century, Sir Albert Howard, assigned to improve conditions at a 300-acre farm at the Indore Institute of Plant Industry in India, discovered a relationship between what goes into the soil and what comes out of it. He noticed that many soil problems—poor tilth, waterlogging, compaction, surface crusting—led directly to the conditions that foster crop diseases and ultimately concluded that it is necessary to feed the soil rather than the plant. To this end, he developed the concept of multilayered compost to provide organic matter that would enrich the soil.

Since then, a great many theories have been advanced on how to produce the best compost. The only real difference among the methods, however, lies in the speed of decomposition, i.e., the length of time it takes the material to reach the compost stage.

Slow (Passive) Compost. This is the method for the gardener who is in no particular hurry for results. A slow compost pile, virtually nothing more than a pile of grass clippings and other garden debris and vegetable scraps from the kitchen allowed to decay in its own time, requires no work other than adding new material to the pile when at hand. Within several months, depending on the size of the pieces of compostable material, the pile will break down into black, crumbly, fertile compost.

Faster Compost. To speed up the process, the Indore method recommends layering the compost pile like a torte: a layer of leaves, weeds, and other vegetation, alternating with a thin layer of manure, in a ratio of 3:1 (three times as much vegetation as manure). The volume of dry brown material (carbon) and green material (vegetative kitchen and yard waste) should be about equal. The addition of manure serves two purposes: it speeds up the rate of decay and—if well-rotted manure is used—is a virtually odorless method of recycling animal waste. If you're lucky enough to

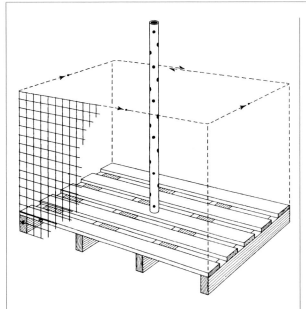

The pole method is a nontraditional but quite effective means of turning the compost pile. Place a wooden pallet on the ground (old ones are often free at lumberyards), and surround it with wire or cloth. Drill a series of holes in a piece of 2"–3" PVC pipe, and insert the pipe vertically into the center of the pallet. Build the compost pile on top. Several times a week, shake the pole as you walk by to create new air pockets.

have a fresh supply of manure (from a dairy farm, riding stable, or a friend who raises livestock), be sure not to add it to the compost pile until it's completely broken down and indistinguishable from other vegetative matter; don't ever apply it fresh. Well-rotted manures are also available at nurseries and garden centers.

Fastest Compost. To produce high-quality compost in the shortest period of time, maintain the center of the heap at a temperature between 104°F. and 131°F. (Use a compost thermometer to check the temperature.) Don't turn the pile as long as it remains between these two temperatures; instead, turn it when the temperature is either lower or higher. Ideally, the pile should be turned when the internal temperature reaches 140°F. This way, it neither gets so hot that it kills off the thermophilic bacteria nor reduces the heat to the point that the decomposition slows down. Obviously, this requires a bit of concentrated attention and work. The pile may need turning as

often as every other day, but the payoff is finished compost in as little as three weeks.

There is much controversy among avid composters about turning vs. not turning (aerobic decay vs. anaerobic decay), large branches vs. small twigs. Ultimately these arguments are variations on the theme of how quickly the raw materials decompose into usable compost. Turned compost piles break down more rapidly than unturned compost piles, aerobic (oxygen-aided) decay is more rapid (and less odiferous) than anaerobic decay, and twigs or wood chips decompose faster than branches. The choice is between more work and less time or less work and more time: the compost will be essentially the same.

COMPOST CONTAINERS

Once you decide to compost, you must provide the environment essential for the microorganisms to thrive, multiply, and break down the organic matter. (Simply piling up vegetable wastes from the kitchen and garden in a corner of your yard, and waiting for them to decompose, is neither aesthetic nor practical; raccoons, squirrels, and other creatures can easily get into such a pile and scatter it as they forage.) The most low-

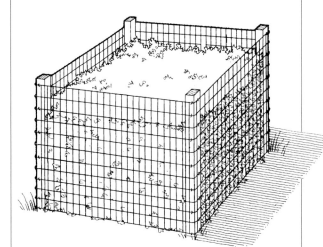

A simple way to contain compost is to enclose it in chicken wire (or hardware cloth), supported at the corners with 48" lengths of two-by-fours pounded 12" into the ground.

Gardeners who have a lot of compostable material are best off with three bins, side by side. If you're content with passive compost, simply fill the bins up one at a time. Usually, by the time the third bin is filled, the compost in the first bin is decomposed and ready to use in the garden. For faster compost once the first bin is filled, move the compost from that bin to the second bin.

tech, low-cost, laid-back approach to compost-making confines the pile in a single container, made with chicken wire or somewhat sturdier hardware cloth. A slightly more elaborate approach involves building a bin from wooden pallets, which are often available free at home and garden centers. One pallet serves as the base, with three other pallets (attached with wire or nails) forming the sides. A hinged front and top help to keep large marauders out of the bin while allowing easy access for adding new material and removing finished compost.

A practical way to compost in a small garden is to have two compost containers: one box can be filled, moistened, covered, and left to rot, while the other box is the active one that you fill with waste. By the time the second container is filled, the first should be completely rotted. If you have a lot of compostable material, you can use three bins placed side by side.

If you're not inclined to build your own composter, many different kinds are for sale—from precut lumber for fashioning a slatted wooden bin to metal "tum-

blers" that are turned daily and can be used only if all materials are shredded first. The middle road is the stackable composter (see also page 121). This method is best suited to households where the scale of contemporary urban and suburban gardens precludes collecting great piles of leaves and letting them decompose in their own good time, and where large-scale wooden bins are equally inappropriate to the gardening space. Stackable composters can be used for the passive method, just to

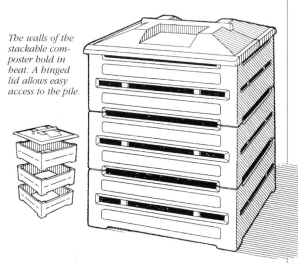

The walls of the stackable composter hold in heat. A hinged lid allows easy access to the pile.

contain the pile, or for the rapid composting method. The three plastic tiers of the unit fit neatly on top of one another and are light enough to be handled easily. When the compost reaches the top of the unit, you simply fork material from the top onto the ground to form the bottom of a new bin. Fork the remaining material from the original stack to the new bin; restack the former middle and bottom sections. Use any completely composted material from the bottom of the original stack.

A tumbler can produce garden-ready compost from shredded organic materials in less than a month.

Peat Moss: An Ecological Debate

In areas of the world where rainfall exceeds evaporation, bogs form in shallow basins and over the years plant debris accumulates under a thin layer of living vegetation. This partially decomposed plant material is usually called sphagnum peat moss, since mosses of the sphagnum species comprise the greater part. The large cell structure of the sphagnum peat moss allows it to absorb air and water like a sponge. Although it contains no nutrients, it does help retain nutrients from fertilizers by storing them and gradually dispersing them throughout the soil.

According to the Canadian Peat Association, Canada has more than 25% of all the peat in the world, and it is accumulating at a rate 70 times faster than it is being harvested. Generally, peat bogs in Canada are harvested for between 15 and 50 years before they are returned to functioning wetlands where the sphagnum can regrow. In the 50 years that peat has been harvested there, about 2,000 acres of peat remain where harvesting has finished. Sources point out that one bog that was harvested until 1968 now has over 18 inches of sphagnum moss regrown on it.

Recent research conducted by the Canadian government and the peat industry indicates that the time it takes for a harvested peat bog to return to a functioning wetland on its own can be shortened from 15–20 years to 5–8 years by restoring the water table to its original level and establishing sphagnum regrowth on the bog. Current projects include transplanting live sphagnum plants, seeding spores of sphagnum taken from live plants, and covering the harvested bog with the top spit from a living bog.

Sphagnum peat moss is, undeniably, one of the best soil conditioners because it provides the right balance of air and water for plants to grow. It reduces the amount of water and nutrients needed to grow healthy plants and lawn. Its low pH makes it an ideal soil amendment for acid-loving plants. Peat moss, like compost, has the ability to loosen clay soil and bind sandy soil. It should always be premoistened and mixed thoroughly into the soil.

Although peat moss is harvested responsibly and with an eye to sustainable supply, gardeners may question whether it's worth all the effort (shipping from Canada to the United States, not to mention the fuel and energy that goes into harvesting, drying, and packaging), the expense, and as-yet-unknown impacts on the environment.

Do the benefits of peat moss outweigh environmental considerations? An equally good substitute is compost; however, most gardeners cannot make enough for their needs. Encouraging local municipalities to compost (leaves, grass clippings) for their population might be an alternative.

"Green Manure"

Using cover crops to provide "green manure" is an organic farming technique that can also be used in gardens, especially for large planting areas. Many organic vegetable gardeners use cover crops to protect and nourish an area left fallow; when dug back into the soil as green manure, they become a relatively inexpensive and efficient way to enrich the soil with organic material. A fast-growing cover crop also controls erosion and suppresses weed growth on cleared ground. Usually the cover crop is a grain or legume. After a season of growth (often over the winter), the crop is dug into the soil, where it decomposes and releases organic matter and nutrients.

Legumes make good cover crops because they are nitrogen-fixing, able to transfer atmospheric nitrogen to their roots and thus enriching the soil. White and crimson clover, large white lupine, fava beans, and winter vetch are common nitrogen-fixing cover crops. Grains such as winter rye, annual rye, winter wheat, winter barley, and

SOIL AMENDMENTS

Choose the best amendments for your soil type and problem from the list below. Generally, if you're buying a prepackaged amendment, a standard 2¼-cubic-foot bagful will cover a 9-square-foot area with 3" of amendment. (Poor soil may require amending up to 50% of the total soil volume.) Always mix amendments thoroughly into the top 8"–12" of soil.

AMENDMENT	EFFECTS ON CLAY SOIL	EFFECTS ON SANDY SOIL
ORGANIC		
Compost	Loosens soil; improves drainage when thoroughly mixed into soil.	Adds texture and volume to soil; contains nutrients.
Humus	Improves soil aeration; allows better penetration of water.	Retains water and soluble nutrients.
Canadian sphagnum peat moss	Allows water and air to circulate freely in soil.	Absorbs water, adding moisture-retentive quality to soil.
Manure	Loosens soil; improves drainage when thoroughly mixed into soil.	Adds texture and volume to soil; contains nutrients.
Leaf mold	Excellent source of nutrients for any impoverished soil. Helps improve soil structure. (Can decompose so rapidly that its nutritional value is short-lived.)	
Organic planting mix	Loosens soil. (Effective only in large amounts—⅓ to ½ of total soil volume.)	Improves texture; adds valuable nutrients.
Ground bark (also sawdust)	Not recommended for clay soil.	Adds texture and volume; decomposes slowly. Should be used in combination with nitrogen-rich fertilizer.
Mushroom compost	Same effects as those listed for compost, but should not be used in areas where acid-loving plants will be grown. Its alkalinity can be offset with the addition of sulfur. Inexpensive in areas where mushroom-growing industry thrives.	
Seaweed	Not recommended for clay soil.	Valuable as a soil conditioner; helps to bind soil particles together. Contains useful trace elements and potassium. (Must be washed first to eliminate salt.)
INORGANIC		
Gypsum	Helps to create larger soil clumps from clay particles. Also provides necessary calcium and sulfur.	Not recommended for sandy soil.
Vermiculite	Not recommended for clay soil.	Improves aeration and moisture retention.
Sand	Improves aeration and drainage problems; should be combined with organic amendment for fertility. Use builder's sand, not beach sand unless rinsed clean of salt.	Not recommended for sandy soil.
Superabsorbent polymers	Not recommended for clay soil.	Increase moisture retention. (Can be expensive; best used in container plantings.)

oats can be used to introduce organic matter into the soil. Seeding a grain and legume together (clover and barley, for example) offers the advantages of nitrogen-fixing from the legume and rich organic matter from the grain.

Cover crops are usually planted during one season so the soil will be enriched for the following one. White clover and winter rye, for instance, can be sown in vegetable plots after fall harvest, left to grow for the winter, and turned under in early spring before it's time to plant. If the crop is very moist, allow it to dry out for a few days before digging it under. Dig the crop down to a depth of 6"–8". Wait 7–10 days after digging in a legume crop and two weeks after digging in a grain crop before replanting. This waiting time is necessary because the soil organisms that decompose the cover crop tie up the nitrogen, which will prevent seeds from germinating and transplants from becoming established.

BOOSTING PLANT NUTRIENTS

When your soil fails to keep up with the nutritional demands of your plants, you may have to provide supplemental nutrients in the form of fertilizers. Most general fertilizers contain the essential elements nitrogen, phosphorus, and potassium. If all three of these nutrients are present, the fertilizer is said to be "complete." The percentage of each is listed on the fertilizer bag as a series of three numbers, representing the percentage of each element in the order N-P-K. For example, a fertilizer labeled 10-20-10 contains 10% nitrogen, 20% phosphorus, and 10% potassium. What's important is the ratio of the elements, since some plants may require a higher amount of one element than another. Thus a fertilizer labeled 10-20-10 contains twice the amount of phosphorus as it does nitrogen or potassium.

In addition to the primary nutrients, the

Applying too much fertilizer can cause plants to "burn." In this case, your only recourse is to water heavily and repeatedly in order to dissolve and wash away as much of the fertilizer as possible. To avoid such problems, be sure to read the label directions and follow them exactly.

secondary nutrients—magnesium, calcium, and sulfur—as well as traces of iron, zinc, copper, manganese, boron, chlorine, and molybdenum need to be present for plants to be healthy.

Even a well-amended organic garden may fail to deliver ample nutrients to meet the demands of a particular plant. The primary nutrients are so named as they are the ones plants need in greatest amounts and need replenishing most often. Most soils contain adequate amounts of the secondary nutrients, which therefore need replenishing less often. Plants require minuscule amounts of the trace elements, so they rarely have to be added to well-balanced soil amended with plenty of organic matter. However, unless you rotate your crops, the soil may become deficient as certain plants (tomatoes and roses are both heavy feeders) deplete the mineral stores.

Remember, fertilizers should never be considered a substitute for organic soil amendments. Fertilizers are appropriate for feeding plants but not for improving the soil. Soil that is fertilized and not amended can become inert and dead, devoid of microorganisms, forcing you to supply the essential nutrients year after year for your plants merely to survive.

Natural vs. Synthetic Fertilizers

Fertilizers fall into two categories: natural (from animal and plant wastes or minerals) and synthetic (man-made). Natural fertilizers are good for plants and will not harm the soil. A synthetic fertilizer, on the other hand, while feed-

NATURAL FERTILIZERS

Complete natural fertilizers come prepackaged, but you can also make your own. For example, equal parts of blood meal and fish meal provide nitrogen; one part bonemeal with two parts rock or colloidal phosphate is high in phosphorus, and a small amount of kelp added to greensand supplies potassium. Mix together and you have a complete fertilizer.

FERTILIZER/N-P-K	USE
Blood meal 15-1.3-0.7	Quick-acting source of nitrogen. Good addition to compost pile to speed decomposition.
Bonemeal 2-14-0.2	Good slow-release source of phosphorus; also supplies calcium. Good for bulbs, fruit trees, flowers.
Colloidal phosphate 0-2-0	Source of phosphorus (18%–20% total phosphate) and calcium (23%).
Cottonseed meal 6-2.5-1.5	Acidifies soil. Good fertilizer for blueberries, citrus, azaleas. May be contaminated with pesticide residue; look for the words "certified pesticide-free."
Eggshells 1.2-0.4-.01	Contain calcium and trace minerals.
Epsom salts (Not N-P-K rated)	Good, water-soluble source of magnesium (10%) and sulfur (13%).
Feather meal 10-0-0	Slow-release source of nitrogen.
Fish emulsion 4-4-1	Liquid fertilizer can be applied to soil or as foliar feed.
Granite dust/meal 0-0-5	Slow-release source of potassium, silica, and 19 trace minerals.
Greensand (mined mineral deposit from seabeds) 0-0-7	Supplies potassium, silica, and 32 trace minerals.
Gypsum (Not N-P-K rated)	Good source of calcium (22%) and sulfur (17%). Lowers soil pH. Should not be applied if pH is below 5.8.
Hoof and horn meal 13-2-0	Good source of slow-release nitrogen.
Kelp meal (from dried, ground seaweed) 1-0.5-2.5	Good source of potassium, iron, trace minerals. Should be used sparingly since it contains growth hormones.
Limestone (calcitic) (Not N-P-K rated)	Raises soil pH. Good source of calcium (65%–80% calcium carbonate); lesser amount of magnesium (3%–15% magnesium carbonate).
Limestone (dolomitic) (Not N-P-K rated)	Raises soil pH. Balanced source of calcium (51% calcium carbonate) and magnesium (40% magnesium carbonate).
Oyster shells (Not N-P-K rated)	36% calcium and trace minerals (add to compost pile or directly into soil).
Rock phosphate 0-3-0	Insoluble; good source of phosphorus, especially in acidic soils. Contains 11 trace minerals.
Soybean meal 7.0-0.5-2.3	Good source of nitrogen. Inexpensive in areas of the country where soybeans are grown commercially.
Wood ash 0-1.2-2.0 (leached) 0-1.5-8.0 (unleached)	Good source of potassium. Leaching (running water through the ashes) removes caustic lye; less risk of burning plants if leached ash is used.
Worm castings 0.5-0.5-0.3	High in nutrients and microorganisms. Castings supply 50% organic matter and 11 trace minerals.

ing the plant, may be detrimental to the soil. Synthetic fertilizers release their nutrients quickly and must be reapplied frequently, taxing the soil. When using such fertilizers, do not allow direct contact with the plant or its roots; the end result may be burning rather than nourishment. Natural fertilizers, like manure, bonemeal, fish emulsion, and blood meal, release their nutrients gradually and contribute to the soil structure.

Wet and Dry Fertilizers

Whether natural or synthetic, fertilizers come in either liquid or dry form. Liquid fertilizers start working immediately upon application. These fertilizers are usually concentrated and need to be diluted before being administered with a watering can. Always water the soil first; never apply liquid fertilizer to dry soil. Foliar feeding, a method in which liquid fertilizer is sprayed directly onto the leaves, was once considered an emergency measure but today is used regularly, especially on hungry plants like annuals and vegetables.

Dry fertilizers, in powder, pellet, or granular form, can be applied by hand or with a spreader and worked into the top 2"–3" of soil with a rake. When water is added, dry fertilizers dissolve slowly, seep into the soil, and begin to work. Those in granular form must be kept off the foliage; otherwise, burning can occur. Always follow package instructions.

Some nutrients, like phosphorus and potassium, are best absorbed at the root zone. Surface application of dry fertilizers that contain these elements (bonemeal, blood meal, hoof and horn meal) are largely ineffective because the phosphorus, once dissolved, rarely gets past the top inch or two of soil and down to the roots. These dry fertilizers should be mixed into the soil at the bottom of the planting holes of trees, shrubs, perennials,

Manure tea turns dry, well-rotted manure into a liquid fertilizer. Wrap a shovelful of manure with several layers of cheesecloth, tie the ends closed with twine, and place the "tea bag" in a pail or bucket of water to steep overnight. (Some gardeners prefer strong tea, steeped up to a week.) Use the tea to give stressed plants a boost of nutrients or as a general fertilizer.

and bulbs to place the nutrients at root level.

Wood ash, which contains 70% calcium carbonate as well as potassium, phosphorus, and many trace nutrients, is best added to the compost pile rather than directly to the soil. It is extremely alkaline and, in any quantity, will raise the soil pH too high.

IN THE LAST ANALYSIS

Once you understand the relationship between healthy soil and flourishing plants, you recognize the immensely satisfying economy in gardening. If the soil is rich in nutrients from organic matter, and the texture of the soil is light and crumbly so that these nutrients can be readily absorbed by the plants, your garden will seem to grow with ease, returning in satisfaction and pleasure what you have offered it by providing the proper environment.

But since soil is alive, a biological site full of individual characteristics, you as the gardener need to restore any depletions that occur as your plants take nourishment. By working organic amendments into the soil and carefully monitoring your plants' nutritional needs, you can achieve the soil quality and thus the garden that will meet your expectations.

PLANTS JUST WANT *to* LIVE

L ike all living things, plants have amazing powers of survival, but sometimes they need a little outside help. Your role as a gardener is to learn all you can about the plants in your care—to recognize their needs and protect them in times of stress. By giving them the best chance in life, you become not only nature's ally but a recipient of her bounty as well.

Responsible gardeners understand the individual characteristics of plants and know how to choose those that will thrive under the conditions their garden offers. Given the proper environment and the benefit of wise preventive management, they will flourish and reward the hand that nurtures them.

Plants just want to live—all they need from you is a little encouragement.

PLANT BASICS

T he more you know about plants, the fewer mistakes you're likely to make and the better your garden will grow. An acquaintance with plant anatomy and physiology also makes the job of caring for plants easier and more gratifying. You don't need a Ph.D. in botany to know that plants require light, water, and nutrients, but you'll be a better steward of your garden if you fully understand their particular habits.

An Anatomy Lesson

Over the millennia, plants have evolved into ever more diverse and complex forms. Of the 260,000 known species, ranging in size and complexity from tiny mosses to giant redwood trees, only a small percentage are cultivated for food and the pleasure we derive from their beauty.

Most plants share the same anatomical characteristics in one form or another and have the same basic needs, with different ways of meeting them. In other words, an agave may not behave at all like an elm tree, but the same components are there.

ROOTS

Plant roots are responsible for absorbing water and dissolved minerals from the soil and conveying these nutrients to the stems and leaves. They also serve to anchor the plant in the soil, holding it upright against the pull of gravity and the force of wind.

Under normal conditions, roots push downward through the soil in search of moisture. A plant's first tiny root, or *radicle*, elongates during seed germination to form the primary root, which then sends out branching secondary roots to penetrate deeper into the soil. Surrounding the growing tips of these roots are nearly microscopic root hairs, which absorb the water and dissolved nutrients essential to the plant's growth. In direct contact with the molecules of soil, the root hairs greatly increase the roots' surface area and thus their capacity for absorption. They also help to retain contact between root tips and soil if the latter starts to dry and contract away from the roots. When moisture is available only near the surface, roots tend to spread horizontally rather than reaching deeper into the soil, and the plant is weakened.

Most annuals and many perennials have *fibrous roots,* which emerge in a dense mass from the base of the stem and branch in all directions. Some plants, such as Oriental poppies and dandelions, have a primary root called a *taproot,* significantly larger and longer than the surrounding secondary roots. Plants such as carrots, parsnips, and beets have *swollen taproots* that constitute an excellent food source for the plants themselves and for the animals that feed on them.

Adventitious roots grow in unusual or unexpected locations along the stem. Those near the base of a corn stem, for example, help to anchor the plant. Those that form higher up on a stem are called *aerial roots* and support or prop up the stem. Banyan and mangrove trees have aerial roots, as do some epiphytic orchids whose roots are modified for quick absorption of rainwater that flows over the bark of the host plants. The aerial roots of clinging vines attach themselves to vertical surfaces. *Tuberous roots,* or root tubers, like those of dahlias, develop from adventitious roots. They are swollen roots, modified for food

storage, and last only one year; the next year's roots do not grow from the old tubers.

Roots grow in temperatures above 45°F. In mild climates, they grow all year round; in cold climates, they go dormant in winter. Generally, the roots of a plant have as much volume below ground as the rest of the plant has above ground and can extend as far out as the ends of the branches. During times of drought, the fine secondary roots (and the root hairs) that grow in the top 6"–8" of soil can die quickly, leaving the plant dependent on its deepest roots. Too little water for a plant that has not yet established a deep, robust root system often sounds a death knell.

Success in planting or transplanting depends heavily on how much care and attention the roots receive. When digging up a plant, the root ball must remain intact and be replanted quickly so that sun, wind, and air will not dry out the roots, killing them with startling rapidity. Plants with taproots are often difficult to transplant because if the root is severed, the plant will die (not true of dandelions, however, which can regrow from pieces of the taproot left in the ground). Plants with fibrous roots are likelier to survive transplanting because it's easier to dig them up without damage to the roots. During planting or transplanting, keeping the roots in intimate contact

COMMON ROOT TYPES

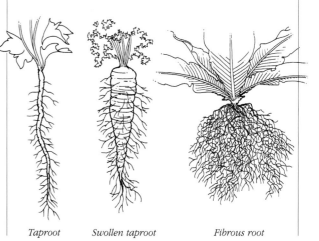

Taproot   Swollen taproot   Fibrous root

RHIZOMES, CORMS, AND TUBERS

Often perceived as roots, these swollen underground stems are actually food-storage organs that also serve to reproduce the plant vegetatively. A *rhizome* is a fleshy stem that grows horizontally below the soil level. Roots grow from its lower portion, and shoots rise from the upper portion. Rhizomes, unlike roots, have nodes, buds, and tiny leaves. They do not die when they are cut; replanted, they yield new plants. Bearded iris is an example of a plant that grows from a rhizome. A *corm* is rounded and thick, producing buds on its upper surfaces and roots from the lower. Gladiolus and crocus are corms. A *stem tuber,* such as a potato or tuberous begonia, is distinguished by buds, or "eyes." The young plants that develop from the buds are nourished from the stored starches in the tubers until they are mature enough to develop root systems and leaves and to perform photosynthesis.

UNDERGROUND STEMS

Gladiolus corm

Bearded iris rhizome

Tuberous-rooted dahlia

Tuberous begonia stem tuber

Narcissus bulb

with the soil is of utmost importance. Avoid air pockets in the hole, and be sure there are no exposed roots on the surface.

STEMS

Roots and stems meet at the crown, or base of the plant. While supporting its leaves, flowers, and fruits, stems also serve the plant by providing channels through which water and nutrients travel to the leaves and dissolved food is transported from the leaves to all other plant parts. This vascular system comprises two different kinds of cell layers: xylem cells deliver water and nutrients, while phloem cells carry nourishment from the leaves to the stems, roots, and storage and reproductive organs. Xylem cells also store food and help to support the plant.

According to the makeup of their stems, plants are referred to as either *herbaceous* or *woody*. Herbaceous plants have soft stems; most die down to the ground each winter. Woody plant stems bear buds that can survive the winter aboveground; these small swellings give rise to new growth (stems or branches, leaves or flowers) in the spring. Growing points called meristems are located either at stem and root tips (apical meristems), where they are responsible for the primary or vertical growth of plants, or on the sides of stems and roots (lateral meristems), where they are responsible for secondary plant growth. Lateral meristems produce the bark and wood in woody plants. Bark contains phloem cells and acts as a protective outer covering, preventing damage and water loss.

True bulbs, such as those of onion, hyacinth, tulip, and lily plants, are actually short underground stems bearing one or more buds enclosed and protected by fleshy overlapping leaves. Large reserves of food in the leaves keep the plant alive during periods when it's unable to make food for itself. Gardeners usually include rhizomes, corms, tubers, and tuberous-rooted plants such as dahlias in the general classification of bulbs.

Stems may be modified to serve other purposes. Thorns and bristles, for example, are useful against predators. In many cacti, the stems act as containers for water storage and may also carry out photosynthesis in the absence of true leaves. The tendrils of plants like Boston ivy and grapes allow the plants to grow and climb. Runners and stolons creep along the surface of the ground and take root, reproducing the plant vegetatively. Runners, such as those on mint plants, root at the nodes, the areas of the stem where buds are present. Stolons, like those on raspberry plants, root only at the tip.

LEAVES

Leaves grow along the stems or branches of plants, or in clumps at the base, connected by narrow *petioles,* or stalks; appendages called *stipules* are commonly present at the stem end of the petiole. Most leaves are green because they contain chlorophyll, the chemical compound that absorbs light and triggers the conversion of carbon dioxide and water into sugars. This food-making process, called photosynthesis, also relies on the small pores, or stomata, that let air (containing CO_2) into the leaves and allow residue oxygen and water to escape. Thus leaves not only provide sustenance for the plant but also exhale the oxygen so vital to other life on the planet.

Most leaves are arranged along the stem or branch in a consistent manner, either directly opposite each other or alternating (with one leaf on one side, the next leaf above it on the other side of the stem). Some leaves grow in rosettes at the base of the plant; some, like those of sweet woodruff, are whorled—with three or more leaves arising at each node. Leaves may be either simple (single) or compound (composed of smaller leaflets like those of roses).

The shape and veining of leaves, and their

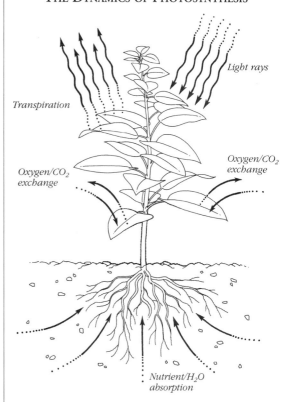

THE DYNAMICS OF PHOTOSYNTHESIS

Light rays

Transpiration

Oxygen/CO$_2$ exchange

Oxygen/CO$_2$ exchange

Nutrient/H$_2$O absorption

In the presence of sunlight, water (taken up by the roots) and carbon dioxide (absorbed from the air by the leaves) are converted into food for the plant. Excess water and oxygen escape through leaf pores in the process of transpiration.

arrangement on the stem, are valuable in classifying and identifying plants; all members of the mint family (Lamiaceae), for example, have opposite leaves on square stems. Leaf texture can be distinctive: shiny and smooth like the leaves of a lemon tree, hairy like lamb's ears, wrinkled like *Rosa rugosa,* or heavily veined like hostas. Frequently a plant's botanical name makes reference to these characteristics.

Variegated leaves are characterized by patches, streaks, or marks of different-colored tissues. Most such leaves are green overlaid with white or cream colors; rarer, and sought after by many gardeners, are tricolor and other multicolor variegations—crimson, purple, orange, red, yellow, pink, apricot, burgundy, mauve—with varying shades and tints of green. Variegations can also take different forms

BASIC LEAF PATTERNS

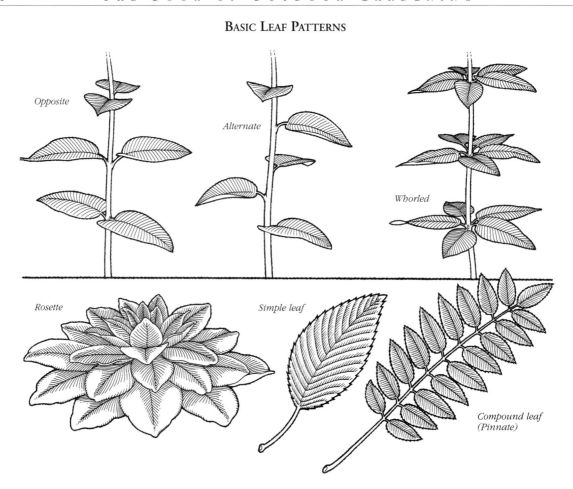

Opposite

Alternate

Whorled

Rosette

Simple leaf

Compound leaf (Pinnate)

on the leaf, including contrasting leaf edging (from narrow to wide, with a regular or irregular edge) and reverse edging (green edge with contrasting color in the center). Even without a single flower, plants with variegated leaves can add special eye-catching interest to the garden.

Like stems, leaves may have modified forms and functions. Some are spines, which protect against predators or, in the case of cacti, cut down on the water lost through transpiration. Succulent leaves, like those of aloes and jade plants, act as reservoirs, storing water for the plant to use in dry periods. Insectivorous plants, like Venus's-flytrap and pitcher plants, have highly modified leaves that trap and digest insects, providing needed nutrients. *Bracts* are also modified leaves, whose bright colors and petal-like shape draw

pollinators to otherwise small, unostentatious flowers like those of poinsettia and flowering dogwood.

Leaves commonly grow, fall off, and are replaced. Plants entering winter dormancy, notably deciduous trees, may lose all their leaves in autumn, remain leafless throughout the winter, and produce new foliage in spring and summer. Evergreens have leaves that stay on the tree year round, although individual leaves may last only a single growing season and drop intermittently. Conifers, or cone-bearing trees, have simple needle-like or scale-like leaves; most are evergreen (exceptions include larches and the dawn redwood). Broad-leaved evergreens like hollies and rhododendron add a touch of green to the stark landscape of winter.

FLOWERS AND REPRODUCTION

The anatomy of a flower, coupled with its appearance and scent, reveals its vital role in producing future generations of plants. The *petals* are the most visible portion of the flower, designed to attract pollinators to the plant and even provide them with a resting place. *Sepals,* usually green in color, surround the outer petals and help to support them; in a flower's earliest stages, they serve to protect the vulnerable bud. (In certain plants, like daylilies, the sepals are indistinguishable from the petals.) *Stamens* (male) and *pistils* (female) grow inside the corolla formed by the petals. Stamens produce pollen, often visible at the top portion, or anther, of each filament; pistils contain the plant's seed-making ovary and are topped by a sticky portion called the stigma, which receives pollen grains.

Most flowering plants have both stamens and a pistil in each flower, but more often than not pollen from one plant winds up on the pistil of another plant's flower. On a *monoecious* plant, such as winter hazel, some flowers produce only female cells while others produce only male cells. The flowers of a *dioecious* plant, such as holly, skimmia, or a ginkgo tree, are one sex only—either all female or all male. Generally, one male plant of the same genus will provide ample pollen for female plants within a range of several hundred feet. However, some plants in this category, such as Meserve, or "blue" hollies, require a specific pollinator; for example, only a Meserve 'Blue Prince' can fertilize a Meserve 'Blue Princess.'

Whether attracted by color, shape, or smell, various insects—bees, butterflies, moths, ants, and flies—as well as hummingbirds and bats visit flower after flower and drink their nectar. Along the way, pollen grains are carried on their bodies from anther to pistil, where, if all goes well, they release male cells that will fertilize eggs in the ovary. (Many trees and some flowers rely instead on the wind to carry their pollen.) After fertilization, the flower petals fade in color and fall off. The energy of the plant is then transferred from flowering into forming seed. The ovary swells and ripens into the fruit that holds the seed and the promise of a new generation.

The seed-bearing fruit, like pollen, must be transported away from the parent plant to a place where germination can take place. Left to themselves, most fruits will ripen and open, releasing their seeds. Many fruits are eaten as food and the seeds discarded; birds and other animals usually eat seeds with the fruit, eventually excreting them often far away from the parent plant. Rodents hide and bury nuts in their burrows. Some seeds, such as those of clematis and dandelions, are carried by the wind; others, such as those of sandbur, tickseed, and foxtail,

VEGETATIVE REPRODUCTION

Some plants reproduce by vegetative (asexual) methods, i.e., with no interchange of genetic material. Blackberry plants, for example, send out runners that develop roots and shoots of their own, becoming separate from the parent plant. Other plants, such as ivy, root at the nodes of stems lying on the ground. Still others, such as rhododendron, will root where branches touch moist soil. Some lilies, such as tiger lily, form tiny *bulbils* between the stem and the leaf; other bulbs, such as daffodils, form *bulblets* underground next to the main bulb. Succulent or semi-succulent plants, such as sedum or geranium, will grow new plants from broken stems where there is loose, moist soil to encourage rooting. Gardeners take advantage of these asexual methods of reproduction to increase the number of plants in the garden.

BASIC PLANT ANATOMY

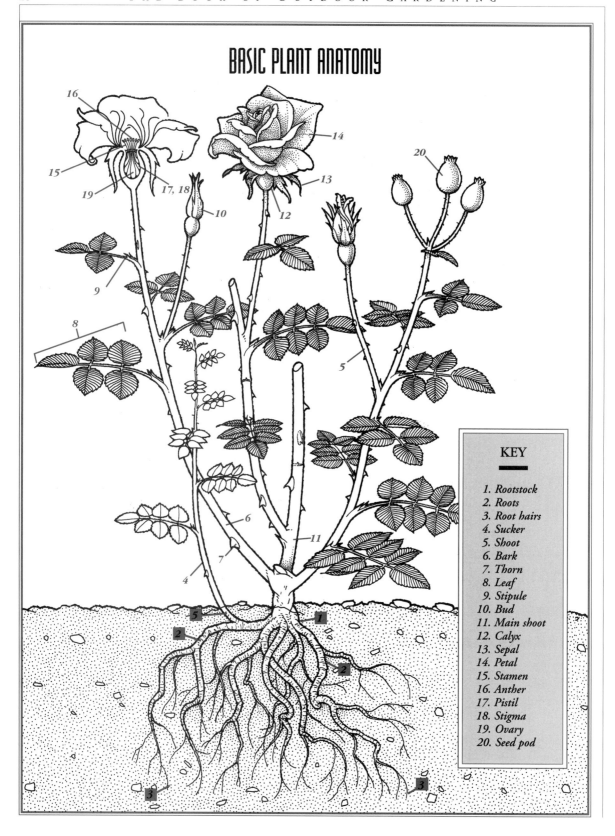

KEY

1. Rootstock
2. Roots
3. Root hairs
4. Sucker
5. Shoot
6. Bark
7. Thorn
8. Leaf
9. Stipule
10. Bud
11. Main shoot
12. Calyx
13. Sepal
14. Petal
15. Stamen
16. Anther
17. Pistil
18. Stigma
19. Ovary
20. Seed pod

HYBRIDS AND HEIRLOOMS

Breeders produce *hybrid plants* by means of controlled cross-pollination, in which one variety of a species is chosen to provide pollen to another variety of the same species. The seeds that develop contain genes from both parent plants and grow into plants known as F_1 (first-generation) hybrids. Frequently, plant breeders use hybridization to control various plant characteristics; they attempt to develop plants that are more colorful, have higher disease resistance, or produce larger and more abundant fruit than either parent. F_1 hybrids often have what is referred to as "hybrid vigor," or healthier, more robust growth than their parents. However, seeds saved from F_1 hybrids will not "breed true," or reliably produce the same plant.

Heirloom plants are time-tested, open-pollinated varieties, primarily of European descent, whose seeds have been passed down from grower to grower for at least 50 years. Heirlooms are the repository of the unusual characteristics such as color and flavor that contribute to genetic biodiversity. For this reason and others, including vigor and local hardiness, they have become garden favorites. Every fall, heirloom growers harvest the seeds from these valuable cultivars in order to ensure their survival for yet another season.

hitchhike on passing animals. Still others, like apples, nasturtiums, and four-o'clocks, simply fall to the ground. One of the largest seeds, the coconut, can be carried by water to a new home.

By any of these means, and with luck, a seed can find its way to fertile ground where it germinates, sprouts, and ultimately develops into a mature plant. In the garden, this is often made apparent by the many surprises that spring up in newly cultivated or mulched soil—seedlings of cultivated plants and pesky weeds alike.

The Importance of Light and Temperature

Plants thrive in varying degrees of sunlight and temperature, and it's up to individual gardeners to choose those that will grow happily in the amounts of each to be had in their particular gardens. Most plants do better in plenty of sunlight than in deep shade and prefer warmer temperatures to extremes.

SUN AND SHADE

In garden books, catalogs, and seed packets, sunlight typically comes in one form: full sun. But the implications of "full sun" vary with location and climate and are worth investigating. Generally, "full sun" means at least six hours of direct summer sun between the hours of 10 A.M. and 6 P.M. Early morning sun (sunrise to 10 A.M.) and late afternoon sun (3 P.M. to sunset) are less intense than midday sun (10 A.M. to 2 P.M.). In the warmest climates, where midday sun can easily scald leaves and sunburn young tree trunks, trees placed to filter or block the sun at high noon create welcome shade for the garden. In climates characterized by summer rain, the combination of lower summer temperatures (which reduce transpiration and moisture lost from soil evaporation), high humidity (which also reduces transpiration), cloud cover (which reduces the intensity of light), and ample soil moisture allows many more plants to grow in full sun without burning or wilting.

Intensity of light is also determined to a large extent by latitude. Sunlight is more intense

SELECTED PLANTS FOR SUNNY OR SHADY SITES

FOR SUN

ANNUALS

Corn poppy (*Papaver rhoeas* 'Mother of Pearl')

Dusty miller (*Senecio cineraria*)

Flossflower (*Ageratum houstonianum* 'Pinky Improved')

Flowering maple (*Abutilon × hybridum*)

Prickly poppy (*Argemone polyanthemos*)

Sweet sultan (*Amberboa moschata* Imperialis series)

PERENNIALS

Baby's breath (*Gypsophila paniculata*)

Black-eyed Susan (*Rudbeckia fulgida* Goldsturm strain)

Blanket flower (*Gaillardia × grandiflora* 'Burgundy')

Butterfly weed (*Asclepias tuberosa*)

Catmint (*Nepeta × faassenii* 'Six Hills Giant')

Lanceleaf coreopsis (*Coreopsis lanceolata*)

Maltese cross (*Lychnis chalcedonica*)

Purple coneflower (*Echinacea purpurea*)

Variegated Adam's needle (*Yucca filamentosa* 'Variegata')

Yarrow (*Achillea millefolium* 'Summer Pastels')

FOR SHADE

ANNUALS

Browallia (*Browallia speciosa* 'Blue Bells')

Forget-me-not (*Myosotis sylvatica*)

New Guinea impatiens (*Impatiens hawkeri*)

PERENNIALS

Fringed bleeding heart (*Dicentra eximia* 'Snowdrift')

Hosta (*Hosta sieboldiana* 'Frances Williams')

Japanese primrose (*Primula japonica*)

Lady's mantle (*Alchemilla mollis*)

Shooting star (*Dodecatheon meadia*)

Wild sweet William (*Phlox divaricata*)

Willow-leaved gentian (*Gentiana asclepiadea*)

FERNS

Hay-scented fern (*Dennstaedtia punctilobula*)

Japanese painted fern (*Athyrium goeringianum* 'Pictum')

Maidenhair fern (*Adiantum pedatum*)

FOR SUN OR SHADE

ANNUALS

Foxglove (*Digitalis purpurea* 'Alba')

Flowering tobacco (*Nicotiana sylvestris*)

Larkspur (*Consolida ambigua* Imperial series)

Pansy (*Viola × wittrockiana*)

Spiderflower (*Cleome hassleriana* 'Helen Campbell')

Sweet alyssum (*Lobularia maritima*)

PERENNIALS

Coral bells (*Heuchera* 'Palace Purple')

Giant rhubarb (*Gunnera manicata*)

Goatsbeard (*Aruncus dioicus*)

Great blue lobelia (*Lobelia siphilitica*)

Hardy geranium (*Geranium* 'Johnson's Blue')

Japanese anemone (*Anemone × hybrida* 'Honorine Jobert')

Milky bellflower (*Campanula lactiflora*)

Monkshood (*Aconitum carmichaelii* var. *wilsonii*)

Wild bergamot (*Monarda fistulosa* 'Violet Queen')

All plants listed here appear in the Plant Guide, pages 276–479.

in the American Southwest than in the North-east, less intense in Seattle than in Los Angeles. A plant that grows in full sun in upstate New York may prefer midday shade in Texas, and vice versa. Latitude also affects the amount of light plants receive per day. "Short-day" plants, such as dahlias and others native to the low altitudes of the tropics, are adapted to about 12 hours of light per day all year long; in more temperate (northern) areas, these plants will bloom only when the days begin to shorten as summer fades into autumn. On the other hand, delphiniums and other "long-day" plants native to higher lat-itudes, where day length varies significantly with the seasons, are adapted to as much as 20 hours of daylight in summer. Gardeners who live in the lower latitudes of the Deep South find that "long-day" plants will not bloom—the day just isn't long enough to trigger flowering. Growers of onions may be familiar with this distinction: short-day onions such as 'Granex' (the famed Vidalia onion) are best suited to Southern gar-dens, while long-day onions like 'Sweet Spanish' thrive in the North.

Plants whose leaves are efficient at absorbing carbon dioxide from the air are termed "sun-loving" plants. Sunlight triggers flowering in these plants, such as ox-eye daisies, and when grown in too much shade they will have fewer flowers. They may also become leggy, with fewer leaves spaced farther apart as they reach for the sun. Plants that are slower to absorb carbon diox-ide derive less benefit from sunlight because their rate of photosynthesis is correlated with the rate at which they absorb CO_2 rather than with the amount of available light. In the garden, such plants are designated "shade-loving" or "shade-tolerant." Many of these plants have adapted, through millennia of growing in an understory, to growing in less light.

Six hours of sun per day, or lightly dappled shade throughout the sunlight hours, is termed *light shade* and is typical of locations under high-

REFLECTED LIGHT

White stucco walls, concrete patios, and side-walks reflect light and heat. Depending on the season and time of day, they can either function as a sun trap, making it possible to grow tender plants that otherwise might not survive the climate, or turn the area into an oven that bakes plants to a crisp. Water also reflects light, so plants growing along a semishaded stream bank or at the edge of a pond often get more light than it would appear from simply tracking the number of hours of direct sun.

branching trees where light is plentiful but lower in intensity than full sun. In warm climates, light shade can be better than full sun because plants are less likely to dry out or to get scorched or sunburned in the heat of the day. Light shade gives the widest range of plant material to choose from, including most sun-loving plants and many plants that will grow in more shade.

Partial or *half shade* (medium shade, semi-shade) means less sun, usually four to six hours a day, or a heavier dappled shade during the day. In partial shade, plants receive some direct sun, but not all day long and none at midday. Ferns, early bulbs, and plants native to a woodland understory do well in partial shade. *Full* or *dense shade* denotes less than four hours of sun a day or heavily dappled sunlight all day. This is often the shade cast by conifers, or the shade on the north side of a building. It can be difficult to grow plants in full shade, so look to mosses and some ground covers for such areas.

Thus it is not a simple matter of sun or no sun. All green plants need light because it is essential for the process of photosynthesis. Plants won't grow in complete darkness—unless they're mushrooms.

A GARDEN LEGEND

✴

CLAUDE MONET'S IMPRESSIONIST LANDSCAPE

A trip to Giverny, Claude Monet's gardens outside Paris, is like diving into an Impressionist painting. One is struck less by the individual plants and flowers than by the unrestrained—even anarchic—mass of light and color.

> *"I perhaps owe having become a painter to flowers."*

First-time visitors to Giverny will likely recognize its gardens from Monet's (1840–1926) prolific paintings of them. Both the Clos Normand flower garden—nearly three acres, including the crowning row of arched, rose-smothered trellies—and the water-lily garden with its wisteria-woven arched footbridge have the friendliness of familiarity.

Though casual in appearance, Monet's copious plantings were carefully chosen for their paint-ability rather than horticultural rarity (with no fear of clashing hues or common origin) and arranged with precision to catch the morning light or soften into the long afternoon shadows. Beds overflow with flowers from field and cottage—tulips and for-get-me-nots, sunflowers and irises, poppies, rambling roses, lupines, coral dahlias, cosmos, bluebells, carpets of nasturtiums, hollyhocks, scarlet poppies, daylilies, and on and on.

Today, in an age that resists

both formality and conformity, Monet's greatest legacy may be the freedom he granted garden-ers to experiment, to break rules, to choose plant materials based on personal vision rather than prevailing fashion.

THE RIGHT TEMPERATURE

Besides knowing whether a plant is sun- or shade-loving, you must know the temperature range in which the plant thrives in order to decide whether or not you can grow it in your garden. The USDA plant hardiness zone map (see page 480) is a great guide in helping you choose the right plants for your area. Originally developed by the Department of Agriculture to help farmers figure out which crops would do best under the different climatic conditions of the continental United States, this widely used map divides the United States and Canada into 11 regions based on the lowest average temperature, from zone 1 (subarctic) to zone 11 (subtropical). Cold is not the only factor to be considered in plant selection (rainfall, snowfall, and the number of hours of light are also significant), but it is the crucial factor for one reason: cold kills. How much cold a plant will endure determines its hardiness. A zonal designation indicates that the

plant is hardy throughout that zone. Climates tend to overlap and the lines of separation are not as clear-cut as implied here. Many plants recommended for one zone will do well in the southern part of the adjoining colder zone and in the colder portion of the next warmer zone.

Using the hardiness zone map as a guide, gardeners can determine, in an average year, when to plant tender plants (those that will not tolerate temperatures below freezing) outdoors in the spring with reasonable assurance that they won't be killed by frost. By June 1, the North American continent is frost-free, except at high elevations, including the Rocky Mountains, Sierras, and northern Canada. By December 1, the entire United States is susceptible to freezing weather, except for the warmest parts of Florida, Texas, the Pacific coast, and Hawaii.

Even if a plant is hardy in a particular zone, however, it may not grow as anticipated if summer temperatures are too high, the days are substantially shorter, or rainfall is significantly less

DROUGHT-TOLERANT PLANTS

An area of high ground with a southern exposure is apt to be quite dry (especially in summer), as is any spot with unamended sandy soil. Drought-tolerant plants are the best choice for such places (as well as the perennially dry regions of the Southwest, California, and the Rockies). These plants have fleshy, water-retaining roots or other adaptations that allow them to thrive in dry periods when other plants would wilt. Leaves can be thick and succulent, waxy, hairy, gray or silver-colored; because they reflect light, they do not absorb as much heat from the sun as dark-colored leaves and lose less water. Though drought-tolerant, these plants are often intolerant of moist conditions and may rot from too much watering or heavy summer rains.

Owing to water restrictions in many communities, the popularity of drought-tolerant plants is growing. Below is a list of recommended plants from the Plant Guide (pages 276–479). For additional suggestions, consult your local Cooperative Extension service or mail-order seed and plant catalogs where such plants are specifically denoted.

Daylilies (*Hemerocallis* spp.)
Eulalia grass (*Miscanthus sinensis*)
Purple coneflower (*Echinacea purpurea*)
Sage (*Salvia* spp.)
Stonecrops (*Hylotelephium* spp.)
Tickseed (*Coreopsis* spp.)
Yarrow (*Achillea millefolium*)

than typical for that zone. Everyone has heard tales of strawberries from Alaska's Mantanuska Valley that grow to the size of a fist and cabbages that grow to the size of footstools, thanks to days with nearly 24 hours of daylight.

Northerners, on the other hand, much admire the winter-blooming camellias that brighten Southern gardens, the flamboyant bougainvillea and long-blooming oleander that flourish in the sustained summer heat of southern California, and the tender bulbs like amaryllis and crinum lilies that need dry summers and mild winters to thrive and bloom outdoors year after year.

By observing the plants that flourish and the weather that is designated normal in a given area, gardeners can get an excellent idea of which plants can be counted on to do well and which will be stretched to their limits to survive. Obviously, wise gardeners use those that thrive in their hardiness zone.

The Need for Water

Water absorbed by a plant's roots carries nutrients up to its leaves, assists in photosynthesis, and transports food to other parts of the plant for storage. Thus, even in the richest soil, a plant will die if no water is available to its roots.

Most plants need at least an inch of water a week to survive. What nature does not provide, the gardener must supply. Some plants, like turf grass, have shallow roots that grow just below the soil's surface and need frequent watering. Others, like trees and many shrubs, are more deeply rooted and rarely require supplemental watering once they're established.

In judging the amount of supplemental water a plant needs, there are other factors besides rainfall to consider. New plantings require extra water until they are established. Temperature (the hotter the day, the more water plants need),

humidity (higher humidity means less watering), and the amount of wind (breezy weather dries plants out) all determine how much and how often supplemental water is needed. You should also know exactly how well watered your soil is. Even if the plant's foliage and the surface soil are wet, the soil may not be well watered. Water should enter the soil at a slow, steady rate in order to seep down into the soil, carrying moisture and also the nutrients held within the soil to the root system of each plant.

Several waterings of short duration, particularly during the heat of the day, will do great damage to a plant's root system. Since roots naturally seek out water, if only the top few inches of the soil are moist as a result of superficial watering, the roots are encouraged to remain close to the surface. In time, the plant forms a very shallow root system. This is most harmful for trees and shrubs, which are significantly weakened by shallow roots. Not only are these plants deprived of the nutrients they need, but they are also far more likely to be uprooted by strong winds.

Some plants, like Japanese iris, naturally prefer their roots to be anchored in consistently moist soil; others, like silver-leaved santolinas, do better with "dry feet." Still other plants, like many hostas, are easygoing and will adapt to dry or moist soil. A good way to conserve water is first to identify the soil conditions of your property and then to match plants to suit the conditions. Never assume the soil conditions are the same throughout your yard, since this is rarely the case. An area of high ground with a southern exposure is apt to be quite dry (especially in summer), while a low-lying area with an eastern exposure that is shaded most of the day by tall trees is likely to have moist soil.

Do a bit of research before you plant. A juniper that likes a dry, sunny location simply will not thrive in a low, wet spot. Nor will a clump of shade-loving, moisture-hungry ferns do well when planted

PLANTS FOR WET OR DRY GARDENS

If, like many gardeners, you find that your soil is too wet or too dry for what you had planned, you can amend the soil with plenty of organic matter and/or create raised or sunken beds. But a simpler, time- and energy-saving solution is to change your plans and include only plants that will thrive in your garden soil. Using a range of appropriate plants, you can create a garden that is more unique and just as lovely as your original designs. Moreover, choosing the right plant for the right place is environmentally responsible, saving one of our most valuable resources: water. Whether your soil is very moist or desperately dry, appropriate plants will require little, if any, supplemental watering.

PLANTS FOR WET GARDENS

Bergenia (*Bergenia cordifolia*)
Black chokeberry (*Aronia melanocarpa*)
Calla lily (*Zantedeschia* spp.)
Elderberry (*Sambuscus* spp.)
Japanese iris (*Iris ensata*)
Primrose (*Primula* spp.)*
Red maple (*Acer rubrum*)
Skunk cabbage (*Lysichiton americanus*)
Willow (*Salix* spp.)

XEROPHITIC PLANTS FOR DRY GARDENS

Beard-tongue (*Penstemon parryi*)
California poppy (*Eschscholzia californica*)
Coral vine (*Antigonon leptopus*)*
Desert evening primrose (*Oenothera deltoides*)
Mescal bean (*Sophora secundiflora*)
Ocotillo (*Fouquieria splendens*)
Peruvian verbena (*Verbena peruviana*)
Purple prickly pear (*Opuntia macrocentia*)

Included in the Plant Guide, pages 276–479.

ing for them. Group plants with similar water requirements in the same location; otherwise, if you mix thirsty plants with those that prefer dry conditions, you must opt to favor one at the other's expense.

Think of the different areas of your yard as mini-habitats. That high sunny spot might be ideal for a rock garden that showcases drought-resistant plants such as creeping phlox, fragrant dianthus, drifts of thyme, and sprawling sedum; tiny spring bulbs like netted iris and crocus also require very little water. A moist, shady spot would be ideal for a woodland garden filled with wild columbine, exotic toad lilies, Jack-in-the-pulpit, and Japanese painted fern; all these moisture-loving plants require less water and consequently less tending if you put them in an already moist spot.

Sometimes a low-lying area, particularly one with clay soil, collects water and becomes simply too wet for most plants, which would experience root rot in such an environment. You can try to change the soil (a lot of work) or simply accept the environment and work with it as best you can. If the soil is heavy clay, you might add peat moss and compost to create a bog. Grow plants that like to have "wet feet" and require constant moisture at the roots. These plants, which thrive in wet soil near streams and rivers, lakes and pools, include willows, alders, sedges, rushes, Japanese primrose, and pickerel weed. Such plants go into dormancy or die if they don't get enough water.

Most plants, however, are in the middle, requiring enough water to grow steadily but not so much that the roots drown. Grow them in a good, loamy soil enriched with organic material and they'll thrive. Plants that go into winter dormancy, which greatly reduces the need for water, would not be good choices in an area where winter is the main rainy season. Also, a plant that normally goes dormant in summer would not be happy in an area where summer

next to a swimming pool where the sun is reflecting off the water all day. Place your plants where they naturally want to be and you'll have less work car-

rainfall is the norm. Too much water when there's no need for it can rot the roots and cause the plant's demise.

Growth Patterns

Plants can be classified according to their growth patterns as annuals, biennials, or perennials. The term *herbaceous* (non-woody) refers chiefly to perennials but botanically applies to annuals and biennials as well. Bulbs and woody plants are classified as perennials in the technical sense but can also be grouped by form and specific habits.

ANNUALS

Annuals flower within a few months after their seeds are sown, produce a continuous show of color throughout one or more growing seasons, and die the same year, roots and all. As their blossoms fade, the seed ripens and is scattered, thus perpetuating the species. However, some plants that are grown and known as annuals in the Midwest and Northeast are, in fact, perennials in their warmer—possibly tropical—native habitats and will grow as perennials in the South and coastal West. Certain species of impatiens and pelargonium are familiar examples of plants grown as annuals in one region and as peren-

INFLORESCENCES, OR FLOWER CLUSTERS

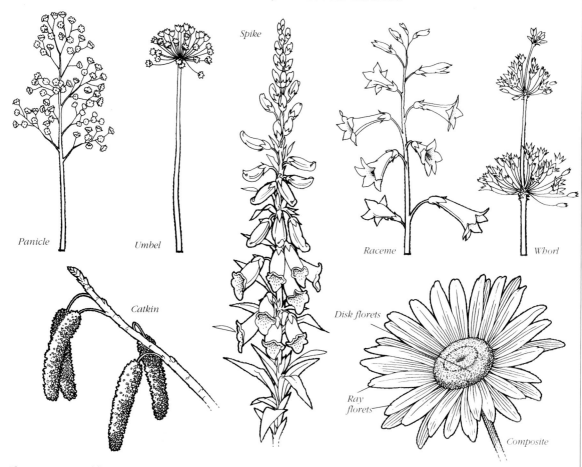

Panicle *Umbel* *Spike* *Raceme* *Whorl*

Catkin *Disk florets* *Ray florets* *Composite*

The arrangement of flowers on their stalks is an important element in plant classification. The large family Asteraceae, for example, includes asters, daisies, and other plants whose flowerheads consist of many small, tightly packed flowers that stand upright on a flat disk. This composite arrangement virtually ensures successful pollination and efficient propagation.

nials in another. Annuals are most often used to serve as bedding plants; fast-growing, they make good fillers between slow-growing perennials or shrubs.

Annuals are further defined by their tolerance to cold. *Tender annuals,* like nasturtiums and busy lizzies, die as soon as night temperatures fall to 32°F. These are also the stalwart plants of the summer garden that do not wilt on the hottest days (provided they have ample water). *Half-hardy annuals,* like cleome and nicotiana, can withstand a very slight drop below the freezing point and still hold their blooms. They will grow in cool, damp weather as well as the heat of the summer. *Hardy annuals,* like calendula and bachelor's button, however, can withstand repeated night temperatures of about 28°F. and bloom into the sun the next day. In Florida, along the Gulf Coast, and in the Southwest and parts of the Pacific Northwest, the flowers of these plants carry the garden through the winter into spring, when they are replaced with tender annuals. The seeds or seedlings of some hardy annuals, like pansies, can be sown directly outdoors in autumn (especially in mild winter areas) or in spring, as soon as the soil is sufficiently thawed. The seeds of half-hardy annuals and tender annuals should be sown outdoors only after all danger of frost is past.

BIENNIALS

The full growth span of biennials extends over two growing seasons; in other words, seeds sown directly in the soil one midsummer will germinate and develop into blooming plants the following year, produce seed, and then die. Although most biennials bloom only once in their lives, some may flower a second time but never with the showiness of their first appearance. In climates where winters are harsh, seeds sown directly in the garden in summer may grow into healthy plants by late autumn, only to be smitten and rotted by winter frosts; starting the seeds in

cold frames helps to protect them through the winter. Many biennials reseed themselves in the summer or autumn, so by the following year they are a year old and ready to bloom. Perhaps this is part of the confusion that causes biennials to be treated as annuals by some gardeners and as perennials by others. By far the most important thing about these plants is their showy presence. Such age-old garden favorites as foxgloves, hollyhocks, sweet William, and Canterbury bells are all biennials, as are many vegetables in the mustard family such as cauliflower, cabbage, and kale.

PERENNIALS

Perennials live and flower from the same roots year after year, although they usually have a shorter bloom season than that of most annuals. Some may rebloom later the same season if the stem is cut back after it finishes flowering. Technically speaking, perennials include the flowering ornamental plants that fill our flower borders, as well as winter-hardy bulbs, some vegetables and herbs, many vines, and grasses (including turf)—all of which have non-woody stems and are ranked as *herbaceous perennials.* Shrubs and some vines such as grapes are *woody perennials.*

Herbaceous perennials, such as lobelia, bee balm, and baby's breath, typically do not begin to look their best until their third year. The tender, fleshy green stems of these plants die down to the ground in autumn, while their roots rest below ground and winter over, gathering the strength and energy to send up new stems and new branches that will flower the following year. Unless growing conditions are less than favorable, the plants repeat this process year after year before becoming overcrowded (in which case you can divide them) or dying out. Many perennial plants let you know that they need dividing when they send up lush foliage but put on a poor show of flowers.

HOW BULBS GROW

Gardeners expect bulbs to come back year after year and to naturalize (multiply in the ground); however, many bulbs neither bloom reliably year after year nor increase their numbers unless very specific conditions are met. Many spring-blooming bulbs are best suited to colder climates because they require winter cold to rebloom.

Northern gardeners who dig up their tulips every spring and replant them in the fall should plant them 2" deeper than recommended—the bulbs will usually rebloom with no fuss. By contrast, many of the summer-blooming bulbs are not winter-hardy in northern gardens and must be either dug up and stored indoors over winter or treated as a one-time luxury.

Half-hardy perennials are on the cold-tender side, with degrees of frost tolerance ranging from minimal to almost frost-hardy. Not only do their stems and leaves die back in cold weather, but the roots may die as well. For best results, half-hardy perennials should be planted just before the last frost date in spring and mulched before a hard frost in autumn. In very cold areas, they may need to be dug up and overwintered indoors or else grown as annuals.

SHRUBS AND TREES

Considered the backbone of the garden, shrubs and trees provide the mass and density around which the rest of the garden can be created. They define spaces and sight lines, frame views, and to a large extent determine the scale of the garden.

By horticultural definition, shrubs are multistemmed woody plants that do not exceed 25' in height and produce branches at, near, or just above ground level. Whether early- or late-blooming, they perform essential functions such as screening out unattractive views, serving as windbreaks, or creating the very sense of enclosure that informs a particular garden. Trees are defined as single-trunked woody plants that usually grow at least 20' tall with branches starting some distance from the ground. However, there are many exceptions: Japanese maples may never reach 20'; saucer magnolia, stewartia, and mountain pine all tend to be multistemmed.

Shrubs and trees are classified as *deciduous* (those that lose their leaves in the fall and grow a fresh set in the spring) or *evergreen* (those that retain their leaves year round). Commonly the term "evergreen" is used as a synonym of "conifer," but not all evergreens are conifers and not all conifers are evergreen. Technically speaking, conifers are cone-bearing, needle-leaved trees such as pines, firs, and spruces; there are a few deciduous conifers, such as the bald cypress, that shed their leaves. Broad-leaved evergreens include English holly, bull bay magnolia, olive, and all citrus and palm trees.

All conifers are trees (none are herbaceous), and they are the world's biggest trees by far. Few broad-leaved trees exceed 180' in height, but quite a few conifers reach heights between 250' and 350'. While many trees can live for a century, some species of conifers commonly live a thousand years or more. Far more than any other act of garden-making, growing trees—of any kind—is a pledge of faith in the future.

VINES

Vines are climbing or trailing plants that must have support to grow vertically. They may be annual or perennial, herbaceous or woody, evergreen or deciduous. Vines can fit into the tiniest spaces (provided their roots are firmly anchored in the soil) and grow vertically and/or horizontally with great flexibility, amid dense vegetation, maximizing space in any garden.

Clinging vines can attach themselves almost anywhere by one of several means. Boston ivy has disklike suction cups that allow it to attach itself easily to almost any surface without damaging it. Climbing hydrangea, English ivy, creeping fig, wintercreeper, and trumpet vine, with their small, rootlike holdfasts, thrive growing up slightly rough surfaces like bricks, wood, or stone. For the gardener, the advantage of these self-clinging vines is that they will grow straight up a vertical surface effortlessly and require only minimal support to get started. They are a superb way to make undistinguished, unattractive, or downright ugly walls appear lovely.

Non-clinging vines have several distinct growth habits. Twining vines spiral their stems skyward around a support—a trellis, pole, string, or wire. Most require a fairly slim support; their turning-circle, as it were, is too narrow for them to climb a thick post. Twining vines curl either clockwise (to the right) or counterclockwise (to the left) by nature. Trying to persuade a right-curving vine to turn to the left is an exercise in futility and frustration; let it twine the way it wants to go.

Vines with twining tendrils wrap them around anything within reach—a wire support, other plants, or themselves. The tendrils grow straight until they touch something, then curl like corkscrews to grab on tight. Grapes and passionflowers have tendrils; clematis, kiwi, Dutchman's pipe, and morning glory have leaf stems that function as tendrils. Some vines, such as bougainvillea, climb by means of hooked thorns but still need additional support and plant ties to be kept within the bounds of order.

Other plants grown as vines have no natural means for climbing and must be tied to or interwoven on a support. They develop long, flexible stems that cast about for something to lie on and are described as scandent, trailing, rambling, or scrambling. A scandent plant is inclined to grow upward; a trailing plant will grow down, over, or out in the process of seeking light. Trailing vines are particularly beautiful draped over high walls. Climbing roses are ramblers; canary creeper is a scrambler.

DORMANCY

Dormancy is a phase of temporary plant inactivity, a resting period for plants during which they usually have neither leaves nor flowers. Not all plants go dormant, but many shrubs, trees, vines, perennials, and bulbs do. The process includes the slowing down of the plant's metabolism and the storage of food in its roots. With the coming of spring, the stored food is drawn upon as the plant breaks dormancy and the leaves break bud. Winter dormancy is common in cold-winter climates. Deciduous hardwood trees such as elms, lindens, and maples, shrubs such as viburnum, hydrangea, and lilac, and perennials such as peonies and astilbe all lose their leaves for the winter and sprout anew in spring.

CHOOSING THE RIGHT PLANTS

Given the vast variety of plants available commercially as well as privately (at local plant sales, from botanical gardens, or swapped over the garden gate), choosing the right ones for your garden can be a daunting enterprise. However, if you approach plant selection with a clear idea of what types of plants you want (annual or perennial, vine, shrub, or tree, deciduous or evergreen), how your garden site meets their needs (type of soil, amount of sun and shade, rainy or dry environment), how much time you want to spend tending them (watering, pruning, deadheading), the problem of choosing becomes far easier.

Botanical Names

The common names of plants, engaging as they may be, are not enough to identify them specifically for gardening purposes. For instance, "daisy" can refer to an English daisy (a name used in the United States, not in England), an African daisy (known as such in America, but not in English-speaking areas of Africa), a Transvaal daisy (also known as African daisy), a seaside daisy, an ox-eye white daisy, or any of a number of other plants. Common names may vary from one region to another, and certainly from country to country. One plant may have a variety of common names; one common name may also refer to a variety of plants. The name gillyflower, for example, has been applied to three unrelated plants—clove pink, wallflower, and white stock—whose one similarity is their intense fragrance.

Botanical names resolve this confusion. The Swedish botanist Carolus Linnaeus (1707–1778) created the now universally accepted system of binomial nomenclature, classifying all plants by their common characteristics into genus and species. Using this system, one can see that no connection exists, in botanical terms, between the above-named daisies (recognized the world over as, respectively, *Bellis perennis, Arctotis acaulis, Gerbera aurantica, Erigeron glaucus,* and *Leucan-themum vulgare,* formerly *Chrysanthemum leucanthemum*). The first part of a botanical name designates the genus (always capitalized and in italics) to which the plant belongs. A genus is the smallest natural group with similar characteristics that contains related yet distinct species; genera do not normally interbreed. *Callicarpa, Aloysia, Caryopteris, Lantana, Verbena,* and *Vitex* are all genera within Verbenaceae (the vervain family). The second part of the name gives the species (all lowercase and in italics), a group of plants within a genus that have common characteristics. Members of one species have distinct attributes that breed true from generation to

generation, reliably duplicating the parent plant when grown from seed. *Verbena bonariensis, V. rigida, V. tenera, V. peruviana,* and *V. canadensis* are all species of vervain.

Plant names may also indicate varieties and cultivars. A variety is a naturally occurring variation that differs in one or more characteristics from the plant species to which it belongs. It will usually breed true, but may revert back to the original species characteristics. *Verbena tenuisecta* var. *alba* is a white-flowered variety of moss vervain. A cultivar (short for cultivated variety and always written within single quotes) is the offspring of two plants of the same species or variety that mankind has bred to produce some desirable characteristic. The seed collected from a cultivar will not grow to produce reliable offspring. Cultivars, however, can be propagated from cuttings or by division. *Verbena rigida* 'Alba' is a white-flowered cultivar of vervain, while the lilac-flowered cultivar is *V. rigida* 'Lilacina.'

A final important distinction is made for hybrid plants, the result of crossbreeding two different species or varieties. Hybrids may be sterile; even if not, they will not reliably breed true. Hybrids between two species are indicated by a multiplication sign. *Verbena × hybrida,* a cross between *Verbena peruviana* and another verbena species, represents many of the modern garden verbenas. Rarely, a hybrid is a cross of two different genera; in the case of X *Fatshedera,* for example, crossbreeding *Fatsia* and *Hedera* created a new, hybrid genus.

Under the International Rules of Nomenclature, the botanical name of standing is determined the first time a plant is described and named in published form. Unfortunately, it sometimes happens that several people find, describe, and name a plant—and they don't all give the plant the same name. Moreover, botanical taxonomists don't always agree on a plant's nomenclature. In this book our references include the Royal Horticultural Society, the

DESCRIPTIVE LATIN TERMS

Often botanical names refer to a particular part of a plant, describing its flower, leaf, or stem characteristics, or impart information about the plant's size or shape. Sometimes the name lets you know a plant's growth pattern or where it originated and what climate it prefers. Familiarity with some basic Latin terms enables you to choose plants for your garden on a knowledgeable basis and helps to eliminate surprises when they reach their maturity.

SIZE/APPEARANCE/TEXTURE

alatus: winged
albus: white
arborescens: treelike, woody
argenteus: silvery
atro-: dark
aurantifolius: golden-leaved
aureolus: golden
aureus: golden
azureus: azure, sky-blue
candicans: white, hoary
candidus: pure white
cardinalis: red
carneus: flesh-colored
cereus: waxy
chryso-: golden
citrinus: lemon yellow
coccineus: scarlet
columnaris: upright
cristatus: crested
cyan-: blue
elatus: tall
erectus: upright
erio-: woolly
flavus: yellow
fulvus: tawny
glabra: smooth
griseus: gray
hirtis: hairy
imperialis: regal, tall
lacta-: milky white
laevis: smooth
leptocaulis: thin-stemmed
leuco-: white
melano-: black

meleagris: speckled (like a guinea fowl)
minimus: very small
mollis: soft
mucosus: slimy
multicaulis: multi-stemmed
muscosis: mossy
nanus: dwarf
niger: black
nitidus: shining
nivalis: white
pallidus: pale
papillosus: with warty protuberances
parvulus: very small
parvus: small
pubescens: downy
pumilis: dwarf
purpurascens: becoming purple
purpureus: purple
roseus: rosy
ruber: red
versicolor: varicolored
virens: green
xantho-: yellow

FLOWER TYPE

asteroides: aster-like
botryoides: clustered
brachyanthus: short-flowered
floribundus: free-flowering
oxypetalus: sharp-petaled
stellata: starry

LEAF TYPE

acaulis: stemless
alternifolius: alternate leaves
angustifolius: narrow-leaved
brevifolius: short-leaved
latifolia: broad-leaved
leptocaulis: thin-stemmed
lobularis: lobed
longispinus: long-spined
monophyllus: single-leaved
ovatus: oval
palmatus: palm-shaped (five-fingered)
pennatus: feathered, pinnate
plumosus: feathery
pubescens: downy
rugosa: wrinkled
tenuifolius: slender-leaved

FRAGRANCE

foetidus: foul-smelling
fragrans: fragrant
moschatus: musky
suaveolens: sweet-scented

HABIT/FUNCTION

aestivus: blooming or ripe in summer
annuus: annual
autumnalis: autumnal
baccatus: berried
biennis: biennial

bulbifera: bulb-bearing
cernuus: drooping, nodding
coccigera: berry-bearing
edulis: edible
flexilis: pliant
fruticans: shrubby
horizontalis: low to the ground, horizontal
humilis: low-growing, dwarf
macrocarpa: large-fruited
majalis: of May, Maytime
noctiflorus: night-blooming
nucifera: nut-bearing
officinalis: medicinal
patens: spreading
pendulus: hanging
procumbens: lying down
radicans: rooting
repens: creeping
scandens: climbing
vernalis: of spring

HABITAT/SOURCE

aquaticus: aquatic
chinensis: of China
japonica: of Japan
montanus: of the mountains
palustris: marsh-loving
pratensis: of meadows
salsuginosus: found in salt marshes
saxitilis: found among rocks

American Rose Society, and the Liberty Hyde Bailey Hortorium.

Nonetheless, botanical names are very useful. They enable you to discuss plants reliably and precisely, and allow you to maneuver intelligently around nurseries, garden books, and catalogs.

What to Look For

Many plant labels include both the botanical name and main common names, although it's always wise to refer to the former when seeking information. In the case of annuals or perennials, labels may provide a plant's eventual height and/or spread, its color, and its preference for sun or shade. *Never* buy plants that are unidentified, even if they stand among a group of labeled plants and look like the others. A rose of our acquaintance, sold from among a group of labeled pink-flowering 'Comtes de Chambord,' was embarrassed into admitting it was a white 'Montblanc' when it bloomed the following year.

Your objective is to choose those plants that have the best chances for survival in your garden. Don't buy plants that are lanky, sparse, and spindly—even if they're the only example of your favorite squash plant or perennial. A plant that is ungracefully thin and spare may not have been groomed or may have had to expend most of its energy in reaching for light. Another explanation is that it may have outgrown its pot and exhausted the nutrient content of its soil. All three problems can exist at once, leaving you with a sickly plant that is unlikely to recover even with the best care and feeding.

The leaves of unhealthy plants may be yellowed, distorted, or spotted with disease. The stems are crooked or broken. The root ball is too small in proportion to the plant or rootbound, with the roots wrapping around themselves or growing out through the drainage holes of its container. Slugs or snails might be curled into the drainage holes; aphids (and other pests) might be visible on the plant itself. The soil is bone-dry, and the leaves are wilted.

Healthy plants have straight, sturdy stems. The leaves are intact and have good, strong color. The plant is bushy and full, but not wildly out of proportion to the size of the root ball. It may be budded but not yet blooming. It is well-rooted, a fact that can be verified either by giving the stem a gentle tug (a well-rooted plant will resist) or by tipping the plant partway out of its pot.

Once you've established that the plant is basically healthy and well-grown, look for a balanced shape. Plants that are nicely leafed out on one side and bare on the other were grown under crowded conditions. Avoid both very small seedlings and plants that are overgrown for their pots—in neither case are the plants likely to transplant well.

The checklist below will help you give your garden the best possible head start:

■ Buy annuals when they are no more than 4"–6" tall, perennials ideally when they are about 5" tall. Always select plants that show healthy green leaves and clear signs of new growth emerging in a paler shade of green. Remember, the plants you select at the nursery are intended to perform their showiest best in your garden, not at the nursery or on the way home in the car. Therefore, never buy plants in full bloom: by the time you get them home and planted, most of the petals will have dropped. Always select plants that are heavily in bud, with only one or two buds giving the slightest hint of color (enough to ascertain that you're getting the color you want).

■ Buy bulbs exactly as you would buy onions at the supermarket. Choose the biggest, firmest ones you can find, with the papery tunic, or "skin," intact. Skip any that have bruises, cuts, soft spots, or black powdery molds.

■ Pick vegetable seedlings that are 6"–8" tall. Tomatoes or beans that have grown the second

VITA SACKVILLE-WEST'S GARDEN ROOMS

From the ruined shell of a Tudor manor house over-grown with weeds, Vita Sackville-West and her husband, Harold Nicolson, created the defining English garden of this century. "A tumble of roses, honeysuckle, figs, and vines," as Vita called it, Sissinghurst is at once modern and nostalgic, abundant and restrained.

Begun in the 1930s, the gardens at Sissinghurst Castle are the living legacy of Vita Sackville-West, an accomplished poet, novelist, and biographer who tempered her bent for unconventionality with an empathy for tradition.

Consisting of a series of invit-ing, interlinking "garden rooms," Sissinghurst presents a profusion of plant varieties within the con-fines of a restrained layout and understated color palette. One moves from the luminous creams and silvers of the famous White Garden to the warmer yellows and oranges of the cottage garden and into the herb garden's sea of light and dark greens. Vita loved old-fashioned flowers, and antique roses are everywhere—mingled with clematis, under-planted with hardy geraniums, and tossed together with lilies, irises, and flowering shrubs.

The genius of Sissinghurst is echoed in the choice of orna-ment, which favors simple over formal. Punctuating the land-scape are earthenware pots, bronze urns, planted stone troughs, and ancient birdbaths pitched at every angle and seeming to grow from the very landscape.

"For the last 40 years I have broken my back, my fingernails, and sometimes my heart in the practical pursuit of my favorite occupation."

set of true leaves will transplant best. Don't ever buy tomatoes that have started to set fruit unless the pot is big enough to sustain them so they won't need transplanting; otherwise, both fruit and flowers are likely to drop off without having the chance to mature.

■ Bare-root rose bushes should be labeled Number 1 and have no fewer than three well-spaced canes, each about as thick as an adult's ring finger and 15"–18" long. Avoid plants whose canes are broken, damaged, or showing new growth.

■ Shrubs and trees are best bought in the dormant stage, while their leaves are still in bud, so they are subjected to less stress when transported and planted; when they emerge from dormancy, they can more quickly adjust to their new garden environment. These plants should be checked for damaged stems and branches. Any kind of damage—be it no more than a small broken twig, or a slight nick or chafe in the bark—may lead to weakening and can also provide a point of entry for pests or disease. Cracked or peeling bark and discolored swellings on the trunk or in the crotch of branches are signs of potentially serious problems that may also have been caused by disease or insect damage. Remember, scarred bark indicates healed damage; unless the scar is large and unsightly, it may be no more significant than a paper cut on your finger.

■ When buying balled-and-burlapped trees, check to be sure the root ball is evenly moist—even brief periods of dryness can harm the roots and set the tree back severely. Check, too, that the root ball is solid; if the soil around the roots is loose and broken up, the tree has probably been dropped or mishandled and the roots may be damaged or torn.

■ Never buy plants that pull out of their pots with the slightest tug. Almost invariably, you'll discover that such a plant has puny roots of a pale dun color. Its growth is probably stunted, and the leaves and stems may be dry and wan. The entire plant could even look like a soggy spinach—a sure sign of doom.

■ Conversely, avoid buying plants that are pot-bound. You'll know them by their pale dryish roots, struggling to escape their cruel confinement and starvation by crawling out through the holes at the bottom of the pot. Often it will be difficult to free the plant from its confines; destroying the pot may be the only way to release the roots from their bounds.

■ Yellowing of leaves and stems is generally a serious warning. It may be the result of a virus spread by insect pests, a prolonged absence of sufficient light, and/or poor air circulation. Nutrient deficiency or too much water could be the culprit. Fungus may cause similar effects. On the other hand, slightly wilted leaves on what appears to be an otherwise healthy plant may need no more than a hearty drink of water in order to make a full recovery from a temporary indisposition. See if you can give the plant a drink of water at the nursery. Then go about your browsing; if it has revived to any degree, you can give the plant a chance and take it home.

■ Carefully examine plants for signs of insects and disease. The undersides of leaves are favorite hiding places for many tiny creatures and their eggs. Some also enjoy lounging in the axil of leaves and stems and not infrequently burrow into the blossoms.

■ Always look for interlopers, usually weeds, that compete not only for space with the plant you want to buy, but also for the food and water on which the plant relies. Interlopers occur most often in field-grown plants (usually biennials and perennials that have been raised outdoors rather than in a greenhouse), lurking amid their host's foliage and distinguished by their different leaf shape. If the stray is small, its removal eliminates further concerns. But if it has comfortably ensconced itself near the stem of the plant, you're better off making another selection.

■ Check the soil moisture of all plants you buy, whether they're potted or balled and burlapped. Don't buy plants if the soil around their roots is bone-dry and crumbles away the minute you tilt the pot or the burlapped ball.

Plant Markets

Where you buy your plants may greatly influence the plant quality you get. As a rule, it's best to buy your plants from an established nursery of good repute—ideally an organic nursery. A nursery's size is not nearly as important as the quality of the plants it sells, and whether or not it grows at least some of its own. In order to provide the broadest possible selection of plant material in an ever more competitive market, most large nurseries buy a portion of their stock, in bulk, from various specialist growers around the country. However, a quality nursery guarantees *all* the plants it sells and sees to it that they are accurately labeled. The people who work there not only know the correct botanical names of the plants and are able to answer your questions, but will also help you select the best plants from those in stock. And if you seek a plant the nursery doesn't have on hand, they will often special-order it for you.

Small local growers are generally reliable sources of quality plants. Many of them specialize in certain types of plants and do all their own work. They tend to be enthusiastic and well informed—and usually refer to plants by their botanical names. Their prices are somewhat lower than those of large nurseries, but their quantities are more limited. The plants you get, however, are healthy and strong, and because they are locally grown outdoors, they are generally suited to your climatic conditions.

OVER THE GARDEN GATE

One of the most intriguing ways to acquire choice additions to your garden is to shop at local plant sales. Annual fund-raising sales sponsored by public gardens, arboretums, and plant societies are good opportunities for finding locally adapted rhododendrons, new tetraploid daylilies, rare white alpine strawberries, heirloom vegetables and flowers, or charming native plants like yellow-eyed grass. Local garden club sales can turn up absolute treasures in the form of hard-to-find old-fashioned varieties of daffodils or the wonderful string beans and sweet corn that someone's grandmother grew and that are no longer commercially available.

Gardening friends and neighbors are also a splendid source of new and fascinating plants. A cutting of French pussy willow in the spring from a colleague at work, a division of lemon daylilies in the fall from your best friend since grammar school, a double handful of iris rhizomes dug up when the family next door built a playhouse—all serve to turn a backyard into a garden of memories, for each plant recalls the friendship of the giver.

Finally, plants on sale at supermarkets, department stores, and discount centers may be cheaper, but they are usually of lesser quality. In such places, they are often dependent on random care by employees who know little or nothing about the needs of plants. Plants may be watered too much or too little, too often or not often enough. They may be massed in the shade of an arcade that acts as a wind tunnel, or they may have to stand in full sun all day—whether they like it or not. Some may lack labels; some may have been grown for different climates and are not suited to the site where they're being sold.

However, sometimes you can find a perfect gem, a plant that is both beautiful and healthy—and just what you want. In that case, it's worth it. Take a chance and buy it.

Catalogs

Mail-order shopping is an excellent way to buy plants. Numerous catalogs offer an astonishing variety of plants, ranging from the familiar to the rare, from annuals to trees. Some specialize in very young, very sturdy plants in quantity, at very good prices. The more reputable the supplier, the more detailed the information about the plants, from botanical names and size or age at shipping time to special features, bloom time, and preferred growing conditions.

Shopping by mail is the answer for people whose time is limited; for some, it is even the preferred method of plant buying. For many elderly, handicapped, or housebound people, or those who live in places where well-stocked nurseries are a day's trip away, it may be a necessity. Whether ordering from a single catalog or several, one thing is certain: mail-order shopping makes it possible to buy anything and everything.

In general, nursery catalogs offer perennials, shrubs, trees, and vines. Seed catalogs offer primarily annuals and vegetables, although some include a few perennials and greenhouse plants to grow from seed, as well as the odd rooted plants of soft fruits such as strawberries, raspberries, and blueberries. Bulb catalogs offer a wide selection of bulbs; some also offer perennials and a selection of potted indoor plants.

Beyond the general catalogs are the specialty grower catalogs, many of which give little more than lists with a sentence or two of description. Specialty growers tend to concentrate on a single genus, e.g., roses, peonies, lilacs, geraniums, daylilies, lilies, or daffodils. Some may offer plants in specific categories such as antique roses, herbs, heirloom vegetables, or dwarf fruit trees. Find

an environmentally responsible grower that suits your needs and budget.

Some catalogs, unfortunately, may be guilty of verbal and pictorial hyperbole in the presentation of their plants, full of alluring pictures of specimens grown to wondrous size and covered in spectacular bloom. There is all the attraction of the newest, the rarest, the choicest. Nursery and seed catalogs can be a long, lovely litany of horticultural temptations in full and flaming color.

Mail-order shopping works best once you're reasonably familiar with the plants you want and understand the language of catalogs—nothing is described as inferior, each plant is superlative. Learn to pick and choose from among the descriptive phrases and the luscious color photographs; use garden books as references to check the facts.

Most companies ship according to the customer's hardiness zone, when danger of hard frost should be past. Plants sent via post may have to travel for several days or more; open and unpack them as soon as they arrive. Granted, the packing of most suppliers is remarkably good and damage-resistant, and the plants may even still be moist. Nonetheless, your new plants will have experienced a certain amount of shock. Disentangle the potted herbaceous perennials carefully, as they will be packed close together—often with damp shredded paper. Water them with a gentle spray to avoid damage to the leaves and stems. Before planting, keep them outdoors in semishade for two or three days to get them adjusted to real life. Ideally, you should set the plants, still in their containers, in an ad hoc bed of loose soil or compost *and keep them watered* until planting time.

Most woody and some herbaceous perennials are shipped "bare root," that is, without soil, and still largely dormant. Although these, too, usually arrive packed in moistened wood shavings or newspaper, it's best to unpack them at once, soak the roots for several hours, then plant them; otherwise, heel them into the soil, and keep them well watered for no more than two or three days before planting them in the garden.

A major advantage of shopping through catalogs is the possibility of obtaining unusual plants that are not otherwise readily available. Choosing a reliable, responsible catalog nursery or mail-order supplier is largely a matter a getting recommendations from gardening friends and neighbors. For specialty nurseries, ask around at garden club meetings or call local specialty plant organizations such as the rose or rhododendron society.

POTENTIAL PROBLEMS

Even though you've done all the right things—amended the soil, provided water, and picked the proper plant for each location—there are still times when plants fail to thrive. Many environmental factors can adversely affect plants, including drought, drainage (too fast, too slow), sun (too much, too little), chemical damage (plants around a swimming pool that are splashed by heavily chlorinated water), and build-up of salts (in seaside plantings and in cold-winter areas along roads and paths where salt is used as a deicer). Any of these conditions will stress plants to the point that they are more susceptible to the pests and diseases all around them.

When plants are in trouble, they let you know. They droop, they wilt, they wither; their leaves turn yellow, develop spots, get crisp around the edges, and drop off. Unfortunately, a plant's distress signals are not easy to interpret; something is wrong and needs attention, but it's not always clear where the problem lies. The challenge in gardening is to figure out why a plant is not thriving and decide what to do about it.

Leaves may wilt because the soil is bone-dry or because it's waterlogged. Give the plant either a good watering or let the soil dry out and water less frequently. If drainage is a problem, you may need to transplant the wilted plant to a drier place, or amend the soil for faster drainage, or turn the area into a bog garden. Repeated wilting stresses and weakens plants, rendering them vulnerable to pests and diseases.

Pest damage, like environmental factors, is readily noticed. Your hosta leaves have an interesting new open-cutwork pattern to them, or a stem on a bean plant is thick with small black insects, or the parsley that had plenty of leaves yesterday has a definite scalped look today. But noticing the problem is easier than identifying the culprit. Experience will help you narrow the list of suspects. It seldom takes more than a season or two to learn that slugs and snails frequent the hosta bed, that aphids favor the bean patch, especially as the weather gets warmer, and that parsleyworms are awe-inspiring in the efficiency of their gluttony.

Diseases can ravage a garden, too. Sometimes their symptoms are obvious: the black spots on rose leaves, a powdery covering on lilac foliage, gray mold on strawberries. All these are caused by fungi. Other diseases may be more difficult to diagnose. But don't get discouraged. Although you may have to deal with a few problems, you can prevent many of them from ever occurring.

PLASTIC BAGS FOR PEST DISPOSAL

In lieu of "stomping," a good way to dispose of insect pests, slugs, and snails is to put them in a zipper-grip plastic storage bag. Carry the bag as you go through the garden, unzipping to add additional pests as you find them. Place the bag (securely closed) in full sun; the pests will be dead within a matter of hours. Empty and wash the bag, and you're ready to go again. Some gardeners prefer a jar filled with soapy water, but insects that are still alive can fly out when you remove the lid to let more in.

WHAT'S WRONG WITH YOUR PLANT?

Sometimes a plant's problem and its cause are obvious: the slime trail leading away from the hole in a hosta leaf is indicative of a well-fed snail or slug; the skeletonized rose leaves are probably caused by a rose caterpillar (you'll likely find the ¼" pale green culprit on the underside of a leaf). The causative agents for other symptoms may not be as evident. Use this chart as a guide to help diagnose your plant's ills.

The slug

SYMPTOM	POSSIBLE CAUSE
Branch dieback	Diseases (fireblight, verticillium wilt, or other vascular diseases); insects (infestation of foliar or root pests, or twig girdlers); nematodes; root stress; soil pH.
Cankers (sunken lesions)	Diseases; insects (especially borers); root stress; sunburn; mechanical wounds (from string trimmers, pruners, lawn mowers, or other equipment).
Discoloration (inside roots and stems)	Wilt diseases; damage from fertilizers.
Holes in leaves	Chewing pests (slime trail—slugs or snails); birds.
Leaf drop	Diseases; bark borers; over- or underwatering; too much/too little light; air pollution; soil pH; seasonal (drop normal for deciduous plants).
Leaf mottling	Viral diseases; pesticide damage; natural genetic variegation on some plants.
Leaf spots	Disease; insects; spider mites; air pollution; pesticide damage; nutrient deficiencies (see chart, p. 11).
Leaf yellowing	Spider mites (pinpoint yellowing); insects (bark borers especially); nematodes (combined with wilting); root rot diseases (affect older leaves first); viral disease; overwatering (affect older leaves first); nutrient deficiencies (see chart, p. 11); soil pH; natural (old age); insufficient light.
Misshapen leaves	Sucking pests; viral diseases; peach leaf curl (peaches and nectarines); underwatering; nutrient deficiencies (see chart, p. 11).
Misshapen roots	Nematodes (often knotted and swollen); diseases (especially crown gall); girdled roots (grown too long in container; roots not released when transplanted); natural (legumes have nitrogen-fixing nodules).
Root rot	Diseases (fungal); overwatering; root stress; soil pH.
Wilting	Under- or overwatering; insects (most likely borers or root feeders); nematodes; diseases (root rots, wilt diseases).

General Control Methods

Spending a half-hour once or twice a week inspecting the garden can prevent a minor pest or disease problem from becoming a full-blown infestation or plague. Once you discover a problem, you have to control it. Environmentally responsible gardening precludes poisoning the planet, so alternatives to contaminants must be sought to deal with these problems. Happily, there are many safe methods of control.

PHYSICAL CONTROLS

Physical controls include the most hands-on approaches. You're one on one with a pest as you hand-pick cucumber beetles, up close and personal with a disease when cutting off rose leaves that have black spots.

■ Hand-picking is one of the best methods for removing snails, slugs, and insect pests from plants. Visit the garden early in the morning to find Japanese beetles or stalk after dark with a flashlight for slugs and snails, which do most of their feeding at night. During the day, slugs are attracted to dark, damp places where they can keep out of the sun, so a few wooden shingles laid down in the garden will generally yield a good harvest by midafternoon. Once picked, the pesky creatures should be placed on the ground and squashed underfoot. Tomato hornworms, cabbage loopers, and other caterpillars can be hand-picked as well; as with slugs and snails, the pick-up-and-stomp method is the most effective. Barriers can also be effective against slugs and snails. A 1"-wide circle of wood ash or diatomaceous earth around the base of susceptible plants works well, desiccating the creatures. Copper sheeting or copper foil around a bed sets up a slight electrical current that keeps these pests at bay.

■ If you don't want to hand-pick Japanese beetles, you can easily shake an affected flower over a plastic bag, letting the sleeping bugs fall inside. Some gardeners become indignant about pests in their flowers and, especially when there are only a few, prefer hand-squeezing their bugs. Others prefer cutting the critters in half with pruners. Whatever method you prefer, get out there and remove any visible pests.

■ A strong spray of water aimed at a plant can be very effective for removing aphids and other small insects. It's the equivalent of a tidal wave: most of the insects will be washed off and killed (look before you squirt to make sure you're not drowning any beneficial insects as well). A few may survive, so you must be ever vigilant, constantly on the lookout for marauders.

■ Pinching and pruning are physical disease controls. When a problem is limited to a few leaves or branches, you may be able to nip it in the bud by cutting or pinching out the affected parts and destroying them. (*Never* add infested material to the compost pile!)

■ Floating row covers (made of spunbonded fabric) are among the most versatile barriers. Placed on top of young spinach plants, they keep flies from laying their eggs on the leaves and disrupt the life cycle of the spinach leaf miner. The material is so light that it doesn't crush the plants and effectively floats atop the leaves. (Floating row covers are also season extenders, warming the air underneath them several degrees and protecting tender plants from spring or fall frosts.)

■ A barrier or fence is the best way to keep many of the larger four-legged pests out of the garden. A 2'-high fence is sufficient to keep hungry rabbits from nibbling the spring lettuce, but it will not keep out dogs, cats, raccoons, or deer. To deter most deer and other large wildlife, you need an electric fence or a 6'-fence. (Some deer can even scale that—if yours are Olympic jumpers, erect an 8'-fence, or two 6'-fences spaced 2'–3' apart.) You can set the height of the wires on an electric fence to best deal with the particular animal you're trying to discourage.

■ Birds, which eat many of the insects that are unwelcome in your garden, can themselves become pests when they eat the fruit you want for yourself. The simplest way to deter them is with bird netting—just throw it over the tree or shrub you want to protect. Or, if you want to spend the time and effort, you can build elaborate walk-in cages for your prized fruit so that birds and animals are barred from entering; but be aware of those smart raccoons who are able to turn knobs and open doors with apparent ease.

BIOLOGICAL CONTROLS

In a well-managed organic garden, pests and their enemies exist together, having achieved a natural balance. However, sometimes the scales get tipped and pests outnumber their parasites or natural enemies. By employing biological controls, you can either encourage predators and parasites or introduce them into the garden. Modern technology brings genetically altered plants, such as those that have pest-fighting bacteria like *Bt* built into them. If crown gall has been a problem, look for plants that have been treated with the bacterium *Agrobacterium radiobacter* to make them resistant to that disease. Hybridization has resulted in new varieties (especially of vegetables) that are disease-resistant. For example, some tomatoes are listed in catalogs with the letters VFT; this means they are resistant to verticillium wilt, fusarium wilt, and tobacco mosaic virus.

Many predators exist in and around the garden, including insect-eating reptiles such as lizards and snakes as well as insect-eating amphibians such as frogs, toads, newts, and salamanders. Salamanders devour aphids, beetles, slugs, and sowbugs. Snakes, once you're over your fear of them, are worth their weight in gold as natural exterminators. Harmless to humans, garter snakes, eastern ribbon snakes, western ter-

restrial garter snakes, green snakes, grass snakes, and brown snakes eat slugs, snails, and many other pest insects. Corn snakes, black rat snakes, and milk snakes eat mice and rats. Many centipedes prey on a variety of soil-dwelling pests. Add to this list the garden spiders whose webs ensnare a wide variety of plant pests. Nocturnal animals, now called urban wildlife, also help out. Raccoons, possums, and skunks all paw through leaf litter to find ground-dwelling pests such as snails and slugs.

Most gardens have both "good" and "bad" insects. See the facing page for a list of insects that you'll want to encourage in order to keep pest populations down to a comfortable level. More and more beneficial insects are available for purchase, including convergent ladybugs (*Hippodamia convergens*), aphid midges (*Aphidoletes aphimyza*), green lacewings (*Chrysopa carnea*), whitefly wasp (*Encarsaria formosa*), and the spined soldier bug (*Podisus maculiventris*). (Skip praying mantises—they eat beneficial and harmless insects as cheerfully as pests.) Mites that eat other mites can be purchased to release into the garden. Some species of mites occur naturally in gardens, but they do their good work invisibly—nearly all of them are microscopic.

Birds, too, are wonderful for pest control. Attracting birds with trees and shrubs for dense cover, plenty of food (seed, berries, and fruit), water to drink and bathe in, and birdhouses is a wise investment for which the provident gardener is repaid many times over. It is estimated that birds eat four times their weight in insects, and in some cases, much more. Hummingbirds, swallows, purple martins, and a number of other birds catch flying insects on the wing. At night bats take over the insect patrol, eating thousands of them while you sleep. The little brown bat, for example, eats moths, caddis flies, midges, beetles, and mosquitoes.

A new deterrent for larger pests is the urine of natural predators. The strategy here is that the

BENEFICIAL INSECTS

■ **Aphid midge larvae.** These legless larvae are light orange to red and hatch into tiny black flies. They feed on aphids. Dried blackened aphid husks are evidence of their presence.

■ **Dragonflies.** The beautiful dragonflies that you see skimming over the water are as beneficial as they are attractive. They keep the water clean by eating mosquitoes, gnats, and midges.

■ **Fireflies.** These beneficial insects eat the larvae of many pest insects as well as slugs and snails. To encourage them, add some tall grasses or a small meadow, or keep your lawn mowed high (3"). They need tall grass to lay their eggs; if you cut the lawn too short, you destroy their eggs.

■ **Ground beetles and hister beetles.** Both are night feeders that prey on cabbage root maggots, cutworms, snail and slug eggs, armyworms, and tent caterpillars.

■ **Lacewing larvae.** The larvae of both the green and brown lacewings feed on soft-bodied insects such as aphids, scale insects, small caterpillars, thrips, and eggs of other insects. The larvae look like miniature gray-green or gray-brown alligators.

■ **Ladybugs (lady beetles).** Ladybugs are typically red-orange with black spots. The larvae, which look like tiny alligators with orange or yellow spots, eat more aphids than the adults do, but both are useful. Small black or gray lady beetles feed on spider mites and whiteflies.

■ **Parasitic wasps.** There are many different wasps, each of which parasitizes a specific insect. Trichogramma wasps parasitize cabbage looper eggs, but must be released before the caterpillars hatch. If cabbage loopers have been a problem in the past, purchase these wasps from a nursery or through a catalog; get them early enough to have them in the garden to destroy the caterpillar eggs. Chalcids, braconids, and ichneumonids control whiteflies, aphids, and some caterpillars. The tiny *Encarsaria formosa* wasp, sold as a control for whitefly, is more effective in a greenhouse than in the garden, where it can escape or be blown away by the wind.

■ **Predatory wasps.** A wide variety of wasps eats other insects, including their larvae. Both paper wasps and yellow-jacket wasps feed caterpillars to their young early in the summer. Wasps have a nasty sting, so avoid them yourself but leave out-of-the-way wasp nests where they are.

■ **Rove beetles.** Rove beetles of various species vary greatly in size, the largest no more than an inch long, the smallest barely visible. All have short wings and look like they're wearing a coat that is much too small. Found on top of soil and garden litter, they are invaluable because they decompose manure and plant material; others eat root maggots, mites, slugs, and snails.

■ **Syrphid fly larvae.** The adult flies, commonly known as hover flies, resemble wasps with yellow and black or white and black markings, but they don't sting. The flies lay their eggs in aphid colonies; the larvae eat aphids, mealy bugs, and scale.

■ **Tachinid flies.** Tachinid flies lay their eggs on cutworms, armyworms, beetle larvae, caterpillars, corn borers, and stinkbugs. The larvae (white maggots) then parasitize the host insect. Adult tachinid flies look like large houseflies.

■ **True bugs.** Assassin bugs attack a great many different insects; they also sting and are best left untouched. Big-eyed bugs feed on small insects, insect eggs, and mites. Pirate bugs are minute, but they eat many kinds of mites and insects, including thrips. Damsel bugs devour aphids, leafhoppers, and caterpillars. The spined soldier bug preys on Mexican bean beetles, imported cabbageworms, and cabbage loopers.

pests will avoid an area that smells dangerous. Three varieties are available: fox urine to deter mice, rabbits, squirrels, moles, and chipmunks; bobcat urine to repel rodents; and coyote urine to keep deer away. Unfortunately, this natural solution has a drawback—the urine can actually attract the predator, especially during the mating season.

Microorganisms that have been pressed into service as beneficials include the bacterium *Bacillus thuringiensis,* more often called *Bt* and sold under the trade names Thuricide and Dipel. When sprayed on leaves or applied in granular form, *Bt* kills caterpillars and larvae by paralyzing their intestinal tracts so that they starve to death. Three different formulas are sold for use with vegetables. *Bt berliner-kurstake* (formerly *BtK*) targets caterpillars such as cabbage loopers, imported cabbageworms, diamondback moth larvae, corn earworms, and hornworms. Javelin, a registered formula of *Bt berliner-kurstake,* works particularly well in combating armyworms and loopers. M-One, a formulation of *Bt san diego,* is effective against Colorado potato beetles. *BtI* (*Bt. var. israelensis*) is effective when used against mosquitoes, black flies, and fungus gnats.

Predatory nematodes eat a variety of insect pests, including carrot weevil larvae, cutworms, Japanese beetle larvae, root maggots, seedcorn maggots, wireworms, and more. *Neoaplectana carpocapse,* more often called *Nc,* is the most broadly useful, but *Heterorhabditis bacteriophora* (formerly *H. heliothidis*), often called *Hb,* is especially effective against Japanese beetle larvae and root weevils because it moves more quickly and burrows deeper into the soil.

Polyhedrous granulosis viruses infect cabbage loopers in late summer, turning them brown or yellow. Leave the infected loopers alone, since they release this virus when they die.

Milky spore disease, a pathogen containing *Bacillus popilliae* and *B. lentimorbus,* can be purchased to apply to your lawn in the spring or fall to control Japanese beetle larvae and other grubs.

It takes a couple of years to wipe them out and works best if the neighbors cooperate and treat their lawns as well. It is totally ineffective, however, if you use any pesticide on the lawn that will kill the bacteria. Once established, milky spore will stay in the soil for 30 years or more.

Even antibiotics, like streptomycin, are used in the battle against plant diseases. However, as in treating human ailments, antibiotics are only effective against bacterial diseases, not viruses.

CHEMICAL CONTROLS

Yes, there are chemical controls that are acceptable to organic gardeners. Dormant (horticultural) oil, included in this group, is one of the most important preventive treatments. In late winter or early spring, before the buds break on trees or shrubs, spray plants (when the temperature is above 40°F.), covering all the branches, to smother any overwintering insects or egg cases.

Even organically derived pesticides, such as pyrethins, sabadilla, and rotenone, may have drawbacks; they may be deadly to fish or cause allergic reactions in some people. They are not pest-specific—that is, they will kill beneficial insects as well as pests—so the advantages of their use need to be carefully weighed.

Elemental sulfur and copper compounds (the classic fungicide, Bordeaux mixture, is a copper compound) are minimally disruptive in the environment but still require similarly thoughtful consideration for essentially the same reasons as the organically derived pesticides. They can harm fish if the residue gets into streams, ponds, or lakes, and some people are allergic to sulfur.

Spraying with plant extracts can stop a pest invasion at the first sign, before it becomes an infestation. Classic home sprays include garlic, onion, hot pepper, eucalyptus oil, and the herb tansy. Some gardeners find that spraying with the pest itself is a deterrent. To use this method, collect some of the bugs or, in the case of very small insects like aphids or psyllids, a portion of the infested plant. Chop fine and mix in a blender with water, several drops of Ivory liquid (so it sticks to the plant), several drops of vegetable oil (to keep the spray on the plant, so you don't have to reapply so often), and a tablespoon or so of vodka (as a preservative). Apparently this works because the bugs are repelled by the stench of their dead relatives.

Pests

As in every other facet of gardening, you need to be involved in deciding how to deal with pests. Integrated pest management (IPM), originally developed for farmers but easily adapted to the home garden, is a highly effective technique. Using IPM precepts, *you* make the choices and decide how to deal with each individual problem that might arise.

The following six simple steps are involved in any IPM program:

1. Monitor plants. Inspect your garden by looking closely at your plants—flowers, leaves (top and bottom), stems, and around the base— at least once a week. You'll get to know your plants and be able to spot the *initial* signs of a pest problem. You may not see the first gypsy moth caterpillars munching on leaves high up in an oak tree, but you'll probably see them traveling down the trunk in the morning in quest of a cool, shady place to spend the day before climbing back up to feast on the leaves all night.

2. Identify pest. Catch the culprit in the act. It's not safe to assume that the holes in your rose leaves are from Japanese beetles; early in the season, these beetles may not even be present in the garden. The holes could be caused by a caterpillar (one of many different kinds, including gypsy moth larvae), or even a snail or slug munching away. If you don't find the culprit during the day, go out at night with a flashlight. That's when you'll catch nocturnal pests like taxus weevil (on

yews and rhododendrons), gypsy moth caterpillars, and slugs.

3. Assess damage. Based on what you've observed in steps 1 and 2, and how bad the damage is, decide whether or not you can live with it. A couple of Japanese beetles on a single rose in an entire garden may not eat much; however, if you see your favorite plants denuded by beetles gorging themselves on petals and leaves, you may decide to act.

4. Choose the least toxic control. Many people mistakenly think that IPM is strictly organic; it is not. However, its precepts recommend starting with the *least* toxic control—physical, biological, or chemical. After treatment, reassess the damage and monitor the number of pests. If there is little or no improvement, try something stronger. In some cases, depending on your mindset and the extent of the pest problem, you may want to resort to a chemical solution. Again, go for the least toxic first. The aphids on roses may be eliminated with a strong spray of water from the hose; if they return quickly, try spraying with some insecticidal soap, being sure to spray all surfaces of infested roses only.

5. Reevaluate pest damage. Wait a week or so after applying the control, then check the plants to see if there are still pests present.

6. Determine the cause of plant stress. A healthy plant does not attract pests or diseases. Once you have the pest problem under control, take a good look at the plant and try to determine what might be causing the stress. Is it getting too much water? Too little water? Not enough light? Too much sun? Is the soil good enough for the plant? Or is it too rich? Does the plant have sufficient air circulation? Is it too crowded? Perhaps you've chosen the right plant but it's growing in the wrong place.

Some pest problems are immediately discernable, but others occur below ground. Both borers and nematodes, for example, can damage plant roots. To make matters worse, some pests have adapted themselves so well that there are specific species of pests for particular species of plants.

BORERS

Among the most prevalent of all insect pests, borers are the larvae (caterpillars or grubs) of moths or beetles that are specific to a certain type of plant. Like other pests, borers are often attracted to weak plants—those newly set out in the garden, or those that are stressed and thus vulnerable.

Many borers overwinter in the soil, emerge as adults in the spring, and lay their eggs on stems and low-growing leaf stalks. The newly hatched larvae make their way into the stem of the plant, feeding for up to six weeks. After they've had their fill, the larvae pupate in the soil. Some types of borers can go through several life cycles in a single year.

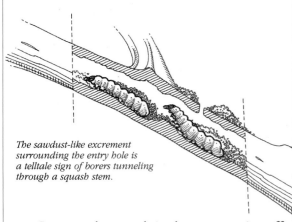

The sawdust-like excrement surrounding the entry hole is a telltale sign of borers tunneling through a squash stem.

Borers make tunnels in the stem, cutting off the flow of nutrients and water and causing the plant to wilt. The tunneling not only damages the plant, but also provides a perfect entrance-way for bacterial infection, fungus, and disease. Dealt with quickly, the damage from borers is minimal, and you can often save your plants from further infestation.

In trees, borers tunnel beneath the bark or bore into live wood. Some borers can bore deep into a branch, weakening it so that a strong wind can snap the branch off. Borers can also tunnel around the trunk of a tree, effectively girdling and killing it. The borers that make their tunnels below the soil line are not as obvious as those on stems and branches.

The most common sign of borers is the sudden wilting of a branch or other plant part. (If the wilting does not respond to watering, then borers are most likely the culprits.) Look for a hole in the stem of the plant. On squash vines, you can see green sawdust-like excrement piled around the entry holes. In trees, holes are often bordered with sawdust, sap, or excrement; some tree borers have a distinctive tunneling pattern that a trained arborist can recognize, giving positive identification to the pest without even seeing it.

Prevent borer damage by regularly inspecting susceptible plants in your garden. Once part of a plant has wilted or yellowed, it is unlikely to revive, so remove the part and destroy it to avoid spreading disease (bacteria or fungus) that may be introduced by the borer. If you suspect a borer problem, use a hand cultivator or hoe to gently aerate the soil around the base of the plant (this is especially important around trees). The cultivation exposes larvae and also allows you to examine the inch or more of trunk just below the soil surface for any signs of borers.

When you're sure the problem is caused by borers, take steps to eliminate them. The easiest way to remove them is to stick a flexible wire up the hole, impale the pest, and remove it. Another solution is to purchase beneficial nematodes, which parasitize and feed on the borer pupae, disrupting the life cycle of the borer. Follow package instructions and inject the nematodes into borer holes in trees and cultivate them in the ground around the base of plants. Physical barriers (floating row covers over small plants, white paint, or burlap loosely wrapped around tree trunks) will foil the adult insect from laying eggs on the plant.

The best defense against borers is a strong offense. Feed your plants well with the nutrients they require. Borers, like other pests, are less likely to attack strong, healthy plants. Place bird

BORER CONTROL

PLANT	CONTROL
Clematis	Clematis borers feed on crowns and roots, stunting plant growth; top may die back. Cut out and destroy affected stems; dig larvae out of the crown. Destroy severely infested plants.
Corn	Encourage natural predators such as Braconid wasps, tachinid flies, and soldier beetles. *Bt* works well when sprayed on leaves or applied in granular form on the tips of the ears.
Dahlia	Remove and destroy affected stems. In late fall, remove and destroy any dead leaves and stems. As a preventive measure, spray *Bt berliner-kurstake* every 7 to 10 days in early summer.
Fruit trees	Borers can invade trees at or just below soil level. Keep mulch at least 3"–4" away from the trunk. Do not grow grass or ground covers at base of susceptible trees. Gently cultivate around base to expose borers and holes.
Fruiting canes (blackberry, raspberry)	Raspberry crown borers lay eggs at cane base. Grubs feed on crown, root, and cane. Dig out and destroy infested plants. Rednecked and other cane borers lay eggs near the tops of canes, causing wilting of tips. Apply rotenone before canes bloom.
Iris	Iris borers enter the fan of leaves at the top and tunnel their way down toward the rhizome. At the first sign of tunnels, squash borers by running your fingers down the leaves. When dividing rhizomes, inspect for borers; destroy any infested rhizomes.
Ornamental trees	Protect the trunks of young trees. Paint the lower half of the trunk with white latex paint (diluted with equal parts of water) to prevent adults from laying eggs in the bark. Or wrap paper or burlap (not too tightly) around the trunk as a deterrent.
Potato	Rotate crops on a 3- to 5-year rotation so that any borers pupating in the soil will not have a host plant on which to feed the next growing season.
Rhododendron	Prune branches below damage. Destroy affected limbs. Seal cut branches with grafting wax. Keep plant well watered and fertilized to aid recovery.
Roses	Rose canes may be attacked by raspberry cane borer, causing tips to die back. Cut back and destroy affected canes.
Squash	Cover vines with floating row covers soon after planting. Remove covers as plant begins to flower so pollinating insects can get to the blooms. Inject stem with *Bt berliner-kurstake*. Apply beneficial nematodes as a control. Look for borer holes. Make a slit just above the hole and, using a flexible wire, impale and remove the borer. Cover joints from which the leaves grow with a layer of damp soil to encourage the vines to root at these joints. Thwart borers by adjusting the time you plant. A later planting of summer squash will often miss the feeding larvae. In warm climates, an early planting avoids these pests. Borers do not lay their eggs until July, when plants are large enough to withstand any attack.
Strawberries	If the whole plant wilts, cut crown in half and look for telltale tunnels of strawberry crown borers. Destroy infested plants and replant the bed in a new site. Adult borers can travel a good distance, so relocate the bed at least 500' away from the old one.

GARDEN PESTS AND CONTROLS

PESTS	DAMAGE	CONTROL METHOD
Aphids	Suck plant juices, weaken leaves and stems.	Encourage natural predators such as lady beetle larvae, small wasps, syrphid fly larvae, lacewings. Use a strong spray of water, insecticidal soap, or horticultural oil. Remove and destroy infested part of plant if small.
Cabbage root maggots	Seedlings of cabbage family plants wilt and die soon after planting. From underground, maggots burrow into stem and eat both stem and roots, killing or weakening plant. 	Pull up plant to see ¼" white maggots. Destroy plant. Rotate plantings to rid soil of pests. Good fall cleanup. Cultivate soil well before planting. Use floating row covers to prevent moths from laying eggs.
Cabbage-worms (cabbage loopers)	Moth larvae eat leaves of cabbage in late spring and early fall.	Apply *Bt* weekly during infestation. Use floating row covers to prevent moths from laying eggs.
Caterpillars	Eat leaves; may defoliate plant.	Spray with *Bt* when less than 1" long. Remove and destroy egg masses when they are laid. Spray trees and shrubs with dormant oil in early spring to smother any overwintering insects or egg cases.
Colorado potato beetles (black and cream striped beetles)	Orange-red larvae emerge from orange eggs on undersides of potato leaves and eat leaves voraciously. 	Mulch heavily with straw. Hand-pick small larvae; wear gloves since they can pinch. Spray larvae with *Bt san diego*. If larvae and adults appear simultaneously, use sabadilla dust. Protect plants with floating row covers. Practice crop rotation.
Cutworms	Moth larvae bite newly transplanted seedlings where stem and roots join. Seedlings wilt and die. 	When planting, make protective collar from cardboard, or tuna or cat food cans. Place around seedling so half the collar is below the soil surface.

PESTS	DAMAGE	CONTROL METHOD
Grubs	Beetle larvae may live 1–3 years underground, eating roots of turf grass and other plants.	Use milky spore disease in lawn and garden to control grubs. Cultivate soil well, and let birds feast on fat white grubs.
Japanese beetles	Eat leaves and flowers in summer, making irregular holes; rest in soil when not eating.	Hand-pick beetles. Traps may attract beetles from neighbors unless placed 30' from garden. Treat same as for grubs (above).
Leaf miners	Tiny fly larvae eat inside the leaf (trails are visible as light-colored lines on leaves).	Damage is more cosmetic than harmful, but affected leaves should be picked off and destroyed.
Parsleyworms (celeryworms, carrotworms) (green, black, and yellow caterpillars)	Can eat their way through a stand of parsley, dill, or carrot foliage (any member of carrot family).	Let them live if possible—they turn into black swallowtail butterflies.
Scale	Sucks sap from the undersides of leaves or stems.	Remove by hand or with soft brush and soapy water. Prune out infested limbs of citrus and destroy. Spray with horticultural oil.
Spider mites	Cause plants to drop leaves. (You may see webs or ashen, light green leaves with hundreds of very small yellow dots that give a bleached effect to the leaf.)	Purchase and apply predatory mites. Spray fruit trees with dormant oil in late winter. Mites thrive in hot, dry weather; keep dousing or spritzing plant with water.
Tarnished plant bugs	Inject toxins into stems and leaves, leaving discolorations.	Apply sabadilla dust early in the morning. Use floating row covers on susceptible plants.

feeders and birdbaths near the garden to attract birds year round. They will peck around the base of trees and plants, eating the pupae and larvae of borers and many other pests. Many flowering weeds, such as butterfly weed and goldenrod, attract native parasites that will kill borers before they can become a problem. Plant borer-resistant varieties, especially of corn, squash, and tomatoes.

NEMATODES

These tiny, wormlike, soil-dwelling creatures are not related to true worms, the majority of which are beneficial in the garden. Of the many different kinds of nematodes, most are not harmful and some actually help out in the garden by attacking pests. A number of nematodes, however, can cause major problems; unhappily, you need a microscope to see them. Some munch on the outside of the plant; others burrow into the plant tissue. Soil nematodes have pointy mouthparts with which they can cut the individual cell walls of the plant, inject saliva into a cell, and then suck out the material from within the cell.

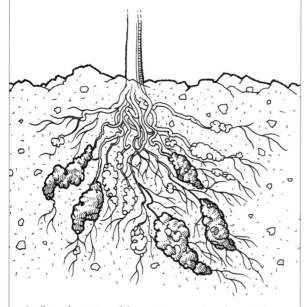

Swelling of a portion of the roots is a sure sign of nematode infestation. At this stage, remove and destroy the plant.

The plant's first response to this attack is swelling. Deformed growth soon follows; eventually areas of the plant die altogether. In addition to the problems nematodes themselves cause, they can also carry viruses that infect the plant when the nematodes inject their saliva into the cells. To make matters worse, the tiny openings the nematodes make are also a perfect route for bacteria and fungus to enter the plant.

The symptoms of nematode damage, including yellowed leaves and wilted or stunted growth, often mimic those of other plant problems caused by viruses, air pollution, or nutrient deficiencies. If you think the nematodes are attacking the roots, gently pull the plant out of the ground. Wash off the roots. If there is root rot, excessive root branching, small lesions or swellings on the roots, or injured root tips, your problem is most likely soil nematodes. The infected roots are swollen, often with galls (abnormal growths on a plant, caused by the parasitic attack of fungi, insects, bacteria, or nematodes) two to three times larger than the healthy roots. Continued infestation results in roots with a clubbed or knotted look. For a definitive diagnosis, call your local Cooperative Extension service and have your soil tested.

Prevent soil nematode damage by changing the environment in which plants have been affected. Nematodes cannot move very far by themselves. However, they are good swimmers and can move quickly in water and in moist soil. If your plants have already been seriously infected, remove and destroy them. Keeping the bed dry will keep the nematodes from spreading into other areas of the garden. If you live in an arid climate, you will be less likely to have a problem with soil nematodes, as long as you can keep the soil dry. Grow plants that will thrive in dry conditions rather than those that need a lot of water, and you may never experience nematode problems.

If nematodes have been a problem, choose

BUTTERFLIES IN THE GARDEN: ARE THEY ALL GOOD?

Butterfly gardening is all the rage. But before you go out and plant a garden for those ethereal winged creatures, think it through carefully. Appearances to the contrary, butterflies do not just appear out of thin air. Before they take that beautiful shape, they are caterpillars, or garden pests. Ask yourself if you're willing to sacrifice part of your garden so that later in the season you can enjoy the beauty of butterflies (assuming you have the nectar plants that will attract them). Before you squash that ugly caterpillar munching away on your plants, identify it. An elementary guide to butterflies and moths will help you see the positive side of caterpillars. For instance, the striped parsleyworm, or celeryworm, which voraciously eats parsley, celery, dill, and carrots, eventually turns into the lovely black swallowtail butterfly. Unaware of this transformation, you may unwittingly kill off the potential butterflies by spraying plants with *Bt.* Instead, plant a large patch of parsley in another garden plot for the hungry larvae, and if they get out of control among your vegetables, hand-pick them and move them to their new feeding ground. Another majestic transformation is the hornworm (host plants include beets, currants, grapes, melon, pears, and plums) that turns into a white-lined sphinx moth, a delicate creature resembling a small hummingbird. The tomato hornworm becomes a five-spotted hawkmoth; the tobacco hornworm, a Carolina sphinx moth.

nematode-resistant varieties of plants if you can find them. Try planting marigolds one year in the garden, then digging them under after the plants die in fall or mix in marigolds with your regular plantings to prevent nematodes from growing in the area. A three-year crop rotation can also help control nematodes. Keep susceptible plants out of the garden area for three years. In the intervening time, grow nonsusceptible crops such as members of the grass family (ornamental grasses, corn, sugar cane, wheat, oats) and the cabbage family (cabbage, Brussels sprouts, broccoli, kale, kohlrabi, cauliflower).

Practice garden hygiene. Avoid spreading nematodes from your shoes or tools by washing them off after being in an infected area. Add chitin, which comes from the shells of shellfish and insects, to the soil. Chitin stimulates the growth and multiplication of the many beneficial soil fungi that will attack nematode eggs. Mix the crushed lobster, crab, or shrimp shells with bloodmeal for balanced fertilizing while providing nematode prevention. Dig lots of organic matter into the soil every fall. During the growing season, dig in freshly cut grass to stimulate the fungi that feed on nematode eggs.

Diseases

Plants are susceptible to a wide range of diseases, most of them lurking in the background, waiting to attack a stressed and weakened plant. Compared to our relatively clean environment, plants live in constant filth, literally surrounded by pests and disease. In fact, many of the insect pests not only injure plants but are also vectors, carrying diseases from one plant to another. Other pests make plants more vulnerable to disease by leaving openings for disease to enter.

Of the three types of organisms responsible for the range of diseases and maladies of plants, *fungi* cause the most problems. Though technically small plants, fungi do not contain chloro-

BAKING SODA SOLUTION

To control black spot and powdery mildew, mix 1 gallon of water with 1 tablespoon of baking soda, 3 drops of Ivory liquid, and 3 drops of vegetable oil. Mix well and spray on the tops and bottoms of the affected plant's leaves or stems. Clean up the soil around the plant, and keep leaf litter away.

phyll and therefore cannot make their own food. They survive by parasitizing other living organisms. All fungi, including molds and mildew, produce spores that can live from several days (in summer when they are most active) to years (in cold weather they have a hard coating to protect them). These spores are like seeds that germinate in the dampness. Once you see, for example, the black mark on a rose leaf that indicates black spot disease, there are already thousands of spores that will be released when a drop of water hits the leaf. These spores will bounce upward, infecting the next set of leaves. One of the best ways to control fungi is to keep the leaves dry. Water early in the day and at soil level.

Bacteria do not cause the same problems for plants as they do for humans. However, a few bacterial diseases are very serious. Fireblight, which affects pears and apples, is caused by bacteria that are spread by wind, rain, and insects from one plant to another, quickly multiplying and killing young twigs. Luckily, most bacteria cannot survive cold winters, so a problem one year will probably not be a problem the next.

Viruses, the smallest of the disease causers, most often do not kill the plant; rather they cause crinkled leaves, specks of yellow in leaves, and twisting of leaves or stems. Viruses are usually carried to plants by hosts, including thrips, leafhoppers, whiteflies, and aphids. Some plants

themselves are carriers—they are unaffected by the virus but can spread it to susceptible plants. Tiger lilies, which carry a virus that can affect other lilies, are best planted alone or at least 30' from other lilies.

Sometimes, despite all your good intentions, diseases strike. The following chart lists some of the more common diseases that attack garden plants, symptoms to watch for, and methods of controlling them. If a problem is recurrent, one of the easiest controls (especially for annuals and vegetables) is to destroy the plant and substitute a disease-resistant variety.

Diseases can be more problematic in the vegetable garden, where there is less diversity of plants. Check with your local Cooperative Extension service to learn which crops are most problematic in your area. Consider growing disease-resistant varieties of those particular vegetables.

There are times when attempts at controlling a disease (be it viral, bacterial, or fungal) fail and the same disease reoccurs season after season. When facing a chronic disease problem, it may be necessary to sterilize the top several inches of soil by using the heat of the sun in a process called *solarization.* In May, remove and destroy any plant material from the infested area. Pull up all roots and rake the entire area smooth. Gently water the entire area, slowly wetting the soil to a depth of at least 12". This may take overnight or a day. Don't drench the soil, just get it lightly moist. Cover the entire area with a layer of plastic by pulling it from both sides so that it loosely covers the soil, leaving some air space between the soil and plastic. Place stones or bricks (you can also use clean soil) around the edge of the plastic to hold it in place. Leave the plastic on until September to completely sterilize the infected soil.

Once you've removed the plastic, plant only disease-free plants. Try not to introduce plants that have been growing elsewhere in the garden into a solarized area unless they are completely healthy with no signs of disease.

COMMON DISEASES

DISEASE	PLANTS AFFECTED	SYMPTOMS	CONTROL
Anthracose	Beans, cucurbits, other vegetables, ash, native dogwood, elm, maple, oak, sycamore, other trees.	Cankers (sunken lesions) on leaves, fruit, stems. Masses of spores (resembling pale, pinkish slime) can ooze from cankers. Leaves drop prematurely; diseased stems and branches die back.	Grow resistant varieties. Practice crop rotation and good garden hygiene. Buy certified, disease-free seeds. Prune out and destroy affected parts. Apply baking soda solution (facing page) as soon as symptoms appear, or use Bordeaux mixture. Don't work among wet plants.
Bacterial wilt (bacteria)	Vegetables (especially corn, cucurbits, eggplant, peppers, potatoes, tomatoes), flowers, herbaceous plants. Survives in soil for years.	Plants wilt and dry (first just leaves, then shoots and larger branches). Initially, plants appear to recover partially at night. To be sure it's bacterial wilt, cut a stem in half, put the cut ends together, and gently squeeze; as you pull the ends apart, a white mucusy thread will indicate that the disease is present. Fatal.	Incurable. Plant resistant varieties. Remove and destroy all infected plants, then wash hands and tools in 10% bleach or alcohol solution. Control flea beetles and cucumber beetles that spread the disease.
Black spot (fungus)	Roses.	Circular black spots (sometimes with a yellow border) on leaves. Leaves may drop off plant.	Grow resistant varieties. Provide good air circulation. Remove and destroy infected parts. Spray with baking soda solution (facing page). Water early in the day; avoid wetting leaves.
Brown rot (fungus)	Apricot, nectarine, peach, and other stone fruit.	Fruit has characteristic soft brown spots (may get bigger and rot, becoming covered with spores). Blossoms wilt and decay, then twigs crack and may ooze sap. "Mummies" of shriveled fruit hang on tree.	Bird netting keeps birds from spreading disease. Pick and destroy infected fruit (also any fallen on ground). Prune out and destroy infected branches; prune to open tree up to more sun and air. When plant is in bloom, spray with fungicide, again 2–3 weeks before harvest.

COMMON DISEASES (CONTINUED)

DISEASE	PLANTS AFFECTED	SYMPTOMS	CONTROL
Club root (fungus)	Cabbages, cauliflower, broccoli, alyssum, and other brassicas.	Swelling or distortion of roots.	Practice crop rotation on a 5-year schedule. Remove diseased plants.
Crown gall (bacteria)	Roses (and other plants in the rose family), marigolds, chrysanthemums, euonymus, and other plants.	Tumor-like growths on roots or stem near soil level (looks worse than it is). Plants weakened or stunted. Gall can split open, providing entryway for other diseases or pests.	Grow resistant varieties. Solarize soil (diseases can live in soil or on dead tissue 2–3 years). Grow plants treated with *Agrobacterium radiobacter* (bacteria).
Fireblight (bacteria)	Pear, quince, apple, crab-apple, pyracantha (sometimes other rose family, e.g., hawthorn, spirea, cotoneaster, serviceberry).	Leaves, shoots, and developing fruit wilt and look like they've been blackened by fire. Large branches may develop dark sunken cankers.	Prune and destroy affected growth. Cut at least 6" below infection and disinfect pruners between each cut in 10% alcohol solution. Plant resistant varieties. Apply Bordeaux mixture or streptomycin when flowers start to open; repeat every 5 days until flowering stops.
Fusarium wilt (fungus)	Many herbaceous plants. Each strain of fusarium is plant-specific.	Leaves and stems wilt, turn yellow, then die. Often plant shows symptoms only on one side.	Remove and destroy infected plants; solarize soil. Crop rotation (at least 5-year rotation; fungus can live up to 10 years in soil). Plant early when soil is cool—fungus is active in warm soil.
Mosaic viruses (virus)	Many plants. Each strain of mosaic virus is plant- (or family-) specific.	Mottled or streaked leaves. Distorted or stunted growth. Reduced yields (vegetables and fruits). Poor fruit quality.	Plant resistant varieties. Don't smoke around plants in the nightshade family (Solanaceae)—if you do, wash hands before touching plants. Control aphids and other virus-spreading insects.

DISEASE	PLANTS AFFECTED	SYMPTOMS	CONTROL
Powdery mildew (fungus)	Roses, cucurbits, phlox, dahlias, lilacs, zinnias, beans, peas, grapes, small fruits, euonymus, fruit trees, bluegrass lawns.	Initially leaves get small, circular gray or white patches. Then entire leaf has powdery coating and becomes distorted. Leaves may drop; then plant weakens or dies.	At first symptoms, spray with baking soda solution (p. 62). Or spray with sulfur or lime sulfur or Bordeaux mixture. Unlike other fungal disease, this one thrives in dry air, so mist leaves with water regularly. Prune to promote good air circulation. Plant resistant varieties. Cut out and destroy any infected parts.
Rust (fungus)	Roses, hollyhocks, snapdragons, lawn, and many other plants. Most rusts are plant-specific. (Cedar apple rust, however, requires two hosts.)	First yellow-orange (sometimes brown or purple) pustules appear on undersides of leaves. Then upper leaf surfaces are mottled with yellow. Severe infections result in stunted growth or death.	Plant resistant varieties. Cut out and destroy infected leaves. Provide good air circulation. Water at ground level—if overhead watering is unavoidable, water only early in the morning on sunny days.
Sooty mold (fungus)	All plants.	Black coating on leaves. Often secondary to infestation by aphids, leafhoppers, mealybugs, psyllids, scale, and whitefly. (Fungus thrives on honeydew secreted by these pests.)	Control insect pests. Wipe or hose mold from plant.
Southern blight (fungus)	Peanuts, tomatoes (other members of nightshade family), lawn, many flowers and vegetables.	White cottony growth on stem near soil level (may spread to soil). Plant wilts, then dies.	Remove and destroy infected plants and 8" of soil around them. Crop rotation on a 3-year schedule. Add nitrogen to soil (fungus thrives in nitrogen-deficient soil).
Verticillium wilt (fungus)	Tomatoes, potatoes, strawberries, and 200 other species.	One branch or side of plant wilts. Leaves yellow (starting at edges, working inward, then brown and die). Disease progresses upward and outward. Plant may die.	Prune out affected branches. Remove and destroy infected plant. Solarize soil (do not till first; fungus in top 6" of soil). Grow plants in raised beds or containers with new, clean soil. Don't overfertilize with nitrogen (verticillium thrives in excess nitrogen).

AN OUNCE OF PREVENTION . . .

It is far easier to prevent a potential problem than to deal with pests and diseases once they've gained a foothold in your garden. Start out with good soil and amend it with plenty of compost or other organic matter. Nurture your plants. Good organic gardening practices provide the basis for strong, healthy plants that will not be susceptible to pests and diseases.

Follow the rules of good garden hygiene. Avoid spreading disease by clearing out any infected plants. Wash your tools and shoes off when going from an infested area of the garden to a healthy one. You can forestall a lot of pests and diseases by eliminating the places where they live and/or hide. At the end of the gardening season, do a thorough cleanup. Cut back and remove the tops of perennials and bulbs after they have browned; pull out dead annuals, roots and all. If there is any evidence of pests or disease, do not compost the affected material. Even hot compost may not kill off all bacteria, viruses, and fungi. Rake up any leaves from healthy plants that may have fallen on the ground and compost them.

Water the soil, not the leaves, by means of drip irrigation systems or soaker hoses. Wet leaves are an easy target for a number of fungal diseases; mildews, rusts, and black spot all need moisture to spread. If you use a sprinkler, water early in the day so that the leaves can dry out in the sun. Watering late in the day, unless done at ground level, results in leaves that remain damp all night. Even if you live in an area where summers are hot and humid, you may still be vulnerable to these problems. Too little water also invites problems. Wilted, thirsty plants are choice targets for aphids, spider mites, and diseases. Pay close attention to the specific water requirements of your plants.

THREE-YEAR ROTATION PLAN

To keep track of your garden plan from year to year, draw your basic garden design on a piece of heavy white paper. Each year or growing season, overlay the design with tracing paper and fill in the plants you grow in specific areas. Be sure to label and date the paper. The plan below, based on a four-area layout, lets you see at a glance what crop should be planted in each area for the following season. Area A includes heavy feeders and most root vegetables: potatoes, carrots, beets, parsnips, onions, leeks, garlic, tomatoes, eggplant, peppers, squash, celery, cucumbers, melons. Area B is for peas, beans, corn, okra, spinach, Swiss chard, lettuce, chicory. Area C is the mustard family: cabbage, Chinese cabbage, Brussels sprouts, cauliflower, broccoli, mustard, kale, rutabaga, turnips, radishes, kohlrabi. Area D is for permanent crops, such as rhubarb, artichokes, Jerusalem artichokes, asparagus, seakale, perennial herbs.

The first year the garden is laid out A-B-C-D; the second year, B-C-A-D; the third, C-A-B-D. The fourth year returns to the starting design.

First Year

Second Year

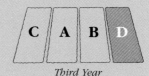

Third Year

ROTATING VEGETABLE FAMILIES

Family Name	Vegetable Crops	Rotation Rationale
Apiaceae (Carrot family)	Carrots, parsley, dill, fennel, celery, coriander	Moderate feeders. May be preceded by any other plant family. Add compost to soil before planting. Follow with heavy mulch or legumes.
Brassicaceae (Mustard family)	Broccoli, Brussels sprouts, cabbage, cauliflower, kale, radish, turnip	Require a lot of soil maintenance. Heavy feeders. Precede with legumes, follow with crop.
Cucurbitaceae (Gourd family)	Cucumber, melons, squash, pumpkin, watermelon	Precede with winter rye or wheat for improved weed and insect control. Follow with legumes.
Fabaceae (Pea family)	Beans, peas, clover, vetch	Fix nitrogen to the soil, adding to soil fertility. Beneficial to soil; few pest problems. May be rotated alternately with all other garden crops.
Liliaceae (Lily family)	Onions, garlic, leeks, shallots, chives, scallions	Rotate with legumes. Never plant in soil that contains uncomposted or undecomposed organic matter.
Poaceae (Grass family)	Wheat, oats, rye, corn	Plant to control weeds and improve soil drainage. Grow before nightshade or gourd family crops.
Solanaceae (Nightshade family)	Eggplant, peppers, tomatoes, potatoes	Heavy feeders; have many fungal diseases and pests. Precede with grass family; follow with legumes.

CROP ROTATION

Crop rotation can be effective in discouraging pests and preventing soil-borne diseases (especially those that are attracted to specific plants) in vegetable gardens and annuals beds. For example, if you grew tomatoes in the same spot year after year, the soil would quickly become depleted of nutrients. Any pest or disease that is particular to tomatoes would thrive in the soil, overwintering from year to year. Crop rotation, combined with adding organic matter each season, helps the soil replenish those depleted nutrients. When practicing crop rotation, you don't grow the same plant (or even related plants like peppers, eggplants, or potatoes) in the same place for at least three consecutive years. The second year, by planting something else in the soil, any tomato pests and diseases that survived the winter would find no tomatoes to feed on. Ideally with several years between planting of the same crop, the pests and diseases will die off from lack of a host plant. In addition to vegetables, there are several flowers (including gladiolus, asters, and tulips) that need to be rotated to avoid an accumulation of pathogens in the soil. For crop rotation to work, the same plant should not be grown within a radius of 10' from where it was previously planted. This means that if you plant corn, for example, in four rows, you must keep corn at least 10' away from the edges of the planting in successive years.

BENEFICIAL HERBS IN THE VEGETABLE GARDEN

HERB	PLANT NEAR:	BENEFIT
Basil (*Ocimum basilicum*)	Tomatoes Any plant in the garden	Enhances growth. Repels flies and mosquitoes.
Bee balm (*Monarda didyma*)	Any plant in the garden	Better flavor; enhances growth.
Borage (*Borago officinalis*)	Tomatoes Strawberries, apples, peas, squash	Repels tomato worms. Improves flavor and growth; increases yield.
Calendula (*Calendula officinalis*)	Tomatoes Asparagus Carrots	Repels tomato worms. Repels asparagus beetles. Repels carrot flies.
Caraway (*Carum carvi*)	Any plant in the garden	Attracts beneficial insects.
Catnip (*Nepeta cataria*)	Edge of garden; crucifers (members of cabbage family) Peaches Any plant in the garden	Repels flea beetles. Repels aphids. Attracts beneficial insects.
Chamomile, Roman (*Chamaemelum nobile*)	Cabbage, onions	Better flavor; enhances growth.
Chervil (*Anthriscus cereifolium*)	Radishes	Better flavor; enhances growth.
Chives (*Allium schoenoprasum*)	Carrots (between rows) Any plant in the garden	Better flavor; enhances growth. Repels aphids.
Coriander (*Coriandrum sativum*)	Anise Any plant in the garden	Better flavor; enhances growth. Repels aphids.
Daisy (*Leucanthemum vulgare*)	Any plant in the garden	Attracts beneficial insects.
Dill (*Anethum graveolens*)	Crucifers (members of the cabbage family) Any plant in the garden	Enhances growth. Attracts beneficial insects.

Fennel
(*Foeniculum vulgare*)
	Edge of the garden
	    (Plant away from the garden.)
		Attracts beneficial insects.
		    (Can also stunt growth.)

Flax (*Linum perenne*)	Potatoes (between rows)	Repels potato bugs.
Garlic (*Allium sativum*)	Roses, raspberries Any plant in the garden	Repels Japanese beetles. General insect repellent.
Horseradish (*Armoracia rusticana*)	Potatoes	Repels potato bugs.
Hyssop (*Hyssopus officinalis*)	Cabbage Grapes Any plant in the garden	Repels cabbage moths. Enhances growth and flavor. Attracts beneficial insects.
Lavender (*Lavandula* spp.)	Any plant in the garden	Repels aphids.
Leeks (*Allium ampeloprasum*)	Celery Carrots	Better flavor; enhances growth. Repels carrot fly.
Lemon balm (*Melissa officinale*)	Any plant in the garden	Attracts beneficial insects.
Lovage (*Levisticum officinalis*)	Any plant in the garden	Better flavor; vigor. Attracts beneficial insects.

Marigold (*Tagetes* spp.)	Any plant in the garden	Repels nematodes, cucumber beetles,
		    Mexican bean beetles, and other
		    insects. Great companion.

HERB	PLANT NEAR:	BENEFIT
Marjoram, sweet (*Origanum majorana*)	Any plant in the garden	Better flavor; vigor.
Mint (*Mentha* spp.)	Cabbage	Enhances flavor; repels cabbage moth.
	Crucifers (members of cabbage family)	Repels flea beetles.
	Tomatoes	Better flavor.
	Any plant in the garden	Attracts beneficial insects; repels ants and aphids.
Nasturtium (*Tropaeolum majus*)	Radishes, cabbage, cucurbits, fruit trees	Repels aphids, squash bugs, striped pumpkin beetles.
Onion (*Allium cepa*)	Carrots	Repels carrot flies.
Parsley (*Petroselinum crispum*)	Tomatoes	Enhances flavor.
	Any plant in the garden	Attracts beneficial insects.
Pennyroyal (*Mentha pulegium*)	Carrots	Repels carrot flies.
	Any plant in the garden	Repels flies, ants, aphids, and mosquitoes.
Radish (*Raphanus sativus*)	Peas, leaf lettuce	Better flavor; repels beetles.
	Cucumber, squash	Repels cucumber beetles.
Rosemary (*Rosmarinus officinalis*)	Cabbage	Repels cabbage moth.
	Beans	Repels bean beetles.
	Carrots	Repels carrot flies.
Rue (*Ruta* spp.)	Roses, raspberries (Plant away from basil.)	Repels Japanese beetles. (Can also stunt growth.)
Sage (*Salvia officinalis*)	Cabbage	Repels cabbage moths.
	Rosemary	Enhances flavor.
	Carrots	Repels carrot flies.
Savory, summer (*Satureja hortensis*)	Onions	Better flavor; enhances growth.
	Beans	Repels bean beetles.
Southernwood (*Artemisia abrotanum*)	Crucifers (members of cabbage family)	Repels cabbage moths and flea beetles.
	Apples, peaches, plums, pears	Repels fruit tree moths.
	Any plant in the garden	Better flavor; enhances growth. Repels ants.
Tansy (*Tanacetum vulgare*)	Roses	Repels Japanese beetles.
	Beans	Repels bean beetles.
	Raspberries	Repels ants and other insects.
	Peaches	Repels aphids.
	Squash and melons	Repels squash bugs and cabbage worms.
	Any plant in the garden	Repels flies.
Thyme (*Thymus* spp.)	Cabbage	Repels cabbageworms.
	Carrots	Repels carrot flies.
	Any plant in the garden	Attracts beneficial insects.
Wormwood (*Artemisia absinthium*)	Crucifers (members of cabbage family)	Repels flea beetles and cabbage moths.
	Any plant in the garden	Better flavor; enhanced growth.
Yarrow (*Achillea millefolium*)	Any plant in the garden	Attracts beneficial insects.

COMPANION PLANTING FOR VEGETABLES

Plant allies help other plants to grow better. Generally they make good neighbors. Plant enemies, conversely, hinder each other's growth, so keep them well away from each other in the garden. The following is a list of common vegetables and their allies and enemies.

VEGETABLE	PLANT NEAR:	KEEP AWAY FROM:
Beans (*Phaseolus* spp.)	Beets (only bush beans), broccoli, cabbage, carrots, corn, cucumbers, peas, potatoes, radishes, Swiss chard	Onions (will stunt plant growth)
Beets (*Beta vulgaris,* Crassa group)	Bush beans, broccoli, cabbage, lettuce, onions	Pole beans (will stunt plant growth)
Broccoli (*Brassica oleracea,* Botrytis group)	Beets, cucumber, lettuce, onions, potatoes, spinach	–
Cabbage (*Brassica oleracea,* Capitata group)	Beets, cucumber, lettuce, onions, potatoes, spinach, Swiss chard	–
Carrots (*Daucus carota* spp. *sativus*)	Beans, lettuce, onions, peas, peppers, radishes, tomatoes	Dill (will retard plant growth)
Corn (*Zea mays*)	Beans, cucumber, peas, potatoes, pumpkins, squash	Tomatoes (will attract worms that feed on corn)
Cucumber (*Cucumis sativus*)	Beans, broccoli, cabbage, corn, peas, radishes, tomatoes	Sage (will retard plant growth)
Lettuce (*Lactuca sativa*)	Beets, broccoli, cabbage, carrots, onions, radishes	–
Peas (*Pisum sativum*)	Beans, carrots, corn, cucumbers, radishes, turnips	Onions (will stunt plant growth)
Peppers (*Capiscum* spp.)	Carrots, onions, tomatoes	–
Potatoes (*Solanum tuberosum*)	Beans, broccoli, cabbage, corn, peas	Tomatoes (attacked by same blights)
Pumpkins (*Cucurbita* spp.)	Corn, squash	Potatoes (will inhibit plant growth)
Radishes (*Raphanus sativus*)	Beans, carrots, cucumbers, lettuce, peas	Hyssop (will inhibit plant growth)
Spinach (*Spinacia oleracea*)	Broccoli, cabbage	–
Squash (*Cucurbita* spp.)	Corn	Potatoes (will inhibit plant growth)
Swiss chard (*Beta vulgaris,* Cicla group)	Beans, cabbage, onions	–
Tomatoes (*Lycopersicon esculentum*)	Carrots, cucumbers, onions, peppers	Corn (attracts worms that feed on tomatoes); dill (will stunt growth); potatoes (attacked by same blight disease)
Turnips (*Brassica rapa,* Rapifera group)	Peas	Potatoes (will inhibit plant growth)

COMPANION PLANTING

Companion planting, a practice long used by organic vegetable gardeners, espouses biodiversity in the garden. Rather than a monocrop of rows and rows of the same plant, flowers, herbs, and vegetables are intermingled, resulting in higher yields, better flavor, more beneficial insects, and fewer pests. Besides, a mixed planting is much more appealing than uniform rows in any garden.

Companion planting is based on the relationships between plants and organisms, as well as among various different plants. *Attractant crops* are the plants that attract beneficial organisms (usually insects) that you want in the garden. These beneficials prey on pest insects and supplement their diet with the nectar and pollen of the attractant crops. *Repellent crops* discourage pests. Aromatic marigolds, for instance, exude a substance from their roots that repels eelworms (root-sucking nematodes). Many gardeners plant a border of marigolds around their garden to keep these pests away from precious edibles. Garlic is a good all-purpose pest repellent. Grown in humus rich soil, it gives off sulfur compounds (what makes it smell) that will kill aphids and onion flies.

Companion plants also include *allies*, those that help adjacent plants by nourishing them. Any legumes, like peas or beans, fix nitrogen from the air, adding nutrition to the soil. When planted with root vegetables, including carrots, turnips, radishes, rutabagas, and beets, these plants provide fertilizer to neighboring plants. Plants that make good neighbors don't compete for space, sun, or nutrients. Interplanting corn and lettuce, for example, maximizes the use of space in the garden; the corn shields the lettuce from the sun's glare and the plants have no pests in common. Some plants, like basil, enhance the growth of any plant in close proximity.

The last group of plants to consider in companion planting are *plant enemies*. These are plants that may have a negative effect on other plants when grown in close proximity. An enemy may be too aggressive, competing for the same sun and soil nutrients of a neighboring plant. Another may attract or be a host plant for a pest or disease that also affects the other plants you want to grow. Some plants inhibit the growth of specific plants or all plants in general. Black walnut trees and sunflowers have a substance in their roots (and seed coats) that inhibits most other plant growth. Fennel often stunts the growth of other plants, but it attracts beneficial parasitic wasps and can be given space near rather than in the garden.

Armed with all the information on companions, you can plan your garden so that it will benefit from allies, attractant crops, and repellent crops while avoiding plant enemies. Pests come in all shapes and sizes, from microscopic nematodes to 1½" cabbage loopers, 8" banana slugs to large deer. Whatever their status, they can wreak havoc on a garden if they are not controlled. Diseases, too, come in various guises—molds and mildews, wilts and blights, curls and burns. Depending on the disease, its manifestation and effects may be merely unsightly or at worst can destroy an entire garden. Insects—both good and bad—will vary from one garden to the next; each habitat is unique. Experiment with companion plants in your garden to see how they work for you.

EVERY GARDEN COUNTS

Planting a garden is an act of creation, an opportunity to use nature's palette to increase our pleasure in the world. Be it humble or lavish, involving inches or acres, a beautiful garden reflects the imagination and style of the gardener. It makes a personal statement and expresses the gardener's individual aesthetic, defining all that is pleasing to look at, tend to, and live with.

Look at a row of identical houses, and you'll see that the front yards differ markedly, each expressing the owner's individual style. One house will have a neatly mowed lawn, some carefully trimmed shrubs at the foundation, and a tree or two. The house next door might have a white picket fence with an old-fashioned garden gate, roses climbing over the arch, and a cottage garden in exuberant bloom. And down the street a tall hedge protects a brick patio decorated with wooden benches flanked by urns cascading with English ivy. There are as many wonderful gardens as there are gardeners, and naturally no two are ever quite alike.

The pleasures of a garden are endless, and you can let your imagination soar. Perhaps you daydream about leisurely Sunday brunches in a closed courtyard, serenaded by the sound of water playing in a fountain. Or you yearn to spend weekends poking about in a potting shed, quietly transferring tiny seedlings from flats to their first pots in anticipation of a bed filled with summer color. It could be that you believe it's not properly autumn until you've raked the leaves into brilliantly colored drifts and into piles destined for the compost bin. Or, with a culinary passion for freshness and flavor married with a respect for history, you want to grow heirloom vegetables from seed in a lovely large container.

Sometimes gardens are a way to transform the world, a way to say how things ought to be. You can, for instance, insist on imposing some order in a world that feels chaotic. Dwarf boxwood hedges offer shape, create a pattern, and define boundaries, as does an intricate knot garden of carefully sheared and shaped fragrant herbs; a bouquet of pastel summer annuals—pale cosmos, bachelor's buttons, and larkspur—introduces a bit of whimsy when planted within the perimeter. On the other hand, in reaction to the rigidity and structure of life, you might want to indulge yourself in a luxurious profusion of tumbling colorful plants.

Even beyond the beauty of a garden, beyond the profound contentment afforded by gardening, you have the opportunity to influence the ecology of your surroundings. By planting trees, you increase the number of places available for birds to nest. Shrubs with berries make more food available to birds and wildlife. Vines with nectar-filled flowers encourage both hummingbirds and butterflies. By expressing yourself, and by respecting nature, you will be rewarded with enormous pleasure.

GRAND DESIGNS

One of the most creative, and fun, parts of gardening is deciding what type of garden to have: large or small, formal or wildly exuberant. The purpose the garden will serve in the life of the gardener is a major element in its conception and design. Gardens designed as private retreats are very different from gardens that are built for outdoor entertaining. Whereas a private garden may have a sequestered bench or two, the garden for entertaining calls for areas furnished with chairs and carts, tables and broad market umbrellas—plenty of places for friends to sit and stand and mingle. The private garden may have casual paths lined with wood chips; the garden for entertaining works best with paths of flagstone or brick, which are easier to walk on and much better at keeping shoes clean and dry.

Certainly a garden need not be big to be beautiful. The smallest city garden can create a sense of refuge or become an urban oasis. If you have minimal space, you can pack it with pretty pots and planters filled with flowers and perhaps even grow

SMALL-SPACE FAVORITES

Small gardens are enhanced by shrubs and trees that give more than one season of pleasure. You want plants that bloom an exceptionally long time, give summer shade and brilliant autumn color, and have an intriguing winter silhouette or interesting bark pattern. Most hollies have glossy green leaves all year round and colorful berries in fall and winter that attract birds. Citrus trees are evergreens with aromatic flowers and delicious fruit. The classic antique rugosa rose 'Blanc Double de Coubert,' introduced in 1892, grows under the toughest circumstances, is seldom troubled by pests or diseases, and has exquisite, richly fragrant white flowers, attractive leaves that turn clear yellow in autumn, and handsome scarlet rose hips (very rich in vitamin C) in the fall. None of these plants is especially small, but any one of them would be a satisfying choice virtually every day of the year.

some vegetables. You can attach trellises to walls and grow flowering vines, or send self-clinging vines like Boston ivy or Virginia creeper up the sides of buildings. A small windowsill filled with potted herbs, or a window box overflowing with bloom, can give as much pleasure to the gardener—and the passerby—as any other kind of garden.

Deciding on the kind of garden is only the beginning; there still remain myriad choices. Do you want a long perennial border with seasonal sweeps and swirls of bloom? If so, you'll need to know when and for how long each plant will flower, and what will bloom around it while it's coming on or take its place when it fades.

You may delight in growing flowers simply for the sheer romance of their names: kiss-behind-the-garden-gate, morning glory, love-in-a-mist, honesty, bleeding heart, forget-me-not. If your passions extend to literature, you can re-create

A SUNNY SUMMER BORDER

In a relatively small space (10' × 3') this border gives the feel of a country garden, whether situated at the edge of a lawn, bordering a patio, in a suburban backyard, or even within the small yard of a town house or condominium. With proper planning, you can enjoy its beauty throughout the seasons.

The ornamentation and the hardscape play a vital role in creating the ambience of the space. The flagstone path helps to delineate the garden, while the plantings between stones extend it outward. Both the thyme and chamomile will spread onto the stones as time goes by; gently stepping on them releases their fragrance into the air.

The rustic plant supports at the back set the tone of an informal country garden. Wattle trellises like these were originally handmade; today, they are available commercially, or you can try your hand at creating your own. Not only are the trellises functional, providing inconspicuous support for the asters, bee balm, dahlias, gas plant, and clematis, but they also lend interest to the garden when the plants are not in season. Even in winter, when the only plant you see is the creeping thyme, such trellises are lovely to look at. With several inches of snow on the garden, you can enjoy the serenity from a warm spot indoors, or you can bundle up, dust off the bench, and sit down to contemplate the stillness. The

PLANT KEY*

1. *Aster × frikartii* 'Wonder of Staffa'
2. *Scabiosa caucasica*
3. *Nepeta × faassenii* 'Six Hills Giant'
4. *Monarda fistulosa* 'Violet Queen'
5. *Veronica austriaca* ssp. *teucrium* 'Crater Lake Blue'
6. *Heuchera* 'Palace Purple'
7. *Dahlia* 'Betty Bowen'
8. *Verbena canadensis* 'Homestead Purple'
9. *Chamaemelum nobile*
10. *Dahlia* 'Athalie'
11. *Erigeron × hybridus* 'Rotes Meer'
12. *Dianthus plumarius*
13. *Dictamnus albus*
14. *Lavatera thuringiaca* 'Barnsley'
15. *Echinacea purpurea* 'White Swan'
16. *Clematis* 'Henryi'
17. *Zephyranthes grandiflora*
18. *Thymus vulgaris*

*All plants listed here appear in the Plant Guide, pages 276–479.

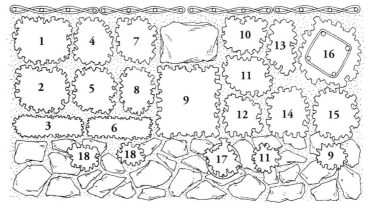

stone bench is the finishing touch, giving you a place to relax and enjoy your garden. The advantage of a wide, backless bench is that you can comfortably face in any direction and delight in the panorama of the border.

Though chosen primarily for a summer border, the plant selection allows for color interest from spring to fall. In spring, perennials emerge from their winter dormancy. The purplish foliage of the heuchera is a welcome contrast to all the spring green. Before long the dianthuses are in bloom, perfuming the air with their spicy-sweet aroma.

As spring turns to summer, the garden bursts into bloom in Jekyllesque style from left to right—blues blending to purples going to pinks that finally fade into whites. The color continues into fall, with the asters and dahlias dominating the scene. Many of the other flowers, including the nepeta, scabiosa, and verbena, will often give a second burst of color if the flowering stems are cut back as soon as possible after they finish blooming.

a "Shakespeare" garden by planting flowers that were extolled 400 years ago. Or you can decide to surround yourself with the fragrance of lilacs and mock orange, antique roses and peonies, jasmine and honeysuckle, mint and melissa, in a garden designed to perfume the air as much as to delight the eye.

Vegetable gardens offer great rewards, from a children's garden with radishes and scarlet runner beans to the most extensive kitchen potager. Herbs can be grown simply in strawberry pots or more elaborately in a knot garden. Peach and plum trees can be relegated to the far corners of the backyard, where fruit drop is not a problem, or heirloom apple trees espaliered against a stone wall. Consider the beauty of many edibles and incorporate them in other areas of the garden; they need not be segregated from the ornamentals. 'Ruby' chard is gorgeous with the sun illuminating its red ribs; lettuces, especially those slow to bolt, are lovely edging a border. The plumes of bronze fennel are elegant as they emerge in spring and make a bold statement in summer.

A cactus and succulent garden can feature anything from such strikingly sculptural cacti as night-blooming cereus and white-haired old man cactus to the pale silver-pink rosettes of *Echeveria crenulata* or the flamboyantly exotic blooms of orchid cactus, a spineless tropical cactus with flowers up to 10" across.

A foliage garden is both soothing and serene, a subtle symphony in shades of green. You can create a tranquil summer shade garden by combining the willow-green, maidenhair-like leaves of inside-out flower (*Vancouveria planipetala*), the silvery leaves of lady's mantle, the broad, blue-green leaves edged in gold of *Hosta sieboldiana* 'Elegans,' the tripartate leaves of wake-robin, the leathery dark green leaves of Christmas rose (*Helleborus niger*), the soft, maple-like leaves of Japanese anemone 'Honorine Jobert,' and the bright, fresh green leaves of *Rodgersia aesculifolia*.

While all of these plants bloom, they do so in quiet colors. The drama here is produced by the foliage.

Garden choices can also be influenced by what you've seen in your travels. Perhaps you admired the traditional English garden, with its softly inviting herbaceous borders and trellises of old cabbage roses; or a Mediterranean garden with lavender and bougainvillea; or a Japanese garden with delicately leafed bamboo, Japanese iris, and a hand-carved deer-scare spilling water over shining black river rocks.

A garden to meditate in, a garden to grub in; a garden to stroll in, a garden to picnic in; a garden for gathering bouquets, a garden for gathering salad for dinner; a garden for children to plant their first beans in, a garden for growing rare species of orchids and ferns—the choices are infinite, alluring, and every one lovely. Whether big or small, casual or formal, sustaining or ornamental, every garden counts.

PRACTICAL CONSIDERATIONS

Gardens need planning before they need planting. One of the first considerations should be how much time and energy you're willing to devote to the garden. If mowing the lawn, trimming the hedge, and deadheading the flowers seem more like chores than pleasures, then plan a garden that requires minimal maintenance. If your greatest joy is found in poking seedlings into the ground and you get into the zen of weeding, daydreaming about how the garden will look when mature and glorying in a beautifully successful effect, then design a garden without regard to the amount of time it may take to tend. A garden is a long-term project; indeed, most serious gardeners would call it a lifetime undertaking. It's foolish—and no fun—to put in more garden than you can realistically manage.

A SHRUB BORDER

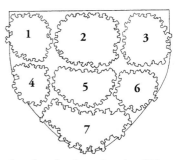

This bed is a wonderful answer to the problem of plantings that end up hiding the front of the house. All too often, gardeners forget to take into account the plants' rate of growth and eventual size—and the ability of the house's occupants to see out the first-floor windows.

The proportion of the plants here is perfectly suitable for use around the foundation. Most of the plants are evergreen, with an interesting variety of leaves from the needled yew and small, rounded leaves of the boxwood to the crenated edges of the holly and the yellow-edged leaves of the daphne. Flowers add continuous bursts of interest. Creamy white clusters of pendulous andromeda flowers bloom in early spring, followed by white rhododendron trusses in late spring; the sweet perfume of daphne fills the air in late winter (in cooler zones, plant *Daphne tangutica*), while the inconspicuous flowers of the heavenly bamboo are followed in fall by bright berries. The new growth on the andromeda is a

PLANT KEY*

———

1. *Rhododendron* 'Loder's White'
2. *Nandina domestica* 'Compacta'
3. *Ilex × meserveae* 'Blue Princess'
4. *Pieris japonica* 'Mountain Fire'
5. *Daphne odora* 'Aureo-marginata'
6. *Taxus baccata* 'Repandens'
7. *Buxus microphylla*

*All plants listed here appear in the Plant Guide, pages 420–433.

striking red in spring, while the heavenly bamboo waits till fall to show its splendid leaf color.

Unlike many other hollies, the blue Meserve hollies need specific males as pollinators. You can just enjoy the leaves and bluish-purple stems of the lovely but hardy 'Blue Princess,' or add a male 'Blue Prince' and watch the female bear fruit. The male can be as far as 50' away and the bees will still do the job of pollinating the female.

All the shrubs here are acid-loving plants. Check your soil pH before you plant, especially if your house has a concrete foundation that leaches calcium into the soil. A good mulch of pine needles, shredded bark, or oak leaves will help to acidify the soil so your evergreens will thrive.

Having a garden forces you to keep an eye on the future. As you plan your garden, its scope and its effects, imagine what it will look like two or even three decades from now. Will the maple's shade be dappled or dense when it's mature? Make a mental note that the gallon-size camellia will someday stand 20' tall with a 10' span. Be aware that perennials like peonies, iris, and hellebores are long-lived, some flourishing for many generations; trees and shrubs can also last a century or more. If you're planning to add on to the house in a couple of years, don't put in permanent plantings where the new family room will go; instead plant annuals or a kitchen garden there. You'll have color or tomatoes until the construction starts, and no loss of valued trees, shrubs, or established perennials. If you have a sense of how your garden will mature, it will be much easier to decide what to plant and where to plant it.

The Inherited Garden

Many gardens are inherited—the lawn, the shrubs, and the trees were planted long ago and came with the house. Most gardeners need to work within the limits of what is already present on the land where they garden: the location and orienta-

EDIBLE LANDSCAPING

Typically, vegetables and fruits are segregated from the rest of the garden, often hidden away behind a fence. Even an herb garden, decorative though it may be, is rarely the front garden. But many edibles can be very showy, and there's no reason not to capitalize on their beauty. Growing them close to the house means you're right there to see when the fruits are ripe and to pluck them at the peak of perfection. In addition, integrating vegetables with the rest of your plantings saves time, energy, and that valuable resource—water.

You can do this in a variety of ways. Include shrubby herbs such as sage, rosemary, lavender, and thyme in your perennial border, where their year-round foliage will provide winter interest when the perennials have died back to the ground. Blueberries, figs, and even prickly pear cactus make handsome foundation plants. Lettuce, parsley, chives, and *fraises des bois* are lovely edging plants. If you use lettuces, grow loose-leaf types and don't harvest the entire plant at once. Instead, pick several outer leaves from each plant as you need them; the plants will continue to produce new inner leaves, often all season long. For summer, choose a slow-bolt variety that can stand the heat, or grow lettuce and other greens in a partially shaded area.

Fruit trees—pear, apple, lemon, orange, and the like—are lovely enough to be used as shade trees on the front lawn. Peppers, eggplants, and tomatoes, especially the European and heirloom varieties in rainbow hues, add wonderful splashes of color in a sunny border.

Edible flowers round out the edible landscape. You may discover that you're already growing some in your garden without having realized how tasty they are. More than 70 flowers are safe (be sure you know what you're eating—there are also poisonous flowers). Their delicious flavors range from sweet to bitter, fruity to anise, oniony to beanlike. You'll have newfound appreciation for your tulips, nasturtiums, roses (in particular, *Rosa rugosa* and many of the old-time roses), daylilies, calendulas, pansies, Johnny-jump-ups, honeysuckle, and other flowers when you indulge in eating them. Used as a garnish or incorporated in a dish, they add flavor and color that you can't get anywhere else. And when not on your plate, they grace the garden with their beauty.

When purchasing new shrubs or trees from a nursery or catalog, be sure to find out their mature heights if you plan on planting them near the house, outbuildings, or pathways. Almost before you know it, your small boxwood may all but hide a window or the branches of your delicate sapling may threaten damage to the roof. Mature heights of the plantings shown here are indicated by light shaded areas.

tion of the house, the number and position of mature trees and established shrubs and perennials.

Before you design your garden, it's a good idea to identify what's already there and get some notion of how much maintenance the existing landscape requires. The next step is to decide what elements you want to add—a collection of antique roses, a children's garden, half a dozen dwarf fruit trees. And finally you need to determine where a new garden can be placed without seriously interfering with what is already growing.

In any inherited landscape, it's wise to wait a year before putting in any plantings in order to observe the garden in every season. This helps to prevent those moments of anguish when you discover, for example, that the huge bare shrub you

ripped out was in fact a rare century-old lilac, the glory of the neighborhood, and a living link with the past. Less dramatically, observing your property in all seasons lessens the likelihood of digging up dormant bulbs and perennials. Spend the first year charting what is already there and satisfy your desire to grow things by planting window boxes, pots, and planters.

The Alternative Lawn

Rather than remove established trees or shrubs, in most cases you can increase the size of your garden simply by reducing the size of the lawn. Large expanses of well-conditioned turf grass are expensive and labor-intensive; they also consume water at

FOR CONTINUAL BLOOM IN THE GARDEN

Especially for those who live in cold-winter climates, one of the greatest pleasures is having flowers for as much of the year as possible. When you plan your garden, intersperse a diversity of plants—from bulbs to trees—that flower at different times to provide a continuity of bloom. All of the plants listed below are included in the Plant Guide (pages 276–479).

LATE WINTER

Giant snowdrop (*Galanthus elwesii*) (B)
Christmas rose (*Helleborus niger*) (P)
Siberian squill (*Scilla siberica*) (B)
Winter daphne (*Daphne odora* 'Aureomarginata') (S)

SPRING

Common shooting star (*Dodecatheon meadia*) (P)
Dove tree (*Davidia involucrata*) (T)
European cranberry bush (*Viburnum opulus* 'Compactum') (S)
Golden columbine (*Aquilegia chrysantha* 'Silver Queen') (P)
Redbud (*Cercis canadensis*) (T)
Virginia sweetspire (*Itea virginica*) (S)
White Chinese wisteria (*Wisteria sinensis* 'Alba') (V)
Wood anemone (*Anemone nemorosa*) (B)

SUMMER

Anise hyssop (*Agastache foeniculum*) (H)
Canary creeper (*Tropaeolum peregrinum*) (A)
Common yarrow (*Achillea millefolium* 'Summer Pastels' Mix) (P)
Crape myrtle (*Lagerstroemia indica* 'Natchez') (T)
Golden rain tree (*Koelreuteria paniculata*) (T)
Prickly pear cactus (*Opuntia humifusa*) (C)
Sunflower (*Helianthus annuus*) (H)
Trumpet creeper (*Campsis × tagliabuana* 'Madame Galen') (V)

LATE SUMMER–EARLY FALL

Belladonna lily (*Amaryllis belladonna*) (B)
Black snakeroot (*Cimicifuga racemosa*) (P)

Butterfly bush (*Buddleia davidii* 'White Knight') (S)
Dahlia (*Dahlia* spp.) (B)
Franklin tree (*Frankliniana alatamaha*) (T)
Moonflower (*Ipomoea alba*) (V)
Silver lace vine (*Polygonum aubertii*) (V)
White boltonia (*Boltonia asteroides*) (P)

FALL–EARLY WINTER

Ivy-leaved cyclamen (*Cyclamen neapolitanum*) (B)
Japanese camellia (*Camellia japonica*) (S)

(A) *Annual* (B) *Bulb* (C) *Cactus* (H) *Herb*
(P) *Perennial* (S) *Shrub* (T) *Tree* (V) *Vine.*

---

alarming rates and usually require pest control. The concept of the rolling lawn came from England, where rain is usually plentiful and flocks of sheep keep it looking like a world-class putting green. Here in America, we must provide a tremendous amount of supplemental water to keep the grass green. During hot, dry summer months, innumerable gallons of potable water are depleted from our reservoirs (we realize this drain on our resources when restrictions are issued), and with limited water come dry, brown lawns and unhappy gardeners.

Since the purpose of a lawn is to provide an area where people can walk or play, and since lawns made of turf grass use so much water, it's time to shift to a more conservation-minded concept. If you want a place where children can play or if you have a high-traffic area, choose plants that are tough and durable but don't trail (vines can snag the foot). Bugleweed and clover are both good choices. Design often dictates a lawn, and it's certainly a pleasure to have a visually tranquil area in which to juxtapose trees, shrubs, and flowers, but this bucolic area doesn't have to be turf grass. Any ground cover can be used as a monoculture (an area made up of only one type of plant) to provide the same visual effect. Consider fescue or crested wheatgrass, both of which are very durable and much more drought-resistant than typically used bluegrasses. Native grasses—little blue stem, big bluestem, and buffalo grass—are deep-rooted and drought-resistant, requiring no fertilizers or other chemicals; they can be quite lovely if left as unmown dry grass during dormant winter months. Sowing handfuls of wildflower seed mixtures adds counterpoints of color and texture in contrast to the uniformity—and boredom—of perfectly shorn grass.

Many low-growing plants easily serve as ground covers and are an ecologically sound alternative to grass lawns. Some are evergreen in cold climates, and all require less water, fewer or no chemicals, and far less maintenance. Ground covers can also be mixed to create drifts of plants with different textures and color. See "Grasses" and "Ground Covers" in the Plant Guide at the back of this book for the right plants for your soil, sunlight, and climate.

Formal or Casual?

Gardens have style, just as architecture does. Indeed, the architecture of a house can influence the style of the garden that accompanies it. In general, formal homes tend to have formal grounds, defined by straight rows of trees, geometrically shaped lawns and flower beds, and paved paths that lead directly from one point to another. Informal dwellings usually have landscapes with softer edges and more curves than angles: meandering paths, winding here and there among free-form flower beds, thick, shaggy hedges, and clumps or groves of trees, maybe grass, pea gravel, or stepping-stones interplanted with moss.

Just as a formally furnished room differs markedly from an informally furnished room, the decorative elements of formal landscapes are readily distinguished from those of informal landscapes. A formal garden may have broad staircases, antique artifacts, or elaborate fountains; informal gardens may include rustic rose arches, weathered wooden garden seats, and birdbaths. The water feature in a formal garden is likely to be rectangular and paved around the edges; in an informal garden, this feature will probably be a naturalistic stream, a small waterfall, or a pond, the edges planted with yellow flag, primroses, and ferns.

Formal gardens have terraces, often stone or tile, typically overlooking the garden, drawing the eye to the far horizon and clearly revealing the outline and patterns of the garden. Beds are geometric and plantings well manicured. Terraces are often furnished with tables and chairs for dining alfresco. In informal gardens, long, open views are blocked by lined paths that twist and turn and lead eventually to secluded clearings, furnished simply with a rustic wooden table and benches or a comfortable Adirondack chair, more suited to a casual picnic or tall glass of lemonade than to a proper meal.

Informal gardens are particularly well suited to "garden rooms," sections planted or furnished quite distinctly from other areas. For example, one "room" might be concealed behind hedges that create an enclosed cloister garden filled with fragrant herbs; another might feature heirloom shrub roses and a series of arches and trellises covered with climbing roses; a third might be no more than a two-tiered fountain centered in a circle of cobbles, kept shiny and moist by the splash and spray of the fountain.

WHY PERENNIALS?

Perennials are of special value in any garden because they return to flower year after year with increasing profusion. They save time because you plant them only once (unlike annuals, which need to be replaced yearly or even, in warm climates, seasonally). Perennials are also economical because many of them can be divided every few years—and should be when they get crowded and produce fewer, smaller flowers. The various divisions can be planted in your garden, passed over the garden gate, or swapped for a division of a plant you admire in a friend's garden.

GERTRUDE JEKYLL'S ORDERLY DISORDER

Doyenne of the quintessential lush and leafy English garden, Gertrude Jekyll sparked a quiet revolution from Munstead Wood, her cottage in Surrey. Jekyll's enemy was artifice; and her ammunition, the trusty, mostly hardy plants of the local countryside.

An artist and craftswoman as well as a garden designer, Gertrude Jekyll (1843–1932) painted her garden and those of her clients with asymmetrical drifts of flowers and bold strokes of color and texture. In place of contrived patterns and pristine rows to be dug up each year, she meticulously planned and planted wild herbaceous borders that would flourish for decades.

No armchair designer, Jekyll scoured the countryside in her pony cart, studying cottage gardens and ancient farmhouses. She worked the soil with enthusiasm and placed as much value on her roughened hands and worn boots as on the final results (her own herbaceous border was an astonishing 200 feet long).

Far from haphazard, the classic Jekyll garden is infused with a thoughtful informality. "I hold the heresy of not minding a little moss on the paths, and of rather preferring a few scattered cluster rose petals on its brown-green velvet," she wrote. And despite its Victorian roots, her aesthetic is intensely fresh and modern, just as her preference for native plants over exotic imports is in keeping with current environmental thinking.

> *"I try for beauty and harmony everywhere, and especially for harmony of colour. A garden so treated gives the delightful feeling of repose...."*

PROTECT THE PAST FOR THE FUTURE

Think long and hard before removing a tree or shrub that cannot be replaced in your lifetime. Trees take many years to achieve maturity, as do large established shrubs. Substituting a skinny sapling or a shrub in a one-gallon pot is not an equal exchange. Twentieth-century suburban development has so often consisted of bulldozing everything in sight that communities across the nation have passed "heritage tree" laws to protect large old trees. One prominent dendrologist, a man who has spent his whole life studying trees, bemoans the fact that we have become a nation of what he refers to as "trinket trees"—small, tidy street and patio trees with gumdrop-shaped crowns that will never inspire the awe of the massive oaks and spreading chestnuts, the magnificent elms and towering pines that were the legacy of the 19th century.

A great many "weed trees"—trees that are fast-growing but weak-limbed and short-lived—were planted in those scraped-to-the-subsoil housing developments. If the trend is not reversed, there will be no trees sturdy enough to support a tree house or a child's swing, no tree large enough to shade a family picnic in the summertime. Consider, too, the financial aspects. Mature trees and shrubs add substantial value to a property, while the expense of moving or removing them is shockingly high. It's often much smarter to garden around mature trees and shrubs than to take them out.

Both formal and informal gardens may use many of the same plants but with different approaches. In the formal garden, a boxwood hedge will be neatly trimmed to a uniform height and width along its entire length. In an informal garden, the same hedge will be allowed to billow naturally, trimmed more to keep it out of the paths than to achieve a precisely uniform appearance. Roses in a formal garden are often planted in blocks—identical cultivars pruned to the same height, all blooming simultaneously to create a mass of single color. In an informal garden, roses are more likely to clamber up trees or along fences, to form shrubby masses covered with summer bloom, or to be included in a perennial border. Vines in a formal garden assume a disciplined, orderly appearance. English ivy, for example, can be trained in neat diamond shapes along the length of a wall. In an informal garden, the same ivy may tumble enthusiastically over a stone wall or drape luxuriously from hanging baskets.

The order and precision of formal gardens work extremely well for both large and small spaces. In a large garden, the formal design takes advantage of spacious views. In a small garden, it organizes the space to create a coherent effect. A walled urban garden, no more than 25' × 45', might have espaliered fruit trees along the long walls and the far wall covered in Boston ivy, Virginia creeper, or variegated porcelainberry vine. A formal fountain placed a few feet in front of the end wall draws the eye to the long view. Paved in stone or herringbone brick, the space can be decorated with a pair of urns on pedestals and formal pots of topiary or dwarf evergreens at each corner. Beneath the fruit trees, white daffodils and narcissus can bloom in the spring, followed by hostas and Japanese anemone in the summer. The scene wants only a table draped in white linen, and cushioned chairs, to make an elegant and enticing garden.

Formal gardens are more likely to use color

to establish patterns. A typical example is a square space divided into quarters, with opposite quarters planted identically, two in red and two in white. Informal gardens tend to mix colors, as in a daylily bed featuring many different shades of soft apricot, salmon, and yellow. Broadly speaking, formal gardens are monochromatic or use color in a very restrained way, while informal gardens tend to use combinations of bright colors.

The Question of Color

Color is a comparatively new aspect in gardening. The color of the great European gardens of the 17th and 18th centuries came from form and mass, light and shade, from the textural and visual contrasts of water, stone, and green. Had all the plants been removed there still would remain the powerful architectural presence of broad terraces and handsome staircases, lakes and ponds, fountains and pavilions.

The more recent fascination with elaborate combinations of shades and tones of color was first popularized to a large extent by Impressionist painters such as Monet, whose garden outside Paris at Giverny has become a mecca for gardeners around the world. In England, Gertrude Jekyll, who had studied painting during the Impressionist period, created herbaceous borders with intricate drifts and ribbons of color.

Much has been written about the process of devising attractive color combinations. Harmonious effects are most easily achieved with combinations of pastel colors; the most startling, with primary colors. A simple and sensible way to see if a given combination pleases you is to test arrangements at the nursery, grouping pots of blooming plants together before bringing them home to the garden. You can also visit other gardens and observe which combinations work well. Seed catalogs usually suggest color combinations, complete with photographs, so you can judge for yourself how certain combinations would look in your garden.

Many plants are sold in "mixed" colors, both in seed packets and as seedlings, particularly annuals and short-lived perennials such as lupines, snapdragons, delphiniums, pansies, and impatiens. A "riot of color" may strike one observer as bright and cheerful; another, as confused and jar-

PLANTS FOR MULTISEASONAL INTEREST*

Beautiful flowers make way for luscious fruit; leaves turn brilliant hues, then drop to reveal bark color and forms; sculptured twigs and pods cast shadow patterns on the snow. Below is a selection of plants that offer visual appeal through more than one season.

Staghorn sumac (*Rhus typhina* 'Laciniata') (T)
Interesting flower heads, clear fall color. Good shape for shadow patterns on snow.

European cranberry bush (*Viburnum opulus* 'Compactum') (S)
Good flower display, fall color, opulent berries.

Holly (*Ilex × meserveae* 'Blue Princess') (S)
Year-round foliar beauty, fall berry production.

Japanese maple (*Acer palmatum*) (T)
Good leaf shape, strong fall color, lovely growth habit for shadow play.

Red twig dogwood (*Cornus stolonifera*) (S)
Fairly interesting flowers, nice foliage and fall color. Fabulous twig color for winter display.

Scarlet oak (*Quercus coccinea*) (T)
Great for color. Acorns feed wildlife. Summer shade provider.

Sedum (*Hylotelephium spectabile*) (P)
Long-lasting flower heads persist through winter, giving lovely shadow patterns.

Serviceberry (*Amelanchier canadensis*) (T)
Flowers, fruit, great fall color.

Variegated Adam's needle (*Yucca filamentosa* 'Variegata') (P)
Summer flowers provide interesting pods for dried arrangements. Evergreen variegated foliage stunning in winter.

All plants listed here appear in the Plant Guide, pages 276–479.
(P) *Perennial* (S) *Shrub* (T) *Tree*

ring. The only hard-and-fast rule is that you must be happy with the garden you've created.

For gardeners who are drawn to the challenge of attempting innovative effects, it's a good idea to "practice" with annuals first. If the color combination turns out to be pleasing, then you can put together the same colors with perennials or flowering shrubs the next year. For example, you might start out by combining perennial red poppies and annual yellow coreopsis; if the colors look good enough to be used as a permanent feature, pull the coreopsis in late summer or early fall (it will be dead or dying anyway, since it's an annual), and add yellow yarrow or perennial coreopsis. You'll have an effective color combination that will come back year after year.

Another way to experiment before making a long-term commitment is to try different color combinations in a pot or planter to see if the reality is as pleasing as the idea. To practice with primary colors, plant Pacific hybrid primroses in pots and move them around until they look right. Once you've achieved an arrangement you like, put it into the garden in fall or the following spring. You can also experiment with shades of one color. To work with pinks, for example, choose a plant that comes in several shades from shell pink to hot pink, from clear pink to salmon. If the color scheme works in a window box, try it in the mixed border next year. If it doesn't, no harm done—annuals are short-term and inexpensive.

In sunny spots, bright or deeper colors show up well; in shady places, pale colors are most effective. Classic combinations are blue and yellow, blue and white, red and yellow, and pink and white. Choice combinations are apricot and pale blue, purple and gold, and clear yellow and cream. Colors that often look best massed alone are purple, magenta, and orange. Vita Sackville-West created a white garden at Sissinghurst, England; suited for evening viewing, it remains green much of the year, with a fabulous white splendor of bloom in June and July.

It is well known that certain colors "recede" and others "advance." Garden designers use this fact to make small gardens seem larger or to foreshorten the perspective to make a large space feel smaller. Planting a mass of blue flowers like delphiniums in the background makes a garden seem to recede into the distance, a useful stroke in a small space. To make a large area feel more compact, plant a red-leaved or red-flowered perennial or shrub, like cardinal flower, in the distance; it will appear to be much closer than it is. A mass of blue and yellow flowers (try bright yellow daffodils or tulips interplanted with blue forget-me-nots) surrounded by large, dense shrubs creates the effect of a splash of spring sunshine, of dappled light and shadow.

Some colors work consistently to smooth the transition from one intense color to another. White always works; cream-colored plants usually do, too. So do silver-leaved plants such as *Artemisia stellerana* 'Silver Brocade'; *Lychnis coronaria; Centaurea cineraria;* and *Senecio cineraria.* Other possibilities are *Artemisia absinthium* 'Lambrook Silver'; *Artemisia arborescens* 'Powis Castle'; *Verbascum bombyciferum* 'Silver Lining'; lavender cotton (*Santolina chamaecyparissus*); *Senecio maritima* 'Cirrhus'; and *Stachys byzantina* 'Silver Carpet.' Sometimes, in certain lights, white flowers or silvery foliage placed adjacent to colorful plants cause the eye of the viewer to "mix" the hues, creating the tints and tones where there are none.

The way the light hits the garden, or the times of day when you observe your garden, may influence what colors you choose. Some colors can wash out in bright sunlight, but oranges and yellows always shine through. If your schedule is such that you see your garden most often by the pale pearly light of dawn and the blue-tinged light of twilight, consider planting the white or very pale flowers and silver-leaved plants that show up best in low light.

FLOWER COMBINATIONS

PALE COLORS FOR SHADE

Bleeding heart (*Dicentra eximia* 'Luxuriant') (P), pink

False spirea (*Astilbe × rosea* 'Peach Blossom') (P), rose-carmine*

Flowering tobacco (*Nicotiana sylvestris*) (A), white*

Impatiens (*Impatiens walleriana* Confection series) (A), pink-carmine

Japanese anemone (*Anemone × hybrida* 'Honorine Jobert') (P), white*

Japanese primrose (*Primula japonica* cvs.) (P), pastels*

Wishbone flower (*Torenia fournieri*) (A), white-pink-blue

FOR BLUE-AND-YELLOW MIXES

BLUES

Bearded iris (*Iris germanica* 'Matinata') (P)

Delphinium (*Delphinium elatum* 'Blue Bird') (P)*

Flossflower (*Ageratum houstonianum* 'Blue Danube') (A)

Hybrid sage (*Salvia × sylvestris* 'Blue Hills') (P)*

Mealy-cup sage (*Salvia farinacea* 'Victoria') (A)

Swan River daisy (*Brachcome iberidifolia*) (A)

YELLOWS

Bearded iris (*Iris germanica* 'Sun Miracle') (P)

Calendula (*Calendula officinalis* 'Kablouna') (A)

Goldenrod (*Solidago* 'Goldenmosa') (P)*

Nasturtium (*Tropaeolum majus* 'Alaska') (A)

Sunflower (*Helianthus annuus*) (A)*

FOR BLUE-AND-WHITE MIXES

BLUES

Aster (*Aster × frikartii* 'Wonder of Staffa') (P)*

Browallia (*Browallia speciosa* 'Blue Bells') (A)*

Wild blue indigo (*Baptisia australis*) (P)*

Italian alkanet (*Anchusa azurea* 'Loddon Royalist') (P)*

Love-in-a-mist (*Nigella damascena* 'Miss Jekykll') (A)*

Pansy (*Viola × wittrockiana* 'Azure Blue') (A)

WHITES

Sweet alyssum (*Lobularia maritima* 'Little Dorrit') (A)*

Astilbe (*Astilbe × aarendsii* 'Bridal Veil') (P)

Gas plant (*Dictamnus albus*) (P)*

Oriental poppy (*Papaver orientale* 'Perry's White') (P)*

Stock (*Matthiola incana* 'Grant Imperial') (A)

Texas sage (*Salvia coccinea* 'Lady in Red') (A)

Note: West Coast gardeners should not fail to consider these blue-flowered perennials:

Asiatic poppy (*Meconopsis betonici-folia*) (P)

Lily-of-the-Nile (*Agapanthus* Headbourne hybrids) (P)*

FOR RED-AND-YELLOW MIXES

REDS

Daylily (*Hemerocallis* 'Stafford') (P)

Lobelia (*Lobelia cardinalis* 'Queen Victoria') (P)

Verbena (*Verbena × hybrida* 'Showtime') (A)

YELLOWS

California poppy (*Eschscholzia californica*) (A)

Ligularia (*Ligularia stenocephala* 'The Rocket') (P)

Thread-leaf coreopsis (*Coreopsis verticillata*) (P)

Yarrow (*Achillea filipendulina* 'Coronation Gold') (P)

FOR PINK-AND-WHITE MIXES

PINKS

Candytuft (*Iberis umbellata* Fairy series) (A)

Cleome (*Cleme hassleriana* 'Cherry Queen') (A)

Cranesbill (*Geranium endresii* 'Wargrave Pink') (P)

Foxtail lily (*Eremurus robustus*) (P)

Lupine (*Lupinus regalis* 'The Chatelaine') (P)

Meadowsweet (*Filipendula rubra*) (P)

WHITES

Fringed bleeding heart (*Dicentra exima* 'Snowdrift') (P)*

Foxglove (*Digitalis purpurea* 'Alba') (A)*

Goatsbeard (*Arunucus dioicus*) (P)*

Meadow rue (*Thalictrum aquilegi-folium* 'Album') (P)

Tree mallow (*Lavatera trimestris* 'Mont Blanc') (A)

*Included in the Plant Guide, pages 276–479.
(A) Annual (P) Perennial*

Climate and Microclimate

The endless diversity of gardens is influenced in large part by climate and the lay of the land, and a key issue for gardeners is to determine what will thrive in their own small corner of the earth. Plants are, by nature, adapted to certain parame-ters of temperature, moisture, and light. Within those parameters they flourish; outside them, they become what the British call "a difficult sub-ject." The hardiness zone map (page 480) indi-cates the minimum temperatures for each region, but within any given area there are a variety of microclimates created by local topography. Even

A WILDLIFE GARDEN

Everyone in the family can enjoy this garden, which hosts a broad spectrum of wildlife from the smallest pest-eating insects to butterflies and moths, from turtles to hummingbirds and perhaps even the neighborhood rabbit.

This is an easy garden to create and one that brings almost instant gratification. Even before the plants start to flower, the birdbath will invite a variety of feathered friends to drink, bathe, and frolic. Birds need fresh water, especially in winter when it's so scarce, so if you live in a cold climate consider adding a heater cable in late fall to keep the water from freezing. In late summer, the birds will eat the rich sunflower seeds after you've enjoyed the golden splendor of the flowers all season long.

Butterfly weed attracts butterflies, and hummingbirds will come to the pineapple sage—so lovely in fall when it sends up its stems of bright red tubular flowers. (In northern gardens you can substitute red bee balm, which blooms in summer.) Step carefully! The luscious *fraise des bois* will attract box and wood turtles. Lay a clay pot on its side in a shady spot to make a home for a garden toad—he'll feast on mosquitoes and other pests that show up in summer.

Be sure to visit the garden after nightfall. Walk quietly and slowly; sit down and keep watch, and you may see a majestic luna moth among the night pollinators drawn by the sweet perfume of the nicotiana.

PLANT KEY*

1. *Fragaria vesca* 'Migonette'
2. *Thermopsis villosa*
3. *Digitalis purpurea* 'Alba'
4. *Delphinium elatum* hybrids
5. *Helianthus annuus*
6. *Nicotiana sylvestris*
7. *Salvia elegans*
8. *Asclepias tuberosa* 'Hello Yellow'

All plants listed here appear in the Plant Guide, pages 276–479.

AN HERB GARDEN

This charming herb garden can be situated at the end of an allée or in the center of a lawn, but not too far from the house. You're much more likely to use the plants, especially those culinary herbs, if they're within reach.

The brick pathway gives the garden a formal air, creating visual stability for the plethora of plants that surround it. Remove several bricks here and there, and you can grow some creeping herbs in the pathway. Be sure to plant low-growing varieties, or you'll be jumping hurdles instead of strolling casually around the garden. Include the herbs that you like and will put to good use. Many of the herbs are annuals, so you can try different varieties each year, adding new ones or eliminating those that serve no purpose. The shrubby perennial herbs—sage, tarragon, lavender, oregano, and rose—give some architectural form to the garden in winter. You'll discover that some of the herbs (calendula, cilantro, comfrey, and borage in par-

ticular) self-seed, so you may have to rogue out unwanted plants or let the planting become less defined.

PLANT KEY*

1. *Pelargonium crispum* 'Variegatum'
2. *Cymbopogon citratus*
3. *Laurus nobilis*
4. *Rosmarinus officinalis*
5. *Ocimum basilicum* 'Opal'
6. *Calendula officinalis* 'Apricot Sherbet'
7. *Borago officinalis*
8. *Petroselinum crispum* var. *neapolitanum*
9. *Heliotropium arborescens*
10. *Agastache foeniculum*
11. *Symphytum officinale*
12. *Rheum × cultorum* 'Victoria'
13. *Mentha × piperita*
14. *Salvia officinalis*
15. *Artemisia dracunculus* var. *sativa*
16. *Aloysia triphylla*
17. *Levisticum officinale*
18. *Chamaemelum nobile*
19. *Lavandula angustifolia* 'Provence'
20. *Coriandrum sativum*
21. *Ocimum basilicum* 'Italian Leaf Large'
22. *Rosa* 'Frau Dagmar Hartopp'
23. *Thymus vulgaris*
24. *Hyssopus officinalis*
25. *Origanum vulgare*
26. *Satureja hortensis*
27. *Allium tuberosum*
28. *Allium schoenprasum*

All plants listed here appear in the Plant Guide, pages 353–371.

a natural dip in the terrain can cause variations in temperature, sunlight, rainfall, and wind, all of which can affect the plantings in an individual garden.

Temperature affects not only the survival of a particular tree, shrub, or flower, but also where and in what season it can be planted. Certain microclimates allow the gardener to cheat a little on the hardiness zone. There might be a spot in front of a sunny stone or brick wall where the heat absorbed from the sun is enough, when released, to raise the temperature sufficiently for the survival of a plant that normally would have no place in the garden. This is what is referred to as "a protected spot." If the wall also blocks the wind, the air temperature may be warmer since wind makes the air temperature feel cooler than it actually is (what is called the wind chill factor in winter). Other methods of protecting plants from protracted, intense cold include wrapping them in burlap and straw, sheltering them with layers of newspaper or plastic, or insulating them under a blanket of snow.

Examine your own landscape with minute attention, noting each microclimate. Follow the path of the sun across the garden to establish where it's sunny or shady and for how long. Get an idea of how the patterns of sun and shade shift with each season. A south-facing slope warms up faster than level ground or a north-facing slope. The southern exposure of a house or garden is usually the sunniest and the north side the shadiest; the west is most often the warmest and the east the coolest. Temperatures are cooler under large shade trees, light intensity is lower, and soil tends to stay moist longer than in open, exposed locations. Cold air flows like water, seeking the lowest point, and frost pockets can occur where there are no solid walls or hedges to interrupt the stream.

In colder climates, cloud cover during the day reduces the amount of direct sun that plants receive; at night it acts as insulation, preventing frost by keeping warmth close to the ground.

Clear nights are most likely to have a sharp frost, because there is no cloud cover to prevent the earth's heat from being released to the sky.

If wind is a problem, there are simple and ecologically sound solutions to consider. Windbreaks of tall trees lift the air up and over the garden. Hedges and openwork fences break the force of the wind significantly. While solid walls and fences block the wind, they can cause air turbulence and downdrafts that batter and flatten plants at their base. Where the problem is more on the order of strong or gusty breezes, sturdy stakes can help support the tall spires of plants like gladiolas and hollyhocks.

Local radio stations, newspapers, or weather stations may have records that reflect local temperatures and precipitation (a combination of rainfall and snowfall) over a period of many years. Most informative, though, is to identify what trees, shrubs, and perennials thrive in your own microclimates. Nurseries, public gardens, nearby arboretums, and your local Cooperative Extension service can all provide helpful information.

Don't Plant a Problem

Gardeners who respect the local natural landscape are amply rewarded with robust growth. Woodland gardens, for example, are appropriate in much of the Northeast and Northwest because these regions were once virtually covered with trees. Meadow gardens filled with prairie wildflowers and graceful ornamental grasses do well in much of the Midwest because the Great Plains once supported a vibrant native grassland. Cactus and succulent gardens and groves of drought-tolerant trees are well adapted to much of the Southwest. Moist soils are naturally the ideal place to put in spectacular bog gardens. A gentle stream, perhaps even a small, still pond, would be the perfect site for a water garden with Louisiana iris and fragrant water lilies.

NATIVE PLANTS

From coast to coast, demand for our indigenous plants continues to grow. Having evolved in North America, these plants are inherently compatible with regional soil conditions, climates, pests, and diseases of our continent and thus represent an ecological approach to gardening. North America can be divided into "Floristic Provinces," or native habitats; look for the plants that are native to a habitat like yours, and they will undoubtedly thrive in your garden. (An asterisk indicates that the plant is listed in the Plant Guide, pages 276–479).

The perennials and annuals listed here are just as lovely as imported plants or modern cultivars. In fact, you may find the return of some animal life, including birds and butterflies, that has been missing from your garden.

COASTAL PLAINS

Boltonia (*Boltonia asteroides*)*
Butterfly weed (*Asclepias tuberosa*)*
Prickly pear cactus (*Opuntia compressa*)*
Royal fern (*Osmunda regalis*)*
Wild blue indigo (*Baptisia australis*)*

EASTERN DECIDUOUS FORESTS

Bee balm (*Monarda didyma*)
Geranium (*Geranium maculatum*)
Great blue lobelia (*Lobelia siphilitica*)*
Northern maidenhair fern (*Adiantum pedatum*)*

CENTRAL PRAIRIES AND PLAINS

Common shooting star (*Dodecatheon meadia*)*
Lanceleaf coreopsis (*Coreopsis lanceolata*)*
Ozark sundrops (*Oenothera macrocarpa*)*
Purple coneflower (*Echinacea purpurea*)*
Queen of the prairie (*Filipendula rubra*)*

WESTERN MOUNTAINS AND PACIFIC NORTHWEST

Cutleaf fleabane (*Erigeron compositus*)
Pussytoes (*Antennaria parviflora*)

Rocky mountain columbine (*Aquilegia caerulea*)

WESTERN DESERTS

Coral bells (*Heuchera sanguinea*)
Dudleya (*Dudleya arizonica*)
Golden columbine (*Aquilegia chrysantha*)*
Mealy-cup sage (*Salvia faranacea*)

CALIFORNIA

Blue sage (*Salvia clevelandii*)
California poppy (*Eschscholzia californica*)
Matilija poppy (*Romneya coulteri*)*
Seaside daisy (*Erigeron glaucus*)

Making use of plants that are well adapted to the garden environment is a recipe for success, but some imported ornamental plants may be *too* well adapted. While they may have advantages, they may also have an unfortunate tendency to crowd out other plants in the garden or to leap the garden gate, as if making their escape, and turn into horticultural bullies that threaten the neighborhood.

You're probably already familiar with many of these plants, which are so commonly found growing "wild" that you assume they're natives. You won't find their names on any endangered plant list because they're imported plants, mostly of European and Asian heritage. They may have "escaped" from cultivation and their seeds or the runners from garden plants happily took hold in the wild. Over time they not only survived but thrived, often crowding out the true natives. There's no reason not to include them in your garden—just be sure to keep them in their place and don't let them go to seed, unless you're prepared for a population explosion. One or more of them may be used as a quick fix for a barren swale or to prevent an unplanted slope eroding. Examples of such invasive plants range from eucalyptus trees on the West Coast to kudzu vines in the South to Japanese honeysuckle in the Northeast. The lovely Queen Anne's lace, often regarded as a native wildflower, is, in fact, an

A POTAGER

A bit of class comes to the vegetable garden in this European-style potager, which can easily keep a family of four happily munching on all the fresh produce they need from late spring through fall.

When planting edibles, it's important to grow what you like. If you're undecided about zucchini, give the unusual 'Ronde de Nice' a try—at least it won't turn into those horrid baseball bats overnight. Remember, a healthy zucchini plant (grown organically with the help of compost made from all the vegetable peelings, roots, stems, and leaves from the garden) yields fruit every day.

This potager was designed with 2'-wide paths between the beds so that you can reach into them to plant, mulch, water, and, most important, harvest the fruits of your labors without having to step onto the soil and risk compacting it. The plants are shown in an adolescent stage; full grown, they will completely fill the beds. (Artistic license

has been taken: asparagus is shown growing in early summer at the same time that tomatoes are on the vine.) You can grow earlier crops in spring, before some of the hot-weather plants are planted out. Peas and broccoli, for instance, or other cool-weather vegetables, can be planted in the space where the tomatoes and zucchini will go in once the weather is warm.

In this plot, you can grow all of one tomato variety or choose to grow four different types. Remember, tomatoes don't have to be red; they come in a rainbow of colors, sizes, and shapes. The second bed provides the salad greens—lettuces and chard bordered with endive. Make successive sowings so that you can pick delicious greens throughout the entire season.

Here you have your own bed of asparagus. If you don't double-dig any other portion of your garden, you should at least double-dig the asparagus bed. This vegetable bed is an investment in the future. For the first two years you just watch the asparagus grow, turning lovely and fernlike in summer. Then, in the third or fourth year, you get to harvest it, and you'll be surprised at how delicious it tastes. Whether you like pencil-thin or finger-thick stalks, they're right there in your garden. And they will be for at least 15 years.

Artichokes are for West Coast and warm-climate gardens only. If you live in a cooler area, substitute pole beans or corn in summer with pumpkins or watermelons trailing along the ground.

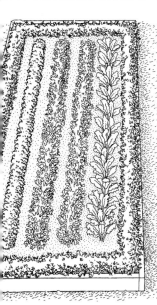
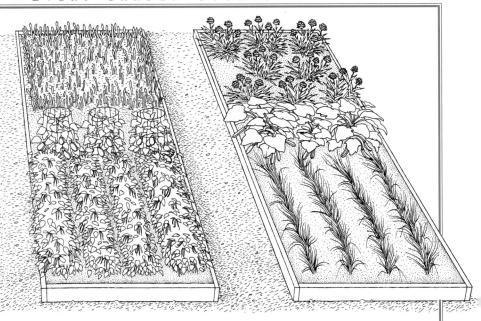

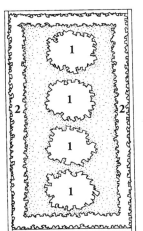
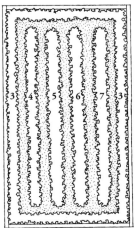
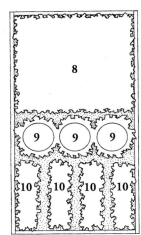
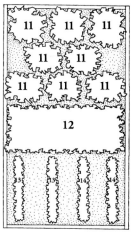

PLANT KEY*

1. **Tomato**
   'Super Marmande'

2. **Radish**
   'D'Avignon,' followed by carrot
   'Artist' and 'Red Russian' kale

3. **Endive** 'Gros Bouclée'

4. **Lettuce** 'Lollo Rossa'

5. **Lettuce**
   'Merveille de Quatre Saisons'

6. **Lettuce** 'Oakleaf'

7. **Swiss chard**
   'Rainbow Chard'

8. **Asparagus**
   'Jersey Knight Improved'

9. **Eggplant**
   'Violette di Firenze'

10. **French, or filet, bean**
    'Marbel'

11. **Globe artichoke**
    'Green Globe'

12. **Zucchini** 'Ronde de Nice'

13. **Onion**
    'Alisa Craig Exhibition'

14. **Leek** 'Bleu de Solaise' or
    garlic 'Spanish Roja'

*All plants listed here appear in the Plant
Guide, pages 276–479.*

escapee carrot of a variety brought to America by the colonists. In streams and ponds, purple loosestrife can easily edge out more desirable or less aggressive species.

If you see plant descriptions like "naturalizes easily," "reseeds," "self-sows," "spreads quickly," "aggressive," "invasive," or "rampant," consider them red flags. Invest in such plants only if you're sure you want them to naturalize, as you may with daffodils, or if you want them to spread, as with ground covers. Some plants have even been declared pernicious or noxious weeds in several regions, and selling them is illegal. If there's any question in your mind, double-check your choices with your local Cooperative Extension service.

A MASTER PLAN

Once you feel that you have a sense of place about your landscape and understand its possibilities and limits, it's time to make the move from what it is to what it can be. You know what kind of soil you have and how it can be improved. You know which plants should thrive in your garden, what absolutely will not grow, and what might grow if given a special place and extra time and attention. You've determined where your garden is sunny, where it's shady, and for how long. You probably have a good grasp of what you intend to use your garden for: to entertain, to meditate, to grow flowers for the house or vegetables for the table.

The next step is lists. A list of trees, shrubs, and perennials you especially want to grow. A list of decorative elements you want: a rose arch, a grape arbor, a teak bench, a Pawley Island rope hammock. A list of things you want to do in the garden: pick *fraises des bois* for breakfast, cut flowers for bouquets, sit in the shade and read, listen to a fountain splash. A list of what you want your plants to accomplish: provide privacy from the neighbors, offer shade, perfume the air, attract birds and butterflies.

Walk around the garden, lists in hand, to get an idea of where some of these things might go. Think about where you'll view the garden from most often—from the house, an entryway, or some point in the garden itself—and at what time of day. Then decide what you'd most like to see from your vantage point. A cedar arch covered in heirloom roses might frame the view. Perhaps a fountain in the center would make the best focal point, or a long perennial border would add interest along the side of the house.

Once you have a feeling for where to put a patio, a garden bench, a table and chairs, figure out what will be required to make these comforts accessible. Stepping-stones may be necessary to keep feet dry and clean, or grassy paths may be sufficient. A fence may be required to keep out dogs and deer. If much of the plant material is started from seeds or slips, a potting shed or area set aside in your home for such purposes may qualify as a necessity. Steep slopes may need retaining walls. A stream might be modified to create a small waterfall. Front gardens can be transformed into courtyards by tall hedges or, for greater security, high vine-covered walls. Large properties may profit by assigning space for an orchard of dwarf fruit trees, a kitchen potager, an herb garden, a cutting garden, and flower beds.

Consider, too, all the people who will be using the garden. Young children may be happiest with a rope swing suspended from a tree limb or a playhouse tucked in a quiet corner. An elderly parent may find great comfort in growing vegetables in a waist-high raised bed that doesn't require bending. Adults and children alike often find that a gently swaying hammock is the perfect place from which to watch the fireflies on a warm evening. A child fascinated by astronomy could use the corner of a deck to set up a telescope for stargazing on summer nights.

Put all these possibilities down on your wish list. Then make a master plan for the garden (see facing page). Remember that gardens evolve over

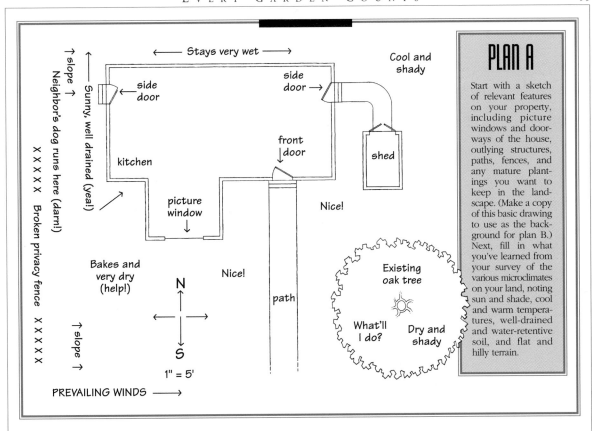

PLAN A

Start with a sketch of relevant features on your property, including picture windows and door-ways of the house, outlying structures, paths, fences, and any mature plant-ings you want to keep in the land-scape. (Make a copy of this basic drawing to use as the back-ground for plan B.) Next, fill in what you've learned from your survey of the various microclimates on your land, noting sun and shade, cool and warm tempera-tures, well-drained and water-retentive soil, and flat and hilly terrain.

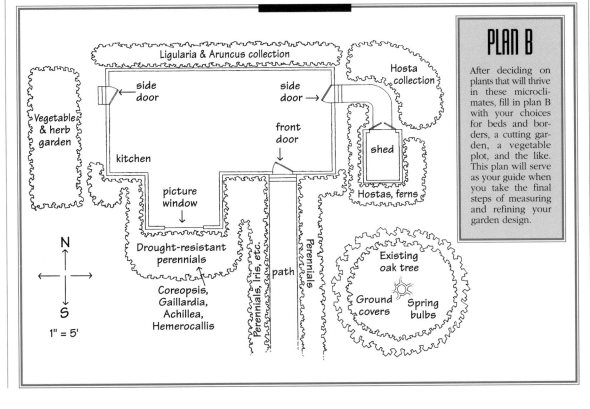

PLAN B

After deciding on plants that will thrive in these microclimates, fill in plan B with your choices for beds and bor-ders, a cutting gar-den, a vegetable plot, and the like. This plan will serve as your guide when you take the final steps of measuring and refining your garden design.

A Xeriscape

Taken from the Greek *xeros,* meaning "dry," the term "Xeriscape" was first coined in the 1980s in Denver, Colorado, where drought-tolerant gardens were being planned. The purpose of xeriscaping is to promote plants that grow naturally in areas of normally low rainfall so that no undue irrigation is required.

Formal in a way, edged in rough, light-colored stone, this simple garden provides varied form and texture using only five plants. Smaller, coarse stones serve as a mulch, setting off the strong form of each plant. The one agave is shown in bloom, but this truly memorable and magnificent sight takes many years. Nonetheless it will be stunning just as a foliage plant for decades before it finally, in a burst of self-perpetuation, sends up its flower stalk and dies. Don't despair. When the main plant dies, suckers often grow from the rootstock. In the meantime, *Agave victoriae-reginae* reigns supreme with its bold geometric form. This is a wonderful plant for meditation—you can just sit and gaze upon its voluptuous shape, with layer upon layer of overlapping, white-edged, deep green leaves. The muted tones of the agaves set off the deep bronze-purple leaves of the *Aeonium.* And the *Sempervivum* (also known as cobweb house leek) adds an odd note of interest, its minute hairs making it look as if a spider has woven its magic all over the plant.

Although this garden is designed for the hot, arid Southwest, you can modify it for colder winter areas by using sedums, yucca, and prickly pear cacti that are hardy into zones 5 and 6. It becomes a little more work in wetter areas, where the soil must be amended to provide ample drainage for plants that cannot tolerate wet feet.

PLANT KEY*

1. *Dudleya brittonii*
2. *Sempervivum arachnoideum*
3. *Agave attenuata*
4. *Agave victoriae-reginae*
5. *Aeonium arboreum* 'Zwartkop'

All plants listed here appear in the Plant Guide, pages 310–320.

time, so plan for the future. If the baby is not yet a toddler, for example, the rope swing or children's play area can wait a year or two. And perhaps that accessible terrace for the parent who will one day be elderly can be put off for a while.

Ordinarily, the hardscape—fences, retaining walls, paths, terraces, and potting sheds—goes in first simply because it's easier and less expensive than having to move major plantings, take out trees, shrubs, and perennials, or dig up the lawn to install it later. Water features—pools, ponds, streams, waterfalls, and fountains—also need to be installed early on; otherwise, this process, which typically involves trenching and laying pipe, can be very disruptive. For the same reasons, electrical wiring for lighting paths or running recirculating water pumps is best installed in the first phases of building a garden. Water and electricity can be a dangerous combination, so it's best to consult a contractor or landscape architect.

Benches and other decorative elements can usually be added at a later time since their installation generally involves less disruption and likelihood of damage to existing plantings. However, arches, arbors, and treillage are best constructed before planting the vines and climbers that will later festoon them with flowers.

Refining and editing are an essential part of the planning process. Remember, many things can be done in phases. Perhaps grassy paths, which are comparatively easy, quick, and inexpensive, will one day be replaced by stepping-stones, and the stepping-stones replaced in turn by herringbone brick paths. Possibly the pond can go in one year and the water garden the next year.

MAPPING THE GARDEN

Before the first spadeful of earth is turned, you want to get a sense of what the composition will look like as a whole. One way to accomplish this is to walk around the area with a measuring tape, stakes, and string, laying out the future location of various elements. A great advantage of such a survey is that it becomes instantly apparent what will work and what won't.

Paths must keep their promises, which is to say they must lead somewhere, whether to a comfortable bench, a secret garden, or a quiet woodland. They must also be wide enough to allow two people to stroll together side by side. And they must be smooth and level enough so that your garden cart full of compost can get through. A stream-fed pond must be placed at the lowest point in the garden, where water would flow naturally, or it will always be a problem. A spot that turns out to be too small for an adequate pond may be perfect for a fountain, which takes up more vertical than horizontal space. The measuring tape clarifies what elements can realistically go where.

Another method is to take measurements of the garden and then draw everything to scale on graph paper. This has some very important advantages. Graph paper is divided into small squares to which you can assign a value in proportion to the square footage of the garden—for example, one square per square foot. It allows you to see clearly the composition of the garden and helps keep the various elements in scale with each other and with the size of the lot. You can also determine if the parts and pieces of the hardscape—the paths, the arbor, the fountain—achieve a sense of proportion and balance. Landscape architects and professional garden designers use templates that make it easy to draw in trees and shrubs, fences and hedges, or to indicate the space that must be allowed for the swing of a garden gate. Such templates are readily available at drafting supply shops.

Graph paper has some drawbacks, however. For one thing, it's difficult to take slope into account. Also, because your rendering is two-dimensional, it's hard to visualize how the garden will look in three dimensions. Though useful for

A SHADE GARDEN

Trees can define a garden—and this particular tree puts on a show of its own in the last two weeks of May. Look up into the branches of the *Davidia* and you may think hundreds of doves have come to nest. The white "wings" are the large bracts, or specialized leaves, that surround the small flowers.

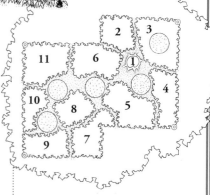

The rest of the garden is a play on form and texture, with most of the interest coming from the foliage of the variety of plants. Color from bloom is an added bonus, not the main enticement. In spring the delicate flowers of the *Epimedium* rise above its elongated heart-shaped foliage. The leaves of the primrose disappear by summer and are echoed in the larger leaves of the late-blooming hardy begonia. The cloak-shaped leaves of the lady's mantle are magical in the early morning dew, changing from silver to gold in the first rays of the sun. The hakonechloa, with its gently swaying, pendant, grassy leaves, looks like a river of gold and green.

This is not a garden you can just quickly walk through. The placement of the stepping-stones allows you to pause and take note of the handsome foliage of the plants as you meander among them.

PLANT KEY*

1. *Davidia involucrata*
2. *Alchemilla mollis*
3. *Asarum caudatum*
4. *Dicentra eximia* 'Snowdrift'
5. *Astilbe × rosea* 'Peach Blossom'
6. *Hakonechloa macra* 'Aureola'
7. *Epimedium × youngianum* 'Niveum'
8. *Rodgersia aesculifolia*
9. *Primula japonica*
10. *Begonia grandis*
11. *Anemone × hybrida* 'Honorine Jobert'

*All plants listed here appear in the Plant Guide, pages 276–479.

"CUT-AND-COME-AGAIN" GARDENS

It is truly one of life's horticultural and aesthetic pleasures to have a space in our gardens that harbors plants grown strictly for cutting. Store-bought flowers pale compared to those we've lovingly sown, nurtured, and selected for cutting. These favorites earn their keep by virtue of their "floriferousness"—and thus are called "cut-and-come-agains."

PASTEL BLOOMERS

California poppy (*Eschscholzia californica* 'Apricot Flambeau') (A), double apricot*

Corn poppy (*Papaver rhoeas* 'Mother of Pearl') (A), mixed pastels*

Cupid's dart (*Catananche caerulea*) (P), lilac blue

Gloriosa daisy (*Rudbeckia hirta* 'Irish Eyes') (A), golden yellow with green disk*

Hardy geranium (*Geranium pratense striatum* 'Speckled and Striped') (P), light blue with white

Lisianthus (*Eustoma grandiflorum* 'Double Eagle Mixed') (A), mixed double pastels

Sunflower (*Helianthus annuus* 'Pastiche') (A), mixed evening shades

Sweet pea (*Lathyrus odoratus* 'Fragrantissima') (A), wide range of pastels*

Thread-leaf coreopsis (*Coreopsis verticillata* 'Moonbeam') (P), pale yellow

Verbena (*Verbena* 'Sissinghurst') (P), rose pink

BOLD BLOOMERS

Garden heliotrope (*Heliotropium arborescens* 'Marine') (A), royal purple*

Larkspur (*Consolida ambigua* Imperial strain) (A), double red, blue, and white*

Pincushion flower (*Scabiosa caucasica*) (P), blues*

Sneezeweed (*Helenium* 'Bruno') (P), crimson-mahogany

Stock (*Matthiola incana* 'Excelsior Mammoth Red') (A), red

Summer phlox (*Phlox paniculata* 'Starfire') (P), brilliant red

Tickseed (*Coreopsis verticillata* 'Grandiflora') (P), bright yellow

Yellow cosmos (*Cosmos sulphureus* 'Ladybird Red') (A), scarlet

UNUSUAL BLOOMERS FOR DRYING

Edelweiss (*Leontopodium alpinum*) (P), furry, whitish gray

Globe thistle (*Echinops ritro*) (P), blue

Sea lavender (*Limonium latifolium* 'Violetta') (P), violet

Statice (*Statice limonium* 'Pastel Shades') (A), pastel mixture

Unicorn plant (*Proboscidea fragrans*) (A), fragrant purple blooms followed by unusual horned pods

Included in the Plant Guide, pages 276–479. (A) Annual (P) Perennial

---

laying out hardscape, scale drawings are limited when it comes to the plants themselves and how they'll look in future years. Another disadvantage is that the point of view is always from an aerial perspective, which is not the way most people see their gardens.

Modern technology offers an alternative way to get a sense of how everything will work together. Using a computer program specially designed for garden planning, you can see how planting a particular perennial, shrub, or tree will affect the garden over time by looking at its rate of growth over 2 years, 5 years, 10 years, and more. The program will also calculate the circle of shade a tree will cast based on the sun's path over the property, which is determined by your latitude. It will let you see your proposed garden from every possible angle. You can explore how it might look with a picket fence, a brick wall, or a hedge; how a deck would work, or possibly a flagstone patio; whether the path would look better with stepping-stones or cobbles.

Whichever method suits you best, refining your garden plan cuts down the number of possible errors and consequently can save you the trouble of having to make time-consuming, expensive, and frustrating rearrangements in the future.

A CONTAINER GARDEN

Versatile as well as movable, container gardens are equally at home on an urban terrace or suburban patio. A wall fountain with a fig tree trained around it in a gentle V-shape gives this one a formal look, reminiscent of Versailles.

PLANT KEY*
—
1. *Ficus carica* 'Brown Turkey'
2. *Stachys byzantina* 'Silver Carpet'
3. *Rosa* 'The Fairy'
4. *Coreopsis lanceolata*
5. *Tropaeolum majus* 'Peach Melba'
6. *Rosmarinus officinalis*
*All plants listed here appear in the Plant Guide, pages 276-479.

The fun, of course, lies in the variety of containers, from simple stone or well-weathered terra cotta to the most elaborate urn from generations ago.

Wonderful styles turn up at tag sales, or you can add a bit of whimsy with one of the new cast-resin "beaux faux" pots that look like antiques.

This garden design combines form and function. The handsome espalier provides delicious figs in late summer. The rosemary topiary, especially lovely when its pale blue flowers bloom, can be lightly snipped and added to a chicken dish or chopped up on garlic bread. Cascading 'Peach Melba' nasturtiums hide the edges of the terrace railing.

'The Fairy,' a petite rose well suited for container culture, bears pale pink blooms from late spring to frost. The stachys will bring people up close to the plants—few can resist petting the silver lamb's ears that soften the edges of each pot.

The fig is quite hardy; well wrapped in winter, it can happily grow in zone 6. Or substitute a grape, such as red 'Foch,' or an espaliered apple or pear. West Coast and Southern gardeners might consider growing an espaliered bay tree or a 'Meyer' lemon.

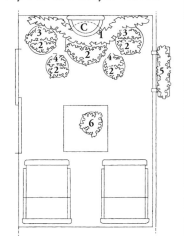

TIME AND THE GARDEN

Advance planning allows you to anticipate problems, and even better, figure out their solutions. For example, if you know how tall a tree will grow, how wide a shrub will spread, or how greatly a perennial will increase *before* you plant, you can easily avoid common problems.

Many gardeners find that when the perennial border looks a bit bare, they want to put in a few more plants. Only a year or two later, they discover that their lovely border has become an unmanageable tangle. There are better ways to manage the problem of bare spots. One is to fill in around perennials with annuals that will cover for a year and die away, leaving sufficient space for the perennials to spread. Another is to interplant with short-lived perennials, such as lupine or baby's breath, which will last two or three years before bowing out gracefully to make room for the peonies or daylilies to increase in size.

The same technique applies equally well with trees. The most desirable and valuable trees, such as oaks, are often slow-growing. The trees that provide quick shade are often short-lived or weak. A nice solution is to plant both at the same time. In this way the fast-growing tree provides shade while the slower-growing tree is coming along. When the slower tree has sufficient size to it, the fast-growing tree can be removed and transplanted.

Time is the garden's, experience is the gardener's. Time brings the loveliness of trees grown tall and handsome, of a wisteria-covered arbor or a weathered garden gate. But it is thoughtful planning that gives a landscape its grace and scope, proportion and balance. And only experience teaches us that old roses are worth growing because they make June glorious, even if they bloom but once a year. It is experience that persuades us to plant the heirloom tomatoes for their rich flavor instead of the tasteless genetically engineered varieties that seem to grow on supermarket shelves. From experience we learn that apple trees are most beautiful in old age—as is any garden that has been well tended and well loved.

The GARDENER'S TOOLS

I magine, for a moment, a garden without tools. No spades to turn the earth in preparation for planting. No rakes to level a planting bed or create furrows to safely harbor seeds. No pruners to tame the barberry or clippers to trim the flowering quince.

A gardener might, for a time, enjoy the exuberant growth as well-mannered plants shook off their restraints and returned to the ways of the wild. But soon, without the benevolent touch of trowel or loppers, the gifts of the garden would dwindle.

Apples would mature, but only as shadows of their former buxom selves. Aphids and black spot would drain the vitality from the hybrid tea roses. There would be no new crops of sugar snap peas or harvests of sweet corn, no bouquets of sweet peas or bushels of squash. Before long, only the hardiest specimens would remain—a gnarled lilac, a thicket of 'Old Blush' roses—adrift in a sea of weeds. To garden is to cultivate; to coax from the earth with hoe and spade and watering can more than nature, left to her own devices, appears willing to supply. Without the implements of cultivation, gardens themselves would cease to exist.

Deprived of familiar tools, no doubt each gardener would soon invent some. Try to turn even the smallest patch of uncultivated earth with your bare hands and you would soon pick up a stick to poke and lever in the dirt, as people have been doing since gardening first began. Try to banish tenacious weeds from around a precious squash vine, using only your hands, and you would soon find a sharp rock or bone to bind to that digging stick and begin to hoe away. Try to carry water to a thirsty seedling in your cupped palms and you would soon scoop out a gourd from which to pour. Your hands, unaided, are no match for bramble patch or hardpan.

But with the proper tools at your side, your garden can take root. Tools allow you to foster the land's fertility, enhance its achievements, and encourage its productive character. "Tickle the earth with a hoe," wrote Douglas Jerrold, "and she laughs with a harvest." Tools expand your reach, augment your strength, and extend your endurance; with their tireless help you will be able to double-dig a garden bed, prune the limbs of the lankiest plum tree, or aerate a mountain of compost. In short, tools are your ticket to the garden of your dreams.

WORKING WITH THE BEST

Pick up a hoe or spade, and you hold history in your hands. Similar implements cultivated gardens in ancient Rome, Greece, Egypt, and China, tended monastery gardens in northern Europe during the Middle Ages, aided in the flowering of the Renaissance, and broke virgin ground on the lush shores of the New World. Wherever humanity ceased wandering and planted fields and gardens, garden tools became the keys to a good life; without them, hunger and deprivation were likely to prevail.

It was a poor gardener who entrusted the vital task of gardening to a shoddy rake or shovel. Early garden tools were far from fancy—their beauty arose from their pure utility—but they were made to last and carefully maintained to extend their useful life. Few gardeners were unwise enough to let their hoard of precious tools succumb to rust or otherwise come to naught; such neglect was akin to biting the hand that fed them.

Then came new methods of manufacturing, modern materials, and the bargain-happy mind-set of the 20th century. When gardening became more hobby than livelihood, gardeners combed store shelves and catalogs bright with inferior tools and gadgets. Why buy an expensive forged trowel, the reasoning went, if you can buy a new, inexpensive sheet-metal version every year?

Today, however, after struggling with trowels that bend, fork handles that split, and shovel blades that wear at the tip, gardeners once again are seeking worthy helpmates in their labors.

Much can be gained from such a partnership. A top-quality tool does its job, and does it well, but there is more to gardening than efficiency. A fine trowel becomes a fast friend, perfectly suited to your grip. Its wood handle is

THE BASIC TOOL KIT

"A multiplicity of tools is an expensive folly," observed the author of *Johnson's Gardener's Dictionary*, first published in 1847. But there is a bottom line. Most gardeners wouldn't lift a finger without the following:

- **Garden or spading fork**
- **Garden spade**
- **Long-handled shovel**
- **Trowel**
- **Weeding hoe** (collinear or oscillating)
- **Steel rake**
- **Bamboo or flexible-tined rake**
- **Hand weeder** (cutting type)
- **Fishtail weeder** (for tap-rooted plants)
- **Watering can**
- **Curved bypass pruning shears**
- **Pruning saw**

smooth as a sea-tumbled stone; its blade, polished by decades of adventures in the dirt, gleams like antique pewter and slips into the soil with a whisper.

You're hardly likely to abandon such a treasure in the damp of the vegetable beds; instead, by its very nature, it inspires your devotion and care and, when not in use, a place of honor in the potting shed.

Gardeners who invest in well-made implements have learned a vital lesson. It's far cheaper to buy one heirloom-quality tool that will last a lifetime—and beyond—than to buy a dozen lesser versions. Fine tools pay off not only in the growth of your garden and the efficient use of your time and money, but also in your own pleasure while performing even minor garden tasks. Like a loving spouse, they lighten your labors, hold up under stress and strain, and stand ready to help whenever help is needed.

Just as important, the decision to invest in heirloom-quality tools reaps dividends in the health and vitality of the world around you. Unlike cheap tools that must be replaced again and again, squandering wood and steel and power, good tools waste no resources; during their long lives they may nurture countless flowers, fruits, and vegetables, along with the growth of a forest's worth of trees. They are a statement of your intent, a tangible commitment to beauty and productivity and the responsible stewardship of a tiny portion of the earth, now and in the years to come. The spade you buy now may still be turning the earth late in the 21st century.

WHAT MAKES A GOOD GARDEN TOOL?

The definition of a good tool may change from gardener to gardener, but some hallmarks of construction and use remain constant.

UTILITY: Good tools are objects of pure utility, the means to a specific end. There is no need in the garden proper for a pipe wrench or toilet plunger, a corkscrew or fountain pen: what are fine tools in other realms are like fish out of water around the compost and the asters. In the garden, good tools directly address the gardener's need to cultivate, plant, propagate, prune, water, and tidy up. An inappropriate tool soon identifies itself as a slouch, lazing season after season untouched upon the shelf.

CLARITY OF PURPOSE: The design of the tool itself will teach you about its proper use and aim. The tread of a shovel says "Put your foot here" in order to more easily thrust the blade into the earth. The hooked lower lip of a pair of loppers says "Use me to cradle the branch" before you squeeze the handles together and cut cleanly through the wood. The narrow tongue of a poacher's spade says "Use me to dig in tight spots," while the yard-wide stance of the broad fork says "Let me help you in open spaces." Listen, and your tools will guide you.

FORTITUDE: In tools, strength is a relative thing. Shovels, spades, and digging forks—the draft horses of the garden—boast stalwart blades or tines and hefty handles to help them pull their weight. Other tasks call for tools with different sorts of staying power. Good pruners and loppers have sharp blades with handles designed for ample leverage, yet are light enough to hold above your head if your pruning tasks tend skyward. Scythes and grass hooks have lightweight blades that both take and hold a keen edge, so they slice through grass and weeds with ease. A good rake for lawns has tenacious yet flexible fingers; a brawny rake with iron teeth would only rip up the grass.

All good tools are made from durable materials and, when properly cared for, have the fortitude to perform their garden roles without complaint. Yet even the strongest tools, like gardeners, have their limits. Push your tools beyond what they are meant to do and you will, most likely, shorten their lives as well as detract from the pleasure of your work.

EASE OF USE: Repetition and rhythm are as common to the garden as they are to music: the clip, clip, clip of the anvil pruners, the back-and-forth sighing of the pruning saw, the thrust and heave of the spade and shovel. As instruments of this garden concert, good tools must be comfortable for the gardener to use, not just with the first snip of the shears, but with the hundredth. Good tools are designed with handles that fit securely in the hand, with their weight distributed to aid your tasks and with parts that won't poke or splinter or rub. Good tools won't entirely eliminate the sweat from gardening, but they will cut down the wear and tear on your back, legs, wrists, and shoulders.

OVERLOOKED GARDEN TOOLS

Say "garden tool" and nearly all within earshot will think of a spade, trowel, or fork. But what of a camera? A rain gauge? A jeweler's loupe or Coddington? These and other overlooked tools will magnify the pleasures of your gardening.

■ **Camera:** An inexpensive point-and-shoot camera, loaded with film for color prints, puts your memory in the palm of your hand. Use it to record that bed of perennials you just planted and next year you'll see exactly how much they grew. Capture that pleasurable pairing of euphorbia and solanum, or poppy and linaria. Can't remember five years from now how you artfully arranged those annuals? Look through your pictures and let them guide you. And don't forget to spy on other people's gardens, then commit their planting secrets to film.

If you have a video camera, you'll be able to make a whole production of your garden survey—or at least provide useful narration in place of written notes. With a cup of tea, a VCR, and your new seed catalog, you're set for a happy winter morning of planning.

■ **Magnifying glass, jeweler's loupe, or Coddington:** Get to know the insects in your garden's life. By learning to identify particular butterfly eggs, you'll be better able to welcome swallowtails and banish cabbage whites. The same goes for other insects: a magnified look will help you identify garden friends or potential pests.

■ **Reference books:** There's no substitute for experience, but you can shortcut the years it takes to gain it with a good set of garden reference books. Particularly helpful are volumes that directly address a single garden topic—insects, pruning, propagating, or design—or that focus on the culture of a single type of plant. Look for information relevant to your local climate and soil, too.

■ **Rain Gauge:** Keep track of how much water nature gives your plants to drink, and you can better adjust your watering schedule to suit their needs.

WHAT'S NEEDED?

You don't need a heavy overcoat if you live in Tucson; you don't need a wheel hoe if you're planting a single flower bed. Whether you're new to gardening or your hands are permanently marked with dirt, remember this basic rule: Buy only what you need, and buy it when you need it.

Fledgling gardeners, in particular, will benefit from this advice. It's easy to be seduced by all the shiny tools in catalogs or at garden centers and end up with a light wallet and a crowded garden shed. Instead, before splurging on four types of hoes, three sizes of spades, and a binful of hand tools, think carefully about what you're hoping to do. If you're planning to start out by filling flowerpots with colorful pansies or petunias, all you will need is a trowel to set your nursery transplants in their spots and a watering can to quench their frequent thirst. Hoes, spades, pruners, and sprinklers are hardly required.

As your garden grows, your shopping list of gardening tools naturally will keep pace. Begin to cultivate any amount of earth and you'll decide you need a digging fork. Buy one, right then, and get to work. Plant a greengage plum tree and you'll come to need a pair of loppers. Seek out the best you can find and begin to prune away. Plot out a perennial bed and you'll find you need a garden spade to bring your plans to life. Heft a few, then bring home the one that suits your frame the best.

A GARDEN LEGEND

ELIOT COLEMAN'S ORGANIC ODYSSEY

From the time he first picked up a hoe at the age of 26 to turn 50 acres of sandy, rocky Maine soil into a profitable organic market garden until today, growing salad greens all year round in one of the country's coldest climates, Eliot Coleman has made a career of defying conventional agricultural wisdom.

Inspired by Helen and Scott Nearing, who motivated a generation of homesteaders with their book *Living the Good Life,* Eliot Coleman bought a plot of their land and soon began producing vegetables famous for their abundance, color, and taste. In 1978 he left to run an experimental organic farm in Massachusetts and then directed the farm program at The Mountain School in Vermont, where he "managed to feed 65 kids and faculty like kings" on just a few acres. Returning to Maine, he devised an ingenious system of cold frames and hooped tunnels that allows him to harvest vegetables all year long.

Coleman's experiences led him to improve upon standard gardening tools by making them more user-friendly. (His collinear hoe, for example, allows the user to remain comfortably upright.) Among his books are the classic *The New Organic Grower* (1989) and *Four-Season Harvest* (1992). "I'm not concerned with how to 'do' organic farming," says Coleman. "What interests me is how we can convince others to farm this way."

"If I had earned a degree in agriculture, I would have been convinced that everything I now do is impossible and never would have tried it."

While you work, tending the berry vines or double digging a new asparagus bed, watch for places where you struggle: such garden battles signal the need for a new tool. If you strain to force your curved bypass shears through that one-inch branch, you should probably graduate to loppers. If you spend hours pulling tiny weeds up by their roots, there's probably a tool—a collinear hoe or sharp-bladed hand weeder, for instance—that will do the job in a fraction of the time. If you find yourself worn out after turning only half your compost, perhaps you need to put down your heavy digging fork and pick up a composting fork, whose five slender tines will make quick work of the pile.

Gardening has been a part of life for so many centuries that a tool has been designed to hasten each and every garden task. If you have a need, no doubt there is a tool perfectly suited to meet it.

Different gardeners, however, may prefer different tools for the same tasks. One may choose an oscillating hoe to slice weeds off just below the soil surface; another may prefer the stable action of a Dutch hoe. One may opt for a trowel for planting tulips between the peonies and the iris; another might be partial to a dibber or a bulb planter. One might swear by his garden spade for digging, and another stand by her shovel for the same job. Imagine yourself at work, then choose your implement. If it works for you, then it's the right tool for the job.

WHAT TO LOOK FOR

"It is quality rather than quantity that matters," wrote Lucius Annaeus Seneca during the first century A.D., and his words still ring true today. Unlike shiny surfaces or bright paint colors, however, quality isn't always apparent to the untutored eye.

What makes one shovel better than another, one trowel or hoe more likely to endure?

MATERIALS: Tools are only as strong as the materials that go into their construction. Ever since the mid 1800s, the business-ends of the best garden tools have been made of steel—a welcome replacement for the heavy, iron blades of earlier times. Today, tool manufacturers forge carbon steel, stainless steel, and carbon-manganese steel into tough blades, then temper them to add to their resilience.

Top-quality handles for shovels, spades, and forks are made from ash, with a straight, smooth grain (look for lines that run the length of the handle) and no knots. The tighter the grain, the stronger the handle. Because these tools often are used as levers, for better or for worse, their handles must possess the utmost strength as well as a bit of flexibility.

You'll rarely put the handles of tools like rakes or cultivators to such severe tests, so the wood type is not as crucial. Ash is the best choice, but other hardwoods are fine. Hand tools like trowels and weeders may have handles of hickory, ash, birch, or even synthetic resins; what counts most here is a smooth, comfortable grip.

Whenever possible, find out what you're buying. Avoid painted handles, which can camouflage inferior wood. Ask questions about the materials; manufacturers (and tool retailers) should be able to tell you exactly what their tools are made from.

METHODS OF MANUFACTURE: The steel heads of most fine garden tools today are forged, either by traditional hand methods (hammer against anvil) or by mechanical drop forging (in which a massive hammer drops from above and forces the steel into the desired shape). The heads of the best tools are forged in a single piece that includes both the blade or tines and the handle socket or straps.

Manufacturers die-cut and shape lesser-quality tools from sheet steel; these types, which are a single thickness throughout, are far more prone than forged tools to bend, break, or rust. Other inexpensive tool heads may be fabricated from more than one part and welded together. If the welds are poorly made, or located at a stress point, the tool can easily break under strain. This is less of an issue with small hand tools than with larger implements such as hoes and spades and shovels, which must endure great stress and strain.

JOINTS: Even tools made from high-quality materials may fail you if their parts are poorly joined. The joint between handle and head is a tool's Achilles' heel, the spot where trouble is most likely to occur—particularly in such hard-use tools as shovels, forks, spades, and hoes. Though it's a challenge to join a heavy steel head to a shaft of wood, over the centuries tool-makers have devised a few enduring methods. Look for a solid socket joint, in which the handle is inserted in a socket 6"–12" in length, formed during forging as an integral part of the tool head. Such sockets encase the wood of the lower handle and reduce contact with dirt and moisture. The handle is riveted in place through the metal socket.

Forged straps extending from the head of the tool up the handle on both its front and back

GETTING A GRIP

The handle is what connects you to your chosen tool: the point where power is transferred, at least in part, from you to the tool in use.

■ **Straight handle:** The most basic handle type is a straight shaft of turned hardwood, 40"–72" in length. Most frequently found on shovels, rakes, and hoes, this type is sometimes available on spades and forks. Straight, full-length handles increase the leverage of a tool and extend its reach.

■ **D-handle** (also called a Y- or YD-handle): To form a top-of-the-line version of this favored handle type, the maker splits a straight shaft of turned wood at the end opposite the tool head, steams it to make it flexible, then forces it into a slingshot-shaped mold to dry. A short section of turned wood is secured between the arms of the Y to form a comfortable grip. On some heavy-duty tools, the valley of the Y is filled with a wood brace; this construction is called a filled D-handle.

■ **T-handle:** The T-handle dates back to earlier centuries, when spades were thrust into the earth with the weight of the gardener's body rather than with a foot on the blade's tread. Some gardeners still prefer this style, which has a horizontal grip (like the top of a T) at the end of the handle.

D- or T-handles usually measure 26"–32" in length and are found on spades, forks, and short-handled shovels.

■ **Trigger grip:** In recent years, gardeners with arthritis or an otherwise weakened grip have become fans of hand tools with a hook or "trigger" beneath the handle, allowing them more control with less effort. Most trigger-grip tools are cast from an aluminum alloy and will not rust, bend, or break.

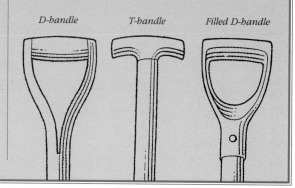

D-handle   *T-handle*   *Filled D-handle*

TOOLS FOR ODD JOBS

Once you've put together a hardworking collection of basic implements, you're free to seek out specialty tools and helpful accessories designed to facilitate occasional garden tasks. Some of the items listed here may come to be your favorite implements, preferred above more standard tool types. Others may be as out of place in your garden as a plow would be in your perennial beds.

Here's a brief lineup:

■ **Broadfork:** An 18"-wide, double-handled cultivating fork that breaks and crumbles soil with an easy rolling motion. Vegetable gardeners with large plots may consider this essential.

The double-handled broadfork is ideal for reworking garden beds.

■ **Bulb planter:** Like an oversize apple corer, this tubular tool lifts a plug of earth, leaving a hole perfect for planting bulbs. Available in short- and long-handled versions.

■ **Dibber:** A tapered hand tool designed for poking holes in prepared soil and useful for setting out transplants, seedlings, and bulbs. Available with a trigger or T-style handle.

■ **Grading rake:** Some gardeners prefer this classic hay rake to a steel garden rake for leveling soil and shaping garden beds. It boasts a lightweight wood head and wood or nylon teeth.

■ **Hand fork:** A pint-size version of a spading fork that works soil to a depth of 4". Helpful when transplanting.

■ **Picks and mattocks:** Use these for making a dent

in cement-like, rock-laden soil, or when digging narrow trenches. A mattock, which has a wider head than a pick, is particularly adept at chopping through thick roots.

■ **Plant markers:** Keep track of your garden's occupants by tying long-lasting copper or painted wood plant tags to their limbs, or by planting zinc markers at their feet.

■ **Plant supports:** These range from simple wood or bamboo stakes for supporting sagging blooms to metal or wood arbors designed to hold up a cloud of climbing roses. Buy what's needed: trellises or wall anchors for climbing vines, wire cages for tomatoes, metal A-frames or bamboo tepees for your beans. Tie up loose ends with twine or raffia.

■ **Poacher's spade:** A narrow-bladed tool that's a cross between a small spade and shovel, great for working in confined beds.

■ **Pole pruner and pole saw:** High branches out of reach? Use these cutting tools, which are mounted on 6'-long jointed or extendable handles, to conquer them.

■ **Riddles and sieves:** Wood-rimmed riddles and sieves, made from various gauges of galvanized-metal mesh, sift soil and compost to a fine tilth, strain out rocks or sticks, and aid in winnowing dried beans or seeds.

A traditional English riddle

■ **Scoops:** Metal scoops come in handy for measuring and spreading soil amendments or mixing potting soil. Look for stainless-steel types so you needn't worry about rust.

- **Scythes and sickles:** Once standard tools for transforming meadows into lawns, razor-sharp scythes still star in mowing tall grasses and grain or dispatching grassy weeds. Use sickles or grass hooks—pint-size scythes—for trimming grasses in tight or awkward spots.

- **Shears:** To supplement your curved bypass pruners, choose from a variety of lightweight, straight bypass shears for trimming flower stems, deadheading the penstemon, or harvesting pears. Different types include Ikebana shears (with large looped handles and short blades), thinning shears (with small pointed blades and a spring-action handle), deadheading shears (with small pointed blades and narrow looped handles), and fruit and flower shears (with stubby blades and a spring action handle). Many models are multipurpose.

- **Spiking fork:** A short-tined garden fork, used to aerate lawns and aid water in reaching roots through thick turf.

- **Sprayer:** With the help of a pump sprayer, which works under pressure, it's a simple task to bathe your roses with insecticidal soap or treat them to a nutritious seaweed cocktail.

- **Square-mouthed shovel:** In the garden, square-mouthed flat-backed shovels make quick work of clearing sand, gravel, or soil from concrete walkways, patios, or other hard surfaces.

- **Wheel hoe and cultivator:** The wheel hoe, a light, human-powered push-plow that balances on a single forward wheel, works with interchangeable blades that efficiently cut off weeds, break up the soil crust, and create furrows for planting or irrigation. And it does all this without disturbing your rows of vegetables.

sides and riveted in place form a somewhat flexible joint that's even stronger than a socket. Many professional gardeners prefer handles that are fashioned this way.

On smaller hand tools, the head is usually joined to the handle with a tang and ferrule. The tang, a narrow extension of the tool head, is embedded in the core of the handle. The cupped metal ferrule squeezes the wood where the tang enters, holding it tightly in place while keeping the wood from splitting and protecting it from moisture.

SIZE AND WEIGHT: Most tool manufacturers make basic tools in more than one size to accommodate the frames of different gardeners. If possible, try a tool on for size before you buy it. Pick it up and pantomime the garden task it will help you perform. Imagine doing the task again and again. Does lifting a six-pound spade tire you out even before the blade is laden with dirt? You may be better off with a spade designed specifically for use in the flower border—an implement that weighs in at just over three pounds. Does a garden fork with a 28" handle force you to stoop while you work? Seek out a taller one, better suited to your height. Similarly, give pruners a dozen squeezes to make sure the grip fits your hand. And if you're one of the world's beleaguered lefties, make sure you track down a true left-handed pruner, such as Felco's No. 9 or No. 10.

FOCUS: The design of a good tool is perfectly suited to the task it performs. For this reason, multipurpose tools (a combination hoe and rake, for instance) rarely perform as well as their single-focus relatives. Initially such tools may appear to be a bargain both in price and convenience, but they usually disappoint. It's far better to invest in several tools that each do a single job perfectly than in a single tool that does every job poorly.

The Right Tools for the Job

But where to start and what to buy? Garden tasks sort easily into categories, from digging and weeding to pruning and watering. Most gardeners soon find they need at least one good tool designed for each primary garden task. More often, both a full-size and a hand-size version of a task-specific tool (such as a spade and a trowel) find their way into the tool closet or potting shed.

Here are the basic tools you're most likely to need as your garden grows, organized by the garden job they're designed to undertake.

Digging

THE TROWEL: Gardeners cherish their trowels for a simple reason: these are the tools that get them closest to the earth. Perfect for digging small holes and easing transplants or bulbs into their new homes, trowels are what you use when the hardest part of your garden work is done and the pleasures of planting begin. (If you find yourself turning the trowel backward and hacking to make a hole big enough for a 4" transplant, serious soil preparation is in order.) Trowels are available in many shapes and sizes, designed for tasks as various as weeding, potting, or tucking alpines into the crevices of a rock garden. A good all-purpose choice boasts a cupped, carbon steel blade, approximately 3" wide and 6" long, with a somewhat rounded tip and a solid, forged or welded shank.

Trowel

THE FORK: Forks bring out the farmer in a gardener. Designed with heavy steel tines for turning the soil, working in soil amendments, breaking up clods, unearthing old roots, dividing perennials, and digging up plants without slicing through their roots, forks can do most of the things that spades and shovels can do and many that they can't. In heavy clay soils, a *spading fork* actually digs more efficiently than a spade or shovel because its separate tines penetrate the sticky soil more easily than a blade.

The best all-around fork is the *English garden fork*, with either a D- or T-style grip, a short handle, and a carbon-steel head with four square tines. Spading forks, which are more familiar in America, have a lighter head with broad, flat, or triangular tines. Most forks range between 40" and 44" in overall length.

Spading fork

THE SPADE: The primary job of a spade is to prepare soil for planting in a technique called spading, or simple digging. The spade's squared-off blade and lack of cant aid the gardener in making vertical cuts in the soil, and in turning or loosening the soil as deeply as the spade's blade is long (creating a spit). The double digging so vital to French intensive gardening essentially is deep spading: a method of prepa-

MEASURING UP

For comfortable use, the top end of the handle of a garden fork or spade should be on a level with your elbow when your arm is bent to a 90° angle and the blade or tines of the tool are touching the floor or ground. Gardeners who are taller than 5'8" will work more efficiently with a fork and spade 44" and 43" in length, respectively.

FORKS AND THEIR TINES

The all-steel garden fork, introduced by Francis Parkes at London's Crystal Palace Exhibition in 1851, probably didn't cause much of a stir among exhibition visitors. Overwhelmed by the decorative and technological marvels of their age, from ornate machine-loomed carpets to the soaring frame of the place itself, they likely weren't paying much attention to tools. But from that year forward, throughout England and beyond, the steel fork competed with spades and shovels for the role of favored digging implement.

Unlike the earlier iron forks (which had two or three clunky tines that derived their strength from their bulk), the forged steel of Parkes' new fork made possible light, narrow tines that were slightly flexible, allowing them to bend safely rather than break when encountering a buried rock or tenacious underground root.

Today, the descendants of Parkes' landmark fork continue to yield to underground obstacles, which is the key to their endurance. It's not a good idea, however, to put all your weight on your fork if you meet strong resistance while working the soil. If one of the tines does happen to get bent out of line while you work, clamp the fork securely in a vise, slip a 3'-long section of iron pipe over the bent tine, and lever it back into its proper place; it will lose no strength in the process.

ration in which the topsoil is removed, the subsoil loosened and amended, and topsoil added from an adjoining hole.

Gardeners often enlist spades for other jobs. A spade readily digs straight-sided holes for planting trees, shrubs, and perennials, helps with transplanting, and can be used in a pinch for edging lawns, slicing sod, attacking monster weeds, hammering stakes, or chopping through ice.

In general, spades have straight-sided steel blades with squared-off ends, short handles with D- or T-style grips, and measure 39"–44" in length.

Garden spade

THE SHOVEL: America's wide-open spaces and uncultivated soil made shovels the digging tools of choice early in this nation's history. These long-handled tools perform arduous digging tasks with ease and offer the best means of actually moving dirt, gravel, sand, and similar heavy materials. Like spades, they also can be used in garden beds to dig holes for transplants and new plantings, but their dished blades and acute cant make them unsuitable for spading, digging straight-edged trenches, cutting through a clump of daylilies, or slicing neatly through the ajuga to keep it in bounds. If you plan to use your shovel frequently in the confines of the flower border, choose a short-handled version with a D-grip.

The best shovel for general digging tasks is a long-handled version with a dished blade and slightly pointed or rounded tip. Shovel blades that are stamped out of sheet steel can be identified by a V-shaped ridge called a frog, in the upper part of the blade near the handle, which lends strength to the blade. Top-of-the-line forged shovels are naturally strong and have no need of a supportive frog. Because long-handled

Straight-handled, round-point shovel

THE CANT

For heavy-duty garden jobs, such as loosening compacted soil, spading heavy clay, or moving dirt from one spot to another, look for spades or shovels with a wider angle between blade and handle. This angle, called the *cant*, determines the amount of leverage inherent in the tool. If you insert the blade of a tool with a lot of cant vertically into the soil, its handle will lean away from you rather than standing straight up; when you pull back on the handle, the head of the tool will move from a vertical to a horizontal, good-for-lifting position before the handle parallels the ground.

In general, shovels tend to have more cant than spades; their full-length handles also add to their superior levering and lifting abilities.

shovels are often used to lever objects out of the earth, ash handles with a tight grain are a must. (A 4'–5' crowbar, with a board as a fulcrum, is a safer, more effective tool for such jobs, and you won't risk breaking your shovel.)

Cultivating and Weeding

THE HOE: The very first gardener probably wielded a makeshift hoe to break through the surface of the earth before planting his grain; since that ancient time, gardeners and inventors have had ample time to expand on the concept. Today, hoes come in more designs and are sold

The versatile warren hoe excels at grading, furrowing, and backfilling to cover seeds.

by more different names than most other garden tools combined.

At its simplest, the hoe is a flat steel blade attached at an angle to a long, straight handle. It is used primarily for cultivating, that vital task of churning up the soil around plants so they're better able to drink, breathe, and grow without competition from weeds.

The more perpendicular the blade to the handle, the better the hoe is for cultivation, chopping at heavy weeds, and pulling loose soil into ridges or hills. Examples of this type include the traditional *garden hoe*, which has a broad, deep blade joined to its handle by a gooseneck shank; the heavy-duty *eye hoe*, named for the "eye" in the blade through which the handle is attached; and the *warren hoe*, with a heart-shaped or arrowhead-

Eye-hoe handles come in various lengths.

shaped blade designed for forming rows and furrows in the vegetable garden.

The more severe the angle of blade to handle, the better the hoe is for sliding on top of or just beneath the surface of the soil to cut off annual weeds. Once called "scarifiers," hoes that fulfill these requirements include the *shuffle hoe*, or *swoe*, which has an offset blade that somewhat resembles a golf putter; the *stalham hoe*, or *swan-neck hoe*, based on a traditional garden hoe design but with an angled blade that can be pulled beneath the soil surface; and the *scuffle hoe*, or *Dutch hoe*, whose flat blade is attached to its handle with a horseshoe-shaped shank.

Some scuffle hoes have a single-edged blade and cut on the push or thrust stroke only; others are sharp on two or more blade edges, allowing them to cut weeds on both the thrust and draw strokes, or when moved from side to side. Yet another good scuffle-hoe type is the *oscillating hoe*, or *hula hoe*, which has a stirrup-shaped blade

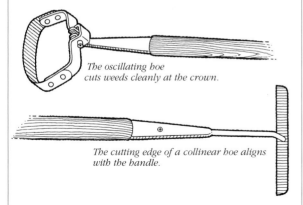

The oscillating hoe cuts weeds cleanly at the crown.

The cutting edge of a collinear hoe aligns with the handle.

that pivots slightly on each back-and-forth stroke to maintain an optimum cutting angle.

The *collinear hoe,* one of the finest weeding hoes, doesn't have a steeply angled blade. But because it's wielded more like a broom than a typical draw hoe, its thin, keen blade sweeps neatly beneath or at the soil surface.

Unless you're breaking new ground in your garden, you can get along quite well with just one hoe, designed for weeding and light cultivation. Every experienced gardener has his or her favorite design: the one that puts no strain on the back, that can cultivate large areas in a short amount of time, and that slides easily under or just on top of the soil surface, making weeding more like sweeping or mopping than wielding a battle-ax.

Remember, although hoes with wide blades look like they would get work done at a faster pace, they take more strength to wield effectively than those with a relatively narrow blade.

THE HAND WEEDER: Weeding in a flower border or raised beds with a full-size hoe is akin to trying to dance the tango in a broom closet—you're bound to step on some toes. A hand weeder allows you the ultimate control and will keep you from inadvertently hacking down your precious columbines or slicing through their roots.

One of the best hand weeders is designed like a miniature hoe, with a sharp, steeply angled triangular blade that cleanly cuts weeds just below the soil surface. (If you wield it or any other sharp-bladed weeder with one hand, keep track of what your other hand is doing. It's easy to get caught up in your weeding and find your fingers in harm's way.)

HOW TO HOE

The most important step in wielding a hoe is taken long before you set foot in the garden. To avoid an aching back, be sure to buy a hoe with a handle suited to your height—one that allows you to stand upright while you work. For gardeners taller than 5'6", this means a hoe 64" long.

Wield lightweight weeding hoes similarly to other draw hoes, using the forward hand to apply the slight downward pressure that gives the blade its bite. The exception is the collinear hoe, which should be drawn across the front of your body in a sweeping motion, much as you'd use a broom; your thumbs will point up toward your chin or wrap around the handle. Stand upright and keep your knees slightly bent.

An oscillating hoe requires a slightly different technique. Push the hoe away from you with the hand at the handle's end, then use your other hand to power the pull stroke and apply pressure as needed.

When working with any hoe, switch hands now and then to avoid tiring the muscles on just one side of your body.

Innumerable tools of similar design have fought the good fight against weeds over the past century and remain available today. Some are versions of the traditional English daisy grubber, with its long, narrow blade, V-notched end, and fulcrum for added leverage in lifting tap-rooted weeds. (Look for *fish-tailed weeders* or *dandelion weeders*.) Others, like the modern hand weeder, aim to cut off weeds at the ankles; they go by names as various as the *collinear hand hoe*, the *farmer's weeder*, the *hot bed* or *Hazeltine's weeder*, and the *Noyes* or *V weeder*. Many do an excellent job; gardeners usually develop unflagging loyalty to one type.

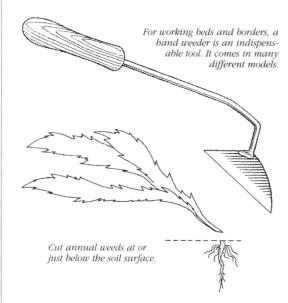

For working beds and borders, a hand weeder is an indispensable tool. It comes in many different models.

Cut annual weeds at or just below the soil surface.

RAKING IT IN

Steel bow- or flathead rakes improve soil tilth before you plant or sow seeds. After spading, use the rake teeth in a chopping motion to break up stubborn clods. Then push and pull the teeth through the soil to further refine its texture. For final smoothing (or for spreading amendments), turn the rake on its back, and push and pull the flat edge lightly over the soil surface.

If you plan to broadcast seeds of grass, wildflowers, or a cover crop, draw the teeth of the rake lightly over the smoothed soil to create shallow drills. Sow the seeds, then rake lightly at right angles to the original drills to cover.

You might prefer a wood *grading rake* (also known as a *hay rake*) for the final smoothing of garden beds; their light weight, 32" width, and 72"-long handle broadens and extends your reach. Pull toward you with long, smooth strokes. If you're gathering up leaves or hay, apply moderate pressure as you rake.

Flexible *lawn rakes* once were called lawn brooms, and for good reason. Draw leaves toward you with a pulling stroke, then use a sideways sweeping motion to move leaves or grass clippings along or gather them into neat piles.

THE STEEL RAKE: Like a judge's gavel, a steel rake brings a garden to order. Its short steel tines are essential for breaking up clods, working soil to a fine tilth, drawing up neat drills for sowing seeds, stirring the soil surface, sifting out rocks and loose roots, and raking up twiggy garden debris, while its flat back expertly smooths the soil surface.

Two standard designs prevail: the *bowhead rake*, which is forged or stamped out of a single piece of steel and includes a bowed pair of shanks that extend from each end of the rake head and join at the handle; and the *flathead* or *levelhead rake*, in which individual steel teeth are fitted into a flat steel bridge, which attaches by socket directly to the handle. If possible, seek out a steel rake with a solid-socket joint; if you can't find one, opt for a pinned tang-and-ferrule type.

Flathead steel rake

THE CULTIVATOR: Cultivators are the garden's masseurs, keeping the soil around plants relaxed and in tip-top shape. Their long fingers loosen the earth, allowing more air, water, and amendments to reach the roots of plants. At the same time, they disturb sprouting weed seeds and prevent them from taking root. In general, cultivators have three to five fingers, although a version known as the *biocultivator*, which stirs the soil to a 6" depth, has only one. Hand cultivators also are available.

The bent tines of this cultivator allow weeding and cultivating in one operation.

Pruning, Shaping, and Harvesting

PRUNING SHEARS: A pair of basic *hand pruners* (or *secateurs*) will see you through a wide range of garden tasks, from cutting roses for a heady bouquet to keeping your espaliered apple trees firmly in line. For the most versatility and the cleanest cuts, choose *curved bypass shears*, which have a scissor-like blade action. The hooked lower blade stabilizes the branch; when you squeeze the handles, the upper curved blade slides past the hooked counter-blade and cuts the branch off cleanly. Stop squeezing and a spring forces the blades and handles to open in preparation for the next cut.

If you buy only one top-of-the-line tool, this should be it. The Swiss company Felco makes pruners that are often the tool of choice for professional gardeners and nursery workers. There is

a model suited to every gardener. A threaded pivot allows the blades to be replaced; other parts also are replaceable.

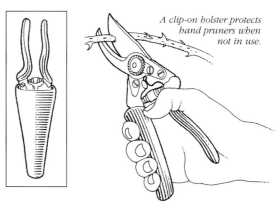

A clip-on holster protects hand pruners when not in use.

Anvil pruners have a single blade that closes against a flat anvil (like a knife on a breadboard) and work best for light pruning jobs and cutting crisp or woody stems such as those on roses. *Ratchet anvil pruners* readily tackle the big stuff; the ratchet mechanism increases their cutting power. If your hands don't have much gripping strength, these will be a welcome helpmate. When cutting off branches close to trunks, use bypass shears or pruning saws.

LOPPERS AND SAWS: Branches larger than $1/2$"–$3/4$" thick call for more power than a pair of pruners and a squeeze of the hand can supply. *Loppers*, or *two-handed pruning shears*, make quick work of slicing through branches up to $11/4$" (most packaging will indicate the largest size branch the pruners or loppers are designed to cut). *Ratchet loppers*, whose cutting mechanism allows shearing through branches up to 2" thick with minimal effort, also are available.

Two-handed pruning shears allow greater leverage as well as higher and deeper reach.

SCRUBBING UP

Gardens are about as far from a sterile operating room as you can get. But there's one place where gardeners need to observe operating-room rules, and that's when pruning their plants. It's all too easy to spread viral, fungal, and bacterial diseases from one plant to another—or one section of a plant to another—via the innocent-looking blades of your pruning shears or loppers. (Bacterial gall and fire blight are just two of the serious problems that can be spread by this method.)

If you have any doubts at all about the health of your plants, dip the blades of your pruners into a solution of 70% ethyl alcohol and 30% water, a mixture of 10% household bleach and 90% water,

or a commercial disinfectant (follow label directions) between each and every cut you make. Leave blades immersed for 30 seconds. Prune obviously diseased plants last, then sterilize your shears again. To prevent damage to your shears, rinse and dry them thoroughly when you're done, then lubricate the blades and pivot point with lightweight machine oil.

Felco manufactures a pair of pruners (No. 19) equipped with a canister and pump that automatically sprays the cut and the blades of your shears as you prune. If you grow a lot of roses or fruit trees, this specialized tool may be a welcome addition to your family of tools.

For banishing heftier branches, your best bet is a *pruning saw*. Particularly convenient are compact folding saws that close up like a jackknife, protecting both the blade and the gardener when the saw is not in use.

HEDGE SHEARS: If your bushes need a haircut rather than a major pruning, hedge shears are in order. These shears, like giant scissors, clip through dozens of tender stems and leaves at once, enabling gardeners to give crew cuts to their boxwood or smoothly shear their cotoneaster. Long-handled versions offer more reach.

THE KNIFE: Every working gardener ought to carry a knife, wrote John Claudius Loudon early in the 19th century, so that "he may be ever ready to cut off pieces of dead, decayed, or injured plants, or gather crops independently of other opera-

Hedge shears

tions." Today, you'll find that a sharp knife still comes in handy for cutting twine, doing light pruning, and harvesting the cabbages and kale. A folding type slips neatly in your pocket and is always close at hand. Specialized knives for grafting and budding also are available.

Watering

THE WATERING CAN: Though farmers often entrust the growth of their crops to nature's watering whims, most gardeners must create their own rain if they want their plants to thrive. The earliest gardeners probably scattered water drops with their fingers; as centuries passed, gourds, baskets, pierced clay vessels, wooden buckets, and tin water pots all were used to carry life-giving water to thirsty plants and seedlings. By the late 19th century, watering cans had evolved into their familiar friendly form: a round or oval reservoir of galvanized or tinned steel with a bowed handle, upturned spout, and round rose (the pierced metal head that turns a would-be torrent into a gentle shower).

For today's watering chores, choose a can with good balance in a size large enough to keep return trips to the faucet or rain barrel to a minimum. Keep in mind, however, that each gallon of water weighs eight pounds; an extra-large can may be too heavy for you to lift and carry when it's full. When you've finished watering, remember to turn the can upside down so it can drain and dry completely between uses. Well-designed plastic cans

Old-fashioned watering can (left) and Haws watering can

add little of their own weight (look for one with a removable brass-faced rose). But if you're a traditionalist at heart, opt for a high-quality old-fashioned watering can of sheet steel that's been hot-dipped in molten zinc (the heavy zinc coating should cover all seams and joints). Avoid cans that have been cut out and pieced together from pregalvanized metal.

Set aside certain watering cans for special jobs and label them appropriately. This way you won't chance contaminating a watering can with some previous solution. Those gardeners who use herbicides and mix them in a watering can should never reuse the can for watering plants. When you're finished watering, turn the can upside down so it can drain and dry completely between uses.

Many gardeners treat themselves to the Rolls-Royce of cans: a *Haws watering can* with a long-reach spout. Designed in the 1880s by Englishman John Haws, who wanted a can that could be easily carried and tipped with one hand (thereby allowing gardeners to water with two cans at once), the Haws watering can has a rigid bar that acts as both a brace for the spout and an easy-to-grip handle. Still made in England, Haws cans are superbly balanced and come with an oval, upturned brass rose that softly showers seedlings with no danger of washing them away. Copper, galvanized steel, and plastic models are available.

If you need to do a lot of hand watering, you can use two cans of equal size, one in each hand to keep yourself nicely balanced as you walk to your destination.

THE HOSE: Gardeners swear by their watering cans for moistening tender seedlings, coddling recent transplants, delivering manure tea to their roses, and quenching the thirst of their potted pansies, but any garden larger than a postage stamp also needs a hose.

Choose the best-quality hose you can afford, preferably rated at high psi (pounds per square inch) burst strength and reinforced with three to four layers of mesh, heavy brass couplings, and a stiff collar to keep the hose from kinking where it's attached to the faucet. Top-quality rubber or vinyl is the best hose material. Do battle just once with a cheap garden hose, as it twists and struggles like an unruly python, and you won't question this investment.

Soaker hoses (sometimes called "weeping" hoses) are perfect for watering beds of herbs, flowers, or shrubs, as well as fruit and vegetable gardens. They ooze water at a very slow rate through tiny pores over their entire length, delivering it right at ground level so there's no waste. Soaker hoses (often made from recycled rubber) come in many lengths; they attach to each other and then to your garden hose, which connects to the spigot. A soaker hose is usually left on for two to three hours; a timer can turn it on and off even if you're not there. Because it's a low-pressure hose, a flow disk is recommended for regulating water output. Snake the hose through the flower, shrub, or vegetable bed in an S-curve or laced back and forth through hedges or rows of plants, keeping it as close to the plants as possible.

Flat, tape-shaped *porous hoses* are slightly different. More water is emitted at a faster rate, in little spurts, so watering takes less time. Since the shape makes them less flexible, they are best used on long, straight runs rather than looped around

plants. Lay the porous hose with the holes facing down so the soil is moistened (not the leaves). You may want to anchor the hose with several small stones to keep it from flipping.

THE SPRAY LANCE: A spray lance, or water wand, turns your hose into a long-spout watering can with an endless supply of water. Depending on the design of the

A spray lance with a Haus oval rose turned upward is useful for watering seeds and flower beds.

AUTOMATED SPRINKLER SYSTEMS

Automated sprinkler systems are high-tech, highly automated, and expensive. Once restricted to the agricultural industry, these systems allow home gardeners to water large numbers of plants without a lot of manual labor. Custom-made for your garden, an automated system saves you time and delivers water efficiently to as many landscape areas as you choose.

These irrigation systems are entirely underground—except for controls, valves, and sprinkler heads—so installation should be done professionally. Review your garden with the contractor and make sure he or she knows the location of gas lines, underground utility lines, and the septic system.

You can have a number of sprinkler heads (pop-up, or stationary and aboveground) for different landscape features, each set for different ranges and volumes of water. The time of day, number of minutes each head is on, and sequence of activation are controlled by a timer box. All good automated systems have a "rain override" button so you can shut off the system when it

rains; or a rain sensor can be set to do this automatically. You'll want to adjust the water output of your system as temperature and humidity rise and fall, and to make sure that sprinkler heads are calibrated to water only the areas they're intended for (watering other areas is a waste, and may kill plants by overwatering).

Many gardeners opt for a service contract, so any problems (leaks, malfunctions, damaged sprinkler heads) can be easily resolved. Where winters are freezing, the contractor will come to blow out water from pipes in autumn and reactivate the system in spring.

A word of caution. You've chosen and set your fully automated system with care; it does the job with maximum convenience and efficiency; you forget it's there! But because most systems are set to run during the night, a malfunction (clogged head, cracked underground pipe) may go unnoticed. Check your system on a regular basis during the day—in the morning, if possible, when it does the garden most good.

lance's head, you can treat your plants to anything from a gentle mist to a soaking shower. A lightweight spray lance looks like a showerhead on the end of a metal tube; it's great for general garden watering and has a shut-off valve on or near the handle.

If you start lots of seedlings, in either the garden or the greenhouse, you may want to invest in a brass spray lance; it comes with a Haws brass oval rose that delivers the gentlest of rains.

SPRINKLERS: *Oscillators* pivot back and forth, shooting fine streams of water high into the air, losing lots to evaporation and wind drift. A better choice is the *rotating* or *whirlybird* sprinkler, which spins out water through two curved bars with holes at the ends; less water is lost because it comes out closer to the ground.

The best choice is an *impulse sprinkler* (used typically on golf courses). Its hard, even spray shoots out very near to ground level in a circular or semicircular pattern, with a higher volume than the other sprinklers, reducing watering time. "Towers" are available to set the mechanism up high if need be, and direction is easier to control. Heavy-duty brass will stand up to the rough dragging around that busy gardeners inflict on their tools.

Composting

THE COMPOST BIN: While it's possible to create rich compost with no equipment at all, most gardeners prefer to corral their compost-in-progress either in home-built wood or wire bins or in a commercial composter. Many kinds are available, from large metal or plastic *drum composters* or *compost tumblers* that turn and aerate debris to speed up the decomposition process, to inexpensive *perforated plastic cylinders* that fence in 15 bushels of raw materials. The key to success is a design that lets oxygen reach the compost and that allows you to turn the compost without undue sweat and toil.

One of the simplest models is the *stackable composter*, consisting of plastic tiers topped with a lid that opens to admit new materials. To turn the pile, remove the lid and place the top tier next to the stack, fork compost from the top of the pile into the tier on the ground; continue moving tiers and compost until the bottom layer becomes the top. (See page 16.)

THE COMPOSTING FORK: Both garden and spading forks work for turning compost, but a *compost fork*—a light, short-handled pitchfork with five long, narrow tines—will do the job faster and with less effort on your part.

THE COMPOST AERATOR: If there's no time for turning, a *compost tool* aids decomposition by introducing oxygen deep into the compost pile. Poke its pointed metal shaft into the pile and the blades fold up tight; pull it out and the blades open out like wings, lifting and stirring the pile from within.

Lawn Care

THE LAWN MOWER: Turf grass, environmental prima donna that it is, must have its mowing (seemingly the day after it greens up). It invites the nostalgic whirring of a classic *reel* or *push mower*—a far better accompaniment to a morning's mowing than the roar of an electric or gas-powered rotary machine. Push mowers require no fossil fuel, are easy to maneuver, make a cleaner cut than their powered counterparts, and create little noise; also, you won't make enemies of your neighbors if you mow early on a weekend morning.

A good hand mower is a precision machine that cuts with ease.

If your grass is tender, a five-blade mower will do the job; if your greensward is planted with a tough turf variety, look for a mower with six to eight steel blades. No matter what kind of lawn mower you use, be sure it has a mechanism that adjusts the cutting height. It's best to keep turf grass at a height of about 3". Never cut more than a third of the length of the grass at a time.

THE SHEARS: Regular *grass shears* make short work of stray grass, but better yet for quick trim jobs are *sheep shears,* or *singing grass shears,* still used in much of the world for shearing sheep. These venerable low-tech shears have scissor-like blades with straight handles, joined by a single or double loop of metal that gives the shears their spring. Squeeze the blades closed to cut the grass or to deadhead spent flowers; loosen your grip and the blades instantly spring open. An added bonus—they make a rhythmic singing sound while you work.

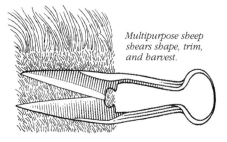

Multipurpose sheep shears shape, trim, and harvest.

THE EDGER: A sharpened spade will neatly edge small swatches of lawn, but a *lawn-edging knife* is the tool of choice for long stretches of edging. A sturdy, long-handled tool with a flat, half-moon blade, it edges lawns in 8" bites, making quick work of a tedious job.

For the straightest edges, tie a string between two stakes as a guide for your cuts. Insert the blade of your lawn-edging knife with the handle at a slight sideways angle, then step down on the opposite side of the blade.

Cleaning Up and Hauling Around

THE LAWN RAKE: Spread your fingers and pull your fingertips across the ground, and you've created the most basic of rakes, a handy tool wielded daily by millions of gardeners. If you have more than a few scattered leaves or just-pulled weeds to gather into a pile, however, you'll want to equip yourself with a bona fide lawn rake.

Differentiated from the steel garden rake by its flexible fingers, the lawn rake—in a multitude of designs—has proliferated since lawns became popular for suburbanites late in the 19th century. "The ordinary steel tooth rake should never be used on a fine lawn, as it tears up and injures the roots," warned one 1890s tool catalog.

Once called lawn brooms, lawn combs, or broom rakes (they're often used in a sweeping motion), lawn rakes also make short work of cleaning up driveways and pathways, while in smaller, narrower widths or hand-size versions they're perfect for cleaning leaves and litter from garden beds. Rakes that fan out from the handle, such as the classic *bamboo rake* or *wire rake,* are best for gathering bulky leaves. Rakes with short curved rubber prongs attached to a wide, flat head (one is known as the *Wizard lawn rake*) readily tackle finer debris. This latter type is a relative newcomer to the garden scene; its quiet demeanor when raking across concrete or paving has won it a host of converts.

The tines of a bamboo rake are bent at the tips for constant and uniform contact with the ground.

Whichever type of rake you buy, test it to be sure that the tips of all the tines meet up with the ground.

THE TARP: A canvas, burlap, or polypropylene tarp can go wherever wheelbarrows and garden carts can travel, and many places they can't, making it the gardener's most versatile hauling tool. Pile bulky leaves or clippings in the center of the tarp, then gather up the corners and haul it to the compost pile.

For extra ease, look for a tarp with strap handles sewn to each of its four corners.

THE WHEELBARROW OR GARDEN CART: Put one of these hard workers to use if you plan to haul mounds of compost, manure, sand, or soil around the garden.

If you must wheel your loads down narrow garden paths or maneuver in tight, inconvenient

A sturdy wheelbarrow is good for transporting, dumping, and collecting garden materials.

spots, buy a wheelbarrow (which balances on a single forward wheel). Otherwise, treat yourself to a two-wheeled garden cart with a plastic or wood-sided body and pneumatic tires. Far more stable than a wheelbarrow, a cart bears heavy loads (up to 500 pounds on level ground) without complaint.

Protection

GLOVES: Plunging your naked hands into rich, sun-warmed soil while you transplant your seedlings of tomatoes or foxglove is one of gardening's most sensual pleasures. But for many other garden tasks, you'll want protection: bare hands are all too easily blistered, cut, scratched, or pricked with nasty thorns.

No one type of garden glove does each and every job well, though most gardeners tend to develop a favorite.

Leather gloves protect against friction, abrasion, and thorn brambles. Cowhide and unsplit goatskin are the most durable choices, while deerskin, pigskin, sheepskin, and goatskin are the softest and most supple. Look for gloves with long gauntlets (the part that extends up your arm) if you'll be pruning lots of berries or roses. Although some leather gloves will regain their flexibility after you've gotten them wet, they're not intended for soggy jobs.

Cloth gloves keep your hands blister-free and out of the sun while you're performing light garden tasks; those with rubber dots on the palms and fingers won't slip on your trowel or rake. Cotton gloves, which don't last long with repeated use, are not recommended.

Rubber-coated or *latex gloves,* designed especially for gardening, protect your hands when the weather is wet or the soil is damp, or when you're doing a messy job such as picking up wet leaves or squeezing out the "tea bag" in your manure tea. Many gardeners develop a "green thumb fungus" that leads to painful cracking; this can be healed or at least managed by consistently wearing rubber or latex surgical gloves while handling soil. Look for heavyweight cloth-lined gloves with a textured surface.

If possible, try on both gloves in a pair before you buy them. To check size, make a fist. Gloves should fit snugly when the hand is closed and be slightly loose when the fingers are extended. If your skin is sensitive, look for gloves with seams turned to the outside.

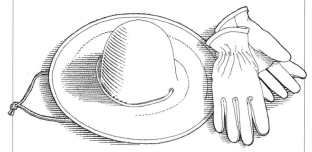

Essential accessories for the gardener: a hat for shade and gloves to protect against dryness and abrasion.

THE HAT: In the chill of fall and early spring, a good wool cap keeps you toasty until your garden labors warm you up. In wet weather, an oiled or waxed cloth hat sheds water like a duck; in summer, a broad-brimmed panama or canvas hat shields you from the sun's burning rays and at the same time helps you to maintain your cool. For breezy days, look for a hat with leather thongs and a sliding bead to cinch them tight beneath your chin.

FOOTWEAR: Mudrooms are made for gardeners, who fill them with rows of dirt-caked tennis shoes, muddy Wellingtons, and assorted other grungy-looking footwear. While gardeners differ in their preferences, most keep footgear on hand that's suited to heavy digging and spading (shoes or boots with a stiff shank or reinforced arch), working in sloppy weather (knee-high Scottish Wellington boots or other waterproof boots), or light garden work (plastic or rubber clogs, rubber and canvas flats, or old tennis shoes). Some gardeners wear their fabric-lined Wellingtons for nearly every garden task—wet weather or dry. They're quick to slip on and off for a brief foray into the garden, and they rinse off neatly with the garden hose.

THE CLOTHES: Line up five gardeners in a row and their clothes will be as varied as their flower beds. Some prefer shorts and T-shirts, some jeans and tank tops; others opt for baggy overalls and plaid flannels or roomy vests or smocks. All their garments, however, have this in common: they are as durable as a well-made spade and as comfortable as a second skin. Look for long-lasting natural materials such as cotton denim (or chambray in summer) and construction details such as double-stitched seams, elastic pant cuffs that keep insects at bay, built-in knee pads, and plenty of pockets in which to cache your pruning knife, bundle of twine, or tube of sunscreen and lip balm.

Plan to layer your clothing, shedding outerwear when spading works up a sweat and donning it again when you're weeding in the shade of the garden.

A gardening vest has pockets and pouches for storing tools and keeping hands free.

SAFETY GOGGLES: Protective plastic goggles are a must-have gardening item, whether you use power tools or not. Even implements as innocent as loppers can endanger your eyes: clip off a heavily weighted branch on a garden shrub and the section still attached to the bush springs up with amazing force and speed. Try goggles on for size when you buy them, and wait a few minutes to ensure they won't fog up. If they do, look for another pair.

Boots and clogs for dry, comfortable feet.

HOTELS FOR TOOLS

Fine tools deserve a safe resting spot for the night, and a place to lodge as the garden sleeps through winter. They're not that picky (a little dust and plummeting temperatures won't bother them a bit), but they do have several preferences.

■ **Shelter:** Whether you keep your tools in a converted mudroom, a corner of the garage, or a full-fledged potting shed, make sure the storage spot stays dry during rough weather and has adequate ventilation when the humidity rises. Avoid storing wood and metal tools in the greenhouse or a dirt-floored shed; the dampness will encourage rust and rot.

■ **Blankets:** Even tools tucked safely in the driest of spots may succumb to rust if their blades are left exposed to air. Avoid the possibility entirely by giving metal parts a light coat of oil, particularly before winter storage.

■ **Single beds:** "Have a place for everything, and everything in its place," wrote Mr. Barnes of England's Bicton Gardens in the middle of the last century, and good gardeners continue to heed this dictum.

Tools much prefer a resting spot of their own, where their sharp blades won't clash against their neighbors, scrape against the floor, or accidently trip up their owner. You'll benefit, too: no more time wasted searching for misplaced tools and less time spent sharpening dull ones.

Provide specially designed plastic clip-holders that grip shovels and other long-handled tools; add double tool hooks, pairs of wood pegs, or a wood peg rack for D- or T-handled tools such as spades and rakes. If the wall studs of your potting shed or garage are open to view, hang the blades of hoes and steel rakes over the exposed wood top plate of the wall to keep them out of harm's way. Provide ample shelf space for small hand tools, pots, and other gardening implements.

■ **Carry-ons:** When you head into the garden, tuck your hand tools into portable accommodations such as a canvas tote bag, apron, or a leather holster. When you're done pruning the pyracantha or weeding the herb garden, slip the tools back into their spots. You'll be less likely to leave them overnight in the damp of the garden.

Preservation Practices

"A little neglect may breed great mischief," wrote Benjamin Franklin, and so it is with tools. Store your spade in a damp shed or stacked in a jumble with other garden implements, and moisture and abrasion soon will dull the keenness of its edge. Leave your shovel caked with dirt from your garden beds and rust will gain a foothold, corroding and roughening its polished blade. Neglect to oil the parched handle of your rake and splinters will quickly remind you of the error of your ways. And as your tools tarnish, the joys of gardening dim.

Give your tools the care they need, however, and they will not fail to reward you with the greatest of pleasures. The pleasure of power, as your spade slips cleanly through the earth. The pleasure of pride, as you survey your trusty tools, arrayed like works by Degas or Matisse on the potting-shed wall. The pleasure of the senses, as you caress the satin-smoothness of a worn ash handle or glimpse the cool sheen of a worn steel blade.

Like good deeds, such pleasures perpetuate themselves. And before you know it, caring for your tools will become an unquestioned routine.

A place for everything, and everything in its place. A tidy tool area takes advantage of all available space and means finding the right tool for the job with no fuss or waste of precious gardening time.

CLEANUP: At the end of each gardening day, when you gather up your tools, brush clinging dirt from their blades with your fingers, a stick, a stiff bristle brush, or a wood man (a wood spatula designed just for this purpose). Or, scour them clean by plunging their blades up and down in a bucket of sharp builder's sand; then wipe them dry with a rag and check them over for signs of rust.

RUST REMOVAL: Remove rust as soon as it appears, using a wire brush or pliable sanding block (a spongelike block of rubber impregnated or coated with abrasive grit). Sanding blocks work best when lubricated with a little water; dry the blade after it's clean.

RUST PREVENTION: Keep rust at bay by oiling the metal parts of your tools on a regular basis. Rub down blades of spades, hoes, shovels, trowels, forks, and other carbon-steel implements with a rag moistened with mineral oil or light vegetable oil. (Motor oil, used by gardeners for decades, harms microorganisms in the soil.) Vegetable oil forms a sticky surface; avoid getting it on tool handles. Wipe blades of pruners, loppers, and mowers—and occasionally lubricate their springs, pivot points, and other moving parts—with lightweight machine oil.

SHARPENING: Tools made from high-quality carbon steel hold an edge through many cutting or slicing jobs, but their original sharpness won't last forever. Hoes, spades, and other tools that continually meet up with pebbles and grit benefit from regular sharpening. Clamp the tool securely in a vise, with the beveled side of the blade facing you. Grip the handle of a 10" mill bastard file with one hand and place the heel of your other hand on the file itself. Sharpen the blade by pushing the file away from you and to the side in short, quick strokes, following the angle of the original bevel. Finish with a few light strokes on the back side of the blade.

Pruners, knives, axes, and scythes are more challenging to sharpen and require the use of a whetstone. Take them to an expert (check in the Yellow Pages under "Sharpening Services") and watch how it's done, then practice up at home.

HANDLES: To increase the resiliency of painted or varnished handles, sand off the original finish and rub them down yearly with a coat or two of boiled linseed oil. When dry, smooth the surface with fine steel wool.

THE TOOLS YOU WERE BORN WITH

Although it puts you on the right path, a tool-shed filled with the finest implements available, kept in the best of shape, does not a garden make. Trowels and spades and forks are essential to planting and cultivating, but they do not provide you with what you need the most: the will to garden. The will to break through the crust of earth and plant a seed, or to nurture a plant—through drought and deluge and insect plagues—until it flowers or fruits. The will to bring beauty into being.

Those who have the will to garden manage to coax forth life no matter what their circumstances, using the most important tools of all: their hands, their head, their heart.

These are the tools you were born with—the vital implements from which the act of gardening springs. Use them well, and your garden will flourish.

DIGGING IN:
from CLEARING *to* PLANTING

A large part of all gardening work consists of digging. In fact, from the standpoint of your garden's good health, proper digging is probably the single most important activity. Digging cultivates the soil, loosening and aerating it at the same time. It also exposes those troublesome large stones, or other debris, and helps in their removal. And there is no better method to prepare the soil than turning the surface vegetation under so that it can decompose into nature's own humus.

There may be days, especially at the beginning of your gardening life, when you wonder if you'll ever do anything other than dig holes—large holes, small holes, wide and shallow holes, narrow and deep holes, round holes, even trenchlike holes. But holes must be dug in every size, shape, and depth to create a proper home for plants, be they tiny cosmos seedlings or strapping young Japanese maples.

So take heart: in due course, your work will create a loose, friable soil that supports healthy plants. Good digging and planting techniques always reward the gardener with robust growth. Shortcuts simply don't work; without proper planting procedures, you risk a garden full of slow-growing, sickly plants. But choose the right location, prepare the soil well, set your plants in the ground correctly, give them careful, consistent watering, and you will ensure them a good start—whether in a tiny pocket garden, on a patio of blooming containers, or in a vegetable bed providing garden-fresh nutritious salads.

WHAT'S WRONG WITH HERBICIDES?

We cannot, with a clear conscience, advocate the use of any chemicals to clear the land or eliminate weeds. Although organic herbicides (with fatty acids that quickly break down) do exist, their effects on soil ecology remain questionable.

Any herbicide is surreptitious; the first sign that it's doing the intended job often comes days or even weeks after its application, when the plants turn brown and die. And although the offending plants have been annihilated, they still need to be physically removed. Moreover, planting must be delayed for at least 6 weeks and as long as 12 weeks because the dead roots and surrounding soil contain enough herbicide to kill off any tender new planting.

For both the short and long term, removing unwanted plant material by hand—with or without the aid of tools—is more efficient and environmentally sound than resorting to chemical methods.

CLEARING THE LAND

It takes some effort to turn a dream into a real garden. Often, your future planting site is overgrown, either with an unkempt tapestry of weeds and/or grasses or with the plants put there by the previous owner. You need to clear away all existing top growth, like weeds and other vegetation, either before or after outlining the individual beds. Only in rare instances is existing vegetation limited to a handful of shrubs that you may want to include in your garden plan.

As you clear the site of each bed, you'll be able to judge the condition of your soil and determine what improvements it needs. And once

you're done, there's a bonus: freed of vegetation, the plot offers an honest perspective that lets you get a sense of the proportions and boundaries of your garden designs.

Traditional Methods

A well-designed mattock and digging fork are the most efficient tools for removing unwanted growth, especially in small or narrow spaces. The mattock helps you expose and remove large roots and deeply embedded rocks; the fork lets you loosen and lift firmly entrenched taproots of weeds like dandelions, Canada thistle, and burdock. A spade, in this instance, would likely chop through the roots, leaving small pieces behind to grow into more weeds.

For larger garden sites, notably those with long-neglected, heavily overgrown, or thickly grassed areas, other methods are more practical. Let an expert help. A professional arborist, for example, has the equipment and staff to fell trees larger than saplings, cut them up, and remove the stumps. Stump removal may seem costly, but in the long run it saves time and aggravation. In addition, the professional, equipped with a chipper, can turn a felled tree into wood chips for you to use later as mulch in the garden.

If you're confronted with a thick, tangled cover of grasses, clumps of weeds, or mounds of

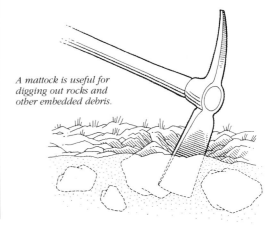

A mattock is useful for digging out rocks and other embedded debris.

overgrown perennials, the first step is to cut them as low to the ground as possible with a sickle, scythe, nylon-line weed trimmer, or mower. You may have to make more than one cut until the growth is uniformly reduced to ground level. Rake up plant debris immediately and remove it from the site. The less opportunity you give weeds to multiply, the fewer survivors and offspring you'll have to remove next year.

Once the overgrown area is cut, the largest clumps of roots should be reasonably easy to dig out. Be alert to plants such as bindweed and couch grass, whose slender root systems form extensive underground networks. You'll need a garden fork to gently dig these thugs out, deterring dozens of potential new weeds.

Smothering Vegetation

A less strenuous, but more time-consuming way to remove unwanted growth is to smother the vegetation—*provided* you do not intend to develop the site within the next year. The objective of smothering is to prevent any light from reaching the soil, so that even the most dormant plants and seeds will not start to grow. The complete smothering process requires 15 months or more.

The best time to prepare a bed for smothering is in early spring, while plants are still young and tender, and quicker to succumb than in their hardier stages later in the year. Begin by closely mowing the outlined garden area and raking away the debris. Divide the site into quadrants or wide bands. On a calm, windless day—and with somebody to help you—cover these quadrants with overlapping layers of moistened newspaper 10 sheets thick. Wet the papers thoroughly and repeatedly to flatten and bind them; weight them at intervals to keep them from becoming windborne as they begin to dry.

As you complete each section, and while the paper is still wet, cover it with overlapping sheets of black plastic. Place enough weights (rocks, boards, or gallon jugs filled with water) along the overlapped seams of the plastic and around the outer borders to keep the sheets from billowing. Since you have no reason to disturb the plastic/newspaper cover for more than a year, consider further securing it by laying weighted boards

The smothering method is a good way to clear large or very difficult areas that can be left unplanted from the spring of one year through the next spring and on into autumn. Throughout that period, the coverings prevent light from reaching the soil, causing all vegetation to die out.

around the periphery and across the center, especially if your land is exposed to frequent high winds. A thick layer of wood chips atop the plastic adds weight, keeps the soil temperature from getting too high, and prevents the soil from becoming heat-sterilized. When carefully prepared, the smothered site may not resemble a work of art but neither will it be an eyesore. It can, in fact, prove an ideal place to carry along containers of nursery plants until such time as they can be further planted or potted on.

By the autumn of the second year, when you rake away the chips (for use elsewhere) and remove the weights and plastic sheets, the newspapers will have decomposed to create a surface of dark, moist earth—with dozens of worms diving for cover—ready for preparing your garden beds.

LAYING A GARDEN BED

Although any time of year is acceptable for laying a new bed, provided the soil is neither frozen nor waterlogged, most experienced gardeners advise scheduling the project for autumn. With each shovelful of soil you turn over at the end of the growing season, you also turn under the surface vegetation that decays and changes into valuable humus during the winter months. Autumn is also the time when you can safely apply a layer of fresh, or "hot," manure to a new, unplanted bed. By the time the soil is dry enough to be lightly cultivated the following spring, the manure will be well rotted and will pose no danger to the roots of the plants you bed there.

Conversely, if you add fresh manure to a garden bed that you dig in the spring, it will be at least one month or more before the manure is sufficiently decomposed and has cooled enough to plant the bed. Why waste precious planting time by leaving a new bed fallow in spring, letting it fall prey to airborne or animal-carried weed seeds?

PUTTING SOD TO WORK

If a proposed bed site is in the midst of a healthy, well-kept lawn, you can remove the sod and use it in the smothering process. Cut and roll up the grassy layers with either a spade (hard work) or a sod-stripping machine (for rent at garden and hardware stores). Unfortunately, the mechanical approach, though fast and tidy, can lift a lot of topsoil. Either way, unroll the sod and lay it soil side up in the area from which it was taken. By the time you're ready to work the site, after 15 months or more, the grass and roots will have long since broken down and turned into humus.

Alternatively, you can use pieces of sod to repair worn patches of lawn. Or, if you're coincidentally double digging, chop weed-free sod into small pieces with a spade and toss some into the bottom of each double-dug trench.

Choosing Shapes

Before deciding on the shape of any garden bed, consider the landscape as a whole, including pathways and any nearby hardscape. You can follow existing lines, curved or straight (as when a bed conforms to a driveway), or create a free-form bed to break up a larger area such as a rectangular lawn. If you want to set your bed apart from an adjoining section of the garden, see "Edging a Garden Bed," page 134.

Unless your aim is to fashion a bit of whimsy or make a stark contrast, stick to one style—informal or formal. Generally, curved and free-form shapes are informal, while stricter geometric shapes (circles, squares, diamonds) are more formal. That said, however, rectangles are most often found in informal plantings.

AIDS FOR OUTLINING

The tools needed for delineating garden beds are an odd assortment: 2 or more (depending on the size of the bed) lengths of garden hose; a quantity of stakes at least 1' long; 2 pounds of flour (lime or baking soda are equally useful), ideally in a pour-spout container; a tape measure; a spool of sturdy twine; a large spoon; a mallet; a utility knife; a pocket calculator; a wheelbarrow or garden cart; and a spade.

A garden line is also handy; if you don't have one, however, two 3' wooden plant stakes (or an old broom handle cut into two 3' lengths) will serve the same purpose. Drill a small hole through the center of each stake and thread one end of a 20' length of twine or nylon string through each and tie securely. Wind the twine around one of the stakes, which will act as a spool.

In various combinations, the tools will enable you to outline, measure, align, and calculate garden beds of any shape or size. Even so, the most important tools for the task will be your eyes—the final arbiters of what looks right and what will work best.

The basic tools for outlining a garden bed are readily available.

LINEAR: Garden beds that follow the contours of the house are easy to lay out. For a 5' bed, all you have to do is sprinkle a spoonful of flour at regular intervals, 5' away from the house wall. Ignore architectural features such as chimneys, but you may want to make the entire bed wider to adjust for a deep bay window.

CURVED: To create a series of curved beds, use coupled hoses to outline the curves and crescents. It's not necessary to cling to your designs as they exist on paper; in reality, a particular site might look more attractive with a single bold sweep rather than a series of undulations, or vice versa. Keep adjusting the hoses, sharpening or broadening the arcs, until you're completely satisfied with their lines. Step back often, even walk away so that you can look at the beds from a distance and, more important, from different directions. Imagine the beds filled with the plants you've planned. If you're still not sure you like the outline, simply leave the hoses in place overnight and look at it with a fresh eye the next day. When you're satisfied, follow the line of the hoses with flour markings, twine, or a series of stakes or dowels to outline the shape. Keep the twine fairly low to the ground so it will be easier to make "moating" cuts.

CIRCULAR: Of all the geometric beds, the circle is by far the least difficult to mark. Using a garden line, firmly press one stake into the proposed center of the circle, then play out the spool until the length of twine equals the circle's radius (half the diameter). If you want to create a circular bed 10' in diameter, for instance, the length of twine should be 5'. Walk the spool around the stationary stake, marking the boundary with flour at regular intervals. The result is a perfectly round circle.

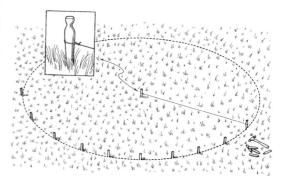

To delineate the boundary of a large circular bed, measure from the center at regular intervals no more than a few feet apart and insert markers at each radial point.

RECTANGULAR: Straight-sided beds are usually not difficult to place and measure. However, when used for kitchen and vegetable gardens, they demand more preparation—double digging or raised beds.

If square or oblong garden beds are to be located close to the house, or near a fence or hedge, it's best to align them with an existing line. To mark the outline of a 20' × 20' bed, for example, measure two lines 20' apart and parallel with the house, fence, or hedge. To avoid creating a parallelogram, measure the diagonal lines between opposite corners. If these two lines are equal in length, and all four corners appear to be right-angled, you have a rectangle. (If all four sides are the same length, you have a square.) For a more perfectionist approach, a T-square is helpful in assuring right-angled corners. The same principles apply if you decide to set a square on point—the diamond shape is merely laid out from a different perspective.

If you want a free-standing rectangular bed measuring 20' × 8', mark a straight line of 20' with the stakes of the garden line. Using this line as a guide, measure and mark a parallel line at an 8' distance. Be sure the two sets of opposite sides are equal in length and that the corners are right angles.

You can also create a circular bed within a square (and vice versa) or plant a triangle in a place of special interest such as a knot garden or maze. Or you might design a serene, hedged-in garden, paved and pebbled with stones of earthen colors, in a mosaic of intertwined circles and rhomboids. The possibilities are boundless and, luckily, so are the combinations of bedding and perennial plants.

FREE-FORM: As for curved shapes around the house, use coupled hoses or heavy rope to outline a free-form bed. Rope is more flexible than hose, although it is also more likely to be inadvertently moved out of place by people or pets. Keep widening or lengthening the bed's outline or adjusting a curve until you're pleased with the shape. Walk the perimeter to see if the perspective encourages the placement of a bench, or perhaps a peripheral grouping of birches, or a focal pergola of wisteria vine nearby. Be alert to any heavy shade cast on the bed by trees, in which case you might want to move the bed's outline several feet in one direction or another. Review the outline from all directions; take a break from your work and then, as you return, observe it with a fresh eye from a distance. If you like the shape of the bed and its proportion to the surroundings, from every perspective you try, consider the die cast. Mark and cut the edge.

Types of Beds

To determine whether you want a flat bed or a raised or sunken bed, consider the bed's location, its function, the requirements of the plants you want to grow, the type of soil you have, and your climate. A raised bed in an Arizona desert garden would overheat the soil and require more water than might be available. A sunken bed in the moist Pacific Northwest would collect too much water and quickly become a bog or quagmire. On a hillside, the rich topsoil in a flat bed would wash away—but a partial raised bed, terraced into the hillside, would thrive.

FLAT BEDS: These are planting areas where the worked soil is level with the surrounding ground. They are slow to dry out in spring, and they hold moisture well in summer heat. Flat beds can be single- or double-dug. Ideally, they should be between 2½' and 5' wide, so that you can easily reach into the bed to plant, weed, mulch, and harvest without stepping on the soil. If you want wider beds, create a path or series of stepping-stones (large enough to stand on and weed com-

EDGING A GARDEN BED

Many gardeners like the finished look that edging gives to their beds, but edging contributes more than polish. It visually and physically separates the bed from adjacent areas. It keeps the lawn from insinuating itself into the bed and makes mowing easier. Proper English gardens often have a small barrier moat of soil, 1"–2" wide, to divide the lawn from the flower bed.

It's easy to create a simple miniature moat to delineate a bed from a surrounding lawn. Once you've marked the outline of the bed with flour, use a spade to cut a V-shaped trench to the width and depth desired. This helps to keep a reasonably crisp line once the bed is dug. However, you will have to maintain the boundary or the moat may fill in.

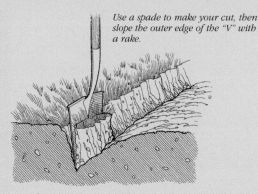

Use a spade to make your cut, then slope the outer edge of the "V" with a rake.

A low-maintenance alternative is to install a permanent edging. Aluminum, steel, and plastic edges are readily available in varying heights. Once sunk into the ground, they can be virtually invisible. Depending on the setting of your bed and your garden aesthetic, you may prefer an edging of bricks (placed vertically, horizontally, or at a 45° angle), stones, paving blocks, shells, or tiles to add visual interest to the garden while creating a boundary. If you choose wood as an edging, avoid the types that have been treated with toxic preservatives such as creosote or pentachlorophenol, which can kill your plants. Although a 4" depth will keep most lawn

grasses and shallow weeds at bay, an 8" edge is better. If you want to keep roots of trees and shrubs out of a bed, opt for an edge 2' deep.

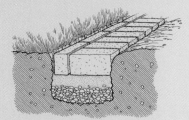

For a more formal edging, set bricks on a bed of gravel topped by sand; level and tamp, then water in. Finish by filling the gaps between bricks with sand.

The best time to install a permanent edge is when you initially prepare the bed. Begin by digging a narrow ditch down to the proper depth. Sink the edging vertically into the ditch, making sure the top is level with the soil line; otherwise it will wreak havoc with the lawn mower. Some edgings, however, are meant to rise above the soil level and may even serve as a guide for the wheel of the mower.

You can create a living edge with plants, but they require a great deal of maintenance to look perfect and will not prevent weeds from entering the bed. Small hedges made of dwarf boxwood or other dwarf evergreen shrubs look attractive year round. Obviously, edging with annuals or perennials is effective only during the growing season.

Some types of commercial edging are fitted with a piece at the top that sits just above soil level and acts as a guardrail for lawn mower wheels.

fortably) at intervals throughout the bed, allowing you access to all the plantings.

RAISED BEDS: Higher than the surrounding soil, raised beds are particularly well suited to areas with problem soil. Once formed, and amended with sufficient amounts of organic matter, they will require minimal cultivating and digging.

A raised bed may be a few inches high or up to 3' high—a comfort to those who would rather stand than stoop and kneel to work. For vegetable gardeners, raised beds with well-worked, double-dug soil allow intensive planting, which means greater yields from less space than in a conventional flat bed. A further benefit is that roots can penetrate deep into the amended soil of a raised bed instead of spreading sideways; the deeper they penetrate, the less they have to compete for soil nutrients. Also, close spacing of plants creates a microclimate under the leaves: the shaded soil holds moisture and precludes the sun-baking problems found in row growing. Raised beds are preferred by gardeners in northern climates because the soil warms more quickly and dries out earlier in spring than it does in flat beds, allowing them a head start on a limited growing season.

Unfortunately, although it would seem that raised beds are ideal for growing the most bounteous gardens imaginable, they are not appropriate for all soils. Sandy soil, which drains quickly, and heavy soil where drainage is clogged do not work well in these beds.

After outlining the sides of each raised bed, use a rake to pull soil toward you from the far side of the bed. In the process, you create a convenient walkway.

Enrich beds with compost or other organic matter, then level off with the back of a rake. The sides should slant at a 45° angle.

Raised beds allow plant roots to penetrate deep into amended soil, drawing sustenance from their own supply of water and nutrients.

To make a simple raised bed 3"–8" high, begin by marking off the sides of the bed with a garden line. Using a rake, stand on the far side of the bed and reach across to pull soil from outside the opposite edge toward you into the center of the bed. Walk the length of the bed, pulling soil into the bed. When one side is finished, go to the other side (where you've created a sunken path) and pull soil from the opposite side into the bed. (Obviously you won't get enough soil to fill a high raised bed from the surrounding area—you'll have to bring some in.) When done, smooth the soil with the rake.

The higher you make the bed, the more important it is to slant the sides outward from the top at about a 45° angle; when you water the soil, you don't want the water to run off the bed into the paths. For a bed higher than 8", build a wall or frame to support the soil. You can use any type of wood (cedar and redwood are among the longest-lasting); the thicker the wood, the longer the beds will last. If you decide on railroad ties, a traditional favorite for raised beds, try to find ties that have not been treated with toxic chemicals. Another option is faux wood, composed of recycled plastic milk containers that can be painted to look like the real thing

A word of caution for gardeners in moist areas like the Pacific Northwest and Texas gulf coast: framed raised beds can become a paradise for slugs, which love to congregate between the wood and the soil of the bed. A solution is to make an easily disassembled bed. Use 2" × 6" boards put together with nuts and bolts instead of screws or nails so you can take it apart once a month, clearing out any slugs and slug eggs. Not only will this help to eliminate these pests, but it will also give the wood a chance to dry out so it will last longer.

SUNKEN BEDS: Used for millennia by Native Americans of the Southwest to grow crops, these beds are ideal in warm, desert-like climates with sandy soils that heat up during the day and drain well. A bed below soil level has a lower soil temperature than the surrounding soil and acts as a catch basin for water. To make a sunken bed, mark off an area 4' by any length you need. Shovel out the soil to a depth of at least 12", then single-dig the bed.

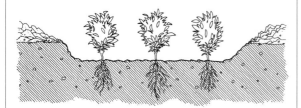

The sandy soil of warm desert climates remains cooler in a sunken bed, whose basin shape also serves to retain moisture.

TERRACED BEDS: These beds protect new plantings on sloped terrain from falling downhill, the natural effect of gravity. To create a series of broad terraces connected by steps, begin at the lowest level, digging into the hillside and moving the soil to a broad terrace. Depending on the soil, you may have to shore up the dug area

before you move up to create the next level. If you're planting no more than one or two plants on the hillside, you can easily create a small terrace for each plant so that its stem is perpendicular to the ground. Build a basin with an inch or so of soil around the periphery of the plant to hold water and to keep it from sliding down the hill. You may want to call in a professional if the slope is very steep and the area to cultivate very large.

THE BASICS OF DIGGING

Digging provides one of the strongest connections to your garden, its past and future, as you make contact with the soil and break through the crust. You can tell a lot just from the amount of resistance the soil gives to your trowel, shovel, or spade. The sound of a tool digging into rocky soil is very different from the sound it makes in clay; different, too, are the sounds of digging in moist and dry soils. Digging also connects you to the sensuality of gardening—to the earthy, rich smell and the dark, friable look of freshly turned soil in spring.

More important than deciding when to dig a new garden bed is making certain that the soil is ready to be dug. A simple test can tell you if the soil is ready to work, regardless of the season.

By choosing the proper tools and learning the correct stance, digging becomes less a tiresome chore than a productive and rewarding exercise.

SAFE DIGGING

When using either a shovel or a spade, place one foot (clad in a sturdy shoe or boot) on the tread of the tool and press down with the weight of your body to thrust the blade into the soil. Don't jump on with both feet—it's easy to slip.

Pull back on the handle to loosen the chunk of soil you've bitten off. Then, bending slightly at the knees and keeping your back straight, reach down with one hand and grasp the handle near the blade. Press down on the end of the handle to lever up the soil, then step and turn your whole body to place or throw the soil where you want it to go. With a long-handled shovel, you'll be able to rest the midpoint of the handle on your thigh as you lift the dirt, using it as a fulcrum and adding to your leverage.

Digging is probably the most tiring of all gardening tasks—exactly how tiring depends on your spinal and muscular condition, as well as on the size, weight, and type of tools you use. All gardeners develop a particular discipline and pace for digging. For many, digging becomes a rhythmic motion that engages the entire body, with the strenuous work done by the shoulder, arm, and leg muscles. This overall effort reduces fatigue and back strain and minimizes stiffening of the spine and joints. Your body needs to adjust slowly to unaccustomed motions. If you push yourself beyond your physical limits, you're likely to be so achy the next day that you won't be able to work in the garden at all.

Always keep a bottle of cool water on hand, not only for sipping but also to sprinkle on your face and the nape of your neck in warm weather. Take regular, periodic breaks, especially if you're new to the work. Stretch yourself, shake your arms and legs, rotate your hands and feet, loosen your neck muscles. You'll be amazed how rested you'll feel in a matter of minutes.

Firmly squeeze a handful of soil. Open your hand and gently press the ball of soil with your forefinger. If the soil mass breaks up easily, it's ready to dig. If it holds together firmly, breaks into only a few solid bits, or is moist to the touch, it's too wet and should be tested again after several sunny days. On the other hand, if it doesn't hold its shape at all and slips right through your fingers, it's much too dry. In that instance, water the soil thoroughly to moisten it to a depth of 6" or more and wait several days. If the soil still isn't right, it needs help—add plenty of organic matter.

Four Techniques

The four basic methods of digging are forking, simple digging (spading), single digging, and double digging. Each is intended for a slightly different purpose; one requires a garden fork, the other three a spade or shovel. Whichever method you choose, spread soil amendments evenly over the soil surface *before* you dig. As you dig, the amendments will be blended into the soil.

When turning over the soil of a large bed, divide the area into manageable sections (halves, quarters, or eighths) each about 5' × 10', depending on the size of the bed. Subdivide each of these into strips the width of the digging tool's blade. Mark the strips either with stakes at each end or with a garden line. Working row by row, methodically dig and turn the soil of each strip or row. Keep a rake and compost, rotted manure, or other amendments you need close by in a wheelbarrow or cart, in a large plastic bag, on a tarp or old shower curtain, or on the ground where you won't be doing any digging.

FORKING: This method is used to loosen topsoil that has become compacted through repeated alternate drenching and drying out, and to pry through clay and other dense soil. It's particularly useful for freeing the roots of established plants in an area about to be single- or double-dug, and for loosening and removing stubbornly rooted weeds. Puncture the soil with the tines of your garden fork and give it a slight twist; such a simple movement can aerate the soil and assure proper drainage. An English garden fork is preferable, especially when spaces among dense plantings are limited. Insert one or two of the fork's tines into the soil and turn to lightly loosen the soil without harming the surrounding plants or their roots.

SIMPLE DIGGING: Also known as spading, this method is most often used in small, confined spaces to aerate and cultivate the soil and to simultaneously add small amounts of compost and other soil amendments, especially amid plants that are needier or greedier than their neighbors. It's also used in the creation of free-form beds and in narrow borders of irregular shape, particularly among shrubs and trees or hardscapes. Simple digging is ideal for "seasonal" soil, as in vegetable gardens or annual beds, both of which require more frequent soil amendments than do perennial and mixed beds. Not least, simple digging creates surface tilth and cleans the soil surface of last year's partly rotted leaves and other debris, turning them under to gradually decay and become one with the soil.

Simple digging requires only a bit more effort than forking and can be done fairly quickly, depending on the type of soil. What makes it so easy is that the soil you dig up is turned over in place. The best tool for this type of digging is a garden spade, whose blade is narrower and flatter than that of a shovel.

SINGLE DIGGING: This method cultivates the soil better than simple digging and is most appropriate for areas that have not been recently used as gardens. Single digging aerates the soil and effectively introduces "new" soil into each row. Although it requires more work than simple digging, the end results prove that it's well worth the effort.

Once you've marked the area to be dug, start digging the first strip. Dig a spit of soil (the depth of a spade's blade, about 10") along the first strip of the first section to create a trench, and drop the soil on a tarp on the ground next to the digging area or into a wheelbarrow. When you've finished the first strip, move the wheelbarrow full of dug-up soil to the far end of the section. Then go back and begin to dig a second trench immediately next to the first. From now on, however, turn each spadeful or spit of earth into the previously dug trench. As you work, be sure to remove any large stones and any perennial weeds you meet along the way—these weeds are often the ones

1. Position your foot (forward of the arch) on the tread of the tool, and use the weight of your body to push the blade into the ground.

2. With bent knees and one hand low on the handle, lift out the soil.

3. For the simple-digging method, turn over the blade and deposit the soil in the hole you created.

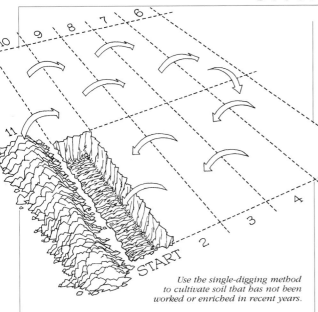

Use the single-digging method to cultivate soil that has not been worked or enriched in recent years.

Remove the topsoil, loosen the exposed subsoil, and cover it with a shovelful of organic matter. Transfer the topsoil from the next trench you dig onto the subsoil of the first trench, and continue working the length of your marked-off area. Some gardeners spread compost over the entire bed when they're done.

with tenacious taproots that may reach 2' down. When the last trench is dug, fill it with the soil dug up and saved from the first trench.

DOUBLE DIGGING: Most often used to correct poor drainage, to cultivate predominantly sandy or clayey soil, or if the ground shows signs of not having been cultivated before, double digging works the soil to a depth of 2'—a little more than two spits.

Mark off the area you plan to dig, and water the soil well. A few days later, remove weeds and loosen the top inch or so. The next day, begin digging by creating a trench 1' wide and 1' deep.

Double digging loosens the soil to a depth of 2' below the surface. This method requires more work than the others but creates a fertile planting area that's well worth the effort.

After you've finished digging, smooth and level the soil with a garden rake. This will break up small clods of earth and give the soil good tilth, rendering the top layer almost silky fine and crumbly, even-textured, and ready for planting. Raking also gives the area a nicely finished look.

Avoid walking in your garden beds: you'll compact the soil, eliminating the air held between its particles and depriving future plants of necessary water and nutrients.

Creating Soil for a Garden Bed

If your ground is so tough that you can't dig down four inches, much less three feet, you can create a serviceable garden bed by layering organic material onto it in late summer and early fall; this will decompose over the winter and form useful soil, ready for planting in spring. Measure out and mark off the area for the garden, including any paths. To create the beds, cover the ground with 8 or 10 sheets of moistened newspaper and add a 1"–3" thickness of each of the fol-

A GARDEN LEGEND

JOHN JEAVONS, MASTER DIGGER

When John Jeavons became convinced that the earth's topsoil reserves were being depleted at an alarming rate—and with it the space required to grow food for millions of people—his response was to pick up a shovel and start digging.

A graduate of Yale with a degree in political science, Jeavons was weary of posing a question that no one could answer: "What is the smallest plot of land required to grow a complete and balanced diet?" In 1970 his quest led him to Ecology Action, a non-profit environmental group that had recently leased a garden near Stanford University. Here, on four acres of inhospitable soil, Jeavons devised his three-section mini-farm comprising one section for food, one for compost crops, and one for income-generating crops. The earth responded by offering vegetables at rates 2 to 15 times the national average. His model for a highly efficient "food factory," which not only maximizes crop yields but also boosts soil health, has been adapted in Mexico, India, and Africa.

In 1980, Jeavons moved his living laboratory to Common Ground, a precipitous hillside plot in Willits, California, that poses many of the same challenges as gardens found in poorer countries. At first the earth was so unyielding it could barely be dented with a spade, but today, says Jeavons, "you can sink your arm in almost up to the elbow."

"The earth is a large garden, and each of us need only care for our own part for life to be breathed back into the planet, into the soil, into ourselves."

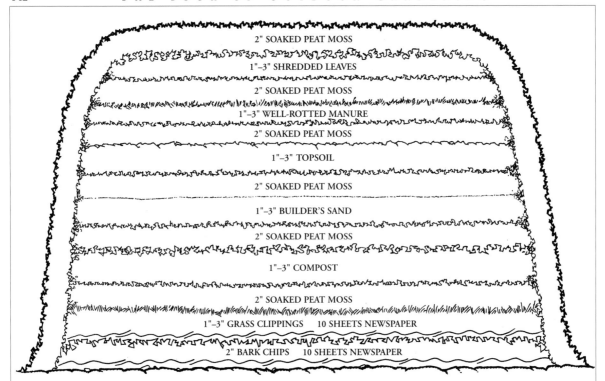

2" SOAKED PEAT MOSS

1"–3" SHREDDED LEAVES

2" SOAKED PEAT MOSS

1"–3" WELL-ROTTED MANURE

2" SOAKED PEAT MOSS

1"–3" TOPSOIL

2" SOAKED PEAT MOSS

1"–3" BUILDER'S SAND

2" SOAKED PEAT MOSS

1"–3" COMPOST

2" SOAKED PEAT MOSS

1"–3" GRASS CLIPPINGS   10 SHEETS NEWSPAPER

2" BARK CHIPS   10 SHEETS NEWSPAPER

If your soil is too poor to cultivate, you can create your own garden planting medium as suggested by Pat Lauza of New York. The organic matter will decompose over the winter, forming new soil in time for spring.

lowing: untreated grass clippings (no more than 1" deep if freshly cut), compost (at any stage of decomposition), builder's sand, topsoil, manure, and leaves. Water and cover each layer with 2" of well-soaked peat moss before adding the next ingredient. Top it with a final layer of soaked peat moss. (The peat moss provides organic matter and gives your garden-in-progress a finished look.) In fall or winter, sprinkle some wood ash on the top. The final creation will be about 18" high. For paths, lay down 8 or 10 sheets of moistened newspaper and cover with 2" or more of wood chips; do not top with any of the other layers.

In spring, after the snow melts, don't be dismayed to see that the bed may be only about 5" high. While you thought the garden was asleep, hundreds of earthworms and other soil dwellers and millions of microbes were at work, breaking down the layers and several inches of the hardpan below. The nutritious soil of the bed is now ready to plant with annuals, perennials, and bulbs. If

you keep adding organic matter to the beds, in a couple of years the good soil should be deep enough to support trees and shrubs.

No-Dig and Low-Till Gardening

Proponents of the no-digging method of gardening contend that soil is stratified and balanced with its own ecology; if you dig the soil in any way, friendly microorganisms are killed and the naturally achieved equilibrium is destroyed. To keep plants thriving in a no-dig garden, you need to continually maintain 3"–6" of compost on top of the soil. The compost decomposes and becomes humus; during watering, its nutrients trickle down through the soil to nourish the plants. Further, when harvesting vegetables or removing annuals at season's end, you don't pull them up. Instead, you cut them off at soil level, leaving the roots to decompose in the soil and form tiny air passages that keep it from compacting.

Low-till gardeners prefer an initial intensive digging to prepare the soil, then no digging at all after the bed is formed. Some are content with a preparatory double digging; others initially trench down a depth of three spits and add 6" of compost to the soil from the bottom of the trench; they then add topsoil and top it all off with the soil from the middle layer. Like no-dig gardeners, they maintain a thick layer of compost on the surface. Depending on the size of the bed, this can require elephantine quantities of compost.

In their vegetable beds, low-till gardeners plant cover crops of legumes to fix nitrogen in the soil. Thus they set up a feeding cycle for the soil by following a nitrogen-hungry crop like potatoes with fava beans or other nitrogen replenishers.

PLANTING THE GARDEN

Ideally, planting should be a peaceful activity—leisurely, not harried, nor shoehorned between grocery shopping, telephone calls, and lunch. Plants seem to respond to the manner in which you set them into the earth, reflecting, through good performance, your considerable care. They don't like being homeless even for a little while, so set them in the prepared soil as soon as you bring them home or directly after they arrive from a mail-order source. Be sure you know the pH of the soil so you'll choose the right plants to grow there. If you decide to alter the pH to meet a certain plant's preference (see page 7), wait about a month and recheck to see that the pH is at the desired level.

The optimum time for planting is in the early morning hours, late in the afternoon, or on a cool, overcast day when plants face the least risk of shock and derive the greatest benefit from watering in. If you just can't do everything at once, give priority to young annuals and

seedlings that are rapidly outgrowing their containers and to bare-root plants, which can withstand the least stress.

Before setting any plant in the ground—perennial, annual, tree, shrub, or bulb—consider its mature size. When growing from seeds, just follow the recommended spacing on the seed packet. Remember that growing plants can thrust horizontally as well as vertically, so they need enough room to spread out and thrive. Your garden may look a little sparse at first, but you'll be glad you planted prudently when those tiny plants fill up the space you provided for them.

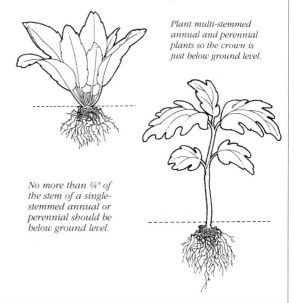

Plant multi-stemmed annual and perennial plants so the crown is just below ground level.

No more than ¼" of the stem of a single-stemmed annual or perennial should be below ground level.

B₁ VITAMINS FOR TRANSPLANTS

Several brands of vitamin B_1 solution are commercially available for use in sowing and transplanting. This solution encourages root growth, making for a smooth transition during and after transplanting and is especially valuable for transplanting root-bound plants from commercial cell packs. Mix the solution as directed on the package and use it to water the hole just before planting.

THE BEST TIME TO PLANT

Plants prosper when started at times that match their growing cycles. Thus daffodil bulbs are planted in the fall, when the cooled-down soil encourages root growth in preparation for the winter cold that will break their dormancy. Summer vegetables are sown in spring, when the soil warms up. Although bare-root roses are best planted in early spring, as soon as the ground can be worked, rose bushes sold in containers can be set out from spring through summer. In cold-weather climates, container-grown plants need to be in the ground by midsummer so they can settle in and establish themselves before the weather turns chilly. In areas with limited seasonal rain, it's smartest to plant before the rainy season to take advantage of the natural watering.

TYPE	WHEN TO PLANT
Annuals (flower seeds and seedlings)	Spring (after last frost) to summer. (In mild-winter climates, sow hardy annuals in fall and winter for spring bloom.)
Vegetables	Spring (after last frost). Sow again in midsummer for fall and early winter harvest.
Bare-root vegetables and fruits (asparagus, horseradish, strawberries, fruit trees)	Early spring, as soon as the ground can be worked.
Bulbs Spring-flowering Summer-flowering Fall-flowering	Fall (smaller bulbs earliest), before ground freezes. Early spring to early summer. Summer to early fall.
Bare-root shrubs and trees	Early spring.
Balled-and-burlapped shrubs and trees	Early spring or fall.
Container-grown shrubs, trees, and perennials	Spring, summer, or early fall.

And smart spacing will help you avoid the need for thinning, a time-consuming procedure, and for rigorous pruning, which can be hard on a young plant.

In the case of permanent plantings of perennials and/or shrubs, the sparse look can be improved by interplanting (filling in the empty spaces) with annual flowers or vegetables. Be careful to choose annuals that won't overwhelm the small perennials as they grow and bloom. At the end of the season, when you remove the annuals, you'll be amazed to see how well the plantings have filled in the garden.

Be cautious when planting near structures. Skinny young trees don't stay that way for long. Massive root systems of trees that were planted too close to the edge of the house can lift or crack the foundation. Trees that hang over rooftops may look dramatic, but they can damage the roof by rubbing or breaking limbs. Leaves falling from deciduous trees can clog gutters, resulting in rot and leaks in the eaves or roof. And, although good

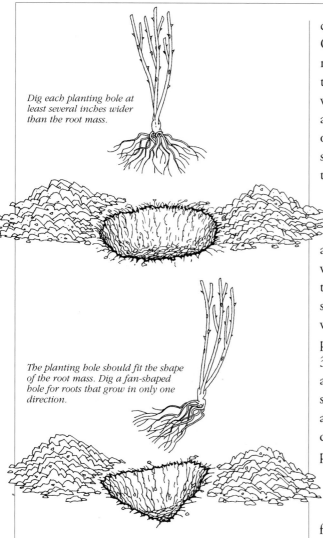

Dig each planting hole at least several inches wider than the root mass.

The planting hole should fit the shape of the root mass. Dig a fan-shaped hole for roots that grow in only one direction.

can, taking care not to disturb the basin's edges. Once the water has seeped into the ground, mulch well around the plant, keeping the contour of the basin. Give annuals and other plants without watering basins a gentle watering, using a watering can with the fine rose turned upward or a water wand attached to a hose. Try not to splash soil on the foliage or disrupt the root system when watering.

The ensuing days and weeks are critical in establishing the plant in its new location. To encourage root growth, keep the soil evenly and lightly moist—never let it dry out, but don't waterlog it, either. If in doubt about the soil moisture, stick your finger one or two inches into the soil. If the soil feels dry to the touch, you need to water small transplants (those that were transplanted from flats, cell packs, or pots smaller than 3") without delay. Depending on the time of year and daytime temperature, you may have to water small plants as often as twice a day. Water the soil around the plant, not the leaves, or you risk fungal disease. In fact, wetting the leaves of tender transplants in the midday heat of summer can actually harm the leaves by causing sunburn. Always water gently, yet give the plants ample water so that it can slowly seep down below the root level. Don't flood the area or wash away the soil.

Bare-Root Plants

A wide diversity of plants ordered through catalogs, including roses, grapevines, strawberry plants, some perennials, and many deciduous trees and shrubs, are shipped when dormant, with bare roots rinsed free of all soil and wrapped in moistened wood shavings, peat moss, or shredded paper. Give these bare-root plants priority over potted plants when they arrive. It's a good idea to wear rubber gloves when handling roots wrapped in peat moss, since this a primary source of sporotrichosis.

fences make good neighbors, large trees planted inappropriately do not. They can obstruct views, screen out precious sun, or simply behave like trespassers. Vines that climb by aerial rootlets can damage stucco or brick walls and therefore are better grown on wood fences. Other vines may force their way between shingles, causing damage to the walls or roof of a building. Wisteria grows so large and heavy that it can end up pulling down a lightweight lattice. It's always best to anticipate such problems and put the right plant in the right place.

Once a plant is settled in its new home in the ground, give it a good, long drink of water. If the plant has a watering basin, slowly and gently fill the basin with water from a hose or a watering

HEELING IN

If bare-root plants arrive before you've readied the garden, or if you can't plant them until the weekend, it's best to heel them in. Dig a trench in a cool, shaded, moist area—under a tree, for example—or in a protected north-facing spot. The trench should be wide and deep enough to accommodate the size of each plant's root system. Cut the trench so that one of its sides is vertical, the other at a 45° angle. Lean the plants individually (never bunched together) against the slope, with the juncture of roots and stems just barely below soil level. Thoroughly moisten the roots, then cover them completely with the soil. Gently tamp down and water thoroughly. For trees or larger shrubs, create a mound of soil below the main trunk or stem to support it in this position.

Although plants can remain heeled in for some time (as long as they're watered regularly), it's always wise to plant them in the garden as soon as possible. Otherwise they'll reach up for more light and become lopsided.

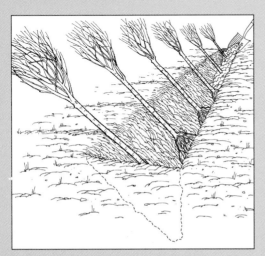

A technique developed by garden professionals, "heeling in" lets you put your planting on hold without causing any damage to the plants.

In nurseries and garden centers, where bare-root plants are sold only from late winter to early spring (before they begin to leaf out), you may be able to examine the roots; if so, choose the plant with the plumpest and fattest ones. Often, however, the roots are wrapped with sawdust or damp newspaper and encased in plastic to prevent drying out, so it may be difficult to examine them thoroughly. Try to feel them through the plastic to determine if the roots are solid (not mushy) and firm yet pliable.

A bare-root plant is virtually naked; don't let it dry out or it will die of exposure. Before planting any bare-root nursery plant or a mail-order bare-root shrub or tree, unwrap the roots, remove any packing material, and soak the roots (you can also immerse a portion of the stem) in a bucket of tepid water for 6–12 hours. If you can't plant it right away, heel it in.

To get the plant properly embedded, dig a hole twice as wide and a little deeper than the roots. Fill the hole with water or a vitamin B_1 solution and allow it to seep in. Amend the soil from the hole with organic matter. Make a mound of this amended soil in the center of the hole, high enough so that the plant's crown will be at ground level. Prune away any broken roots. Position the plant and carefully splay the roots out around the mound, then carefully backfill the hole with the remaining amended soil. Tamp down the soil with the palms of your hands, and water thoroughly to eliminate any air pockets. Add more soil, if necessary, to cover the roots and fill the hole; keep the crown at soil level. Make a watering basin around the plant and water thoroughly. (For planting bare-root roses, see page 155.)

Annuals

Most annuals, despite their shallow roots, require at least 6"–8" of rich soil with a fine tilth. Generally, they prefer a soil pH between 5.5 and

7.0, depending on the particular plant, and at least 6–7 hours of sunlight. Avoid planting annuals where they will compete with large tree roots for nutrients and moisture.

The amount of space needed between plants is largely influenced by their mature height and width and by the preferences of individual annuals. (Labels or seed packets offer this information.) Some plants, like alyssum, do well when crowded; others, like zinnias, need more breathing room. Annuals planted too far apart, however, run the risk of being slower to produce mass (showiness) and may fall prey to strong winds and rain or dry out between waterings. In general, if the soil is healthy, friable, and well nourished, most annuals do best at a *minimal* distance of 4"–6" from their neighbors. When massed at such close quarters, they create a warm, moist atmosphere, almost like that of a greenhouse, that helps to reduce the danger of dehydration during hot weather. Given the energy that annuals exert throughout their short lives, with their continuous blossoms and exuberance, these demands seem modest enough.

Annuals are usually sold when they're 8–12 weeks old and come in small flats of 4–6 seedlings each, in cell packs, or in small individual pots. Annuals grown indoors from seed should be at least 2"–3" tall before you consider planting them outdoors.

To free young plants from individual containers, lace the fingers of one hand through the stem of the plant with one finger on the soil, turn the container upside down, and tap it gently at the bottom. If several plants are growing in the

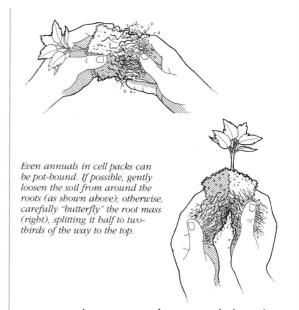

Even annuals in cell packs can be pot-bound. If possible, gently loosen the soil from around the roots (as shown above); otherwise, carefully "butterfly" the root mass (right), splitting it half to two-thirds of the way to the top.

same container, remove them as a whole and pry the young plants apart with your thumbs. Don't be concerned if a few of the roots break. Separate the seedlings by carefully breaking or cutting the root mass into halves, then quarters or sixths, making sure that each seedling retains its own clump of soil and roots. Roots may be so intertwined that they are impossible to tease apart. Separate the plants with the aid of a sharp knife, cutting straight down through the soil and root mass (see page 148) and be sure that each plant is centered in its own clump of soil and roots. Loosening the roots and thoroughly moistening the soil encourages the plant's rapid recovery from any shock due to transplanting.

Using a trowel, make a hole about double the length and breadth of the root mass, work in a handful of compost, and fill the hole with vitamin B_1 solution to encourage good, quick root growth. Hold the plant upright between your thumb and your first two fingers, gently loosen and spread the roots, then set the plant slightly deeper in the hole than it was in the container. With your fingertips, gently tamp down the soil to stabilize the plant, and add enough water to fill the saucer-like indentation produced by the tamping.

Never try to speed up the planting procedure by unpotting all the plants for a given bed at one time. Particularly in the case of annuals, the result could be mass death from dehydration or heat exhaustion.

POT-BOUND PLANTS

Plants that have been growing too long in a container often become pot-bound, their roots so densely matted that they inhibit all growth. Gasping for air, water, and nutrients, the roots crawl out of the bottom holes of the pot or else push their way up toward the surface, where they wind themselves several times around the top of the root ball. Give pot-bound plants extra attention by untangling some of the larger roots and splaying them out as you plant or repot them. Spreading the roots helps all plants toward a speedy recovery from transplant shock. In the most troublesome cases, the root ball can be split with a knife to encourage the growth of new feeder roots.

1. Support the root mass and stem with one hand when removing the plant from its container.

2. Gently loosen the roots and tease them apart.

3. If the plant is severely rootbound, make several cuts in the root ball, 1/4"–1/2" deep from top to bottom, to promote feeder root growth.

Bulbs

When choosing bulbs (or rhizomes, corms, and tubers, which are generally planted in the same fashion), look for those that are firm and unwrinkled. Shop early—don't wait for the season's leftovers. Once in hand, keep the bulbs cool and dry, and plant them as soon as the ground can be worked. Most of the bulbs planted in the fall for spring bloom are hardy and can remain in the ground, undisturbed, for years, whereas the majority of bulbs planted in spring for summer bloom are tender in cold-winter areas and must be dug up and stored before the cold sets in. In zones 8–10, where winters are mild, it's necessary to prechill some spring-blooming bulbs, especially tulips and daffodils, to induce bloom. Refrigerate these bulbs (keeping them away from apples and pineapples, which produce ethylene gas that inhibits flower production) for 8–12 weeks. Some catalogs and nurseries offer prechilled bulbs, ready to plant.

Bulbs need loose, porous, well-drained soil, amended with plenty of organic matter or peat moss. Many gardeners like to mix a small amount of bonemeal with the bottom inch or two of soil in the hole to encourage root development. Plant bulbs at a depth three times their diameter (measured from the *top* of the bulb to soil level). Generally, small bulbs such as crocus and snowdrop should be covered with 1"–2" of soil, while larger bulbs like tulips and daffodils are best planted 6"–8" deep. In mild-winter areas, plant larger bulbs 2" shallower than recommended. Position bulbs according to the effect you're trying to create, allowing at least twice the bulb's diameter between each one. Natural-looking swaths rather than soldierly rows make the most effective design. Consider color, too, when spacing bulbs; plant the softer colors in front and the more vibrant in the background. Group bulbs according to height and in sequential bloom pattern for a long-lasting show of color.

A bulb-planting tool is handy for removing the right amount of soil to plant a single bulb.

Drop the bulb in the hole (pointed end up); cover with the soil in the tool.

the proper depth. Loosen the soil at the bottom of the hole and drop in the bulb, making sure its bottom rests firmly on the soil, then cover with the soil removed from the planting hole. This technique is effective for planting small bulbs in a lawn area to create a naturalistic spring scene or for planting bulbs in a cultivated bed. For small bulbs and especially for massed plantings, it's more efficient to dig a free-form hole to the correct depth and lay down a large group of bulbs, spacing them at regular intervals. Cover the bulbs with the soil removed from the planting hole.

Planting bulbs in layers of various depths extends the bloom period; you can plant two or

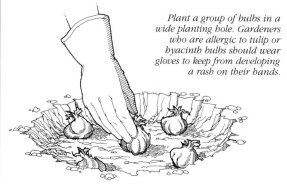

Plant a group of bulbs in a wide planting hole. Gardeners who are allergic to tulip or hyacinth bulbs should wear gloves to keep from developing a rash on their hands.

Bulbs are easy to plant—once you know that the pointed end goes up. On some bulbs, little roots may indicate the bottom. If you can't figure out which end is the top, plant the bulb on its side.

Label bulbs as you plant them, using markers long enough so that a good 2"–3" is below the soil surface. (Smaller labels can be heaved out of the soil during winter freezing and thawing.) Labeling also prevents you from accidentally digging up bulbs out of season when no foliage is showing. Do not rely on your memory; labeling is much more trustworthy.

Cover the planted bulbs with soil, water well, and mulch with shredded leaves. If the weather is dry, water the bulbs during their growing period. If squirrels and other critters like to dig up your newly planted bulbs, thwart them by laying chicken wire over the planting; be sure to remove it in early spring before any foliage emerges.

You can plant bulbs in three different ways: individually, as a group in a large hole, or layered in a large hole. To plant single bulbs, use a dibber, narrow trowel, or bulb-planting tool to make a hole a little wider than the bulb and to

A VITAMIN BATH FOR BULBS

If your bulbs appear a bit shriveled or show a touch of mold, don't be too quick to throw them out. As long as a bulb is still firm, not soft or squishy, it will probably grow—especially if you pretreat it with vitamin B_1 solution.

Gently scrape off any mold; if it's only on the paper skin, remove the skin and discard. Soak the bulb in vitamin B_1 solution (prepared according to package directions) for 2–4 hours, then plant immediately. The solution will stimulate root growth essential to getting any bulb off to a good start.

PLANTING BEARDED IRIS

Bearded iris thrive in full sun in well-drained soil. Plant the rhizomes horizontally, with the leaves up and roots down, so that the rhizomes are never more than 1" deep; in fact, the top third to half of the rhizome may be above soil level with no adverse effects. Plant with the fan of the leaves pointing in the direction you want the iris to grow. Never mulch over the rhizome.

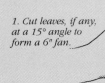

1. Cut leaves, if any, at a 15° angle to form a 6" fan.

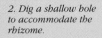

2. Dig a shallow hole to accommodate the rhizome.

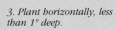

3. Plant horizontally, less than 1" deep.

4. Replace soil and gently tamp down.

three different kinds of bulbs within the same large hole. Plant the largest bulbs at the deepest level, cover with several inches of soil, then add another level of bulbs, trying to place them so they are not directly above the ones in the lower layer. You can even top these layers with a third layer of small, early-blooming bulbs. Combinations that work well are lilies on the bottom, tulips or daffodils in the middle, and crocus, snowdrops, or winter aconite on top. In this way, you get the greatest yield from a small space, with the foliage of each succeeding layer covering the ripening leaves of the earlier-blooming layers.

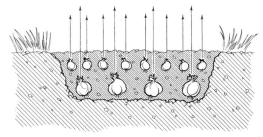

Create a longer season of interest by growing two different kinds of bulbs in the same planting hole.

Cacti and Other Succulents

No matter the size, shape, or cultural requirements of the particular plant, well-drained soil is essential for success in growing any succulent. Most large cacti and other succulents require full sun, although many smaller ones will thrive in the partial shade of shrubs or trees in your garden, much as they would in nature. A great diversity of succulents will prosper as long as the temperature stays above 25°F.; a few are completely winter-hardy, so even gardeners in northern regions can enjoy some of these charming, under-utilized plants.

By their nature, succulents store water in their leaves or stems; they do not need frequent watering. They transplant easily and, in fact, can endure bare-root conditions for weeks or even months before you plant them. Unlike other plants that need judicious watering to keep their soil evenly moist after planting, succulents need a good drink of water only at planting time. From then on, allow the soil to dry out completely between waterings.

In hot desert areas, a sunken bed is ideal for growing succulents. The basin may collect sufficient moisture so that the plants need only occasional supplemental water—if any.

Ferns

Before you plant, it's important to consider the mature size of your new fern and whether it grows from a crown or a rhizome. Crown-forming ferns generally grow slowly and form a vertical crown of fronds; some are short, while others may be 3' tall or more. Ferns with widely creeping rhizomes need ample room to grow and spread. You may want to install 6" metal or plastic edging to keep them from spreading into places where you don't want them.

Spring is the best time to plant ferns in areas where winters are cold and wet. Fall planting is preferred in warmer climates to give the plant plenty of time to establish itself before the stressful heat of summer. If the fern is in active growth, cut the fronds back by half to reduce stress from water loss.

When planting a potted fern, knock the plant out of the pot and remove as much of the potting soil as possible (unless you potted it with garden soil originally—as a division, for example) and gently tease the roots apart. Typical potting soil is light and peaty and will dry out faster than the soil around it, leaving the fern dry even when the surrounding soil is wet.

Dig a hole a bit larger than the root ball of the plant. In the hole, mix compost, a small amount of bonemeal, some of the potting soil, and the soil from the hole. Fill the hole with vitamin B_1 solution. After the liquid has been absorbed, spread out the roots, planting the fern so the crown is at the surface level—never below ground. Fill in around the plant with soil and compost, tamp down, and water. Mulch with compost, dry leaves, or wood chips to help keep the soil evenly moist. Water regularly until the fern is established. Since both the fronds and roots grow directly from the rhizome, do not disturb the fern once it's planted.

Perennials (and Biennials)

Although they may be found at nurseries throughout the growing season, most perennials do best when planted in spring. (Two notable exceptions are peonies and iris, which prefer to be planted in early fall.) Perennials are available in containers or as bare-root plants. Depending on the size and age of the plants, containers range from cell packs to 2-gallon pots. Most nurseries

Mulching puts the finishing touch to the planting process, effectively preventing weed seeds from germinating, maintaining even soil temperature, and conserving soil moisture. Newly transplanted seedlings need at least two weeks to adjust to their environment and grow tall enough to be in no danger of premature burial in the mulch. Leave at least an inch between the mulch and the stems of plants, since the decay of the organic matter may cause injury or introduce pests or disease. Add more mulch, an inch at a time, as the plants grow larger, ending with about 4"–6" of mulch. To mulch beds of tightly planted annuals (vegetables or flowers), sprinkle on about 1" of the mulch when the seedlings are about 2" high. (See pages 176–179 for an in-depth discussion of mulch.)

LENDING SUPPORT

Although it may be tempting after the hard work of digging holes and lifting containers on a hot afternoon to put off staking your plants, don't. Think of the support work as part of the planting process—one of the chores that must be done as you set new plants into the ground.

It's sometimes hard to imagine how quickly new plants start reaching for the sky, but in no time at all, it seems, they're covered with flowers or vegetables. Like proud parents taking pleasure in their lanky adolescents, we may forget how vulnerable the new stalks are. A summer thunderstorm, for example, can easily beat the plants over and leave them drooping in the mud. Rather than be confronted with that kind of disappointment, discover the advantages of staking and providing the support that weak-stemmed plants need to stand straight and tall.

It's important to match the type and size of support to the plant. A support that prevents a stately dahlia from toppling over in high winds is different from those that pole beans scamper up or that hold 50 pounds of ripe tomatoes.

In the vegetable garden, stakes, poles, and cages can be less decorative than in the main portion of the landscape. In the flower garden, stakes and supports generally should be a backdrop to the real stars of the show—the plants themselves. The exceptions are arches, arbors, pergolas, and trellises, whose decorative appearance actually enhances the look of whatever plant is growing on them. (For more on supports, see pages 186–187.)

nials are generally sold in spring (having been sown the previous fall) and should be treated the same as perennials in containers.

As soon as you get them home, give containerized perennials a good soaking. Dip each potted plant into a bucket of vitamin B_1 solution so the liquid just covers the soil. The air bubbles that rise to the surface indicate that the liquid is being absorbed by the potting soil. When the bubbling has stopped, remove the plant from the bucket. This thorough wetting helps the plant make a smooth transition from pot to ground.

Mail-order perennials are often shipped bareroot. Plant these perennials as soon as you've unpacked them and removed their wrappings. If this is not possible, heel them in (see page 146). Failing that, set them at once in water (room temperature, not cold) deep enough to cover their entire root system. The roots of small plants recover from their journey within an hour or two; those of larger plants like roses need immersion for several hours. Don't leave them too long or you'll suffocate the roots.

Horticulturists have found that bare-root perennials fare better in the long run when planted in a pot and grown for several months rather than planted directly in the garden. Their delicate roots develop better in the lighter potting soil than they would in the ground. Also, plants in containers are likely to get more individual attention. Choose a pot 2" wider and deeper than the root system; place a handful of compost in the bottom, fill with a good potting soil, and plant the perennial so the crown is just below soil level. In 6–10 weeks, you can transplant it into the garden.

Be sure you know exactly where the plants will go before you begin planting. While they're still in their containers, separate them according to whether they'll live in a shady or sunny bed, then group them by their mature heights. (If the information is not on their tags, you'll readily find it in plant and seed catalogs or in the Plant Guide

sell perennials that are in their second year, ostensibly ready to bloom—albeit modestly—during their first year in the garden. Look for "field-grown" varieties, which are locally grown and likely to be well suited to your area. Potted bien-

at the back of this book.) Arrange the potted plants on the prepared bed (preferably double-dug), in whatever design or pattern, texture, and color you have visualized. Move the plants around until you're satisfied with their placement—it's far better to do it now than to dig them up once they're planted. If you don't know the spacing requirements of a particular perennial, allow at least 12" between plants.

In a border, tall plants should be in the background; in a free-standing bed, they look best in the center, with the shorter plants graded downward toward the edges. For instance, upright delphiniums can be interspersed in the background with the billowy flowers of a crambe or the fullness of a phlox or heliopsis. Most perennials pre-

sent a pleasing density when grouped in threes. For large beds, or for plants that remain small at maturity, groupings of five or even seven may be preferable.

Whereas annuals demand instant and constant gratification of their needs, perennials, when secure in the enriched, friable depth of a double-dug bed, approach life at a somewhat more leisurely pace. True, they also depend on a reliable supply of necessary nutrients, but they're not in a mad rush to get them. Their roots are capable of searching far more extensively and over a longer period of time.

A trowel is the most commonly used tool for digging holes for perennials, but you may be better off with a garden spade if a plant's root system

PLANTING TIPS FOR SMALL GARDENS

Segregating flowers and vegetables in different areas is a luxury of large gardens, but planting the two together in small garden spaces can result in a pleasingly rich tapestry of colors, leaf textures, and shapes. A garden bed with violas and iris interplanted with a border of parsley and rosy-leaved lettuce looks charming and provides both beauty to the eye and food for the kitchen. Make successive plantings so that the space in the garden is never lying fallow. Plant peas early in the season with lettuces at the base of the plants. As these are maturing, start beans or tomatoes in the same space.

Pair plants with complementary growth habits. One of the classic combinations is the pairing of climbing roses with clematis. Plant the clematis just outside the rose's watering basin, but close enough so the clematis can easily reach into the branches. Choose colors that go together well, such as pink roses and purple 'Jackman' clematis or flowers in the same shades. By selecting plants with different bloom periods you can also increase the flowering

time of your garden. Plant early spring-blooming bulbs beneath later-blooming deciduous shrubs or trees. The bulbs have the benefit of full sun before the flowers and leaves of the larger plants shade the growing space.

Use architectural elements like pyramids, trellises, pergolas, or fences to grow larger plants. Look closely at your space and match it appropriately with the plant that will grow just to that size. The small garden benefits from striking changes of height, so don't be afraid to try out some shockingly tall plants to create garden rooms or the illusion of spacious walkways.

Concrete driveways or patios provide space for container gardens along the edges—a great way to experiment with new plants—and expand the amount of available growing areas. Whether you use this extra space as a nursery to start new stock, a holding zone before setting in new plants, or a display point in your garden, a large number of plants can be grown in a small space.

is especially large. Tip the plant out of its pot and into your hand. While holding the plant upright with one hand, half-fill the hole with soil, gently tamping down until the plant stands securely on its own. Fill the hole with water or vitamin B_1 solution to promote quick root growth. When the liquid has completely seeped in, fill the hole with the remaining soil, tamp down with the palms of your hands, and water the plant. Prune off any faded flowers, broken or bent branches, and wilted or damaged leaves. Water in and apply mulch. (For planting bare-root perennials, see page 145.)

Roses

Like reigning royalty, roses used to be isolated, grown apart from other plants as if intermingling would corrupt them. Today, however, many gardeners include them in a mixed border with other shrubs and perennials. Roses need a lot of elbow room; air must circulate around them to prevent fungal diseases. Space them to allow easy access for cutting: at least 12" between miniature roses, 24" between hybrid teas, 30" between grandifloras, 36" between floribundas and old garden roses, 7' between climbing varieties. It's best to keep roses at least 18" from the edge of a bed; otherwise, their arching stems may prick an innocent passerby.

Roses require full sun and well-drained soil with a pH of 6.0 to 6.5. The soil should be richly amended with organic matter in the form of compost, leaf mold, well-rotted manure, or shredded bark.

CONTAINERIZED ROSES

Nurseries and garden centers carry an array of containerized roses. Miniature roses are available year-round, while other varieties are sold only during the growing season. Containerized plants offer fewer choices than bare-root plants; they are also more expensive. The upside is that containerized plants are available later in the season, so you can see them actually in bloom.

No matter what the container, whether plastic pot, metal can, cardboard, corrugated paper,

GRAFTED AND SELF-ROOTED ROSES

Some roses are grown on their own roots; others are grafted. Gardeners in cold climates should seek out self-rooted roses, which are hardier in winter than grafted roses. Most miniature roses, despite their dainty stature, are self-rooted and hardier than many of the other modern hybrids. To tell whether a rose is grafted, look near the bottom of the stem to see if there is a swelling, or bud union, where the top variety was grafted onto the rootstock. All containerized grafted roses bought at a nursery have the bud union above the soil level.

When planting roses, it's important to know at what depth to place the bud union of grafted and self-rooted roses.

	COLD-WINTER AREA	MILD-WINTER AREA
Grafted rose (bare-root or containerized)	Bud union 1"–2" below soil level	Bud union 1"–2" above soil level
Self-rooted rose (bare-root)	Crown just below soil level	Crown just below soil level

PRESERVING CONTAINER SOIL

The soil in which nursery plants are potted, whether field- or container-grown, is the mixture best suited to each plant type. (Ferns are an important exception. See page 151.) Mix as much of the potting medium as possible into the garden soil at planting time. When plants move from one location or soil to another, they like to take along a piece of familiar ground.

fiber, even "plantable" box, remove it before planting the rose. Dig a planting hole somewhat larger than the container. Amend the soil with plenty of organic matter. Many gardeners recommend mixing a handful each of bonemeal and rock phosphate with 5"–6" of soil in the planting

hole, then adding a tablespoon of boric acid to promote strong stem growth. Fill the hole with vitamin B_1 solution or water. When the liquid has seeped in, remove the rose from its container; keep the soil surrounding the roots intact, unless the rose is rootbound. Position the rose at the proper depth and fill the hole halfway with amended soil, gently tamping it down. Slowly pour in a bucket of water, which will eliminate air pockets and moisten the roots. When the water has dissipated, add the remaining soil and tamp down with your hands. For efficient watering, create a watering basin around the rose. Water well and mulch. Keep well watered until the plant is established.

BARE-ROOT ROSES

As soon as your bare-root rose arrives, unwrap it and soak it in muddy water for at least 8

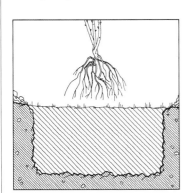

1. Dig a hole wider and deeper than the root mass.

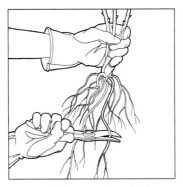

2. Prune back any overlong, broken, or dead roots.

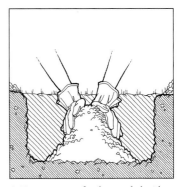

3. Form a cone of soil amended with plenty of organic matter.

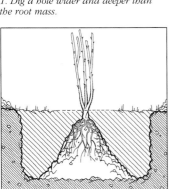

4. Set plant with stem at proper depth; splay roots evenly around cone.

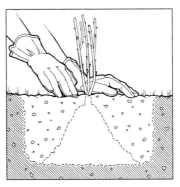

5. Fill hole with soil; gently tamp down.

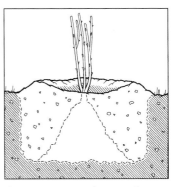

6. Create a watering basin, and water well.

THE WATERING BASIN

Before setting your shrub or tree in the ground, take time to consider how you're going to water it. If you live in a mild-winter climate, you can install a drip irrigation system at planting time. However, it's often easiest to create a watering basin. Once the plant is in the ground, make a low wall or berm of soil, 2"–3" high and 3"–5" wide, that encircles the filled-in planting hole. When you water or when rain falls, the basin will hold the water, allowing it to seep slowly down to the roots. Although any new plant will benefit from a watering basin, it is most important for roses, shrubs, trees, and the larger perennials. Never make a watering basin for cacti or other succulents.

If you live in a relatively dry area, where you'll be providing water for the plant rather than relying on nature's rain, it's preferable to make a moat instead of a basin. Dig a ring several inches wide and deep, just outside the filled-in planting hole, to hold the water. This keeps the base of the plant dry, preventing the possibility of rot (especially in tree trunks) from several inches of water in the basin on a regular basis. It also directs the water downward, just beyond the reach of the root mass, encouraging roots to grow into the surrounding soil.

A watering basin catches the water and directs it to the root zone of each individual plant.

hours before planting. If you can't plant it within 24 hours, rewrap it in wet burlap or newspaper and store in the refrigerator for up to a week. If at that time you still aren't ready to plant, resoak the rose and then heel it in (see page 146), covering the entire plant completely with several inches of moist soil. A bare-root rose can remain entrenched for up to six weeks.

To plant, dig a hole to accommodate the roots of the plant with several inches to spare—at least 12"–18" deep and 12" wide. Fill the hole with vitamin B_1 solution and let it soak in. Meanwhile, amend the dug-up soil with at least a spadeful of well-rotted manure or compost and a cup of rock phosphate; mix well. Cut back any roots that are damaged or too long. Prune the top back to three or four healthy canes, removing any canes that are thinner than a pencil.

Form a mound of soil in the middle of the hole to support the roots. If the rose is grafted, position it so that the bud union is at the proper level for your climate; if self-rooted, the crown should be just below soil level. Spread the roots down over the mound. Add amended soil, filling two-thirds of the hole, then pour in a bucket of water; when the water has been absorbed, fill in the hole with the remaining amended soil and gently tamp down with your hand. Cover two-thirds of the plant with moist (unamended) soil to protect it from wind and weather and to provide extra moisture so the rose can develop properly. Check the plant weekly. When new growth is 1"–2" long, gently remove the extra soil from around the plant to form a watering basin. Mulch well, keeping the mulch at least 1" away from the rose canes.

Shrubs and Trees

Shrubs and trees support and accentuate the main features of your landscape because of their size and permanence. Seldom do these plants go

HOW TO STAKE A TREE

The latest studies by professional arborists and dendrologists show that most trees should not be staked when first planted—that staking actually weakens the tree. However, a newly planted tree in a windy site, or one that has a small root ball with a disproportionately large canopy of leaves, will benefit from staking during the first six months to a year. This gives the roots a chance to grow deep enough to anchor the tree securely.

Depending on how much support the tree requires, you can use either two tall stakes or three shorter ones. With both methods, two-by-fours (2" × 4" lumber) make the best staking material.

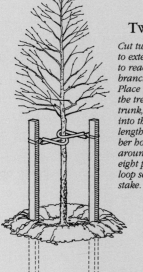

TWO-STAKE METHOD

Cut two two-by-fours long enough to extend 2' into the ground and to reach just below the lowest branch of the newly planted tree. Place the stakes on either side of the tree, 18"–24" away from the trunk, and pound them firmly into the ground. Cover two lengths of heavy wire with rubber hosing. Loop the hose around the trunk in a figure-eight pattern. Attach one loop securely to each stake.

THREE-STAKE METHOD

Cut three 2½' lengths of two-by-fours. Pound them into the ground, angled away from the tree, about 2'–3' from the trunk and equidistant from each other. Attach the ends of heavy guy wires to the stakes. Cover the other ends of the wires with rubber hosing and loop them around the trunk and lower branches of the tree.

Check the stakes every few weeks to make sure the loops are not rubbing the tree or pulling too hard in one direction.

into prepared garden beds; generally they're destined for grassy areas, in groups or alone as specimen plants. Once shrubs and trees have grown a few feet, it's unlikely that you'll want to move them elsewhere, so choose their sites carefully. (Of course, exceptions do occur: For transplanting evergreens, see page 167.) In addition, the soil they're in can rarely be easily worked and enriched, so their individual planting holes should be prepared with particular attention to proper drainage.

Nurseries usually carry a full range of shrubs and trees suited to the locale. Young shrubs are sold in containers as large as the 5-gallon size; young trees are often sold balled-and-burlapped, in late winter and early spring only. Trees that are taller than 12'–15' are generally sold in oversize, wire-supported biodegradable baskets. (In most instances, the baskets and the root balls they contain are too hard to remove and therefore planted together. Roots grow through the supporting wire, and the basket disintegrates in due course.) Submerging balled-and-burlapped trees and shrubs or those in wire baskets in buckets of water is impractical, so thoroughly soak the root ball with a hose or watering can—but be careful

A GARDEN LEGEND

THOMAS JEFFERSON'S AMERICAN POTAGER

Thomas Jefferson's gardens at Monticello are a verdant reflection of their creator—a man driven by science, passion, imagination, and democratic ideals. His acres were at once a vast laboratory for horticultural experimentation and a fanciful refuge filled with grottoes, ornamental groves, and flowers in profusion.

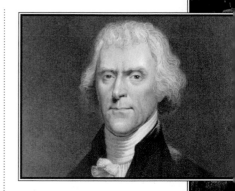

At Monticello, the house and gardens exist in near-perfect harmony with one another and with the sweeping Virginia countryside. When he set about planning the grounds, Jefferson did not look to the contrived colonial garden then in fashion, but instead sought a style appropriate to the spirit of a newly independent America.

"The greatest service which can be rendered any country is to add a useful plant to its culture," Jefferson wrote. To this end, he devoted many years to the introduction of new crops like olives and rice that could improve the living standards of American farmers and the poor. A hands-on gardener and a prodigious planter, he cultivated more than 250 vegetable varieties in his 1,000-foot-long kitchen terrace and at least 170 distinct fruit varieties in the eight-acre orchard.

Many of Jefferson's efforts are documented in his Garden Book, a meticulous record of plans, plants, experiments, agricultural observations, and the wisdom gleaned from years spent with his hands in the soil.

"If heaven had given me choice of my position and calling, it would have been on a rich spot of earth . . . near a good market for the productions of the garden."

HOW TO DIG A HOLE FOR A CONTAINERIZED OR BALLED-AND-BURLAPPED PLANT

All permanent planting, whether for a shrub, tree, or perennial, begins with digging a hole. You are creating an environment that will give the plant all the water and nourishment it will need for good root growth.

With a shovel or garden spade, dig a hole about half again as wide and the same depth as the root system. Keep the center of the hole at this depth, then dig the sides deeper still so that they angle down and outward into the soil, giving the roots room to expand. The sides of the hole should be rough, not smooth; use a hand fork to roughen them if necessary. You may want to amend the soil from the hole with compost or well-rotted manure and use it to fill in around the plant; however, many experts now agree that container-grown or balled-and-burlapped plants will often do better in unamended soil.

not to wash away the soil. If planting must be delayed for more than a day, set the plants in a semishaded location, where they can't be assaulted by high winds. Keep them well moistened; their root hairs are particularly vulnerable to drying out, which could greatly retard the plant's recovery.

CONTAINER-GROWN SHRUBS AND TREES

After you've dug the hole, remove the shrub or tree from its container. If the roots are loosely packed, dig your fingertips into the base of the root ball to loosen or untangle the mass as you set it in the hole. Pot-bound roots need a somewhat more radical approach. If the roots are so enmeshed that unwinding and spreading the roots by hand is out of the question, use a utility knife to make four fairly energetic slashes down the sides of the root mass. This will sever some roots but loosen up others so they gradually spread over the larger space you've created for them.

Once the plant is set in the hole, lay a broom handle across the top of the hole to determine that the plant is sitting no deeper or higher in the ground than it was in the container; adjust by adding or removing soil as necessary. Begin filling the hole with soil, firmly holding the plant upright. When the hole is half to two-thirds filled, water it well. After the water is absorbed, fill the hole with soil, tamping down the top to create a watering basin (see page 156).

BALLED-AND-BURLAPPED SHRUBS AND TREES

Never remove the burlap covering the root ball until the shrub or tree is properly set upright on a level base in its hole, with the sides of the hole adjusted to the depth and width required by its roots. Lay a broom handle across the hole, against the tree's stem, to see whether the soil line of the root ball or the tree's bud union (if grafted, as are many ornamental and edible fruit trees) is even with the ground level. Bud unions should always be aboveground; soil lines of the root ball, at ground level.

If the root ball is too low, tilt it slightly and push or shovel more soil under the ball. Often, a handful of soil wedged under the root ball is sufficient. Walk slowly around the plant at a distance to check that the stem or trunk is on an exact vertical line. Only when the tree is upright and set at the proper depth should you unfasten and very carefully remove as much of the twine and burlap as possible from around the root ball.

Add soil to fill the bottom third of the hole, then pour in the first of three buckets of water. Tiny bubbles across the water surface indicate that water is filling in large air pockets in the soil, which left untended could lead to serious problems for the tree, even death. Evenly spread more soil, and tamp it down until the hole is about two-thirds filled. Be sure the tree remains upright, and slowly continue watering in. If you've sufficiently tamped the soil, only a few bubbles might appear near the outside of the hole; keep tamping if the bubbles are near the center. With the remaining soil, fill the hole to within an inch of the surrounding surface, tamp down, and form a watering basin. Complete the watering in and mulch.

The Vegetable Garden

Anyone who has grown vegetables knows the satisfaction of watching the first tomato gradually ripen from green to orange to the deep red that only vine-ripened tomatoes achieve. The first zucchini plucked and cooked, corn so fresh and sweet you can eat it raw in salads, the sun-sweet fragrance of herbs—anticipating these subtle pleasures makes the gardener's heart quicken when spring approaches.

Vegetable gardening has a specific goal: high production of fruit and vegetables in a plot that may change its plantings with every season. The bed itself can be raised or flat, single- or double-dug. Most vegetables are annuals and best grown from seed, that is, sown directly in the garden at the proper time.

Locate your vegetable garden near the house if you can—it's so convenient to step from the kitchen into the vegetable plot when you need lettuce, tomatoes, or herbs for dinner. With your gardening space in mind, make a list of your favorite fruits and vegetables and then choose those varieties best suited to your climate and zone. For cool-summer areas, pick types with the shortest harvest dates; for long, warm summers, plant those with early-, mid-, and late-season maturity dates so your harvest extends all summer long. Most catalogs and nursery tags (and, of course, seed packets) cite the number of growing days from sowing seed or transplanting to harvest for each variety. When in doubt, check with local nurseries or call the mail-order catalog for information; these sources can be helpful in suggesting appropriate varieties to match your growing season.

To save space and increase production, many gardeners grow vining vegetables such as beans, peas, and tomatoes on supports. You can use cages of wire, tripods of poles, or string netting to allow these vines to grow upward. Keeping the vines off the ground results in more fruit production from better exposure to sun and pollinating insects,

"PLANTABLE" CONTAINERS ARE NOT FOR PLANTING

Any plant that arrives in a container should be removed from it just prior to planting. Even though some containers purport to be biodegradable, experience shows that they seldom disintegrate quickly enough to satisfy the spreading roots of the plants they hold. This is especially true of roses in "plantable" boxes—they'll do much better if you cut away the box, remove any soil from around the roots, and treat them as bare-root plants. Trees may come in large containers or wire baskets, or else bagged in burlap and tied with string. (Some trees are wrapped in a synthetic burlap that's nearly indistinguishable from the real thing except that it won't decompose in the soil.) Get another person to help you remove the container or burlap.

WARM-WEATHER VEGETABLES

Warm-weather vegetables need night temperatures of 60°–65°F. and day temperatures of 75°–85°F. to thrive. Soil temperature must be at least 50°F. for seeds to germinate outdoors. Plant seeds indoors 4–6 weeks before the last frost for a jump start, or seed directly in the ground when the soil has warmed up.

All annual herbs
Beans (*Phaseolus*)
Corn (*Zea mays*)
Cucumbers (*Cucumis sativus*)
Melons (*Cucumis melo*)
Okra (*Abelmoschus esculentus*)
Peppers (*Capsicum*)
Squash (*Cucurbita pepo*)
Tomatoes (*Lycopersicon*)

COOL-WEATHER VEGETABLES

Cool-weather vegetables are hardy, tolerating temperatures down to 28°F. Start seeds for fall-weather crops in July in cold-winter areas, in August in mild-winter areas. They can also be grown as early spring crops; often the seeds are started indoors 6–8 weeks before outdoor planting.

Asian greens
Beets (*Beta vulgaris*)
Broccoli, kale, Brussels sprouts, cabbage (*Brassica oleracea*)
Leeks (*Allium ampeloprasum*)
Lettuce (*Lactuca sativa*)
Onions (*Allium cepa*)
Peas (*Pisum sativum*)
Potatoes (*Solanum tuberosum*)
Spinach (*Spinacia oleracea*)
Turnips (*Brassica rapa*)

less mildew from improved air circulation, less damage from pests and weather, and easier harvesting.

Most vegetable gardens need at least six hours of sun a day, but a partly shady area with midday and afternoon sun can be planted with a few sun-loving crops such as squash and beans. Lettuces and other leafy greens will thrive in partial shade, especially as the weather warms in summer. Consult your local Cooperative Extension service for information about varieties that are best suited to your area.

PLANTING IN BEDS

Row planting brings order to the vegetable garden, and for some types of vegetables—climbing peas and cucumbers, for example—a line of netting stretched between two posts works efficiently. Row planting also gives the gardener space to control weeds by surface hoeing or mulching between rows. Soaker hoses or drip irrigation also work efficiently in rows, and harvesting is easier.

To plant in a row, make a line through the prepared moist soil with your finger or a warren hoe to create a shallow furrow ¼" deep. Space the rows 4" apart for a tightly planted area, or follow written guidelines on the seed packet. Sow seeds in the furrow, spacing them about 1" apart. Cover the furrow with soil, and pat down firmly. Water gently but thoroughly, using a fine rose on a watering can or water wand.

Wide-row planting, an intensive gardening technique often used in raised beds, results in a greater yield. A bed 3' wide and 10' long (smaller than a traditional row) planted with a single row of lettuce growing down the center, with the plants spaced 12" apart, will yield 10 plants. Planting a wide-row bed in a 2-1-2 pattern allows you to grow 11 plants in a bed only 2' wide and 4' long. (It's called a 2-1-2 pattern because for every two plants on each side of the bed, one is planted in the center; looking down on it, the pattern is shaped like an "X.") For example, plant the first four lettuces only 6" from the side of the bed but spaced 12" from each other. Add four more lettuces along the opposite side of the bed in the same fashion. Finally, add three lettuces in the center of the bed. Even plants like beans and peas will produce up to four times as much as when they're planted singly in rows. This method cuts down on weeding, since the plantings are so thick that the soil is shaded and weeds are generally choked out.

PLANTING IN HILLS

Heavy feeders like vining melons and squash are grown in hills enriched with organic matter. Mix several shovelfuls of compost into a 6"–8" area, creating a hill of amended soil about 6" high. Insert five or six seeds around the center of the mound, at the proper depth.

After the seeds have sprouted and at least one set of true leaves has appeared, thin to two or three plants per hill. As the vines grow, train them in different directions. The enriched soil in the hill will help nourish the plants as they develop.

PLANTING IN TRENCHES

Certain vegetables, such as asparagus and potatoes, must be planted in trenches for the greatest success. Order year-old roots ("crowns") of asparagus and seed potatoes from catalogs or get them at your local nursery in early spring. Dig each trench 1' wide and about 10" deep, with about 2' between trenches. Fill the bottom with about 2" of equal parts compost and soil. Spread out the roots of the asparagus plant and place them so they are about 8" below the surface and spaced 1' apart. Place the potato tubers the same way. Cover them with 2" of soil and water thoroughly.

Let the stems grow up through the soil and gradually fill in the trench, always keeping the newly emerging tips above soil level.

SUCCESSION PLANTING

The challenge for a vegetable gardener is to keep the vegetables growing and producing, with a smooth transition into each new season with crops well suited to changing seasonal conditions. A well-organized gardener plants cool-weather crops in early spring, has warm-weather plants ready to go in when those spring crops are spent, and is prepared for the autumn harvest as summer cools into fall. Mild-winter gardeners can extend their planting and harvest even into January and February.

For maximum yields, you can use a combination of methods and techniques. Start seeds early indoors so the seedlings are ready to put into the garden as soon as the soil can be worked. Use a hot cap or Wall o' Water to get an extra-early start on the season. Protect early plantings from unseasonable weather with cloches or floating row covers. Plant young summer vegetables in areas with spring crops so that when you harvest the spring plants, the summer plants will have room to expand and grow. You can intercrop with both seeds and plants. Sow seeds every few weeks in order to harvest over a longer period of time.

INTERCROPPING AND DOUBLE CROPPING

Careful spacing affords each plant the best light exposure and room for good root development. Especially in small gardens, space is at a premium and you may be reluctant to leave perfectly good garden space unplanted for several months until small plants reach maturity. Just as quick-growing flowering annuals, vegetables, or herbs are often planted between slower-growing perennials in a border to make the most of a given space, planting quick-maturing vegetables between season-long crops maximizes yield and uses space to its best advantage. Zucchini takes several months to spread to mature size; in the meantime, you can bring small starts of lettuce to harvest in the space between plants. As the weather warms, the lettuce will appreciate the cooling shade of the large zucchini leaves. Lettuce is not a heavy feeder, so it does not compete with the zucchini for vital nutrients in the soil.

Traditionally, gardeners sow radishes with slower-germinating carrots. The fast-growing radishes mark the space where the carrots will grow. By the time the radishes are harvested, they will have loosened the soil so the carrots have more room to grow. Squash, beans, and corn are often interplanted. The beans can twine up the corn stalks, while the squash provides a living

mulch for the soil around the corn. The corn is tall and slender enough not to overshadow the squash.

Herbs

Growing herbs brings great pleasure both in the garden and in the kitchen. Besides their culinary uses, many herbs attract beneficial insects—from tiny wasps that prey on larger bug pests to bees that increase pollination of fruits, vegetables, and flowers.

You can tuck herb plants among your vegetables, fruits, and flowers, grow them in containers, plant them at the end of your rows or beds, or, for a French country garden look, plant them between flagstones or bricks on the patio. It's nice to grow the most often-used herbs in a large (18"–24") container convenient to the kitchen, so the cook can easily take snippets, and keep the main planting of herbs in a formal herb garden.

Herbs are either perennial or annual and are planted as such. Most of them are not fussy about soils and are drought-tolerant. In fact, many of the herbs native to the Mediterranean, including sage, oregano, and thyme, have a more concentrated flavor when grown with a minimum amount of water. With the exception of sweet woodruff, most herbs prefer full sun.

Vines

To decide where to plant a vine and what kind of support to give it, you need to know its type. Clinging vines attach themselves physically to almost any surface by suction cups, hold-fasts, or similar means. Non-clinging vines can have tendrils or twining stems that aid them as they wind their way skyward. Unlike shrubs and trees, vines are not genetically constrained to a prescribed form and so can fit into the tiniest

WATCH OUT FOR CROSS-POLLINATION

To reduce pollen transfer by bees, other insects, or the wind, which may result in undesirable hybrid crosses, squash, melon, corn, cabbage, cucumbers, and other cross-pollinating plants should be isolated from each other. Breeders recommend separating these crops by 200'—an impractical distance for most gardeners. A more practical solution is to loosely cover the blooms of plants to be used for seed with muslin, spun-bonded fabric, or a paper bag before the flowers open. Once they open, shake pollen onto them from flowers of the same crop, then cover them again. You can also plant at intervals so that sources of pollen do not flower at the same time. The hazard of cross-pollination does not exist among self-pollinating plants, such as beans, tomatoes, lettuce, and peas.

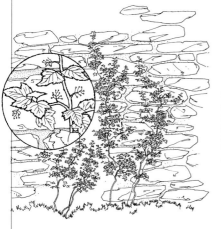

Clinging vines such as Boston ivy easily scale a stone wall with their "suction cup" disks.

Ivy's aerial rootlets will cling to a brick wall, but must be kept from working their way into old masonry.

VINES IN CONTAINERS

Many vines make great container plants. Be sure the container is large and sturdy enough for the vine's root system. Train the vine upward on supports; a small bent-twig trellis adds bucolic charm, while tuteurs give a look of elegance. In window boxes or hanging baskets, let vines trail down.

of spaces, provided that their roots are firmly anchored in the soil.

Supports can be purely functional or supplied by existing structures in the landscape. For showy perennial or woody vines and large annual vines, consider sturdy, permanent features to play the supporting role: fences, trellises, arbors, arches, pergolas, gazebos—even the walls of your house, garage, barn, or doghouse. Many vining vegetables and annuals will grow on supports that can be added or taken away as needed, including cages, stakes, tepees, wires, strings, and netting. If you decide on a permanent support for an annual vine, choose one that allows easy removal of the dead vine in fall or winter. If you pull strong, twining vines like moonflowers off a lattice, you risk breaking the lattice apart; such vines have to be painstakingly cut away instead. Be sure the support you provide for a young plant can hold the weight of the mature plant. The small vine you plant today hardly seems the precursor of a 30' vine that can topple a

fragile arbor with its heavy limbs.

Before planting, anchor the vine's support firmly about 12" in the ground (deeper if the support is very tall and heavy). Plant the vine according to its type—annual, perennial, or bulb—by providing the soil, light, water, and spacing that the species demands. Annual vines like scarlet runner beans, morning glory, peas, and sweet peas should be planted right next to their support. Perennial vines need to be planted at least 3"–6" from their support. The stems of woody vines, like wisteria and trumpet vine, can reach several inches in diameter; plant these vines about 12" from their support to keep them from pushing against it as they grow.

If a vine is in active growth, with at least 6" of stem, gently guide it to the support to encourage it to grow vertically. On a lattice, begin to weave the stem in and out of the support. To train a large non-climbing vine, such as a tomato on a stake, a climbing rose on an arbor, or bougainvillea on a pergola, tie it to the support with horticultural ties or soft cloth pieces. Use loose loops (a figure-eight pattern is the least harmful to the vine) so that the stems will have room to expand as they grow. Even clinging vines need a little help getting started on their journey upward. Wires firmly anchored in a wall every 8"–24" help support these vines and keep them from becoming dislodged in heavy winds or rain.

Non-clinging vines need three-dimensional supports to wrap their stems or tendrils around. Stems can wrap around a post, but tendrils require a narrower support such as wire, string, or netting. A twining vine will happily grow up a stout string attached to the top of (or above) a wall. Anchor one end in the soil so a strong wind cannot whip the plant around. You can create a lovely illusion by fastening a length of bird netting to a concrete or brick wall so your morning glories can wind their way up, greeting the day with their showy flowers. Nail-in and stick-on clasps adhere to most surfaces and can hold a beautiful annual vine like a canary creeper aloft all summer long.

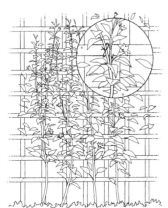

Provide interest on both sides of a fence by weaving a non-clinging vine through the opening, or tie loosely to lattice crosspieces to create a handsome, one-sided screen.

TRANSPLANTING WITHIN THE GARDEN

Every gardener at some time finds it necessary to dig up a plant and move it. Perhaps the new extension to your home requires whole garden beds to be moved, or your favorite planting has outgrown its space. A vine may suddenly swallow up your porch space; a group of bulbs multiplies and no longer fits the container; or the plant that was labeled white blooms outrageous purple. And no matter how carefully you site your plants, they may receive too much or too little sun or suffer a soil-borne disease.

Although you can transplant all year long, the optimal time is during the plant's dormant stage (usually in cool weather) when moving it is less hazardous to its health and any root loss is not critical. Don't transplant when the ground is overly wet or you'll compact the soil, compromising good root growth. Deciduous plants like roses and other shrubs can be dug during their dormancy and transplanted with their roots bare. Be sure the hole in the new location is ready before you dig out the plant to be moved; you don't want the bare roots to dry. If, for some reason, you cannot get the plant moved into its new home immediately, treat it like a bare-root plant bought from the nursery (see page 145).

If you're transplanting a large shrub or tree from a corner of your property to a lawn area, you can use the turf (weed-free) you dig out to anchor and feed the new planting. The sod will decompose into valuable humus. After setting the plant in the hole and loosening the roots, arrange the pieces of sod upside down and close together like mosaic tiles on and around the lower roots. While holding the plant upright, firmly tamp down the pieces of sod with your hands. Slowly begin the watering-in process. When the water is absorbed, fill the hole with soil, tamp down, and water again.

Place your less hardy plants in the most protected spots in your garden, and mulch to insulate from the cold. South-facing, freestanding walls absorb the winter sun, and south-facing walls under the roofline of a building are even warmer and often the most protected spot in the garden. You can also grow tender plants in containers and move them inside to a sunny porch or west-facing window in fall until warm temperatures return in the spring.

TRANSPLANTING EVERGREENS

Evergreen plants should be moved with as large a root ball as possible. Leave as much soil around the roots as you can manage, and encourage the growth of feeder roots close to the base of the tree by root-pruning it at least three months (even up to a year) before you want to transplant it. Root pruning means cutting through all the roots at a prescribed distance from the trunk. By the time you actually dig the tree out, a healthy system of new roots will have developed and will help to lessen the shock from the loss of any deep roots severed during the moving process.

To prune the roots: Measure the tree's diameter and multiply that number by 10. Use a piece of string or twine to measure that distance from the tree trunk and mark it on the ground with flour, continuing until you've made a full circle. Using a spade, cut down into the soil a full spit deep all the way around the circle. Root pruning is that easy. Months later, when you're ready to dig out the tree, dig just outside the root pruning circle. Root pruning can also be done on both deciduous and evergreen trees and shrubs to control their growth.

To transplant: If a large plant needs to be moved during active growth, not in its dormant stage, the greatest care must be taken. Two or three days before you plan to transplant, soak the area around the plant to make digging easier and to help keep the root ball together. Dig a trench around the plant just at the drip line (the outside edge where the plant drips when the leaves are wet). Dig down as deep as the root ball is wide. If the root ball is wider than 3'–4', use burlap or heavy brown paper to wrap the entire root ball and tie the top with string to keep it intact. If the root ball is smaller, you may not need to enclose it, but be sure to keep it intact. A brown grocery bag is an easy way to enclose a smaller plant when the root ball threatens to fall apart; the bag will disintegrate in the ground over time.

Lift the plant out of the original hole and lower it into its new one. Backfill around the root system. When you have the new hole half-filled with soil, water generously and let the soil drain. Continue to fill the hole with soil. Press down the soil gently but firmly. Make a watering basin (see page 156) with a berm of soil all around the plant. Until the plant shows new growth, water at least once a week, more if the weather turns unseasonably warm. Stake the plant if necessary.

Larger trees and older shrubs may have root balls too large for an individual to move without physical strain to both gardener and plant. Estimate the size of the root ball from the drip line, and don't hesitate to call in a friend or a professional landscaper if it looks like too big a job to handle alone.

PLANTING IN CONTAINERS

Containers not only provide the perfect solution to limited garden space but serve many other purposes as well. For homes with patios and decks, container gardens soften expanses, provide shade, and showcase specimen plants from the most delicate orchid to a robust tree. Vegetables and even dwarf fruit trees can be grown in containers, while flowers and fragrant flowering vines fill hanging baskets. Anyone can successfully garden in containers by heeding a few planting requirements and tips.

PLANTING AESTHETICS

You can create a sense of flow and continuity throughout each garden bed by repeating groups of species, textures, and colors. Try to avoid clustering all the mauves or reds at one end and the whites or deep blues directly opposite. Keep in mind that some plants need not be grouped at all; showstoppers such as rugosa roses, butterfly weed, and *Achillea* 'Coronation Gold,' with their continuous bloom on dense, shrubby plants, provide highlights or special effects when planted alone. The blooming times of different plants in a bed should also influence your groupings. A constant flux of subtly changing hues is far more effective than isolated seasonal patches of color.

FIRST STEPS

Containers can be made from clay, wood, terra cotta, stone, concrete, plastic, or wire. Whatever container you choose, it must have a drainage hole in the bottom, or several holes, to keep the plant's roots from suffocating. If you have a cherished container with no drainage hole, grow your plants in a smaller, plain pot and use the decorative container as a cachepot; use rocks or pebbles to elevate the inner pot several inches. Plants in containers resting on catchment saucers may drown in summer rain, so use the saucers indoors only. Keep "self-watering" containers inside as well; they have no drainage holes, so the pot can flood in a heavy rain. Raise large containers an inch or more above the ground on stones, bricks, boards, or specially made pot feet so water can drain freely from the bottom hole. If you're using containers in a hot area or one that receives reflected sunlight from a wall or flagstone path, keep your plants happy by planting them in a smaller container and placing it on several inches of gravel in a larger container. This will provide insulation and keep the soil cooler. You can disguise the edges of the double container with a handsome decorative moss mulch.

Prepared potting mixes work better in containers than plain garden soil because they allow better drainage and offer a clean growing medium. How often you'll need to water, especially in summer, depends on the type of potting mix you choose; sterile (soilless) mixes tend to dry out faster than live mixes. It is not necessary, as we were once told, to add pot shards, rocks, or gravel to the bottom of the container; in fact, these can create a drainage problem.

To plant, fill the container with thoroughly dampened mix. Make sure the soil level is ½"–1" below the rim of the container to allow room for watering. Many container gardeners find that a mulch helps keep the potting mix moist. If you decide to add mulch, leave 2" of space between the top of the soil and the rim of the container when you pot your plants.

REPOTTING CONTAINERS

Repot your container plants every two or three years, or sooner if the plant is a vigorous grower. Repotting prevents the plant's roots from running out of room and encircling the pot's interior, thus stifling plant growth. If you see roots coming out of the container's bottom, slip the plant out of the pot and look closely at the roots. Roots that are clearly visible around the sides of the root ball indicate that the plant is ready to be repotted. Before you repot, however, check on the requirements of the individual plant. Some plants and bulbs, such as amaryllis and clivia, like to be crowded in their pot and bloom better when pot-bound.

If the plant has reached its mature size, or if it's a size you wish to maintain, repot it into the same container. Withhold water for a week before repotting to let the root ball dry out slightly. Trim back the foliage to make it manageable, then carefully tip the plant out of the container onto a piece of plastic. With a sharp knife, cut 1"–2" from the sides and base of the root ball, less if the container is smaller than five gallons. Clean the container by washing it with a 10% bleach solution. Add fresh, moistened potting mix to the bottom of the container, slip the root ball back so that it sits an inch below the rim of the con-tainer, and add more fresh mix around the sides. Center the plant in the container. Tamp down the sides firmly and water the container thoroughly. Add more mix until it's level with the top of the root ball.

If the plant is still growing, you need to repot into successively larger containers. Each time, choose a container an inch or two larger than the root ball. With just a slight amount of space around the root ball, the plant will grow faster and healthier.

TENDING *the* GARDEN

T he big jobs are complete. You've designed your landscape. The right plants are growing in each section, rooted in soil enriched by your own hand. Now come the lighter tasks of anticipating and tending to the needs of your garden, preparing your plants for each change of season.

Often it's the little things, done in a timely manner, that matter most in gardening. Digging up and destroying a dandelion before it develops its puffball of seeds can prevent dozens of little yellow flowers from popping up in the lawn and garden next spring. The reward for faithfully picking mature green beans every day, even though you may occasionally want to be doing something else, is twofold: the freshest possible beans on your table and a continuing harvest that will last for weeks. Staking a peony when its pink shoots begin to emerge in spring means you won't have to see the flowers facedown in the mud just as they reach their full beauty.

While it's certainly true that there's always something to do in a garden, don't let this daunt you even if you're short on spare time. The few moments it takes to spread an organic mulch in the flower border will be returned to you because you won't have to water nearly as often and there will be far fewer weeds to pull. And pinching off faded dianthus flowers on your way to the mailbox or car will yield a plant that keeps blooming profusely.

Tending the garden, then, is quite simple—a matter of doing the right thing at the right time. The Garden Care Calender at the end of this chapter (pages 211–215) provides specific information about maintenance schedules for each plant hardiness zone.

WATERING BASICS

E veryone knows that plants need water. But they need it in the right amount at the right place and time. Too much water in a poorly drained soil can drown plants by rotting their roots; too little can make them so dry that they won't revive when moisture is applied.

With well-prepared soil, a nice blanket of natural mulch, native plants, and adequate rainfall, you might not have to water at all during the growing season. But for the rain to be efficient, it must be a good long rain that saturates the soil. A summer shower is quickly evaporated by the sun's rays, and a hard deluge runs off almost as quickly as it arrives. Neither one does the plants much good, since the water may never actually reach the roots. Whether from rain or cans, hoses or sprinklers, water must penetrate several inches so that not just moisture but also nutrients held within the soil are carried to the root system of each plant. Water that is not absorbed by the roots is virtually useless.

To be an efficient water provider, you need to know your plants' requirements and growth habits. You must also keep track of the temperature (how hot is it?), wind conditions (have the plants dried out?), and precipitation (how much rain has fallen and when is more expected?). No one ever gets this right all the time, but with a good watering program in place you can make every little drop count.

When to Water

The best time to water your garden is early in the morning after the plants have had a good night's sleep, when the air temperature has cooled and the plants are not yet stressed from the heat of the day. Morning is also a good time for the gardener. An early inspection of your garden lets you know right away if a certain plant, bed, or border needs attention, if the eggplant is ready for harvest, or the hollyhocks need a little less water, the sweet peas a little more.

If you can't water in the morning, the second-best time is late afternoon. Avoid nighttime watering; wet foliage in the cool darkness promotes the growth and spread of fungal diseases. Gardeners with automated irrigation systems should set them to start just before sunrise for the best effect.

Systems in which water is applied directly to the ground, such as drip irrigation, soaker hoses, or hoses set to a trickle, may be used day or night. These systems pose no danger of foliage damage, nor do they promote pests and diseases.

MEASURE THE WATER

Plants need a minimum of one inch of water a week. Using a rain gauge, you can measure the amount of weekly rainfall and calculate how much supplemental water your plants need. But how do you really know how much water your plants are getting from a hose, sprinkler, or irrigation system?

If you have an irrigation system or use sprinklers attached to hoses, set out coffee cans or other straight-sided containers all the same size (at least 4" across) 1' apart in a line beginning 1' from the sprinkler or irrigation head and going out as far as the water reaches. Run the system for 30 minutes. Measure the water level in the containers. If it hasn't reached a depth of 1", turn the system back on and time how long it takes for 1" of water to accumulate in the containers. Ideally, if the system is working properly, the water level in all the containers will be the same; if not, take the discrepancies into account when watering. Have the system adjusted by a professional.

Watering Requirements

Water must enter the soil at a slow, steady rate, as close to the root zone as possible to limit the chance of evaporation and to direct the water where it's most needed. Slow watering gives the soil a chance to absorb every drop. Watering should also be infrequent—as seldom as once a week

Carrying a watering can in each hand balances the load and cuts down on refilling trips to the faucet or rain barrel.

during dry weather—to give the soil a chance to drain and dry a little before more water is added. Your aim is to develop sturdy plants that have sent their roots deep into the soil in search of water.

The best way to find out if you've watered enough is to dig down and turn over a shovelful of soil in different parts of the garden. Is only the top inch or so moist? Most plants will not thrive in less than 8"–9" of moist (not wet or soggy) soil. Either you or nature will have to supply this amount of water on a regular basis. Since conditions change, dig into your soil several times during the gardening season to be sure you and nature are providing ample moisture.

SEEDS AND SEEDLINGS

Newly planted seeds need to be kept moist until they germinate—usually in one to three weeks, depending on the type of seed. Seeds planted in dry soil will not sprout. Use a mister or watering can with a fine rose upturned, and water gently (in order not to disturb the topsoil or wash the seeds away) once a day or once every two days until the seeds germinate. You can water seeds in a container by immersing it in 1" of water; this method will not disturb the seeds or tender seedlings. Then reduce watering to every two to three days once the seedlings are established.

ANNUALS AND PERENNIALS

When transplanting annuals and perennials, water them thoroughly at first and then twice a week until the plants are established. Water them once a week from then on (or less if you get adequate rainfall).

Established annuals and perennials appreciate a deep watering, with the soil moistened 2' down to encourage long, strong roots. To water a 4' × 5' bed of loam, calibrate your hose to deliver 2–3 gallons per minute and sprinkle the bed evenly for 20 minutes. For clay soil, sprinkle a total of 30 minutes (if there is runoff, pause for a while to give water a chance to seep in). For shady soil, sprinkle for 10 minutes. Be sure both sides of the bed get the same amount of water.

SHRUBS AND TREES

Lack of water is the number one cause of death in the first two years of growth for shrubs and trees. The roots of large shrubs and trees grow at least 2' below the soil surface, making it much more difficult to get adequate moisture to the lowest portions of the root zone. During the first year, water deeply once a week to encourage long roots. Place a hose, with the water running at slow trickle, at the base of the shrub or tree and let the water soak in for an hour. If you have a watering basin 4"–6" deep at the base of the plant, fill it up with water and let it drain completely; fill again and let drain.

In organic loam, filling the watering basin should moisten the soil to a depth of 6'. In clay soil, you'll need to fill the basin a total of four times; in sandy soil, only once. If the water soaks in so quickly that the basin doesn't fill, leave the hose on full for 10 to 15 minutes.

Watering shrubs and trees is crucial from late summer through the fall, especially if the weather is dry. These plants need to be fully hydrated before they enter the winter months, which can sap the moisture out of them—particularly in areas where the ground freezes and plants are unable to get reserve moisture from the soil.

Evergreen shrubs and trees transpire even in winter, which means they lose moisture and can become vulnerable to drought. If you're experiencing a dry winter, water your

Even if you have an automated irrigation system, you'll need the classic watering can for planting and other individual gardening activities.

one- or two-year-old evergreens when the temperature stays above freezing for a couple of days in a row to provide them with moisture during this critical time.

During the second year, water shrubs and trees once every two to three weeks, less if there is adequate rainfall or more if drought conditions exist. Once established, these plants can usually survive on natural rainfall, requiring supplemental water only when drought threatens.

ROSES

Water newly planted roses once a week for the first year so that, combined with rainfall, they receive an inch of water weekly. It's important to keep your roses evenly moist during the first year, when they are struggling to get established.

During the second and subsequent years, you'll need to water your roses very little or only if drought conditions jeopardize their existence. (They'll grow, but blooms will be smaller.) Roses use water the most when they're blooming. In most cases, old garden roses bloom only in the spring and early summer, when rainfall is usually adequate.

Everblooming roses flower in spring, then on and off during summer and profusely again in early autumn, when rainfall generally returns. Most of the old and shrub roses will survive and bloom quite well during a normal summer with little or no supplemental water.

FRUITS AND VEGETABLES

Fruit trees (apples, pears, plums, and the like) and fruit bushes and vines (blueberries, raspberries, grapes) are watered in the same fashion as other trees and shrubs (see above). If they don't have a watering basin, you can water them deeply by placing a hose with water trickling out at the base of the plant for an hour once every two weeks (less often if it rains, more if there is drought).

A combination of spring rains and heavy mulch usually provides enough water for strawberries. If dry weather persists, however, run a length of soaker hose through your berry patch and water at least 30 minutes once a week.

The seeds of melons need to be kept evenly watered until they germinate, after which they need watering once a week while they send out their running stems covered with leaves. Once the melons establish themselves and begin to flower and set fruits, it's best not to water unless drought sets in. Melon vines produce sweet fruit in hot, dry weather.

Vegetable seeds have to be kept evenly moist until they germinate; seedlings must be kept well watered until they are established. There is much controversy among gardeners as to how much water the vegetable garden needs. One approach is to keep the soil lightly but evenly moist (many vegetable plants, like lettuce and tomatoes, may be 90% water) with 1"–2" of water a week. At the other end of the spectrum are gardeners who prefer to moisten the soil deeply when planting, apply a thick layer of mulch, then water only if the plants show signs of water stress. Wilting leaves can be a sign that watering is needed, but for vegetables and melons wilting is normal in the late-day summer sun. Wait until the next morning to see if the leaves have perked up overnight; if they haven't, water the plants. Always water the vegetable garden early in the day and avoid wetting leaves. In many cases, you won't have to water your garden at all if you have well-drained crumbly soil and a good mulch.

BULBS

Be sure to water bulbs well when you plant them. They will quickly absorb the moisture from the soil and begin to grow roots. Fall-planted bulbs, which have to establish roots before a winter freeze, need an inch of water a week until hard frost, then no supplemental water until they produce blooms. Spring-planted bulbs (including dahlias and gladiolus) need an inch of water a

SARAH HAMMOND'S ENGLISH IMPORTS

Sarah Hammond's gardening epiphany occurred as she rested on a bench in the Oxford Botanical Garden. When she looked up and noticed the white drifts of *Lysimachia ephemerum*, she jotted down the words "excruciatingly beautiful"—and knew that finding and sharing such plants with others would be her life's work.

Sarah Hammond, founder of the original Smith & Hawken nursery, resides in a house she rebuilt herself on a windswept mesa on northern California's coast. She is sought out for her vision as a garden designer and for the new and unusual plants she tracks down in England and imports for propagation (she once drove 2,800 miles through the countryside to secure a fine form of white lavender).

Hammond approaches garden design not as a plant collector but rather as a plant selector. She also believes that some cultivars are clearly better than others—with superior bearing, bloom time, and fragrance—and are worth the effort even though it may take years to separate the wheat from the chaff.

Hammond's own garden, a never-ending work in progress where she tries out many of her imports, is a melding of low, mounded, green and silvery herbaceous Mediterranean natives (whose virtues she discovered during the years of the California drought) and deliciously fragrant old roses that nod and beckon from the tall wooden fences.

"People too often focus on flower color rather than on a plant's shape and texture—all those wonderful shades of green and gray."

week until they bloom. Because of their very small root systems, more bulbs die from overwatering than from lack of water. Don't plant them in an area watered by an automated irrigation system unless you can manually omit watering the section where the bulbs will go into the ground.

HARVESTING WATER

A resourceful gardener finds all sorts of ways to augment the water supply. Runoff from rooftops, driveways, patios, and other flat, nonporous surfaces can all be "harvested" for watering plants, taking otherwise wasted water and putting it to good use. Using "gray water" from sinks, washing machines, and diswashers also makes good sense if the proper precautions are observed.

You can collect rain from a rooftop by directing it through gutters or downspouts, channeling it via underground pipes, and evenly dispersing it through a French drain (a long pipe with a series of holes), thereby irrigating a high water demand area such as a vegetable plot. A simpler method is to channel water directly into rain barrels for future use. Modern barrels come with a spigot inserted in the bottom third of the barrel, making it simple to fill watering cans. (Rain barrels should be kept covered to keep mosquitoes and other insects from breeding in the water.)

Runoff from any smooth, paved areas can be collected and stored in an underground holding tank called a cistern and retrieved by a sump pump. From paved areas, rain may also be directed through subsurface clay drain tiles or PVC pipes into leach fields beneath lawns or other growing areas. Such a system requires grading to keep water from pooling. The drains must also be sloped or pitched at a rate of at least 1" per 10'. Consult a landscape architect for advice.

CONTAINER GARDENS

Plants grown in window boxes, hanging baskets, or any other types of containers need to be watered every day or at least every other day when receiving full sun. Depending on conditions, containerized plants growing in shade may go two or three days without watering. Soilless mixes can be difficult to rewet, so avoid letting pots dry out completely.

If the soil feels dry yet water runs right through it, place the container in a bucket (or even a saucer) and fill halfway with water to allow roots and soil to take up the moisture. Leave it for at least an hour. At the same time, sprinkle water on the top of the soil to slowly wet it from the top down.

It's a good idea, especially for large pots, to use pot feet or materials like bricks to raise containers slightly (1"–3") off the ground. This not only allows excess water to drain away, particularly important in areas with summer thunderstorms, but also keeps pots from absorbing heat from concrete and similar surfaces.

MULCH: THE GREAT GARDEN COVER-UP

A few inches of organic mulch cuts down on the need for watering (a big advantage in dry climates), improves the soil's structure, insulates plant roots against summer's heat and winter's cold, prevents erosion, keeps plants from being heaved out of the soil in winter by alternate freezing and thawing, and can all but eliminate weed problems. In the vegetable garden, mulch also keeps sprawling plants from getting dirty on the ground and provides a mud-free walkway in wet weather.

A mulch is simply a covering spread over the top of the soil. Leaves and twigs are the natural mulch on the forest floor. The home gardener, however, is more likely to use grass clippings, wood chips left from power-line tree trimming, or even the Sunday newspaper. These organic mulches eventually break down and add to the fertility of the soil.

Synthetic mulches, such as black plastic and landscape fabrics, are also available. Black plastic warms the soil, allowing eager gardeners to plant early in the spring, but it's a liability in the middle of a hot summer when roots prefer to be cool. And while it discourages the growth of some very tenacious weeds, it also prevents air, water, and nutrients from reaching the soil. In addition, it causes shallow root growth owing to poor aeration at greater depths.

Landscape fabrics, invented to overcome these drawbacks, are geotextiles that allow food, water, and air to reach plant roots. Some look like woven black plastic, others like thick cloth. Both kinds have to be covered by a layer of organic mulch to improve their appearance and to keep them from breaking down because of exposure to sunlight. Moreover, landscape fabrics are far from care-free. If a weed germinates in the mulch on top, you'll usually have to tear the fabric to remove it. A similar problem arises when shrub roots grow up into the fabric. Perennial weeds that spread by underground runners will often sneak through the holes in a loosely woven landscape fabric.

Because black plastic does not break down and landscape fabric is equally unkind to the environment, natural mulches are preferable to these synthetic materials.

Since no single mulch is best for all situations around the garden, you'll want to base your selection on appearance, availability, and cost. The choices are many, including commercial pine bark mulch, grass clippings, and hay. A coarse mulch like straw is fine in the vegetable garden but has an unattractive look in a perennial border. On the other hand, cocoa hulls are delightful in the rose garden but too expensive for a large pumpkin patch. In many parts of the United States, various hulls and shells that are agricultural by-products are available at little cost or free for the taking; when composted, these often make the best mulches because they're the least expensive.

Timing can make a difference. Don't rush to apply a mulch around vegetables or flowers in the spring. If the soil has not completely warmed up, the mulch will keep it cool enough to delay growth by a couple of weeks. Nor does it pay to be too eager to apply a winter mulch in autumn; you'll insulate the soil, keeping in warmth. The best time to apply a protective winter mulch is after the first hard frost or before winter rains that can cause erosion.

The first step in mulching is a thorough weeding of the ground to be covered. While a mulch prevents weed *seeds* in the soil from germinating and growing, it has no effect on weeds that are already in place so you must get rid of them first. Then water the soil if it isn't already moist.

Don't assume that if a little mulch is good, a lot more will be better. An extra-thick layer can prevent water from getting through to the soil, depriving the roots of necessary air and nutrients. Careful application is a must; dumping a bag of bark chips on a flower bed could smother tiny seedlings. When you mulch around trees, especially young ones, start several inches away from the trunk. Mulch piled up against the trunk can lead to rodent damage and provide a haven for insects or disease.

Never apply mulch to poorly drained soil. Covering soils that stay wet will only aggravate the situation.

Although it's sometimes said that mulches like pine needles and bark chips will make your soil acid, there doesn't seem to be much basis for this belief. According to most experts, these mulches have little effect on soil pH when used on top of the soil rather than tilled in as a soil amendment.

THE BEST NATURAL MULCHES

Most natural mulches break down slowly, improving your soil in the process. Renew them as needed by adding enough to maintain the thickness recommended in the chart on these pages. For light and airy mulches such as pine needles, use approximately 2" more for the initial application; within two weeks they will have settled to the correct thickness.

MATERIAL/THICKNESS	ADVANTAGES	DISADVANTAGES
Bark chips *2"–4"*	Nice appearance. Readily available. Easy to apply.	Expensive for large areas. Large pieces may harbor insects or slugs. May wash away on slopes. Can develop an unattractive (though harmless) slime.
Buckwheat hulls *2"–4"*	Small, dark brown, attractive. Slow to break down.	May blow away. Expensive for large areas.
Cocoa hulls (cocoa bean shells) *3"–4"*	Delightful chocolate aroma when first applied. Mild fertilizer. Absorbs quite a bit of water. Color doesn't fade. Neat appearance.	Easily tracked into the house on shoes. Will wash away on slopes. May mildew. May contain insecticide residues or fungicide.
Compost *3"–4"*	Free, if homemade. Natural-looking.	In visible areas, must first be pressed through a coarse screen. If not hot, may contain weed seeds. Airborne seeds will easily germinate in fine compost used as a mulch.
Corncobs, ground *3"–4"*	Free or inexpensive. Sugar content helps increase microorganisms in soil. May be effective against nematodes.	Appearance best suited to vegetable plots.
Cornstalks *3"–4"*	Free.	Must be shredded for best appearance.
Cottonseed hulls *3"–4"*	Free or inexpensive (in regions where available). Lightweight. Add nutrients to soil.	May blow away. Possible pesticide residue; not for use in a certified organic garden.
Evergreen boughs *(one to several layers)*	Good for erosion control and winter protection. Good use of healthy prunings and discarded holiday fixings.	May turn brown and become a fire hazard (not commonly used as a year-round mulch).
Grass clippings *2"*	Free. Decompose quickly. Look neat.	When fresh, must be spread in a thin layer and kept several inches from desirable plants. May contain weed seeds or, if from someone else's yard, insecticide or herbicide residues.
Grasses, ornamental *2"–4"*	Free (dead stalks have to be cut down each year anyway). Long-lasting.	May contain seeds. Stalks of taller grasses may have to be cut in half.

MATERIAL/THICKNESS	ADVANTAGES	DISADVANTAGES
Hay or straw 6"–8"	Readily available. Easy to apply. Natural appearance.	May contain weed seeds. Fire hazard. Best for the vegetable garden.
Leaf mold (rotted leaves) 3"–4"	Adds nutrients to soil. Looks nice. Free if you or your community composts the leaves.	Requires a huge quantity of leaves and at least a year to make.
Leaves, shredded 4"–6"	Free. Contain nutrients.	Leaves from a variety of trees must be gathered and shredded. Cannot be spread close to stems of delicate plants. Never use black walnut leaves.
Newspapers 4"–6" (when shredded)	Free. Readily available. Great for preventing weeds.	Time-consuming preparation: 1) wet soil before putting newspapers down, then wet paper thoroughly; 2) anchor edges to prevent blow-away; 3) except in vegetable garden, top off with a layer of another mulch to improve appearance. Don't use colored newsprint or magazines.
Peat moss	Natural-looking. Adds organic matter to soil.	Not recommended because it dries out on the surface of the ground and prevents water from passing through.
Pine needles 3"–6"	Won't wash away on slopes. Natural appearance. Easy to obtain. Light and airy.	Need renewing more often than wood chips or bark. Fire hazard when dry.
Salt marsh hay 3"–6"	Free or inexpensive. No weed seeds. Long-lasting.	Environmentally irresponsible to use (harvest upsets the ecology of the marsh). Okay to use what has been washed ashore.
Sawdust 2"	Free or inexpensive. Neat appearance.	Has to rot 6 months before use. Fire hazard when dry. Can clump (avoid this by mixing with shredded leaves). Light color can call attention to itself in the landscape.
Seaweed 2"–4"	May be free or inexpensive. Excellent fertilizer. Contains growth-producing hormones.	May contain salt. Use of harvested seaweed is environmentally questionable because some seaweed habitats are under stress. Okay to use what washes up on beaches.
Stones, gravel, pebbles 1"–1½"	Top surface dries quickly; for plants whose foliage may rot when kept moist. Beautiful in Oriental garden schemes. Ideal for areas subject to wildfires.	Do not break down and improve the soil. Can be expensive; not easily moved if you change your mind.
Wood chips, fresh 3"–4"	Inexpensive or free. Long-lasting. Good for paths.	Appearance varies. Look best when composted 6 months before using. Can harbor insects and slugs

WEEDING MADE SIMPLE

As you tend your garden day by day and get to know and appreciate the trees, shrubs, flowers, fruits, herbs, and vegetables that have become part of your landscape, you're helping them reach their beautiful, productive potential. This is what gardening is all about, and weeding is part and parcel of the life-enhancing experience.

Far from being the tiresome drudgery you might imagine, weeding is a wonderful way to stay in touch with the natural rhythms of life. Visitors to a noted garden were once surprised to see daisy fleabane, often considered a weed along roadsides, growing at the back of an otherwise elegant flower border. The gardener explained that she left the fleabane there because she thought they were pretty. This should be every gardener's goal—beauty, not perfection.

Weeds are simply plants that are growing where the gardener would rather they weren't. Lamb's-quarter isn't a weed to someone who picks its tender young shoots to include in a salad, but it certainly is to the homeowner who sees dozens of plants popping up throughout the perennial border. If you want a good-looking yard, it's impossible to take a live-and-let-live attitude toward weeds. They're interlopers (some are outright bullies) that crowd out good plants by taking over their space, competing with them for sunlight, and stealing their moisture and nutrients. The right thing to do to a weed is to get it out of the garden as quickly as possible, and the best time to do this is when the weed is small and the soil is moist. After a rain is a wonderful time to weed your garden—everything looks and smells refreshed and the weeds come out of the soft ground easily with less risk of disturbing nearby plants. If the soil is dry and hard, and the weed is mature, you may need to dig around it with a trowel before pulling it out.

The more you know about the different kinds of weeds, the easier it will be to keep them from taking root in your garden or to get rid of them should they appear. Weeds, like flowers, can be annuals, biennials, or perennials. Most annual weeds, such as crabgrass, are summer annuals; their seeds, which have lain dormant since fall, sprout in spring and grow in summer. Before they succumb to fall frost, they will have dropped more seeds that will germinate the next spring

IF YOU CAN'T BEAT 'EM, EAT 'EM

A number of weeds have edible parts, but you have to know what you're eating—some are extremely poisonous. Below is a list of plants you may want to sample if they appear in your yard.

PLANT	EDIBLE PART
Burdock (*Arctium* spp.)	Root
Chickweed (*Stellaria media*)	Leaves
Dandelion (*Taraxacum officinale*)	Root, leaves, flowers
Dock, curly (*Rumex crispus*)	Leaves
Kudzu (*Pueraria lobata*)	Leaves
Lamb's-quarter (*Chenopodium album*)	Leaves, shoots
Plantain (*Plantago* spp.)	Leaves
Purslane (*Portulaca oleracea*)	Flowers, leaves
Red clover (*Trifolium pratense*)	Flowers
Sheep sorrel (*Rumex acetosella*)	Leaves, seeds
Shepherd's purse (*Capsella bursa-pastoris*)	Leaves, seeds
Sweet violet (*Viola odorata*)	Flowers
Virginia strawberry (*Fragaria virginiana*)	Fruit
Wild rose (*Rosa* spp.)	Flower petals

ROOTING IT OUT

The basic equipment you'll need for weeding is simple: a hoe, a trowel, possibly a hand fork, and perhaps a mattock for big jobs. For long taproots, however, no tool is as effective as a dandelion weeder (sometimes called an asparagus knife). If you have trouble getting down on your knees, look for a long-handled model with a fork on the end that grasps the taproot while you lean on the handle to lever it out safely—with no troublesome pieces left in the ground.

and continue the cycle. A winter annual, such as henbit or annual bluegrass, completes its life cycle the same way but appears in fall and disperses seeds the next spring.

Biennials, like wild carrot, grow from seed one year but do not bloom and produce seeds until the next year. Perennial weeds, which come back year after year, are often difficult to control. Some spread by runners or rhizomes, while others have roots that grow deep into the ground. Bindweed and quackgrass are examples of tenacious perennial weeds.

It pays to heed the old saying, "Seeds one year, weeds seven years." You can prevent many future weed problems by never allowing a weed to develop seeds. Snapping off seed heads, even when you're not able to dig up the weed immediately, is weed-prevention insurance—especially where annuals are concerned. One annual weed can produce hundreds if not thousands of seeds.

Annual weeds are generally the easiest to banish from the garden. Cut them off at ground level with a hoe or the edge of a trowel, or pull them out by grasping their base and giving a sharp upward tug. This is a wonderful way to get exercise and work off your everyday frustrations.

When you sever an annual weed from its roots, you can usually be confident that you've killed it. This doesn't hold true, however, for perennial weeds. When they're very small, you can often hoe them down like annual weeds. But once they've grown larger, it's vital to dig up the entire root system with a trowel, dandelion weeder, or hand cultivator. If you don't get it all out (if even a speck is left), the weed will grow back. The most effective way to get rid of perennial weeds with spreading roots is to pull up the tops and sift through the soil with your hands, removing every bit of the roots you can find. If you cut the roots without removing all of them, each one of the severed pieces can sprout, producing an explosion of new weeds. The process of getting rid of tenacious perennial weeds sounds tedious, but it isn't if you do it a little at a time. And when you succeed, you have a great sense of accomplishment knowing you have finally vanquished every vestige of bindweed or burdock from your vegetable garden.

You may want to investigate two organic products currently on the market. Superfast Weed & Grass Killer is a natural, fatty acid-based product that kills annual weeds when they're tiny. It works only on young plants, however, and it kills just the top of the plant so it's not effective against perennial weeds. An interesting crabgrass preventive is maize gluten meal, the by-product of corn syrup manufacture; spread on the lawn in early spring, it stops feeder roots from developing and kills the crabgrass.

Research has shown that a strong defense against lawn weeds is thick, vigorously growing grass that's mowed high. Three-inch-tall grass prevents weed seeds from getting the light they need to germinate, and thick turf leaves no opening for a weed to intrude. Similarly, plants growing close together in the flower border or vegetable garden produce a canopy of leaves that also reduces weed seed germination and weed growth.

Weeds will never get the upper hand in your garden if you weed often and weed when the

WEED CHART

WEED	DESCRIPTION	HOW TO GET RID OF IT
Bindweed (*Convolvulus* spp.)	Vining morning glory relative that will twine around your good plants and kill them. Both perennial and annual species.	Cut it off at ground level. After the top has died, untwine it and pull it off the host plant. If it reappears, cut it off again and dig up as much of the root as you can find. It may be necessary to do this again and again during the summer. Eventually the plant will weaken and die.
Burdock (*Arctium* spp.)	Biennial or perennial with fuchsia-colored flowers and sticky burrs.	In loose soil, it can be pulled up. Otherwise, dig so that you remove all of the long, slender root.
Chickweed (*Stellaria media*)	Annual with white flowers and delicate foliage. Spreads by seeds and stolons.	Easily pulled out by hand.
Crabgrass (*Digitaria sanguinalis*)	Coarse annual grass with thick, hairy stems. Spreads by stolons.	Don't let this plant go to seed. Dig out while small. In the lawn, keep grass mowed high and turf thick to discourage its establishment. Sprinkle maize gluten meal on lawn as a pre-emergent treatment when forsythia begins to bloom or crocuses finish flowering.
Dandelion (*Taraxacum officinale*)	Perennial with long taproot and yellow flowers that ripen to spread hundreds of seeds.	Pick all flowers to keep plant from seeding. When digging out taproot, take pains to get it all.
Dock, curly (*Rumex crispus*)	Perennial with narrow leaves 6"–12" long; can grow 2'–4' high. Long taproot.	Dig out root before plant blooms.

WEED	DESCRIPTION	HOW TO GET RID OF IT
Dodder (*Cuscuta* spp.)	Annual vine that twines around and becomes a parasite on desirable plants. Spreads by seeds.	Pull it off garden plants as soon as you see it, then slice off at ground level.
Henbit (*Lamium amplexicaule*)	Cool-season annual or biennial that spreads by both seeds and rooting stems.	Don't let this plant go to seed; begin digging it out as soon as it appears.
Johnson grass (*Sorghum halepense*)	Tall grass with creeping roots; also spreads by seeds. Perennial in warmer climates.	Don't let it go to seed; dig up roots whenever new plants appear.
Kudzu (*Pueraria lobata*)	Deep-rooted perennial vine.	Eradicating a stand of kudzu can take several years. Begin the attack each spring as soon as growth has started. Pull up top growth, then dig out as many roots as you can find. Repeat throughout the growing season.
Nut grass (nut sedge) (*Cyperus esculentus*)	Tenacious perennial grassy weed.	Once past the small stage, when it can be pulled out, this plant is very difficult to eradicate. It will even come up through landscape fabric. Cut off blades at ground level and dig through the soil to remove as many of the roots as possible. Be persistent.
Plantain (*Plantago* spp.)	Cool-season perennial weed with broad or thin leaves. Quickly forms colonies.	Easily hoed up in spring when small. Be sure not to let plantain go to seed.

WEED CHART (CONTINUED)

WEED	DESCRIPTION	HOW TO GET RID OF IT
Poison ivy (*Rhus toxicodendron*)	Vigorous perennial vine. All parts can cause rash. Recognized by rhyme: "Leaves of three, let it be."	Keep plants cut to the ground, or try a fatty-acid organic herbicide to keep the tops killed back; both methods will eventually weaken roots. Deep mulches can help. People who don't seem to be affected by poison ivy may want to grub out the roots. Otherwise, don't touch these plants even when they're dead. Never burn them (the oil that causes the rash is carried in the smoke).
Purslane (*Portulaca oleracea*)	A relative of the garden portulaca, with fleshy stems, rounded leaves, and little yellow flowers. Spreads by seeds.	Don't let it to go to seed. It's easily pulled up, but don't leave it around—pieces left on the ground can root.
Quackgrass (**witchgrass**) (*Agropyron repens*)	Cool-season perennial grass that spreads by seeds and underground runners.	Cultivate frequently to keep top growth removed. Dig out and remove as many stolons as possible. Infested non-lawn areas may need a thick layer of mulch covered by black plastic.
Shepherd's purse (*Capsella bursa-pastoris*)	Tall annual or biennial weed with arrow-shaped leaves and small white flowers.	Dig up long, thin taproot.
Wild onion (**wild garlic**) (*Allium canadense*)	Looks like green onion. Highly noticeable in early spring.	Dig up when plant is young and soil is wet. Be sure not to leave bulb in the ground.

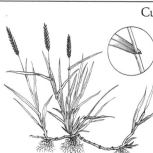

plants are small and the ground is wet. But remember, prevention is the best form of weed control. The best all-around preventive is a thick organic mulch. Remember, it's easier to prevent weeds from moving into your yard than it is to banish them once they've taken hold.

SUPPORTING PLANTS IN STYLE

Plants have a way of taking gardeners by surprise, growing quickly from tiny delicate seedlings to heights and widths that often seemed inconceivable when they were first put into soil. Those that have weak stems are vulnerable to heavy winds and rain, and require support in order to maintain their stature.

Match the type and size of support to the plant, making certain it's strong enough and tall enough to do the job. Stakes, poles, and cages can be more utilitarian in the vegetable garden than in the main portion of the landscape, where looks matter. However, arches, arbors, and trellises, chosen for their decorative qualities, enhance the look of whatever plant is growing on them. (For plants that need supports right from the start, see page 152.)

Begin tying plants to their supports when they reach a height of 6"–8" tall. Use soft materials such as cloth strips and twine, which won't harm tender stems. Twist ties with a metal wire in the center can cause damage, as can tying a plant so tightly to its support that the stem is squeezed by the tie or harmed by being rubbed against the support. To avoid this, secure plants to stakes with a figure-eight loop.

Staking is a summer-long activity—you'll need to continue tying tall plants to stakes and supports as they climb upward throughout the growing season. This pleasant task lets you watch the growth of your garden and enjoy the beautiful results of your efforts.

Supports for Flowers

The number of different kinds of flower supports rivals the number of different kinds of flowers you can grow. Bamboo stakes are ideal for single-stemmed annuals or perennials. They come in several lengths, may be green or beige, and are relatively inexpensive.

Even more economical for areas where appearance doesn't matter—an out-of-the-way cutting garden, for instance—are tomato stakes. Use them full size for tall-growing dahlias; saw them shorter for smaller plants.

Metal stakes are more expensive and longer-lasting. Especially handy are those with a loop at the top; you don't have to tie the plant to them—simply slip the stem through the loop. They come in a range of heights suitable for many tall, single-stemmed plants like delphiniums, hollyhocks, or foxgloves.

Hoops work well to support perennials with multiple stems. These are round rings attached to wire legs, some of which have a metal

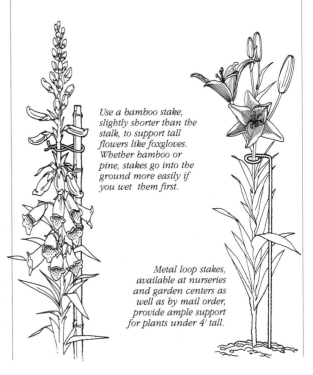

Use a bamboo stake, slightly shorter than the stalk, to support tall flowers like foxgloves. Whether bamboo or pine, stakes go into the ground more easily if you wet them first.

Metal loop stakes, available at nurseries and garden centers as well as by mail order, provide ample support for plants under 4' tall.

FLOWERS THAT NEED SUPPORT

African marigolds
(*Tagetes erecta*)

Asters (*Aster* spp.)

Baby's breath
(*Gypsophila* spp.)

Bellflowers
(*Campanula* spp.)

Carnations (*Dianthus caryophyllus*)

Chrysanthemums
(*Dendranthema* spp.,
Leucanthemum spp.,
Chrysanthemum
spp.)

Cosmos (*Cosmos* spp.)

Dahlias (*Dahlia* spp.)

Delphiniums
(*Delphinium* spp.)

Foxgloves (*Digitalis purpurea*)

Hollyhocks (*Alcea rosea*)

Larkspurs (*Consolida ambigua*)

Lilies (*Lilium* spp.)

Peonies (*Paeonia* spp.)

Roses, climbing and rambling (*Rosa* spp.)

Snapdragons
(*Antirrhinum majus*)

Tickseed
(*Coreopsis* spp.)

grid across the top for more control. Put the support in place by pushing the legs into the ground. The plant grows up through the circular support, which is virtually invisible once the foliage has filled out. Peonies in particular benefit from support by hoops.

Some do-it-yourselfers like to fashion a wire cage (much like those tomatoes are grown in, but shorter) to place around their peonies. It needs to be anchored with side stakes and will not be noticeable once the leaves hide the cage.

A homemade support fashioned from stakes and turkey wire will be hidden from view when the plant's foliage fills out.

You can also make a simple but effective support for multistemmed flowers like coreopsis or a group of single-stemmed plants such as cosmos, which tumble over after they reach their mature height. Pound four stakes of the

appropriate height into the corners of the bed and run string from stake to stake (about 1" from the top) to make a box that will keep the flowers upright.

Low-growing sweet peas can be brush-staked, using twigs and deadwood as support. This technique adds the kind of casual look that befits a cottage garden.

Supports for Vegetables

Plants in the vegetable garden require a little help to grow straight and tall. All climbing or sprawling plants—pole beans, tomatoes, peas, cucumbers, gourds—need something to lean on. Up in the air, vegetables also stay drier and cleaner, have less chance of rotting, are less damaged by slugs, and take up much less space than if allowed to spread out all over the garden, swallowing everything in their path.

Unlike flowers, vegetables are usually staked after the plants are up and growing. The exceptions are peas, which grow quickly, and tomatoes, if you plant them lying on their sides.

POLE BEANS

As their name implies, pole beans are usually grown on poles, which should be at least 7' tall, since these vining beans are some of the vegetable kingdom's most vigorous growers. The vines climb rough poles more easily than smooth ones but will also happily scurry up strings. The traditional support for pole beans consists of three to four poles arranged tepee-style and tied together at the top. You can also space stakes 3' apart, connect

A tepee-style support made of strong bamboo poles becomes an attractive garden feature when beans are in full flower.

them with twine or wire at the top and bottom, and every 6" tie a string vertically between the horizontal wires for the beans to climb. Another option is to construct bean trellises that look like A-frames covered with fruit netting.

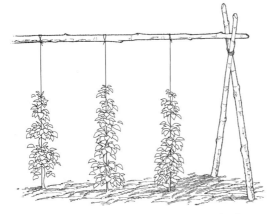

Lengths of nylon twine tied to a horizontal pole allow bean plants to climb straight up. The twine is anchored by the root ball of each plant.

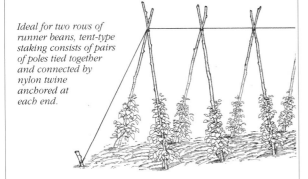

Ideal for two rows of runner beans, tent-type staking consists of pairs of poles tied together and connected by nylon twine anchored at each end.

Whichever types of supports you pick, be sure to anchor them firmly so they won't blow over in windy weather, especially when weighted down by vines.

PEAS

Grow peas along a fence made of chicken wire or fruit netting spread between posts. To make the most of your space, plant peas on both sides of the fence. For regular varieties, pea fences should be at least 5' high. Try a 2' fence for dwarf varieties. Low-growing pea plants can also be brush-staked or allowed to sprawl if you have the

space. No matter what kind of support you choose, handle the delicate vines as little as possible as you tend to their needs.

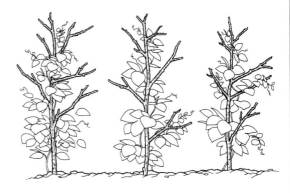

Brush-stake low-growing varieties of peas, using winter's tree prunings to support the vines.

TOMATOES

You can tie tomatoes to stakes or grow them in cages. The big advantage of wooden tomato stakes is that they're inexpensive and easily obtained. (Cut one end to a point so you can insert it into the soil more easily.) Often one stake isn't enough for a tomato vine, as you may learn to your dismay halfway through the summer when the plant is loaded with fruit. It's a good idea to start with two stakes, one on each side of the plant. Some gardeners install heavy poles in the row between every two plants and connect them by heavy twine or wire. To control the size of a staked tomato, remove the suckers (the sprouts that grow in the crotches of the larger stems). Simply pinch them off once a week as you're tending the garden or picking ripe tomatoes.

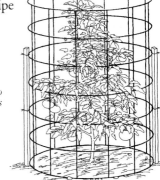

Making your own tomato cage with turkey wire lets you tailor it to the mature size of the plant. Two sturdy wooden stakes keep it secure.

University tests have shown that tomatoes grown in cages produce more fruit than those grown on stakes, but the fruit ripens earlier (by a week or so) on staked plants. Commercially available tomato cages are almost always too short unless you're growing a determinate variety, and often the openings are not large enough for a hand grasping a tomato to fit through. To overcome these limitations, make your own tomato cages by cutting concrete reinforcing wire to form a circle 20"–24" in diameter and at least 60" high. You can spray the cages with green enamel before using them, or let them rust naturally. To keep the cages from falling over in a strong wind, drive two 4' stakes a foot into the ground on opposite sides of the cage. They'll last a long time if you store them out of the weather over winter.

CUCUMBERS

Cucumbers aren't picky about their supports. If you're growing only a few, try planting them around a 24"-diameter tomato cage. Otherwise, a fence or an A-frame works fine. If you use plastic mesh as part of the support, get the kind with 6" holes for easier picking.

GOURDS

Gourds have a growth gene that just won't quit. Like Jack's beanstalk, these vigorous vines get longer and longer—and longer—as the season progresses. For this reason, they should be grown along a fence or allowed to creep along a wire strung between posts. Where thunderstorms are prevalent, or the gourds are large, the support needs to be especially sturdy.

Supports for Vines

Vines are versatile. When grown on an arbor, they provide shade; trained on a trellis, they become attractive elements in the landscape. But without some support, whether stake, string, arbor, trellis, or pergola, your vine won't be an asset because no one will see it. Depending on how the vine clings, choose the right kind of support to show it off and allow it to grow vigorously.

Vines that twine do well when climbing a wire, string, or single pole. These include five-leafed akebia, bittersweet, black-eyed Susan, cardinal climber, Carolina jessamine, clematis, honeysuckle, kolomikta vine, mandevilla, moonflower, morning glory, nastur-

A trellis not only provides an ideal climbing surface for vines but also enhances both the plant and the garden site.

tium, scarlet runner bean, and silver lace vine. Wisteria, an exception to the rule, is not suited to a single support because of the large size it eventually attains; even with yearly pruning, this twining vine needs a very sturdy arbor, trellis, or pergola.

Climbers such as cathedral bells, marble vine, sweet peas, and passionflower, all of which put out tendrils that wrap around whatever they touch, need supports no wider than 1" in diameter so the tendrils can encircle them.

Boston ivy, creeping fig, cross vine, English ivy, climbing hydrangea and trumpet creeper, Virginia creeper, and wintercreeper, all vines that climb with holdfasts or aerial roots, will make themselves at home on any kind of support or flat surface.

As bougainvillea reaches skyward, you'll have to tie it loosely to a support because it does not have its own means of clinging.

Supports for Climbing Roses and Ramblers

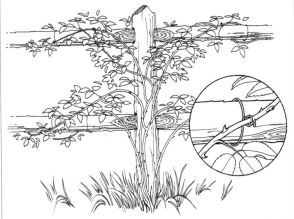

Training roses horizontally on a fence encourages the growth of lateral, flower-producing branches. Just tie the canes loosely along the fence for a picture-perfect effect.

You may think of climbing roses as flowering vines, but they don't actually climb. Instead, their very long canes only look like vines when tied to supports such as trellises, arbors, and arches. Pillar roses are smaller and stiffer varieties that are usually grown on a single post or pillar. Ramblers are the most vigorous growers, requiring the strongest support.

You can train any climbing rose onto a pillar by wrapping the canes around the post in an upward spiral as they grow, securing new growth to the post with sturdy twine. This approach is particularly suited to a garden with limited space.

Trellises and arches for luxuriant climbing roses are usually chosen for their decorative features, which fit gracefully into the landscape. The best are those constructed of long-lasting materials that don't need frequent painting. Trellises should be spaced a foot away from a house or other building; if possible, they can be hinged for easy removal when the house needs painting or the rose needs winter protection. Before you build or buy a trellis or arch, find out the ultimate dimensions of the vine. Ramblers, for instance, look especially nice on arbors but, because of

their exuberant growth, need an archway 5'–6' wide and 8' tall. Keep in mind that a decorative support must be tall enough and wide enough for people to walk through comfortably once the plants reach their full, mature size.

PRINCIPLES OF PRUNING

If you're like most gardeners, pruning is the task you feel most uncomfortable about. It's one thing to cut a dead limb off a tree, or clip a hedge that has grown a bit out of bounds, but the need for pruning a perfectly good plant—perhaps one you've been growing from its infancy—can seem incomprehensible.

Pruning doesn't hurt a healthy plant; rather, it stimulates new growth and enhances the plant's vigor, beauty, and disease resistance. And that's not all. Pruning can improve a plant's appearance, correct or repair damage, direct growth, improve health, rejuvenate, control size, and increase production of flowers and fruits. In other words, proper pruning—at the proper time—is good for your plants and your garden in general.

Moreover, pruning is not confined to large plants like fruit trees and forsythia shrubs. Removing the faded blossoms from ageratum is pruning; so is cutting back petunias by half in summer before you go on vacation so they'll be bushy and full on your return.

TOO CLOSE TO BUD | TOO FAR AWAY FROM BUD | WRONG DIRECTION OF ANGLE | ANGLE TOO SEVERE | A PERFECT CUT

A pruning cut must be correctly angled at 45° away from the bud, leaving 1/4" – 1/2" of stem. Cutting at the wrong angle or leaving too much stem invites rot.

CHOOSING THE RIGHT PRUNING TOOL

More gardeners than would care to admit it have been guilty of using the wrong pruning tools. Usually, it's a matter of using hand pruners on too large a branch. Not only can this damage the plant (resulting in a ragged cut and perhaps tearing the bark), but it can also dull the blades of your pruners, put them out of alignment, or, at the worst, break them. You can also hurt yourself when you have to wrestle a sharp tool wedged into a branch. Using the right tool saves time, money, and aggravation.

Tool	Maximum Cutting Diameter *
Hand pruners	¾"
Pole pruners	1"
Loppers	1¼"
Ratchet loppers	2"
Hedge shears	½"
Pruning saw	2"
Pole pruning saw	2"

Note that these figures indicate maximum diameter. Inferior-quality tools will not cut as much.

It's important to know the right way to make these cuts, especially on woody plants. Using the proper tool for the size of the branch you're pruning results in a clean, smooth cut. Always cut at a 45° angle about ¼" above a bud. When pruning in fall or winter, especially in cold-winter climates, make the cut ½"–¼" from the bud so it won't dry out. Angle the cut down and away from the bud; rain and water can then run down the bud rather than pool at its base, causing the bud to rot. Keep in mind, whenever pruning, that a bud grows in the direction it faces, so prune to outward-facing buds if you want to encourage an open habit.

The exception is the removal of an entire limb or shoot. In this case, make the cut parallel to the main stem, holding the saw or pruners with the cutting edge flush against the trunk at the top of the limb or shoot that you're cutting.

PRUNING CUTS

There are various pruning methods but only two kinds of pruning cuts: thinning and heading. *Thinning cuts* (cutting the branch all the way back to the trunk or its origin) are used to reduce the

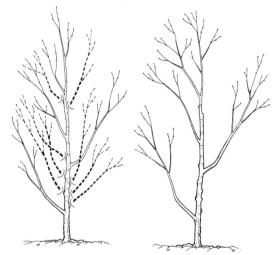

Thinning is a pruning method in which no more than a third of the branches are cut back to the main stem, or trunk. The result, after a season's growth, is a configuration that allows more light and air to reach the plant.

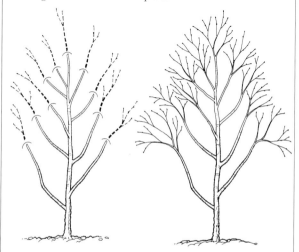

Heading cuts, or cutting branches back to a bud, encourage branching and ultimately produce a plant with thicker growth while strengthening existing branches.

THE BASIC STRUCTURE OF A TREE OR SHRUB

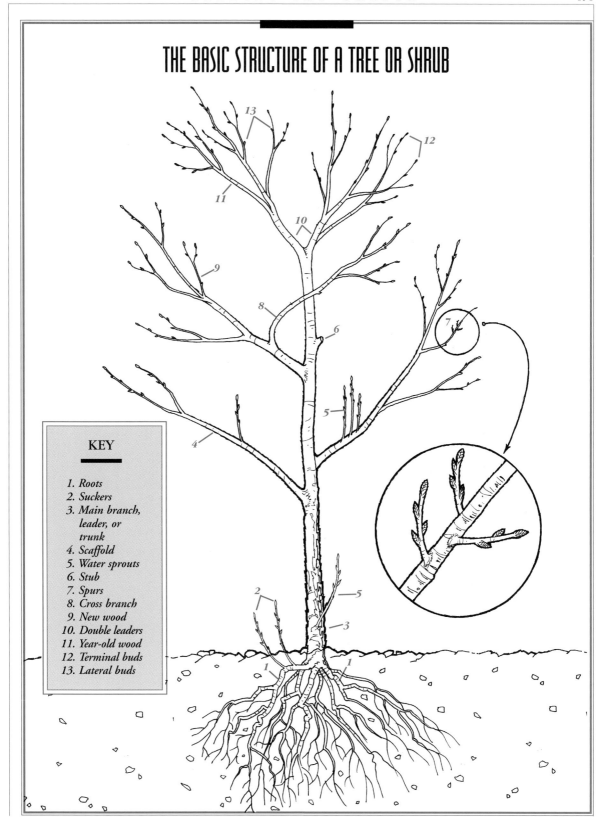

KEY

1. Roots
2. Suckers
3. Main branch, leader, or trunk
4. Scaffold
5. Water sprouts
6. Stub
7. Spurs
8. Cross branch
9. New wood
10. Double leaders
11. Year-old wood
12. Terminal buds
13. Lateral buds

number of shoots and direct growth. By opening up the plant, thinning allows more light and air to reach its center. *Heading cuts* are made by cutting a branch back to a bud or to another branch. This stimulates dense growth and stiffens the existing branches.

There are several heading techniques. *Pinching* is a method of pruning the soft growth of herbaceous plants. Use your thumb and forefinger to break off several inches of the current season's growth. Pinch back naturally tall-growing chrysanthemums several times during the growing season to produce more compact, floriferous,

later-blooming plants. This technique is commonly used on pines; pinch off half the length of the candles (new growth) for fuller, bushier growth. *Snipping* is similar to pinching except that it removes the previous season's growth.

Pinch back the tops of annuals before you plant them to encourage bushier growth.

Shearing is nonselective heading, which involves making many cuts along a single plane with hedge clippers or shears. This technique is best saved for hedges and topiary. More judicious pruning that allows a natural form is preferable for most shrubs and trees.

OTHER PRUNING TECHNIQUES

Deadheading is removing faded flowers from a plant either with your fingers (on soft-stemmed plants such as black-eyed Susans) or with hand pruners (on harder-stemmed plants like roses and rhododendrons). This technique prevents the plant from setting seed and, in many cases, encourages it to bloom longer. Deadheading also keeps aggressive self-seeders from sowing themselves all across the garden, saving you the effort of weeding them out when the seeds sprout.

The simplest way to deadhead is to remove only the spent flower or group of flowers (as a truss of a rhododendron). You can quickly deadhead the day's faded blooms from a bed of daylilies, leaving the buds that will be the subsequent days' flowers. However, if there are no

UNDESIRABLE GROWTHS: SUCKERS AND WATER SPROUTS

Originating from the lower portion of the stem or roots of a woody plant, suckers are fast-growing, upright secondary branches that sap the plant's energy. Cut them back to the trunk or roots with hand pruners or loppers. You may notice vigorous growth coming from the rootstock (the area below the graft) of a rose bush or fruit tree. If not removed, these suckers will quickly take over and crowd out the desirable part of the rose bush or tree. Rose suckers are most undesirable because they produce small blooms of a different color or shape from the regular roses on the bush.

Water sprouts are weak vertical shoots on tree branches that are often caused by improper pruning, including tree topping. If there are only a few, cut them off at their base; if numerous, remove one-fourth to one-third each year until they're all gone. If they become a recurrent problem, wait until summer to prune them out—sometimes spring pruning actually encourages regrowth of water sprouts.

other buds on the flower stem, a more aesthetic approach is to cut off the bare stem, cutting down to its base (if it's leafless) or to a bud, leaf, or set of leaves.

Deadhead rhodo-dendrons immediately after they finish blooming. Take care not to disturb the forming bud.

Disbudding is removing smaller flower buds to concentrate the plant's energy to the buds that remain. Because one bud is left on each disbudded stem, the plant won't produce as many flowers, but those that bloom will be much larger. Camellias, chrysanthemums, dahlias, peonies, and roses are frequently disbudded to produce bigger blooms. The best time to disbud is when the buds are very small.

You can disbud by snipping or pinching off the unwanted buds. On some plants, like camellias, the buds are so close together that the best way to disbud them is to rub or twist off the young unwanted buds with your thumb and forefinger.

Hard pruning (also called *rejuvenation*) involves cutting a shrub or vine back to within a few inches of the ground in early spring. This is usually done on overgrown or neglected shrubs that have many latent buds and may be attempted as a last-ditch effort since some shrubs will not survive the shock. Other shrubs, like buddleia and caryopteris, thrive on a hard pruning each spring. Gardeners sometimes use this term to mean pruning or cutting back more severely than usual.

Pruning Flowering Annuals and Perennials

The tools you'll use most often for pruning your flowers are hand pruners and your fingers; most annuals and perennials are pruned by dead-heading and pinching. Removing faded flowers encourages the plant to bloom longer, so for the glory of your garden you'll want to deadhead all annuals and perennials (except those that drop their old blossoms naturally and those whose seed heads you'd like to leave for the enjoyment of the birds). Some plants get leggy if you don't pinch them back several times during their growing season, beginning in early spring. Perennials that benefit from pinching are artemisia, aster, bee balm, boltonia, chrysanthemum, helianthus, lobelia, lychnis, salvia, and sedum. Annuals that you'll want to pinch back occasionally include ageratum and petunias. For fewer but larger blooms, disbud dahlias, peonies, zinnias grown for cut flowers, hibiscus, and large-flowered chrysanthemums. This kind of pruning can be done a little at a time when you're outdoors watching the butterflies flit from flower to flower in your garden or listening to the birds sing their cheerful melodies.

Pruning Bush Fruits, Brambles, Grapes, and Strawberries

Blueberries, gooseberries, currants, and other bush fruits require little pruning, making them some of the easiest fruits to grow. Each year, once the plants have started to bear, cut back a few old or thin canes to ground level to stimulate the growth of new canes. On blueberries, watch out for twiggy growth that needs to be thinned. On gooseberries and currants, cut back to ground level any canes that are more than three years old.

On the other hand, bramble fruits like raspberries, blackberries, boysenberries, and loganberries need yearly pruning; otherwise, they will decline until they produce few if any berries. (The roots are perennial and the tops biennial, so they come up and grow one year, then bear the second year.) Cut down canes that have finished producing fruit. This not only makes room for the new canes that will bear the next year but is necessary because canes that have borne fruit dry out and become magnets for insects and disease. At the same time, remove weak canes and thin other canes to about 6" apart to permit plenty of air circulation. During winter, cut off the floppy top portion of the stems.

Everbearing raspberries are an exception to the rule. Because they bear in summer and again in fall, their canes should be cut only after the summer fruiting. The fall crop will be borne on new canes, which will bear again the next summer.

A thick mulch around the bramble patch will cut down on sucker production, but you'll have to prune out any suckers that pop through. The very long canes of some raspberries and blackberries arch over and root as they touch the ground. This is fine within the rows, but it's a nuisance when they spread outside the bed. Keep them controlled the same way you do suckers (see page 192).

Grapes are pruned yearly in late winter to get rid of all but year-old wood on which the fruits are produced. There are numerous ways to grow grapes, and your local Cooperative Extension service can provide information about each of them. The Kniffen system is most popular for American grapes and muscadines. The first summer, let the vine grow naturally, then in the winter prune it back to a single stem. The following summer, allow the stem to develop four canes, and train them along two wires 36" and 60"–66" high. By the third year, the top two canes should have five buds and the bottom two should have six. Wrap the canes around the wire to encourage growth that will become the following year's fruiting canes. To prevent weakening the vine, don't allow

much fruit to ripen the first year it bears. Each subsequent year, prune off all but four canes with 6 to 10 buds each. Train these along the wires and they will produce fruit. From the old fruiting canes, select two or three canes and prune them to two buds each to produce next year's fruiting vines.

The three methods of pruning strawberries depend on which growing method is used. In the hill system, all runners are kept pinched off. The matted row system lets strawberry plants develop two runners in each direction. After the row is full, extra runners (and the plants they're developing) are pruned off. In a combination method, each plant can develop two runners in each direction, with all others being pruned off.

Pruning Fruit Trees

In mild-winter climates, you can prune fruit trees anytime in winter or even in late fall. If your winters are harsh, however, wait until late winter to prune—after the coldest weather has passed and while the trees are still dormant but the wood isn't frozen. With fewer limbs, dwarf trees and spur-type trees (which produce fruit on short, compressed branches) will need less pruning.

Fruit trees are usually pruned to one of three shapes or styles. The *open-center shape* has a short trunk and three or four main limbs, each of which has several branches. This permits a lot of air and light to get to the center of the tree, which, in turn, will produce more fruit on the lower branches and in the interior of the tree. Another benefit of a short tree is that it's easy to harvest and prune. Apricots, crab apples, cherries, nectarines, peaches, plums, and sometimes apples and pears are trained to the vase shape.

If you want to train a young fruit tree to an open-center shape, cut off the trunk or central leader 2'–3' above the ground and prune lateral or side branches back to two buds. During the first winter, reserve four lateral or side shoots,

6"–8" from each other vertically, that are evenly spaced about the trunk, with the lowest starting at least 18" above ground level. These are called the primary scaffold limbs. The following winter, select four secondary scaffold limbs about 18" above the primary scaffold limbs. From then until the tree bears, prune off crossing branches and broken or damaged limbs but leave the twiggy growth, which will bear the fruit.

The *central leader* pruning style has one strong trunk and is therefore most suitable for apples and pears, which can produce heavy crops. Thin the limbs that come from the trunk so there will be plenty of space between them. Also prune the smaller branches that grow from the limbs to allow air and sunlight to reach the center of the tree.

The *modified central leader* style is used to train apples and pears as well as dwarf fruit trees. Prune the same as for the basic central leader style until the scaffold limbs have formed; then head back the central leader.

Pruning Herbs

In early spring, remove any winter damage from perennial herbs and shape them so the herb garden's appearance is as attractive and inviting as possible, complementing its sweetly enticing aroma. Otherwise, herbs need little attention— usually the pruning takes place as you harvest them throughout the growing season. Herbs grown as ornamentals should be pinched back occasionally so they'll look neat and fulfill their garden potential.

Pruning Roses

Most gardeners hate to cut back the queen of flowers, but after a couple of years of observing the less-than-beautiful results of *not* pruning, they realize that yearly pruning of rose bushes is essential for healthy, vigorous growth and abundant flowers. Exceptions to the rule of annual pruning are shrub roses and old garden roses; these are

The open-center pruning style permits air and light to reach the center of the tree, encouraging fruit production.

Most suitable for apple and pear trees, the central leader style opens up the space between limbs that grow from the trunk.

In the modified central leader style, the central trunk branch is allowed to form several scaffold limbs, ensuring lighter fruit at the top.

PRUNING DIFFERENT TYPES OF ROSES

Hybrid teas, floribundas, grandifloras, and polyanthas. For hybrid tea roses, begin in early spring by cutting back diseased or winter-killed growth. Make the cut ¼" above an outward-facing bud about 1" below the dead or diseased area. Then remove all canes that are thinner than a pencil, and cut off any sucker growth from below the bud union of grafted roses. Prune out canes that are deformed, grow toward the center of the bush, or grow straight out and then up; when two canes cross, remove the weaker one.

The job is done when the rose has three to six uniformly spaced canes that form a vase shape. This allows necessary sunlight to reach the interior of the bush and provides good air circulation, which cuts down on fungal diseases. How tall you leave the canes depends on the extent of winter damage you must remove, how vigorous the canes are (weak canes are usually pruned more heavily than strong ones), and whether you want fewer but larger roses (produced by shorter canes that have been pruned hard so that they grow more vigorously). Heavy pruning results in canes that are about 12" tall; moderate pruning leaves canes 18"–24" tall; a light pruning removes about a third of the growth.

Some gardeners like to leave all healthy, outward-facing canes about 24" tall on floribundas, grandifloras, and polyanthas; in warm climates, old canes should be removed and newer ones shortened so that the plant is about half the size it was before pruning.

Climbing roses and ramblers. Wait until climbing roses and ramblers are two or three years old to start regular pruning, then remove only dead, diseased, or weak wood in early spring. Do all other pruning on climbers after they finish blooming. Remove faded flowers on rebloomers, and cut all old, gray canes back to the bud union. Be sure to leave four vigorous canes, tied securely to their support. Also cut back each shoot to four sets of leaves. Because they're such vigorous growers, ramblers usually need harder pruning than climbing roses.

Shrub or old garden roses. When to prune depends on whether the bush blooms once or several times during the season. If you're not sure, wait until after the first blooming period ends to shorten over-long canes and cut out old, unproductive wood. On very vigorous growers, thin some of the canes to keep the plant in bounds. Other pruning, which is usually minimal, shapes the shrub so it will look attractive in your landscape.

Species roses. These wild, natural roses require pruning only to remove old or dead wood once the plant reaches its mature size. Prune in early spring. *Rosa banksiae* and other species roses with exuberant growth may be pruned to keep them within bounds.

Tree roses or standards. Prune tree roses to about 12" beyond the bud union, spacing the canes as evenly as possible for a more symmetrical shape. Cut all suckers back to the base as soon as they appear.

Miniatures. These are the simplest roses to prune because they can be clipped like hedges to about half their original height.

pruned like deciduous shrubs and may not need cutting back every year, although they look and grow better when you remove winter damage and deadhead the faded blossoms.

Climbing roses bloom on previous years' wood; to ensure abundant bloom, wait until after they finish flowering. Cut all other roses back in early spring, using hand pruners, loppers, or a pruning saw, depending on the thickness of the canes. (You may want to invest in a pair of thorn-proof gloves and wear a long-sleeved jacket or shirt made of heavy fabric to protect your hands and arms from scratches.) Make your cuts at a 45° angle and seal any cut cane more than ¼" in diameter with Elmer's glue or a similar white glue to prevent borers and rot.

Cutting a rose stem is, in effect, pruning the plant. Cut down to a leaf with five or seven leaflets. Be sure to leave ¼" above the point where the leaf meets the stem.

Unless you want rose hips, those wonderful "fruits" that can develop when a pollinated flower (especially of species roses) is left on the bush, you'll want to remove all flowers as they fade. This gives the rose garden a neater look; in addition, most plants respond by producing more beautiful blooms. When snipping off blossoms that are past their prime, or cutting roses for an arrangement, cut to just above the next seven- or five-leaf cluster that points outward; this is where the new growth will start.

When you've gathered your courage, taken pruners in hand, and cut your roses back to what looks like a handful of bare sticks, it's heartening to know that within a few short months the miracle of renewal will have taken place—and the sight and scent of romantic roses will fill your garden once again.

Pruning Shrubs

The technique and timing of pruning shrubs vary depending on whether the shrub is deciduous or evergreen, flowering or not. Summer-flowering shrubs bloom on the current season's growth and should be pruned in early spring. Spring-blooming shrubs, which form their buds during the previous year, are best pruned right after they flower. Use hand pruners or loppers, and begin by removing branches that are broken, dead, or cross other branches.

Always prune to a natural shape. Too many homeowners shear all their shrubs as if they were hedges, producing the look of little green lollipops dotting the landscape. In addition to being unattractive because they look unnatural, shrubs pruned this way are also more subject to problems. A round ball of a shrub has only a shell of foliage. This heavy canopy of leaves on the surface won't let the inside of the plant dry out after rains and dews, rendering the plant more susceptible to insects and diseases. Instead of uniformly clipping the entire surface of a shrub, which causes a rash of random growth, shorten individual branches to a bud or to a lateral branch. When necessary, you can remove a branch completely, cutting back to the trunk.

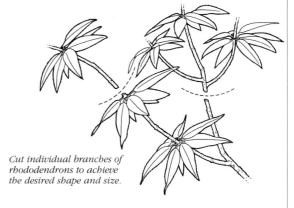

Cut individual branches of rhododendrons to achieve the desired shape and size.

Deciduous shrubs are more vigorous and therefore can be pruned more severely than evergreens. When a healthy deciduous shrub or hedge is heavily overgrown, you can cut it back in late winter to a foot tall and allow it to regrow. Admittedly, it will be several years before the plant regains its full form. Many broad-leaved evergreens (in zone 6 and warmer) can also be severely pruned. A less drastic method is to prune the branches over a period of three years, cutting back one-third of the old wood to soil level each year. Slow-growing shrubs that have become too large need more judicious pruning; remove one-fifth of the growth each year for five years. If you consistently remove the suckers from lilacs and other suckering shrubs, you'll have less strenuous pruning to do later on.

Broad-leaved evergreen shrubs usually need pruning only for shape and size control. Dead-head flowering evergreens like azaleas and rhodo-dendrons after they've bloomed.

Pruning Hedges

Because the foliage of hedges is so dense, al-most every pruning cut is near a growth bud. Shear small-leaved or evergreen hedges with hand pruners each time they put on 4" of new growth. Prune large-leaved hedges one branch at a time with hand pruners. Don't shear off the top and ignore the sides. Shape the hedge so that it's wider

The top of an improperly pruned hedge (left) shades the lower portion so the leaves receive too little light. A correctly pruned hedge (right) gets sun on all its leaves.

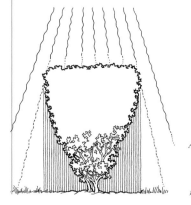 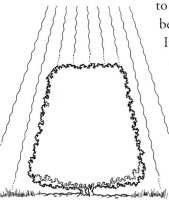

at the bottom and narrower at the top, allowing the sun to shine on the lower foliage and thus promote growth.

Needled evergreens are generally sheared in late spring or early summer. But if more extensive pruning is called for, be careful never to cut past the green wood in the interior of the plant. Only green wood can produce new growth.

Pruning Trees

Training young trees from the time they're planted cuts down on pruning time and effort. If you wait until a tree is full grown, it's too late.

In the past, gardeners were advised to prune back the tops of bare-root trees by a third at planting time to compensate for root damage that occurs in digging and transplanting; how-ever, such pruning is no longer recommended. Through experiments, horticulturists have learned that keeping as much leaf surface as possible helps build larger root systems. So don't automatically prune a tree at planting time. Confine your cuts to removing any damaged wood or water sprouts that spring up on the trunk.

DECIDUOUS TREES

When a deciduous tree has been growing in your garden for more than a year, you may want to begin removing some of the lower limbs (up to a height of 7'–8') so that later on you'll be able to mow or walk beneath the tree. It's easier to do this when the limbs are small. Don't cut off all the lower limbs at once; remove them over a three-year period so that ample leaf area remains to nourish the tree.

Some trees develop limbs that cross each other and rub in the wind, producing sores that can be entrance points for diseases or insects. In time, the limbs may even fuse. When you notice crossed limbs, remove one of the offending branches (usually the smaller limb).

Promptly cut off any damaged or diseased branches to preserve the health of the tree. When disease is the problem, disinfect your loppers or saw by dipping the tool into rubbing alcohol or a 10% solution of bleach between cuts to avoid spreading the disease.

When removing an entire branch, always cut back to the main trunk. And when cutting off unwanted growth from the sides of a live limb, cut all the way back to the limb. Leaving a stub invites rot, which can damage the branch and the tree.

Don't worry about sealing the cuts with pruning paint. Most experts believe this is unnecessary; in fact, some of the paints may do more harm than good. A correct cut will heal itself naturally within a year.

Prune summer-flowering trees in late winter (as you do shrubs) and spring-flowering trees as needed just after they finish blooming. Prune inconspicuous or nonflowering deciduous trees on a sunny day in late winter. The exceptions are maples and birches, which are pruned in summer.

EVERGREEN TREES

Broad-leaved evergreen trees are pruned with loppers or a saw during the dormant stage. Needled evergreens require a different approach. Don't wait until they've grown too large before you think of pruning; instead, shear or give a "haircut" to these evergreens to shape them in late spring or early summer. Start shearing (with hedge shears) when the plant is young. The ideal

A rule of thumb for pruning trees: Never remove more than one-fourth to one-third of a tree's branches at a time.

TREE TOPPING

Don't confuse tree pruning with tree topping. Topping is heading back a tree, cutting its branches so that stubs are left—a practice condemned by all competent tree professionals. It's detrimental, disfigures the tree, encourages masses of ugly water sprouts, reduces a tree's vigor, and leaves entryways for diseases and insects through the stubs that are left. Topped trees don't add to the beauty of your property; they detract from it. You can avoid this problem altogether by planting trees whose mature height is suitable without pruning.

time is right after a rain. Should major pruning become necessary, do it when the tree is dormant in the fall or winter. To promote bushier, thicker growth on needled evergreen trees or shrubs, pinch back half the new growth in spring. Pines are particularly easy—just pinch back half of each lighter-colored candle.

When new growth appears at the branch tips of firs, pines, or spruces in the spring, encourage denseness by pinching off a half or two-thirds of each candle.

Pruning Vegetables

Vegetables are usually pruned for very specific purposes. When tomatoes are grown on stakes rather than in cages, the side shoots (sprouts or suckers that grow in the crotches of the larger stems) can cause the plants to grow so heavy and unwieldy that the stakes can no longer support them. Each time you're in the vegetable

CATHRINE SNEED'S WORKING GARDEN

Back in 1982, when San Francisco County Jail counselor Cathrine Sneed passed a serious hospital stay by reading *The Grapes of Wrath*, she was struck by how Steinbeck's characters drew strength from the soil. Her response was to begin teaching organic gardening to the prisoners in her charge—an experience that she credits with enriching her own life.

Part botany class and part work therapy, Sneed's Jail Horticultural Program brought a new sense of purpose to inmates who had known only pain and violence. As they transformed a defunct farm on the jail grounds into a flourishing fruit, vegetable, and herb garden, the participants experienced—many for the first time—the satisfaction of nurturing living things.

As a result of that success, in 1990 Sneed went on to found the Garden Project, a horticultural and job-skills program for former prisoners located on a derelict, garbage-strewn half-acre lot. Today that land is a market garden overflowing with lettuces, broccoli, spinach, garlic, beets, radishes, and culinary herbs—all raised by biodynamic French intensive methods. Once a day, participants gather to enjoy the fruits of their labor; the rest is donated to charities or sold to fine restaurants to provide money for maintenance. Many will go on to find employment in the larger community.

"Gardening has the potential to make people whole again. I want them to have that opportunity . . . I want my children to live in a healed world."

garden, check your tomato plants for side shoots and pinch them out with your fingers. (If you live in a climate with a long growing season, you may want to root these side shoots, which will grow into plants that produce a welcome late crop of tomatoes.)

To encourage more Brussels sprouts to develop along the stem, break off the leaves between the lower sprouts. In cold climates, other vegetables may be pruned to hasten ripening near the end of summer. Pinch off the growing tips of melons, cucumbers, tomatoes, squash, and pumpkins when the plants have plenty of fruit on them to direct the plant's energy to ripening the fruit, rather than producing more stem or leaf growth. The fruit will be larger than if the plant continued growing, plus you'll be able to harvest before frost.

Pruning Vines

When perennial vines have been cut back hard, they look so puny that you wonder if they'll ever recover. Not only do such vines rebound, however, but they grow vigorously and bloom better than ever. If pruning is neglected, most perennial vines become an unsightly mess.

Trim nonflowering vines as needed to control their size in springtime. The time of year for

WHEN TO PRUNE

Winter is the major pruning season for most deciduous trees, fruit trees, and nonflowering deciduous shrubs. Certain plants, however, are best pruned at other times of the year.

EARLY SPRING
■ Prune bush roses, summer-flowering shrubs that bloom on new wood, overgrown plants, evergreen hedges (in mild-winter climates), and broad-leaved evergreens that do not flower or berry.
■ Remove dead or diseased wood from any plant.

LATE SPRING
■ Prune spring-flowering shrubs and trees *after* they have bloomed.
■ Pinch one-third to one-half of new candles on pines and other needled evergreens to promote compact growth.
■ Remove new suckers or water sprouts on any plant.

SUMMER
■ Shear needled evergreens to control shape in early summer; pinch pines to control shape in early summer (if not done in late spring).

■ Prune maples and birches if necessary.
■ Correct obvious defects in the way limbs or branches are growing.
■ Deadhead annuals, perennials, and blooming shrubs.
■ Prune bush roses slightly when removing spent flowers; prune climbing or rambling roses when necessary after they bloom; remove suckers.
■ Prune summer-flowering shrubs as soon as they finish blooming.

FALL
■ Lightly cut back excessively long rose canes (in both mild- and harsh-winter climates) that could be whipped about in the wind.
■ Remove any diseased or dead wood on shrubs or trees.

LATE WINTER
Whenever possible, prune on a sunny, relatively warm day.
■ Prune deciduous trees (except birches and maples, which could "bleed," or exude sap); fruit trees; deciduous shrubs that don't flower and berried shrubs or trees such as holly; deciduous hedges.

pruning flowering vines depends on whether they bloom on new wood (the current season's growth) or old wood (the previous season's growth). Give those that produce blooms on new wood (such as silver lace vine and trumpet vine) a severe pruning in late winter to encourage new growth. Wait until after flowering to prune those that bloom on old wood (such as bougainvillea and wisteria), cutting as necessary for appearance and control. If the vine is large, you can prune at planting time. To encourage new growth from the bottom of the vine, choose three to five strong shoots, cut each back by half, and prune out any other shoots. Rejuvenate overgrown vines by cutting them back to three or four short stems. You'll find it much easier to prune vines if you remove them from their trellis or support.

The Right Time to Harvest

Harvesting is the most enjoyable part of gardening, the time when you get to reap the rewards for all the hours spent carefully planting and nurturing your crops. What a treat to bite into a crisp red apple plucked from your very own tree and savor the rich sweetness. Or to have guests at a backyard cookout rave over the unparalleled taste of home-grown corn on the cob, picked minutes before in your vegetable garden.

Just as there's a right time to sow each crop, there's a right time to reap everything from corn to coriander, potatoes to peaches. All fruits, vegetables, and herbs will be tastier, better-looking, and richer in nutrients when harvested at the peak of perfection. But that's not the only reason to pick them at their prime. A timely harvest can also prevent problems in the garden. Overripe crops often attract birds, insects, and diseases that can wreak havoc.

Once you've harvested your home-grown produce, you'll want to use it or preserve it imme-

diately. When supermarket fruits and vegetables are trucked in from thousands of miles away, they look and taste tired. So will yours if they're not consumed, canned, frozen, or dried the same day or the next.

Harvesting Fruits

When trying to determine if fruit is ready to eat, use your senses. First, look at the fruit. Is it larger than it was last week? Has its color changed? Next, gently feel it. Is it slightly soft or very firm? Now sniff the fruit. Has it developed a fruity aroma?

If all the indicators point to ripeness, pick one and bite into it. If it's ready, you'll be able to enjoy a flavor impossible in fruit that has been gathered far away.

Harvesting Vegetables

If flavor and nutrition are your main reasons for raising vegetables, you'll want to guarantee those qualities by picking your crops just as they reach their prime. When possible, harvest in the morning before the sun and heat affect the plants. In the case of beans, wait until the dew has dried; working among wet bean plants can cause and spread fungal rust.

When the vegetables have been bearing abundantly, and you've eaten, frozen, or put up all you can, keep on picking them every day. Resist the temptation to let some of those zucchinis stay on the vine. If you think you just can't face one more cuke, or you're tiring of the tomatoes you couldn't wait to pick in the beginning of the season, keep harvesting. Vegetables left to rot on the plant attract damage-causing insects and birds to your garden. Also, when you stop picking, the plant stops bearing. Plants bloom and fruit in order to produce seeds, thereby reproducing themselves. When you pick the vegetables, the plants put more energy into flowering and fruiting in an effort to set seeds.

HARVESTING FRUITS AT THEIR BEST

FRUIT	WHEN TO HARVEST
Apples	Ready when full color develops and fruit is easily plucked from the tree. Another indicator is the darkening of the seeds. The only foolproof test, however, is to pick an apple and bite into it.
Apricots	Wait until entire fruit is golden, with no trace of green. For eating ripe, be sure it gives easily when gently squeezed. For canning, choose firmer fruit. Although they will continue to ripen after picking, apricots never taste as sweet as they do when left on the tree to ripen fully.
Blackberries	Ready when they fall off in your hand in response to a gentle tug. Blackberries are sweetest after their color changes from shiny to dull. If possible, don't pick berries when they're wet.
Blueberries	Don't be fooled into thinking blueberries are ripe when they turn deep blue; it takes about 5 to 7 days longer for them to mature. Wait for a powdery blue patina to develop. Unlike most fruits, ripe blueberries can remain on the bush several days without loss of quality.
Cantaloupes, honeydew melons, Crenshaw melons	On cantaloupes, look for prominent green ribs with heavy, beige-colored netting. Ripe honeydew melons are silvery green with a tinge of yellow. Crenshaw melons turn yellow when ripe. Ripe melons of any type slip easily from the vine with no pressure and have a characteristic melon aroma.
Cherries	Different types of cherries turn varying shades of red or yellow when ripe. Know whether yours are supposed to be dark red, bright crimson, yellow, or blush (pinkish yellow). Pull gently on the stem, twisting upward. Ripe fruit separates readily from the tree. Taste-test one to be sure.
Citrus fruits	It's essential to know what variety you're growing; different citrus fruits ripen at various times. Your local Cooperative Extension service can provide the maturation information for each variety. Sometimes the color changes, but the only sure test is to taste the fruit.
Figs	Ready when the neck bends over. If milky sap oozes out of the stem after a fig is picked, the fruit is not ripe. Handle with care to avoid breaking the skin (this sours the flesh). For drying, let figs stay on the tree and drop off naturally; gather the fallen fruit and let dry in the sun.
Gooseberries	The skin color changes from green to pale pink to the reddish purple that tells you when the fruit is ripe; however, berries can remain on the bush for up to 2 weeks after they ripen, getting sweeter all the while. Many gardeners use green gooseberries of a mature size in pies, jams, and jellies. Plants are thorny, so wear a heavy glove on one hand to hold back the branches as you pick the fruit with a thinly gloved or bare hand.
Grapes	Stems turn brown and shrivel, the vine's ripe wood turns reddish brown, seeds become brown, and the fruit changes color and is easy to pick. Wait for a sweet, mellow taste.
Kiwis	Both hardy and regular kiwis change color as they ripen. Hardy kiwis become paler green; fuzzy kiwis develop a more intense brown coloration. Both become slightly less firm.

FRUIT	WHEN TO HARVEST
Passion fruits	Fruit is ripe when it falls to the ground. It's highly perishable, so it should be picked up and eaten within a day.
Peaches, nectarines	The background color is a much better indicator of ripeness than the fruit's redness, which can vary from variety to variety and from year to year. The background color should be white for white-fleshed peaches, yellow for yellow-fleshed peaches and nectarines. Any greenness means the fruit is not ready to be picked. Don't squeeze to determine softness, or you'll bruise the fruit. Peaches and nectarines continue to ripen after picking; however, they taste much better if they ripen at room temperature rather than in the refrigerator.
Pears	Unlike other fruits, most pears are harvested before they're completely ripe; when left to ripen on the tree, they develop a mealy texture and soft core. The proper time for harvest is when you pull gently on a pear and it separates easily from the branch. Allow fruit to ripen slowly in a cool room. An exception is Asian pears, which are delicious and crisp when allowed to ripen on the tree; judge their edibility by tasting.
Persimmons	Oriental persimmons are of two types: astringent (tart) and nonastringent. Astringent persimmons (including all American persimmons) are ripe when they feel soft. Depending on the tree, this can be early in the season, late, or even in winter; frost has nothing to do with it (nor does fruit dropping from the tree). American persimmons are especially variable. Some gardeners freeze astringent persimmons several days before cooking to give them a sweeter taste. As soon as the nonastringent varieties turn orange, they have a texture like that of a sweet, crisp apple.
Pineapples	Ready to cut from the stalk when the fruit turns golden yellow and has a rich, fruity fragrance, and you can easily pull a leaf from the crown. Don't remove the crown until you're ready to eat the fruit.
Plums	Plums develop their full color 20–30 days before they're ready to harvest. The fruits that receive the most sun will ripen first. The sign that they're sweet enough to pick is a slight softening. The fruits of a plum tree with a very large crop are usually not as sweet as those of a tree whose yield is more moderate.
Quinces	Look for yellow to orangish coloration. Pick the fruit before the first frost and store in a cool spot away from apples or pears, which will absorb its flavor.
Raspberries	Look for even color overall as well as berries that part from the plant at the slightest tug. Raspberries that mature in wet weather are less tasty than those that ripen in sunshine. Place berries in a single layer in the container to avoid crushing them.
Strawberries	Usually ready a month after blossoming; should be firm and plump, with an even, bright red color. Pick as soon as they're ripe, and handle carefully to avoid bruising. Leave the green "caps" on until you're ready to use the berries—they'll stay more flavorful.
Watermelons	Several clues let you know when a watermelon is ready. The underside, where the melon touches the ground, will be yellow; the curly tendril just below the point where the fruit is attached to the vine will change in color from green to brown and will shrivel up; and the melon will produce a dull (rather than metallic) sound when you thump it.

HARVESTING VEGETABLES AT THEIR BEST

VEGETABLE	WHEN TO HARVEST
Asparagus	When the spears are 5"–9" above the ground, use a sharp knife to cut the stems at an angle just below soil level. Or break off spears just above the ground. Don't begin harvesting until plants are 3 years old.
Beans, lima	When the pods look full and feel spongy, and the seeds (beans) are green.
Beans, snap	When the pods snap readily. Frequent picking produces more beans. When growing beans for shelling or dry use, wait until the pods turn dry and brittle, then shell beans and allow to dry on a screen before storing. For best flavor and texture, don't let yard-long beans grow more than 12" long.
Beets	Highest quality when small to medium-size. (Ideal is about the size of golf balls). Pull them out of the ground by hand.
Broccoli	The traditional way to harvest broccoli is to cut the stem 4"–5" below the tightly formed, dark green head. For a longer harvest, cut the stem near the base of the head to stimulate growth of side shoots. As you cut off the little heads that appear on the side stems, several more will form. In cool weather, your harvest can continue for weeks. When yellow flowers form, the heads are past their prime. (Flowers are edible, with a flavor like that of broccoli raab.)
Brussels sprouts	When sprouts are 1"–1¼" in diameter. Many gardeners feel the flavor is improved by a frost. Harvest individual sprouts from the bottom of the plant up. Break off the leaves between the lower sprouts to let sprouts develop along the stem.
Cabbage	When solid heads form. Cut from the stalk with a sharp knife and remove the loose outer leaves. If you cut off the head of early varieties and leave the stem, several smaller heads will form on side stems.
Cabbage, Chinese	Harvest heading Chinese cabbage the same as regular cabbage. For bok choy and other nonheading Chinese cabbages, cut off either individual leaves or entire plants. Always harvest the older, outside leaves first.
Carrots	When firm and crisp. Carrots taste tough or woody when allowed to reach giant size, whereas fingerlings have a delicious flavor. In loose soil, grasp the base of the green top to pull the carrots out. In heavy soil, ease them out with a trowel or garden fork so they won't break off. Right after digging, cut off all but an inch of the leafy green tops to preserve the carrots' moisture and sweetness.
Cauliflower	When the florets are still tight and white, before the curd becomes discolored and loose.
Celery	Begin removing outer stalks as soon as they're large enough. This encourages new stalks to form in the center of the plant, extending your harvest.
Corn	When the silk begins to turn brown and dry, or when piercing a kernel with a fingernail releases a milky juice. If no liquid appears, the corn is no longer fresh.
Cucumbers	Optimum size depends on the variety. Pick before they lose their fresh green color and firmness. Cucumbers for pickling are usually no longer than 1"–2".
Eggplants	When fully colored but before skin turns dull. Cut from plant with garden shears.
Kale	Younger shoots and leaves are sweetest; they should be crisp and bright green. Older leaves can be bitter. Some think the flavor improves after a frost. Lengthen your harvest by removing outer leaves as needed rather than cutting the entire plant at once.

VEGETABLE	WHEN TO HARVEST
Kohlrabi	Harvest standard varieties when 2" across, newer hybrids at 3"–4". The leafy green tops are also edible.
Lettuce	Cut head lettuce when mature and firm. For an extended loose-leaf lettuce harvest, cut the leaves one by one from the outside of the plant. In warm weather, lettuce loses quality quickly. As they get past their prime, leaves will elongate. To see if they're still edible, break a leaf from the plant and look at the base. If liquid is milky instead of clear, the lettuce will taste bitter and is no longer edible.
Okra	When the pods are 2½"–3½" long. Cut, rather than pull, the pods from the branches; wear gloves and long sleeves to avoid getting pricked by spines.
Onions	For green onions, or to use fresh, dig up after the bulb has grown to at least ½" in diameter. For storage, wait until the tops have died down. Let onions dry in the sun for a week, then indoors 20–30 days before storing.
Parsnips	In late fall or early winter—cool weather improves the flavor.
Peas	For English peas and sugar snaps, pick after the pods fill out, but before they turn yellow. Begin daily harvest about 3 weeks after flowering. Pick snow peas when the pods have reached mature size but remain flat, with no bumps.
Peas, Southern	For fresh use, when easily shelled. For dried beans, when pods are dry and brittle.
Peppers	Orange, yellow, and other non-green peppers start out green; pick them when they develop their true, full color. Those that are supposed to be green will turn red if left on the vine past maturity. The flavor will change and the vitamin C content increase. Hot or chili peppers can be picked at any size if they are used fresh, but should be full size for drying. Wear gloves when handling hot peppers.
Pumpkins	For fresh use, when full-grown with a uniform, slightly dull color. For storage, after the shell hardens but before frost. Cut pumpkins from the vine with a knife, leaving 4"–6" of stem attached to the pumpkin.
Radishes	When firm with bright color. Round types should be less than 1" across. When left in the ground too long, they become woody and strong-flavored.
Spinach, Swiss chard	When leaves are dark green, crisp, and tender. For an extended harvest, break off outer leaves; new leaves will grow in the center.
Squash, summer	Pick squash when young and tender, with shiny skin. Ideal size for yellow squash is 4"–6" long; pattypan, 4" across; zucchini, 6"–7" long.
Squash, winter	When the rind has become hard enough that it can't be pierced by a fingernail. Leave several inches of stem attached.
Tomatoes	After they develop their full mature color. Never refrigerate tomatoes. Leave at room temperature, stem side up, out of the sun.
Turnips	For greens, when the leaves are crisp, tender, and the size you like. For roots, dig white varieties when they reach the size of a golf ball. Purple ones taste best at 2½"–3½" in diameter. Remove all but ½" of the tops after harvest.

Harvesting Herbs

The best time to harvest herbs is when their fragrant oil content is highest—after the flowers have formed but before they've opened. The day before picking, gently hose off the plants to wash away any dust or dirt. Cut the herbs, with shears or a sharp knife, in midmorning, after the dew has dried on the plants but before the sun has gotten hot, or in late afternoon.

To harvest seed heads, such as anise, caraway, or dill, pick the stems when the seedpods are mature but still green (before they open and spill the seeds into the garden).

When harvesting annual herbs, allow at least several inches of the stem and some leaves to remain on the plant so it can grow back and be harvested two or three more times. The larger and bushier an annual herb, the more you can remove at any one time. In cold-winter areas, cut annual herbs all the way to the ground before the first frost. Remove no more than one-third of the stems of perennial herbs at a time; to avoid winter damage, make the final, light harvest in early fall.

Drying is the easiest way to preserve herb leaves for later use. Cut the stems as long as possible and remove any damaged or yellow foliage. Rinse gently with water and place on a towel to remove excess moisture, then tie the stems together and hang them upside down in a dark, dry, warm spot for a week or two. When drying herbs for their seeds, enclose the seed heads in a paper bag to catch the seeds if they fall. The seeds are dried when they've changed from green to brown. Another drying method is to spread the seed heads, or the herbs with stems removed, in a single layer on a screen. Elevate and place the screen in an airy spot out of direct sunlight; turn the herbs every few days to make sure they dry evenly.

Not all herbs are suitable for air drying. Salad burnet, chervil, chives, dill, fennel, and garlic chives lose color and flavor when dried. Parsley needs high temperatures to dry well.

Some gardeners preserve their herbs by freezing; however, this may cause the herbs to turn brown or black. To prevent discoloration, chop the leaves finely in a blender, add some water, then freeze in an ice-cube tray. Herb cubes give winter soups or pasta a welcome burst of summer flavor.

If you weren't able to harvest an herb before it flowered, don't despair. You can cut the blooms of most herbs (parsley, anise, caraway, and salad burnet are the exceptions) for pretty edible flowers that add color and flavor to your cuisine.

WINTERIZING YOUR YARD

As the long summer days grow shorter and evenings become chilly, gardeners in cold-winter climates embark on the last and most important tasks of the garden year—the ones that may make the difference between whether some plants will live or die. Just as in early autumn you make sure your car has plenty of antifreeze to protect the engine, this is the time to provide protection for your plants.

In addition to low temperatures, the ravages of winter can include windburn, sunscald, snow damage, salt injury, alternate freezing and thawing (which can heave plants out of the ground), and animal damage. To make conditions less stressful for sensitive plants, don't wait until north winds howl. Around Labor Day, begin soaking the soil around perennials, shrubs, trees, and vines once or twice a week when rainfall is less than an inch. Watering is particularly important for evergreens, which continue to transpire all winter; when the ground is frozen, their roots cannot deliver moisture to the foliage to replace that given off, so the leaves dry out and look as if they've been sunburned. This is less likely to happen to plants that have stored up enough water before winter.

Some gardeners use antidesiccant sprays to slow down the rate of transpiration and help

Rabbits, rodents, and deer can pose problems in any season, but they can cause severe damage during winter in cold-climate gardens. To protect tree bark from rabbits and mice, encircle trees with quarter-inch mesh hardware cloth from 3" below the ground to 1½'–2' above the expected snow line. Plastic tree guards are effective deterrents for small trees. Protect shrubs and other plants from rabbits with 2'-high chicken-wire fences. Fences to keep deer out must be strong and at least 6'–8' high.

Organic repellents, available in garden centers, are less expensive and time-consuming. They're sprayed on trees and shrubs to make them smell or taste bad and must be reapplied frequently—especially after heavy precipitation. Some gardeners have concocted their own home-made deer repellents (like hanging bags of human hair or soap scraps in the vicinity of threatened plants), but these are of varying effectiveness. When they're hungry enough, deer will find a way to dine in even the best-protected gardens.

plants avoid winter foliage injury. Antidesiccants are made of lightweight vegetable wax, and a thin coating on the foliage of a broad-leaved evergreen like rhododendron can reduce evaporation by as much as 80%. One coating of wax lasts six to eight weeks. Such sprays should be used in fall, while temperatures are still moderate, and must be reapplied once in winter. Be sure to read the manufacturer's directions, since antidesiccant sprays cannot be used on all plants and should be applied only when the temperature is within a specific range—neither too hot nor too cold.

Listen carefully to evening weather forecasts as the seasons change. Often the first couple of fall frosts are light. If you cover vegetables, annuals, and perennials with a sheet, blanket, or piece of spun-bonded fiber, they'll be protected against a few degrees of frost and continue blooming and bearing for a few weeks more. In cold climates, spread a thick layer of mulch (12" or more) such as straw or hay over carrots and parsnips and you can harvest them all winter.

Immediately after a killing frost, empty all ceramic or clay containers and take them indoors so they won't be damaged by freezing. Then dig up tubers, bulbs, and rhizomes of tender plants such as dahlias, gladiolus, and cannas that will not survive if left in the ground. Wash them off, let dry, and store in a dry, cool place. In cold climates, untie perennial vines, lay them on the ground, and cover with mulch. A good fall cleanup makes the garden look better and gives insects and diseases no place to overwinter. Pull up dead annuals and vegetables, and toss them on the compost pile.

You may also want to cut your perennials back close to the ground. In climates where perennials will not be covered with heavy mulch, many gardeners like to leave them if any flowers or seed heads remain. The birds love them, and it's fun to watch acrobatic goldfinches perch on coneflowers and rudbeckia throughout the winter, pecking at the seeds.

The next protective task of autumn is mulching to prevent frost heaving. In zones 6–7 and warmer, add just enough mulch to make sure it's as deep as when first applied in spring. In colder climates, wait until the ground is frozen, then cover the soil around perennials, shrubs, and young trees with a 4"–6" layer of mulch. This helps to maintain a constant soil temperature. When the soil alternately freezes and thaws during the winter, young transplants and perennials can easily be heaved up out of the ground; this exposes their roots, which will be killed by the cold. Mulching around the base of vulnerable evergreens also helps to thwart sunburn by keeping the soil from freezing so deeply that roots can't function.

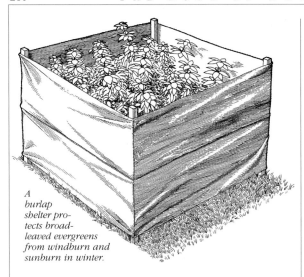

A burlap shelter protects broad-leaved evergreens from windburn and sunburn in winter.

Winter winds can cause plant tissue damage called windburn. A windbreak, or screen of trees or tall shrubs planted at right angles to the prevailing winds, slows down the wind and diminishes its effects. Shelters constructed around the south, west, and windward sides of shrubs are also helpful. A variety of materials are suitable for framing the shelter: wooden or metal stakes, chicken wire, or a tomato cage covered with burlap, which allows necessary air and moisture to penetrate (which plastic will not).

Burlap shelters also protect shrubs against damage by salt spray from passing cars. But the only sure way to avoid injury from de-icing salt is not to plant trees and shrubs in heavily salted areas or where salt runoff can be absorbed by the roots.

It seems odd to think of sun damage in winter, but a brightly shining sun followed by a bitterly cold night can cause tree trunks to thaw during the day and refreeze at night, resulting in bark cracking. To avoid this, wrap the trunks of young trees with a light-colored tree wrap that extends from the base to just below the first branches. As an alternative to wrapping, the trunks of fruit trees are often painted with white latex (never oil) paint to prevent sunscald.

To protect evergreen shrubs from sun, wind, and snow, prop discarded Christmas greenery and

trees over or against them. Prevent snow and ice from bending or breaking the limbs of small evergreen shrubs and trees by wrapping them with strong cloth strips in a crisscross pattern from top to bottom around the outside of the plant.

Roses also need winter protection anywhere that temperatures fall below 20°F. In zones 6–8, place a mound of organic mulch 6" over the bud union of grafted roses. Dig up tree roses, place them in a tub of soil and let them spend the winter in the basement or garage.

In colder climates, two methods are commonly used to protect roses from low and fluctuating temperatures: mounding soil and leaves around the bushes, or tipping them into a trench that extends out from the base of the bush and covering them with soil and leaves.

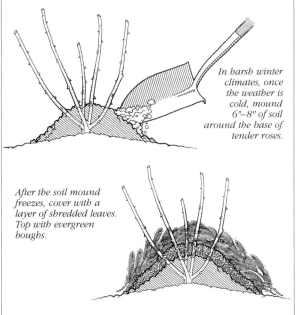

In harsh winter climates, once the weather is cold, mound 6"–8" of soil around the base of tender roses.

After the soil mound freezes, cover with a layer of shredded leaves. Top with evergreen boughs.

Once you've done all you can to prepare your plants for winter, you'll have time to think about next year's landscape. Start a notebook, if you don't already have one, and write down everything you want and need to remember about your garden—from new plants to wish lists to what not to grow again. Reading catalogs, recording your successes and failures, and noting new ideas is the best way to plan the coming garden year.

GARDEN CARE CALENDAR

Use the plant hardiness zone map on page 480 to identify your temperature zone and determine the approximate range of temperatures within its geographical limits. This information will help you schedule your seasonal grooming and maintenance tasks throughout the year.

ZONES 3–4

EARLY SPRING

- As weather moderates, remove winter protection from roses and prune them.
- When bulbs start to grow, remove mulch to warm up soil where earliest crops will grow.
- Prune berry and fruit trees before growth begins.
- Prune winter damage to shrubs.
- Fertilize all fruits.
- Apply dormant oil to trees and shrubs when the temperature is above 40°F. but before buds open.

LATE SPRING

- Fertilize trees and shrubs before growth begins.
- Clean up perennial beds to prepare for planting. Remove dead foliage and divide perennials that need it.
- Don't forget to label new plants and those moved to new locations.
- Watch for pests, which are more easily controlled when caught early.
- Begin weeding.
- Fertilize hardy annuals as you plant.
- Renew mulches.
- Deadhead bulbs, but don't remove foliage.

SUMMER

- This is the prime time for maintenance tasks in the garden: weeding, watering, fertilizing, and controlling insects and diseases.
- Deadhead annuals, perennials, and roses to promote more blooms. Tie roses, vines, and tomatoes to their supports as they climb. Pinch back mums and asters until the middle of July to promote more compact plants. Prune hedges.
- Harvest fruits and vegetables. Put netting over fruits to protect from birds.
- Cut herbs and flowers for drying.
- Mow lawn regularly.
- The first of August, stop feeding roses and cut off any new growth to help the bushes harden off.

EARLY AUTUMN

- Harvest ripe fruit promptly. Begin fall cleanup of yard and garden.
- Fertilize when planting bulbs and mulch well afterward.
- Be sure all plants are well-watered going into winter.
- Fertilize and renovate lawns.
- When first frosts are predicted, cover vegetables and any annuals you want to save.
- After a hard frost, remove all plant debris to the compost pile.
- Dig dahlias and glads after frost; store bulbs in a cool place where the temperature remains above freezing.
- Rake leaves regularly.
- Clean out terra-cotta containers and store them out of the weather.

LATE AUTUMN

- When temperatures will remain above 40°F. for 24 hours, you can apply an antidesiccant spray to evergreens.
- Rake up the last of the leaves; shred and add to the compost pile.
- Prepare plants for winter. Paint trunks of young fruit trees with white latex paint, or install light-colored tree guards. Be sure perennials, perennial herbs, and bulbs are well mulched.
- Take down, clean, and store stakes and supports for use next year.
- Clean, sharpen, and oil tools before putting them away for the winter.

WINTER

- Check all winter protection to be certain it's secure.
- Gather berries, cones, and evergreens from the yard for indoor decorations.
- Spray an antidesiccant on evergreens again if late-winter temperatures rise above 40°F.
- Check stored bulbs and tubers; remove any that have rotted.

GARDEN CARE CALENDAR (CONTINUED)

ZONES 5–6

EARLY SPRING

- Remove wraps, screens, and other winter protection as weather moderates.
- Finish harvesting root crops left over winter.
- Fertilize bulbs when their shoots get to be 1"–2" high. Turn under cover crops in vegetable garden. Set up supports for peas.
- Prune and fertilize fruit trees and vines before growth starts; when temperature is above freezing for 24 hours, apply dormant oil spray.
- Prune trees and summer-flowering shrubs. Prune out winter damage from other shrubs.
- Remove heavy mulch from roses; prune and fertilize.
- Remove debris from lawns and ground covers. Have soil tested if not done within past 3 years.
- Put peony supports in place.
- Remove faded ornamental grass foliage before new growth is evident; divide plants if needed.
- Clean, oil, and sharpen tools. Begin weekly weeding.

LATE SPRING

- Cover vegetable seedlings if frost is expected.
- Trim ground covers as needed. Prune spring-flowering shrubs after they bloom.
- Set up supports; start to train plants up trellises.
- Watch for signs of insects and disease; both are more easily controlled when caught quickly.
- Divide fall-blooming perennials and those that have already flowered.
- Hoe down annual weeds when they're small; begin digging up roots of perennial weeds. Water when rainfall is less than adequate.
- Deadhead bulbs and perennials. Begin pinching back mums and asters.
- Clean out water gardens; divide and repot plants.
- Thin vegetables and herbs.
- Feed roses monthly.
- Turn compost pile occasionally, if possible.
- Gradually remove mulch from flower beds and lightly fertilize perennials.
- Don't forget to label new plants. Side-dress vegetables as they begin to grow.
- Mow grass at 3" high; if clippings are thick, add to compost pile.

SUMMER

- As soon as soil is reliably warm, put mulches in place.
- Prune climbing roses when they finish blooming.
- All summer long, regular weeding, watering, and controlling insects and diseases will be necessary. Don't let weeds go to seed.
- Pick vegetables and herbs at the peak of perfection; serve or preserve them right away.
- After raspberries have finished bearing, cut canes back to ground (except everbearing varieties).
- Take cuttings of ground covers you would like to increase.
- Be sure to frequently water and feed container-grown plants.
- Tie plants to stakes and trellises as they grow.
- Add to compost pile and turn it occasionally if you can.
- Even in hottest weather, mow grass 3" high. Leave light clippings on the lawn to serve as a mild fertilizer.
- Divide perennials that flowered in spring or early summer if they have grown crowded together. Mulch well after replanting and be sure they get sufficient water.
- Trim hedges and prune shrubs as needed.
- Deadhead annuals and perennials weekly. When annuals aren't blooming well, shear them lightly to encourage new growth and flowering; fertilize lightly at the same time.
- In August, stop fertilizing roses so they will stop growing and harden off for winter.

EARLY AUTUMN

- Divide daylilies.
- Cut and dry flowers and herbs.
- Water all plants deeply if rainfall is inadequate.
- Begin fall cleanup. Pick up and remove fallen rose foliage to prevent spread of disease. Keep after weeds and insects, with particular attention to the vegetable garden.
- Deadhead perennials and annuals.
- Fertilize bulbs when planting.
- Dig up gladiolus and caladiums when they finish blooming, and store indoors.
- Rake up early leaves.

ZONES 5–6 (contd.)

LATE AUTUMN

- After ground has frozen, mound soil 6" over bud union of rose bushes to protect from cold.
- Set up winter shelters for shrubs and small trees.
- Mulch perennials, bulbs, shrubs, and young trees. Prevent winter sun damage with light-colored tree guards or paint trunks of fruit trees with white latex paint.
- Rake up and compost all leaves except those you shred and use as mulch.
- Take down vegetable and flower cages and supports, clean, and store out of the weather.
- Spray evergreens with an antidesiccant.

WINTER

- Keep snow brushed off evergreens.
- Check that screens, wraps, and other winter protection remain secure.
- Don't use salt near the roots of plants.
- When temperature remains above 40°F., reapply antidesiccants to broad-leaved evergreens. Prune trees.
- Check for perennials or bulbs that may have heaved out of the ground; put them back in place and mulch.
- Discard stored bulbs that have rotted.

ZONES 7–8

EARLY SPRING

- If fruits weren't pruned in late winter, do so before growth starts. Prune any winter-damaged shrubs and crape myrtles that need shaping.
- Overseed bare spots in lawns. Begin mowing when fescue grass is 3" high.
- Plant, prune, and fertilize roses.
- Begin weeding and insect control.
- Cut back ornamental grasses before they start to grow; divide if needed.
- Fertilize trees, shrubs, vines, and perennials. Divide overgrown perennials that flower in summer or fall; mulch well.
- Stake plants that will need it.
- Deadhead bulbs, allowing foliage to mature and turn brown. Feed and deadhead pansies. Edge flower beds.
- Remove and compost leaves that fell over winter.
- Harvest last of collards and kale, and clean up vegetable garden. Put up pea fences. Rig row covers for early crops that need protection. Thin onions and carrots. Prune perennial herbs. Remove mulch from strawberries.
- Turn compost pile. Amend soil with organic matter.

LATE SPRING

- Stake tall-growing and floppy flowers. Begin training vines and tying climbing roses to trellises.
- Mulch vegetables, annuals, perennials, shrubs, vines, and trees, keeping mulch several inches from plant stems.
- Deadhead late bulbs, pansies, and perennials. Feed and support vegetables as they begin growing. Harvest early crops; watch out for cabbage loopers.

- Move houseplants and tender plants taken indoors for winter back outside; water and feed.
- Control weeds and insects when first noticed.
- Mow grass as needed.
- Cover strawberries with netting to deter birds.
- Prune spring-flowering shrubs and climbing roses when spent; water if weather is dry.
- Begin pinching mums. Shape needled evergreens as needed. Begin trimming hedges.
- Feed azaleas, camellias, and rhododendron.
- Thin excess fruit on trees.
- If spring-flowering bulbs need to be moved, do so after the foliage has turned brown.

SUMMER

- Keep all plants mulched and watered. Water first thing in the morning to avoid wetting leaves (can cause fungal diseases). Use a rain gauge to tell exactly how much rain has fallen on your property.
- Deadhead perennials and annuals regularly. Mow grass as needed.
- Keep ahead of weeds; never let them develop seeds.
- Look for signs of insects or diseases; control quickly.
- Feed annuals and container plants. Harvest vegetables, herbs, and fruits as they ripen; protect from bird damage.
- Trim hedges and prune shrubs that require shaping.
- Cut herbs and flowers for drying.
- Divide spent perennials if needed.
- Roses need weekly attention throughout the summer (water, fertilizer, fungus and insect control).

GARDEN CARE CALENDAR (CONTINUED)

ZONES 7–8 (contd.)

EARLY AUTUMN

- Trim hedges one last time.
- Renew all mulches.
- Water deeply when rainfall is less than 1" weekly. Control insects and weeds (more important now than ever); if not killed, they'll be back next year.
- Feed pansies.
- Fertilize and renovate cool-season lawns as needed. In zone 7, overseed warm-season lawns with annual rye.
- Stop fertilizing roses; pick up and remove all fallen leaves to avoid fungus diseases next year.
- Divide overcrowded perennials; mulch well after replanting. After mums finish blooming, leave them alone; cut back next spring instead of in fall. Continue to deadhead flowers that are blooming.
- Pick ripe apples and keep fallen fruit cleaned up.
- Protect vegetables from possible early frosts.

LATE AUTUMN

- Rake leaves; shred and add to compost pile. Secure climbing roses, ramblers, and vines to their supports. Remove unneeded vegetable and flower supports.
- In zone 8, fertilize and overseed warm-season lawns with annual rye.
- Cut back perennials, if desired, for appearance's sake.
- Improve drainage where poor.
- Fertilize all bulb plantings, old and new. Clean up beds, borders, and vegetable plot.
- Harvest greens and other cool-season crops. Protect vegetables from first frosts.
- Water newly planted trees at least weekly if rainfall is deficient. Fertilize established trees after they go dormant.

- Cut back extra-long rose canes that could whip about in the wind. Move tender perennials and tropicals indoors.
- After frost, dig up dahlias and other summer bulbs and tubers, or mulch heavily. Fertilize pansies; water regularly. Mound 8" of soil over roses that are especially tender.
- When temperature is above 40°F., apply dormant oil spray to fruit trees and shrubs affected by scale. Apply antidesiccant to evergreens on the east side of the house. Cover camellias to protect flowers from frost (never use plastic—it will burn the leaves).

WINTER

- Protect less hardy plants.
- Finish vegetable garden cleanup; till vacant areas for February or March planting if soil is not too wet. Harvest late crops.
- Check stored bulbs and tubers and toss out any that have rotted.
- Remember to water porch plants regularly.
- Test soil and apply lime early in winter so it will have time to become effective.
- Fertilize spring bulbs that have grown 1"– 2", and any bulbs planted in December or January.
- Fertilize before planting late-winter crops in the vegetable garden.
- Fertilize trees in February.
- Prune shade and fruit trees.
- Apply a dormant oil spray to shrubs or roses affected by scale or numerous insects when temperature is over 40°F.
- If weather is favorable, mounded mulches can be removed from roses during February and the bushes can be pruned.
- Add fireplace ashes to compost pile.

ZONES 9–10

EARLY SPRING

- Prune spring-blooming shrubs after they've finished flowering. Fertilize trees, shrubs, vines, and roses if not done earlier; water well afterward.
- Mow grass as needed. Start lawns from seed or sod.

- Deadhead faded flowers to keep plants blooming. Begin weeding. Thin seedlings.
- Water when rainfall is insufficient.
- Put up stakes and trellises (if not done earlier).

ZONES 9–10 (contd.)

- Take steps to control any insects or diseases.
- Start shearing hedges.
- Spread mulch around shrubs, trees, and flowers.
- Edge beds. Begin to train and tie vines to trellises.
- Harvest fruits and early vegetables.
- Turn compost pile occasionally.
- Fertilize fruits as needed.

LATE SPRING

- Continue harvesting vegetables. Fertilize young crops lightly.
- Renew all mulches.
- Weed regularly. Watch for insects and control organically.
- Deadhead flowers. Lightly fertilize summer bulbs. Keep tying vines to supports. Prune spring-flowering shrubs when spent. Harvest herbs and flowers.
- Lay sod of warm-season grasses and fertilize established warm-season lawns.
- Plant tropicals.
- Feed summer bulbs when shoots appear.
- Check containers often to see if they need water.
- Dig up tulips grown as annuals and discard.
- Put stakes in place if not done earlier.
- Harvest perennial herbs.

SUMMER

- Water, weed, and feed as necessary. (Watering may be the most critical task to be done all summer.)
- Add grass clippings to compost pile if you don't feed the lawn with them.
- Fertilize citrus fruits.
- Feed and water roses regularly; cut faded roses back to just above the next 5- or 7-leaf cluster.
- Prune summer-flowering shrubs that have finished blooming. Mow grass regularly except when under stress from heat and drought. Deadhead annuals frequently. Cut back perennials after blooming.
- Harvest ripe fruit, keeping plants covered to protect them from birds. Pick up all dropped fruit.

EARLY AUTUMN

- Keep shrubs and trees well watered.
- Continue controlling insects and weeds. Divide and transplant perennials; cut back those that have finished blooming. Deadhead flowers.

- Check dahlia stakes and vine supports.
- Fertilize roses and new plants after they've started to grow.
- Harvest herbs and flowers for drying.
- Turn compost pile; spread compost around garden.
- Fertilize citrus trees, shade trees, and spring-blooming shrubs.
- Overseed warm-season lawns with annual rye.
- Fertilize spring-flowering bulbs and hardy annuals when planting.
- Pull spent vegetable plants and harvest other crops.
- Tidy up beds, borders, and vegetable garden.

LATE AUTUMN

- Fertilize trees and shrubs; prune summer and fall bloomers.
- Harvest vegetables, herbs, and fruits.
- Prune back extra-long rose canes so they won't whip around and be damaged.
- Overseed warm-season grass with rye if not done in October; continue mowing as long as grass grows.
- Water if weather is dry.
- Add all yard debris to compost pile.
- Deadhead hardy annuals; fertilize as needed.
- When pulling up spent plants and replacing them, enrich soil with compost or other organic material.
- Continue weeding. Pick up fruit that has dropped off trees. Be vigilant in controlling insects.

WINTER

- Continue harvesting citrus fruits and winter vegetables and herbs.
- Water as needed when temperature is above freezing.
- Prune shrubs, trees, and vines when dormant. Lightly fertilize overseeded lawns. Prune hybrid tea and other bush roses. Renew mulch around rosebushes and clean up bed if needed.
- Cut back ornamental grasses before new growth begins.
- Feed perennials and winter annuals as they start to grow; deadhead as necessary.
- Protect marginally hardy plants whenever a frost is predicted.
- Keep bougainvillea tied to its trellis.
- Fertilize early vegetable crops. Prune fruits when dormant; fertilize plants.

START SMALL, THINK BIG: PROPAGATION

Starting plants by propagation offers an abundance of exhilarating options. Just for the adventure of it, you can decide to grow an exotic blue Himalayan poppy from seed. Or you might experiment with layering a witch hazel or taking a cutting of your finest penstemon. You select the specimen, and you initiate and supervise the reproductive process. As creative director and midwife, you become an active partner in the birth and growth of nature's offspring.

All types of propagation, except growing from seed, are asexual. These vegetative methods result in plants exactly like their parents. Think of it as cloning, using a piece of a plant as a starter.

By propagating different genera, species, varieties, and hybrids at home, without resorting to synthetic fertilizers and pesticides that nurseries may use, you work in harmony with nature to perpetuate the complex universe in which microbes, insects, small animals, and plants all play a necessary part. The more varied your choices, the better for your garden.

Choosing to propagate plants also benefits you as the gardener. A packet of about 50 seeds typically costs less than one or two nursery seedlings; since most packets contain too many seeds for one season, you can store the remainder in a seed envelope in a dark, dry place to use next year or to share with friends. Hundreds of flowering perennials and shrubs can be started from cuttings for next to nothing.

Moreover, as you learn to rely on your own skills in overseeing the birth-death-rebirth cycle, you'll direct your time and energy to where they can do the most good. Fewer gas-consuming trips to the garden center will be needed because the material required for an entire season's propagation is minimal. You'll happily recycle cell packs or flats to start seeds, and reuse garden tools time and again, glad to touch base with old friends.

GROWING PLANTS FROM SEED

To grow from seed takes a leap of faith that careful nurturing will turn a handful of drab seeds into a riot of greenery, color, taste, and scent. The diversity of choice extends from flowers to fruits and vegetables; from seed you can grow varieties—especially heirlooms—that may be unobtainable through other means. These seeds are treasured by gardeners for providing a living link to and taste of our past. Their patchwork of antique genes, which would otherwise be lost forever, is a gift of biodiversity to the garden. Not incidentally, seed-starting increases the gardener's respect for nature's unhurried pace. With time and patience, you can grow even a tree from seed.

Novice gardeners may think seed germination is complicated, but in truth most seeds require only the right temperature, moisture, and darkness to sprout their first tiny roots and leaves. Give them the right temperature, depth of planting, and a good medium to grow in, and the success rate is high. Responsible gardeners grow flowers and vegetables from seeds that have not been treated with synthetic chemicals. Untreated seeds add no toxins to the environment in their preparation and produce chemical-free crops if grown organically.

Growing from seed gives you an early start in the season on most of your vegetables and many flowers, from tomatoes to alyssum, peppers to pansies. You are able to work your garden and continue planting long after commercially grown seedlings have disappeared from local nurseries. And you can grow what you want—the choices, particularly of flowers and vegetables, are much greater among seed offerings than among seedlings. (A purple or white tomato, for instance, is only available as seed.)

Starting from seed further assures control over chemical-free fertilizers and soil composition through the plant's life cycle. While commercial seed breeders have been attempting to perfect fast-producing, thick-skinned, easily transportable fruits and vegetables by subjecting them to the chemical wonders of science, home gardeners have concerned themselves with beauty, color, fragrance, and flavor. These qualities may be found in heirloom seeds or modern hybrids—but be aware that seeds saved from heirloom plants will grow true to form while those produced by a hybrid plant will not. If you're growing for hybrid vigor, you'll have to buy new seeds every year.

Seed Packets: Read with Care

Whether you purchase seeds off the rack or from a mail-order catalog, your most reliable source for specific information about when and how to start and grow seeds comes from the packet itself. Like a field guide, the seed packet points the way and offers sound advice to keep

CHEMICAL-FREE SEEDS

Synthetic chemical fungicides such as Thiram and Captan are commonly used by commercial seed producers to develop a disease-resistant product. These chemicals ward off fungal diseases during seed germination and in the seedling stages.

To purchase chemical-free seeds, seek out small, regional mail-order catalogs that grow and sell chemically untreated, responsibly harvested seeds. These companies will often carry an imaginative (if limited) selection of seeds suitable to the weather and soil conditions of your area. Specify "untreated seeds" when ordering.

you from getting lost; paying attention to it decreases the chance of a serious misstep but doesn't guarantee success. Seed packets usually provide the basics: the hardiness zone for successful growth, when to plant (outdoors or indoors), how long it takes the seeds to germinate, how far apart to space plants in the garden, and how long until the plant matures (flowers or fruits). Be sure to read carefully. For plants like tomatoes and peppers, seed packets indicate the number of days to maturity from the time of transplanting the seedling into the garden rather than from the sowing date. Because every garden is unique and nature unpredictable, days to maturity will vary from one garden to the next—and even from one year to another in the same garden. Microclimates also affect the cultural information, especially watering needs and growing conditions.

Instructions to sow the seeds outdoors indicate that the plant in question doesn't transplant well. Heed the advice and don't start the seeds indoors unless you grow them in a soil block, peat pellet, or peat pot, which can be planted directly into the garden without disturbing the roots. This is especially true of many fast-growing plants: beans, corn, peas, nasturtiums, sweet peas, and those with taproots such as carrots, radishes, and Iceland poppies. Sow these seeds directly in the garden (direct-seed) at the appropriate time.

Some seed packets contain more information than others; they may even give suggestions on how to use the harvested plants. Still, few packets tell you in clear bold type whether the seeds inside are untreated, or hybrid, or open-pollinated. For this reason, many gardeners prefer to order seeds from mail-order catalogs, establishing long-term relationships with a few suppliers whose seeds deliver on their promise. Generally, seed companies respond to phoned-in questions and are more than pleased to make personal contact with their customers.

Starting Seeds Indoors

Indoor germination has many advantages. In cold climates, you'll be transplanting sturdy seedlings outdoors when your neighbors are sowing seeds. Moreover, seeds started indoors often germinate faster than those planted directly in the ground; seedlings grown on a shelf or table are at a comfortable height for thinning, eliminating that backbreaking chore in the garden, and can be properly spaced in the garden when it's time to transplant them. In addition, starting seeds indoors at different times before and during the growing season assures a continuity of flowers and vegetables over the months.

EASY TO GROW FROM SEED

While some seeds require a lot of attention and nurturing, the annuals and vegetables below are easy to grow from seed—the perfect plants for beginners.

ANNUALS

Calendulas (*Calendula officinalis*)*
California poppies (*Eschscholzia californica*)
Corn poppies (*Papaver rhoeas*)*
Cosmos (*Cosmos* spp.)*
Love-lies-bleeding (*Amaranthus caudatus*)
Marigolds (*Tagetes* spp.)
Moss roses (*Portulaca* spp.)
Nasturtiums (*Tropaeolum majus*)*
Sunflowers (*Helianthus annuus*)*

VEGETABLES

Beans (*Phaseolus vulgaris*)*
Corn (*Zea mays*)*
Peas (*Pisum sativum*)*
Radishes (*Raphanus sativus*)*
Squash (*Cucurbita* spp.)*

Included in the Plant Guide, pages 276-479.

For gardeners who want to grow vegetables for fall harvest, or for those in mild climates who want a nice variety of annuals and vegetables for winter, indoor germination is a must. These cool-loving plants would be extremely stressed if started outdoors in the harsh heat and sun of summer.

Freed from restrictions of climate and location, you can create an ideal environment for the early growth of your plants. You'll need to know what medium to plant your seeds in, what kinds of containers to use, and what conditions the seeds prefer for germination. Remember that you'll need to monitor and nurture your seedlings; don't start seeds indoors if you've planned a weeklong vacation during that time, unless you have a reliable plant-sitter who will care for the planted seeds on a daily basis.

On average, seeds take one to three weeks to germinate. The seedlings grow for several weeks before they reach a size where they may be potted on, if necessary, to a larger container indoors. A few weeks later they're ready, weather permitting, to be hardened off and subsequently transplanted out in the garden.

PLANTING MEDIUMS

For best results, start seeds in a medium that is both moisture-retentive and porous. A good planting medium keeps seeds evenly moist without becoming compacted or waterlogged—conditions that invite rot, mold, and fungus. The medium needs to be light and loose enough for air and water to circulate freely and for small, young roots to penetrate it easily. Because seeds contain their own nourishment, the medium need not supply nutrients; as seedlings, however, they will need regular fertilizing or will have to be transplanted into a more fertile medium.

Gardeners have different opinions on the composition of planting mediums for starting seeds indoors, focusing on whether to use a sterile or "live" mix. Some insist on a sterilized mix-

SEED-STARTING MIXES

Live mixes, containing unsterilized compost, can be enriched by adding nutrients such as kelp meal, bonemeal, or blood meal to the basic recipe below; lime can also be added to lower the pH level, if desired. Sterile mixes ensure a germ-free environment for germinating seeds and minimize the risk of damping off.

Live Mix
1 part well-sifted (screened) compost
1 part milled sphagnum peat moss
1 part perlite or builder's sand

Sterile Mix
1 part horticultural-grade vermiculite
1 part perlite or builder's sand
1 part milled sphagnum peat moss

It's always best to have the planting medium slightly moist when you sow seeds. Planted dry, a pot filled with sterile mix is next to impossible to moisten thoroughly. If you don't mind a little mess, and you have to moisten a lot of mix at once, do it in a dishpan, a bucket, or even a wheelbarrow. Keep adding small amounts of water and mix thoroughly—get in there and use your hands—until the mixture is uniformly damp, not wet. For small amounts, a zipper-seal plastic bag works well. Add about one part water to four parts mix; seal the bag and gently knead it until the water is uniformly incorporated.

ture to ensure a germ-free environment for the germinating seed and to minimize the risk of damping off, a lethal fungal disease that causes seedling stems to collapse at the soil level. Others assert that a mix containing unsterilized compost is perfectly safe if the compost itself has been prepared from chemical-free vegetation and isn't

DEPTH AND LIGHT

Most seeds prefer to stay warm, moist, aerated, and undisturbed while germinating, usually under a light, loose coat of planting mix. Depth requirements for seeds are given on seed packets. Generally, they should be planted at a depth three times their diameter. This is easy to judge with corn, watermelon, or other large seeds: just push the seed into the planting mix with your index finger, a pencil, or a dibber, and sprinkle or gently press mix over it, up to the surrounding level.

For small seeds, calculating three times the diameter of a tiny point isn't easy. Instead, sow these seeds on top of the planting mix, then sift over them a fine layer (about ⅛" deep) of dried sphagnum peat moss or planting mix to keep them moist.

Most seeds will germinate in the dimness of their thin cover of planting mix, but some very small seeds—such as lettuce, dill, begonia, and bellflower—require light to germinate (the seed packet will note this). Sow these seeds on top of the mix, gently pressing them down or spritzing with tepid water so they make contact with the mix. Put them under lights or on a sunny windowsill.

A few seeds, like parsley, need complete darkness. Either start them in a closet (don't forget they're there!) or cover the planted seeds with several sheets of moist newspaper. Check every few days to see if they've sprouted.

---

mildewed; they argue that such a live mix provides some nutrients necessary for the seedling's growth as well as helpful microorganisms.

All-purpose commercial sterile (soilless) planting mix is composed of vermiculite (made from mica deposits), milled sphagnum peat moss, and sometimes perlite, which is heat-expanded volcanic rock that resembles plastic but comes from a natural source. Special seed-starting mixes are also readily available at nurseries and from catalogs.

A live mix can be as simple as equal parts of well-sifted, well-rotted compost and vermiculite. Any sterile mix can be enlivened by adding compost to it. Never add soil straight from the garden to planting mixes; even if the soil is rich in humus, watering packs it down too densely to allow roots to take in oxygen. Nor should you try sterilizing your own compost in your oven or microwave. Too much time and space are needed to sterilize sufficient amounts, and even more important, cooked compost or soil leaves a lingering aroma like that of wet dog hair mixed with a little burned rubber and rotten eggs.

SEED-STARTING CONTAINERS

Starting seeds indoors requires a container of some sort to hold the planting mix. Anything with a drainage hole that holds at least 2" of planting mix without contaminating or waterlogging will do. You can use nursery seed trays, flats, cell packs, homemade soil blocks, peat pots, peat pellets, recycled milk cartons, even folded newspaper formed into a biodegradable pot—whatever you find most convenient. Reused containers should be sterilized before use. (To sterilize any recycled container, wash it in a solution of one part bleach and nine parts water. Rinse thoroughly with plain water. Any contaminants that can create problems will be killed by this solution.)

An advantage to starting seeds individually in soil blocks, expanding peat pellets, peat pots, or newspaper pots is that the seedlings can be transplanted directly into the garden without disturbing their tender root systems.

Flats germinate the greatest number of seeds in the least amount of space and are ideal if you don't have much room to work in. With flats, you can start several hundred plants at once; however, you'll have to thin and pot on the seedlings at least once to give them growing room before they can be transplanted out in the garden.

Commercial seed-starting systems, available from nurseries and catalogs, come with a tray that has drainage holes along the bottom, 3"-high sides, and a clear, rigid, tight-fitting lid. The snug lid creates a mini-greenhouse, maintaining even heat and minimizing evaporation during germination. Seedlings have room to grow about 1" tall in a moist, warm environment.

Seedlings started in a commercial seed-starting system benefit from the "greenhouse" atmosphere provided by a clear plastic lid, which retains warmth and moisture while allowing room for plant growth.

FLATS: If you're sowing seeds in a slatted-bottom wooden flat, line the bottom with a sheet or two of newspaper to keep the planting mix from spilling or leaking out. Check commercial flats to be sure there are drainage holes in the bottom; if not, poke holes into them with an ice pick, awl, or similar sharp object. Pour lightly moistened planting mix into the flat to a depth of about 2" (the mix should be about ½" from top of flat), level it, and tamp it down lightly—a cardboard box-flap makes a good trowel to level and tamp.

Depending on the variety of plants you want to grow, and how much space you have, your flats can be used in different ways. If space is limited and you want to start a lot of plants, divide the flats into "rows." Using a popsicle stick, pencil, dibber, ruler edge, or your finger, create furrows or recessed rows about ⅛" deep and spaced about 2" apart. You can sow different types of seeds in each furrow, labeling each row. Seeds started in flats will have to be thinned and transplanted into

individual pots or other larger containers within several weeks after they sprout.

To sow a lot of seeds of the same species, simply broadcast (evenly scatter) the seeds over the entire surface of the planting mix, and label. Once these seedlings grow, they too will need to be thinned and transplanted.

If you want to start seeds without having to pot on before transplanting into the garden, choose a live mix rather than a sterile mix. Such a planting medium will supply nutrients to the seedlings while they're growing in the flat. Using a dibber or pencil, make shallow indentations in

SOWING SMALL SEEDS IN A FLAT

To make small seeds easier to handle, mix them with an equal amount of builder's sand (available at a hardware store or nursery) in a salt shaker and broadcast by lightly shaking over the flat. (Don't use beach sand unless it's been thoroughly rinsed.) The salt shaker method produces fairly even spacing so that thinning is kept to a minimum. Another method is to sow directly from the seed packet by pinching its sides together, creating a funnel down the center of one flap; this seems to allow more control than sowing seeds out of a corner of the top.

To sow small seeds by hand, drop them one by one with a rotating motion of your thumb and forefinger to spread them over the planting medium.

the mix, spaced about 2" apart, then sow one or two seeds in each hollow.

After sowing seeds in a flat, cover them to the proper depth with moistened planting mix or finely sieved peat moss (the latter requires light misting). Then slip the flat into a large plastic bag, close, and place in a warm spot away from direct sunlight—unless, of course, the seed packet stipulates that your seeds require light.

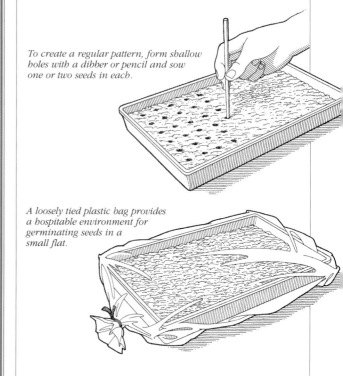

To create a regular pattern, form shallow holes with a dibber or pencil and sow one or two seeds in each.

A loosely tied plastic bag provides a hospitable environment for germinating seeds in a small flat.

SOFT COVERS FOR FLATS

If you're not using a commercial flat with a rigid plastic dome and need to cover your germinating seeds, don't just lay plastic over a large flat; as tender seedlings emerge, they won't have the strength to lift the plastic and may become flattened. The best solution is to rig up a frame over which to hang the plastic, creating a mini-greenhouse. Wire coat hangers are readily accessible and do the job. Cut them with the wire cutter found beneath the teeth of most household pliers and bend them into a U-shape. Insert at least three upside-down U's from end to end across the planting mix so that each straddles the width of the flat, creating a covered-wagon look. Drape plastic over them, being sure to secure the sides and ends to maintain moisture.

In the absence of such a frame, use a flat deep enough so that the rim is at least 2" higher than the surface of the planting mix. Pull the plastic taut across the top of the flat, from one side to another. With a deep flat, there is adequate space for seedlings to emerge without hitting an impenetrable barrier.

A "covered wagon" frame raises the plastic covering, allowing seeds to sprout with plenty of growing room.

CELL PACKS AND INDIVIDUAL CONTAINERS: The advantage of cell packs and individual containers, especially when growing small or medium-size seeds, is that you don't have to pot on before the plants are ready to go into the garden. Cell packs, available with four, six, or eight cells, are especially handy for growing several different varieties of the same plant, such as pansies. One cell pack gives you enough plants for a modest planting of one color variety. With four or five cell packs sown with different pansy cultivars, you'll have enough plants to create a riot of bold color or paint a Jekyllesque palette of muted tones.

Individual containers such as peat pots, 2" or 3" plastic pots, or pots made from newspaper are good if you only want to grow one or two plants of a particular type or a single type of vegetable like tomatoes or peppers. They're also useful when starting large or fast-growing seeds like cucumbers or melons. Or you can be creative and recycle other biodegradable products into bottomless pots. The cardboard rolls from paper towels or toilet or wrapping paper, cut into 2"–3" lengths, make good pots. You can also use milk containers, paper cups, or the like, but be sure to make small drainage holes.

Using a live planting mix rather than a sterile mix, fill the cell pack or container with moist mix, tamp down lightly, then refill to within ½" of the top. Sow one or two seeds per cell or con-

1. Fill with moist mix; compress lightly, then add to refill.

2. Poke one hole in each cell, and sow two seeds for guaranteed results.

3. Cover the seeds with a thin layer of mix.

4. Label each cell before enclosing the container in plastic.

PRETREATING SEEDS TO SPEED GERMINATION

Some seeds benefit from treatment before sowing to induce or hasten the germination process. Sometimes germination is controlled by chemical inhibitors that respond to temperature, preventing the germination process until the seed is warmed in spring. In other cases, seeds are protected by a hard coat that must rot or crack before they can grow. Some seeds must even be subjected to alternating cold and warm periods before they begin the first stirrings of life. If a seed requires pretreatment, the seed packet will say so.

Soaking. As a rule, soaking seeds in tepid to hot water overnight before sowing encourages rapid germination. Presoaking is necessary for seeds with chemical inhibitors that must be leached out before sowing and is recommended for larger, thick-coated seeds like parsley. Soaking seeds of trees such as redbud and honey locust mimics the spring rains, which soften the seed coat in nature.

Scarification. Another way to speed up germination is by scarification—breaking the seed coat so the seed can receive moisture. Nick or chip large seeds (like wisteria) with a sharp knife, removing a small sliver from the end of the seed, or rub the ends with sandpaper. To scarify small seeds, place them in a jar lined with coarse sandpaper, cover, and shake vigorously

Stratification. The seeds of many hardy shrubs and trees, as well as certain perennials such as gas plant and roses, will germinate only after exposure to several months of continuous cold, usually between 32°F. and 45°F. You can simulate winter by covering the seeds with damp peat moss and refrigerating them in a plastic bag for the specified time.

A GARDEN LEGEND

✳

JOHN BARTRAM'S BOTANICAL GARDENS

More than 250 years ago, Quaker farmer John Bartram was plowing his fields when he was stopped in his tracks by a daisy. The flower's beauty and simplicity inspired him to spend the next 40 years exploring the countryside, collecting plants and writing about nature.

"Nature is my telescope to God."

From their farm on the banks of the Schuylkill River near Philadelphia, John Bartram and his son William traveled north to Lake Ontario, south to Florida, and as far west as the Ohio River in search of seeds, roots, bulbs, and cuttings for what is the continent's oldest extant botanical garden.

The Bartrams ultimately propagated more than 4,000 native and exotic species and set up a thriving commercial nursery and catalog, supplying collectors at home (eventually including Jefferson and Washington) as well as specimen-thirsty clients in Europe.

A self-taught botanist and naturalist, John Bartram was also one of the earliest advocates of the "right plant, right place" use of native species, ranking botanical correctness well ahead of aesthetics. He situated his plants according to their cultural and ecological needs and allowed them to grow as they would in nature—with competition from invasive weeds. The result was healthier stock and a somewhat sprawling and overgrown landscape that looks surprisingly fresh to contemporary eyes.

Generations ahead of their time in recognizing the need to balance the concerns of both conservation and commerce, the Bartrams not only left a legacy of vital information about native plants and habitats but also inspired later naturalists such as Henry Thoreau, John Muir, and Rachel Carson.

tainer. Planting two seeds doubles your chance of success: just in case one doesn't germinate, you have an extra. Cover the seeds with mix, label, and bag the cell pack or container as described for flats.

PEAT PELLETS: Like peat pots and biodegradable homemade pots, peat pellets can be planted directly into the garden once the seedlings have reached a respectable size. Soak the pellets in a

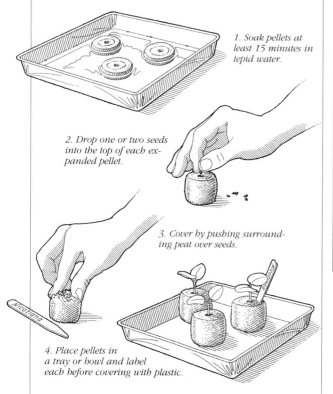

1. Soak pellets at least 15 minutes in tepid water.

2. Drop one or two seeds into the top of each expanded pellet.

3. Cover by pushing surrounding peat over seeds.

4. Place pellets in a tray or bowl and label each before covering with plastic.

shallow bowl or pan of water for about 15 minutes, or until they expand completely. Many peat pellets come with a ready-made planting hole—a small dimple in the top. If yours doesn't have one, poke a small hole ¼"–½" deep in the pellet and sow one or two seeds. Push a bit of the moistened peat from the top of the pellet to cover the seeds. Place on a small tray or shallow bowl, label, and place in a plastic bag.

SOIL BLOCKS: Using blocks of soil for starting seeds is a technique that has been around for

SEED SAVERS EXCHANGE

The social and botanical significance of heirloom seeds is the specialty of the Seed Savers Exchange in Iowa. Devoted to saving open-pollinated vegetables that might otherwise be long extinct, Seed Savers maintains a diverse genetic pool. Among the unusual varieties they have preserved: 'Stump of the World' tomatoes (an Exchange favorite among their 510 varieties), 'Montezuma Red' beans, and 'Old Time' Tennessee muskmelon.

As its name indicates, Seed Savers is an exchange, not a commercial venture; those who join are obligated to grow out and save the seeds they obtain and to share them with others—more a privilege than a chore for the many who get to plant varieties available nowhere else. For an informative two-page newsletter, write: Seed Savers Exchange, 3076 North Winn Road, Decorah, IA 52101. Enclose a SASE.

some two thousand years. Because a soil block is simply a cube of your own live planting mix, it serves as both the medium and the container for the seed. Although making soil blocks may require more time at the beginning of the sowing process, you save time later. While seeds that germinate in flats must be potted on before they can be hardened off and planted in the garden, seedlings in soil blocks can go directly into the ground.

Soil blocks can be made in various sizes to hold a tiny seed, a large seed, or even another, smaller block. A graduated series of blocks enables you to begin seeds in a small block, move that block into a larger one, and, when ready, place that larger block directly into the garden without any danger of root shock. Moreover, unlike some varieties of peat pots, soil blocks make a seamless transition into the garden soil; the plant's roots grow undisturbed, without having to work their way through any barrier.

Using a soil-block tool, it's easy to produce rows of neatly compacted cubes of planting mix, each with a dimple in its top ready to receive a seed. Tools for making soil blocks come in three sizes suitable for home gardening. "Cubers" produce 20 ¾"-cubes at a time; brass "blockers" make four 2" blocks at a stroke; and extra-large blockers create 4" blocks. An investment in two sizes, under $50, lasts a lifetime and usually pays for itself over the first few seasons.

A well-grown seedling in a soil block is ready to transplant directly into the garden. Soil blocks are ideal for plants that prefer not to have their roots disturbed.

1. Press the soil blocker into the planting mix by its handle and fill the blocks.

2. Release the soil blocks by squeezing the plugger. You now have four individual cakes of mix ready for planting.

You can prepare soil-block mix in a clean bucket, wheelbarrow, or old dishpan. The mix itself can be as simple as three parts peat moss to one part well-sifted compost. Use a ¼" screen to sift out all lumps and semicomposted matter to give the mix a fine, granular texture. Water in two or three stages, turning the mix over each time until it takes on the consistency of firm mashed potatoes. Be generous with the water—peat moss absorbs large quantities of moisture. Let the mixture sit at least 15 minutes before using.

To make blocks quickly and efficiently, push the soil blocker down into the mixture by its handle. Then tilt it at a 45° angle and use a trowel to tamp the bottom and to help lift out the blocker. Or, as an alternative method, turn the blocker sideways over the mixture, scoop up the planting mixture, and fill the blocks.

When the blocks are filled, place the blocker's bottom firmly on a hard, clean surface such as a tray or even a commercial flat. Squeeze the plunger to lift up the exterior mold that forms the blocks. If the blocks slump, they're too wet; add more peat moss to the mixture in small increments. Try again until the blocks come away cleanly and maintain their shape.

Once you've made the blocks, drop one or two seeds into the top of each one and cover to a depth of no more than three times the width of the seed. To isolate small seeds, place them in water and use a toothpick (the seed will adhere to it) or tweezers to transfer them individually to the small block dimple. Time-constrained gardeners can simply sprinkle small seeds over the blocks before covering.

If using a commercial flat, cover the tray with the airtight hard plastic dome; otherwise, secure a plastic bag tightly around the tray rim, preferably supported above the blocks by wire-hanger hoops or arches. Place away from direct light to let seeds germinate, monitoring their moisture content to maintain constant dampness.

THE GERMINATION PROMOTERS: MOISTURE, WARMTH, AND AIR

A continual and even supply of moisture, warmth, and air are required for seeds to sprout. Seed embryos rely on a combination of oxygen and carbohydrates that becomes available to them as ample food reserves only when there is sufficient air and moisture. A flat with a raised, rigid roof or a container slipped inside a loose-fitting clear plastic bag, tied shut, supplies the required oxygen and keeps moisture constant.

Since all activities concerning germination involve a chemical reaction of one sort or another, and since most chemical reactions speed up at higher temperatures, a warm planting mix (70°–90°F.) germinates seeds more quickly than a cool one (with a few notable exceptions). Keep germinating seed flats warm on top of a refrigerator, or use electric heating cables to warm flats from below.

Some seeds take up to several weeks to germinate. During this time, it's a good idea to monitor them at least once a day to make sure the planting mix is moist but not soggy. Sterile mixes dry out faster than live mixes. You can tell from the weight of the container whether or not watering is needed. Pick it up and feel its heaviness after you've planted and moistened the seeds thoroughly. If the container becomes lighter at any time during the germination process, add room-temperature water from above, using a watering can fitted with a fine rose, or from below until it feels as heavy as it did initially. Do not overwater: seeds can suffocate and drown.

Germination begins as moisture seeps slowly through the seed coat, providing oxygen and creating pressure in the interior of the seed. The embryo swells until it ruptures the softened seed coat and a root erupts. The stem breaks ground, bearing the cotyledon leaves, and a seedling is born. In time, the cotyledon leaves disappear, and the first true leaves remain on the plant as it grows.

DAMPING OFF

Damping off is a fungal disease that can kill seedlings in a single day. If your seedlings are wilted and you find a dark, rotted area at the base of the stem at the soil line, remove them at once and destroy them. Inspect neighboring seedlings growing in the same container and remove at first sign of disease. Cut back on watering, and be sure the seedlings are getting enough light and air circulation.

Prevention is really the best cure for damping off. The conditions that foster the lethal fungus are poor ventilation and excess moisture, so monitor your plants daily. Sterilize all seed containers before use. Thin overcrowded flats or pots to maximize air circulation around each seedling. Water from below to keep the planting mix from getting too wet. Excess nitrogen (from fertilizer) can stimulate damping off—wait until three true leaves appear before you start fertilizing. Sphagnum peat moss has a mild fungicidal effect. Covering the newly planted seeds with a thin layer of finely sifted sphagnum peat moss is a good prophylactic action.

Seedlings

A seedling is a sprouted seed in search of moisture for its roots and light for its leaves. As soon as plants have germinated, they need both—*immediately*. The fragile-looking sprouts pop up like slender green periscopes searching for a light source. If they fail to find one, they will soon collapse or grow leggy and pale and never fully recover. Be alert for the first signs of life. Since they never break ground all at once, it's helpful to know that the cover can be left on for a day or two after the earliest ones show themselves to give the slower seedlings time to emerge.

Not surprisingly, the most critical time in seedlings' lives is when they first break ground. In addition to light, they thrive on a steady supply of room-temperature water throughout their early stages to stimulate root growth. Because newly emerged seedlings are not sturdy enough to stand up to normal watering, misting them—as often as twice a day—is the best way to keep them evenly moist. Once they're strong enough, gently water, using a fine rose turned upward, around the base of the seedlings and not on the leaves themselves. Or water from below by placing the flat, cell pack, or container in a clean pan filled with tepid water to a level below the rim of the container. Use the fine rose to water around the base of soil blocks and peat pellets, making small puddles of water for them to wick up. If you see mold on the planting mix, or if the seedlings wilt and the soil is damp, decrease the amount of water and be sure there is sufficient light.

Watering from below is recommended for wooden-slatted flats but can also be used for any container with proper drainage holes.

Ideally, seedlings should get 16 hours of light a day, but 12 hours of light is acceptable. The light can come from fluorescent tubes, grow lights, or the sun, indoors or outside, depending on temperature and time of year. Seedlings require less warmth than do germinating seeds—

60°–70°F. in the daytime, about 50°F. at night—and fare better if not kept in hot rooms when started indoors. (A Farmer's Almanac adage: Start seeds warm, keep seedlings cool.) Generally, a seed has enough food reserves to keep it alive until the true leaves appear and the seedling can start producing food for itself.

Set seedlings on a sunny windowsill fitted with shelf brackets and a board on which to seat the containers. Curtain the window or move the seedlings at night in cold climates to prevent

FLUORESCENT LIGHTING

There really is no need to spend money on expensive grow lights; fluorescent lights produce healthy seedlings at less cost. Two or three 48"-long, cool white tubes in a fixture suspended on chains can illuminate a 5'-square area. After seeds have sprouted (never before), remove their cover and position the fluorescent tubes about 3" above the top of the seedlings for the first weeks. After that, raise the lights to 6" above the seedlings. The chains provide a practical way to move the lights, maintaining the proper distance as the seedlings grow. Keep seedlings under light 12–16 hours a day, until it's time to harden off.

Fluorescent lighting can be adjusted by fixtures on chains as seedlings grow.

chilling. Turn containers regularly to keep plants from leaning to one side toward the light. Many gardeners prefer to install fluorescent fixtures as a more controllable light source. Electric bills go up; frustration, on the other hand, usually decreases.

Once it has three true leaves, the seedling needs additional nourishment. Always feed plants after you've watered them. Seedlings grown in a live medium can be fed with half-strength liquid fertilizer twice a week for the first three weeks, then full-strength every 10 to 14 days. Seedlings started in a sterile mix, especially in a flat, usually have to be potted on before they need to be fed. If not, give them a half-strength solution of liquid fertilizer twice a week until you transplant them. Too much nitrogen can stimulate damping off, so be sure to wait until three true leaves have developed before using fertilizer.

Seedlings grown in flats usually need to be thinned before potting on so that there is less competition for nutrients and more room for roots to grow. Thin after the first set of true leaves appears. Don't try to pull seedlings out by the roots; all the other seedlings' roots will be disturbed. Instead, using manicure scissors, nip off the stems of overcrowded seedlings at soil level. Thin to allow 1½"–2" between each plant. Although it may seem counterproductive to kill off seedlings that you've been nurturing, it really is necessary. Reducing competition for moisture, light, and air produces healthy survivors spaced far enough apart to prevent their roots from entangling as they extend out into new territory like foragers. Crowded plants become weakened and will be more prone to pests and disease. Sacrificing one or two seedlings in order to grow one strong healthy plant is far better than having two weak plants that fail to thrive, flower, or even produce fruit.

The following abbreviated list of do's and don'ts will simplify the task of keeping your seedlings in the best of health.

■ Be careful not to overwater. A soggy planting medium encourages damping off and root rot.

■ Plants that look spindly, weak, and pale, with leaves that are not compact, probably need more light.

■ Be sure to keep seedlings in an environment that is not too warm. Never put them on top of a covered radiator; too much heat will weaken the young plants.

■ Don't start seedlings too early in the season, or they'll be too far along when it's time to plant them outside—they'll be spoiled by the luxurious life they enjoyed indoors. If you can't plant out in the garden when anticipated, use a cold frame for several weeks rather than keeping plants going indoors. Plants at this stage may have overgrown their containers; if you have to postpone planting out in the garden, it may be worth the effort to pot on to the next larger size container.

■ Remember to harden off seedlings so they can gradually adjust to garden conditions.

Potting On: Transplanting Seedlings into Larger Containers

Although two-week-old seedlings may look too fragile to move, they are surprisingly adaptable and can adjust to relocation with minimal discomfort if properly handled and supplied with their basic needs. There are several sound reasons to move seedlings to a larger container before setting them out in the garden. Plants that germinated in a sterile mix can take advantage of any micronutrients in a potting mix and benefit from increased air circulation for their root systems. Those that are growing in rows or that were broadcast in a flat will get the room they need to grow when transplanted into cell packs or 4" pots. If small seeds were started in 2" soil blocks, they can stay put: they don't need additional room to grow. Place those in ¾" blocks into 2" blocks, if necessary. Larger seeds, or fast-growing plants like tomatoes, will need potting into larger containers.

Fill the clean, sterile container with moistened potting mix and let it sit for about 15 minutes. Next, using a pencil, popsicle stick, or dib-ber, loosen the mix completely around the seedling as you support it gently by its leaves with your other hand. Carefully pry the seedling from the mix, keeping its root system intact, dirt and all. Poke a depression into the moistened potting soil about as deep as the plant's roots and wide enough to accommodate them without disturbance. Gently lower the seedling into the hole, then firm the soil around its stem with your fingertips. Add a small amount of water around the

COLD FRAMES

By controlling weather conditions, cold frames can extend a growing season or, more commonly, begin one earlier than outside conditions allow—a boon for starting seeds and for hardening off. In areas with not-too-severe winters, cold frames enable gardeners to grow hardy crops (like lettuce and spinach) in winter. When seated over flower beds, they also provide winter protection for tender perennials. In summer, topless cold frames placed in a shaded area can be used to start cold-weather seeds for fall crops.

These enclosed structures consist of a framed transparent lid that sits on top of a bottomless rectangular box whose sides slope down toward the front at a 45° angle. Glass or Plexiglas is used for commercial lids; old sash-type windows or storm windows are traditional in homemade cold frames. If home-constructed, the banked wood base (¾" plywood is an acceptable lumber) should be treated with linseed oil and caulk to ensure a water-tight seal. Portable cold frames come in models that collapse when not in use; larger ones obviously remain in place.

The cold frame collects solar heat, warming its interior when exposed to full sunlight. An interior painted white or lined with foil will increase reflective light, useful in the coldest climates. A site facing south prolongs sunlight exposure and is recommended. An old blanket is useful for covering the frame during a prolonged winter freeze.

A cold frame requires monitoring to prevent plant-burning and disease. The inside temperature can get very hot. One warm day with the lid closed can steam your plants. Maintain a favorable temperature (a thermometer is essential), and provide ventilation by opening and shutting the lid. If you're short on time, look for a cold frame with an automatic vent that opens and closes, adjusting to changes in temperature. You can also buy such a mechanism to attach to a homemade cold frame.

Water early in the day, and frequently; the heat in a cold frame quickly evaporates moisture. Pests, snails, and slugs that may enter as stowaways on flats or other containers thrive once inside and can create havoc. Be sure to check for them thoroughly and remove them—along with any diseased or wounded plants—at once.

base, taking care that the seedling is planted at the same depth as it was in the original container. (Tomatoes are the exception. They can go deeper—almost up to their leaves.) Transfer the label, adding date of transplant.

Lift a young seedling with care, supporting its roots and surrounding mix as you transfer it to a larger container.

Place the seedling in moistened potting soil, gently lowering it into the hole prepared beforehand. Firm the soil around the stem.

Newly transplanted seedlings must be handled delicately. Keep them out of direct light (sun or fluorescent lighting) for at least the first day. If they seem stressed or start to wilt, check the moisture. If necessary, go back to misting them twice a day to maintain soil moisture. After about a week, you can water the transplants—this is best done in the morning—by putting the containers in a pan or tray of water that will be absorbed from below without creating any root disturbance. You may not need to water more than twice a week, but check the transplants daily. Feed with diluted half-strength solution of liquid organic fertilizer (kelp is excellent) twice a week for the first 3 weeks after transplanting. Then continue to feed every 10 days to 2 weeks

PREVENTING PEST DAMAGE TO YOUNG TRANSPLANTS

Fresh, young transplants may need extra protection against a whole host of garden pests. A simple paper or metal collar around a plant will thwart slugs, snails, and cutworms. A paper cup or tuna can is perfect—just remove the bottom of the cup or can and slip it over the new transplant in the garden. Be sure that at least 1" of the collar is below soil level, with the rest sticking above the soil. Ideally, there should be no more than an inch of space between the collar and the stem of the plant.

Another way to discourage slugs and snails is to make a circle about 1" wide and ¼"–½" high around the plant with diatomaceous earth (available inexpensively and in large quantity at pool supply stores, more costly at garden centers). It abrades the soft bellies of these creatures when they crawl across it, drawing moisture and desiccating them.

Some birds and rabbits find young plants irresistible. New transplants can easily be protected with a loose covering of chicken wire or bird netting. Form several hoops from wire hangers and slip the chicken wire or netting over them. Be sure the covering goes all the way to the ground—some critters can be persistent!

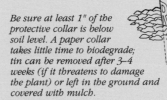

Be sure at least 1" of the protective collar is below soil level. A paper collar takes little time to biodegrade; tin can be removed after 3–4 weeks (if it threatens to damage the plant) or left in the ground and covered with mulch.

SEED-SAVING: A NATURAL ECONOMY

The seeds of many non-hybrid (open-pollinated) fruits, vegetables, and annuals can be saved, dried, stored, and germinated at home. Seed-saving harks back to the time when gardeners had to use every available local resource to regenerate their crops—generally seeds started from their own plants in soil amended with home-grown decayed vegetation (compost). They entered into a pact with their garden, replenishing its needs in return for its bounty. Much has changed since then, but the garden remains a place to stay in touch with the earth's cycles of birth, death, and rebirth.

There are also practical benefits in saving seeds. Heirlooms can be shared with and given to friends, often in exchange for other hard-to-find varieties. The seeds germinated from home-grown plants in your organic garden will be free from synthetic chemicals. In addition, saved seeds seem to produce corn that tastes sweeter, tomatoes that burst with juice, and flowers that shimmer with vigor and color.

The time to harvest flower or vegetable seeds approaches when the pods that contain them become dried out and appear ready to crack open, or when the fleshy vegetables or fruits containing them ripen fully on the vine (before rot can begin).

The fleshy seeds found in melons, eggplant, tomatoes, cucumber, and members of the squash family must be separated out and washed off thoroughly. They must then be soaked for a few days in airtight, labeled glass containers filled with water until they sink and detach themselves from the surrounding pulp, which floats to the top and appears to ferment. Pour the mixture through a fine sieve or mesh, discard the (odoriferous) water, and dry the seeds.

Moisture is the stored seed's adversary. To eliminate it, spread out all your seeds—pod-dried and fleshy—to dry for a week or more, preferably on a screen in a non-windy place where air freely circulates. Don't pack the seeds until they have dried completely (the time will vary with the humidity). If you're unsure about dryness, put the seeds in a small, airtight glass jar and place in a sunny spot for about five minutes. Any sign of condensation means back to the drying screen. In an area of high humidity, you may have trouble getting seeds to dry thoroughly; try running a dehumidifier in the house, with the seeds on mesh nearby. Don't be in a hurry: total dryness is crucial.

Finally, store the dried seeds in waxed paper or paper envelopes. Seal and label each packet, and store in a cool, dark place in an airtight container impervious to dampness and household pests. Be forewarned: mice love seeds. Many gardeners store seeds in the freezer in moisture-free containers. Most seeds will last for years—peas, parsnips, and beans are exceptions. Freezing before planting also helps some plants, like clematis and gas plant, to germinate quickly.

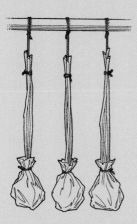

One way to guarantee a seed harvest is to cover the seed heads with cheesecloth as they begin to brown. When the pods are completely dry, cut the stems to a uniform length, tie them in bundles, and hang them upside down; the cheesecloth will catch the seeds when the pods break open. Remove the cheesecloth bag and shake the seeds onto newspaper or plastic before packaging them.

with full-strength fertilizer until you plant them in the garden. Transplants usually stay indoors for another 4 weeks, until after the last spring frost.

Young plants require a smooth transition from their protected environment indoors to their outdoor growing conditions. You can introduce them to outdoor conditions, gradually and gingerly, through a process called "hardening off." First cut back (but don't cut out completely) their watering and feeding for their final week indoors. Then move them to a sheltered, lightly shaded spot outside for a few hours to begin the hardening-off process. Increase their exposure to outside conditions for an hour or two each day for one or two weeks before planting them outside; always bring them inside for the night. Water as needed and feed once during this period. During their last few hardening-off days, leave the plants out day and night, and expose them to direct sunlight for about four hours each day.

Transplanting into the Garden

After hardening off, your plants are ready to go into the garden. By now you've cultivated and amended the soil in preparation for the transplants. For about three days before transplanting, "charge" the soil—that is, saturate it with water to stimulate rapid root growth and diminish the possibility that a peat pot or soil block, if used, will dry out and cake.

Transplant in the late afternoon or on an overcast, drizzly day. Dig a hole about twice as wide and deep as the plant's root system. Fill the hole with water and let it sink down into the surrounding soil. Remove the plant from its container, spreading the fingers of your free hand to catch the plant as it slides out. Take the potless seedling in hand, spread its root system gently apart (see page 147), and insert it into the hole at the same depth it was growing. (Do not bury the

COLD-WEATHER PROTECTION

The first cloches, or miniature greenhouses in the form of glass bell jars, were placed over individual plants by French farmers more than a century ago and have been used to extend the growing season ever since. They keep the soil and air warm, protect plants from frost, and can be moved around at will. They also shield seeds and seedlings from harm; wind, birds, and airborne insects cannot penetrate them. Moreover, when not in use as a mini-greenhouse, they make lovely garden ornaments.

Although none of the newer products approaches the etched French bell jars in elegance of design, they provide a serviceable alternative.

Most popular is the "Wall o' Water," a series of interconnected vertical plastic tubes that fill with water and act as a solar blanket, transferring the heat collected during the day to the plant they surround at night.

Available commercially, the "Wall o' Water" is a modern-day version of the cloche; the water absorbs heat during the day and slowly releases it at night, keeping plants alive even in freezing weather. Homemade cloches can be fashioned from plastic, spunbonded fiber (such as Reemay), or waxed paper.

A "covered wagon" frame raises the plastic covering, allowing seeds to sprout with plenty of growing room.

stem.) Fill the hole with loose soil, tamp down firmly, and add water around the stem, being careful not to wet the leaves. Water daily until the transplant becomes established, usually within 10 days, and feed weekly with diluted kelp or fish emulsion. After a month or so, you can use a full-strength fertilizer.

Because of their high peat moss concentration, soil blocks, peat pots, and peat pellets must be thoroughly moistened before being planted in the garden. For peat pots, remove the rim above the soil and slit the sides and bottom to prevent root-binding when planting. Soil blocks, peat pellets, and peat pots should be completely buried—just below soil level—in the garden. If any portion is above soil level, they will dry out and wick moisture away from the plant.

The same simple, reliable, and efficient techniques for transplanting home-grown seedlings into the garden also apply to nursery-grown seedlings.

Sowing Seeds Outdoors

Seeds sown directly into the garden sprout and grow into healthy seedlings under the same conditions as indoor seeds, i.e., with sufficient moisture, air, and warmth. Rely on seed packets for information on where and when to plant as well as how far apart seeds should be.

Soil temperature determines when seeds can be planted safely. Seeds do not germinate if the soil is too cold; if it's both cold and wet, seeds are more likely to rot than sprout. Air temperature determines whether or not the sprouted seedlings will survive. This is why many seed packets advise against planting before all danger of frost is past. Most seeds can be sown outdoors once the soil temperature reaches 60°F. If you feel insecure about judging the soil temperature, a soil thermometer is a good, inexpensive investment. If you try to sow when the ground is still cold, the

PLANTS TO DIRECT-SEED IN THE GARDEN

The flowers and vegetables listed below do not transplant well and are best seeded directly into the garden once the soil is warm enough and workable in spring. If you want to start these plants indoors, sow the seeds in soil blocks or peat pellets, so their roots aren't disturbed when transplanting.

Baby's breath (*Gypsophila paniculata*)*
Bachelor's buttons (*Centaurea cyanus*)
Beans (*Phaseolus vulgaris*)*
Beets (*Beta vulgaris*)*
Butterfly weed (*Asclepias tuberosa*)*
Calendulas (*Calendula officinalis*)*
Carrots (*Daucus carota*)*
Corn (*Zea mays*)*
Cosmos (*Cosmos* spp.)*
Cucumbers (*Cucumis sativus*)*
Flossflowers (*Ageratum houstonianum*)*
Flowering tobacco (*Nicotiana* spp.)*
Four-o'clocks (*Mirabilis jalapa*)
Larkspur (*Consolida ambigua*)*
Love-in-a-mist (*Nigella* spp.)*
Nasturtiums (*Tropaeolum majus*)*
Okra (*Abelmoschus esculentus*)
Peas (*Pisum sativum*)*
Spiderflower (*Cleome hassleriana*)*
Stock (*Matthiola incana*)
Sweet peas (*Lathyrus odoratus*)*
Turnips (*Brassica rapa*)*
Verbena (*Verbena* spp.)*

*Included in the Plant Guide, pages 276-479.

seeds may germinate poorly, if at all.

Soil preparation is crucial when you sow directly into the garden. While many seedlings can survive the bacteria and fungi that thrive in garden soil, few can withstand oxygen deprivation and waterlogging. Your goal is to produce a

DIVIDING PERENNIALS

Some perennials need to be divided every year, while others resent being divided at all; the majority of perennials fall between the two extremes. Before dismissing the more vigorous plants as too much work, remember that their rapid growth makes them very effective for filling in areas inexpensively over the course of several years.

DIVIDE YEARLY

Big-root geranium (*Geranium macrorrhizum*)

Obedient plant (*Physostegia virginiana*)

Ribbon grass (*Phalaris arundinacea*)

Spiderwort (*Tradescantia virginiana*)*

Yarrow (*Achillea* spp.)*

DIVIDE EVERY 2–3 YEARS

Aster (*Aster* spp.)*

Bee balm (*Monarda* spp.)*

Evening primrose (*Oenothera* spp.)*

Painted daisy (*Tanacetum coccineum*)

Sneezeweed (*Helenium* spp.)

DIVIDE AS NEEDED

Artemisia (*Artemisia* spp.)

Astilbe (*Astilbe* spp.)*

Bellflower (*Campanula* spp.)*

Blanket flower (*Gaillardia* spp.)*

Cranesbill (*Geranium* spp.)*

Dahlia (*Dahlia* spp.)*

Daylily (*Hemerocallis* spp.)*

False rockcress (*Aubrieta* spp.)

Hosta (*Hosta* spp.)*

Lamb's ears (*Stachys byzantina*)*

Larkspur (*Delphinium* spp.)*

Lily of the valley (*Convallaria majalis*)*

Pampas grass (*Cortaderia selloana*)*

Pincushion flower (*Scabiosa* spp.)*

Pink (*Dianthus* spp.)*

Purple coneflower (*Echinacea purpurea*)*

Snow-in-summer (*Cerastium tomentosum*)*

Speedwell (*Veronica* spp.)*

Stonecrop (*Hylotelephium spectabile*)*

Sweet woodruff (*Galium odoratum*)*

Tickseed (*Coreopsis* spp.)*

DO NOT DIVIDE

Bleeding heart (*Dicentra* spp.)*

Carolina lupine (*Thermopsis villosa*)*

Christmas rose (*Helleborus niger*)*

Cinnamon fern (*Osmunda cinnamomea*)*

Columbine (*Aquilegia* spp.)*

False indigo (*Baptisia* spp.)*

Foxtail lily (*Eremurus* spp.)*

Gas plant (*Dictamnus albus*)*

Lupine (*Lupinus* spp.)*

Oriental poppy (*Papaver orientale*)*

Included in the Plant Guide, pages 276-479.

---

soft and pliant planting medium for seeds, one that will provide sufficient air and moisture for germination. The soil should be worked at least one foot deep, if not deeper. Once the bed is properly prepared, you're ready to plant your seeds.

DIVISION

For the resourceful gardener, division constitutes an easy, effective, and inexpensive way to proliferate favorite perennials and bulbs, especially when they outgrow their space and their flowering is diminished. It's the best way to propagate plants that multiply by means of suckers, rhizomes, underground growths, or offsets, and is the method of choice for many plants with woody crowns and fibrous roots, like most perennials. Division is handy for filling out ornamental gardens with minimum effort and expense.

Perennials

While perennials can reproduce from seed, many of them are cultivars that will not breed true (reliably produce offspring that resemble their parents) when started from seed. In addition, it may be three years before a perennial grown from seed is large enough to bloom.

Most perennials can be divided; indeed, division is necessary from time to time as a means of rejuvenating a plant and encouraging more blooms. You can divide when you want more of a particular plant, or you can wait until the plant tells you it's time to be divided—the plant will look crowded and its blooms sparse and smaller than in other years. Some plants, like chrysanthemums, may need rejuvenative division every couple of years, but others, including some iris and peonies, can remain undivided for decades. Most perennials fall between those extremes, needing division every three to five years.

Divisions are made from mature plants, usually in the fall, and should bloom the next season. In cold-winter areas, divide your perennials four to six weeks before the first frost date so the new divisions have time to get established before the weather gets too cold.

Many perennials can be divided right in the ground with a sharp spade before removing and replanting one section.

Water the plant the day before dividing, then wait to remove it until late afternoon or until the plant is shaded. Dig out the plant with care, making a wide, deep hole with a spade or fork in order to take out its entire root system, which may extend laterally at least a foot beyond the crown of the plant. Shake off any embedded soil and clip away dead growth and any tall stems.

A practiced foot is often your best division tool. Step down firmly on a sharp spade to split an older root system cleanly into two halves, each one like the original plant. If this method is too daunting, you can lift the plant out of the garden before dividing. As you divide any perennial, look at the plant's center to see how it has grown. If the roots are old and tough in the center of the plant or the crown is woody, cut out that portion, sav-

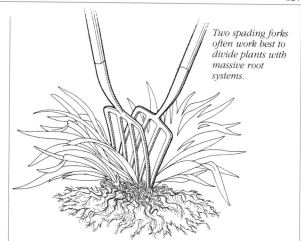

Two spading forks often work best to divide plants with massive root systems.

ing only newer, more vigorous roots and crown from around the center.

Depending on the size of the plant, you may get three or more divisions from it. If the plant has a cluster of crowns, pull the clump apart or cut it with a knife; be certain that there are growth buds or eyes on each new division where new shoots will form. Replant each clump immediately in a fresh hole whose soil has been amended. Plant the clump at the same depth as the original plant. Fill the hole with the soil, tamp down, and water well.

Small plants like primroses are easily separated by hand, but larger plants with more tightly massed roots and crowns call for more serious tools. A large mass of crowns separates most easily with two spading forks pushed back to back in the center of the clump. Rock the handles of the forks back and forth until the roots and crowns release and separate. Phlox and many ornamental grasses form such tight, thick clumps that you

Smaller plants often can be dug up and divided easily by hand.

may have to use a sharp spade or hatchet to separate them.

Peonies, daylilies, and other perennials with fleshy roots require special attention. Look closely at the roots, and you'll see the growth buds. Pull or cut apart the roots so that each new section has several buds, then replant each section.

Some perennials, like irises, have fleshy rhizomes that grow underground or just barely above the soil. Pull or cut them apart so that each new division contains at least one bud on its rhizome. Replant each division at the same depth it was planted before.

Bulbs

Many bulbs, like tulips and daffodils, multiply naturally in the soil, producing bulblets that grow into new bulbs. In time, the bulblets will compete with the main bulb for water and nutrients, and your bed of tulips or daffodils will be lush and green—but without bloom. This is the time to divide. After the leaves have turned yellow, in late spring or early summer, dig up the bulbs, pull off the bulblets, and replant them at the same depth as the parent bulbs.

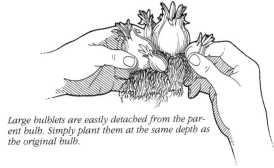

Large bulblets are easily detached from the parent bulb. Simply plant them at the same depth as the original bulb.

Some plants, like crocus, gladiolus, and iris, grow from corms, not true bulbs. The original corm dies each year, and a new one takes its place. Small cormels form around the base of the new corm. To divide, dig up the corms after the foliage ripens and turns yellow—crocus in late spring, gladiolus and iris in fall. Discard the old

corm, and replant the new corm and cormels. In cold-winter areas, store the corm and cormels in a cool, dry area, packed in sawdust or dry peat moss, until time to plant in spring.

Scaling is an easy way to increase your supply of lily bulbs. Planted in a container, scales produce new bulbs that go in the ground come spring.

Lily bulbs, which resemble bulb garlic with scales that surround the mature bulb, offer another means of propagation called scaling. Because scaly bulbs do not develop protective membranes, they must be handled delicately to ensure that their root systems do not drop off during division. The best time to scale lilies is in the fall. Dig up a mature bulb, then carefully separate the outer scales. Plant the scales in a flat or pot filled with a moist mix of equal parts peat moss and sand. The scales will grow over the winter, producing new bulbs that can be planted in the spring. Some lilies propagate by producing bulbils, which are small bulbs that look like little black or brown jelly beans and grow in the leaf axils along the stem. Plant bulbils in the ground or as described above for scales. Depending on the type of lily, it takes one to four years before bulbils or scales produce plants mature enough to flower.

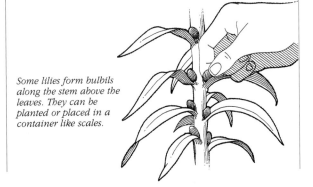

Some lilies form bulbils along the stem above the leaves. They can be planted or placed in a container like scales.

Most bearded irises need to be divided every three to five years. In preparation for dividing, prune them in late summer or early fall (if you didn't do this earlier). Using a sharp knife or scissors, cut the foliage 8"–10" above soil level, trimming it into a fan shape. Carefully dig up the old clumps. Divide the rhizomes with a sharp knife, making sure that each new division has a strong root section and a single fan of leaves. To avoid spreading disease, dip the knife in rubbing alcohol or a 10% solution of household bleach between each cut. Discard the oldest (center) part of the rhizome. Check for evidence of disease or borers. Destroy (do not compost) any infested rhizomes. Dust the cut surface of the rhizomes with powdered sulfur, which acts as a fungicide and averts disease and pests, and allow to dry for one or two days. Replant the horizontal rhizome with the top third or half of the rhizome showing above the soil.

CUTTINGS

Cuttings are small fragments of stems, leaves, or roots that form new roots of their own. That these chips off the old block somehow grow to become the block itself is equally as thrilling as a seed's journey into planthood. As a method of propagation, taking cuttings is an effective and inexpensive way to grow numerous popular flowers and shrubs, including geraniums, veronica, azaleas, dogwoods, and hollies. Taking cuttings also enables you to propagate many hybrid plants that would not come true from seed. Only a sharp blade, a delicate hand, and patience are required.

In addition to the real economy of duplicating or cloning plants in this fashion, you may begin to see the universe of growing plants as a vast resource for your home garden. A snipped stem from a neighbor's bellflower is all you need to grow your own, and since most propagation succeeds with little effort, you'll find yourself justifiably eager to try a wide assortment of flowers, vines, and shrubs. Several years later, walking through your garden, you may stop to push back a sprawling barberry branch laden with foliage, and realize only then that the vigorous, berried plant began life as a nondescript 6" stem stuck in a pot. Such moments serve as reminders of the extraordinary life force at work in your garden.

Cuttings require a water-retentive yet light planting medium, preferably containing vermiculite and peat moss. (Garden soil, which packs down densely when wet, is not recommended.) Depending on your climate, you can grow your cuttings outdoors, in a cool, shady location, or indoors, in the same conditions you would use to start seeds. Cuttings also need moisture, both in the soil and in the air. Large quantities of cuttings may require a greenhouse or a cold frame. For a small number of cuttings, the simplest way to create an ideal environment is to construct a mini-greenhouse, using a clear plastic bag that minimizes evaporation by completely enclosing its well-watered planting pot. Open the bag every day for an hour or so to allow air to circulate, add water only if the soil feels dry, and remove the bag after the cuttings have become well rooted (the duration varies depending on the species). Gently wiggle the cutting when you first plant it. Initially, it will feel very loose; as it roots, it becomes increasingly difficult to wiggle.

Herbaceous Stem Cuttings

Creating new plants from stem cuttings is a technique generally used on the young vigorous growth of herbaceous plants—annuals and perennials. For annuals and summer- and fall-blooming perennials, the best time to take stem cuttings is in the spring. You can also take cuttings of annuals (to winter over indoors) and spring-blooming perennials in summer or early fall.

PLANTS TO PROPAGATE FROM STEM CUTTINGS

HARDWOOD STEM CUTTINGS

Andromeda (*Pieris japonica*)*
Beauty bush (*Kolwitzia amabilis*)
Bougainvillea (*Bougainvillea* spp.)*
Boxwood (*Buxus* spp.)*
Butterfly bush (*Buddleia* spp.)*
Cotoneaster (*Cotoneaster* spp.)*
Dawn redwood (*Metasequoia glyptostroboides*)
Firethorn (*Pyracantha* spp.)
Forsythia (*Forsythia* spp.)*
Grape (*Vitis* spp.)*
Holly (*Ilex* spp.)*
Honeysuckle (*Lonicera* spp.)*
Japanese aucuba (*Aucuba japonica*)
Kolomikta actinidia (*Actinidia kolomikta*)
Mountain laurel (*Kalmia latifolia*)*
Poplar (*Populus* spp.)
Raspberry (*Rubus* spp.)
Rose of Sharon (*Hibiscus syriacus*)
Spirea (*Spiraea* spp.)*
Virginia creeper (*Parthenocissus quinquefolia*)

HERBACEOUS STEM CUTTINGS

ANNUALS

Begonia (*Begonia* spp.)
Coleus (*Coleus* spp.)
Impatiens (*Impatiens* spp.)*
Larkspur (*Delphinium* spp.)*

PERENNIALS

Baby's breath (*Gypsophila paniculata*)
Bee balm (*Monarda* spp.)*
Bellflower (*Campanula* spp.)*
Blanket flower (*Gaillardia* spp.)*
Butterfly weed (*Asclepias tuberosa*)*
Lavender (*Lavandula* spp.)*
Mint (*Mentha* spp.)*
Periwinkle (*Vinca* spp.)
Pink (*Dianthus* spp.)*
Speedwell (*Veronica* spp.)*
Sundrop (*Oenothera* spp.)*
Thyme (*Thymus* spp.)*

Included in the Plant Guide, pages 276-479.

SOFTWOOD STEM CUTTINGS

Abelia (*Abelia* spp.)
Barberry (*Berberis* spp.)*
Beauty bush (*Kolkwitzia amabilis*)
Birch (*Betula* spp.)
Blueberry (*Vaccinium* spp.)*
Broom (*Cytisus* spp.)
Cinquefoil (*Potentilla* spp.)*
Cherry (*Prunus* spp.)
Clematis (*Clematis* spp.)*
Deutzia (*Deutzia* spp.)
Fothergilla (*Fothergilla* spp.)*
Fuchsia (*Fuchsia* spp.)
Heath (*Erica* spp.)
Hibiscus (*Hibiscus* spp.)
Hydrangea (*Hydrangea* spp.)*
Maidenhair tree (*Ginkgo biloba*)
Maple (*Acer* spp.)*
Mock orange (*Philadelphus* spp.)*
Privet (*Ligustrum* spp.)
Rose (*Rosa* spp.)*
Russian olive (*Elaeanus angustifolia*)
Spirea (*Spiraea* spp.)*
Trumpet vine (*Campsis* spp.)*
Viburnum (*Viburnum* spp.)*
Weigela (*Weigela* spp.)

Using a sharp knife or a single-edge razor blade, cut a 3"–5" length off the end of a flexible stem. Make the cut just below a node (the place where the leaf is attached). Carefully cut off and remove the lower leaves to expose two or three nodes. This is where most of the new root growth will occur. If you want, you can dip the stem into rooting hormone, covering all the cut surfaces with the powder. Fill the pot with moistened perlite or coarse sand. Use a dibber or pencil to make a hole in the medium, and insert the cutting so that the bare portion of the stem will be completely covered. With your fingers, gently press the medium around the cutting. You can root six to eight cuttings (of the same plant) in a 6" pot.

Cover the pot with plastic, and set in a warm, well-lit place (not in full sun, or the cuttings will steam) for about six weeks. Check the moisture weekly; mist to remoisten. After six weeks, most cuttings will have rooted. When transplanting the rooted cuttings, use a dibber to create a hole in the planting mix, then insert the cutting; don't press the cutting into position, or you risk compromising the fragile roots.

Softwood Stem Cuttings

The best time to take softwood (green) cuttings is before the new growth hardens—when the stems are neither too soft nor too woody.

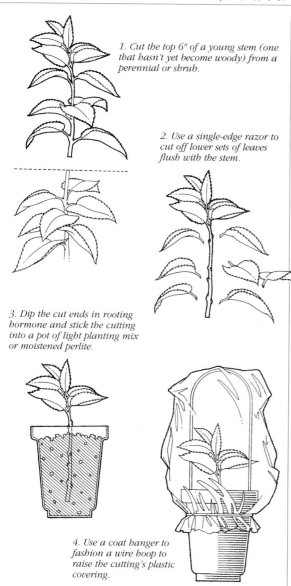

1. Cut the top 6" of a young stem (one that hasn't yet become woody) from a perennial or shrub.

2. Use a single-edge razor to cut off lower sets of leaves flush with the stem.

3. Dip the cut ends in rooting hormone and stick the cutting into a pot of light planting mix or moistened perlite.

4. Use a coat hanger to fashion a wire hoop to raise the cutting's plastic covering.

Most trees and shrubs are best propagated from June to August. You may want to take cuttings from tender perennials treated as annuals in early fall, growing them indoors over the winter to get a jump start on the season the following spring.

Water the parent plant well a day or two before taking cuttings. Choose stems that are strong and healthy, but avoid those that are the largest or most prolific. Generally, side shoots that are firm but flexible are best—neither so pliant that they crush easily, nor so hard that they

break. However, there are individual differences among plants; lilacs and azaleas are best propagated when very soft and young, while weigela and hydrangea are best cut late in the season, when they are at their sturdiest.

Use side shoots from 2" to 6" long, cut cleanly at the base—taking care not to wound the main stem. If there are no good shoots, take the cuttings from top shoots 6" or longer. Take three or four cuttings to build in a margin for error.

The procedure itself is uncomplicated. Cut the shoot below its terminal (end) bud, then cut off a 6" length just below a leaf node (the stem juncture). Remove all buds and flowers, then prune off the bottom two sets of leaves at their nodes, dip the bottom few inches in rooting hormone, and plant, leafless end down, in a 2" or 4" pot filled with a moistened, light, sterile planting medium. Be sure to bury at least one node—this is where new roots will form. If the cutting isn't going immediately into the pot, wrap it in moist burlap or wet newspaper and keep it away from direct sunlight.

Place the pot indoors, out of direct sun but in bright light, wrapped in a plastic bag for the first month or so to maintain constant humidity and monitored every few days for evaporation. You can use wire hoops made from coat hangers to raise the plastic off the plant. Keep the planting medium moist but not soggy. Uncover the container every day for an hour or so to prevent mildew. Fluorescent lights, 8"–9" above the tops of the cuttings, provide sufficient light when kept on for 12 hours a day. Once its roots are established, harden off the cutting by removing its protective bag for several hours a day. Repot into a larger container, in a planting mix containing nutrients, or plant directly into a prepared garden bed within a few days.

You can also root softwood cuttings outdoors in a cold frame. Do not wrap the pot in a plastic bag; instead, provide moisture by misting several times a day. Keep the cuttings shaded with cheesecloth or shadecloth for the first 7–10 days.

Once the cuttings are established, gradually remove the shade.

Cuttings taken in the spring are often ready to be planted in the garden by fall. Those taken in summer, or those slow to root, can be wintered over in a cold frame and planted out the following spring.

Hardwood Stem Cuttings

Hardwood cuttings, including those from deciduous trees and shrubs, are taken from woody stems that are a year old and fully firm. They do not require high humidity and all the care that softwood cuttings do. They need a cold rest period until early spring and then can be planted outdoors in a cold frame or sheltered nursery bed. Cuttings are best taken during the plant's dormant stage, preferably in fall after the leaves have dropped. Ideally, the cuttings come from a parent plant that has been rigorously pruned back the previous year, stimulating hormones in its stems that will promote root growth when planted.

Choose a pencil-thin stem up to 30" long, and cut it off near its base. Don't use spindly branches or canes that have grown from the base of the plant. Remove any leaves from evergreen stems. Cut the stem into pieces between 6" and 10" long. Make the top cut straight across just above a bud or node (which appears as a slight protrusion on the stem). Make the bottom cut at an angle ⅛" below a bud or node, where the stem is less susceptible to fungal rot. The angled cut will clearly indicate the lower end, which should always be planted in your medium.

In mild-winter areas, hardwood cuttings can go directly into the ground. Dig a large hole, add compost to the soil, mix well and refill, then water well. Moisten and dip the lower portion of each cutting into rooting hormone. Insert the cuttings into the refilled hole, leaving three buds

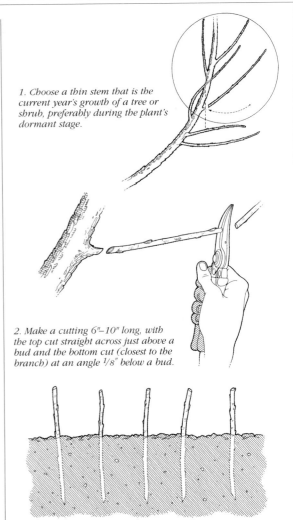

1. Choose a thin stem that is the current year's growth of a tree or shrub, preferably during the plant's dormant stage.

2. Make a cutting 6"–10" long, with the top cut straight across just above a bud and the bottom cut (closest to the branch) at an angle ⅛" below a bud.

3. After dipping the stem into rooting hormone, plant in enriched soil with at least 3 buds below ground level to produce roots.

at least an inch above ground level; space cuttings about 6" apart. Label the cuttings, using stakes or popsicle sticks and indelible ink. Continue to water, since drying out is the primary cause of propagation failure. A year later (the following autumn—and no sooner) carefully lift out the rooted cuttings and transplant them into the appropriate location.

In cold-climate areas, wrap the cuttings in heavy paper surrounded by damp peat moss, and store at 32°–40°F. over the winter. The meat or vegetable drawer in an extra refrigerator will do for this purpose. Another method of winter storage takes a bit more effort. Dig a trench 8"–12" deep in well-drained soil, stand the wrapped cuttings in the trench with the tops down and bottoms up; fill in with sand and cover completely, with the cuttings no deeper than an inch below soil surface. Over the winter, the cuttings form a callus, or protective tissue, at the base.

In spring, choose an area in full sun with loose, porous, well-drained soil that has been amended with peat moss, sand, and vermiculite. Plant the cuttings so the top bud is above the soil level; space the cuttings 4"–6" apart. Water well initially, then water whenever the soil dries out. The cuttings should root within three months, but leave them in place for at least a year. After that time, transplant them into a spot where you can show off the product of your patience and determination.

LAYERING

Layering is a method of propagation suitable only for woody plants. Part of a branch, still attached to the parent plant, is bent toward the ground and partially buried in soil, where it remains until it roots. Layering is the simplest propagation technique, requiring no tools, no pots, no space in the house, and little or no attention after you've buried the branch—until it roots. Layering is best done on one-year-old shoots of trees or shrubs in the early spring.

Simple Layering

Select the branch you want to layer, and twist and bend it gently toward the ground in the opposite direction from which it normally grows. (If a branch grows toward the right side of the plant, bend it over to the left side.) Mark the spot where the portion of the branch that is about 6" from its tip touches the ground, and dig up to 6" of soil from that area, creating an oval-shaped hole to

hold that portion of the branch. Since you're digging near the root system of the plant, work carefully to avoid destroying any roots. Amend the removed soil with compost, peat moss, and sand to create a rich, moisture-retentive, well-drained, well-aerated home for the buried portion of the branch. Replace 1"–2" of soil in the hole, and bend the branch, making it as flat as possible. Trim off any leaves from the section that will be buried, leaving the other foliage intact. (At this point, some gardeners choose to girdle the branch, removing about a 1"-wide strip of bark all the way around the branch; others make a diagonal cut halfway through the underside of the portion that will be underground, then dust it with rooting hormone. Both methods speed up the rooting process, but are optional.) Anchor the branch to keep it in place. Large staples designed for this purpose are available at garden centers, or you can use one or two pieces of heavy wire, a coat hanger bent in a U-shape, a heavy stone, or a strong forked

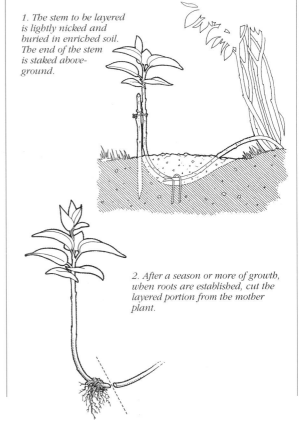

1. The stem to be layered is lightly nicked and buried in enriched soil. The end of the stem is staked aboveground.

2. After a season or more of growth, when roots are established, cut the layered portion from the mother plant.

PLANTS TO PROPAGATE BY LAYERING

SIMPLE LAYERING

Apple (*Malus* spp.)*
Bellflower (*Campanula* spp.)*
Blackberry, raspberry (*Rubus* spp.)
Clematis (*Clematis* spp.)*
Crabapple (*Malus* spp.)
Cranesbill (*Geranium* spp.)*
Euonymus (*Euonymus* spp.)*
Forsythia (*Forsythia* spp.)*
Grape (*Vitis* spp.)*
Hawthorn (*Crataegus* spp.)
Honeysuckle (*Lonicera* spp.)*

Hydrangea (*Hydrangea* spp.)*
Ivy (*Hedera* spp.)*
Jasmine (*Jasminum* spp.)
Pink (*Dianthus* spp.)*
**Rhododendron and azalea
    (evergreen)** (*Rhododendron* spp.)*
Wisteria (*Wisteria* spp.)*

AIR LAYERING

Cotoneaster (*Cotoneaster* spp.)*
Crabapple (*Malus* spp.)
Fig (*Ficus* spp.)*
Flowering dogwood (*Cornus florida*)

Holly (*Ilex* spp.)
Japanese zelkova (*Zelkova japonica*)
Lemon (*Citrus limon*)*
Lime (*Citrus aurantifolia*)
Magnolia (*Magnolia* spp.)
Smokebush (*Cotinus coggygria*)
Tamarisk (*Tamarix* spp.)
Winter hazel (*Corylopsis* spp.)
Wisteria (*Wisteria* spp.)*

Included in the Plant Guide, pages 276-479.

branch. Refill the hole with the rest of the amended soil, stake the portion of the branch that rises above the ground, if necessary, and water well. Keep the soil moist throughout the growing season or until the branch firmly takes root, about six months later.

In autumn, check the root system by tugging up on the layered section. If properly rooted, it will resist; if not, return the stem and wait another year. When it's ready, cut the layered stem from the parent plant, using a spade to sever the stem. Leave it in place and water it regularly until the first frost. The following spring, dig it out, roots and all, and replant in open ground or in a pot. Grapevines, hydrangeas, and other woody plants can be successfully propagated in this manner.

Air Layering

Air layering is a technique invented by the Chinese four thousand years ago. Used most often to propagate large indoor plants like ficus and rubber plants, air layering is also good for some outdoor trees and shrubs, including wiste-

1. Girdle the selected branch or make a small nick in the bark, exposing the wood below.

2. Pack the area well with moistened sphagnum peat moss.

3. Cover at least 1" on either side of the sphagnum with air-permeable polyethylene plastic; tape securely.

4. After a season, when roots have formed, cut off the rooted end of the branch and plant out.

ria, smokebush croton, Chinese hibiscus, and winter hazel.

Select a healthy branch and remove any leaves growing 6"–12" from the end. Carefully girdle the branch just below a bud, removing a ring of bark ½" to 1" wide, then gently scrape the thin cambium layer of soft tissue (which may be white, reddish, or green) directly under the bark, exposing the wood without wounding it. Dab a small amount of rooting hormone on the upper portion of exposed bark. Pack the area, covering at least 1" on either side of the exposed wood with moist peat moss, then wrap it securely with polyethylene plastic (air-permeable plastic that holds moisture in but allows the area to "breathe"). Tape the top and bottom of the plastic tightly to the branch to keep rain from getting in. At the end of the growing season, roots should have formed. Cut the stem below the layering point, remove the plastic, loosen the moss ball and roots, and plant in a pot or cold frame.

With Time, Abundance

Division, cuttings, and layering are the major methods of propagation that will allow you to produce as many new plants as you wish. There are other, more complex methods, like grafting, budding, and additional types of layering, that you may wish to explore. But for most gardeners, the methods described here will be adequate for creating a small nursery of desirable plants from your garden. Rather than spend hundreds of dollars buying plants, you can propagate your own at very little expense, and in time you'll have an overflowing garden.

ADDING *the* FINISHING TOUCHES

There is something unfinished about a garden without ornament—rather like a sentence that lacks punctuation. Objects have had a natural place among trees and flowers since ancient times, when gardens were more sculpture than greenery. Ornament provides a garden with inflection, emphasis, and spark. It tells the eye where to pause and the body where to linger. While appearing to be randomly placed, it is as integral to the overall scheme as a perennial border or a bed of antique roses.

A birdbath placed in the corner of a peony bed, an arch for climbing roses, an antique washtub planted up with succulents, a weathered teak bench—all constitute garden ornament. From the mundane to the sublime, its domain encompasses everything from humble terra-cotta pots to elaborate wrought-iron sculpture.

Ornament can be elemental to the architecture of a garden, comprising its hallways of arbors, or as small and decorative as a clutch of stones retrieved from a hike. It doesn't compete with plantings; rather, it acts as their foil, balancing soft curves with harder surfaces and sharper edges, reinforcing their beauty through contrast. A garden that artfully integrates ornament and plantings is a balm for the spirit.

DEFINING THE GARDEN

Ornament gives a garden depth and character, providing perspective and evoking emotion in those who view it. A backyard adorned with secluded benches on which to linger within earshot of a fountain becomes a place of quiet contemplation. Without much work, ornament can establish a historical or geographic style. A

An attractive ornament during the day, a stone lantern softly illuminates a portion of the garden at night. It can also be hung from an eave or placed beside a pathway.

bed of low-mounding heather may suggest an Asian aesthetic; add a grouping of boulders and a votive stone lantern, and the space becomes "Japanese." Tucking a white wrought-iron bench within a perennial cottage garden labels the garden "Victorian." And nothing seems more "formal" than a replica of Diana set on a plinth and ringed by a circle of English box.

Not everyone is fortunate enough to begin a garden from scratch—an empty canvas on which to sketch beds, draw pathways, and site ornament. For those of us who inherited our gardens, or who have already plunged our shovels into the dirt without much thought to an overall design, ornament can play a unifying role. It can actually pull disparate elements together by establishing focal points, creating rooms and pathways through the space. Moreover, ornament is often portable and can be moved about as the mood strikes, as the seasons change, or when the garden undergoes design review.

Historical ornament opens windows onto our past relationship with nature. Decorated with images of Pan, goddesses, and satyrs, terra-cotta pottery recalls the medieval belief that these spirits ensured fertility and protected the harvest.

GARDEN ART

Ironically, much of the literature on garden ornament is limited to the classical sculpture of Roman gardens—or the modern equivalent by Henry Moore. Statuary, sculpture, and other art objects are placed in the garden for their decorative appeal. Just as the overall garden design reflects your personality, the artwork you place in the garden should be a tribute to your individual tastes. Many people find an idiosyncratic, personal piece much more rewarding than a mass reproduction of Michelangelo.

If you want a sculpture to be a focal point, give it some breathing space so that others can appreciate it without distraction. Staying with a single theme and type of art—be it classical grandeur or flea-market funky—may have a more pleasing effect than mixing styles. But then again, with the right attitude and vision, even the most eclectic collections can appear cohesive.

Your search may start with a visit to the local nursery, but can also take you to secondhand stores, salvage yards, flea markets, and garage sales—all surprisingly rich sources for unique pieces of garden art.

The Green Man, an ancient symbol of fertility and renewal, keeps a watchful eye on the garden as a reminder of all that has gone before and all that is to come.

A LEGACY OF WIT

In the 18th century, no English country estate was complete without the addition of a folly: a downscale Greek temple, an instant Roman ruin, a crumbling hermitage, a faux pagoda. Existing more for their sense of fun and the desire for historical symbolism than for any utility as shelter, these fanciful buildings seemed to exaggerate human control over the natural landscape, turning the arcadia into a sort of early theme park. Their quirky legacy survives on a smaller scale in the form of gargoyles, gnomes, mirror balls, trompe-l'oeil trellises, and other humorous ornament found in modern gardens. The same may be said of topiary, which treads the line between plant and ornament. It conjures up a world through the looking glass where, thanks to artistic trimming, greenery seems to come alive, bringing unexpected whimsy to the garden.

The archetypal Green Man, thought in Gothic times to be reborn each spring following winter in the Underworld, continues to cast a protective eye over some modern gardens.

Certain kinds of ornament descend from fanciful roots, such as the British folly or the topiary of colonial America. At a writers' retreat endowed by author and cartoonist James Thurber, giant stone dogs romp in the garden like comical characters come to life. Sprites, gargoyles, and mirrored orbs show up in the most formal of gardens, softening their symmetrical severity and casting smiles into dark corners. Plastic pink flamingos and rows of ceramic chickens, popular in the American Southeast, can be blatantly tongue-in-cheek or signify a deliberate wink on the part of the gardener.

Some designers warn against a "promiscuity" of ornament, but in fact there is no right amount, no particular formula to follow. One individual's overabundance is another's paradise, and the only guide that matters is your own aesthetic preference. The layer upon layer of ornament in a "folie de grandeur" such as Anthony Noel's London garden may be lovely to some, while to others the stark beauty of a single well-placed urn is a perfect delight.

Often the most powerful accents are those that speak privately to the gardener, summoning memories through association. A handful of sand dollars, placed beside a favorite Adirondack chair, may recall a happy day of beachcombing; a weathered stone frog, peeking through liriope leaves, may become a secret companion for the gardener who hid it there. Such personal ornament reflects our lives—and exposes our human desire to make our mark on the landscape.

Because the ornament of a garden is likely to outlive even the hardiest perennials growing there, pieces made from natural materials—stone, wood, ceramic, iron—represent more than good value. Over the years, these pieces seem to become part of the garden, sinking into its embrace. Hard lines are softened by rain and sun

Look at everyday objects with an eye toward recycling them into yard art. Here, a rusted antique pump, born of utility, adds whimsy and a touch of color to a shaded fern garden.

Containers are decorative objects in themselves but also allow the gardener to introduce plants to soilless areas such as patios, steps, and terraces. Terra-cotta planters blend well, particularly with a brick pathway.

and yearly frost. Moss creeps between the fissures created by heat and ice. Lichen mottles new patterns on surfaces. In this way, nature merges with ornament, slowly becoming indistinguishable from artifact.

Points of View

Before setting foot in a garden, one picks up subtle clues about its content and style from the entrance itself. The ornament placed at the gar-

ANTHONY NOEL'S "FOLIE DE GRANDEUR"

In some gardens, ornament plays a supporting role. Not so in Anthony Noel's "folie de grandeur," his 17' × 40' jewel box of a garden in Fulham, London. Sharing space with the ramblers and climbers, hostas and peonies, are painted flowerpots striped with sky blue, acid green, Schiaparelli pink, black, and white ("rather like the chairs on Brighton Beach"), a Brobdingnagian 8' terra-cotta pot, a spitting lion fountain framed by a fireplace surround, golden urns, orbs, pineapples, pyramids, tompe-l'oeil tents, swags in profusion—and a good deal more. But somehow, though, the profusion of ornament and the cheekiness of the colors do not upstage the plant life, which itself is anything but understated. An actor by training and a garden designer by trade (undertaking everything from a single window box to a 150' conservatory), Noel claims that his approach is basically formal—with a twist. His secret? "Distress the hardscape and make it look bold, old, and slightly crumbly. Anything growing around an ancient wall will look as if it dropped from heaven—and the ornament becomes pure poetry."

LIVING ORNAMENT

Certain elements of a garden fail to fit the neat categories that divide man-made accents from organic plant material. Is a stone bench entirely overtaken by moss an ornament or an organism? Topiary, parterres, and espaliers are living works of art—hybrid creations of a human artistic vision and nature's constant and forgiving growth. Gardeners have long held a fascination with shaping greenery according to the human imagination.

Topiary. Clipping trees and shrubbery into fanciful shapes dates at least back to ancient Roman times, as recorded in Pliny the Elder's first-century *Historia naturalis*. Revived in the Italian Renaissance, topiary dotted villa gardens with oversize animal shapes formed from yew, while spheres and squares were guideposts and anchors for the corners of flower beds. With the later inclusion of geometric shapes on a grand scale in French and English gardens, topiary became a fully established garden art.

Much topiary, from simple ivy cones to unicorns clipped from holly, begins with a wire framework to guide the gardener in shaping the finished piece (adding a pleasing ornamental element to the landscape in the meantime). Tightly leaved shrubs such as yew and boxwood are the preferred choice, as they provide a dense, richly textured surface. Leaving the base wider than the top ensures that the necessary sunlight and air will reach all surfaces. Creating topiary requires patience, but simple shapes don't involve as much work as you might think; periodic clipping is sufficient to maintain the desired form.

Parterres. The term *parterre* (from a French phrase meaning "along the ground") refers to the practice, begun in Renaissance days, of planting in strong geometric patterns. Low-growing shrubs are planted to form a swirling outline on a ground of colored sand and gravel. The ornate patterns are loveliest when viewed from above, where sun and shadow highlight the contrast between solid hedging elements and smooth ground treatment. In English gardens, turf or bedding plants form the background and a sculpture is often placed at its center. At Colonial Williamsburg, entire gardens were laid out like a parterre, with vegetables and flowers filling the empty spaces and evergreen topiary spiking the corners.

One evolution of the parterre is the knot garden, a rectangular space outlined in boxwood, rosemary, germander, or other small-leaved evergreen plants. Continuous bands of two or three different colored shrubs form a complex "knot," carefully trimmed to give the illusion of one shrub passing over or under the other. The interstices are often planted with herbs or flowering plants, creating a bed as useful as it is worthy of marvel. Like topiary, a knot garden or parterre requires patience and regular maintenance, but once fully established can become a signature piece. Parterres and knot gardens add special interest when their strong geometric patterns take center stage in the bare garden.

Espalier. This technique of training plants into a flattened configuration is used to grow fruit trees and flowering shrubs against a wall or other horizontal surface. Front and back shoots are clipped, while lateral growth is often tied to a framework. The results are dramatic as the plant continues to bloom and bear fruit prolifically in its ever-evolving shape. Forming a free-standing border between sections of the garden—on a post and wire framework—espaliered fruit trees provide a constantly changing curtain: blossoms in spring, leaves in summer, fruit in fall, and a tracery of empty branches in winter.

den gate casts an indelible impression about what is to come. Consider the mood set by a haphazard arrangement of lime-stained pots on worn brick steps, with rosemary and thyme spilling languidly in the sun. This is an invitation to a garden that values a naturalistic display, marked perhaps more by vigor than precision, in a space free of pretension. On the other hand, an entrance flanked by brick gateposts and surmounted by a precisely trimmed arbor sends a message that the garden inside will be more symmetrical and ordered—a showplace.

Just as a favorite plant is often moved to the prime location in a sunny border, a special ornament should also be displayed to best advantage. A copper washtub discovered at a local auction, for example, warrants a position front and center in the cottage garden and a planting of bright penstemon and cascading sapphire lobelias. In a small patio garden, a series of paint-splattered half-pots planted with aloe and set on a sunny ledge may lend an air of tidy abundance—and a welcoming first glimpse.

When placing ornament, remember that it will be seen from a number of points in the garden. How it looks from the street, driveway, or parking area should also be taken into consideration. And before siting a piece, consider the scene from favorite viewpoints inside the house, such as the desk, the kitchen sink, or the balcony off the bedroom.

Ornament can also be used to direct the eye away from a potentially unfavorable view. Arches and pergolas are often used to mask a neighbor's carport or a utility pole by calling attention to the garden and away from objects outside the frame. A grouping of enameled pots planted with rose standards creates a central focus while ingeniously shielding the toolshed from the dining area. Sculpture and containers can serve a similar purpose. Placing a bronze statue, or a grouping of rusty watering cans planted with lantana, on a 90° axis to heat pumps, water spigots, sprinkler

boxes, and other eyesores can make them all but vanish from view.

Pathways

Ornament can encourage forward momentum. A cobblestone path or artfully placed flagstones, a herringbone brick walkway or even a yellow-stone road—all offer a way of getting inside the garden, serving as an implicit invitation to roam. Even small gardens benefit from a 4'-wide path that curves out of sight, offering the promise of new discoveries just around the bend.

Reduced to bare bones, a path is simply a way to get from one spot to another, and as such it should feel reassuringly stable, firm, and slip-proof underfoot. But it also provides a surface for adding texture and pattern at ground level. A garden path can be fashioned from almost any hard

For an alternate pathway, simply remove sod to form natural stepping-stones. Such a path reduces lawn care and gives the garden a relaxed, restful atmosphere.

Stone steps are visually exciting as they invite the garden visitor to ascend and explore.

material, including block, brick, gravel, flagstone, slices of timber, old millstones, cast-stone pavers, crushed oyster shells, or merely packed earth. (In truth, lovely if impermanent paths may be made from soft organic material like pine needles or bark, or from turf itself, such as a walkway mown through a meadow of wildflowers and tall grasses.) If possible, the material should echo the home. Stone pavers and flagstones are well suited to wood or stone houses; brick is generally associated with colonial architecture; and polished surfaces often surround structures that are starkly modern.

As garden design elements, pathways yield strong clues to the character of the garden. Straight paths composed of carefully laid marble or brick can reinforce the structure of a formal garden, while a meandering walkway of random crosscut logs highlights a more carefree planting style. The classic gardens designed by Edward Lutyens and planted by Gertrude Jekyll demonstrated the loveliness of geometric pathways contrasted with asymmetrical drifts of flowers. A combination of hard lines and soft curves is often the most satisfying to the eye.

Pathways or edging limited to a single material can bring neatness and unity to a garden, providing a common thread between different flower beds or garden rooms. Alternatively, changes in materials—like changes in levels—can be used to signal a transition to a different part of the space. Moreover, the layout of a walking surface often signals where to speed up, pause, or stop. Bricks laid end to end in a "running course," for instance, have a tendency to increase the pace, while a static basket-weave pattern implies that a destination has been reached. Straight, wide, smooth pathways lengthen the stride, whereas stepping-stones force one to slow down and admire the view along the way.

A wide area devoted to one material such as brick, slate, or concrete can be tiresome in its uniformity. Varying the materials and patterns or leaving spaces in which creeping plants may grow will heighten the visual interest of a patio or expansive walkway. Embedding pebbles or pottery shards in concrete before it sets turns a plain material into a colorful carpet. But highly textured surfaces—such as crazy paving, mosaic, or small cobbles—are often better suited to small areas. By themselves, they are sufficient ornamentation; adding containers or other accents may detract from the beauty of the paving pattern.

Ideally, pathways are laid out before the first

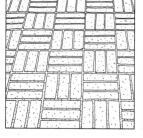

Bricks can be used in a wide variety of designs. Two popular patterns, the herringbone (top) and basket weave (bottom), give a different look, depending on the viewer's perspective.

plant is placed in the soil. But in many cases gardeners will decide to add or change a path through an existing garden as trees overtake beds, families grow, or a house changes hands. Taking a photograph of the garden with you when you buy materials will help you choose those that won't clash with your planting scheme or palette.

A strong, graceful cedar pergola frames a view in the distance while serving to separate one garden space from another.

Structural Ornament

Along the way, arches, arbors, and pergolas present thresholds that beg to be crossed. They extend the perspective of a small area, making it appear deeper and more generous than its dimensions would suggest, and practically force people to stroll beneath them. The pull is even more magnetic when the structure frames a clear focal point, such as a sculpture, a distant mountain range, or a water vista. A bench is especially suitable as a destination, as it suggests a reward for the trip and promises a view back down the length of the span.

Structural ornament was often used to lead a visitor from one area into the next in the classic gardens of the 19th century. At Giverny, the *grande allée* forms a tunnel of pink roses that deposits visitors, nearly drunk with scent, at Monet's front door, while the green, humpbacked Japanese bridge begs exploration of the lily pond, one side to the other. At Hidcote, visitors are guided through the space by a series of archways, gateposts, and hedges.

Ornament may be used to direct garden roamers in subtler ways. A piece of sculpture set at midground catches the eye and leads the feet forward. Tree roses planted in Italianate pots mark a stairway landing, indicating an impending change in level. From the bottom, a stone seat is glimpsed off to one side, which in turn puts visitors within earshot of a gurgling fountain. As each ornament comes into view, a new destination is presented.

A grand-scale structural ornament often becomes the ultimate focal point and destination of a garden. A gazebo or summerhouse lends a dramatic aspect, evoking feelings of mystery and romance. Such a structure takes on multiple functions—as a trysting place, a picnic site, a shady refuge, or simply a vantage point from which to view the garden, grounds, and house.

Water is no prerequisite for a bridge. The arch can span a path, link two flower beds, or cross a stream of small, dry pebbles.

A GARDEN LEGEND

EDWIN LUTYENS' GARDEN ARCHITECTURE

The collaboration of Sir Edwin Lutyens and Gertrude Jekyll forever changed the face of garden design. Their great achievement was the aesthetic integration of house and garden—the creation of a setting harmoniously conceived and a pleasure to live in.

Architect Edwin Lutyens met Gertrude Jekyll when he was 20 and she several decades his senior ("We met at a tea table, the silver kettle and the conversation reflecting rhododendrons"). She hired him to build her house at Munstead Wood in 1894, and over the next 17 years the two collaborated on some 70 house and garden commissions—for which he worked out the siting, vistas, and hardscape while she planned the intricate plantings.

Both designers were influenced by the Arts-and-Crafts movement, with its appreciation of honest craftsmanship and emphasis on the natural over the contrived, and both believed that every site should dictate its overall scheme. After 1912 Lutyens' style became more classical as he accepted larger-scale commissions (such as planning the New Delhi capital complex in India), but the fruits of their partnership still seem fresh and continue to inspire.

"A garden scheme should have a backbone— a central idea beautifully phrased."

Boundaries

Hard boundary lines that separate a neighbor's parcel from your own—including property lines, walls, fences, and driveways—carry a rich potential for ornamentation. Any sort of fence can be softened and made more naturalistic with the addition of climbing vines. A low post-and-rail fence twined with blowsy pink roses, for example, acts as a cheery demarcation; with a perennial border in front, it also serves as a colorful backdrop. Walls made of stone, brick, block, or other dense materials have a textural appeal as sunlight plays over their crags, but adding a series of grand pots of lemon trees or a pair of curving trellises doubles the visual interest of these blank spaces, especially as shadows fall.

Clever placement of ornament can actually make a small garden seem larger. An arbor that divides a space in two can make each half seem larger by providing a grand window into the adjacent space. Seen from the house, patio, or pool, a

Rustic supports lend architectural grandeur to a natural setting and provide ample room for tendrils of sweet pea, thunbergia, or clematis.

pathway tapered toward the back gives the illusion of depth. Rows of pots on either side of the space enhance the effect when graded from largest in front to smallest behind. A series of arches, each one slightly narrower than the last, may extend the perceived length of a pathway. Each of these tricks causes the eye to see a vanishing point beyond the dimensions of the garden.

Even impenetrable physical boundaries may be turned to your advantage. Trompe-l'oeil painting can transform a garage wall into the Spanish Steps, or the neighbor's fence into a view of the Cotswolds. On city patios, a wall trellis constructed in forced perspective—with all crosspieces pointing toward a single vanishing point—gives the illusion of depth to a one-dimensional surface. (Specialty garden stores offer premade versions of such trellises.) In the same way, a mirror hung on a fence or angled behind a piece of sculpture promises a landscape that never ends. Using such illusions to turn a boundary into a grand vista is sure to elicit double-takes and bring laughter to the garden.

Planters of different sizes, shapes, and heights soften the hard lines of a narrow entryway.

Often one boundary of the garden is the home itself. By blurring the borders between home and garden, ornament establishes continuity between indoor and outdoor pursuits. Manmade accents add pleasing layers of texture and color to the garden, much as a potted palm or the scent of forced hyacinths embellishes the landscape indoors. By referring back to the objects found inside the home, the ornament of a garden creates a sense of familiarity and welcome outdoors.

The landscapes by Edwin Lutyens and Gertrude Jekyll are still sources of inspiration for ways to integrate house, hardscape, and garden. Lutyens used brick and timber pergolas to link two wings of a building or to connect a house to its outbuildings with a tunnel of greenery. To reflect the architecture of the home, he designed structural garden elements crafted of the same local materials and laid them out in a logical yet friendly way that encouraged outdoor living.

Lutyens' stone, brick, and wood framework, employing straight lines with 90° angles, looked crisper than free-form boundaries, particularly between the flower beds and adjacent gravel paths and lawns. The result might have appeared too regimented without the addition of Jekyll's asymmetrical drifts of flowers and naturalistic groupings of color, flopped here and there outside Lutyens' lines. A pleasing tension resulted between the order imposed by man and the irrepressible nature of flowering plants.

Today, container-grown plants, wall fountains, window boxes, or an arbor extending from the back door help to anchor a house to the earth. Ornament that echoes the materials, design motifs, and scale of the house creates an unbroken flow between home and garden, erasing any

Much of the appeal of a garden pool lies in the way it reflects the day or night sky as well as surrounding vegetation.

THE GARDEN ALIGHT

Lighting the garden at night increases its value both as an extension of the living area of the home and as a dramatic visual element when viewed from indoors. Ornament that is well lighted does round-the-clock duty as a focal point.

Garden lighting generally serves two purposes: safety and aesthetics. Exterior lighting should provide security from prowlers, yet allow people to walk through the garden safely after dark. Intentionally bright and glaring, security spotlights are ill-suited to show plants and ornaments at their best; equipping these lights with motion sensors that can be turned on when you're away from home offers a good compromise. The source of step and pathway lighting should be located close to the surface to be walked on, rather than overhead, to avoid casting shadows. Low-voltage lights, shaded to cast light downward, provide a more pleasing effect than a few bright bulbs at eye level.

The purpose of aesthetic lighting is not to replicate the brilliance of daylight, but to emphasize the contrast between light and dark while highlighting the dramatic textures of greenery and ornament. Garden lighting should never call attention to itself. Spotlights, for example, should be positioned out of sight; you should not have to look directly into their beams or walk through them. Fixtures can be mounted in trees, on poles, or on the side of the house; ground-mounted fixtures are even more inobtrusive.

Selective lighting is often more successful than attempting to illuminate the entire space. Begin by picking out the most attractive features of your garden, from architectural ornament to specimen plants or trees. A white birch, for example, takes on a sensuous loveliness when a light shines up its papery pale trunk. Bathed in halogen spotlights, a bronze sculpture looks other-worldly when viewed from the house. Water splashing from a fountain becomes a glittering cascade with light playing over its surface. An added benefit of lighting only the best features of the garden is that less attractive elements are hidden in darkness.

Once you've decided which elements you want to illuminate, consider where the lights will go and how strong they should be. Uplighting, the technique of pointing ground-mounted spotlights into trees, often provides the right glow for dining as the leaf canopy seems to capture and reflect light. The alternative, shining a strong light source down from above, is practical for barbecue areas, wet bars, and other work spaces; in most cases, however, light shining down from a great height gives a garden the eerie feel of an Edward Hopper painting and is unflattering to both plants and people.

Permanent electric lighting for the garden should be installed by a licensed electrical contractor. Ideally, the wiring and housings should be invisible, buried if possible, and metal conduits should be used to avoid damaging wires with shovels or clippers. All boxes and outlets should be waterproof, childproof, and grounded. Low-voltage lighting, on the other hand, is easy and safe for a do-it-yourselfer to install. Rapidly gaining in popularity over the past decade, the lights are available in many styles.

Garden lighting need not be permanent. A walkway lined with Mexican luminaria—votive candles set in sand inside decorative paper bags—can guide guests through the garden while casting flickering shapes through their cut-outs. Tiki torches and Chinese paper lanterns lend a festive air, as do tiny white Christmas lights strung along tree trunks. Indoor table lamps or torchieres, run outside on extension cords, offer and provide welcome light enough to read by. And sharing a summer meal outdoors by candlelight is one of life's true pleasures.

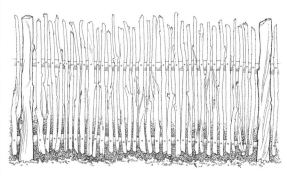

A nontraditional picket fence lends a bucolic look to a garden landscape.

hint of boundary between the two. Shingle and clapboard houses seem to sprawl happily into the landscape when surrounded by arbors, benches, and flower-bed edging made of wood. Stone houses benefit from the placement of stone horse troughs and seats at their flanks, with stone pathways stretching fingers into the garden. Similarly, a house with Mexican tile in the kitchen seems to continue outdoors if the colors in the tile are repeated in glazed pots on the deck.

Garden Rooms

The concept of subdividing an outdoor space into distinct sections was popularized by English gardens such as Tintinhull and Sissinghurst, where acres of land and a staff of groundskeepers were on hand to separate flaming red flowers from delicate pinks and whites, and the kitchen garden from the formal cutting garden. Laid out like the foundation of a great mansion, these outdoor garden rooms reflected a scale and budget unreachable today.

Modern gardeners want all the elements of those big gardens to fit into their small backyards, with additional room for outdoor entertaining, a place for children to play, and space for growing vegetables. The result can approach chaos, with tomatoes spilling into the area set aside for perennials and the family spaniel sleeping in the hosta bed because no structure exists to mark it off.

INSTANT ANTIQUITY

Rather than waiting centuries for rain, snow, and sun to sculpt the surfaces of the hardscape, you can create the pleasingly lived-in look of antiquity by hastening the process of decay. Applying yogurt, buttermilk, or a bath of diluted manure to stone or clay encourages a lush growth of moss and lichen. Rubbing lime into water-soaked terra cotta softens its color, while painting it with a poultice made from old comfrey leaves and water adds mossy green highlights. Many a too-new pot or bench has benefited from a few careful blows with a hammer—not to the point of mortality, but enough to suggest the ravages of a life well lived.

Ornament comes to the rescue by allowing even modest backyards to be logically organized. When placed outdoors, furniture creates a vantage point from which to enjoy a repast or revel in the solitary contemplation of nature. It blurs the

Covered with climbing roses, an English arch both connects and separates, puffing up each side with importance.

boundaries between house and garden, and allows elements of surprise to creep into the most ordered day. A grouping of a bench, container, and trellis neatly separates a grassy swath for children from a specimen rose bed. A low iron fence, like those surrounding street trees on urban sidewalks, discourages pets from exploring the garden bed. An arbor of flowering jasmine forms a fragrant backdrop for an outdoor eating area as it hides browning iris stalks and daylily leaves from view. Set near the middle of the garden, an arch can separate a bed of tree roses from a pleasant—though potentially distracting—tangle of asparagus plants and raspberry canes. A small garden divided into distinct rooms appears grand, especially when each room offers a different purpose, mood, or theme.

There is an art to creating a garden a within garden. How can the space be divided without making each room feel cramped and oppressive? While no rule exists for how many interior "walls" a garden should have, the number should be dictated by what functions you wish the garden to perform.

■ If your goal is simply to have a wildflower patch, a place to enjoy brunch with the Sunday paper, and an herb garden near the kitchen, segmenting your available space will be a straightforward task. But what if you also want to grow peppers, feed songbirds, store firewood, and have a place for the children to play? Rather than cut the space up into ever-smaller sections, consider using each room of the garden for double duty. You can grow herbs in half-barrels or large tubs and use the tubs themselves as a border around the brunch area. A cord of firewood can be stacked in a square shape, creating a "playhouse" for the children, while today's

When the ceiling is a wisp of cloud or a wash of stars, and the air trails a rumor of jasmine or roses, even the simplest refreshments seem to explode on the palate.

sandbox can be turned into a raised vegetable bed in future years. The birds may be fed in winter, the feeder removed in spring, and the ground beneath it sprinkled with wildflower seeds for a profusion of summer color that will overwhelm the sprouting birdseed.

■ Hedges are without equal as interior walls for the garden. They add structure and architectural unity, form a velvety backdrop for flowering plants and artistic ornament, block wind and noise, confer privacy, lend visual interest to the garden in winter, and offer birds a place to nest. In North America, solid, impenetrable hedges consist most often of yew, boxwood, holly, beech, hornbeam, privet, and cypress, each endowed with its own qualities. (Beech is deciduous, for example, but retains its brown leaves in winter. Boxwood is evergreen, but may not survive a dumping of snow. The local nursery is your best guide.) No matter which plant you choose, allow a 3' margin on either side of the hedge for maintenance and to keep flowers from having to compete for root space and sunshine. Alternatives to evergreen hedges include flowering shrubs such as forsythia, spirea, autumn olive, and rambling rose.

■ Look to other options to create garden "walls." Espalier a row of apple or pear trees on wire strung between posts. Over time, the trees not only provide an impenetrable hedge-high division but also blossom sweetly and bear fruit. Another option is to build a 3' fence of wood or wire upon which ivy or some other rapid climber can be grown, creating a low, solid wall with a narrow footprint. Even one-gallon shrubs form a hedge-like partition when planted in oblong planter boxes; the bottoms can be cut out of the boxes to root the plants there permanently.

■ To avoid turning a backyard into a sort of prison, interior garden walls of all kinds should be short enough to see over, narrow enough to walk around, and provided with generous openings (think "doors" and "windows"). At Hidcote, garden rooms limned by tall yew hedges and brick walls were designed with both entrances and exits. Through these apertures one can see—and be drawn into—the adjacent rooms. Other 18th-century English gardens had large windows deliberately cut in their surrounding hedges, offering views of other rooms or neighboring farmland, framed in rich green. Ideally, one should be able to get a sense of the garden's size while happily ensconced in any one of its rooms.

Whether made from wrought iron or wood, a gate should complement the hedge, fence, or wall through which it gives access.

■ Internal divisions needn't be entirely impenetrable nor solid. A lineup of four boxwood spheres in Versailles planters, though spaced far enough apart to walk between, still suggests an unbreachable line. An archway in a low picket fence gives the appearance of cleanly separating one room from another. An airy lattice panel twined with climbing roses appears opaque with the sun shining on it; when the sun lights the area behind it, the panel becomes a scrim through which the rest of the garden can be seen. Even such insubstantial dividing lines as these give the illusion of well-defined outdoor space. And though the backyard may include areas designated for children, pets, vegetables, cut flowers, barbecues, water plants, and tool storage, we quite happily "see" primarily the room we are in.

■ Don't neglect the backstage views of the sets you create. If you choose to arrange a seating tableau at the back of the garden for reading and quiet contemplation, think about what the view from that location will be. If a pathway studded with Cretan water jars leading to a bench suits your fancy, consider the perspective found at the end of the path. Will the scene be as compelling when you're sitting down and the plants (and water jars) are at eye level? Be sure not to create a view that leads to dead ends, mediocre vistas, or an eyesore. Once explorers reach the destination suggested by your carefully placed ornament, they should be rewarded, not disappointed, with the view.

The addition of a simple chair turns an otherwise empty space into a garden nook.

■ Consider also how the appearance of ornament will change throughout the seasons, particularly in autumn and winter. An ornament that was just one of many features in the summer garden suddenly becomes prominent when coated with brightly colored fallen leaves or tangled in bare vines. As the days grow shorter, ornament either

light or dark in color will stand out, while tones of gray or tan may disappear. In the relatively bare winter garden, benches, statuary, trellises, and arbors often become the main attraction—especially when lighted at night or seen against a backdrop of evergreen hedges and trees—and each new rain, frost, or snowfall transforms the scene anew.

A garden overcrowded with too many rooms, vignettes, or scenes may end up being overwhelming. But one that mingles a few props among the plants to balance the composition, especially when some of these elements are revealed through discovery and chance, will always delight. Wrote Gertrude Jekyll, "A little garden, if too simply treated, soon exhausts our curiosity. The more the designer lacks space, the apter should he be in making us forget his garden's limitations. Ingenious pleasantries of treatment here and there arrest the interest. By concentrating it, they make the visitor oblivious of the smallness of the theatre which yields so much diversion."

OLD AND NEW

Though born of utility, much ornament is possessed of an elegance that has outlived its original purpose—and has developed new uses and a richer presence through time. Consider the sundial, which for centuries marked the hour; in our digital age, it is still valued for its graceful shape. Or the craggy stone troughs excavated from the grounds of Sissinghurst by Vita Sackville-West; employed in a bygone age to feed and water farm stock, the troughs were given new life as flower-bedecked planters along one wall of the house. The armillary, a remnant of the Renaissance, was originally made to reflect interplanetary relationships, but as its scientific rationale was usurped by the deep-space telescope it has emerged as a piece of historical ornamentation.

Objects with a heritage of utility can infuse a

SUBTLE ACCENTS

Within each room of the garden are opportunities to create small vignettes and focal points, especially in spots at first hidden from view. A fruit tree may go unnoticed on its own, but suspend wind chimes from a low-hanging limb and it becomes a destination for the eye while adding music to the garden. In a corner too dark for all but ferns and sweet woodruff, consider placing a broad-based watering bowl to transform the space into a mossy, cool vignette—and a refuge for toads and newts. A few flats filled with vegetable starts beside the garage turns into a scene of patient serenity when surrounded by stacks of terra-cotta pots, upturned and waiting for planting.

A generous container like this old cistern makes a wonderful planter and garden centerpiece.

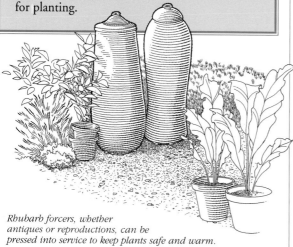

Rhubarb forcers, whether antiques or reproductions, can be pressed into service to keep plants safe and warm.

garden with their legacy, providing a link to ancient ways of living. In the kitchen garden at Chatsworth, for example, bean stalks sprout from cast-iron kettles—an ironic twist on their original use as pots to boil beans for animal feed. Another corner reveals sections of chimney liner from the castle roof, brought to earth and planted with sunny annuals.

Many a gardener has discovered that salt pans—the broad stone vessels once used to feed

FORM VS. FUNCTION

Some historical pieces still perform their original functions. In biointensive market gardens outside Paris, centuries-old cloches extend the growing season for lettuces and other frost-tender plants by concentrating heat and moisture under glass. Rhubarb and sea-kale forcers, used since the 19th century in working vegetable gardens such as Hidcote, also allow plants to grow in warmth and safety through the winter. Elsewhere, these large terra-cotta vessels are valued more for their heroic size and splendid shape. At Tintinhull, Penelope Hobhouse has turned an old lime-stained sea-kale forcer upside down and planted it with a sizable tree; in the same way, tuteurs and topiary forms may be used as intended—to support living sculpture—but may also be left bare to reveal a pleasing architectural framework, the skeleton of the garden.

Much ornament with historical roots is being skillfully replicated and can be found in gardening shops and catalogs. Facsimiles are available in the original materials (at a price), or in materials that are lighter, more portable, and longer-lasting, including cast stone and fiberglass.

PENELOPE HOBHOUSE, TRADITIONALIST WITH A TWIST

Penelope Hobhouse is proof-positive that a legendary gardener need not have been born with a trowel in one hand and a seed packet in the other. She was 25 years old when her interest in gardening was first piqued by a visit to Tintinhull House.

"I read everything I could get my hands on and began gardening like mad," explains Hobhouse, who almost 30 years later assumed responsibility for Tintinhull's National Trust garden.

To Hobhouse, one of the world's most esteemed garden designers, there is room for variation in style, but only within certain parameters. The design must be appropriate for the locale. The house and garden should complement one another. And plants must be selected for their suitability to both soil and site. Structure is crucial, and there is no place for anarchy: "I like to show nature that I'm in control!"

Today Hobhouse tends a one-acre plot in Dorset, with a woodland, meadow, formal allée, walled garden, evergreen shrubs, and flowers—but not too many. The focus here is on foliage, shape, texture, and the interplay between sunlight and shadow.

"Whether the effect you seek is formal or relaxed, a garden is not meant to duplicate nature."

A BIRDBATH IN BLOOM

Familiar garden ornament gains new appeal when used in an unexpected way. While birds may depend on a birdbath for water during the dead of winter and the heat of summer, early spring rains bring welcome puddles—and free the bath for other uses. Try filling it with stones and paperwhite narcissus bulbs (forced over the winter) to create a dramatic display. For weeks, the bath will be alive with unexpected texture and spiked with scent before returning to its noble calling as a watering hole for birds.

A large urn is an ideal container and looks best when filled to overflowing. For a more dramatic effect, place the urn on a pedestal surrounded with bedding plants.

salt to farm stock—are just the right depth to accommodate herbs for snipping. Likewise, a lead cistern reborn as a water garden may recall in its dented surface a gathering of quarterhorses vying for a drink. This is not to say that one must scour estate sales in Provence to find the original pieces. A cast-stone facsimile from a specialty garden store or catalog may resonate with the same tones as an original after a season or two of settling in (and will be all the more impervious to frost).

Of course, ornament doesn't have to be centuries old to be pressed into service in a new way. A clawfoot bathtub overflowing with cosmos and clarkia can become the centerpiece of a walled city garden. A wheelbarrow with a broken handle may be recycled into a portable planter for annuals. An old potbellied stove is easily transformed into a focal point when used as a pedestal for strawberry pots.

Choosing newly made benches, pots, and birdhouses can engage the aesthetic senses as surely as the selection of a treasured antique. Because even the newest of ornament will one day have a history of its own, keep an eye toward a future time, when you will look back on your purchase from a perspective deepened by the intervening years. A plastic lawn chair, for example, may provide the same support as one made from teak, but it doesn't offer the same tactile pleasure, weather as gracefully, last as long, or biodegrade at the end of its life.

CONTAINERS

Containers are essential to a successfully ornamented garden. Pots, urns, planter boxes, and troughs extend planting areas to porches, patios, decks, and steps, softening their hard surfaces with texture, color, and scent, and making a seamless transition between home and garden. Within the garden, containers may control the flow of traffic or define boundaries between a water garden, kitchen garden, child's sandbox, or some other division of the space. And as part of a perennial border, they can be used to show off greenhouse bloomers, fill in with a sequence of bright annuals, or add species (such as camellia or citrus) with specific soil needs.

Container-grown plants make ideal movable

Terra cotta is a porous material and should therefore be soaked before planting, watered regularly, and taken indoors to prevent cracking in freezing weather.

A cast-stone fountain offers an oasis for sparrows and finches— and, when burbling, a soothing mask for noise.

have been planted, it's easy work to rearrange them for a fresh look.

Like the layout of a perennial border, containers look best staggered with low-growing plants at the front and taller specimens behind. Setting a small pot on a tabletop or on a pedestal formed by another overturned pot will raise it up to a prominent position. Remember that large plants may steal sunlight from smaller ones, which can result in stunted flowering. Container trees and vines grown on trellises, however, can be used to form a windbreak, which may allow smaller and more delicate species to flourish.

Types of containers are as various as the plants used to fill them. Terra cotta suits a wide variety of plants and comes in several grades of quality and price, from the hand-thrown to the mass-produced. Unfinished clay weathers nicely and gains visual appeal as it chips and new patterns are etched on its surface by mosses and lime. Pots with bas-relief decoration add a textural effect that can amplify the best features of the plants they contain.

walls for alfresco dining or garden parties. Use them to break up a uniform expanse of lawn or patio, or anchor a lone bench, table, or pedestal to the landscape. An arrangement of flowering plants, even in the most humble terra cotta, forms an eye-catching focal point to a backyard seating area. Potted geraniums, ablaze with bloom from sitting in the summer sun, may be moved to splash color into a dark corner or to enliven a shaded deck for a party, then happily returned to their sunny home. Pots also allow fragrant flowers to be brought to the table to perfume an outdoor luncheon or indoors to scent the living room.

Wherever space is at a premium, containers can play a definitive role. Terraces and balconies, roof gardens and fire escapes, entryways and alleys come alive with plantings and the decorative effect of the vessels themselves. In these spaces, groupings of different-size pots present pleasing layers of texture and color. Although each container may support only a single plant, the massed effect forms a rich tableau. And once the pots

Containers in concert create a garden of harmonious colors, shapes, and scents.

To protect wooden decks and tar rooftops from wet pots, consider resting them on pot feet. These decorative wedges—often in the shape of lion's paws—raise the pot off the surface to allow water to drip through and evaporate. They also add a whimsical charm to the plainest of clay pots.

Glazed clay containers add bright, reflective surfaces to the garden. Taking the color and pattern of the pot into account when pairing it with particular plants can create a synergistic effect. A favorite lily will take on one character when placed in a multicolored Mexican pot and another in a celadon Chinese urn or stark Italian cachepot. Light glazes keep plant roots cooler; dark glazes absorb heat, which some plants crave. Though less porous than their terra-cotta counterparts, glazed containers are equally prone to damage from frost.

Wooden containers, including half-barrels, window boxes, horse troughs, and Versailles-inspired box planters, have an organic advantage: they were once living, breathing plant material. Teak and cedar are the longest-lasting and worth the premium price. Wood insulates well, but adequate drainage is a must because it will decay if left untreated. Drop-in plastic liners offer the best protection for window boxes and other wooden planters while allowing continual rotation of blooming plants. (Be sure the liners have drainage holes; some look solid at first glance but have easy punch-out holes.)

Concrete sinks and antique stone troughs make delightful containers for groupings of alpine or water plants. Reproductions of stone pieces are now fashioned from cast stone, a cement composite that can be distressed to emulate the time-etched surfaces of limestone and granite. Cast stone is lightweight, impervious to cracking from cold, and capable of growing moss and lichen like the real thing, and it blends into the landscape with surprising ease.

The cool blue-gray tones of metal containers

such as coal scuttles, verdigris copper tubs, lead planters, and galvanized bins offer a handsome counterpoint to bright flowers. Cast-iron containers, with their jet-black luster, are particularly striking when paired with drooping plants such

Container gardening transforms a small urban backyard into a refuge from the hustle and bustle of city life.

FIT THE PLANT TO THE CONTAINER

The plant and its root ball determine the proper size and shape of the container. Plants with deep taproots will benefit from tall pots; spreading plants thrive in wide, low vessels; and those with generous roots prefer containers with a bulbous shape. Tall plants tend to call attention to their containers, while those with drooping leaves can be used to mask a more humble pot. A combination of plants with erect, bushy, and trailing leaves creates a well-balanced arrangement. A good rule of thumb is to devote one-third of the overall size to the container, allowing plantings to take up the remaining two-thirds.

as erigeron, whose wispy flowers become sharply silhouetted. Care should be taken to paint or treat cast-iron pieces in order to avoid the leaching of toxic salts into the soil. And for all metal containers, proper drainage is essential: be sure to drill holes in watering cans and other watertight containers before using them. Keep in mind that plants susceptible to changes in temperature may not thrive in metal, which reacts quickly to heat and cold.

Most container-grown perennials need regular care, including pruning, fertilizing, and dividing when overgrown. Removing a root-bound plant from a hard-sided pot can be arduous work, but the rewards double once it's been planted in a new home as the former container is now ready for a new tenant. Keep a supply of empty pots on hand so you'll have the right-size container for replanting.

An alternative to putting plants and soil directly into containers is to pot them in lightweight plastic nursery pots that fit snugly down inside. Using this method, a ceramic urn at the front door, for example, can become a cachepot filled with color year round. In January, a plastic pot of cyclamen is tucked into the urn, while a dozen tulip bulbs are potted up in the basement. In April, the cyclamen is planted in the garden, to be replaced by tulips just sending up their stalks. When the tulips fade, instead of gazing out on their shriveling leaves, replace them with a hydrangea on the cusp of bloom, and so forth throughout the year. Substitutions may be kept in an out-of-the-way place in the garden, greenhouse, or potting shed until their time comes.

Ironically, the largest and most ornamental of containers can flourish without plants. Terracotta Ali Baba pots, for instance, patterned after the sinuous water and oil vessels used by the Moors, have a sculptural presence when left unplanted. An Edwardian urn set on a slate-topped wall may appear so resolute that a plant would seem to mock its purpose. Amphorae and other oddly shaped containers are often sufficiently beautiful on their own—and in any case may not support plant life adequately.

OUTDOOR FURNITURE

Though utilitarian, garden furniture undoubtedly carries decorative potential and is usually the largest artifact in most gardens. In practical terms, furniture creates additional living space outdoors. A wicker chaise offers an invitation to curl up with a book in the shade; a grouping of French bistro furniture provides an opportunity for an alfresco brunch on the deck. A hammock oriented toward the setting sun becomes a place to release the cares of the day.

A Variety of Uses

Providing a common thread between a life lived within four walls and the freedom of the infinite sky, garden seating tends to meet several goals: conversation, dining, reflection, and temporary rest. These activities frequently coincide, yet the choice of seating and its materials and placement dictate the primary use.

Conversational seating should create a sense of intimacy and comfort. People who have to shout to be heard by their companions or who are constantly squirming are unlikely to settle in for a chat. If tea or cocktails are enjoyed on the deck, end tables or furniture with broad arms encourage relaxation. If privacy and quiet are the main concern, seating placed far from the neighbor's swing set or balcony best serves the purpose.

Benches and swings, usually designed for two, have an inherent intimacy. A bench placed away from the house (but still within transmission range of the portable phone or baby monitor) lends itself to quiet conversation and can even serve as a romantic hideaway.

Furniture designed for snacks and meals

should not be placed too far from the house. No one wants to hike long distances when burdened with trays of food and glassware. Proximity to the kitchen, particularly if sliding doors and generous windows allow conversation with the cook, is a plus; so is closeness to the barbecue grill. Don't forget to consider prevailing breezes, as well as sun and other natural elements. What meals will likely be taken out of doors, and at what time of year? An umbrella portable enough to be moved with the sun, yet not so light as to invite liftoff, enhances outdoor dining in almost any climate. And if the eating space is subject to stiff winds, adding trellises, arbors, and other windscreens allows leisurely dining without chasing napkins.

Because eating alfresco is so delightful, it's tempting to choose lightweight pieces that can be picked up to follow pockets of sun around the yard through the seasons. But remember that comfort tends to match heft. The best compromise is to site your heaviest table and chairs in the spot most conducive to warmth, quiet, comfort,

and shade—and to keep a lighter-weight, folding dining set on hand for impromptu meals and additional guests.

Often seen only in the context of entertaining, outdoor seating is also vital to lounging and private reflection in the edens we create. A lone chair and ottoman provide a personal source of pleasure—a place to keep a journal, nap, nurse a baby, watch a chipmunk at work, or simply enjoy the garden. An out-of-the-way spot gains purpose when a comfortable chair is put there; it becomes a secret destination and an ideal place for quiet reflection.

No less important is a spot to pause during the garden workday. A Saturday afternoon spent dividing irises or mulching raspberries usually leaves one's boots and clothes in no condition for collapsing onto fabric furniture cushions. For many gardeners, a rough-hewn wood bench set simply on grass or gravel becomes the preferred resting spot at midday. Every working garden should have one.

THE HEIGHT OF CONTAINERS

Rebecca Cole, a New York rooftop gardener, has created an urban oasis of herbs, roses, fruit trees, and perennials potted up en masse in unusual containers—from an old wooden toolbox to an antique tin baby bath and a porcelain sink rescued from a Soho sidewalk. Other found objects in her Greenwich Village roof garden include a metal headboard used as a trellis and a reclaimed iron gate that frames a twining orange clockvine. Throughout the summer, Cole adds annuals to the pots for color; in winter, she packs them with bubble wrap and covers them with burlap for frost protection. The view from her kitchen window—even as snow falls and the plants become shrouds of white—changes with each passing day.

Choosing Pieces That Last

Purchasing furniture for the garden is a long-term investment, not unlike furnishing the rooms of the home. Pieces that are well built of strong materials not only pay for themselves many times over but may one day find use in the gardens of one's descendants. Outdoor furniture is available in materials ranging from plastic to metal and stone. Wood and cane pieces are favored for their biodegradability, and within these categories exist many levels of quality.

Benches made of teak still offer a welcome seat in venerable places such as Hyde Park, Kew Gardens, and Sissinghurst a century after they were first placed there. A dense hardwood with a high oil content, teak is as well suited for garden use as it was for the decks of clipper ships, where it withstood years of salt spray and direct sunlight without rotting, splitting, or buckling. Left untreated, it will weather to a soft and silvery gray that blends beautifully into the garden.

Cypress, pressure-treated pine, clear-grained cedar, and kiln-dried oak, though not as long-lasting as teak, are much more durable than untreated soft wood. Hardwoods may be allowed to weather naturally or, for greater longevity, may be painted or varnished yearly. Reclaimed redwood, whose tight grain is naturally resistant to rot, is another excellent choice for outdoor furniture.

When choosing wooden furniture, first ask about the origins of the wood. Look and feel for a smooth, dense grain and a generous thickness, especially at the joints. Pieces constructed with mortise-and-tenon or pegged joinery are strongest, and seams should be solid and wiggle-proof. Turn over tables and chairs, if possible, to

TEAK AND THE OUTDOORS

Teak thrives outdoors. You don't have to cover it, coddle it, or store it every time a squall darkens the horizon. An extremely dense hardwood with a high oil content, teak is almost impervious to rotting, splitting, and buckling—which is why it has long been prized for making both seafaring vessels and earthbound furniture. The only effect of sun, snow, fog, or frost is to soften the color of the wood to a silvery gray. (While most people prefer to leave the wood untreated, occasional applications of marine oil will preserve the original color.) Not only is teak furniture lovely to behold, solid to sit on, and longer lived than most of us, but it can also impart a pleasant feeling of history and permanence to even the youngest of gardens.

In a well-appointed garden, furniture reflects the mood and style of the larger structural pieces.

A WORD ABOUT THE ENVIRONMENT

Back when teak first became popular for park and garden furniture, the world and its resources were viewed as something like that magic stewpot in the fairy tale—the one that fills up instantly as soon as it approaches depletion. Today, with so many of the earth's resources threatened with extinction, we know better. When contemplating a teak furniture purchase, it's critical to find out where the wood is grown.

Teak is a tropical deciduous hardwood that grows throughout Southeast Asia. In some regions the trees are cut down indiscriminately, victims of rampant clear cutting. A notable exception is Java, one of the few places in the world where responsible teak forestry is practiced. Here, trees have been cut and planted at the same rate for more than a century, and there is actually more teak in production today than 100 years ago. Due to increased demand for sustainably raised resources, this teak may cost slightly more than competing wood, but the benefits are priceless. You might also inquire if the teak has been granted Smart Wood™ certification by the Rainforest Alliance—proof that it has been raised through well-managed forestry practices.

examine their joints and look for any metal braces or screws. Ideally any hardware should be brass, not steel, which can rust and loosen within a few seasons. Painted, oiled, or varnished pieces will eventually require refinishing.

The longevity of any outdoor furniture can be extended by bringing it indoors, onto porches, or under the eaves in winter. This is especially true of furniture made of willow, wicker, or rattan.

Metal furniture outperforms many alternatives over the long haul, but rust is its Achilles' heel. When selecting metal pieces, examine them for chips in their surfaces and burrs at their soldered joints, which can become places for corrosion to gain a toehold. Pay special attention to joints near the leg bottoms, which are most vulnerable to water damage; these joints should be soldered cleanly and smoothly to allow the rust-resisting applications to adhere properly. Even if you like the look of a delicate tracery of rust on your metal pieces, it spells eventual decay and should be held at bay as long as possible to secure your investment.

The glass tops found on many metal tables not only provide a smooth, stable surface for dining, but reflect candlelight and flower arrangements beautifully. They must be cleaned regularly to look their best, however, and are susceptible to cracking in cold weather and getting nicked when moved about. When adding a glass top to an existing outdoor surface, use thick, tempered glass with beveled edges for safety.

Furniture made of stone is a good investment; it lasts virtually forever and is quick to look like an organic part of the garden. Because of their weight and heft, stone pieces can be difficult to find secondhand or have made anew, and may require heavy equipment to be placed in a backyard. Stone can be cold to the touch, so it should be placed in sunlight whenever possible.

WILDLIFE VISITORS

Ornament can work in tandem with plantings to attract and accommodate living creatures. Salvia and buddleia draw butterflies on their own, and dense trees and vines entice finches and sparrows to nest, but strategically placed sources of food, water, and lodging make their invitations even more irresistible. The redness of a cardinal, striking against a snowy backdrop, seen from your living room window can turn a drab winter day into a delight.

Bird feeders come in a multitude of clever

shapes and sizes, but the differences among them are more than cosmetic. Find out exactly what species of birds live in your area, during which season, and which ones may be expected to visit during migration. (You can find out from an Audubon guide or local bird center.) A feeder that dispenses only millet and other small seeds may not attract grosbeaks or cardinals, which prefer to crack open sunflower seeds. One designed to be placed close to the house may scare off skittish species. Tailor your purchase to the birds you want to attract. (The same is true for birdhouses.) You'll want to keep feeders away from flower beds and lawns where seed will germinate. The cast-off hulls of sunflowers can kill plants in the immediate area, especially lawn and ground covers.

Hummingbirds are often sustained through periods of drought and cold by drinking sugar water from a well-placed feeder. Garish to the human eye, these devices resemble gigantic blossoms to the birds, and the pleasure of watching them dip their long spouts into the nectar more than offsets the appearance of the feeder. (Butterflies and dragonflies will sometimes be attracted to the colorful cylinders, too, although a mud puddle seems to provide a much more potent lure.) Place the feeders where you will be able to watch the birds coming and going.

The water needs of birds are often overlooked. Larger species—robins, thrushes, jays, and the like—prefer a broad, deep birdbath to splash around in and don't mind if it's placed amid shrubbery. Sparrows, finches, and other small birds prefer shallow baths that are lower to the ground and less susceptible to ambush by cats. Doves enjoy water at ground level, for some reason, while hummingbirds seem to delight in darting through the moving water of fountains and sprinklers. Again, be sure to choose a birdbath that will accommodate the species you want to attract to the garden.

In addition to the pleasure they offer, living creatures are beneficial to the health of the garden. Birds and bats, for instance, consume insects that can prey on plants (and humans). Toads and turtles help keep snail and slug populations in check. Bees, moths, and butterflies pollinate flowers, fruit trees, and vines. And many a flotilla of mosquito larvae has been consumed by hungry goldfish in the lily pond. Anything you can do to attract wild things to the garden will improve the overall ecology of the place—as well as present a living display of color, movement, and song.

Keep in mind that pets and other animals are likely to utilize your garden ornament, too, and that you may encourage or discourage their involvement depending on where you place it. Cats are drawn to sunny seats and any features related to birds. Dogs often prefer to sleep in the shade—beneath a bench if you're lucky, instead of beneath the boxwood. Lizards and geckos like to lounge on stone seats placed in the sun.

Herb beds radiate from a glazed ceramic birdbath where feathered friends take center stage.

ORNAMENT THROUGH THE YEAR

Ornament's role in the garden changes with each passing season. In spring, movable pieces reveal their value: containers can fill in blank spots in beds, and sculpture can be placed to draw the eye away from immature plantings.

Summer growth seems to strike the strongest of garden accents; the eye is drawn more toward the bright color of blooming plants and a lush palette of greens. Often ornament is literally taken over, as plants robe their containers with flowers and a thunbergia turns a prized armillary into a Medusa head of tangled growth. At this time of year, you may want to trim back plantings or move objects to reestablish the balance between ornament and greenery.

Ornament seems to reassert itself in autumn. The birdbath and reflecting pool are seen afresh when fallen leaves float on their surfaces. Clipping back rose canes, you might come across a Spanish tile hanging on the garden wall, all but obliterated since May, and be cheered by the discovery.

Ironically, the ornament of a garden is often at its most robust in winter, when the competing influence of greenery has retreated for a time. Consider this when selecting pieces and siting them in the garden. What will your sundial look like wearing a cloak of snow? Might ice crack the birdbath? Will the shadow of the neighbor's wall leave your prized bronze cherub in the dark until March? Pondering these eventualities on a

CANE FURNITURE

When selecting furniture crafted from wicker, rattan, or bamboo, check for cracks where the skin bends (which point to poor curing), loose strings, or ends that are only glued instead of tied or nailed in place. Under the surface scrim, joints should be wrapped or secured with nails. Chairs should be braced beneath the seat and the back, tables beneath the horizontal surface to provide a solid foundation for heavy vases and perhaps even champagne flutes. Wicker, rattan, and bamboo pieces will require periodic brushing to remove spiderwebs and any bugs, and may need to be sponged clean before storage.

summer day may save regret come winter.

Winter dieback reveals the bones of the garden, and the stark beauty of metal and wood and stone in silhouette against snow and evergreen. As the sun drops low on the horizon, shadows lengthen and colors are painted with a dusky palette. Although the exuberance of summer greenery is gone, a garden enhanced with ornament is never fully dormant. One still gazes out on the scene and finds in a frost-dusted stone orb or the gentle curve of a barren rose arch objects lovely to behold—and as vital to the fabric of the garden as the first crocuses that will soon push their way to the surface.

A gazebo helps to erase the threshold between home and garden.

A Guide

to Garden

Plants

ANNUALS AND BIENNIALS

Annuals are the stalwarts of our flower gardens. These energetic plants germinate, grow vegetatively, flower, set and disperse seed, and then die—all in one year. Their popularity reached a pinnacle in the 19th century, when they were used in great bedding schemes for Victorian gardens. With the discovery of so many perennials in the 20th century, the role of annuals was modified to enhance other flowers, rather than be the star of mass plantings.

Today, annuals are once again gaining favor with expanded uses that take advantage of their versatility. In the Gulf Coast, Southwest, and coastal California, where winter frosts are rare, hardy annuals can provide color from fall to spring. Tender annuals carry these gardens through the heat of summer. In cold-winter areas, annuals are the workhorses that put forth incessant flowers all summer through. The vast number of annuals from which we may choose allows us to fill every planting niche, from sun-scorched strips to shady corners that receive little or no direct sun.

Diversity among annuals is almost limitless. Heights can range from tall and stately, weaving a quilt among tall perennials, to minute foliage of only a few inches, bringing color to a planting's edge. The form of the plant can range from strongly vertical, giving backbone to a planting, to low and rounded, for the middle or front of a border. Foliage texture is an important consideration when creating plant compositions. Leaves can be bold and wide, occurring along the stem or growing in low basal rosettes. Or plants can have delicate ferny foliage that demands quantity to make a state-

ment. The majority of annuals fall somewhere in between, with flowers being the dominant feature of most. Colors span the rainbow. Choose from solid, bicolored, tricolored, striped, blotched, or picoteed blooms. Intense brilliant colors evoke energy and can be used to portray a tropical theme or to accent areas that are viewed from afar. Soft pastels are gentle and impart a romantic feeling; use them to enhance a cottage garden or create an Impressionistic composition.

The shape of flower can denote a specific feeling in our gardens. Cheery bell-like blooms, such as digitalis, remind us of fairy-tale gardens. The flat-topped, picoteed flowers of *Dianthus barbatus* take us back in time to Victorian patterned gardens of riotous color. Prickly pincushions composed of protruding stamens wave like miniature space satellites on the wiry stems of scabiosas— good for whimsical or children's gardens. Daisy-like blooms are common to a large group of annuals that share the same structure: ray flowers, which are the rows of "petals" surrounding the central disk flowers. Bees and butterflies flock to this nectar-producing central portion. Red flowers attract hummingbirds.

Other plant types can also be grown as annuals. Biennials, such as Canterbury bells, grow vegetatively one season, go dormant for the winter, return the next growing period to flower, set and disperse seed, and then die. They are usually started in late summer for bloom the following year. Some can be started in late winter and have time to bloom the first season after germination. Perennials, which grow quickly, can be used as annuals by starting the seed early in the year. Some plants from warmer climates, like browallias, which winter over where they naturally grow, can be used as annuals in more extreme locations. Tropical plants such as abutilon adapt well to steamy summers. Use them in abundance as seasonal accents. They can be discarded at the end of summer or, if space allows, brought inside to continue growing in a sunny window.

You can easily grow most annuals from seed, either by direct-seeding in the garden at the appropriate time or by starting seeds indoors. In fact, nurseries and garden centers are limited in the varieties they offer as young plants, and most mail-order companies offer only seed. Most annual seeds germinate best at a relatively warm soil temperature (65°–89°F.). Optimum temperatures can be maintained by using a thermostatically controlled heating cable or mat placed under the seed-starting medium.

Once in the garden, some plants need more care than others. Removing spent flowers stimulates more blooms. Many flowers like ageratum and impatiens, which do this naturally, are often called self-cleaning as they need little help from the gardener. Others, such as antirrhinum, cosmos, and nicotiana, take a long time between flowering periods if the faded blooms are not physically removed. Generally, plants covered with browning flowers are unsightly and detract from the general garden aesthetic. Annuals such as centaurea, *Coreopsis tinctoria,* and viola, with thin stems and many flowers, need much dead-heading—these are good choices for people needing to improve their dexterity and are often included in "enabling" gardens. Fertilizer needs vary with the plant, but most benefit from regular feeding with a balanced fertilizer during the growing season to keep them thriving with an abundance of blooms. Keeping plants in good health also helps them fend off insect and disease attacks. Observation on a regular basis can nip a potential problem in the bud, and a good stream of water can control many insects. Start with the safest control possible if spraying becomes necessary.

Uses for these seasonal wonders span all the facets of gardening. Tall, loosely branched annuals, such as cleome, cosmos, and coreopsis, can be planted in front of walls or fences to soften the backdrop, or mixed with tall perennials to create the look of a cottage garden. Intermingled with perennials, annuals provide constant color, while perennials usually have a limited season of bloom. Wildflower gardens can contain many annuals wildly planted for a glorious jumble of color. Summer forget-me-nots, sweet alyssum, and violas make good companions for spring-flowering bulbs. Planted alongside or among the bulbs, they prolong the flowering season. Planting a new landscape with annuals allows you to observe the garden space and formulate ideas for its permanent use. Facing or edging annuals in a shrub border gives textural and floral variety to a mostly green landscape, adding excitement to the planting space. Cutting gardens almost always contain a large percentage of flowers such as cosmos, scabiosa, antirrhinum, and cleome. Lush floral arrangements or loose country bouquets rely on the constant bloom of many annuals. Everlastings, or dried flowers, add prolonged color to indoor decorations. Nigella, with its striped seedpods, is produced commercially and can be grown in home gardens as well. Their ferny foliage also provides contrast in an indoor creation.

Beautiful, tenacious, energetic, enduring, versatile—these are the annuals! What would the garden be without them? And if all else fails, and the picture still isn't perfect, the promise of these plant wonders is that next year you can start with a new canvas and display these beauties in better and better plant compositions.

Abutilon × *hybridum* 'Splendens'
Malvaceae (Mallow family)
FLOWERING MAPLE

PLANT TYPE: *Perennial grown as an annual*
ZONES: *8–9*
HABIT: *To 3' tall; to 2' wide*
CULTURE: *Full sun; well-drained soil*
BLOOM: *Summer to frost*

Flowing maple, a tropical plant, is used to enhance temperate gardens during the growing season. The mounded shape of the plant is composed of hairy, maple-like leaves, which can be solid green or mottled with yellow. Drooping trumpet-shaped flowers occur singly at the ends of the branches. Flower color ranges from yellow to pink, red to white. Blooms have the texture of crepe paper. 'Splendens' produces striking deep red flowers that stand out against solid green foliage.

CULTIVATION: Sow seeds indoors in a warm location at any time. Lightly cover the seed. Germination should occur in 14–21 days. Seed sown in the spring will bloom the following winter. To use outdoors in cool climates, sow in late winter. Transplant outdoors when all danger of frost is past, night temperatures are 50°–60°F., and day temperatures are 70°–75°F. In cold-winter areas, bring your abutilon indoors before frost. With a minimum of 4 hours of good light, it will continue to bloom.

RELATED PLANTS: 'Souvenir de Bonn' has magnificent salmon blooms with red veins. The striking cultivar 'Insigne' has white flowers with red and purple veins. *A. megapotamicum* has long, narrow yellow flowers with toothed leaves that are handsomely blotched yellow.

USES: Besides its traditional use as a pot plant indoors or out, abutilon can be a specimen plant in larger containers, combined with other annuals of finer texture, such as sweet alyssum or lobelia. Vertical

elements such as snapdragons complement it as well. The salmon-colored varieties combine well with the spiky purple blooms of the perennial veronicas.

Ageratum houstonianum 'Pinky Improved'

Asteraceae (Composite family)

FLOSSFLOWER

PLANT TYPE: *Annual*
ZONES: *Not applicable*
HABIT: *6"–10" tall*
CULTURE: *Full sun; well-drained soil*
BLOOM: *Early summer to frost*

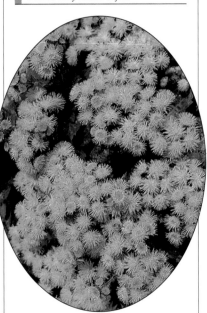

Native to Mexico, ageratum is a longtime garden favorite. The plants are mound-shaped, with oval foliage. The flat clusters of powder puff-like blooms are composed of feathery florets in colors ranging through shades of blue, light purple, pink, and white. In warm-summer areas, the cool colors are a delight in summer. 'Pinky Improved' looks almost bicolored, with lovely pink flowers that mature to fluffy white.

CULTIVATION: Seed may be sown outdoors where plants are to bloom; for earlier flowers, sow indoors in a warm location 6–8 weeks before the last spring frost date. Do not cover, as seeds need light to germinate. Germination takes 5–10 days. When planting outdoors, space plants 9"–12" apart in a warm location. Do not allow the plants to dry out as they wilt easily, and fertilize monthly for the best blooms. These plants are very frost-sensitive and will show blackened leaves where the frost settles.

RELATED PLANTS: 'Blue Horizon' is much taller, growing to 24". The habit is very loose and informal. It makes a wonderful cut flower and can be dried without the violet-blue coloration of the blooms fading. Fluffy blossoms of 'Southern Cross' are bicolored blue-and-white, which is quite unusual and charming. Other cultivars such as the commonly grown blue 'Blue Danube,' deep blue 'North Sea,' violet-blue 'Pacific,' and white 'Summer Snow' add to the many choices for this useful and long-blooming annual.

USES: Flossflower forms wonderful combinations with other annuals, such as pink globe amaranth, white vinca, and the pinky-purples or reds of *Dianthus chinensis*. Use in the rock garden to complement other perennials and annuals of small stature. Combine it with nicotiana and 'Rocket' snapdragons for a stunning planting. Ageratum performs well in containers with zinnias, verbenas, and vertical elements such as cleomes.

Alcea rosea
Chater's Double hybrids
Malvaceae (Mallow family)
HOLLYHOCK

PLANT TYPE: *Biennial grown as an annual*
ZONES: *Not applicable*
HABIT: *5'–6' tall*
CULTURE: *Full sun; well-drained, alkaline soil*
BLOOM: *Summer*

This old-fashioned favorite has been grown in Europe since Medieval times and came to America with the colonists. Tall flower spikes bloom on heavy stalks of rounded, lobed leaves. Frilly double flowers of the Chater's Double hybrids last longer than the single varieties. They come in a good mix of bright colors—yellow, maroon, salmon, scarlet, and white. The plants look their best early in the season, becoming tired as the summer wears on.

CULTIVATION: Sow seed indoors in a warm location up to 2 months before the last spring frost date. Barely cover the seeds as they need light to germinate. Germination should occur in 10–14 days. When danger of frost has passed, transplant into the garden, 18" to 3' apart.

Water and fertilize regularly during the growing season. It may be necessary to stake the heavy plants. Many will self-sow, but trueness of color is not guaranteed in the seedlings. Sow new seed each year for a much better display.

RELATED PLANTS: The Majorette strain is also a mix of brightly colored ruffled flowers. Double 'Powder Puffs' blooms on a 4'–5' stalk more reliably the first year. 'Zebrina' has lavender flowers with dark purple veins. Self-sown seeds of this variety most likely come true to color.

USES: Plant in bold masses for the best effect. Hollyhocks make a handsome annual screen. You can create an old-fashioned garden using them with foxglove, larkspur, and flowering tobacco.

Amberboa moschata
(syn. *Centaurea moschata*)
Imperialis series
Asteraceae
(Composite family)
SWEET SULTAN

PLANT TYPE: *Annual*
ZONES: *Not applicable*
HABIT: *18"–24" tall*
CULTURE: *Full sun; any good soil*
BLOOM: *Mid summer to frost*

Originally native to the Far East, this was a colonial favorite. The tall, well-branched plant adds richly colored flowers and fragrance to the garden. The flowers are shiny and thistle-like, with pincushion centers. Monarch, fritillary, and skipper butterflies are attracted to the honey-scented blooms. The Imperialis series produces fluffy blooms in pink, purple, and white.

CULTIVATION: Sow indoors in a warm location 4 weeks before the last spring frost date. Cover seeds; darkness is needed for germination, which takes 7–14 days. Transplant outside just as soon as the soil can be worked—these are frost-tolerant plants. In mild climates, sow seed outdoors in the fall for bloom the following spring.

RELATED PLANTS: 'The Bride' bears silky white flowers. 'Dairy Maid' has 2" sunflower-yellow flowers. *Centaurea cyanus* (bachelor's button) has fewer fringed petals on wiry stems with gray-green leaves. The flowers can be bright blue, pink, or white. These plants do not like heat and humidity and bloom longest in cool climates.

USES: Sweet sultan is a good filler in the flower border when many perennials are past their peak of bloom. Handsome combined with foliage of lavender and santolina, this plant adds a burst of color.

Anchusa capensis 'Blue Angel'

Boraginaceae (Borage family)

SUMMER FORGET-ME-NOT

PLANT TYPE: *Biennial grown as an annual*
ZONES: *Not applicable*
HABIT: *8"–10" tall*
CULTURE: *Full sun; average, light soil*
BLOOM: *Early summer to late fall*

Native to South Africa, these showy, compact plants have long-flowering stems. The name comes from anchusin, the red dye derived from the plant's roots that is used commercially for rouge and for dyeing wool. Brilliant ultramarine-blue flowers with a white "eye" are truly eye-catching. Free-flowering in cool climates, anchusas dislike heat and humidity. The striking color of the blooms is a natural companion to other flowers of either pinks or purples. It also calms hotter groupings of oranges and reds.

CULTIVATION: Sow directly in the ground after all danger of frost is past, or sow indoors in a warm location 6–8 weeks before the last spring frost date. Germination takes 14–21 days. When planting outdoors, space the plants 10"–12" apart. Transplant early—the plants form a taproot and are harder to establish when more mature.

RELATED PLANTS: The taller 'Blue Bird' grows to 18" and has clusters of vivid indigo-blue flowers. *A. azurea* 'Dropmore,' a perennial, is a gorgeous plant that can take some shade. Clusters of brilliant blue flowers bloom on 4'–5' stems.

USES: These attractive flowers with their spreading habit are useful in a rock garden, tumbling over stepping stones and walls. They are best planted in drifts in the borders or planting beds. Summer forget-me-nots are wonderful in containers along with *Nicotiana sylvestris;* or for a pretty wildflower effect, combine them with California poppy (*Eschscholzia californica*).

Antirrhinum majus 'Giant Forerunner Mixed'

Scrophulariaceae (Figwort family)

SNAPDRAGON

PLANT TYPE: *Annual*
ZONES: *Not applicable*
HABIT: *To 36" tall*
CULTURE: *Full sun to light shade; sandy, rich, well-drained soil*
BLOOM: *Summer to frost in cold-winter areas; fall to spring in mild-winter areas*

The flowers of this popular plant consist of an upper and lower lip; it is said they are a dragon's jaws waiting to spring open. Flowers are borne on spikes and open from the bottom of the spike, progressing upward, emitting a light, spicelike scent. The new cultivars are rust-resistant, unlike their ancestors, which barely made it through the growing season without succumbing to rust. 'Giant Forerunner Mixed' are F_1 hybrids in a rainbow of colors—white, yellow, red, rose, pink, purple, bronze. The narrow foliage is sparse, and each stem culminates in a flower spike. This particular series is very uniform in habit, branching at the base for a bushy appearance.

CULTIVATION: Sow outdoors when danger of frost has passed. To jump-start the season, sow indoors in a warm place (70°F.) 6–8 weeks before the last spring frost date. Do not cover—the seeds need light to germinate, which takes 10–14 days. After germination, place the seedlings in a cooler place for stronger plants. They should be staked at a young age or planted close together to prevent toppling.

RELATED PLANTS: Many dwarf hybrids, such as 'Floral Carpet' and 'Floral Showers,' have an excellent range of colors and a low habit of 6"–12". The medium-height 'Rembrandt,' bright orange with yellow lower lip, and bicolor purple-and-white 'Popette,' at 14"–24" tall, may not need staking and are good for cutting. Taller varieties include 'Madame Butterfly Mixed,' with double florets on stems 24"–30", and the Rocket series, with stems reaching to 36".

USES: Combine with flowers of a similar vertical habit, such as cosmos and larkspurs, for a cottage garden theme. Or use snapdragons as the focal point in urns or containers with plants of contrasting rounded or cascading habit, such as petunias, vincas, and begonias. Snapdragons are indispensable for cutting gardens, providing a strong vertical accent to the garden and bouquets. They will last longer if cut when only half the buds are in flower.

Argemone polyanthemos
Papaveraceae (Poppy family)
PRICKLY POPPY

PLANT TYPE: *Annual or biennial*
ZONES: *Not applicable*
HABIT: *2'–4' tall*
CULTURE: *Full sun; well-drained, alkaline soil*
BLOOM: *Summer to fall in cold-winter areas; spring in mild-winter areas*

Dramatic, pleated white flowers with bright yellow stamens are borne on slender stems of deeply lobed leaves. The many branches of this graceful plant can topple over to the ground, but sprawling does not diminish its overall beauty. Native to the arid portions of the U.S., it develops a long taproot to find moisture. This species has smooth leaves without prickles on the top. The prickly seedpods are yet another aspect of the beauty of the plant, a favorite of bees.

CULTIVATION: Sow indoors 4–6 weeks before the last spring frost date. Germination takes 10–15 days. Space 2'–3' apart. Feed with nitrogen fertilizer for best growing results.

RELATED PLANTS: *A. grandiflora* grows to 2' tall with white flowers.

A. mexicana, which grows to 3', bears yellow flowers. *A. mexicana* 'Alba' is white, and the showstopper 'Sanquinea' bears red blooms.

USES: Argemone commands attention and can be used as a specimen plant in any scheme. The yellow stamens complement yellow-flowered rudbeckia and gaillardia. It's lovely in containers, combined with sunny trailing lantana. Plant with other drought-tolerant plants, such as euphorbias and sedums.

Browallia speciosa
'Blue Bells'
Solanaceae
(Nightshade family)
BROWALLIA

PLANT TYPE: *Perennial usually grown as an annual*
ZONE: *10*
HABIT: *10"–12" tall*
CULTURE: *Full sun to dappled shade; humusy soil*
BLOOM: *Summer*

Native to tropical America, browallia is a lovely, much-branched plant often grown in pots or hanging baskets. Its virtues are now taking it into the main garden. The velvety blooms, most often in blue, white, or lavender, are bell-shaped. The plants are rounded with a semi-open habit. Browallia loves the heat of the

summer. In some of the more northern climates, summer may be too short for the plant to bloom, but it can be grown indoors in good light, providing color during gray winter months. The flowers of 'Blue Bells,' one of the Bell series, look like indigo-blue stars.

CULTIVATION: Sow seed indoors in a warm location 6–8 weeks before the last spring frost date. Do not cover—the seeds need light to germinate. Germination takes 10–21 days. After all danger of frost has passed, transplant into the garden, allowing 8"–10" between plants. Keep the soil moist by mulching, and feed with a balanced fertilizer at planting time.

RELATED PLANTS: 'Blue Troll' has abundant clear blue flowers on a compact 10" plant. 'Jingle Bells' comes in shades of blues, lavenders, and white. 'Compacta Major' has dark blue flowers; 'Silver Bells' has silvery-white blooms.

USES: Plant browallia in shady borders with pink astilbe and white begonia. Combine in a sunny spot with dusty miller 'Silver Lace' and dianthus 'Ideal Crimson.' Good for hanging baskets.

Campanula medium 'Calycanthema'
Campanulaceae (Bellflower family)
CANTERBURY BELLS

PLANT TYPE: *Biennial grown as an annual*
ZONES: *Not applicable*
HABIT: *To 2' tall*
CULTURE: *Full sun to light shade; rich, moist soil*
BLOOM: *Early summer*

This cottage garden favorite has satiny, bell-within-a-bell flowers up to 2" across. The color range includes deep violet-blue, dusky-rose, and white. Dainty double flowers with ruffled rims grow on pyramid-shaped plants. The foliage, with medium to bold texture, combines well with many different plants. Blooms of 'Calycanthema,' nicknamed cup-and-saucer, are usually larger than those of other cultivars.

CULTIVATION: Sow Canterbury bells outdoors in late spring or early summer for blooms the next year (some may bloom the first season). Or sow indoors in a warm location 6–8 weeks before the last spring frost date. Don't cover—the seeds need light to germinate, which takes 10–14 days. Set plants in the garden 18" apart. Keep the soil moist by mulching, and deadhead to prolong the flowering period.

RELATED PLANTS: 'Canterbury Musical Bells' have mixed colors. Blue *C. spicata* grows 18"–24".

USES: A must for cottage gardens or old-fashioned themes, delightful in the perennial border as a vertical effect, and a good cutting flower for country bouquets. Mix with larkspur and foxglove for a classic combination. Use in semi-shade with *Brunnera macrophylla* and pink astilbes.

Clarkia pulchella 'Snowflake'
Onagraceae (Evening primrose family)
FAREWELL-TO-SPRING; GODETIA

PLANT TYPE: *Annual*
ZONES: *Not applicable*
HABIT: *12"–15" tall*
CULTURE: *Full sun to partial shade; average, well-drained soil*
BLOOM: *Summer to frost*

Native from the Rocky Mountains to the Pacific Coast, this charming flower was named after Captain William Clark of the Lewis and Clark expedition. Delicate 1" blooms grow along the 2'–3' stems. Most commonly seen are double-flowered varieties, but single-flowered clarkias are charming wildflowers. The cultivar 'Snowflake' has sparkling white flower spikes that look best when massed. Their frilly double flowers are poppy-like and have a long growing season, lasting well into the fall.

CULTIVATION: Sow the seeds directly in the garden as soon as soil can be worked in the spring. In mild climates, sow seed in the fall for blooms the following spring. Transplanting is difficult because of the taproot, so indoor sowing is not recommended. Cover the very fine seeds lightly. Germination should occur in 5–10 days. Thin plants to 8"–10" apart. Flowering will occur 3 months from seed. Clarkia grows well in cool climates but languishes in heat and humidity.

RELATED PLANTS: *C. concinna*, native to California, grows to 2' with pink to lavender flowers. *C. unguiculata* (syn. *C. elegans*), a taller variety at 3', is the most popular species with blooms in white, rose, red, lavender, or purple.

USES: Hillsides and slopes of breezy wildflowers are perfect for the glistening white blooms of 'Summer Snowflake,' as well as all other clarkia colors. These plants look best when massed to give body to their delicate structure. Use them in rock gardens among other plants of small size, or in front of the perennial border for continual bloom all season.

Cleome hassleriana 'Helen Campbell'

Capparidaceae (Caper family)

SPIDERFLOWER

PLANT TYPE: *Annual*
ZONES: *Not applicable*
HABIT: *3'–6' tall*
CULTURE: *Full sun to light shade; ordinary garden soil*
BLOOM: *Mid summer to frost*

A native of the Caribbean, cleome has been grown since the 1830s. It gets its name from the 4 clawed petals that are complemented by 2½" stamens that protrude outward, giving the flower its "spidery" look. Each afternoon a new spiral of flowers opens. Long, slender seedpods form "whiskers" underneath each one, giving the entire plant an exotic look. Spines occur at the base of each leaf and on the stem. Cleome seeds itself profusely and may winter over. Self-sown seedlings appear late in spring. The bloom emits a pungent odor, which is not enjoyed by some but is a favorite of hummingbirds. 'Helen Campbell' has sparkling white flowers.

CULTIVATION: Sow seeds directly in the garden after all danger of frost has passed and the soil has warmed. Or sow indoors in a warm location 4–6 weeks before the last spring frost date. Germination occurs in 10–14 days. Cleomes are easy to maintain; feed lightly and don't overwater.

RELATED PLANTS: The Queen series is most common and comes in cherry, pink, rose, white, and lavender.

USES: Place spiderflowers in the background against a wall or fence, or dot them among perennials to enliven the mid-summer blooming period. Use with other vertical annuals, such as cosmos and *Verbena bonariensis*. Cut the flowers when clusters are half in bloom for informal arrangements.

Consolida ambigua Imperial series

Ranunculaceae (Buttercup family)

LARKSPUR

PLANT TYPE: *Annual*
ZONES: *Not applicable*
HABIT: *36"–48" tall*
CULTURE: *Full sun to partial shade; rich, well-drained, slightly alkaline soil*
BLOOM: *Late spring to summer*

A native of the Mediterranean, larkspur prefers cool temperatures; the blooming season may be shortened in hotter climates. Low branches of feathery foliage support the strong flower spikes of this old-fashioned plant. The Imperial series supplies brilliant large flowerheads in lilac, rose, white, and blue.

CULTIVATION: For best results, use only fresh seed. Direct-sow in

the garden in the early spring, or sow indoors in peat pots placed in a warm location 6–8 weeks before the last spring frost date. Cover the seeds as they need darkness to germinate, which takes 8–15 days. Plants bloom about 17 weeks from germination. In mild climates, sow the seeds ⅛" deep in the fall for bloom the following year. Space the plants 10" apart in the garden, and mulch the soil to keep it cool and moist. The erect plants are quite sturdy and seldom need staking.

RELATED PLANTS: 'Sublime Mixed' has been reselected from the Imperial series, chosen for the fully double blooms and strong erect stems; this cultivar makes good dried flowers. 'Frosted Skies,' a recent introduction that grows only 12"–18" tall, bears large, semi-double white flowers that are broadly edged china-blue. The species *C. ambigua* has more horizontal branches. Delphinum 'Connecticut Yankees' is a 2½' plant in colors of blue, white, purple, and lavender.

USES: Include larkspur in the perennial border as a vertical element. The Imperial series is shown off to its best advantage when planted in groups or with other old-fashioned flowers such as foxgloves and snapdragons. The spiky blooms make striking, long-lasting cut flowers.

Coreopsis tinctoria
Asteraceae (Composite family)
CALLIOPSIS; ANNUAL COREOPSIS

PLANT TYPE: *Annual*
ZONES: *Not applicable*
HABIT: *12"–36" tall*
CULTURE: *Full sun; sandy, very well drained soil*
BLOOM: *Mid summer to frost*

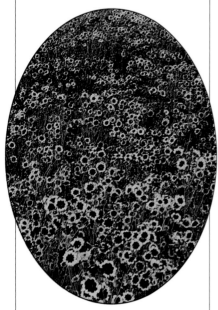

Native to our prairies near the Rocky Mountains, this charming wildflower was discovered by Thomas Nuttall about 1820, and it quickly became a garden favorite. Calliopsis, the common name, means "beautiful eye," referring to the central disk portion of the flower. This disk can be rusty-red or crimson-brown to deep mahogany. The surrounding ray flowers can be the same color or form a band of yellow, pink, or purple, with a red base at the center. These dainty blooms are set atop thinly branched plants with wiry stems. The bright flowers yield a dye used to tint cloth.

CULTIVATION: Sow outdoors after all danger of frost has passed, or sow indoors in a warm location 8 weeks before the last spring frost date. Do not cover—these seeds need light to germinate, which takes 5–10 days. Transplant, spacing plants 8"–12" apart. Scatter seed in mid summer for later blooms, extending the flowering season. Somewhat drought-tolerant—little to moderate moisture is required for the best growing conditions. Rot can result from overwatering. Frequent cutting of the blossoms stimulates new flower buds. Although quite sturdy, a stake will keep stems from toppling in strong wind.

RELATED PLANTS: Most other species of *Coreopsis* are perennials. *C. verticillata* 'Moonbeam' has sulphur-yellow flowers on wiry stems and blooms all summer, more like an annual. *C. grandiflora* has several cultivars, such as 'Early Sunrise,' that bloom in early to mid summer with semi-double bright yellow flowers.

USES: Blooming in mid summer, at a time when many perennials are quiescent, this is a good filler in the perennial border. It is a must in cottage gardens where informality is the theme—wildflower mixes almost always include it for the naturalistic habit. It seeds itself freely; the seedlings may live over the winter if the weather is not too severe. Calliopsis is an attractive, long-lasting cut flower.

Digitalis purpurea 'Alba'
Scrophulariaceae (Figwort family)
FOXGLOVE

PLANT TYPE: *Biennial or perennial grown as an annual*
ZONES: *Not applicable*
HABIT: *To 4' tall*
CULTURE: *Full sun to dappled shade; soil rich in organic matter*
BLOOM: *Spring to mid summer*

Native to the Mediterranean region, foxgloves are much prized by gardeners. Although digitalis, a strong medicine used to treat heart ailments, is derived from foxglove, the plant is considered poisonous. In the garden, its handsome structure and strong vertical aspect command attention. A rosette of round or tapered leaves forms a collar, above which rises a flower spike. Elegant bell-shaped blooms give it a regal appearance opening from the bottom of the stem upward. 'Alba' has white blooms evenly spaced all around the stem.

CULTIVATION: In the garden, you can sow seeds from spring until 8 weeks before the first autumn frost date. You can also sow seeds indoors in a warm location 10–12 weeks before the last spring frost date. Germination occurs in 15–20 days. In fall, transplant seedlings to the place in the garden where you'll want them to bloom the following spring. Provide good air circulation around the crown to keep it from getting soggy in winter. Fertilize with an all-purpose fertilizer, and mulch under the foliage. 'Alba' will reseed, so after the second season, you should have a continual supply of new plants.

RELATED PLANTS: Other cultivars include 'Grandiflora,' with longer flower spikes, and 'Foxy,' which blooms the first season. Both come in an array of colors from pink to lavender, white, and purple. The Excelsior group has flowers all around the stem and exotic mottling on the petals. *D. ferruginea* has a tidy rosette of leaves at ground level and sends up a 4' spike with curious brownish-yellow flowers in mid to late summer.

USES: Wonderful in old-fashioned cottage gardens, or used in the middle or back of the perennial border. The delicate white blooms of 'Alba' light up shady corners of the garden—combine with plumy pink astilbes for textural contrasts. Foxglove is exceptionally good as the vertical element in flower arrangements.

Erysimum cheiri (syn. *Cheiranthus cheiri*)

Brassicaceae (Mustard family)

WALLFLOWER

PLANT TYPE: *Perennial grown as an annual*
ZONES: *7–9*
HABIT: *12"–15" tall*
CULTURE: *Full sun to light shade; well-drained soil*
BLOOM: *Mid spring*

Native to the Canary Islands and Madeira, wallflowers have been a favorite in English gardens and in Europe since at least the 16th century. Thomas Jefferson grew them at Monticello, where they still thrive today. Clusters of tiny florets form the flowers, which come in hues of yellow, red, mahogany, and russet-brown. The heady sweet scent of the blooms is by far their greatest attribute. The plants have medium green foliage, and their compact habit makes them adaptable to both formal and informal settings.

CULTIVATION: This plant grows well where the climate is cool and damp. Sow outdoors in early spring. To get a jump on the season, sow in peat pots indoors in a warm location. Germination takes 5–7 days, and plants will bloom 5 months from seed. Space 12"–15"

---

apart in the garden. When transplanting, remove the very end of the taproot to encourage more side roots. Keep the plants moist at all times. Deadhead to promote new flower formation and to extend blooming time.

RELATED PLANTS: Siberian wallflower (*E. hieraciifolium*), also very fragrant, grows uniformly with orange flowers. The soft blue-green leaves are quite attractive when the plant is not in bloom. 'Fire King' is a brilliant orange, 'Eastern Queen' is orange-red, and 'Tom Thumb' comes in mixed colors.

USES: Historically, wallflowers have been included in formal gardens and parterres. The yellows, reds, and russets are wonderful combined with purple flowers such as sweet alyssum and veronica. Use in mass plantings, taking advantage of the compact foliage. Wallflowers are good in containers on patios and decks, where the sweet scent of the blooms can be enjoyed, and in cut-flower bouquets.

Impatiens hawkeri New Guinea hybrids

Balsaminaceae (Balsam family)

NEW GUINEA IMPATIENS

PLANT TYPE: *Annual*
ZONES: *Not applicable*
HABIT: *12"–24" tall*
CULTURE: *Partial shade; humusy soil*
BLOOM: *Summer*

Discovered in the 1970s by botanists visiting New Guinea and brought back for hybridizing, these plants are prized for their variegated yellow-and-green leaves. The flowers, which bloom all summer with little or no deadheading, are similar to those of garden impatiens.

CULTIVATION: Most varieties can be grown only from vegetative cuttings. Seed cultivars are started indoors in late winter. Sow 6–8 weeks before planting outside. Germination should occur in about 15 days. Do not cover seeds as they need light to germinate. After soil has warmed, space plants 12" apart, and keep them well-watered. Mulching helps conserve moisture in the soil.

RELATED PLANTS: The Spectra hybrids are free-flowering and come in strains of solid red, rose, pink, salmon, and lilac. 'Sunshine' has large flowers on compact plants. 'Sweet Sue,' the first to be grown by seed, has orange flowers and deep green foliage with a touch of bronze. 'Pink Blush,' with blush-pink flowers and dark bronze foliage, is rain resistant. Hybridization has introduced new varieties with all-green foliage. *I.*

walleriana (garden impatiens) is one of the most popular annuals for shady areas. The flowers bloom all summer in a wide range of sizes and colors.

USES: Place in shady borders to light up somber areas under trees. Use with caladiums, cannas, elephant ears, and castor beans to create a tropical mood. New Guinea impatiens are excellent grown in window boxes, hanging baskets and other containers and urns.

Lathyrus odoratus
Fabaceae (Pea family)
SWEET PEA

PLANT TYPE: *Annual vine*
ZONES: *Not applicable*
HABIT: *To 9'*
CULTURE: *Sun with afternoon shade; deep, rich, alkaline soil*
BLOOM: *Spring to mid summer*

The blue-green leaves of lathyrus, a native of Italy, are attractive, but its crowning glory is the wing-petaled flowers. They come in a jeweled assortment of colors such as deep purple, light lavender, ruby-red, pink, white, and bicolors. Some plants climb by means of tendrils along the stem, needing support to twine. Others are sprawling, forming small bushes of brilliant color. The fragrance is legendary, with a sweet perfume that is strongest at dusk and after a rain. Many different types are available, such as the grandifloras, with larger flowers, and the multifloras, with many flowers per stem.

CULTIVATION: Sow in the late summer for fall-to-winter bloom in mild climates, or sow in the fall for bloom the following year. In colder climates, enrich soil with manure in the fall and plant at the

first spring thaw. Soak seeds overnight and plant 2" deep. To get ahead of the weather, start indoors in peat pots in a cool (55°F.) location. Germination takes about 15 days. Space climbers 6" apart and bush types 8" apart. Feed once a month with phosphorus and potassium, as legumes make their own nitrogen. Mulching helps keep the soil cool, extending the life of these cool-loving plants. In areas where the climate is hot and humid, the flowers are very short lived.

RELATED PLANTS: From 'Burpee's Patio Mixed,' which blooms on bushy 9" plants, to ruffled, bicolored 'Sweet Dreams,' which grows 6'–8' tall, there is a sweet pea for every garden. 'Painted Lady,' a bicolor fuchsia-pink and white, has been in cultivation since 1737. 'Pink Performance' has shell-pink flowers on 15" plants. *L. latifolius* (perennial sweet pea), with rose-colored or white flowers, is from Europe and has become naturalized in America. An unruly cousin, it can climb to 10' but is most often seen scrambling on banks and roadsides. With its natural ability to better withstand heat and humidity, blooms are produced on and off again all summer over a wider geographic range of the country. It is effectively used in the more informal parts of the garden.

USES: Use as an annual screen with trellising. View the pealike flowers close-up and enjoy the heady fragrance in containers on a patio or deck. Plant bush varieties in beds with spring-blooming bulbs and flowers such as pansies and toadflax.

Lobularia maritima
Brassicaceae **(Mustard family)**
SWEET ALYSSUM

PLANT TYPE: *Annual*
ZONES: *Not applicable*
HABIT: *3"–12" tall*
CULTURE: *Full sun to partial shade; well-drained soil*
BLOOM: *Late spring to frost*

Composed of many tiny florets, the flower clusters sit atop a much-branched plant with slender leaves. The white blooms emit a lovely scent when warmed by the sun, attracting bees. The minute plants spread during the growing season to form a low mound 12" wide.

CULTIVATION: The plant prefers moisture but will tolerate drought. In mild climates, sow seeds outdoors several weeks before the first autumn frost date. Sow seeds where they are to grow, or in cold frames to be moved into place the following spring. In colder climates, sow indoors in a warm location 4–6 weeks before the last spring frost date. Germination occurs in 8–15 days. Do not cover the seeds as they need light for germination, and provide good air circulation to prevent damping-off of seedlings. Transplant into the garden, spacing the plants 10"–12" apart. Sweet alyssum prefers cool weather and may stop blooming in extremely hot weather. In the heat of summer, shearing the plant back to remove all flowers will help it rebloom when the weather cools. In warm-winter climates, a late summer sowing in the garden can provide a new crop that will bloom the same year, adding to the fall flower palette.

RELATED PLANTS: 'Apricot Shades' is a charming cultivar with a novel, light salmony flower color, but many other varieties are star performers as well. 'Rosie O'Day,' with rose-colored flowers, is more heat-tolerant. The Wonderland series comes in rosy shades, as well as purple and white. 'Oriental Night' is a brilliant purple. 'Carpet of Snow,' pure white, is of a more uniform habit. 'Snow Crystals' has larger flowers and blooms more reliably in hot weather. *Aurinia saxatilis,* a perennial alyssum commonly called basket-of-gold, blooms in early spring. It is good for dry spots—drainage is important to the culture. The tiny flowers, forming clusters in shades of

light yellow to gold, love to tumble over rock walls.

USES: Sweet alyssum makes a wonderful edging plant for perennial borders or annual planting schemes, and is best combined with other plants of bolder texture to offset its delicate foliage. It is superb in rock gardens, among others of the same low habit, and makes a good cover for the ripening foliage of spring bulbs. It can be grown as a ground cover among roses, and as a flower gracefully cascading over hanging baskets.

Machaeranthera tanacetifolia
Asteraceae **(Composite family)**
TAHOKA DAISY

PLANT TYPE: *Biennial grown as an annual*
ZONES: *Not applicable*
HABIT: *12"–18" tall*
CULTURE: *Full sun; prefers sandy or gravelly soil*
BLOOM: *Spring to late summer*

A wildflower of western North America, from the hills of South Dakota to Texas, the Tahoka daisy is a charming addition to domesticated gardens. The blooms sport bright lavender-blue ray flowers. The center, or disk, is vibrant yellow. Fernlike leaves give the whole plant a fine, delicate feeling. The daisies are good companions in any garden, having such a long period of bloom. The Tahoka daisy is short-lived in climates that are hot and humid; it does much better in cool climates.

CULTIVATION: In mild climates, sow outdoors in the early spring. In cold areas, sow indoors in a warm location 6–8 weeks before the last spring frost date. Germination takes 25–30 days. Transplant into the garden, spacing 9" apart. Be careful not to overwater, as Tahoka daisy prefers dry soil.

RELATED PLANTS: *Aster × frikartii,* a perennial, resembles Tahoka daisy and can be grown in hotter climates. The coloration of the blooms is very similar, on larger plants of 18"–24". The leaves are less divided but still maintain an open and airy appearance. The bloom period is from summer to early fall, providing cheery color in the perennial border or containers. *Aster tongolensis,* a native of western China with 2" blue flowers, is similar in appearance. The tufted plants form 6"–12" mounds and bloom in early summer.

USES: Combine with bright yellow marigolds for summer flower beds, plant to fill gaps in the rock garden for annual color, use as a companion for *Allium moly* in double plantings, or plant with sedums in xeriscape gardens. Tahoka daisy is a great cut flower, often used to fill out bouquets.

Myosotis sylvatica
Boraginaceae (Borage family)
FORGET-ME-NOT

PLANT TYPE: *Biennial grown as an annual*
ZONES: *Not applicable*
HABIT: *6"–18" tall*
CULTURE: *Semi-shade; moist soil*
BLOOM: *Spring*

Native to Eurasia, forget-me-not is a cherished plant in gardens throughout the world. Profuse, tiny flowers of blue, pink, or sometimes white with a yellow center bloom charmingly in spring, forming frilly mats. They make wonderful companions to spring-flowering bulbs in deciduous shade. The plants are self-seeding and will beautify the garden for years to come. The diminutive size lends itself to many appropriate sites. Tufted foliage remains neat and tidy but dies back in the heat of the summer.

CULTIVATION: Scatter the seed in early fall for blooms next spring. Indoors, sow seed in a warm location 8–10 weeks before the last

---

spring frost date. Germination occurs in 8–14 days. Do not cover as seeds need light to germinate. Transplant into the garden, spacing 6"–8" apart.

RELATED PLANTS: There are many cultivars, such as 'Blue Ball,' with rounded flowers, 'Carmine King,' with rosy blooms, 'Compacta,' which is a dense grower, 'Robusta Grandiflora,' a more vigorous plant, and 'Victoria Blue,' a mound-shaped plant 6"–8" tall with gentian-blue flowers. *M. scorpioides* is a perennial with bright blue flowers and much the same habit as *M. sylvatica,* but it flowers in summer.

USES: A mass planting of forget-me-nots makes a charming ground cover. Plant along the front of the border with pink astilbes for a soft, gentle effect. Use in shady rock gardens among stepping stones. Combine with pansies and toadflax to fill planters and baskets.

Nicotiana sylvestris
Solanaceae (Nightshade family)
FLOWERING TOBACCO

PLANT TYPE: *Annual*
ZONES: *Not applicable*
HABIT: *To 5' tall*
CULTURE: *Full sun to partial shade; well-drained soil*
BLOOM: *Summer*

Named in honor of Jean Nicot, who introduced tobacco to France, this stately native of Argentina has long been enjoyed by gardeners. A powerfully built plant, it has had a surge of popularity in recent years with gardeners' heightened interest in old-fashioned and fragrant flowers. It lends itself to many settings, creating an exotic tropical look or an old-fashioned quality. The bold rosette of large, lyre-shaped grass-green leaves stands upright, and the single flower stalk emerges from the basal leaves. The candelabra of individual drooping white flowers bloom in clusters. Each flower is 4"–5" long, having a slender tube with a ½" flared star at the end. The blooms open at night but stay open during the day if the sun is not too bright. They seem to glow at twilight like a spray of fireworks and emit a sweet, jasmine-like scent.

CULTIVATION: Sow indoors in a sterile potting mix placed in a warm location 6–8 weeks before the last spring frost date. Do not cover as the seeds need light to germinate. Germination takes 10–20 days. Give half-strength fertilizer weekly. Transplant outdoors 2 weeks after the last spring frost date, spacing the plants 2'–2½' apart.

RELATED PLANTS: *N. alata* is also very fragrant with a lower, more informal habit. It is well-suited to evening or cottage gardens.

Hybrids of *N. alata,* such as 'Nicki,' 'Merlin,' and 'Domino,' range through hues of white, pink, purple, and red but have no fragrance. Light salmon 'Apple-blossom' is very charming and different. 'Lime Green' is a unique shade of chartreuse.

USES: Intermingle this bold-textured plant in the perennial border for contrast with those plants that have finer foliage. Use as a specimen or "dot plant" in mass plantings of other annuals, or in containers. Include it with other night-blooming flowers, such as evening primrose and four-o'clocks, in a moon garden. Combine nicotiana with cleome and annual pennisetum for a colorful Victorian look.

Nigella damascena 'Miss Jekyll'
Ranunculaceae (Buttercup family)
LOVE-IN-A-MIST
PLANT TYPE: *Annual*   ZONES: *Not applicable*   HABIT: *12"–24" tall*   CULTURE: *Full sun to light shade; well-drained, moderately fertile soil*   BLOOM: *Spring to mid summer*

Cultivated for over 400 years, love-in-a-mist gets its name from the starry, semi-double, 1½" blue, rose, or white flowers that seem to float in a gentle tangle of pale green ferny foliage. Surrounded by feathery bracts, the double row of petals has an arching green center, adding to the spidery appearance. Another attractive facet is the purple-and-cream-striped seedpods that develop if the flowers are left to mature. Fast growing, they quickly

form globe-shaped pods, which dry naturally and are wonderful for dried arrangements. Planted in drifts or groups, their fine-textured, needley leaves make a statement. 'Miss Jekyll' has bright blue flowers.

CULTIVATION: Sow seeds directly in the garden several times during the growing season for successive blooms. Plants readily self-seed and may winter over as seeedlings in mild-winter areas. Seed may also be started indoors in peat pots in a warm location 4–6 weeks before the last spring frost date. Germination will occur in 10–15 days. Transplant into the garden as soon as possible to avoid damaging taproot, spacing plants 8" apart. Keep young plants moist.

RELATED PLANTS: 'Miss Jekyll Alba' bears long-stemmed white flowers. 'Mulberry Rose' has lovely deep rose flowers. 'Oxford Blue' grows to 30" tall with very double blue flowers. *N. hispanica,* from the Mediterranean, also grows to 30" tall; the flower petals are bright blue with striking red stamens. Its cultivar 'Alba' has clear white blooms; 'Atropurpurea' has purple blooms.

Uses: For a stunning combination of informal habit, pair with *Aurinia saxatilis* (basket-of-gold) and *Phlox subulata* in the rock garden. For contrast use between vertical elements, such as larkspurs, or plants with bold texture, such as foxgloves. The seeds are used to flavor foods; the papery striped seedpods are grown commercially for dried bouquets.

Papaver rhoeas 'Mother of Pearl'
Papaveraceae (Poppy family)
Corn poppy
Plant Type: *Annual*   Zones: *Not applicable*   Habit: *10"–14" tall*   Culture: *Full sun; fertile, well-drained, moisture-retentive soil*   Bloom: *Early to mid summer*

The Shirley poppy, a cultivated version of the scarlet-petaled corn poppy native to the fields of Flanders, was named in 1880 by Rev. W. Wilks of Shirley, England. Like its wildflower ancestor, self-sowing is truly one of the attributes of this plant. It is often shown growing in colonies, carpeting fields of ripening wheat, having naturalized there. The delicate glaucous leaves and stems covered with soft downy hairs are especially attractive when they catch the sunlight. Shirley poppies are easily distinguished from other poppies as the petals always have a white base. The 2"–3" flowers range from white through shades of red, orange, and pink. The pearly undertones of 'Mother of Pearl' soften the bright colors to cool pastel shades. The petals may look like silky crepe paper rustling in the breezes, but they can stand up to wind and some rain.

Cultivation: In mild climates, sow outdoors in fall for blooms the following spring. In colder climates, sow indoors in peat pots in early spring. Cover the seeds as they need darkness to germinate, which takes 10–15 days. Transplant into the garden carefully—corn poppies resent root disturbance—spacing the plants 9"–12" apart. Successive sowings in mild climates will extend the period of bloom. Some gardeners in cold-winter regions successfully sow corn poppy seeds in winter by sprinkling them on top of the snow.

Related Plants: *P. nudicaule* (Iceland poppy) has larger flowers on stems 1'–2' tall. Flowers are fragrant and come in delicious colors of white, red, orange, yellow, rose, and apricot. Although it can bloom from May to August, it languishes in hot weather and is grown to its best in cooler climates.

Uses: Create wonderful wildflower gardens with 'Mother of Pearl' and larkspurs, California poppies, and clarkias. Use as fillers among perennials for spring color. For informal bouquets, corn poppy's goosenecked buds are favorites of floral designers.

Pericallis × *hybrida* (syn. *Senecio* × *hybridus*)
Asteraceae (Composite family)
Cineraria
Plant Type: *Perennial grown as an annual*   Zone: *10*   Habit: *6"–8" tall*   Culture: *Partial to full shade; moist, well-drained soil*   Bloom: *Spring*

Bold hairy foliage is topped with single or double daisy-like flowers in colors of red, scarlet, crimson, pink, blue, purple, violet, or white, some with a light center or contrasting rings. There are basically 3 types: the large form, which grows to 3' tall; the star-flowered, at 1½' tall; and the compact, which is about 1' tall. As a pot plant, cineraria is a longtime favorite of spring flower shows and a choice plant for gift giving.

Cultivation: Sow the seeds indoors in a warm location in the fall for flowers the next spring. Germination occurs in 10–15

days. Once germinated, keep plants cool—about 50°F. When buds form and bloom begins, keep plants well-watered and cool at night. Feed every other week with a balanced fertilizer. Cinerarias do better if they are pot-bound.

RELATED PLANTS: Brightly colored 'Cindy' has a domed habit, blooming quickly and for a long time. 'Dwarf British Beauty Mixed' blooms for 8–10 weeks with 3" blooms on 10" plants. The dainty 'Mint Starlet Mixed', grows only 6" tall and can be grown in a 4" pot.

USES: This brilliantly colored, daisy-like flower is best used as a pot plant. It can be displayed on the patio or deck with other seasonal plants, or in the home if the nights are cool.

Rudbeckia hirta 'Irish Eyes' ('Green Eyes')

Asteraceae (Composite family)

GLORIOSA DAISY; BLACK-EYED SUSAN

PLANT TYPE: *Short-lived perennial grown as an annual*
ZONES: *Not applicable*
HABIT: *To 2½' tall*
CULTURE: *Full sun to light shade; rich, well-drained soil*
BLOOM: *Mid summer to frost*

Gloriosa daisies have an upright, branching habit, growing 3'–4' tall. Stems and leaves are rough and hairy. Flowers are daisy-like, with orange-yellow ray petals surrounding a purplish-black disk. 'Irish Eyes,' bred in 1957, is a novel variety of the black-eyed Susan. Borne above the rough woolly foliage are flowers 4½"–5" wide, with clear green

disks, or "eyes," surrounded by golden-yellow ray petals. The habit is loose with thin flower stalks, giving the plant an informal appearance. Its striking form adds grace and a feeling of gentleness to any border. Gloriosas are less likely to self-sow than other cultivars.

CULTIVATION: In mild areas, sow the seeds outdoors in spring or summer, up to 2 months before the first autumn frost date, for blooms the following year. Indoors, sow in a warm location in mid winter for blooms in the summer. Germination takes 5–10 days. Set plants out in the garden, allowing at least 12" between plants, and fertilize with an all-purpose fertilizer.

RELATED PLANTS: 'Becky' grows 12"–15" tall and has solid yellow and bronze-tinged flowers. 'Goldilocks' is 8"–10" high, with semi-double 3"–4" gold flowers; 'Indian Summer,' an outstanding new cultivar, has 6"–9" single flowers of golden-yellow and grows 3'–3½' tall. It blooms 10–12 weeks from sowing. 'Toto,' 8"–10" tall, has golden-orange blooms.

USES: Black-eyed Susans lend themselves to informal, old-fashioned gardens, especially when mixed with their hardier cousins. Interplant them in perennial borders among plants with shorter flowering periods for all-summer bloom. Fill containers with 'Irish Eyes' and *Nicotiana* 'Lime Green' for a stunning combination. Mass with sedums and ornamental grasses for a classic trio. Black-eyed Susans make wonderful cut flowers.

Scabiosa atropurpurea

Dipsacaceae (Teasel family)

PINCUSHION FLOWER

PLANT TYPE: *Annual*
ZONES: *Not applicable*
HABIT: *To 2' tall*
CULTURE: *Full sun; well-drained soil*
BLOOM: *Mid summer to frost*

The name "pincushion" refers to the many stamens that occur around each floret and stand above the flower cluster. *S. atropurpurea* was known as the mourning bride in earlier times, for the somber coloration of its flowers, but hybridization has replaced the purplish-black blooms with a vibrant dark blue. Blooms also come in white, rose, mauve, and clear purple. When considering other cultivars, this dramatic flower is best chosen in solid hues—the colors of the mixes can be muddled, closely resembling their ancestors. The period of bloom starts with a few flowers and the number increases as the growing season progresses until frost.

CULTIVATION: Sow where plants are to bloom as the long taproot makes transplanting difficult. Or sow seeds indoors, 4–5 weeks before the last spring frost date, in a well-drained, sandy mix placed in individual peat pots set in a warm location. Drainage is very important in winter as the seeds tend to rot. Germination takes 10–15 days. Carefully transplant outside after danger of frost is past, spacing plants 10"–15" apart. (Transplants may never be as tall or bloom as well as those sown in place.) The long wiry stems with divided leaves can be floppy and will need the support of their neighbors or a sturdy stake.

RELATED PLANTS: S. stellata is used for dried arrangements. Standing 18" tall, it has rosy-violet blooms and papery calyxes, which dry naturally. Perennial S. caucasica 'Pink Mist' is 12" high; 'Butterfly Blue,' its counterpart with lavender-blue flowers, cheerfully blooms all summer right up to frost.

USES: These wispy flower stems and fine leaves with cushion-like blooms lend themselves to old-fashioned or cottage gardens. Intermingle them with mid-height perennials, such as veronicas and mulleins, contrasting the rounded

habit of the scabiosa flowers with those having a vertical aspect. The fine texture of scabiosas is attractive in loose, informal bouquets.

Senecio cineraria (syn. *S. maritimus*)
Asteraceae (Composite family)
DUSTY MILLER

PLANT TYPE: *Perennial grown as an annual*
ZONES: *8–10*
HABIT: *4"–30" tall*
CULTURE: *Full sun; very well drained soil*
BLOOM: *Late summer to early fall*

This Mediterranean native, primarily grown for its striking silver foliage, has white matted hairs that give it a woolly appearance. The small ½" flower clusters can be cream or yellow and are produced at the very end of the growing season or not at all. The boldness of the texture varies with the cultivar.

CULTIVATION: Sow outdoors in place 2 months before the first frost in mild climates. Or sow indoors in a warm location 8–10 weeks before the last spring frost date. Germination takes 10–15 days. Do not cover as seeds need light to germinate. Dusty miller

resents overwatering and needs to be fertilized lightly or not at all.

RELATED PLANTS: 'Cirrus' has rounded, shallow-lobed silvery leaves on small plants 10" high. 'Silverdust' is 12" tall and bushy, with dissected leaves giving it a ferny appearance. *Tanacetum ptarmiciflorum* (syn. *Chrysanthemum ptarmiciflorum*) 'Silver Lace,' 6"–8" tall, has very lacy leaves.

USES: The distinctive coloration of the foliage outlines or defines the area in which dusty miller is planted, making it effective as an edging in formal settings. The neutral silvery color acts as a buffer, improving combinations of flowers with incompatible colors. Mixed plantings of flowers in containers and baskets are also unified in design by interspersing dusty miller among them.

Viola × wittrockiana 'Imperial Antique Shades'
Violaceae (Violet family)
PANSY

PLANT TYPE: *Short-lived perennial grown as an annual*
ZONES: *9–10*
HABIT: *6"–7" tall*
CULTURE: *Full sun to partial shade; rich, moist soil*
BLOOM: *Spring to early summer in cold-winter areas; fall to spring in mild-winter areas*

Pansies are loved by gardeners and children for their 2"–3" colorful, cheery blooms. Five petals overlap to create the flat flowers that are seen in a wide range of colors—white, yellow, purple, blue, dark red, rose, and even black. Colors may be single or combined in variations—often with blotches that give the characteristic look of a smiling face. The cultivar 'Imperial Antique Shades' is one of a series. The plants are bushy with large 2½"–3" flowers. The coloration of the flowers is unique—blooms change color, intensifying with maturity. Shades of white, yellow, gold, lavender, and purple blend to make a most unusual pastel palette. They bloom very early in the season and can be combined with narcissus for a sensational combination. Pansies, if grown in partial shade, will often rebloom in the fall—if the summer isn't too hot.

CULTIVATION: Sow seeds outdoors in summer to fall for blooms the following spring. Place the seedlings in a cold frame or plant where they are to bloom. They can also be started indoors in a warm location in late winter to early spring, and will flower the first year. Germination takes about 20 days. Cover the seeds as they need darkness to sprout. Mulch to keep the soil cool and to

prolong bloom. Deadhead faded flowers to keep the plants blooming.

RELATED PLANTS: There are many varieties and cultivars of *V. × wittrockiana.* Colors come in every shade from glistening white to almost black. 'Romeo and Juliet' is a pastel mix similar in appearance to 'Imperial Antique Shades.' 'Black Devil' is truly unique for its black flowers with a spot of yellow at the center. 'Maxima Marina' is light blue with a dark blue face bordered in white. 'Jolly Joker' is a

fun flower with striking colors— deep orange and royal purple. 'Padparadja' is an intense jewel-like orange. 'True Blue' is a lovely medium blue with a touch of yellow at the center. 'Rippling Water' has velvety deep purple petals edged in white. *V. tricolor* (Johnny-jump-up) blooms in the spring with smaller flowers; the typical form is tricolored in shades of yellow, white, and purple. There are also solid-colored cultivars. *V. cornuta,* a perennial in zone 6, can be used as an annual in colder climates. Cultivars come in yellow, blue, purple, red, and apricot; flowers are 1"–2", blooming in early spring.

USES: Pansies look their best when planted in groups and are used extensively in mass plantings. They can be used as an underplanting with spring-flowering bulbs such as tulips. Intersperse them among perennials in the rock garden. Use in hanging baskets for seasonal color.

BULBS

What a joy to have old garden friends herald the coming of a new season. The snowdrops planted 15 years ago have grown into large drifts that you divided, replanted on your property, and shared with friends. The lily your children gave you for your birthday blooms every year, perfuming the summer air. The autumn crocus you picked up on a long-ago trip rewards you with dozens of waterlily-like blooms, a flowering memento.

The term "bulb" is used loosely here to include plants that are true bulbs and others that are actually rhizomes, tubers, and corms. These plants have several characteristics in common: All are perennial—they will come back year after year if grown in an appropriate climate; their bloom lasts several weeks to several months—the flowers are a bulb's raison d'être for most gardeners; lastly, all have an underground food storage mechanism that allows them to be dormant for much of the year, showing neither foliage nor flower above ground.

The key to success with any bulb—which is measured by getting the plant to bloom year after year—is to allow the foliage to remain after the flower has faded.

As photosynthesis occurs in the leaves, food is produced and carried down to the bulb, where it is stored to keep the plant alive during its long period of dormancy. Cutting the foliage down too early, before it dies back naturally, will result in a weakened bulb that may not have sufficient food to get it to the next blooming season. The wise gardener interplants bulbs with other perennials that will hide the ripening and browning bulb foliage.

Choose bulbs that are hardy in your region for a low-maintenance approach to gardening. Plant bulbs in the exposure and soil they prefer, give them ample moisture, and they will perform for many years. Many bulbs will, in fact, naturalize or multiply in

the ground. The only time you need to bother with these bulbs is if they fail to bloom—usually because of overcrowding. Then dig them up, separate the bulbs, replant them at the recommended depth and distance from one another, and the next season you will be enjoying their beauty once again.

As you look through our favorite bulbs, you may find ones that are not hardy in your region. This does not mean that you cannot grow them; in fact, anyone anywhere can grow any bulb—it just takes more effort. If certain bulbs are not cold-hardy, but you live in a region that has cold winters, wait until after the danger of frost has passed in the spring before planting. Then be sure to dig the bulbs after the foliage ripens but before the first frost in autumn. Air-dry in a well-ventilated place for a week. Remove all soil from the bulbs and store them in sand, peat moss, or sawdust—lightly moistened if so directed—in a cool (45°–55°F.) dry place for the winter. Some people store large bulbs or tubers, like dahlias, in discarded pantyhose. (Tie a knot between each bulb so they don't touch one another, and hang in a cool dark place like a basement.) This allows for good air circulation—a must to keep mold and mildew from forming.

Even gardeners in warm climates need to make an effort if they want to grow bulbs that require a cold period to get them to bloom (like many of the early spring flowering bulbs—tulips, daffodils, crocuses, etc.). Either buy precooled bulbs or chill them for at least 8—preferably 10 to 12—weeks. You can do this in the refrigerator, but be sure to keep them away from bananas, apples, and pineapples; these and other ripe fruit give off ethylene gas, which inhibits flower formation in bulbs. After chilling, plant the bulbs out in the coolest part of the garden.

Bulbs run the gamut of size, color, and shape. From delicate white snowdrops, with their bell-shaped flowers that grace the late-winter garden, to spikes of hot red crocosmias 3' long in late summer, there are bulbs for every garden and every color scheme. Many bulbs make excellent cut flowers, so grow enough to enjoy them both indoors and out.

Agapanthus
Headbourne hybrids
Liliaceae (Lily family)

LILY-OF-THE-NILE;
HARRIET'S FLOWER

PLANT TYPE: *Rhizome*
ZONES: *9–11*
HABIT: *36"–48" tall*
CULTURE: *Full sun; rich, well-drained soil*
BLOOM: *Summer*

Native to South Africa, these rhizomatous perennials are evergreen, producing lovely clusters of thick, dark green leaves. In summer, they send up stiff stalks that bear globular umbels of up to 100 blue flowers. The individual funnel-shaped flowers are produced throughout the summer. In areas with no winter frost, agapanthuses are handsome year-round. In cold-winter areas, they are often grown in containers and brought indoors in autumn, when the weather turns chilly. They make a bold statement in the garden—an exclamation point of vivid blue against the summer sky.

CULTIVATION: Plant so the crowns are at soil level. They thrive in pots—use a rich planting medium. Feed monthly with fish emulsion or liquid kelp. In cold-winter areas, bring pots indoors in fall; allow plants to rest, do not fertilize, and give them just enough water to keep them from dying back; keep in partial sun. When new growth appears in spring, increase light and watering, move to a warmer space, and begin fertilizing. Move outdoors only after all danger of frost has passed. These plants rarely need dividing—only if you want to increase your stock.

RELATED PLANTS: 'Peter Pan' is a dwarf that grows only 24" tall but produces exceptional blue flowers. White selections are also seen.

USES: In warmest areas, in the middle of the flower border, they will provide year-round interest. In colder climates, place tubs of plants near a swimming pool or deck for an instant lush tropical look.

Allium christophii
(syn. *A. albopilosum*)
Liliaceae (Lily family)

STAR OF PERSIA;
DOWNY ONION

PLANT TYPE: *Bulb*
ZONES: *4–9*
HABIT: *18"–30" tall*
CULTURE: *Full sun; sandy, well-drained soil*
BLOOM: *Late spring to early summer*

Native to central Asia, star of Persia is an outstanding plant for the summer border. The straplike leaves, 1" wide, have white hairs on the reverse side, giving the plant its other common name, downy onion. The lilac flowers are extremely showy, comprising 100 or more tiny florets that form a ball-shaped umbel 10"–12" in diameter on a 24" stem. Even after blooms fade to brown, they still resemble fireworks in the garden.

CULTIVATION: In spring or fall, plant bulbs 4" deep and 8"–10" apart. You can increase your plants by allowing the seeds that form in the flowerheads to drop to the ground, or by scattering the seeds elsewhere in the garden.

RELATED PLANTS: Equally showy, *A. karataviense*, a lower growing plant reaching 6"–10" tall, has broad, dark blue-green leaves and a silvery-lilac bloom made up of ½" flowers in a loose, ball-like umbel up to 4" across.

USES: A low-maintenance plant that will give beauty for many years. Include it in the middle of a mixed border, or pair with day-lilies to hide allium's ripening foliage after the flowers have faded. A long-lasting cut flower when fresh, it is also beautiful in dried arrangements.

Alstroemeria Ligtu hybrids
Liliaceae (Lily family)
PERUVIAN LILY
PLANT TYPE: *Rhizome* ZONES: *7–10* HABIT: *36"–48" tall* CULTURE: *Full sun to partial shade; moist, well-drained soil* BLOOM: *Summer*

Native to South America, alstroemerias have been catching on as superb plants for the cut-flower garden and the mixed border. They will withstand short periods of 32°F. temperatures, but not prolonged freezes. Resembling true lilies (*Lilium* spp.), they put forth a colorful display in a range of colors—often spotted or streaked in combinations of pink, flame, salmon, and yellow. Each trumpet-shaped flower is 1"–2" wide, perhaps not that showy by itself, but in profusion creating a gorgeous instant bouquet on the plant.

CULTIVATION: Be careful when handling the brittle rhizomes. Plant 2"–4" deep and 8"–12" apart. Water well in summer; provide a winter mulch if temperatures dip below 32°F. for short

periods of time. In colder areas, lift rhizomes after the first frost. Dry and store in a cool dry area for the winter. Check periodically to make sure they do not dry out. Replant in spring. In warm climates, if plants become overcrowded and fail to bloom, divide in spring or fall.

RELATED PLANTS: *A. ligtu,* the species, grows only 36" tall with variegated flowers in mid summer in hues of pink, pale lilac, or off-white with a splash of yellow on the inner petals.

USES: Include Peruvian lilies in a cutting garden for their lovely, long-lasting blooms. Plant them among true lilies and daylilies in a mixed border for continual color all summer.

Amaryllis belladonna
Amaryllidaceae (Amaryllis family)
BELLADONNA LILY; CAPE BELLADONNA
PLANT TYPE: *Bulb* ZONES: *9–10* HABIT: *To 18" tall* CULTURE: *Full sun; rich, well-drained soil* BLOOM: *Late summer*

Native to South America, this bulb is sometimes called naked lady lily because its blooms appear before the leaves. Three or more fragrant, trumpet-shaped, 3½" flowers of perfect pink with a white throat are borne at the top of a deep plum stem. The plant adds a burst of color in the border in late summer, when most perennials have stopped blooming. Leaves then emerge and persist until spring in frost-free areas. In areas where there is no frost, it will naturalize. This unusual plant is bound to grab attention.

CULTIVATION: Plant bulbs in spring after danger of frost is past, in a warm, protected area. Plant 4" deep and 4"–6" apart; do not mulch. In cold-winter climates, either dig up before the first autumn frost and store indoors in a cool dry space, or grow in pots, planting 3 bulbs 1" deep in a 12" pot. Water once. As flowers begin to emerge, increase watering and fertilize. As flower spikes appear, increase water; as leaves appear, feed balanced fertilizer. Don't disturb bulbs. Let dry out when dormant.

RELATED PLANTS: *Lycoris,* another member of the amaryllis family,

also blooms without its leaves. Like *A. belladonna,* it can be grown in pots in cold-climate areas.

USES: Place belladonna lily where you can appreciate the blooms—and mark the space so you don't forget it's there the following spring. Lovely following peonies in summer.

Anemone nemorosa

Ranunculaceae (Buttercup family)

WOOD ANEMONE

PLANT TYPE: *Rhizome*
ZONES: *5–9*
HABIT: *3"–5" tall*
CULTURE: *Partial shade; rich, humusy soil*
BLOOM: *Early spring*

An underutilized plant in America, the wood anemone is native to Europe. It is commonly seen in woodland wildflower gardens, adding its charm in early spring. The creeping rhizomes give rise to attractive, cut-leaf, fernlike foliage. White 1" flowers with a tinge of pink rise on 3"–5" stems. By summer, all traces of the plant have disappeared.

CULTIVATION: In fall, as soon as they are available, plant rhizomes 2" deep and 6" apart. Plants look best in large drifts of 25 or more. Divide as necessary if plants become overcrowded or bloom declines. Keep well-watered until killing frost.

RELATED PLANTS: 'Alleni' has rose-lilac blooms that are bluish inside. *A. blanda* (Greek wind-flower) is a hardy tuberous bulb that grows best in full sun. Daisy-like flowers of white, blue, pink, or bicolors appear in early spring above fernlike foliage. Flowers close in shade, or when a cloud passes overhead.

USES: An excellent plant for naturalizing in large drifts in woodlands. Wood anemonies bloom before deciduous trees leaf out, adding interest and color early in the year. Interplant with daffodils and ferns, which follow these heralds of spring.

Begonia grandis

Begoniaceae (Begonia family)

HARDY BEGONIA

PLANT TYPE: *Tuber*
ZONES: *6–9*
HABIT: *12"–24" tall*
CULTURE: *Partial shade; moist, rich, well-drained soil*
BLOOM: *Summer*

Native to China and Japan, the hardy begonia is becoming recognized as a great flowering plant for shady areas. It may look semi-tropical, but will withstand winter temperatures down to 0°F. Elongated oval leaves with toothed lobes are green on top and red on the underside. Flowers hang in loose clusters on reddish-pink stems. The larger 1½" male flowers are distinguished from female flowers by their 4 petals; female flowers have only 2.

CULTIVATION: Plant hardy begonia tubers in spring after danger of frost has passed, 2"–4" deep and 12"–18" apart. Feed with fish emulsion monthly, once leaves emerge. Stop watering and feeding in autumn. Hardy begonias will sprout bulbils in the leaf axils. Spread the bulbils over the surface of the potting medium in a flat; press down firmly, and cover the flat with a piece of glass or plastic to keep in the moisture. Once the bulbils have sprouted, pot them up in individual pots. When the plants develop several sets of leaves, set them out in the garden.

RELATED PLANTS: *B.* Tuber-hybrida hybrids (hybrid tuberous begonias) are not hardy except in zones 10–11. Their exquisite, large, camellia-like blooms enhance any lightly shaded area. Perfect in pots or hanging baskets, they flower all summer.

USES: Throughout the summer, the leaves and flowers of hardy begonias add color to a shady border. Plant to follow bleeding hearts (*Dicentra* spp.), with their pink and white spring blooms, in a woodland garden.

Claytonia virginica

Portulacaceae
(Portulaca family)

SPRING BEAUTY

PLANT TYPE: *Corm*
ZONES: *4–7*
HABIT: *To 12" tall*
CULTURE: *Shade; moist, neutral to alkaline soil*
BLOOM: *Early spring*

Spring beauty is often called an ephemeral—like many other spring wildflowers it seems to be there in all its beauty one minute, and gone the next. A delicate-looking wilding, it is native to the eastern United States. Its small, 5–petaled flowers are a white that hints of pale pink, with a slightly deeper pink venation. Grasslike, deep green leaves accompany the blooms. Both flowers and leaves disappear by early summer, reappearing in their minute splendor the following spring. A lovely woodland plant, spring beauty is still seen growing wild along some of the nation's scenic roadways, such as the breathtaking Blue Ridge Parkway of western Virginia and North Carolina.

CULTIVATION: Plant delicate tubers as soon as you receive them. Handle carefully. Since it is often difficult to tell which way is up, plant tubers on their sides, ½"–1" deep, 2" apart. Let other plants shade the dormant roots in summer. Spring beauty will naturalize in the garden, forming large colonies from self-sown seeds.

RELATED PLANTS: Carolina spring beauty (*C. caroliniana*) is a Southern species with broader leaves—equally hardy and lovely.

USES: Use spring beauty to provide a naturalistic swath of early color in a deciduous woodland garden. Plant with wake robin, creeping phlox, and oak fern for continuous interest through fall.

Crinum × powellii 'Album'

Amaryllidaceae
(Amaryllis family)

CRINUM LILY

PLANT TYPE: *Bulb*
ZONES: *8–10*
HABIT: *24"–30" tall*
CULTURE: *Full sun; rich, moist soil*
BLOOM: *Summer*

Crinum lilies are tropical bulbous plants. The evergreen foliage is somewhat fleshy and straplike, growing 2'–3' long and 2"–4" wide, and needing a fair amount of space in the garden. Crinums are grown for the fragrant, trumpet-shaped flowers that are borne in heads of up to 15 flowers atop a sturdy 24"–30" flower stalk. Usually only 3 or 4 fragrant pure white flowers open at one time, which extends the blooming season. These plants make a lovely accent in the Southern summer garden. Northern gardeners can enjoy them in pots.

CULTIVATION: Plant so the neck of the bulb is visible above soil level, allowing about 24" between plants. Protect them from wind. Water well throughout the growing season. Crinum lilies dislike being transplanted to new locations; they may take up to 3 years to bloom again after being disturbed. To grow these plants successfully in pots, pot them up in early spring and place where air is warm and moist. Move them outdoors for summer; bring indoors in fall and store in a cool, frost-free place. Crinums must be potted up as they become pot-bound. Rest them in the winter by reducing heat and allowing them to partially dry out. Plants will produce offsets from the base of the bulb—these offsets may be detached and planted separately to increase your stock.

RELATED PLANTS: 'Mystery' has pink flowers; 'J. C. Harvey' grows to 60" tall with coral-pink flowers; 'Ellen Bosanquet' bears lovely red blooms; 'Maureen Spinks' boasts red flowers with a white stripe.

USES: Crinum lilies give an exotic look to the summer garden. They are handsome planted near agapanthus. In pots, they are excellent accent plants and can be moved around the garden as attention grabbers.

Crocosmia × *crocosmiiflora* 'Lucifer'

Iridaceae (Iris family)

MONTBRETIA

PLANT TYPE: *Corm*
ZONES: *5–8*
HABIT: *To 36" tall*
CULTURE: *Full sun; light, well-drained soil amended with plenty of organic matter*
BLOOM: *Late summer*

Crocosmias are cormose plants native to South Africa, generally hardy only in zones 9–10. Their sword-shaped fans of large leaves are attractive even before the slender, branching flower stalk shoots up in late summer. *C.* × *crocosmiiflora* is a hybrid of *C. aurea* and *C. pottsii*. The result is a handsome plant that sends up a zig-zagged flower spike that bears flowers in summer. 'Lucifer' is the hardiest cultivar, known to grow even in parts of Switzerland. Its blooms are a strong red color that stands up well in full sun and can last up to 3 weeks when cut.

CULTIVATION: Plant corms 2" deep and 8"–10" apart in an area where they will not be disturbed and can spread and multiply. To increase your stock of plants, remove any offsets that form and replant them. As soon as seed of this hybrid is ripe, it can be planted—however, it may not grow true to the original plant.

RELATED PLANTS: 'Jenny Bloom' bears deep yellow flowers; 'Firebird' has fiery red-orange blooms.

USES: 'Lucifer' is lovely in the mixed border for its bold foliage and brilliant-hued flowers late in summer, when much of the garden is fading. It is a long-lasting cut flower, excellent in arrangements. Pair with rudbeckia in the garden for a bright late-summer treat.

Crocus tommasinianus

Iridaceae (Iris family)

CROCUS

PLANT TYPE: *Corm*
ZONES: *3–9*
HABIT: *To 6" tall*
CULTURE: *Full sun; light, well-drained soil*
BLOOM: *Early spring*

One of the best heralds of spring, *C. tommasinianus* is an outstanding species native to regions of Hungary and Bulgaria. It glows with pale lavender petals that are silvery on the inside, with a long white throat and brilliant yellow stamens in the center of the flower. The slender, grass-like leaves appear at the same time as the flowers in earliest spring. This crocus is one of the best to naturalize in a lawn.

CULTIVATION: Plant corms in early fall, as soon as they become

available, 3"–4" deep and 2"–3" apart. These plants prefer to be moist during the growing season and dry during the rest of the year. Let the foliage ripen naturally. Never cut the foliage until it turns brown, especially if you are trying to grow this crocus in the lawn. *C. tommasinianus* seeds freely; therefore, you may see different forms and variations within a mature planting.

RELATED PLANTS: 'Barr's Purple' has abundant, purple-lilac flowers; 'Ruby Giant' is a deep violet-purple. The larger hybrid Dutch crocuses bloom in the garden a week or two later than *C. tommasinianus*.

USES: Plant in the lawn to give a lighthearted burst of color in early spring. In the garden, plant to follow snowdrops (*Galanthus nivalis*) and to precede *Iris reticulata*—a low-growing, early blooming garden gem with pretty, deep purple flowers.

Cyclamen hederifolium (syn. *C. neapolitanum*)

Primulaceae (Primrose family)

IVY-LEAVED CYCLAMEN; NEAPOLITAN CYCLAMEN; SOWBREAD

PLANT TYPE: *Tuber*
ZONES: *5–9*
HABIT: *3"–6" tall*
CULTURE: *Partial shade; rich, well-drained soil*
BLOOM: *Late summer to autumn*

Ivy-leaved cyclamen, native to Europe, is a dainty cousin of florist's cyclamen. Grow it where you can appreciate its delicate features from late summer through autumn. First flowers bloom before the leaves emerge. The 1" flowers, borne on 3"–5" stems that rise above the leaves, have the classical recurved petals typical of all cyclamens, in shades of pink or white with a crimson blotch. Leaves up to 5" across vary in form, and may be rounded, heart-shaped, or look like ivy leaves. They are dark green with a white marbling on top and either plain green or deep red underneath.

CULTIVATION: Plant tubers at least 3"–5" apart as soon as you get them, with tops just below soil level. Interestingly, the roots are produced from the upper surface of the tuber. Cover lightly with evergreen boughs or salt hay in the winter to prevent the soil from heaving and thawing. Once planted, cyclamens do not like to be disturbed.

RELATED PLANTS: 'Album' bears pure white blooms. *C. coum* is a spring bloomer, often flowering early with snowdrops.

USES: Makes a handsome edge to a path. Excellent in a rock garden or planted atop a shaded rock wall where you can appreciate its beauty.

Dahlia spp.

Asteraceae (Composite family)

DAHLIA

PLANT TYPE: *Tuber*
ZONES: *9–11*
HABIT: *7"–48" tall*
CULTURE: *Full sun; well-drained, sandy loam*
BLOOM: *Mid summer to autumn*

Originally native to Central America, thousands of hybrid dahlias now add their beauty to fall gardens throughout North America. The tender tubers are often treated as annuals, but many gardeners in cold-winter areas take time to dig the tubers and store them indoors over winter. Dahlias range in size from miniature plants less than 12" tall, with appropriately small flowers, to large exhibition plants that can grow to 5' or more. Flowers come in various sizes and shapes, from single flowers less than 1" across to showy blooms 8" or more in diameter. Gardeners have various motivations for growing dahlias; some prize them for their beauty in the garden, others for their cut flowers in arrangements. And some gardeners like to grow them for competition—these are the people who pinch off all but one or two buds from the plant, directing all its energy to produce a single gigantic flower.

CULTIVATION: Plant dahlias 10 days before the last frost date in spring. Dig soil to a depth of 12" and amend with peat moss or compost. Replace half the soil in the hole; place tuber on its side and cover with remaining amended soil. Space tubers 12"–36" apart. Set stake in the ground when you plant tall varieties. Water well, then don't water again until shoots appear. Increase the amount of water as plants grow. Fertilize sparingly. Disbud dahlias for competition-size blooms. Dahlias can be started indoors in very cold climates. Fill individual 8" pots with a mix of damp peat moss and vermiculite; plant tuber 2" deep. After all danger of frost is

past, transplant gently into the garden. In cold-winter areas, dig the tubers in fall, leaving a 6" stalk. Store indoors in peat moss or sawdust, or dip in paraffin, to keep tubers from drying out.

RELATED PLANTS: Cactus-Flowered dahlias are extremely showy, with starburst-type flowers. Dahlinovas are a new strain of dahlia, with perky blooms that burst forth from diminutive plants only 7"–8" tall. Prolific bloomers with long-lasting flowers, they are excellent in containers or to edge a flower bed or pathway. Dinner Plate dahlias are the largest blooms—in brilliant colors, literally the size of a dinner plate, especially if disbudded; a single stem is awesome. These are the dahlias to enter in flower shows. Pompon dahlias are lovely, with globelike heads of tightly packed petals rising above the foliage, and attractive dark-colored stems. They bloom in abundance and are striking as cut flowers or massed in borders. Magic Carpet dahlias are miniature, only 16"–18" tall, but covered with a mass of colorful single blooms—great for beds, borders, and window boxes. Anemone-Flowered dahlias are very attractive; their large single row of petals surrounds a pincushion center. Large-Flowered or Decorative dahlias, with outstanding double blooms, are also welcome additions to the late summer and fall garden.

USES: Dahlias, along with chrysanthemums, are mainstays of the flower border in fall. Plant different varieties together for a range of flower types and colors. Elegant massed in front of cannas for autumn color. Long-lasting in the garden, excellent as cut flowers, they are equally at home in the cutting garden, the perennial border, or containers.

Eremurus × *isabellinus* (syn. *E.* × *shelfordii*)
Liliaceae (Lily family)
FOXTAIL LILY; DESERT CANDLE

PLANT TYPE: *Tuber*
ZONES: *5–8*
HABIT: *48"–60" tall*
CULTURE: *Full sun; rich, well-drained soil*
BLOOM: *Late spring to early summer*

Foxtail lilies are native to western and central Asia. Not true bulbs, they have brittle, tuberous roots that are shaped like starfish. Long green, straplike foliage appears before the tall, unbranched flower spikes. The top third of the flower spike is covered with hundreds of tiny, closely-spaced, bell-shaped flowers that gradually open from the bottom of the spike upward. In the glow of sunset, it is easy to see how they got the name desert candle. This is one of the most spectacular tuberous plants that you can have in your garden.

CULTIVATION: In September, or as soon as you get the tuberous roots, dig the soil to a depth of 24". Form a large cone of soil in the center of the hole. Gently spread roots so that the crown rests on the cone, 6" from the top of the hole. Fill the hole with soil. Allow at least 36" between plants. Keep well-watered during the growing season. Do not disturb once planted, but divide if crowded by lifting roots as foliage dies down in fall, and carefully separate plants. Mulch with evergreen boughs or salt hay if a late spring frost is expected, to protect the developing flower spike.

RELATED PLANTS: The blooms of 'Shelford Pink' are a lovely salmon-pink; 'Cleopatra,' orange-pink; 'Moneymaker,' yellow-orange. *E. stenophyllus* blooms earlier on shorter flower spikes (only 24"–36" tall) with bright yellow flowers.

USES: Foxtail lilies make a vivid exclamation in early summer gardens. Tall and colorful, they are good for the back of a border and as long-lasting cut flowers. Plant behind daylilies—the colors harmonize well.

Erythronium revolutum 'White Beauty'
Liliaceae (Lily family)
DOGTOOTH VIOLET; TROUT LILY

PLANT TYPE: *Corm*
ZONES: *5–9*
HABIT: *To 5" tall*
CULTURE: *Partial shade; rich soil*
BLOOM: *Spring*

This species is native to the Pacific Coast, where it thrives in moisture provided by the summer fog. Each corm produces 2 handsome, large, broad, mottled

green leaves and a slender flower stalk that bears 4–5 flowers in late April. The blooms are lilylike, hanging from a thin stem, with dainty recurved petals. Flowers range in color from pure white to rose-pink, with yellow to orange centers. 'White Beauty,' a short variety only 4"–5" tall, has pure white flowers.

CULTIVATION: Plant corms in fall, as soon as they become available. Plant 3"–4" deep, 8"–10" apart, where they will not be disturbed. Dogtooth violets need partial shade, especially in the heat of the day. They prefer to be moist throughout the growing season, drier in late summer and fall. The species may be grown from seed, with patience; it can take several months for seeds to germinate, and then up to 3 years until the plant is mature enough to bloom.

RELATED PLANTS: *E. tuolumnense* grows 12" tall, with solid green leaves and deep golden-yellow flowers that bloom in very early spring; hardy in zones 3–9. *E. americanum,* the common fawn lily, has green leaves mottled purple and white. Growing 4"–8" tall, it bears single yellow flowers in April; hardy in zones 3–9.

USES: Dogtooth violets are lovely naturalized in a deciduous woodland or planted in a rock garden. Plant with ferns and species lilies to provide interest after the flowers have faded.

Fritillaria meleagris 'Alba'
Liliaceae (Lily family)
GUINEA-HEN FLOWER; CHECKERED LILY
PLANT TYPE: *Bulb*   ZONES: *5–8*   HABIT: *To 24" tall, usually 12"–18"*   CULTURE: *Full sun to partial shade; deep, lightly moist, humusy, well-drained soil*   BLOOM: *Early spring*

This graceful woodland perennial is underutilized in America. Native to Europe, it is often seen in lawns or meadows, blooming in early spring on the Continent and in England. Its names come from the checkered design of the flower, most visible on the maroon-and-white variety (feathers of guinea hens form a similar design). 'Alba' is more subtle—the design is white on white.

Several narrow leaves are borne along the stem, which is topped with a solitary, nodding, bell-shaped 1½" flower.

CULTIVATION: Do not allow bulbs to dry out; plant them in early fall as soon as they become available. Amend soil with organic matter. Plant bulbs 3"–4" deep and 3"–4" apart, with pointed ends up, in clusters of 7 or more bulbs for best effect. Mulch lightly in late fall. Once they bloom in the spring, allow the foliage to ripen and die back naturally. Do not disturb bulbs and they will bloom for many years.

RELATED PLANTS: Taller *F. persica* 'Adiyaman' has gray foliage and up to 30 drooping, deep purple 1" flowers on a 2'–3' stem; it needs frost protection. Crown imperial (*F. imperialis*) is a unique-looking plant. Growing 3' to 4' tall, the single stem has lilylike foliage with a cluster of 2"–3" bell-shaped flowers crowned by a topknot of leaves. Flowers are red, yellow, or orange. Foliage has a skunky scent—deer will not eat the plant. Hardy in zones 4–8.

USES: Brightens a deciduous woodland before the trees leaf out. Plant with *Anemone nemorosa* or interplant with ferns.

Galanthus elwesii
Amaryllidaceae (Amaryllis family)
GIANT SNOWDROP
PLANT TYPE: *Bulb*   ZONES: *4–9*   HABIT: *4"–11" tall*   CULTURE: *Full sun to partial shade; sandy soil*   BLOOM: *Late winter to early spring*

Native to southeastern Europe, the giant snowdrop is one of the first heralds of spring, often emerging and blooming even when there is still snow on the ground. Each bulb produces two or three dark bluish-green, strap-like leaves that can grow to 8" long and ¾" wide. The nodding, 1"–1½" flowers are solitary, borne at the end of a 4"–11" stalk. The 3 inner petals are tipped with green and overlap the longer, pure white outer petals. Giant snow-drops naturalize easily and form lovely blooming drifts to grace the earliest gardens. Plant them where you can appreciate them from indoors and out.

CULTIVATION: In early fall, plant bulbs 3"–4" deep and 2" apart, with pointed ends up, in groups of 15 or more for best effect. Bulbs can be left for many years to multiply. Divide when they become crowded, just as flowers fade. In fall, mulch with well-rotted manure or compost.

RELATED PLANTS: *G. nivalis* (common snowdrop) grows to about 6" tall and bears solitary 1" blooms. 'Flore Pleno' is inter-esting for its slightly upturned

double flowers that bloom just a little later in the spring.

USES: Long lasting in the garden, they are precious as miniature cut flowers. Plant with *Iris danfordiae* or *Crocus tommasinianus.*

Gladiolus callianthus (syn. *Acidanthera bicolor*)
Iridaceae (Iris family)
ABYSSINIAN GLADIOLUS

PLANT TYPE: *Corm*
ZONES: *7–11*
HABIT: *To 36" tall*
CULTURE: *Full sun; prefers clay soil*
BLOOM: *Mid to late summer*

Native to South Africa, this tender cormose perennial deserves a place in the summer garden. It produces an elegant fan of sword-shaped leaves, and a sin-gle stem that can bear 6–8 flow-ers. Each is majestic—up to 3" across—with 6 pure white petals that are purple at the base. The flower has a pleasant aroma that's more pronounced at night.

CULTIVATION: Plant corms 4"–6" deep and 6"–10" apart in spring, after all danger of frost has passed. In mild-winter climates, leave corms in the ground all year. In zone 7 and colder, dig them up in

fall when the leaves start to yellow. Store indoors in a cool dry space, and replant the following spring.

RELATED PLANTS: Garden gladio-lus, like Abyssinian gladiolus, gives a great show in summer, bearing a spike of blooms that opens from the bottom of the spike upward. Dozens of cultivars come in a rainbow of colors.

USES: Include Abyssinian gladio-lus in an evening garden—the white blooms and sweet fragrance will lure you, especially at night. Plant with galtonias and white dahlias for continuous night inter-est and fragrance.

Hyacinthus orientalis 'L'Innocence'
Liliaceae (Lily family)
HYACINTH

PLANT TYPE: *Bulb*
ZONES: *3–8*
HABIT: *8"–12" tall*
CULTURE: *Full sun to light shade; rich, well-drained soil*
BLOOM: *Spring*

Originally native to the eastern Mediterranean region, mod-ern hyacinths are hybrids, usually bred and grown in Holland. Hyacinths are the most fragrant of all spring-blooming bulbs, producing a single spike of 1" flowers clustered around the stem. They are easy to grow in the garden, and can be forced into bloom indoors in a pot.

CULTIVATION: In early to mid fall, before the ground freezes, plant bulbs in groups of 3 or 5, 4"–6" deep and 4"–8" apart. In zones 8–10, plant 8" deep. In zones 3–4, mulch lightly with straw after the ground freezes. Keep well-watered during the fall and spring. Unlike other bulbs, which will display the same bloom year after year, hyacinths bloom with less-showy flower spikes in subsequent years. After the first year, move the bulbs to a less prominent location and enjoy their perfume and daintier flowers for many years. Some people develop contact dermatitis when handling hyacinth bulbs, so be sure to wear gloves.

RELATED PLANTS: Other delightful cultivars include 'Violet Pearl' (violet-purple), 'Pink Pearl' (deep rosy-pink), 'Delft Blue' (deep blue), 'Amethyst' (violet-mauve), 'Jan Bos' (carmine-red), 'City of Haarlem' (lemon-yellow), 'Hollyhock' (double flowers, crimson-red), and 'King Codro' (double flowers, deep violet-purple).

USES: Excellent as cut flowers or forced for indoor bloom in a hyacinth glass. Plant to follow snowdrops and crocuses in a perennial and bulb bed. Makes a dramatic contrast with *Narcissus* 'Vintage Rose' or grape hyacinth (*Muscari armeniacum*). Plant where you can appreciate the sweet aroma.

Iris 'Vanity'
Iridaceae (Iris family)

BEARDED IRIS;
GERMAN IRIS

PLANT TYPE: *Rhizome*
ZONES: *3–9*
HABIT: *30"–36" tall*
CULTURE: *Full sun to light shade; moderately rich, well-drained soil*
BLOOM: *May to June*

Originally native to Europe, bearded irises have been hybridized and are now prized worldwide for their elegant beauty. The 3 top petals are called standards, the 3 lower ones are called falls. These irises are distinguished from others by the hairlike "beards," 1" long, that emerge from the base of each of the falls. The range of colors spans the rainbow—white to blue to red to nearly black. Flowers may be one color or many—often the falls and standards are of contrasting colors, with the beard adding yet another hue to the display. 'Vanity' is the palest pink with a slight green venation and a lovely peach beard.

CULTIVATION: In early fall, plant the rhizomes horizontally with the top ⅓ to ½ above the soil and the leafy end pointed in the direction you want growth to follow. Allow 24" between plants. In hot climates, plant the rhizomes just below the soil surface, and grow them in partial shade. Never mulch bearded irises, and don't let fertilizer touch the rhizomes. Water plants deeply when they become dry. After flowers fade, trim foliage to a 12" fan. Lightly feed in early spring. Divide after flowering every 3–5 years.

RELATED PLANTS: 'Kiss' has falls that fade from muted purple to almost white, and a soft gold beard; 'Blue Luster' is a glistening medium blue with a matching blue beard; 'Cranberry Ice' has huge ruffled blooms of red-orange-violet touched with amber at the petal's edge; 'Joyce Terry' is a charming bicolor with clear yellow standards and white falls edged in yellow; 'Gay Parasol' has silvery-white standards and lacy rose-purple falls.

USES: Bearded irises are most showy in late spring and early summer, either planted by themselves or mixed in a perennial border. They're equally elegant as cut flowers. For continuous bloom, plant near Dutch irises.

Lilium 'Casa Blanca'
Liliaceae (Lily family)

ORIENTAL LILY

PLANT TYPE: *Bulb*
ZONES: *3–8*
HABIT: *4'–5' tall*
CULTURE: *Full sun; humusy, slightly acid, very well drained soil*
BLOOM: *Mid summer*

Oriental lilies are regal hybrids from Japan that bestow an elegance on the summer garden unmatched by any other plant. A single tall stem may bear up to 8 large flowers, 6" or more across. The blooms are fragrant, especially at night. One of the later-blooming Oriental lilies, 'Casa Blanca' has cool white flowers with slightly recurved petals and very prominent red-orange stamens.

CULTIVATION: Plant the bulbs as soon as they become available—before autumn frost. Prepare soil to a depth of 18"–20", adding humus, compost, or leaf mold plus a handful of bonemeal. Plant bulbs in groups of three, 8" apart with pointed ends up, so that 4"–6" of soil covers them. In late fall to early winter, mulch with salt hay, straw, or pine needles. During the summer, remove flowers as they fade. When last bloom fades, cut the stalk below the lowest flower but above leaves; when the leaves die, cut the stalk down.

RELATED PLANTS: There are many other beautiful Oriental lilies: 'Antonia' has large, delicate pink blooms with a creamy-yellow throat, and grows 24"–36" tall; 'Kyoto' grows 36" tall and has lovely white flowers handsomely spotted with maroon; 'Muscadet' is pure white with pink spotting and a soft pink stripe down the center of the petals; 'Sartre' is deep pink with yellow markings; 'Hot Lips' grows 30"–40" tall and has white petals with a bold, deep pink stripe down the center and deep pink spotting; 'Le Reve,' 3'–4' tall, has soft pink petals with a golden-yellow star at its throat.

USES: With its height, 'Casa Blanca' works well in the middle to back of the border. Pair with gold-banded *L. auratum* for a stunning display. Oriental lilies are excellent cut flowers. Some people remove the stamens because the pollen can stain.

Narcissus poeticus 'Actaea'

Amaryllidaceae (Amaryllis family)

PHEASANT'S EYE; POET'S NARCISSUS

PLANT TYPE: *Bulb*
ZONES: *3–8*
HABIT: *To 18" tall*
CULTURE: *Full sun to partial shade; deep, fertile, well-drained soil*
BLOOM: *Mid spring*

In most parts of the country the daffodil, or narcissus, is synonymous with spring. The earliest species daffodils burst forth even before the snow has melted. And through the winds of March and the showers of April, daffodils keep spring alive with cheerful blooms. 'Actaea' is the last of the daffodils to flower, usually in late April or early May. It ushers the genus out of blooming season in great fashion with the largest flower of any narcissus. This is a charming, old-fashioned flower,

with narrow green leaves and a single, fragrant bloom borne atop a stem that can reach up to 18". White petals surround a yellow cup edged in red—those who know what a pheasant's eye looks like will immediately see the resemblance.

CULTIVATION: Plant the bulbs in early to mid fall, before the ground freezes. (In zones 8–10, precool the bulbs for 6 weeks at 35° to 45°F.) Plant with pointed end up, 8" deep and 6" apart, in groups of 3, 5, 7 or more for best effect. In spring, allow the foliage to yellow and die back naturally, then cut it to the ground.

RELATED PLANTS: There are hundreds of narcissus cultivars, divided into 12 classes. Trumpet daffodils include 'Dutch Master,' a golden classic, and 'Mount Hood,' with long-lasting white flowers. Large-Cupped daffodils include 'Carlton,' a soft yellow bloom with a frilled cup, and 'Ice Follies,' with white petals and a cup that opens yellow and matures to white. 'Mistral' is a lovely, fragrant Split-Corona, or Butterfly narcissus, with a golden-yellow split cup and white petals.

USES: Irresistible in a mixed border, naturalized in a lawn, or planted at the edge of a deciduous woodland. For contrast, plant with yellow lily-flowered tulip 'Lady Bird Johnson.' Bring spring indoors with cut daffodil flowers.

Ornithogalum arabicum
Liliaceae (Lily family)
STAR OF BETHLEHEM

PLANT TYPE: *Bulb*
ZONES: *6–10*
HABIT: *18"–24" tall*
CULTURE: *Full sun; moist, well-drained soil*
BLOOM: *Late spring*

Native to the Mediterranean region, this bulb is an eye-catcher in any garden. It gives rise to 5–8 pale green leaves, 12"–18" long and ¾" wide. In May or June, a single flower stem shoots up 12"–24" with a cluster of 6–12 white, star-shaped, 1" flowers with prominent black pistils (called the black eye). In areas where it is not hardy, it makes an excellent potted plant that can be grown indoors and brought outside when the weather warms in late spring.

CULTIVATION: Choose a sheltered location. In warm-winter areas, plant in fall; in other areas, plant in spring after danger of frost is

past. Set bulbs 2"–5" apart and 4" deep in bold clumps of 7 or more. Do not let bulbs dry out in winter; keep soil evenly moist. In areas with winter frost, dig bulbs before autumn frost and store indoors in a cool dry place; replant in spring.

RELATED PLANTS: *O. saundersiae* (giant chincherinchee) has strap-like leaves and flowering stems 4' tall, with clusters of white 1" flowers with black ovaries. Hardy in zones 7–9. *O. thyrsoides* (chincherinchee) bears dense clusters of ¾" white flowers. Hardy in zones 8–10.

USES: Be sure to include this bulb in a cutting garden and in a mixed border for late spring interest. It's excellent as a cut flower.

Oxalis purpurea
'Grand Duchess'
Oxalidaceae (Oxalis family)
OXALIS

PLANT TYPE: *Tuber*
ZONES: *4–10*
HABIT: *10"–12" tall*
CULTURE: *Full sun to partial shade; sandy soil*
BLOOM: *Late spring*

There are more than 800 species of oxalis. Most are native to South America and South Africa, and a few are native to the United States. Some varieties are prized; others have naturalized, becoming "weeds" in the landscape—the small, yellow-flowered, clover-like plants with fleshy roots that pop up in many gardens. Originally native to Chile and Argentina, *O. purpurea* is a tuberous perennial that makes a charming addition to any garden. Some tender species may be

grown only in frost-free areas or as houseplants, but 'Grand Duchess' grows throughout a wide range of climates. Three leaflets provide the typical clover-like look; in late spring, a cloud of small, star-shaped pink, lavender, or white flowers, 3–9 per stem, seems to cover the plant.

CULTIVATION: In spring or fall, plant tubers 1" deep and 3"–5" apart. With its tuberous roots, oxalis can survive drought conditions but benefits from some summer moisture. Divide as necessary if plant becomes overcrowded.

RELATED PLANTS: *O. tetraphylla* (syn. *O. deppei*), known as lucky clover or iron-cross oxalis, has brilliant rose-pink flowers. Hardy in zones 8–10, it can be grown as an annual in colder areas. *O. depressa* (syn. *O. inops*), growing only 4"–5" tall, is a good rock garden plant for zones 8–10, with its shiny shamrock foliage and pink blooms with a yellow eye.

USES: This lovely plant can be grown singly, or en masse as a late spring blooming ground cover. Plant at the edge of a woodland to follow fritillarias.

Puschkinia scilloides var. *libanotica* (syn. *P. libanotica*)

Liliaceae (Lily family)

STRIPED SQUILL

PLANT TYPE: *Bulb*
ZONES: *4–10*
HABIT: *6"–8" tall*
CULTURE: *Full sun to partial shade; any well-drained soil*
BLOOM: *Mid spring*

Native to Lebanon, this minor bulb is most often seen in cold-winter areas, yet it is suitable to milder climates as well. Each bulb produces several shiny green leaves, up to 10" long and 1" wide. Once the leaves emerge, the flower stem soon follows—so eager to bloom, it seems each flower opens as soon as its bud appears above the soil. Each stem carries up to 8 star-shaped flowers that have a unique, light, grape-like fragrance. Blooms are bluish-white, with a thin, pale blue stripe that runs down the center of each petal. Planted in drifts, striped squill makes a lovely spring display in any garden.

CULTIVATION: Plant in early fall before the ground freezes. Dig soil to a depth of 5" and work in a handful of bonemeal and some compost. Plant bulbs 3" deep and 3"–5" apart with pointed ends up,

in groups of 9 or more for an impressive showing. Bulbs are best left undisturbed to multiply for many years. Lift only to divide, which should be done right after flowers fade.

RELATED PLANTS: *Scilla mischtschenkoana* (syn. *S. tubergeniana*) looks very similar but blooms earlier, and its flowers face downward, whereas striped squill's face upward.

USES: Striped squill naturalizes well in a spring garden. Excellent in a rock garden or deciduous woodland. Plant with early daffodils and *Scilla siberica*. Snip some of the flower stems for an adorable mini flower arrangement of spring blooms.

Ranunculus asiaticus 'Superbissimus'

Ranunculaceae (Ranunculus family)

PERSIAN BUTTERCUP

PLANT TYPE: *Tuber*
ZONES: *8–10*
HABIT: *12"–18" tall*
CULTURE: *Full sun to partial shade; well-drained, slightly acid, sandy soil*
BLOOM: *Late spring to early summer*

Persian buttercups, native to Iran, are often seen as cut or potted flowers in florist shops in the East. In California and other mild-winter areas, they are a standard in the spring garden with their boldly colored blooms. Compound leaves are finely cut and fernlike, attractive both before and after the flower blooms. Up to 4 flowers, 1"–4" wide, may appear on a long stem. Usually fully double, they look as delicate as crepe paper, but in fact are quite tough. Wherever they are

grown—window box or flower border—they add a bright and cheery note.

CULTIVATION: In zones 8–10, plant in fall; in other areas plant as soon as the ground thaws in spring. Thrives in cool weather, so do not wait to plant until the soil warms. Soak the tuber overnight in tepid water. Plant with claws pointing downward, 4" deep and 4" apart. If planted in fall in zones 5–7, mulch heavily. In cold-winter areas, lift tubers after foliage dies back; store inside in a cool dry place, in sawdust or sand, until spring.

RELATED PLANTS: Tecolote hybrids grow 18"–24" tall in a range of bright colors—sunset-orange, yellow, white, rose, red, pink. French peony hybrids, 12"–15" tall, have bright double or semi-double flowers.

USES: Exotic double flowers will dazzle your eyes in late spring. Often treated as an annual, they are hardy in zones 8–10. These are excellent potted plants, handsome in a window box combined with white pelargoniums and trailing *Vinca major,* or planted in the garden with freesias.

Scilla siberica
Liliaceae (Lily family)
SIBERIAN SQUILL

PLANT TYPE: *Bulb*
ZONES: *3–9*
HABIT: *6"–8" tall*
CULTURE: *Full sun to partial shade; moist, well-drained garden soil*
BLOOM: *Early spring*

Native to Eurasia, Siberian squill is a handsome plant for the early spring garden, making a large impact when thickly massed. Sturdy green leaves 4"–6" tall and ½" wide clasp the deep purple flower stem that bears up to 6 brilliant deep blue, nodding, star-shaped ½" flowers. The blooms are unique in having blue stamens and pollen. Bees are attracted to this early bloomer; beekeepers can easily tell when it has begun to flower, as the bees return to the hives with blue legs—covered in Siberian squill pollen.

CULTIVATION: In fall, as soon as you receive the bulbs, dig soil to a depth of 5" and add a handful of bonemeal. Plant bulbs 3"–4" deep and 4"–6" apart with pointed ends up, in groups of 7 to 12 or more for a significant display. A light mulch may be applied in winter. Keep soil moist in spring. Allow foliage to die back naturally, then remove. Siberian squill may be left undisturbed to multiply for years; it naturalizes well.

RELATED PLANTS: *S. bifolia* blooms late winter to early spring, with up to 8 flowers on a 4"–8" stem. A lovely woodland plant with blue, pink, or white blooms.

USES: This garden gem is stunning planted in large drifts in front of yellow forsythia or under flowering dogwoods. Beautiful in a rock garden, or deciduous woodland interspersed with glory-of-the-snow (*Chionodoxa* spp.) and daffodils.

Triteleia laxa (syn. *Brodiaea laxa*) 'Queen Fabiola'
Liliaceae (Lily family)
ITHURIEL'S SPEAR; GRASS NUT

PLANT TYPE: *Corm*
ZONES: *8–10*
HABIT: *20"–28" tall*
CULTURE: *Full sun; well-drained soil*
BLOOM: *Early summer*

Native to Oregon and California, this plant makes a lovely show in June or July. Lofty grasslike leaves appear in late spring, then disappear by late summer; meanwhile, tall stems produce loose umbels of delightful, funnel-shaped, deep blue 1" flowers.

CULTIVATION: Plant the corms in fall as soon as you get them; set 3"–4" deep and 6"–8" apart, in groups of 7 or more for a truly impressive display. If winter temperatures get below 32°F. at night,

protect with a mulch of leaves. Where winters are colder, lift the bulbs in late summer, store indoors in a cool dry area, and replant in spring.

RELATED PLANTS: *Brodiaea coronaria*, hardy to zones 7–8, grows 12"–18" tall with a loose umbel of funnel-shaped, violet-purple 1½" blooms in early summer.

USES: Handsome in a mixed border, or planted in front of climbing sweet peas. These are excellent cut flowers.

Tulipa 'Angélique'
Liliaceae (Lily family)
PEONY-FLOWERED TULIP

PLANT TYPE: *Bulb*
ZONES: *3–8*
HABIT: *14"–18" tall*
CULTURE: *Full sun to light shade; sandy, humus-rich, well-drained soil*
BLOOM: *Mid spring*

Originally native to Turkistan, tulips have been hybridized and cultivated for many hundreds of years. Today, most tulip bulbs are field-grown and imported from Holland; only a small percentage of the bulbs originate in the U.S. Unusual and spectacular, Peony-Flowered (or Double

Late) tulips, with huge double blooms that look like dainty peony blossoms, are surprisingly resilient. Among the last tulips to bloom in spring, 'Angélique' is one of the most beautiful, with light pink petals with varying shades of paler and darker pink.

CULTIVATION: Plant bulbs in fall, in an area sheltered from wind, before the ground freezes. In zones 8–10, precool bulbs at 40°–45°F. for 8 weeks before planting. Dig soil 8"–12" deep and work in bonemeal. Plant bulbs 4"–8" deep and 4"–8" apart with pointed ends up, in groups of 5, 7, 9 or more for a good show. In coldest areas, mulch with straw or hay after the ground is frozen.

RELATED PLANTS: Other Peony-Flowered tulips are 'Mount Tacoma' (white), 'St. Tropez' (brilliant red), and 'Carnaval de Nice' (rose fading to white edges). Hundreds of different tulips bloom from early to late spring in every color and hue.

USES: Excellent as a cut flower. Beautiful planted in large containers. Include 'Angélique' in a perennial bed for mid to late spring color. Plant to follow Double Early tulips 'Peach Blossom' (pink) and 'Schoonoord' (white). Interplant with forget-me-nots for a delicious pairing of blue and pink.

Zephyranthes grandiflora
Amaryllidaceae
(Amaryllis family)

ZEPHYR LILY

PLANT TYPE: *Bulb*
ZONES: *9–10*
HABIT: *To 12" tall*
CULTURE: *Full sun; moist, rich soil*
BLOOM: *Late spring to summer*

Zephyr lily, native to South America, is a handsome tropical plant for warm-climate gardens. The bulbs give rise to flat, narrow leaves up to 12" long. Flowers, usually borne singly atop

a hollow stalk, have an irregular funnel shape. Blooms 3" long may be pink or red.

CULTIVATION: Plant bulbs 1"–2" deep and 3"–4" apart in fall in warm-winter climates. In cold-winter areas, plant in spring after danger of frost is past, and dig up before autumn frost. Store indoors in a cool area in fairly moist sand, so the bulbs do not dry out over the winter.

RELATED PLANTS: *Z. candida* bears crocus-like flowers on 4"–8" stems in early autumn.

USES: Excellent planted with freesias and to follow ranunculus in warm-weather gardens.

CACTI AND OTHER SUCCULENTS

For texture, color, diversity, and drama in the garden, succulents reign supreme. They are an excellent choice for gardeners without much time since they need little maintenance, are not fussy about soils, and tolerate drought. Succulents are plants with thickened, fleshy leaves, stems, and/or roots that store water to carry them through dry periods. Cacti are a special form; their branches are reduced to small cushion-like structures called areoles, supporting spines instead of leaves.

usually slow growing and thus do not often need pruning or dividing. In certain areas succulents seem to thrive on neglect, surviving with no care other than ambient rainfall and well-drained soil—although they'll respond if given more water and fertilizer. In addition, succulents are resilient. They transplant easily and will endure bare-root conditions for weeks, even months, until planted.

A succulent border, varied and rich, presents a sculptural quality unparalleled in perennial gardening. Because succulents come from many plant groups, the gardener has the opportunity of adding unique colors, shapes, and textures. Barrel-shaped cacti and rosette-shaped agaves are arresting, used individually or in groups. Columnar-stemmed cacti and euphorbias provide strong vertical accents. The architectural forms of most succulents create a visual framework for less-structured plants growing around them.

Succulents provide year-round foliage color, from silver-blue and gray-green hues to sunny yellows and splashy reds. And the diversity of floral types offers a whole other dimension to explore. Flower colors may be nondescript or flashy—orange, red, purple, even chartreuse.

Many succulents thrive as potted plants and can provide the ideal landscape solution for courtyards, patios, porches, balconies, and window gardens. Where succulents will not survive outside over the winter, they can be brought inside and planted out again in spring. Others make excellent indoor plants year-round, given bright light and little water.

Many succulents are native to the world's deserts, where water is seasonally unavailable, but some are found near the seashore, where water is saline. Others come from tropical climates, where they cling to exposed rocks or atop tree branches, competing with other plants for water that soon drains away. Most succulents are perennial.

Larger succulents thrive in full sun, but many smaller kinds do better in the partial shade of trees or shrubs, much as they would in nature. Soil with good drainage is the most essential requirement. Microclimates that do not dip below 25°F. will accommodate a great diversity of succulents. A few are able to withstand temperatures well below freezing, so that even gardeners in northern regions can enjoy some of these fascinating plants.

Succulents have certain advantages over many common garden plants. Primarily, they require less maintenance. They are

Adenium obesum

Apocynaceae
(Dogbane family)

DESERT ROSE;
IMPALA LILY

PLANT TYPE: *Succulent*
ZONE: *10*
HABIT: *To 3' or more tall and across*
CULTURE: *Full sun to light shade; any well-drained soil*
BLOOM: *Throughout the warmer months*

Neither rose nor lily, this oleander relative is native from tropical East Africa to Arabia. A caudiciform—a plant with thickened, water-storing roots and trunk but with thin leaves—it thrives in heat and seems equally at home in Arizona's aridity or in the steamy tropics. Its oleander-like flowers are typically a lovely pink and about 2" across, but depending on the cultivar, they vary from 1"–5" across and from white to pink to deep crimson-red. The spineless adeniums are protected by their toxic sap, so take care to avoid contact with eyes or skin.

CULTIVATION: Requires ample moisture and fertilizer during spring and summer, winter protection from frost. Partly or wholly deciduous during cooler winter months, when the plant should be watered only sparingly. Easily grown from seed when available. Selected forms are grown from cuttings set in well-drained planting medium, with high humidity and a high bottom temperature (80°–90°F.). A percentage will root within 2–6 months. Place far enough apart to achieve best mature form.

RELATED PLANTS: Selected forms and hybrids of *Adenium* include 'Asha,' with 5" flowers; 'Crimson Picotee,' with white-throated flowers and an undulate crimson margin; and the 3" flowered 'Crimson Star,' with intense red blooms. Adeniums are spineless relatives of the spiny pachypodiums, which include the so-called Madagascar palm (*Pachypodium lamerei*). Caudiciforms belonging to other families include *Cyphostemma juttae* (in the grape family, Vitaceae), with thick, knobby trunks to 3' or more tall and 1' across, covered with a peeling, parchment-like bark. In late spring it produces fleshy gray-green leaves to 1' long, followed in fall by showy clusters of pinkish-red grapelike fruits. *Dioscorea elephantipes* (in the yam family, Dioscoreaceae) has a hemispherical caudex covered with corky tubercles, which make it look like a tortoise shell. It produces a vine in winter with 1" heart-shaped leaves.

USES: *A. obesum* is widely planted in tropical landscapes such as Singapore and Thailand. An ideal patio container plant in cooler climates—bring inside in winter to protect from frost.

Aeonium arboreum
'Zwartkop'

Crassulaceae
(*Stonecrop family*)

BLACK AEONIUM

PLANT TYPE: *Succulent*
ZONES: *9–10*
HABIT: *Shrub 3'–4' tall; 2'–3' across, less if massed*
CULTURE: *Full sun to partial shade; well-drained soil*
BLOOM: *Late spring*

Native to North Africa and the Canary Islands, aeoniums are adapted to Mediterranean climates with cool wet winters and long dry summers. Most commonly cultivated varieties, however, will tolerate—and in fact require—summer watering to look their best. 'Zwartkop,' also sold as 'Schwarzkopf,' is derived from the North African *A. arboreum* 'Atropurpureum,' and was selected in Holland for its very dark purple, almost black, foliage. Plants will flower only after mature stature is attained; the small, brilliant yellow flowers stand out strikingly against the foliage and are arranged in cones to 1' long and 5" across at the base.

CULTIVATION: This succulent may be planted at any time of year, but most growth will occur during winter in Mediterranean climates. Amend the soil with pumice and organic matter to improve drainage as needed. Propagate black aeoniums by cuttings, which can usually be planted immediately, about 1' apart. Allow cuttings to callus for about a week if planting in wetter conditions or heavier soils.

RELATED PLANTS: The Catlin hybrids incorporate the dark reddish or purple foliage of 'Zwartkop' into various forms: 'Zwartkin' has matte purplish foliage in contrast to the glossy and darker 'Zwartkop'; 'Garnet' has glossy, deep reddish-purple leaves reminiscent of the gemstone; 'Cyclops' has bronzy-purple leaves in rosettes to 1' across. Other species of *Aeonium* range from basal rosettes to cushions to shrubs with leaves of varying degrees of succulence, with or without markings or marginal cilia (fringed edges). Colors vary from shades of green, reddish, or purple. *A. hierrense* has low-growing, glaucous rosettes of leaves with ciliate margins and squat cones of pink flowers. *A. × hybridum* makes small green, compact cushions with showy yellow flowers.

USES: 'Zwartkop' is a striking bedding plant, and when cut and replanted every couple of years, it can be kept bushy and under 1' tall. In colder climates, it can be used as an annual and moved indoors over the winter. Combine black aeoniums with other bedding succulents for long-lasting foliage color.

Agave victoriae-reginae
Agavaceae (Agave family)
QUEEN VICTORIA AGAVE

PLANT TYPE: *Succulent*
ZONES: *8–10*
HABIT: *Stemless spherical rosettes to 1½' tall and across*
CULTURE: *Full sun to light shade; well-drained soil*
BLOOM: *Summer, but only at maturity, after a decade or more*

Native to central Mexico, *A. victoriae-reginae* rewards the patient grower with beautifully symmetrical, spherical rosettes of spiraled green leaves marked with white as if hand-painted. Although endangered in the wild, it is well-established in cultivation. Small plants offset vigorously, but this feature wanes with age as the plant acquires its mature beauty. Remove offsets to favor the largest rosette with freedom from competition for water and nutrients.

CULTIVATION: Will grow in any well-drained soil; one rich in nutrients will hasten growth. Can be planted at any time of year, but should be lightly shaded if planted in hot weather—spring or fall planting is best. Propagate by seed (occasionally available) or division.

Plant rosettes of about 3" across about 6" apart; when clumps fill in, divide further. Cluster large rosettes with smaller ones for a natural appearance.

RELATED PLANTS: The agaves range from the 6" miniature *A. parviflora*, with symmetrical rosettes of stiletto-like leaves with curled fibers on the leaf margins, to the 10' *A. mapisaga*. Similar to *A. parviflora* are *A. filifera*, to 1' across, and *A. multifilifera*, to 5' across. Several smaller species, to 2' or less across, have gray leaves with jagged teeth on the leaf margins. Among the best of this type are *A. colorata* and *A. guadalajarana*. Among medium-size species, the spineless *A. attenuata* is especially popular in mild coastal regions for its elegant, 3' yellow-green rosettes and dramatic arching inflorescences. *A. a.* 'Nova' has straight inflorecences and slightly larger 4' rosettes of a superior glaucous bluish color. *A. americana* (century plant) is the most common of the larger species, with gray-leaved rosettes to 8' across. *A. a.* 'Variegata' has yellow-margined green leaves with whimsically drooping tips. A more refined and smaller cultivar, to 4' across, *A. a.* 'Medio-picta-alba' has gracefully recurved blue-green leaves with cream-colored mid-stripes.

USES: Agaves may be used as accent plants singly or in small groups. They are effective fountaining out of ground covers or standing boldly among the delicate foliage of mesquite (*Prosopis glandulosa*) and other leguminous desert shrubs.

Aloe sinkatana
Liliaceae (Lily family)
ALOE

PLANT TYPE: *Succulent*
ZONES: *9–10*
HABIT: *To 1' tall and across*
CULTURE: *Full sun to partial shade; well-drained soil*
BLOOM: *Year-round, peaking in spring*

Native to Sudan, *A. sinkatana* is perhaps the most freely flowering of any landscape aloe. Most species are more seasonal, typically blooming during the winter months, with orange (more rarely yellow, red, or pink) tubular flowers in heads or more elongated racemes. The smooth spotted leaves have pinkish margins that make it an attractive plant even when not in flower.

CULTIVATION: Plant in masses, 6"–8" apart. Divide offsets at any time of year.

RELATED PLANTS: The genus *Aloe* includes about 300 species native from Africa to Arabia, ranging from 2" miniatures to 60' trees. Flowers are typically orange and arranged in racemes. *A. sinkatana*'s

nearly everblooming qualities are shared by its hybrid *A.* 'Rooikappie,' which has greener foliage and orange flowers in heads. Smaller species include *A. humilis*, with toothy gray-green leaves in miniature rosettes just 3" across, but with orange flowers of about the usual size. *A. aristata* has 4"–5" rosettes of green leaves covered with bristly teeth. It is among the hardiest aloes—to zone 8. *A. brevifolia*, with 5"–6" rosettes of gray-green leaves with teeth on the margins, is one of the commonest landscape aloes since it soon offsets to form carpets. Nearly as abundant are the spotted-leaved 1' rosettes of *A. saponaria* and its close relatives, the best of which is *A. commutata*. *A. virens*, with 8" rosettes, stands out in spring with a profusion of intense orange flowers.

Among the medium-size aloes with rosettes 2'–3' across, some of the most attractive have bicolored floral displays, with red or orange buds opening yellow or white. Notable examples of this sort are *A. petricola* and *A. wickensii*. Some of the larger solitary aloes form rosettes, eventually 4'–5' across, atop a trunk to 10' tall or more covered with a skirt of dried leaves. Three of these species have similar toothy leaves, but when in flower they are easily distinguished: *A. ferox* has orange flowers on erect branches; *A. spectabilis* has yellow to orange flowers contrasting sharply with dark green to black stalks; and *A. marlothii* has horizontal branches, and flowers that lean in one direction, evoking windswept flames. If a tree is what you're after, try *A. bainesii*, which has a grotesquely thickened trunk and tapering branches that make it

look like a character out of a Dr. Seuss story.

USES: Plant larger types in irregular groupings of odd numbers of plants. Use smaller species in mass plantings.

Cleistocactus samaipatanus (syn. Borzicactus samaipatanus)
Cactaceae (Cactus family)
CLEISTOCACTUS

PLANT TYPE: *Cactus*
ZONES: *8–10*
HABIT: *To 2' tall; to 1' across*
CULTURE: *Full sun to light shade; well-drained soil*
BLOOM: *Almost year-round, except for a brief period in winter*

Native to Bolivia, *C. samaipatanus* is one of the most satisfying of landscape cacti, vigorous and easy to grow. Its beautiful golden-yellow spination is especially attractive with back lighting. It blooms freely, with periodic flushes of delicate coral-pink, trumpet-shaped flowers borne not just at the tip but along 6" or more of the upper stems.

CULTIVATION: One of the most undemanding of landscape succulents, but responds to watering and fertilizing with more attractive spination and even more profuse flowering. Easily rooted from cuttings, which should be allowed to callus for a week in summer, up to 4 weeks in winter; plant 6" apart. This ease of propagation makes mass planting affordable and allows for periodic renewal should an old planting start to look scruffy.

RELATED PLANTS: The related cleistocacti share the freely flowering nature of *C. samaipatanus,* but have tubular rather than trumpet-shaped flowers. *C. candelilla,* with tan 2" spines, yields a profusion of crimson flowers. *C. chacoanus* has less spiny, thinner stems and bright orange, gracefully S-curved flowers. *C. dependens* has carmine flowers with a band of yellow, and then green tips. The larger *C. strausii* has stout, erect, organ-pipe-like stems 3" in diameter and completely covered in glassy white spines. It bears 3" tubular burgundy-colored flowers. A host of larger columnar cacti includes the popular night-blooming *Cereus uruguayanus* (sometimes listed as *C. peruvianus*), with usually 5-ribbed, glaucous, nearly spineless stems to 5" across, forming large shrubs. Monstrose forms of *Cereus* have grotesquely knobby stems that appear to be made of molded wax. *Cephalocereus senilis,* the Mexican old man cactus, named for its covering of white hairs, is a favorite container plant as a seedling but also makes a fine landscape specimen, growing to 6' or more, with stems 4" thick. *Oreocereus celsianus* (syn. *Borzicactus celsianus*), the South American old man, has more robust stems with stout caramel-

colored, awl-like spines poking through the white hairs. The best of the largest columnar cacti is *Echinopsis terscheckii* (syn. *Trichocereus terscheckii*), an easier-to-grow South American look-alike of the saguaro. Its solitary stems may be nearly 1' across and over 15' tall.

USES: For container or landscape, singly or in mass plantings.

Crassula perfoliata var. *falcata* (syn. *C. falcata*)

Crassulaceae (Stonecrop family)

AIRPLANE PLANT

PLANT TYPE: *Succulent*
ZONES: *9–10*
HABIT: *To 2' tall and across*
CULTURE: *Full sun to partial shade; well-drained soil*
BLOOM: *Late summer to fall*

Native to South Africa, *C. falcata* has variable foliage—extreme forms hardly look like the same species, except in flower. Some have yellow-green, channeled, chisel-shaped leaves, but the best and most commonly cultivated form has recurved, sickle-shaped silvery-gray leaves arranged in a propeller-like fashion, and flat-topped heads of brilliant crimson, carnation-scented flowers.

CULTIVATION: Divide or take cuttings in summer and allow to callus in partial shade for a week or two or until adventitious roots appear; plant 6" apart. If you have enough, plant groups of 3 about 8" apart.

RELATED PLANTS: One of the largest genera of the stonecrop family, *Crassula* offers a great variety of forms from tiny ground

covers to 10' shrubs. Many are choice miniatures suitable for containers. One of the best of these is a hybrid of *C. falcata* with the miniature white-flowered *C. mesembryanthemopsis* (the smallest plants always seem to have the longest names). The result is a compact, silvery-leaved mound with fragrant pink flowers called *C.* 'Morgan's Beauty' (often mislabeled 'Morgan's Pink'). Good landscape varieties include *C. ovata* (syns. *C. argentea, C. portulacea*), the ubiquitous jade plant. Numerous cultivars of this species exist, though the drab ivory-flowered form is most commonly planted. A better choice is *C. ovata* 'Pink Beauty,' a form with longer-lasting pink flowers. *C. arborescens* (silver jade plant) is the hardy giant of the genus, with silver-dollar-size gray leaves with red edges. In full sun, the leaves of the ground cover *C. capitella* 'Campfire' turn brilliant scarlet, especially in winter, followed in late summer or fall by 1' spikes of creamy, musty-smelling flowers. *C. capitella* ssp. *thyrsiflora* (syn. *C. corymbulosa*) turns a darker shade of red, and bears drooping stalks of similar sweet-musty flowers. Another standout with bright red foliage, especially in winter, is the 3" ground cover *C. pubescens* ssp. *radicans,* covered in spring with tiny pale to pure white flowers in ½" pompons atop slender stalks.

USES: For container or landscape, singly or in mass plantings.

Dasylirion longissimum
Agavaceae (Agave family)
SOTOL

PLANT TYPE: *Succulent*
ZONES: *8–10*
HABIT: *6'–8' rosette of wiry leaves*
CULTURE: *Full sun to partial shade; well-drained soil*
BLOOM: *Summer to fall*

Like a living kinetic sculpture, the Mexican *D. longissimum* forms a rosette of hundreds of slender, wiry leaves that wave hypnotically in the breeze, resembling a giant shaving brush. It has impressive, torchlike terracotta-colored spikes of small creamy flowers.

CULTIVATION: Grown from seed when available. Seedlings look like tufts of grass at first, but will soon round out to form a spherical rosette to 8' across.

RELATED PLANTS: Other dasylirions are smaller but also form spherical rosettes. *D. wheeleri* has flattened, swordlike gray leaves lined with teeth, and forms 4'–5' rosettes. Native to the southwestern U.S. and northern Mexico, it is hardy to zone 8 but seems equally comfortable in tropical climates. The yuccas can also form spherical rosettes of usually more rigid leaves—from the stemless *Yucca whipplei,* to short-trunked species such as *Y. rigida* and *Y. rostrata,* to trees such as *Y. brevifolia* (Joshua tree), *Y. valida, Y. filifera,* and the ubiquitous *Y. gloriosa. Y. filamentosa* is among the hardiest species, to zone 4. *Y. elata* is one of several with green leaves ornamented with marginal white fibers. All have waxy cream-colored flowers on impressive torchlike stalks, with the exception of *Y. filifera,* which has pendent inflorescences. Resembling a yucca rosette atop a bottle-shaped trunk with thick corky bark is *Nolina stricta* (syn. *Beaucarnea stricta*) of Mexico. *N. recurvata* (syn. *Beaucarnea recurvata*), the so-called ponytail palm, is a familiar container plant with a rosette of gracefully drooping green leaves. It can form, after several decades of growth in the garden, a massive bottle-shaped trunk to 6' across at the base. It is especially effective when planted in groups, as small forests. *N. longifolia* is similar to *N. recurvata,* but has a denser tuft of leaves nearly concealing the corky-barked trunk.

USES: As with the similarly bold forms of agaves, *D. longissimum* and its relatives are effectively planted fountaining out of a ground cover or juxtaposed against the delicate foliage of small-leaved shrubs. Many look quite at home when interplanted with desert wildflowers.

Dudleya brittonii
Crassulaceae (Stonecrop family)
DUDLEYA

PLANT TYPE: *Succulent*
ZONES: *9–10*
HABIT: *Rosette to 1' across*
CULTURE: *Full sun to shade; well-drained soil*
BLOOM: *Spring to summer*

The largest and most impressive of the 40 *Dudleya* species native to western North America is *D. brittonii.* Its foliage varies from green to chalky-white, the latter forms seeming to radiate light, providing focal points in the garden. Pinkish stalks bear pale yellow flowers.

CULTIVATION: Easily grown from seed sown in fall. The choicer forms can then be propagated by cutting out the top and removing subsequent offsets. For mass plantings, set 12" apart. Leaves do not root as in related genera (such as *Echeveria*). Old plants that become too leggy can be cut and rerooted in fall.

RELATED PLANTS: The genus *Dudleya* is primarily coastal in distribution, but a few will tolerate more inland conditions. *D. pulverulenta* (chalk lettuce) is a flatter version of *D. brittonii*, with fewer-leaved chalky rosettes. *D. virens* is the most adaptable species for garden use. Its 3" rosettes of gray leaves will blush purplish in bright light or under drought stress, and will offset to form cushions. Closely resembling the dudleyas, but actually in a different subfamily, are the largely Mexican echeverias. The hardiest, which will withstand temperatures in the teens, is *Echeveria agavoides,* with hefty rosettes to 1' across of silvery-green leaves often edged in red or purple. Others are prized for their delicate pastel foliage colors; among the most garden-worthy are *E. subsessilis* (syn. *E. peacockii*), with pinkish-gray 4"–5" rosettes, and the hybrids *E. 'Perle von Nürnberg,'* with its rich pink foliage, and *E. 'Imbricata,'* with symmetrical rosettes of waxy gray leaves. One of the most appealing features of this and other waxy echeverias is their tendency to capture mercurial-looking droplets of water in their rosettes. The *E. gibbiflora* hybrids resemble large ruffled cabbages in various pastel hues. To achieve their maximum size, 1' or more, these must be topped and rerooted at least every other year. *E. 'Pulv-Oliver'* has fuzzy red-tinged leaves in 3" rosettes, and long-lasting orange flowers.

USES: Excellent in containers such as strawberry pots, planted in eye-catching groups with other bedding succulents among rocks, or with drought-tolerant grasses or perennials.

Euphorbia milii var. *splendens*
Euphorbiaceae (Spurge family)
CROWN OF THORNS

PLANT TYPE: *Succulent*
ZONES: *9–10*
HABIT: *Mounding 1'–2' shrub*
CULTURE: *Full sun to partial shade; well-drained soil*
BLOOM: *Virtually year-round*

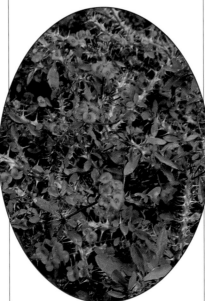

Like some other species native to Madagascar, *E. milli.* var. *splendens* has both succulent stems and well-developed but thin leaves; these are deciduous during the dry winter-dormant period, when the tangled, spiny stems give the effect of a miniature bramble patch. When in leaf, the 2" oblong leaves provide an effective foil for intense red inflorescences with minute flowers at the base of showy red bracts that provide most of the color.

CULTIVATION: Easily grown once established, but the semi-woody stems make cuttings somewhat challenging to root. Take 4"–6" cuttings during active growth, dip

---

in rooting hormone, and plant so they stand firmly about 6" apart. Keep in a warm, humid environment for best results.

RELATED PLANTS: Other varieties and hybrids of *E. milii* range to 6' tall and have floral bracts varying in color from white to creamy-yellow or pink. Another leafy but spineless euphorbia is the Canary Islands native *E. lambii,* which forms a 6' shrub with an umbrella-shaped canopy of branches, and chartreuse-bracted flowers. *E. xantii,* a 6'–8' shrub, is essentially leafless. Its slender, slightly succulent stems bloom throughout the spring with white-bracted inflorescences that blush pink, especially when night temperatures are below 50°F. *E. tirucalli* grows to be a large shrub or tree and is also essentially leafless, with pencil-thick, spineless green stems (its protection from herbivores lies instead in its toxic sap). A choicer form is *E. tirucalli* 'Sticks on Fire,' with bright orange stems. Many succulent euphorbias are superficially cactus-like with thick, spiny stems. *E. resinifera* forms mounds 1' high and 6' or more across of tightly packed gray-green stems; *E. grandicornis,* a shrub to 6' or more, has attractive sinuous-ribbed stems armed with 3" spines; *E. ingens* forms a tree to 40' or more.

USES: The diverse forms of euphorbias offer attractions for nearly any landscape. Some are shade- and drought-tolerant enough to make good houseplants. Just be sure to exercise care and also wear gloves and eye protection to avoid contact with their toxic, milky sap.

Kalanchoe blossfeldiana

Crassulaceae
(Stonecrop family)

KALANCHOE

PLANT TYPE: *Succulent*
ZONES: *9–10*
HABIT: *Shrubby perennial to 1' tall and across*
CULTURE: *Full sun to partial shade; well-drained soil*
BLOOM: *Late winter to early spring.*

Native primarily to the Old World tropics, the genus *Kalanchoe* includes some 200 species of leaf succulents displaying an incredible range of foliage forms and colors. While many are too tender to grow outdoors year-round except in zone 10, some of the South African and Madagascan species are hardier—but all can be planted as annuals. *K. blossfeldiana* is by far the most commonly cultivated species and has become a staple of the florist industry, but few realize that these foil-wrapped potted gifts can be planted out in the garden. Many color forms are now available—besides the typical red are found white, yellow, apricot, and magenta-flowered forms.

CULTIVATION: Easily grown from cuttings taken at any time of year when temperatures are above 50°F. Callus for a few days if not in active growth; plant 6" apart.

RELATED PLANTS: Other familiar species are the sometimes weedy *K. delagonensis* (syn. *K. tubiflora*) and *K. pinnata*. The latter is sometimes sold by the leaf, which within a few weeks will generate several plantlets along the leaf margin nourished entirely by the stored reserves in the leaf. Both species are naturalized weeds in the tropics. *K. delagonensis* (chan-

delier plant) is a curiously colored plant, with cylindrical leaves mottled tan and brown reminiscent of a military camouflage pattern. As a result, the plants tend to disappear in the landscape until they produce their showy, tubular, pinkish-orange pendent flowers. The flowers make a pleasant surprise when interspersed with other plants not in bloom. *K. grandiflora* has glaucous gray leaves and lemon-scented yellow flowers. *K. marmorata* (syn. *K. somaliensis*) has small yellow flowers and reddish-tinged, notched-edged leaves that are reminiscent of crab shells. *K. marnierana,* from Madagascar, has nearly round gray-green leaves in an attractive overlapping arrangement. It is tolerant of dry shade and has an unusual floral color scheme: orange tubular flowers from purplish, bell-shaped calyces.

USES: Easily propagated in quantity for annual bedding, or year-round planting where climate allows.

Lampranthus spectabilis

Aizoaceae (Iceplant family)

LAMPRANTHUS

PLANT TYPE: *Succulent*
ZONES: *9–10*
HABIT: *Ground cover 6"–12" high*
CULTURE: *Full sun to partial shade; well-drained soil*
BLOOM: *Spring*

Native to South Africa, the *Lampranthus* species provide solid carpets of almost fluorescent floral displays in a wide range of colors. Besides the typical red-violet form, several other color forms of *L. spectabilis* have been named: 'Pink Ice' is palest pink; 'Pink Betty' is bright pink; 'Red Shift' opens red, then turns magenta. Individual flowers are aster-like, made up of numerous radiating linear petals.

CULTIVATION: Easily propagated in winter by planting handfuls of fresh cuttings (about 3") directly into the ground 6"–10"apart; they will root within a week or two. The same method can be used to renew plantings that have become somewhat leggy. In zones 9–10, optimally planted in winter; in other areas, wait for spring.

RELATED PLANTS: *L. aurantiacus* has flowers in the yellow-to-orange spectrum: 'Glaucus' is brilliant canary-yellow; 'Sunman' is yellow-orange; and 'Gold Nugget' has fuller flowers of an intense day-glow orange.

Other ground-cover iceplants include *Carpobrotus edulis,* ubiquitous along California freeways, and *Drosanthemum floribundum* (often sold as *D. hispidum,* rarely cultivated), which in early spring colors whole hillsides in southern California hot pink. *D. speciosum* is a hardier, more mounding plant, with red-orange flowers and paler centers. *Aptenia* 'Red Apple' has recently become a popular ground cover, with its rich green foliage dotted with red flowers. To look its best, however, it requires ample water or shade. Tolerance of dry shade makes it useful for planting under root-rot-sensitive oaks. *Cephalophyllum* includes both ground covers and more restrained clumping varieties. Among the trailing kinds are *C. anemoniflorum,* (syn. *Jordaaniella dubai*), with flowers from white to salmon-pink, and *C. stayneri,* with satiny, coral-pink flowers.

USES: These succulents make unsurpassed ground covers with absolutely knockout floral displays. For annual bedding, propagate indoors and plant as soon as danger of frost is past. Smaller clumping varieties can be planted en masse or tucked between rocks.

Mammillaria geminispina

Cactaceae (Cactus family)

MAMMILLARIA

PLANT TYPE: *Cactus*
ZONES: *9–10*
HABIT: *Mounds to 1' high; 2'–3' across*
CULTURE: *Full sun to partial shade; well-drained soil*
BLOOM: *Summer to fall*

*M*ammillaria is a genus of over 200 species of the primarily Mexican pincushion cacti, which are characterized by rings of flowers at the tops of the stems. *M. geminispina* is among the hardiest of the genus—its snow-white spines and copious wool between the stem tubercles make a striking foil for small carmine flowers.

CULTIVATION: Grow from seed, or from cuttings that should be callused until well-healed, 2 weeks or more. Plant 6" apart; thin later for best form. Growing from cuttings allows selection of the choicest, long white-spined forms.

RELATED PLANTS: *M. compressa* and *M. magnimamma* are other mound-formers with more open spination revealing the prominently tubercled stems. A few mammillarias, including *M. karwinskiana,* *M. muehlenpfordtii* (syn. *M. celsiana*), and *M. parkinsonii,* branch dichotomously—resulting in paired heads that often give the impression of eyes staring out of the garden. The Easter lily cacti (*Echinopsis* species and hybrids), can also form mounds of globular stems, but with large funnelform

flowers, some to 6" or more long and nearly as broad, in a range of colors from white through yellow, orange, red, magenta, or a combination of these. Some of the newer hybrids are spectacular and repeat bloom throughout the spring and summer. Easter lily cacti do best with ample water and fertilizer. Other globe-stemmed cacti have solitary stems of impressive proportions, gaining them the general name barrel cacti. *Echinocactus grusonii* (golden barrel), is the quintessential landscape cactus, with multi-ribbed, golden-spined stems to 2' across. Other barrel cacti belong to the genus *Ferocactus;* one of the best of these is *F. wizlizeni* (syn. *F. hererrae*), with flattened, fishhook-like red central spines and wispy white radials.

USES: Most effective when planted in groups of varying-sized plants. These can be creatively combined with columnar cacti or other succulents, grasses, perennials, wildflowers, or shrubs that not only provide textural variety, but also partial shade to prevent scorching in hot climates.

Opuntia compressa (syn. *O. humifusa*)

Cactaceae (Cactus family)

PRICKLY PEAR CACTUS

PLANT TYPE: *Cactus*
ZONES: *3–10*
HABIT: *To 8" tall*
CULTURE: *Full sun to partial shade; well-drained soil*
BLOOM: *Summer*

---

*O*puntia is the largest genus of cacti, with over 250 species ranging from Canada to Patagonia at the tip of South America. Many are extremely cold-hardy and, therefore, popular with succulent enthusiasts in northern regions. Opuntias are distinguished by their flat broad segments, or pads. Spines, few or numerous on the pads, should be treated with respect—handle the pads carefully with tongs or strips of folded newspaper. (Gloves soon become embedded with spines and are rendered useless for handling opuntias.) Hardy virtually anywhere in the U.S. and native to the Eastern Seaboard, *O. compressa* is an attractive, ground-hugging prickly pear. It stands up to cold winters, occasionally appearing a bit shriveled. In August, 2"–3" bright yellow, many-petaled flowers open. They are followed in early fall by 1½"–3" purplish-red edible fruits.

CULTIVATION: Pads can be lopped off and planted in dry soil, immediately or after callusing for a time. While callusing, cuttings are best supported in an upright position to avoid stems' arching upward and distorting the shape of the new plant.

RELATED PLANTS: Another hardy species is *O. polyacantha,* native to the Great Plains, with varied forms, spine colors, and flowers of

yellow but also occasionally white, red, or magenta. The cholla-type opuntias have cylindrical branched stems, and also include many very cold hardy species with beautiful flowers. *O. robusta,* from Mexico, is one of the larger shrubby species, growing to 10' tall, but is easily maintained as a small shrub or container specimen in zones 8–10. The best and most widely cultivated form has gray-skinned, nearly round stem segments or pads, making a classic cactus silhouette.

Another large shrubby type is *O. ficus-indica,* cultivated commercially in some parts for its edible fruits as well as for its edible shoots. Smaller shrubby species include *O. macrocentra* (syn. *O. violacea*), widely grown in desert landscapes for its purple, nearly round pads. Other forms have long black spines lining the margins of the pads. Both species are hardy to at least 10°F. and have yellow flowers, often with red centers. Equally hardy is the grizzly bear cactus (*O. erinacea* var. *ursina*), native to the Mojave Desert. Its pads are covered with long white, hairlike spines.

USES: Prickly pear makes an excellent, impenetrable ground cover for dry sunny areas. Plant it in a rock garden where you can enjoy its sunny blooms. Its unusual forms combine well with most other succulents as well as with grasses, perennials, shrubs, and wildflowers. In addition to their landscape value, many opuntias have delicious fruits, often made into jams or jellies, and the tender new pads of some are used as a nutritious vegetable.

Sedum album

Crassulaceae (Stonecrop family)

SEDUM

PLANT TYPE: *Succulent*
ZONES: *8–10*
HABIT: *Ground cover barely 2" tall*
CULTURE: *Full sun to shade; well-drained soil*
BLOOM: *Spring*

The largest genus of the stonecrop family—with over 600 species worldwide—*Sedum* is, in fact, the inspiration for the family's common name, as many species grow in rock crevices in the wild. The genus is most diverse in the northern temperate regions; many are extremely cold-hardy. Others, especially those from Mexico, are fascinating for their colorful foliage. *S. album,* native to the mountains of southern Europe and North Africa, varies considerably in leaf shape and foliage color, with white or pinkish flowers that at times create a nearly solid carpet.

CULTIVATION: Easily propagated from small stem sections or even from individual leaves, which may be scattered over the surface of the ground and will quickly take root and spread to fill in the gaps.

RELATED PLANTS: More common perhaps than the *S. album* pictured is the pure green form with white flowers. Numerous other forms are available from specialty nurseries. *S. dasyphyllum* has a similar distribution and minute, hairy gray leaves on stems that creep between rocks. Little clumps seem to pop up here and there out of nowhere—all it takes is a single leaf to start a new plant. Golden carpet (*S. acre*), native to Eurasia and North Africa and widely naturalized in northern regions, is named for its bright yellow flowers. *S. spurium,* from the Caucasus, is widely cultivated, especially those forms that turn blood-red in winter. *Hylotelephium sieboldii* (syn. *S. sieboldii*), from Japan, is a deciduous species. In spring it produces graceful arching branches with gray, nearly orbicular, ½" leaves in whorls of three, crowned in fall with clusters of lovely pink flowers. A form with leaves variegated with creamy-yellow is especially choice. *S. kamtschaticum* is a bright accent in the garden with its yellow-and-orange flowers in summer and autumn. *S. rubrotinctum* has jellybean-like leaves that blush a cheery red in winter, giving it its common name—Christmas cheer.

USES: *S. album* makes a good ground cover, especially for seaside gardens or areas with sandy soil. Tuck it into small spaces among rocks in a rock garden. It is especially charming planted in nooks and crevices of rock walls. Use tender species as annual bedding plants in cold-winter areas.

Sempervivum arachnoideum
Crassulaceae
(Stonecrop family)
COBWEB HOUSELEEK

PLANT TYPE: *Succulent*
ZONES: *5–9*
HABIT: *Mat forming rosettes, 1"–2" high*
CULTURE: *Full sun to partial shade; well-drained soil*
BLOOM: *Summer*

Sempervivums have enjoyed a long and rich horticultural history—planted for centuries on cottage roofs as a means of fire prevention (to think we still use shake roofs today!), and grown between roof tiles to keep them from slipping. Sempervivums are Eurasian in distribution and, due to their extreme cold-hardiness, are staples among alpine gardeners for planting in troughs. Extensive breeding has resulted in hundreds of selected forms with considerable variation in color, which typically becomes enhanced during cold weather, and in size, shape, and number of leaves per rosette. *S. arachnoideum* is distinctive in having dense, cobweb-like hairs stretching from leaf

tip to leaf tip. The cultivar 'Cebenense' is one of the hairiest.

CULTIVATION: Easily propagated from prolific offsets divided during the spring or summer growing period. Make clusters of 3–5 offsets, plugging about 6" apart. Many sempervivums will tolerate warm weather but develop their best color only in cooler climates.

RELATED PLANTS: Other variants of *S. arachnoideum* include smaller red-tinged forms, those with varying degrees of hair, and even a white-flowered form differing from the usual pink. *S. tectorum* 'Greenii' has olive-green leaves with maroon tips. It is especially attractive nestled in a bed of *Sedum dasyphyllum. Jovibarba sobolifera* (syn. *Sempervivum soboliferum*) is one of a charming group of houseleeks known as "rollers." These produce small rounded rosettes on the tips of slender stolons; the plantlets are readily dislodged and roll down slopes until they come to rest in a crevice, where a new colony takes root. The temperate Asian genus *Orostachys,* though actually more closely related to *Sedum,* is similar to *Sempervivum* in its small rosette forms and its extreme cold-hardiness. One of the most adaptable and heat-tolerant species is *Orostachys fimbriata,* from China, which in fall produces spikes of white flowers with red anthers. In winter a small compact rosette forms in the center of the longer, fleshier summer leaves, giving a delightful sunburst effect.

USES: As ground covers, or for tucking into small spaces among rocks or even roof tiles.

FERNS

Ferns have thrived on earth since before the age of the dinosaurs. Primitive as they may be, these perennials form a diverse group, native to all areas of the globe. Terrestrial and aquatic ferns are most common in tropical regions; but many ferns are native to and grow in colder parts of North America, Europe, Asia, and parts of the Southern Hemisphere.

Ferns are extremely useful plants in any garden, providing fluid form and lush texture in return for low maintenance. Once established, they generally need little care, coming back year after year. Some ferns are evergreen; others die down when the weather turns cold in autumn.

Fiddleheads emerge from the ground in spring. Blades unfurl, leaves expand, and colors deepen from palest green to rich emerald—in fact, ferns display every hue and tint of green. Some have fronds tinged red, while others have silvery-gray fronds; some show a bronze color in spring, later maturing to green; some keep their color through the year, while others turn golden in autumn.

Ferns may appear delicate, yet they are sturdy, adaptable plants. Although commonly used in shade gardens, some are equally happy in full sun. Ground-dwelling ferns can be found growing in forests, bogs, swamps, meadows, marshes, and open woodlands; these are best suited for the garden. Rock-dwelling ferns, which are more difficult to grow, can thrive growing on cliffs, alongside waterfalls, and even in rock rubble.

To get acquainted with ferns, it is valuable to know the unique terms used to describe their parts. The *croziers,* also known as fiddleheads, are the newly developing fern leaves. Their form can vary from a tightly coiled spiral to a loose shepherd's crook. The portion of the fern that is above the ground is the *frond.* It is made up of the *stipe,* or stemlike portion, which connects the leafy blade to the underground rhizome. The *blade,* or *lamina,* includes the *rachis* (supporting stalk of a compound blade) and the *pinnae* (primary leafy segments). Pinnae may be further divided into *pinnules.* The most distinguishing charac-teristics of any fern are the overall shape of the blade, the outline of its margins, and the number of segments into which it is divided. A *simple* blade is one that is undivided or undissected. *Pinnate* describes a blade that is divided once, completely to the rachis, with each pinna narrowed at the base where it meets the main rachis. A *bipinnate* blade has two divisions—the pinnae, which are attached to the main rachis, and the pinnules, which are attached to the pinna rachis (also known as the *costa*). Some ferns are tripinnate or quadripinnate.

Both the rhizome and frond may have a protective covering, the *indument,* composed of hairs and/or scales. The presence of indument as well as their shape and color helps to identify specific ferns. Not only does the rhizome provide the link between the roots and frond, it also plays an important role in determining the fern's habit. Erect rhizomes hold the fronds in a vaselike cluster, while creeping rhizomes tend to have fronds that rise in an irregular cluster.

In keeping with their ancient origins, ferns don't flower. Instead, they produce spores that give rise to new ferns. Generally, the first fronds in spring are sterile; the fertile fronds that have the spore-producing organs (*sporangia*) emerge later in the season. The clusters of sporangia that you see on the blade are called *sori;* these may be scattered along the veins, on the ends of veins, or on the underside of the frond. For most gardeners, it is easier to propagate ferns from division rather than trying to collect spores and grow them.

Ferns thrive in shade—the

kind of shade that is mixed with sunlight for part of the day, or lightly dappled throughout the day. They don't like strong, direct afternoon sun. Most ferns require consistent moisture all year. Amend the soil with organic matter to improve its moisture-retentiveness. Without ample water, some ferns may simply go dormant, while others may die.

If you start with healthy plants and give them the conditions they need, ferns remain relatively insect- and disease-free. Snails and slugs tend to be the worst problems. Most ferns prefer soil that is evenly moist, not waterlogged, so don't overwater. Allow enough space between plants for ample air circulation. Mulch the plants with pine needles, coarse compost, or leaf mold, and add new mulch each spring. But keep the crown of the fern above soil level and be sure not to cover it with mulch.

Ferns are well-suited to natural landscapes, yet they are also at home in formal gardens. They can be underplanted in front of shrubs, or used in foundation plantings, as ground covers, and even as specimen plants. Polypodies, oak ferns, and beech ferns are graceful in a woodland garden. Hay-scented ferns quickly naturalize and fill in (or take over) a large area.

Use ferns to accent other plants. The graceful fronds of maidenhair fern are lovely combined with columbine, mayapple (*Podophyllum* spp.), or violets. Plant ferns close to rocks, logs, or ornaments to show them off to their best advantage. Or grow them in containers placed where their lushness and distinctive form can be appreciated.

Adiantum pedatum

Adiantaceae
(Maidenhair fern family)

NORTHERN MAIDENHAIR FERN; AMERICAN MAIDENHAIR

PLANT TYPE: *Perennial*
ZONES: *3–9*
HABIT: *12"–24" tall*
CULTURE: *Partial to full shade; neutral, humusy, moist soil*
BLOOM: *Not applicable*

Legend links this fern with powers to enhance hair—thicken, curl, or restore it. It is native to eastern and central North America, from southern Canada to the Gulf Coast. The northern maidenhair fern has airy, delicate fronds that grow singly or in tufts along slender, branching black stipes above a creeping rhizome. The rachis is horseshoe-shaped, bearing long, narrow branches of overlapping pinnae. In early spring, pale green fronds arise, fanning out in arching whorls, and maturing to a deep blue-green. It is a slow-growing deciduous fern that is a lovely addition to any shade garden, adding an interesting form matched by no other fern. One of the few ferns that is somewhat drought-tolerant.

CULTIVATION: Space plants 12"–24" apart. Keep well-watered after planting until established in the garden. Will not tolerate direct sun or intense heat. Remove dead fronds in early spring before new growth appears. Divide the plant in spring or fall when it becomes so dense that you cannot appreciate the delicate foliage of individual fronds.

RELATED PLANTS: *A. capillus-veneris,* (southern maidenhair) bears 12"–24" cascading, bright green triangular fronds composed of fan-shaped leaflets. Growing in moist, alkaline soil, it is native to the Southeast, the Gulf states, and the Rockies into Utah and California; hardy in zones 6–9.

USES: This fern will enhance any area—rockery, woodland garden, or north-facing foundation planting. It's lovely planted singly or in drifts. The delicate pink fiddleheads in spring are especially attractive combined with small bulbs like *Narcissus* 'Wee Bee' or 'Small Talk' and *Scilla siberica.*

Athyrium filix-femina

Woodsiaceae
(Woodsia family)

LADY FERN

PLANT TYPE: *Perennial*
ZONES: *3–8*
HABIT: *To 3' tall*
CULTURE: *Partial to full shade; evenly moist, humusy, neutral to acid soil*
BLOOM: *Not applicable*

To most gardeners' eyes, this is the quintessential fern in shape and habit. It grows worldwide, and is native to eastern North America. A perennial deciduous woodland fern, it bears lance-shaped fronds that grow to 3' long and 15" wide, and taper at both ends. Billowing bunches of lacy fronds grow up from a creeping rhizome. Finely toothed young pinnae are yellow-green, maturing to darker green. New fronds unfurl all summer long. Spore clusters are borne along the central stipe of each frond.

CULTIVATION: This fern spreads rapidly and should be given ample room to grow. Plant in spring or fall, allowing 18"–24" between plants. Provide constant, even moisture. It cannot tolerate drought conditions, but can tolerate sun as long as the soil is moist. Cut back tattered fronds to the ground—new fronds will take their place. Mulch with leaves or evergreen boughs in winter. Divide in spring or fall to keep plants within bounds.

RELATED PLANTS: 'Fancy Fronds' is a dwarf variety with tight, fringed pinnae. 'Fieldii' is an interesting variety, with tall narrow fronds whose paired pinnae form crosses. 'Plumosum Axminster' has finely cut fronds. 'Victoriae' has narrow pinnae tapering to crested tips.

USES: Lady fern is a dense enough plant to hold its own in a shade garden combined with hosta, ligularia, iris, or *Cimicifuga racemosa* (black cohosh). It makes a lovely ground cover along a shaded stream.

Athyrium nipponicum (syn. *A. goeringianum*) 'Pictum'

Woodsiaceae (Woodsia family)

JAPANESE PAINTED FERN

PLANT TYPE: *Semi-evergreen perennial*
ZONES: *4–8*
HABIT: *6"–18" tall*
CULTURE: *Light to partial shade (full shade in the South); moist, well-drained, acid soil*
BLOOM: *Not applicable*

Native to Japan, Korea, and China, this showy variegated fern provides more color interest than most other ferns. From a distance you see dense clumps of silvery-gray fronds with red-purple veins; a closer look reveals even more color—fronds purplish at the base, blending to lavender and then a silvery greenish-gray near the tips. The horizontal rather than vertical growth habit effectively displays this variegation. Growing from creeping rhizomes, the fronds are up to 1½' long and form a tight, slowly spreading clump. In mild areas it remains evergreen; in cooler locations it is a deciduous perennial.

CULTIVATION: In zone 5 and colder, plant in a sheltered spot, protected from the wind. Plant in spring or fall, setting the rhizome just below the soil surface. Allow 18"–24" between plants. Keep soil evenly moist, but avoid a soggy location. Allow fronds, which brown after the first frost, to remain on the plant, acting as a protective winter mulch and sheltering the emerging growth in the early spring. Once the new fronds emerge in spring, cut back any old foliage. Divide plants, when necessary, in spring.

RELATED PLANTS: 'Pictum Red' is a more brightly colored cultivar. *A. otophorum* (English painted fern) is native to China, Korea, and Japan. Leathery triangular fronds are chartreuse when young, maturing to deep blue-green with red rachises and veins. Hardy in zones 4–8.

USES: Japanese painted fern will light up a dark spot in a shade garden and draw the viewer's attention into the area's deeper recesses. Traditionally grown along paths in Japanese tea gardens, this fern is suitable for edging a shady border or accenting a tranquil woodland glade.

Cyrtomium falcatum

**Dryopteridaceae
(Wood fern family)**

HOLLY FERN

PLANT TYPE: *Evergreen perennial*
ZONES: *8–11*
HABIT: *18"–24" tall*
CULTURE: *Full sun to shade; moist, humusy, acid soil*
BLOOM: *Not applicable*

Holly fern is native to warm regions of Japan, Korea, and China. A tender evergreen, it is suited to hot climates in which other ferns would not survive. It is beautiful with coarse, stiff, leathery, arching fronds. The broad, scythe-shaped pinnae grow in a vase form, arising from a stout, scaly rhizome. Despite the dark green color, the glossy surfaces of the pinnae reflect light. Holly fern spreads rapidly in the garden and is tolerant of air pollution.

CULTIVATION: This is one of the best ferns for beginners; it tolerates a wide range of growing conditions. It can be grown in full sun and in drier soil than most other ferns. Plant any time of year, placing the ferns at the same depth as they were originally growing, allowing 18"–24"

between plants. Fertilize with fish meal in spring or mid summer.

RELATED PLANTS: 'Compactum' is a lower-growing form that reaches only about 12" high. 'Rochefordianum' bears deeply toothed pinnae 2" wide, and is hardy in zones 10 and 11.

USES: Place holly fern where you can appreciate its dramatic shape and year-round color. Use as an accent under trees or next to large rocks.

Dennstaedtia punctilobula

**Dennstaedtiaceae
(Cup fern family)**

HAY-SCENTED FERN

PLANT TYPE: *Perennial*
ZONES: *4–7*
HABIT: *10"–18" tall*
CULTURE: *Full sun to shade; moist, neutral to acid, average to humusy soil*
BLOOM: *Not applicable*

Hay-scented fern, native to eastern North America from Nova Scotia to Arkansas and Georgia, gets its common name from the smell of the fronds when crushed. It is a quick-growing, deciduous fern that grows from a thin, creeping rhizome. In spring, it sends up a mat of

bright green, elongated, flexible fronds, which darken to medium green; in autumn, they turn a soft yellow.

CULTIVATION: This is an easy fern to grow, good for beginning fern gardeners as it is tolerant of varying soil, sun, and moisture. Plant 1" deep in spring, allowing 2' between plants. Keep evenly moist until plants are established. This can be a zealous grower—control with barriers of lawn edging or a rock wall. Allow the yellowed foliage to remain on the plant through winter, then cut off just before the new fiddleheads unfurl in spring. Propagate by cutting the mats of rhizomes apart in spring before new growth begins; space 2' apart.

RELATED PLANTS: *D. cicutaria* (common cup fern, or cuplet fern) is hardy in zones 8–11. It bears very large 6'–12' fronds from creeping rhizomes, and grows best in the shade in moist to wet, humusy soil.

USES: Because of its somewhat aggressive nature, hay-scented fern makes a good ground cover under trees and shrubs. Don't try to mix it with delicate plants, as they will be overrun. Lovely planted with *Phlox divaricata*.

Dryopteris erythrosora

**Dryopteridaceae
(Wood fern family)**

**AUTUMN FERN;
JAPANESE SHIELD FERN**

PLANT TYPE: *Evergreen perennial*
ZONES: *5–9*
HABIT: *12"–18" tall*
CULTURE: *Partial to full shade; moist, humusy, neutral to acid soil*
BLOOM: *Not applicable*

FERNS

This evergreen fern, native to China, Japan, and Korea, is rapidly gaining in popularity in this country, and for good reason. Its name is a bit misleading—it is in spring that this fern puts on a show of fall-like color. As they arise from the crown-forming rhizome, the new broad, triangular fronds have a copper color and then unfurl, turning pinkish-green. Fronds mature to a deep shiny green. In the fall, the fertile fronds have bright red sori highlighting the undersides of the pinnae.

CULTIVATION: Grow in shade in warmer climates. Plant in spring or fall, allowing at least 2' between plants. Take care not to disturb the rhizomes once established; the new fronds develop underground one year and the croziers rise and unfurl the following spring. Divide as necessary, or when you want to increase your stock.

RELATED PLANTS: *D. filix-mas* (male fern) is hardy in zones 3–9. Its stiff, dark evergreen fronds form a lovely, somewhat flattened vase-shaped plant and make a handsome garden accent. *D. marginalis* (marginal wood fern) forms 1'–2' stiff arching, drab green fronds. Hardy in zones 4–8, *D. marginalis* is drought-tolerant once established.

USES: Give autumn fern a special place where you can admire its beauty throughout the year—as an accent plant in a shade garden, placed next to a stump or rock for dramatic effect, or as a lovely foilage plant in the perennial border.

Matteuccia struthiopteris

Woodsiaceae (Woodsia family)

OSTRICH FERN

PLANT TYPE: *Perennial*
ZONES: *2–8*
HABIT: *3'–5' tall*
CULTURE: *Partial to full shade; moist, humusy, neutral soil*
BLOOM: *Not applicable*

Native to northern North America, from Newfoundland west to Alaska and British Columbia and south to the Great Lakes and Virginia, the ostrich fern is one of the largest American ferns, growing up to 8' tall in the wild. In cultivation, however, it rarely exceeds 5' in height. Vase-shaped clusters of tall, plume-shaped, sterile fronds rise from a creeping, crown-forming rhizome. The shiny dark green balls of the croziers appear late in spring. Blunt, leathery, sterile fronds unfurl, surrounding the bronze, hard, woody, fertile fronds with stiff pinnae later in summer. The fertile fronds brown but remain erect through the winter, giving vertical interest in the garden at that time of year. It is not until spring that these fronds release their spores. This fern spreads rapidly, with a tendency to become invasive.

CULTIVATION: It is tolerant of full sun if planted in a cool wet location. Allow 2'–3' between plants. Divide plants in fall as necessary to keep control of growth. Ostrich fern thrives in moist to wet locations; do not let it dry out.

RELATED PLANTS: None.

USES: Its robust nature makes ostrich fern excellent for naturalizing in a woodland, or along a stream or water garden. Plant in drifts for best effect. Attractive with spring-blooming bulbs and wildflowers. Use as a vertical accent growing through ground covers like sweet woodruff (*Galium odoratum*) or epimedium.

Osmunda cinnamomea

Osmundaceae (Osmunda or flowering fern family)

CINNAMON FERN

PLANT TYPE: *Perennial*
ZONES: *3–10*
HABIT: *2'–4' tall*
CULTURE: *Full sun to shade; moist to wet, humusy, acid soil*
BLOOM: *Not applicable*

Native to eastern North America from Labrador to Ontario and south to Florida and Texas, cinnamon fern is one of

the most attractive deciduous ferns. In early spring, the tawny fiddleheads are handsome as they emerge from a wiry, stout, crown-forming rhizome. At the center of the clump, bright green fertile fronds arise, which turn cinnamon-brown as they mature, giving the plant its common name. The sterile fronds are a lustrous green, surrounding the fertile fronds in an arching vase form. In autumn, the fronds turn a lovely golden hue. Osmundas are grown commercially for their massive root systems, which when shredded are used as a growing medium for orchids and other epiphytes, including some of the tropical ferns.

CULTIVATION: Tolerates full sun when given plenty of moisture, and thrives in wet, boggy soil. Keep soil moist—extended dryness will kill the plants. Allow 3' between plants. Although slow to get established, they are very long

lived. Their large, clump-forming rhizomes make them difficult to transplant when they are large; start with small plants for best success. Divide crowns in spring before croziers unfurl.

RELATED PLANTS: *O. claytoniana* (interrupted fern) looks similar, but has broader, paler green pinnae. Also, it does not bear separate fertile fronds. Instead, the fertile pinnae are borne halfway up the frond, with sterile pinnae above and below, which creates an interrupted look in summer when the fertile pinnae fall off. This plant is more tolerant of dry conditions than is cinnamon fern.

USES: Plant cinnamon fern where fiddleheads will show off in early spring—handsome accented with a large rock or log. Plant in drifts with fine-textured ferns, or among wildflowers like tiarella or mayapple (*Podophyllum* spp.).

Osmunda regalis
Osmundaceae (Osmunda or flowering fern family)
ROYAL FERN; FLOWERING FERN
PLANT TYPE: *Perennial*   ZONES: *3–10*   HABIT: *2'–5' tall*   CULTURE: *Sun to shade; moist to wet, humusy, acid soil*   BLOOM: *Not applicable*

The osmunda ferns are the link between modern (polypody) ferns and ancient ferns that covered forest floors in prehistoric days. Large crowns with slightly erect stems arise from massive root systems. Native to eastern North America, this deciduous fern has a regal bearing. The stout, wiry, crown-forming rhi-

zome gives rise to new pale pink fronds that mature with dark stipes and deep sea-green pinnae. The fertile pinnae, at the tip of the fronds, produce beadlike sori that resemble a flower cluster—thus the common name, flowering fern. The sterile pinnae resemble leafy stems.

CULTIVATION: Tolerates full sun when given plenty of moisture, and thrives in wet, boggy soil. Keep soil moist—extended dryness will kill the plants. Allow 3' between them. Although slow to become established, these ferns are very long lived. Their large, clump-forming rhizomes make the plants difficult to transplant when they are large; start with small plants for best success. Divide crowns in spring before croziers unfurl.

RELATED PLANTS: 'Purpurescens' is a European variety. The new growth is purple; the stipes are large and dark, and the fertile pinnae are plumelike.

USES: Attractive planted in a boggy woodland or along the banks of a stream or pond. Combine with woodland wildflowers such as aquilegia and sanguinaria.

Polystichum acrostichoides

Dryopteridaceae
(Wood fern family)

CHRISTMAS FERN

PLANT TYPE: *Evergreen perennial*
ZONES: *3–9*
HABIT: *1'–3' tall*
CULTURE: *Light to full shade; moist, humusy, well-drained, acid to neutral soil*
BLOOM: *Not applicable*

Polystichums are robust ferns that form handsome, tufted clumps of stiff, deep green, symmetrical fronds from a creeping, crown-forming rhizome. Christmas fern is native to eastern North America, from Nova Scotia and Ontario south to Florida and Texas. Early settlers in the Northeast prized the 1'–3' fronds for holiday decorations and gave it its common name. This luxuriant evergreen fern has a magnificent spreading form. The one-piece, 3" leaflets have a pointed or rounded bump, called an ear, on their topmost edge close to the stalk. The stiff fronds stay upright until heavy snow knocks them down.

CULTIVATION: Tolerates dense shade and dry soil; will grow in full sun if the soil is amply moist. In preparing a new bed, use a mixture of 1 part garden loam, 1 part builder's sand, and 2 parts leaf mold or peat moss. Keep soil evenly moist, but not soggy. A pH of 5.5–6.6 is best for these ferns. Allow at least 2' between plants. Divide clumps in spring or fall.

RELATED PLANTS: Leather fern (*Rumohra adiantiformis*, syn. *Polystichum adiantiforme*) has coarsely lobed 12"–20" fronds that become very rough and stiff with age. East Indian holly fern (*Arachniodes aristata*, syn. *Polystichum aristatum*) has oval 6"–36" fronds up to 12" wide, with tapering, harsh-textured pinnae that end in spiny segments; lower leaflets are butterfly-shaped. *P. munitum* (Western sword fern) bears pairs of 5", dagger-shaped pinnae that have bristly, prickly edges. They grow 18"–36" tall and are impressive; well-established clumps bear as many as 75–100 fronds. *P. setiferum* (soft-shield fern) has more pliant and arching stalks than other polystichums; finely divided lacy fronds are 1'–2½' long. Unlike most ferns, which have prominent veins on the undersurface of their fronds, the veins of the upside-down fern (*Arachniodes standishii*, syn. *Polystichum standishii*) protrude from the top surface, giving the fern its common name; fronds 1'–3' long are cut into 3 lacy segments. All are hardy in zones 5–10.

USES: The leathery evergreen foliage is often used in floral arrangements and wreaths. These stiff bushy ferns make excellent border and foundation plants.

FRUITS

Botanically, a fruit is the ripened ovary of a flower and usually it contains the seeds. Tomatoes, eggplants, peppers, squash, peas, corn, pumpkins, and other produce that are commonly called vegetables are actually fruits. For our purposes, however, we are dividing fruits and vegetables by their culinary usage. This section encompasses plants having succulent sweet fruit that can be eaten raw.

Fruits are often divided into two groups. Tree fruits, such as apples and oranges, are borne on trees; small fruits, such as watermelons, strawberries, and blueberries, may grow on shrubs, vines, perennial plants, or annual plants. All fruits are the result of pollinated flowers. Some plants, such as strawberries, are self-pollinating and can produce fruit from their own pollen. Other plants, such as apples, require the pollen from a different cultivar in order to produce fruit—this is cross-pollination. Thus a 'Cox's Orange Pippin' apple tree will always bear the same fruit, no matter what other apple is used as a pollinator. However, if you try to plant the *seeds* from that apple, the resulting plants will be widely variable and different from the parent plant.

Although most well-nourished people consume fruit daily, too few of us actually grow and harvest fruits in our own garden or landscape. This is a shame, because most fruits are easy to grow. Planted in the right location, many will produce an abundant crop year after year with precious little effort on your part.

The best thing about backyard fruit growing is that you don't need a baronial estate to cultivate a wide range of interesting plants. The mouthwatering list is limited only by your imagination and space. And if the luxury of enjoying luscious homegrown fruit at its peak isn't reason enough to grow fruits at home, consider their striking ornamental landscape qualities. Many fruits are beautiful themselves, of course, but the plants they grow on also may have fragrant or showy blossoms, brilliant autumn foliage, or a graceful growing habit (or at least they can be pruned or trained to have one). What's more, growing a variety of fruits helps attract native birds and wildlife to your property. In a world where humans occupy more and more space, and where natural habitats are shrinking for many other species, planting fruit trees and bushes may be the single most significant step that homeowners can take to improve their own little parcels of nature.

The following plant entries offer only a sampling of the impressive number of fruits available to the home gardener. From annual plants like melons, which define high summer's bounty in the fruit and vegetable garden, to shrubs and trees that will enhance your landscape for years to come, the world of fruits is rich and various—an almost endless source of pleasure for gardener and gourmand alike.

Citrullus lanatus 'Yellow Baby'

Cucurbitaceae (Gourd family)

WATERMELON

PLANT TYPE: *Annual vine*
ZONES: *Not applicable*
HABIT: *8'–12'*
CULTURE: *Full sun; rich, well-drained, slightly acid to neutral soil*
HARVEST: *Summer to first frost*

The watermelon originally comes from the African tropics, so it's no surprise that some of the biggest, best melons grow in the South, where summers are long, hot, and humid. Gardeners in short-season areas shouldn't be discouraged, however, since many smaller varieties have been bred to yield tasty fruit even under less-than-optimal conditions. The flesh color of watermelons varies all the way from bright red to pale yellow. 'Yellow Baby' has crisp, delicious yellow flesh, few seeds, and a thin rind with hard skin for longer storage. The fruits average 7" in diameter and ripen early, in about 75 days.

CULTIVATION: Start watermelon seed indoors in individual 2"–3" pots or soil blocks, about 3–4 weeks before the last spring frost date. Provide gentle bottom heating until plants emerge. Harden off seedlings and transplant to the garden when weather is warm and settled. Set out plants 3' apart in rows spaced 5'–6' apart. Mix compost or dried manure into the planting hole when setting out seedlings. In cooler climates, mulch around plants with black paper and cover plants with a floating row fabric to provide additional heat early in the season.

In warmer regions, gardeners can direct-seed watermelon outside in the garden, planting seeds 6"–8" apart in rows spaced 5'–6' apart, and later thinning to 3' apart in the row. An alternative is to plant in circular hills spaced 6'–8' apart in the row. Sow 5–6 seeds per hill, later thinning to the best two plants in each hill. Fertilize watermelons by side-dressing with dried manure while the plants are still upright and before the vines start to run on the ground.

Watermelons are ripe if the spot where the fruit rests on the ground has turned yellow, and if the melon makes a hollow "punk" sound—rather than "pink" or "pank"—when you rap it with your knuckles. About a month before the first fall frost date, pinch off the fuzzy growing tips at the ends of the vines and remove

any small fruits that won't have time to develop. This encourages more mature fruits to ripen.

RELATED PLANTS: Round or "icebox" varieties include the heirloom 'Cream of Saskatchewan' (yellow flesh, 4–10 pounds, 78–85 days) and 'Sugar Baby' (red flesh, 8–10 pounds, 76 days). Two early, space-efficient hybrids are 'Garden Baby' (red flesh, 7 pounds, 70 days) and 'Sunshine' (yellow flesh, 8–10 pounds, 75 days). Larger, oblong watermelons include the heirlooms 'Kleckley Sweet' (red flesh, 25–40 pounds, 80–90 days) and 'Tom Watson' (red flesh, 25–40 pounds, 80–95 days).

The most beautiful watermelon is the widely available heirloom 'Moon and Stars,' whose dark green leaves and fruits look like they've been splotched with bright yellow paint. Various strains are available, with pink or yellow flesh; most need a long season, 95–105 days.

The citron melon (*C. lanatus* var. *citroides*) is grown strictly for making preserves, pickles, or candied "citron" from its solid, inedible flesh. 'Red-Seeded Citron' is the most common variety (10–12 pounds, 80–100 days).

USES IN THE LANDSCAPE: Watermelon's running vines make it a fairly effective ground cover, but it is not widely grown outside the vegetable garden proper; try growing this plant in empty spots that have well-drained, fairly fertile soil. The fruits are the main attraction, of course, and many varieties have attractive "rattlesnake" patterns of dark and light green. 'Moon and Stars' is the most ornamental variety available, and like all watermelons, it interplants well with taller garden crops such as corn and sunflowers.

Citrus limon 'Meyer'
Rutaceae (Rue family)
MEYER LEMON

PLANT TYPE: *Tree*
ZONES: *9–11*
HABIT: *To 6' tall*
CULTURE: *Full sun; humusy, well-drained soil*
HARVEST: *Almost everbearing*

Growing citrus trees outdoors throughout the year is a luxury limited to those lucky enough to live in warm climates where winter temperatures rarely dip much below freezing. Some cultivars, like the Meyer lemon, are hardy enough to make good outdoor plants in the warmer regions of the U.S., and excellent container plants in colder climates. A container adds to the plant's versatility—you can enjoy it indoors in winter and outside in summer.

'Meyer' is a fine ornamental plant that bears rounded, slightly orange-colored fruits that lack the pronounced "nipple" common to other lemons. The 3" fruits are borne over much of the year, and their flavor is tangy and less acidic than that of the common lemon —it's almost sweet when fully ripe. The leaves are glossy green and the white flowers are fragrant and attractive. 'Meyer' is the hardiest variety of lemon, withstanding temperatures as low as 17°–18°F. Best of all, it is a natural dwarf, growing to only 6' tall even when grafted on standard rootstock. This makes it very manageable as a container plant.

CULTIVATION: Lemons do not require another pollinator to set fruit. If planting in the ground or in a container outside, choose a sunny, sheltered location. Be careful not to plant the tree too deeply or bury the lower part of the trunk. If the plant's foliage does not shade the stem from direct sun, paint the exposed trunk with white exterior latex paint to protect it from sunburn. Water regularly, but avoid wetting the trunk or the root crown. Lemons planted in containers like growing in a soil mix that is light and well-drained yet has sufficient organic matter to retain some moisture. Fertilize container

plants periodically with a citrus fertilizer that includes iron and zinc. If the tree has been grafted onto another rootstock, remove any suckers that may sprout from the rootstock as soon as they appear. Northern gardeners can grow Meyer lemon in a cool sunny room in winter and move it outdoors in summer.

RELATED PLANTS: Other lemons include 'Eureka,' widely grown and productive but quite sensitive to cold. 'Lisbon' is somewhat hardier than 'Eureka' and is a vigorous, attractive tree. 'Meyer Variegated' is similar to 'Meyer' but with beautifully variegated foliage and fruit.

USES IN THE LANDSCAPE: Meyer lemon makes a great container plant on a sunny patio or porch, especially in cold regions of the country. Whether confined in a container or planted in the ground, the tree can be used to outline a path or walkway in a formal manner.

Cucumis melo, Reticulatus group, 'Jenny Lind'
Cucurbitaceae (Gourd family)
MUSKMELON

PLANT TYPE: *Annual vine*
ZONES: *Not applicable*
HABIT: *To 5'*
CULTURE: *Full sun; fertile, well-drained, slightly acid to neutral soil*
HARVEST: *Summer to first frost*

The two most commonly grown types of melons are muskmelons (*C. melo*, Reticulatus group), which have a corky netting over their surface, and honeydew or casaba melons (*C. melo*, Inodorus group), which have

smooth yellowish-green skin and require a long hot growing season. The heirloom variety 'Jenny Lind' has been rediscovered by home gardeners in recent years. The vines are rather short but productive, forming small fruits, 1–2 pounds, that have a small button or "turban" on their blossom end. The flesh is light green, sweet, and juicy. 'Jenny Lind' is early, maturing in 70–85 days, and does well in short-season areas.

CULTIVATION: Start melon seeds indoors, in individual 2"–3" pots or soil blocks, about 3 weeks before transplanting to the garden. (Starting plants any earlier results in sprawling plants that are harder to transplant.) Provide gentle bottom heat until seeds germinate. Harden off seedlings and transplant after all danger of frost is past and weather is warm and settled. Set out plants 2'–3' apart in rows spaced 5'–6' apart. Provide additional warmth around plants, if necessary, with a black paper mulch and a floating row cover.

Gardeners in regions with warm spring weather can plant melon seeds outside in circular hills spaced 6' apart. Sow 6–8 seeds per hill, thinning to the best

2–3 plants per hill. Fertilize young plants and keep well-watered until fruits are the size of a baseball. Then water only as necessary during dry weather.

To encourage ripening, pinch off the fuzzy tips at the ends of the vines. About 4 weeks before the end of the growing season, remove from the plants any small melons that won't have time to ripen; this directs energy into ripening larger fruits. Muskmelons are ripe when the skin is well-netted and buff-yellow in color. Also, the fruit will "slip," or separate easily from the vine. Honeydews, casabas, and French cantaloupes won't slip when ripe, but the blossom end will crack and smell sweet.

RELATED PLANTS: Other good muskmelons include the orange-fleshed 'Hearts of Gold' (90 days, 3–4 pounds), 'Iroquois' (75 days, 4 pounds), and 'Sweet Granite' (70 days, 2–4 pounds), and the green-fleshed heirloom 'Rocky Ford' (85–95 days, 2–3 pounds). 'Golden Beauty' is an excellent casaba melon (110–120 days, 7–8 pounds), perfect for warmer regions. One of the tastiest Galia types is the green-fleshed 'Passport' (73 days, 5–6 pounds). The true or French cantaloupe known as Charentais is delicious; good varieties include 'Vedrantais' (92 days, 2 pounds) and the hybrids 'Savor' (78 days) and 'Acor' (85 days).

USES IN THE LANDSCAPE: Melon vines, through spreading, are fairly sparse and uninteresting as ornamental ground covers go. To save space, plant them at the base of tall crops such as corn, sunflowers, or quinoa.

Ficus carica 'Brown Turkey'
Moraceae (Mulberry family)
COMMON FIG

PLANT TYPE: *Tree*
ZONES: *8–11*
HABIT: *To 10' tall*
CULTURE: *Full sun; heavy, rich, consistently moist soil*
HARVEST: *Everbearing, 2–3 crops a year in ideal conditions*

Many gardeners are far more familiar with the house-plant known as weeping fig (*F. benjamina*) than they are with the species that bears delicious edible fruit. Dried figs are common in the market, yet growing your own fresh figs is possible even if you don't live in a region that has mild winters. Home gardeners in zones 8–11 can grow figs outside without any special protection, but those living in colder regions can also raise figs successfully. 'Brown Turkey' is a popular, hardy everbearing variety with sweet, fine-grained flesh. It has attractive, glossy green leaves and makes a good container plant. It begins setting fruit in early June.

CULTIVATION: Figs are usually purchased as nursery stock 18"–24" tall; if planted in a permanent location, they can be set outdoors in spring 18'–25' apart.

They can also be propagated from established fig trees, taking woody cuttings 4"–5" long in winter or early spring while the tree is dormant. Plant cuttings with their tips even with the soil surface; transplant the following spring 2' apart in rows. In the third year, plant out in the same manner as nursery stock. Figs need ample water, especially during hot dry weather, and they benefit from mulching.

Gardeners in zones 5–7 can grow figs outside, given adequate winter protection. Dig up the plant in fall, transplant it to a large container, and move it to a cool, moist location indoors for the winter, replanting outdoors in the spring. A less strenuous method involves training the branches in an espalier fashion to grow close to the ground, then gently bending them down in the fall and covering them with soil before temperatures dip to 10°F., mounding soil over the central trunk as well. Some gardeners wrap the trees in burlap for the winter.

RELATED PLANTS: Other good varieties include 'Celeste,' which bears sweet violet-brown fruits and is hardy to 0°F., and 'White Genoa,' suited to growing in mild coastal regions, whose fruit is better fresh than dried.

USES IN THE LANDSCAPE: As landscape plants, trellis figs along the south wall of the house, or grow near a south-facing stone or masonry wall, where the trees will benefit from the sheltered location and additional reflected heat. In colder regions, grow figs in large tubs that you can roll inside during the winter months.

FRUITS

Fragaria vesca 'Mignonette'
Rosaceae (Rose family)

ALPINE STRAWBERRY

PLANT TYPE: *Perennial*
ZONES: *3–9*
HABIT: *To 1' tall*
CULTURE: *Full sun to partial shade; moist, rich garden soil*
HARVEST: *Late spring through fall*

A cultivated form of the European wood strawberry (*fraise des bois*), alpine strawberries produce small, flavorful fruits over a long harvest season. Unsuited to commercial growing, they are ideal for backyard gardeners, with a flavor unmatched by the best large-fruited hybrids. With alpine strawberries, gardeners can grow the closest thing to wild berries, and picking them is a lot less trouble.

Unlike other strawberries, alpine plants produce few runners, forming instead a compact mound of green leaves that sport white blossoms and either red or creamy-white berries. The plants are quite attractive, and since they tolerate partial shade they can be grown as an ornamental edging or ground cover. The variety 'Mignonette' is a prolific bearer, with large 1" red fruits that have a very good flavor.

CULTIVATION: Start seeds in flats in early spring, sowing thinly and pressing them into a moist soilless potting mix. Seeds need darkness to germinate, so cover flats until seedlings emerge (2–3 weeks), watering if the surface of the mix feels dry. Transplant seedlings 2" apart in flats or in individual cells or soil blocks. Alpine strawberries like a moist, rich soil that contains lots of organic material, so build up the planting bed with peat moss or compost before transplanting to the garden after the last spring frost date. Space plants 1' apart, or as close as 6" apart if you want to create a hedgelike effect. Plant so that the root crown sits just below the surface of the soil. Spread an organic mulch around the plants to conserve soil moisture, suppress weeds, and protect the strawberries' shallow roots.

Alpine strawberries self-sow vigorously, so thin out plants as necessary. To revitalize an old bed, dig up plants and divide the roots,

replanting young sections from the outside of the clump and discarding the old, woody central crown. Top-dress with compost or humus-rich soil early each spring to maintain the level of the bed. Established plants are quite winter-hardy, but in colder regions it doesn't hurt to mulch them in late fall for added protection. Alpines will bear fruit beginning either in the fall of the first season, or in the spring of the second season. Plants bear their largest crop in the spring, and continue to produce berries in lesser quantity through the summer, finishing up with a second, smaller crop in the fall.

RELATED PLANTS: Other good red-fruited varieties include 'Alexandria,' 'Baron Solemacher,' and 'Rugen' (hardy to zone 5). Alpines that bear creamy-white mature fruit are also tasty. An advantage is that they are not normally bothered by birds. 'Pineapple Crush' is an early-bearing, prolific variety. A similar small-fruited species with runners, hardy to zone 5, is the musk strawberry (*F. moschata*). The aromatic Italian variety 'Profumata di Tortona' is available in America.

USES IN THE LANDSCAPE: Alpine strawberries make an ideal front-of-border planting, tucked in with just about any other plant. They are particularly attractive when grown just inside the landscaping timbers of raised beds, where it's easy to see and pick the ripening berries all season long. Planted at their closer spacing (6" apart), the strawberries form a neat and productive ground cover. Since the plants don't need much elbow room, alpines are also ideal for containers, especially for a garden with poor soil or limited space.

Malus pumila
(syn. *M. communis*)
'Cox's Orange Pippin'
Rosaceae (Rose family)

APPLE

PLANT TYPE: *Tree*
ZONES: *5–8*
HABIT: *6'–20' tall*
CULTURE: *Full sun; deep, fertile, well-drained soil*
HARVEST: *September to October*

The apple is the classic home-garden fruit tree. With thousands of cultivated varieties available, both heirloom and modern, and more appearing on the market every year, backyard orchardists in most regions of the country can find a type that's perfect for them. Apple trees are usually sold by mail-order nurseries as "bareroot" stock, and by garden centers in balls or containers of soil. In either case, the tree consists of 2 sections that have been grafted together. The top part is the scion, a branch cutting taken from the variety of apple you want to grow. The bottom part is the rootstock, and it is this section that determines the hardiness and eventual height of the mature tree.

Dwarf and semidwarf rootstocks, which result in mature trees 6'–12' tall, are popular among home orchardists who have limited space or who want to have fruit sooner than is possible with standard-size trees. Dwarf and semidwarf rootstocks are not very hardy, however, and gardeners living in zones 3–4 should choose varieties grafted to standard rootstocks to avoid winterkill. Before buying any planting stock, do some research in reference books and nursery catalogs, and ask local orchardists or your local extension service for advice and recommendations as to good varieties and rootstocks for your area.

'Cox's Orange Pippin' is a splendid variety for growers in moderate climate zones. It comes from England, where it was developed around 1830 by a man named Richard Cox as a seedling from 'Ribston Pippin.' It is one of the best dessert and pie apples, with creamy-yellow, highly aromatic flesh. The skin is an unusual

but pretty orange, overlaid with red stripes.

CULTIVATION: For best cross-pollination and fruit set, plant 2 or more trees of different varieties near each other, or plant an ornamental crabapple near the apple as a pollinator. Plant bareroot stock early in the spring in colder regions, to give the tree plenty of time to establish itself before winter; in milder-winter climates or with balled or potted nursery stock, planting can take place in either spring or fall.

Space trees grown on standard rootstocks 25' apart if you plan on pruning them, 35' apart if you'll leave them to grow to full size. Trees grown on dwarf or semidwarf rootstocks are planted closer together. Plant dwarf or semidwarf trees with the graft union (the point where the scion joins the rootstock) 2"–3" above the surface of the soil; plant standard trees with the graft union just below ground level. Prune bareroot trees by about a third

after planting; trees with balled roots or those planted in containers do not need cutting back. Dwarf and semidwarf trees have shallow root systems and require staking.

Young apple trees need abundant water every day for a month or so after planting, and then biweekly watering through mid summer if planted in the spring. To prevent competition from grass, mow and mulch widely around young trees, particularly dwarf types. Place plastic tree guards or cylinders of wire mesh around apples to prevent mice and rabbits from gnawing on the bark. In orchards where browsing deer are a problem, the only foolproof solution is to erect a tall deer-fence.

Most dwarf and semidwarf trees will begin fruiting 2–5 years after planting, while some standard-size trees may take 8–10 years to set fruit. If properly maintained, however, standard trees will continue producing for many years, whereas dwarf trees may need to be replaced in 10–20 years. Dwarf trees don't require as much pruning as standard trees, whose canopies should be opened up when they have reached around 12' to allow sunlight into the tree and limit its final height. Some hand-thinning of developing fruits in late June will prevent overcropping; this is especially important with apple varieties that tend to bear every other year.

Apple varieties vary in their susceptibility to a wide range of insects, including codling moth and plum curculio, and diseases such as scab, rust, and fire blight. Limited spraying with organic controls at specific times of the year can eliminate many of these problems, as can the selection of one of the new disease-resistant varieties.

RELATED PLANTS: Other excellent cultivars that are generally hardy to zone 5 include 'Baldwin,' 'Braeburn,' 'Esopus Spitzenberg,' 'Gravenstein,' 'Jonagold,' and 'Winesap.' Many other apples are excellent for zones 3–4 if grown on hardy rootstock; these include 'Chenango Strawberry,' 'Fameuse,' 'Haralson,' 'Mantet,' 'Westfield Seek-No-Further,' and 'Yellow Transparent.' Two of the best new disease-resistant varieties are 'Freedom' and 'Liberty.' Low-chill apples can flourish in milder winter climates, as warm as zone 9. 'Anna' is good for the Deep South and desert Southwest; 'Beverly Hills' and 'Dorsett Gold' need no pollinators; 'Pearl Pink' has cream-and-green skin and bright pink flesh. New introductions for the small garden include 'Colonnade'; it is fastigiate, growing only 2' wide yet 6'–8' tall, and bears standard-size apples.

Crabapple trees produce tart fruits that are great for jellies and pickling, but many also have beautiful, fragrant blossoms and are good pollinators for other apple varieties. Hardy crabapples include 'Bechtel' (with fragrant, double-pink blossoms) and 'Dolgo' (white blossoms and good fruit that make exquisite, clear red jelly).

USES IN THE LANDSCAPE: The main season of ornamental interest for apples is springtime, when the trees produce their sweet-smelling white or pink blossoms. Apples and crabapples can make exceptional specimen plants on a gently sloping hillside, in the midst of an uninteresting lawn, or even fairly close to the house.

Pyrus communis 'Seckel'

Rosaceae (Rose family)

SECKEL PEAR

PLANT TYPE: *Tree*
ZONES: *5–8*
HABIT: *15'–20' tall*
CULTURE: *Full sun; deep, fertile, heavy soil*
HARVEST: *Early fall*

As a group, pears are more limited in their climate range than apples, although several varieties are hardy enough to try in favored locations as far north as zone 3. Pears are generally planted as 1-year-old nursery stock. Standard-size trees are those grafted to pear seedling rootstock, while dwarf trees are normally grown on quince stock. Dwarf pears are popular for home gardens, although they are typically less hardy and have a shorter lifespan than their standard-size counterparts.

Pear trees reach maturity rather slowly, with dwarf varieties usually bearing fruit in 3–5 years and standard trees requiring up to 8–10 years to produce a crop. The popular variety known as 'Seckel' is an heirloom that came over from Europe around 1790. The fruit is small and russeted. What it lacks in appearance, though, it more than makes up for in productivity and in superb flavor,

---

which is aromatic, spicy, and very sweet. 'Seckel' is somewhat susceptible to scab but has good resistance to fire blight.

CULTIVATION: To get good pollination, it's necessary to plant at least 2 different varieties of pear. In general, any variety will pollinate any other variety, with the exception of 'Bartlett' and 'Seckel,' which are not cross-fertile.

Pears thrive in humid climates. The flowers open a few days before apple blossoms in spring. In locations where late frosts are a problem, site pears on slopes or near bodies of water for extra frost protection. Plant standard-size trees in spring about 20'–30' apart, dwarf trees 12'–15' apart. Protect the young trees from rodent damage with wire-mesh cylinders or tree guards. Spread a thick, rich organic mulch such as composted manure around the trees to nourish them. In general, standard pear trees do not require as much pruning as apple trees. Cut out any crowded or crossing limbs, but leave some of the secondary branches.

Fire blight—a bacterial disease that turns blossoms, fruit, and branches black—is the chief enemy of pear trees. Cut out any infected limbs, dipping pruning tools in chlorine bleach, and select blight-resistant varieties for planting. Prune off any low-growing twigs and spurs, which can become infected. Also, do not stimulate growth through heavy pruning or apply a high-nitrogen fertilizer to pear trees; both actions can stimulate lots of tender new growth that is especially susceptible to blight damage.

Harvest pears when they have reached full size but before they have fully ripened on the tree. Planting different varieties can extend the harvest season from late summer through November, with the later pears keeping well into early winter. Wrap harvested pears in soft paper and store in a cool location, bringing them to room temperature for ripening.

RELATED PLANTS: Classic varieties suited to zones 5–8 include 'Anjou,' 'Bartlett,' 'Beurre Bosc,' 'Clapp's Favorite,' 'Colette,' 'Duchess,' and 'Warren.' Pears that are reliably hardy in zones 3–4 include 'Flemish Beauty,' 'Golden Spice,' 'Luscious,' 'Manning-Miller,' and 'Patten.' Other varieties that exhibit good blight-resistance include 'Kieffer,' 'Magness' (zones 6–9), 'Moonglow,' 'Orient,' and 'Tyson.'

USES IN THE LANDSCAPE: If you have limited space or wish to grow pears along a path in an allée planting, select a tree grown on dwarf rootstock; for the home orchard or as larger landscape plants, choose standard-size pears. You might also consider training a standard-size pear as an espalier. Some nurseries even carry young trees already trained. Standard pears make excellent specimen trees in the landscape, and stand out nicely against evergreens and other dark backgrounds. They grow well and look quite pretty in protected locations near buildings, but as with most fruit trees, you have to clean up "drops" in the fall, which can be unsightly in a formal area such as a patio near the house.

Vaccinium corymbosum 'Berkeley'
Ericaceae (Heath family)
HIGHBUSH BLUEBERRY

PLANT TYPE: *Shrub*
ZONES: *4–8*
HABIT: *To 12' tall; to 6' wide*
CULTURE: *Full sun; rich, acid, well-drained, sandy loam*
HARVEST: *Mid to late summer*

Native to North America, the blueberry is a valuable plant in any home landscape, producing delicious fruit in summer and making a grand exit in the fall with its attractive reddish-orange leaves. The highbush blueberry (*V. corymbosum*) is the most widely cultivated species, although it suffers winter damage in zone 3 and even in colder areas of zone 4. For cold-climate gardeners, the new "half-high" cultivars (2'–4' tall) or lowbush blueberries (*V. angustifolium* and hybrids, 1'–2' tall) are much safer choices than the highbush types. 'Berkeley' is a popular highbush variety introduced in 1949 and still widely available. Bushes are vigorous and spreading with heavy, brittle yellow canes. Berries are large, firm, and pale powder-blue in color.

CULTIVATION: Blueberries require an acid soil to grow well; pH 4.0–5.0 is ideal. If your soil is not that acidic, work in peat moss, composted oak leaves, or elemental sulfur at planting time, and mulch heavily around the plants every year with pine needles or shredded oak leaves.

Plant nursery stock in either spring or fall, digging a hole about 1' deep. Set highbush varieties 6' apart in rows spaced 8' apart or in a roughly circular patch for easier watering and bird protection.

Lowbush blueberries should be spaced 2' apart, and half-high varieties 3'–4' apart. Planting at least 2 different varieties near each other will aid in cross-pollination and encourage heavier fruiting. Provide blueberries with plenty of water, especially as the fruit develops and ripens. Feed bushes with applications of organic fertilizer labeled for acid-loving plants. Cover bushes with netting or plastic mesh as the fruit ripens to protect the crop from birds. Most blueberry varieties will start bearing fruit in their second year after planting, but will require another year or two to produce a good crop.

RELATED PLANTS: Other good highbush varieties for the backyard garden include 'Bluecrop,' 'Blueray,' 'Herbert,' 'Ivanhoe,' 'Jersey,' 'Meader,' and 'Patriot.' Highbush/lowbush hybrids for colder-winter zones include 'Northblue' and 'Northsky'; the latter variety grows to only 18"

high with a 2'–3' spread, and makes an attractive edible landscape border.

The rabbit-eye blueberry (*V. ashei*) is recommended for zones 6–9, especially in hot and droughty conditions where highbush blueberries don't perform well. Cultivars include 'Bluebelle,' 'Delite,' 'Premier,' 'Tifblue,' and 'Woodard.'

USES IN THE LANDSCAPE: The flowers, fruits, and bright autumn foliage of blueberries provide interest all season long, and the tasty berries attract birds and other wildlife to the garden. Highbush blueberries make attractive hedges or specimen plants, even in areas normally considered problem spots. Lowbush blueberries are handsome ground covers and are effective foundation plantings in well-drained areas near the house. Select other acid-loving shrubs such as azaleas and rhododendrons, or low ground covers like bearberries and lingonberries, as companion plants. Be aware, however, that the concrete foundations of many homes leach calcium, which is alkaline, into the surrounding soil. This can raise the soil pH to a level that won't support these acid-loving plants.

Vitis vinifera 'Foch'
Vitaceae (Grape family)
EUROPEAN GRAPE
PLANT TYPE: *Woody vine* ZONES: *5–7* HABIT: *To 12'* CULTURE: *Full sun; deep, well-drained soil* HARVEST: *Late summer through early fall*

The European wine grape (*V. vinifera*) has been cultivated in the Old World for ages, but today it is often grafted to the

disease-resistant rootstocks of various North American grapes. Vinifera grapes require a long growing season and mild winters, which is why the Mediterranean climate of California's famous wine valleys suits them so well.

Even gardeners in relatively short-season areas can grow good grapes, as long as they select one of the hardy vinifera hybrids (such as 'Foch') or one of the hybrids developed from the wild American fox grape (*V. labrusca*). The famous European wine grapes are also not well-suited to areas with hot, humid weather like the South. Gardeners in zones 7–9 should try growing a variety of the muscadine, or southern fox grape, (*V. rotundifolia*) instead. 'Foch' (or 'Marechal Foch') is a bluish-black grape grown extensively in the Northeast to make cherry-flavored fresh juice and a Burgundy-style wine. The vines are hardy and ripen fruit in late summer, making this variety good even in short-season areas.

CULTIVATION: In cooler regions, choosing a warm, favorable site is important—one that is protected from cold northern and western winds and from frosts in late spring and early fall. Planting on a sloping, south-facing hillside is one option; planting close to a sunny wall or near a lake or other body of water will also give a climatic advantage. Grapes can be started from hardwood cuttings taken in early spring or purchased as 1-year-old rooted vines from a nursery. Plant 1-year-old vines 8' apart in rows spaced 9' apart. Plant muscadine grapes 9'–10' apart in the row. The easiest way to support grape vines is to train them on a wire fence. Drive in wooden fence posts 4' from either side of the grape vine and stretch 2 strands of wire taut between the 2 posts, setting one strand 2' above the ground and the other at 3' or higher.

After planting the vine, cut it back so that it has 2–3 good buds. Keep the area around the young vines clear of grass and weeds; mulching around plants is an easy way to do this. Early in the second year, before the buds swell, cut the vine back to a single stem with no branches. Allow 4 side branches to grow, training 2 in each direction along the wires. If the second-year growth is good, vines should flower and bear some fruit in the third growing season. Allow 4 more side branches to grow in the third year to replace the previous year's growth.

To maintain productive grape vines after the third growing season, prune the vines in late winter, cutting out all the old woody branches (canes) and training 4 new shoots to the wires. Grapes produce fruit on new wood every year. Grapes are ready to harvest when individual fruits pull away easily from their cluster, and when the seeds inside are brown. A well-maintained grape vine is long-lived and can produce for 50 years.

RELATED PLANTS: Seeded table grapes include the heirloom 'Concord' (blue-black, late), 'Seneca' (gold, early), and 'Steuben' (black, mid season); seedless table grapes include 'Flame' (red, early, zones 7–10), 'Glenora' (blue-black, early), and 'Reliance' (red, mid season). In addition to 'Foch,' vinifera hybrid wine grapes suited to short-season areas include 'Baco Noir' (blue-black) and 'Chancellor' (blue). Good labrusca hybrids include 'Cayuga' (green) and 'Saturn' (red). Good muscadine grape cultivars recommended for zones 7–9 include 'Cowart' (black), 'Magnolia' (bronze), and 'Nesbitt' (black).

USES IN THE LANDSCAPE: Grapes are handsome ornamental vines, best shown off on arbors, pergolas, or sturdy trellises. They can provide a privacy or shade screen and can even coexist with other climbers such as wisteria or clematis, providing the support is strong enough and the grapes are kept well-pruned. However, grapes are harder to prune when grown vertically, and they're not as productive as when trained horizontally along a fence. Grapes will attract wildlife; protect with bird netting.

GRASSES

Ornamental grasses belong to the family Poaceae (formerly known as Gramineae), which comprises some 7,000 genera, broadly divided into the agricultural grasses (such as cereals and fodder) and the ornamental (grown for our gardens). Ornamentals are meant not for lawn parties and croquet, but to be admired for color, form, and texture in smaller settings.

Members of the grass family vary enormously in size and habit—from the short grasses we grow in lawns to bamboos that grow as tall as forest trees. Ornamental grasses, too, come in all sizes—from a few inches tall to giants that send their plumes 15' into the air. Foliage colors range from medium "grass-green" to blue- or gray-greens, yellow-greens, and variegations of white, yellow, and rose. Many turn red or orange in fall.

These are some of the hardest-working but easiest-to-care-for plants. Once established, an ornamental grass rarely needs fertilizer and is unbothered by insects. Its clean, full foliage is attractive all season long, providing fullness in the garden and a foil for brightly colored plants. Its inflorescence rises above the leaves, adding further interest.

Ornamentals fall into two general groups: warm- and cool-season grasses. Warm-season grasses begin growth in late spring, when the weather is settled. As a rule, these usually bloom in mid fall. Often their foliage takes on an attractive winter color and may be left in the garden throughout the winter as a kind of dried flower bouquet. They require cutting back to several inches high in late winter or very early spring.

Cool-season grasses are those that are either evergreen or that appear very early in the spring. Generally, their blooms appear in late spring or early summer.

Arrhenatherum elatius ssp. *bulbosum* 'Variegatum'
Poaceae (Grass family)
BULBOUS OAT GRASS
PLANT TYPE: *Perennial*   ZONES: *4–8*   HABIT: *1'–2' tall; 15"–24" across*   CULTURE: *Full sun to partial shade; rich, moist, well-drained soil*   BLOOM: *Early summer*

Named for the unusual bulbous nodes at the base of each stem, bulbous oat grass is prized for its wonderfully clean, showy white-and-green-striped foliage. At its best in cool, early spring weather, this plant's bright, variegated foliage is colorful very early and late in the year. It may "brown out" when the weather gets hot, but usually revives in fall. Oatlike flower spikes appear in early summer.

CULTIVATION: Bulbous oat grass grows best in cool climates or during cool weather. Set out divisions or nursery-grown plants in early spring. Avoid a spot that is hot and dry; situate in shade in hot-summer climates. When hot weather causes the appearance to deteriorate, cut back for fresh, new fall growth.

RELATED PLANTS: The subspecies *bulbosum*, without the variegation, is similar in habit, but more robust.

USES: A bright spot in rock gardens. The fresh white-and-green foliage lights up borders, especially early in the season when bulbs are in bloom.

Bambusa multiplex (syn. B. glaucescens) 'Riviereorum'
Poaceae (Grass family)
CHINESE GODDESS BAMBOO

PLANT TYPE: *Perennial*
ZONES: *8–11*
HABIT: *To 8' tall; 2'–3' wide*
CULTURE: *Sun to light shade; moist, well-drained soil*
BLOOM: *Not applicable*

Chinese goddess bamboo grows into a dense clump whose delicate stems only ¼" wide, known as culms, arch over at the top into a graceful vase shape. Leaves are small and carried in lacy sprays. Because of the size of its fine leaves and culms, this grass is prized as a bonsai subject and container plant. This is a clumping bamboo, not a runner.

CULTIVATION: Take divisions or set out nursery-grown plants in late spring or early summer.

RELATED PLANTS: *Sinarundinaria nitida* (syn. *Fargesia nitida*), a clumping bamboo with narrow, willowy, pale olive-green leaves, is hardy into zone 7.

USES: A fine accent or specimen plant for warm-climate gardens. Also used as a screen or hedge.

Briza maxima
Poaceae (Grass family)
QUAKING GRASS

PLANT TYPE: *Perennial often grown as an annual*
ZONES: *9–10*
HABIT: *Clumps 1'–2' tall; to 4" wide*
CULTURE: *Full sun; average to moist, well-drained soil*
BLOOM: *Summer*

Quaking grass bears small, heart-shaped, pale green flowers that dangle on threadlike stems and turn a lovely shade of golden tan as they age. These showy flowers are held above the fine, grassy clumps where they shimmer and quake in the slightest breeze.

CULTIVATION: Sow quaking grass in early spring, planting it where it will grow in the garden.

RELATED PLANTS: *B. minor,* an annual, is similar but smaller; *B. media* is a perennial relative, hardy in zones 5–9.

USES: The shimmering flowers of quaking grass are a good contrasting addition to the front and mid border, and are especially attractive in a dried bouquet combined with the flowers of *Chasmanthium latifolium.*

Coix lacryma-jobi
Poaceae (Grass family)
JOB'S TEARS

PLANT TYPE: *Perennial often grown as an annual*
ZONES: *9–10*
HABIT: *3'–6' tall; 1'–1½' across*
CULTURE: *Full sun; rich, moist, well-drained soil*
BLOOM: *Summer*

Job's tears bears dangling little tassel-like flowers in summer. Female flowers produce beady seeds that range from white through blue- or brown-tinged gray to black. These seeds were once prized in monastery gardens for making rosaries. The broad cornlike leaves, upright habit, and interesting seeds of Job's tears make this a handsome evergreen (in warm climates) accent in modern flower borders.

CULTIVATION: In zones 8 and below, soak seeds before sowing indoors in late winter, then transplant into the garden in spring.

RELATED PLANTS: None.

USES: Handsome enough to stand alone as a specimen plant. Lovely in a mixed or perennial border, especially when paired with purple coneflower. A good cut flower.

Festuca glauca (syn. *F. ovina* var. *glauca*)
Poaceae (Grass family)
BLUE FESCUE

PLANT TYPE: *Perennial*
ZONES: *4–9*
HABIT: *5"–8" tall; 6"–8" wide*
CULTURE: *Full sun to light shade; moist, well-drained soil*
BLOOM: *Late spring*

Blue fescue is much prized by gardeners for its tufted, glaucous blue-green foliage that is attractive year-round. Frothy flowers are held 10"–12" above the plants in late spring.

CULTIVATION: Set nursery-grown plants in the garden in spring or fall. This cool-season grass may sulk in hot dry weather.

RELATED PLANTS: Some cultivars, such as 'Solling,' don't usually produce flowers and are grown solely for their powdery-blue foliage. *F. cinerea* 'April Gruen' is a green-foliage fescue, similar in habit to blue fescue; *F. ovina* 'Glauca Minima' is an intensely blue-leaved sheep's fescue.

USES: Ground cover, accent, front border. An attractive companion for silver-foliage plants such as lavender and santolina.

Hakonechloa macra 'Aureola'
Poaceae (Grass family)
HAKONE GRASS

PLANT TYPE: *Perennial*
ZONES: *7–9*
HABIT: *1½'–2' wide; 2'–3' wide*
CULTURE: *Part shade; moist, rich, well-drained soil*
BLOOM: *Late summer*

This plant is grown primarily for its attractive, nodding yellow-green variegated foliage. Its broad leaves, wonderfully soft to the touch, are reminiscent of bamboo foliage. Its flowers are feathery and delicate. Although Hakone grass spreads moderately, it is slow-growing and never invasive.

CULTIVATION: Plant nursery-grown Hakone grass in spring or fall. Best grown in a cool-summer climate; with shade and prime growing conditions, it will survive in hot-summer areas.

RELATED PLANTS: The species *H. macra,* which is all green, may be easier to grow in hot-summer climates.

USES: Hakone grass serves as a handsome accent in shade. In a rock garden, its yellow-green leaves will cascade gracefully. It combines well with wild ginger.

Helictotrichon sempervirens
Poaceae (Grass family)
BLUE OAT GRASS

PLANT TYPE: *Perennial*
ZONES: *4–7*
HABIT: *Spiky clump 2'–4' tall; 1½'–2' wide*
CULTURE: *Full sun; light soil with excellent drainage*
BLOOM: *Summer*

Blue oat grass produces feathery powder-blue flowers that mature into handsome tan seedheads in summer. When oat grass blooms, its flowers—on long, arching stems—dance in the wind, bringing energy to the garden. The stiff foliage is evergreen in warm, protected areas.

CULTIVATION: Plant nursery-grown plants in spring or fall in soil that is fertile and light. Blue oat grass cannot survive winters in wet clay soil. It likes full sun, good air circulation, and perfect drainage.

RELATED PLANTS: Blue fescue (*Festuca glauca*) can give a similar effect but is smaller.

USES: Ground cover, border, rock garden. A wonderful seaside accent plant. The powder-blue clumps blend well with herbs like lavender and santolina.

Milium effusum 'Aureum'
Poaceae (Grass family)
BOWLES' GOLDEN GRASS

PLANT TYPE: *Perennial*
ZONES: *5–9*
HABIT: *Upright clumps to 15" tall; to 8" wide*
CULTURE: *Partial shade; moist, rich, well-drained soil*
BLOOM: *Late spring to early summer*

The vivid yellow-green of the foliage is unique in the garden and a wonderful accent—at its best in the cool days of early spring. Golden flowers that shimmer and dangle on fine stems blend beautifully with this bright yellow-green color in late spring.

CULTIVATION: Not a grass for hot-summer climates, Bowles' golden grass thrives as a handsome evergreen in cool, mild, moist climates. It can be started from seed sown in late winter and then planted outside, or from nursery-grown specimens planted out in fall or spring.

RELATED PLANTS: *Carex elata* (Bowles' golden sedge), similar in color, does better in hot-summer climates.

USES: Accent, ground cover, rock garden. A fine companion for early bulbs.

Miscanthus sinensis 'Strictus'
Poaceae (Grass family)
PORCUPINE GRASS

PLANT TYPE: *Perennial*
ZONES: *5–9*
HABIT: *Upright to 6' tall; about 3' wide*
CULTURE: *Full sun; moist, well-drained soil*
BLOOM: *Fall*

This is a warm-season grass that begins active growth in late spring and doesn't bloom until fall. Like other members of the genuses *Miscanthus,* it remains attractive in winter when the leaves have turned a warm tan color. It is prized for the yellow horizontal banding on the leaves, and for its distinctly upright habit even in rich, moist soil. In fall, porcupine grass sends up silken copper-magenta plumes that turn to white, on stems that rise about a foot above the clump.

CULTIVATION: Set out divisions or nursery-grown plants in the spring.

RELATED PLANTS: 'Zebrinus' (Zebra grass) is very similar in color but somewhat broader in habit and not nearly as erect.

USES: Porcupine grass is a striking specimen rising out of a field of yellow flowers. It can also be used for spot screens and hedging.

Miscanthus sinensis 'Variegatus'
Poaceae (Grass family)
VARIEGATED EULALIA

PLANT TYPE: *Perennial*
ZONES: *5–9*
HABIT: *Upright to 6' tall; about 4' wide*
CULTURE: *Part shade to full sun; moist, well-drained soil that is not too rich.*
BLOOM: *Mid fall*

Satiny magenta plumes appear late—in mid fall; in cold climates, they may not appear at all. But the handsome foliage is reason enough to grow this plant. Variegated eulalia's clean white-and-green-striped foliage is especially attractive with pastel and gray-leaved plants.

CULTIVATION: Divide existing clumps or set out nursery-grown grasses in spring. Do not fertilize.

RELATED PLANTS: Other variegated cultivars include 'Gracillimus,' whose graceful, slender foliage has a white midrib, and 'Morning Light,' edged in white.

USES: Accent, back border, screen. The wealth of foliage adds fullness and serves as a fine background in a perennial border. Eulalia's summer green is a calming companion to bright orange and magenta flowers.

Molinia caerulea 'Variegata'
Poaceae (Grass family)
MOOR GRASS

PLANT TYPE: *Perennial*
ZONES: *4–9*
HABIT: *Spiky clump to 3' tall; about 15" wide*
CULTURE: *Sun to light shade; moist, well-drained, slightly acid soil*
BLOOM: *Early summer*

Frothy lavender flowers appear above the clumps in early summer. Slow-growing, long-lived variegated moor grass has fine, arching leaves of medium green edged with almond.

CULTIVATION: Set out nursery-grown plants in early spring.

RELATED PLANTS: 'Karl Foerster' and 'Winspiel' have slightly larger clumps with very long flower stalks, making them more suitable for specimens. Var. *altissima* (tall purple moor grass) has mounding foliage and bears an abundance of flowering stems that grow to 6' tall.

USES: Moor grass is a superb tall ground cover whose flowers and seedheads add tremendous drama to a planting. It also serves well in the mid border, where it combines effectively with tall, spiky plants such as lilies.

Pennisetum alopecuroides 'Hameln'
Poaceae (Grass family)
AUSTRALIAN FOUNTAIN GRASS

PLANT TYPE: *Perennial*
ZONES: *6–9*
HABIT: *Cascading clump to 24" high; to 28" wide*
CULTURE: *Full sun to light shade; moist, well-drained soil of moderate fertility*
BLOOM: *Mid summer*

Silky, narrow bottlebrush flowers emerge in pink, then turn to creamy-white in mid summer. Flowers remain on the plants well into late winter, when winds and rains finally shatter them. Although the fine green clumps of grass appear somewhat late in spring, they make up for this in summer, when their cool green makes an excellent foil for colorful perennials and annuals. Australian fountain grass remains attractive throughout the winter after frost has turned its long, cascading leaves a pleasing buff color.

CULTIVATION: Start 'Hameln' from divisions or set out nursery-grown plants in spring.

RELATED PLANTS: The species *P. alopecuroides* (fountain grass, or Chinese pennisetum) is similar to 'Hameln' but grows up to 4' tall.

USES: In rock gardens, massed, or as an accent. A handsome decorative grass for a sunny border.

Phyllostachys nigra
Poaceae (Grass family)
BLACK BAMBOO

PLANT TYPE: *Perennial*
ZONES: *7–11*
HABIT: *Upright to 20' tall; to 15' wide*
CULTURE: *Full sun for best cane color; light, well-drained soil*
BLOOM: *Not applicable*

Black bamboo is grown for its long, thin, willowy leaves and stem joints that turn black with age. Prized for its combination of delicate leaf and interesting architecture, this runner is a sculptural plant that is magnificent when situated where it will be backlighted by the rising or setting sun. If not constrained, it will spread, creating an impressive forest.

CULTIVATION: Plant divisions or nursery-grown plants in spring. In hot-summer climates, some shade is desirable. In colder parts of zone 7, black bamboo needs a protected situation.

RELATED PLANTS: *P. aureosulcata* (yellow-groove bamboo) is hardy to zone 6.

USES: Screen, hedge, accent. The new shoots are edible and the dried roots are used in Chinese medicine. Combine black bamboo with mondo grass (*Ophiopogon* spp.) and moss.

Pleioblastus pygmaeus (syn. *Arundinaria pygmaea*)

Poaceae (Grass family)

PYGMY GRASS; PYGMY BAMBOO

PLANT TYPE: *Perennial*
ZONE: *7–10*
HABIT: *To 12" tall; spreads rampantly*
CULTURE: *Full sun to partial shade; moist, fertile, well-drained soil*
BLOOM: *Not applicable*

It's easy to get too much of this good thing, but pygmy grass plays an important role in erosion control. The upper surfaces of its narrow, bright green leaves, 3"–5" long, are covered by coarse hairs.

Sharply pointed, they have silvery-green undersides. They grow on branched, erect, bright green canes that are 1'–3' tall. Round and increasingly purplish toward their tapering tips, the stems' bamboo-like internodes are distinctively zigzagged.

CULTIVATION: Plant pygmy grass in spring or fall. It's extremely invasive, spreading by underground rhizomes. To keep it in bounds, sink an 18"–24" edge in the soil. Every few years, mow to the ground in late winter to encourage density. Propagate by rhizomes cut in early spring when new growth begins.

RELATED PLANS: *P. auricoma* (syn. *Arundinaria viridistriata*) has attractive yellow-and-green variegated foliage. It prefers cooler climates, and a shady site in areas with hot summers.

USES: Restrict in pots and planters; good for erosion control on steep slopes. Provides textural contrast to other ground covers in large patches if controlled.

GROUND COVERS

I t's often long after we fall in love with plants, in their infinite diversity and mystery, that we come to appreciate their many functions in the garden. In all their forms (trees, shrubs, bulbs, annuals, perennials), the appeal of plants extends well beyond the purely aesthetic—and never more so than when they function as ground covers.

Ground covers provide color, texture, and variety in the landscape. Moreover, they do not require the routine mowing, annual fertilization, supplemental watering, or periodic pesticide applications needed by the long-popular turf grasses. In fact, American gardeners have a new appreciation of the many low-maintenance, environmentally friendly lawn alternatives

Plants that serve as ground covers come from all parts of the plant world. In fact, they are often familiar plants used in a different manner—massed over expanses of ground, forming undulating tapestries of uniform color and texture. Although ivy, pachysandra, and ornamental grasses come to mind, everything

from ferns to roses, blueberries to impatiens, strawberries to daisies, and barberry to juniper can be used as ground covers. All anchor topsoil and prevent erosion. They also protect trees and shrubs, acting as living mulches that retain moisture, suppress weeds, and condition the soil. Ground covers are indispensable to the biodiversity in residential gardens, hosting wildlife and preserving organic material in the soil.

Some ground covers grow in neat mounds; others grow in bushy clumps. They may have tiny thread-like leaves, or big leathery ones, or any size in between. They may be annual or perennial, evergreen or deciduous. They may have woody stems that survive winter weather, or

soft ones that die back in winter and reappear as young shoots each spring.

Ground covers may feature flowers, thorns, berries—or just foliage. They may prefer sun or shade, acid or alkaline soil, humid or dry conditions. Though commonly low-growing, they range in size from mat-forming plants only 1" tall to shrubby ones several feet in height. In short, there is a ground cover for almost every site or situation.

Choose a ground cover that is appropriate to the conditions where it will be sited. Plants do best if you prepare the soil by cultivating it 8"–10" deep and by removing stones and debris. A sprinkling of slow-acting fertilizer will help the plant become established, but is rarely needed thereafter. Depending on the size and habit of the variety you choose, space plants equidistant from one another, about 6"–12" apart, or farther in the case of small shrubs like carpet-type junipers. If you are in a hurry for them to spread and weave together, plant them closer initially. Water and mulch temporarily to keep down weeds.

Take advantage of plants not commonly used as ground covers, and double your enjoyment of their beauty.

Ajuga reptans 'Jungle Green'
Lamiaceae (Mint family)
BUGLEWEED; CARPET BUGLE

PLANT TYPE: *Perennial*
ZONES: *3–8*
HABIT: *Foliage to 3"; spread unlimited*
CULTURE: *Sun or shade; ordinary soil*
BLOOM: *Early summer*

A lthough ajugas show off in spring with attractive 4"–6" spikes arrayed with perky blue

flowers, their foliage is the main attraction. The plant develops a fast-growing, tightly-knit mat composed of rooted leaf rosettes 4"–6" wide and glossy, crinkly, narrow oval leaves that are virtually evergreen. Like many members of the mint family, it tends to become invasive, but it is easily uprooted. 'Jungle Green' is the largest-leaved ajuga. Its leaves are greener, more round-edged, and less mounding than the species.

CULTIVATION: Nursery-grown stock from flats or pots is easy to transplant. To start a patch of ground cover, plant larger-leaved types 12"–18" apart. Don't fertilize. Ajugas spread quickly by underground stems that root and send up new plants. Mow or clip dead flower spikes for appearance. Propagate by division. Beware of overwatering or overcrowding, which may foster root rot.

RELATED PLANTS: The mature foliage of 'Burgundy Glow' is variegated cream, green, and pink;

'Royalty' has strongly puckered dark purple leaves; 'Silver Beauty' is gray-green variegated with cream. Other large-leaved types are 'Bronze Beauty' (bronze-purple) and 'Catlin's Giant' (bronze-green).

USES: Excellent for edging, in patches at the front of the flower border, between paving stones, underplanting trees and shrubs, or covering bulb beds.

Aptenia cordifolia (syn. *Mesembryanthemum cordifolium*)

Aizoaceae (Iceplant family)

BABY SUN ROSE

PLANT TYPE: *Succulent*
ZONE: *10*
HABIT: *2" tall; 2' trailing stems branch and spread indefinitely*
CULTURE: *Full sun; ordinary, well-drained soil*
BLOOM: *Spring and summer*

This plant transforms an area with so-so soil and harsh sunlight into a splash of jaunty pink. It forms a mat of freely branching, succulent, prostrate stems, covered with heart-shaped or oval leaves 1" wide. The bright green fleshy foliage cushions numerous deep pink flowers 1" wide. The small, bright, finely petaled, daisy-like

flowers bloom with gusto over almost the entire growing season.

CULTIVATION: Plant in spring or fall. Once established, this plant needs minimal moisture—in fact, it requires truly dry soil in winter. Propagate by seed or stem cuttings taken in spring.

RELATED PLANTS: 'Variegata' leaves are edged in white.

USES: Welcome as a trailer in rock gardens. Use in hanging baskets or planters.

Arctostaphylos uva-ursi 'Massachusetts'

Ericaceae (Heath family)

BEARBERRY; KINNIKINICK

PLANT TYPE: *Woody perennial*
ZONES: *2–7*
HABIT: *6"–12" tall; spreads at will*
CULTURE: *Full sun; dry, sandy, acid, well-drained soil*
BLOOM: *Late spring*

This slow-growing, vigorous, self-reliant landscape gem has prostrate, crooked, woody stems, weaving flat evergreen mats of bright green leathery foliage for 4-season appeal. It greets the growing season with waxy white, pink-tinged, urn-shaped flowers that eventually give way to red berries resembling tiny apples. With the coming of frost, as birds devour the berries, the foliage turns reddish-bronze. Sturdy enough to handle foot traffic, 'Massachusetts' also has good disease-resistance. Versatile bearberries thrive in New England, the Rockies, and the Pacific Northwest.

CULTIVATION: 'Massachusetts' tolerates salt spray and can handle damp weather better than some other

types. Bearberries are a bit difficult to transplant. Plant large nursery-grown mats or containerized plants in early spring or fall. Space plants 2' apart; because they are slow growers, mulch the plantings to keep down weeds until they fill in. Never fertilize. These plants are tricky to propagate; try layering branches that are low to the ground.

RELATED PLANTS: Drought-tolerant 'Alaska' has darker leaves; 'Vancouver Jade' has glossy, dark green leaves turning deep red in fall; 'Wood's Red' (Royal Horticultural Society Award of Merit winner) is compact with large red fruits and small, dark green leaves.

USES: Rock gardens, hillsides, seaside gardens; erosion control on steep slopes. Looks good with needled evergreens or artfully placed rocks.

Asarum caudatum

Aristolochiaceae (Birthwort family)

WILD GINGER

PLANT TYPE: *Evergreen perennial*
ZONES: *6–8*
HABIT: *3"–7" tall; spreads 10" or more*
CULTURE: *Shade; moist, humusy, well-drained soil*
BLOOM: *Late spring to early summer*

The glossy, dark green carpet formed by the pairs of leathery, kidney-shaped, evergreen ginger leaves is an invitation to enjoy the cool shade on a hot day. From 2"–6" long, rising on stems 7" long, these highly ornamental leaves hide small, pitcher-shaped purplish-brown flowers with interesting 2" tail-like extensions on each of their 3 petals. They nestle modestly among the foliage nearly at soil level by early summer and are relatively inconspicuous.

CULTIVATION: Plant nursery-grown containerized plants in spring or fall. Ginger spreads briskly by creeping rhizomes, so it will need to be corralled after a few years. Control or propagate by division of the rootstocks. The flowers, which are slug-pollinated, self sow. Both the leaves and rhizomes exude a pungent odor when crushed.

RELATED PLANTS: European wild ginger (*A. europaeum*) is hardier, growing 6"–10" tall with glossy, highly ornamental evergreen leaves. Canadian wild ginger (*A. canadense*) is 6"–12" tall and tolerates more heat. Southern wild ginger (*A. shuttleworthii*) has leaves

mottled with silver marks, resembling cyclamen foliage. 'Callaway' has smaller foliage, vigorous growth.

USES: Naturalize in the wild garden, the winter garden, over bulb beds in deciduous shade, or under evergreen shrubs and trees.

Ceratostigma plumbaginoides (syn. Plumbago larpentiae)

Plumbaginaceae (Plumbago family)

DWARF PLUMBAGO; LEADWORT

PLANT TYPE: *Perennial*
ZONES: *5–9*
HABIT: *8"–12" tall; spreads over several feet*
CULTURE: *Full sun to partial shade; any well-drained soil*
BLOOM: *Late summer*

This plant reminds us that good things are worth waiting for. Semi-prostrate green mats of shiny leaves appear a bit late to the spring party but stay around until the season ends. They are slow to emerge in spring, waiting till the soil warms. Leaves are about 3" long with tapered tips. Then cobalt-blue single flowers, ½" across, cluster at stem ends, lasting until frost. The deciduous foliage turns reddish and then drops to close the season.

CULTIVATION: Plant containerized plants during late spring or fall, spaced 8"–10" apart. Mulch them for winter protection in zone 5. Tough, adaptable, and fast-growing, they will prosper. In warmer areas, cut plants back to ground level in spring to foster dense new growth. Propagate from cuttings in summer or by division in the spring only. Hates soggy soil and competition from tree roots.

RELATED PLANTS: Chinese plumbago (*C. willmottianum*) is a small shrub and is more drought-tolerant; *C. griffithii* is more compact.

USES: Under shrubs, at the front edge of a flower border, in rock gardens, or along walks. It will cascade beautifully over walls.

Chelone obliqua
Scrophulariaceae (Figwort family)
TURTLEHEAD; ROSE TURTLEHEAD

PLANT TYPE: *Perennial*
ZONES: *6–9*
HABIT: *2'–3' tall; clumps 2' wide*
CULTURE: *Full sun to partial shade; humusy, acid, consistently moist soil*
BLOOM: *Late summer to early autumn*

This native is at home in several places in the residential landscape. Its coarse, toothed, 6" basal leaves are opposite as they extend up stiff stems 2' tall. Lance-shaped and distinctly veined, they effectively set off the tubular magenta flowers, 1" long, compactly arranged at the stem tips. Resembling snapdragons, the long-blooming flowers have 2 irregular lips that form a hollow tube. Flowers open a few at a time, providing welcome color late in the season. Combine with ferns, lobelias, and irises near water; or with goldenrod, sunflowers, and asters in grassy meadow settings.

CULTIVATION: Plant these low-maintenance standbys in the spring as seedlings or as root divisions from existing plants. Pinch back after a few weeks to encourage compactness, if desired. Staking is not necessary unless the site is too shady. Quite self-reliant, they self-sow and are pest free.

RELATED PLANTS: Pink turtlehead (*C. lyonii*) is best suited to the garden and has rose-purple flowers 1" long. White turtlehead (*C. glabra*) has white flowers with a pink blush.

USES: Ideal for streamside or marsh. Also useful in the middle of the flower border, in wildflower plantings, and in bog gardens. The striking vertical bearing makes good specimens or accents in more formal situations.

Convallaria majalis
Liliaceae (Lily family)
LILY-OF-THE-VALLEY

PLANT TYPE: *Rhizomatous perennial*
ZONES: *2–7*
HABIT: *Foliage 6"–8" tall; spread unlimited*
CULTURE: *Partial to full shade; humusy, acid, moist, well-drained soil*
BLOOM: *Spring*

So delightful is this plant that it is no surprise its fragrance is the very essence of the perfume Joy. In the garden, tender shoots will become pairs of large, oblong bluish-green leaves with pointed tips, rising each spring from rhizomatous root structures called pips. Shortly after, the leaves unfurl, 1"–3" wide, and slender stems peek out from their folds, with waxy, bell-shaped, nodding white flowers arrayed along one side. By mid summer, berries sometimes form just before the leaves begin to age, ripening to yellowish-brown and dying back by late summer. The berries and flowers are poisonous.

CULTIVATION: Site on the north or east side of a building or under shrubs and trees out of the sun. Competes well with shallow-rooted trees. Plant in late spring or early fall, 4"–6" apart. Plan to cut back

or otherwise mask dying foliage toward the end of the season. Thin the bed if flowering becomes sparse. Invasive in colder climates; less aggressive in warmer ones. Propagate by dividing clumps of crowded plants in the fall.

RELATED PLANTS: 'Flore Pleno' has larger, double flowers; 'Striata' foliage is variegated with thin white stripes; var. *rosea* has pale pink flowers.

USES: Along shady borders, under shrubs and trees; naturalize in woodland and undeveloped areas. Cut flowers for charming fragrant bouquets. Combine with other minor bulbs. Prechilled pips are available for forcing in winter, to be planted outdoors in spring.

Cotoneaster dammeri 'Lowfast'

Rosaceae (Rose family)

BEARBERRY COTONEASTER

PLANT TYPE: *Shrub*
ZONES: *5–8*
HABIT: *6"–24" tall; spreads 12'–15' or more*
CULTURE: *Full sun to full shade; any well-drained soil*
BLOOM: *Spring*

This eminently satisfactory, very low-growing shrub spreads with gusto as its prostrate woody branches root everywhere they touch the soil. Notable for fine-textured, glossy deep green leaves, it also bears small inconspicuous white flowers, ⅓"–½" wide, singly or in pairs. These give way to an abundance of bright red ¼" berries that announce the coming of autumn. If the plant has protection, its winter foliage of dullish green to purple remains; the foliage drops if the plant is exposed to harsh weather.

CULTIVATION: Easy to grow. Plant nursery-grown container transplants in spring or fall, about 3'–4' apart. 'Lowfast' is extremely cold-hardy. It becomes unkempt in about 5 years. Very susceptible to fire blight. Propagate from softwood cuttings in June or July, or by layering branches near the soil.

RELATED PLANTS: 'Coral Beauty,' up to and over 2' tall with coral red berries; 'Eichholz,' up to 12" tall with green summer foliage that turns yellow or orangy-red in fall. 'Major' has good winter hardiness; 'Skogholm' is a good spreader and bloomer.

USES: On banks and slopes to hold soil, massed as wildlife habitat or an informal hedgerow, in a shrub border.

Epimedium × youngianum 'Niveum'

Berberidaceae (Barberry family)

BISHOP'S HAT; LONGSPUR EPIMEDIUM

PLANT TYPE: *Perennial*
ZONES: *3–8*
HABIT: *8" tall; clumps spread indefinitely*
CULTURE: *Partial to full shade; humusy, moist, well-drained soil*
BLOOM: *Spring*

The dainty appearance of this semi-evergreen shade garden plant belies its sturdy reliability. Its spring foliage is a shiny reddish-bronze, each leaf having 3 heart-shaped, toothed leaflets up to 3" long near the tops of thin, wiry stems. Nestled among them are ¾" cup-shaped white flowers that often have interesting spurred petals, causing them to resemble a bishop's mitre. This is the latest epimedium to bloom each spring; the medium green summer foliage persists long afterward, darkening to a reddish-purple with frost.

CULTIVATION: Easy to grow and care for, slow to get established, it eventually forms a thick matrix of roots and stems impenetrable by weeds. Transplant containerized plants in spring or fall 12" apart for ground cover. Cut back overwintered stems and foliage in early spring as new shoots emerge. Propagate from division of matted rhizomatous roots in fall or late winter.

RELATED PLANTS: *E. grandiflorum* 'Rose Queen' has red flowers with white spurs; 'Snow Queen' is vigorous with showy white flowers. Red alpine epimedium (*E.* ×

rubrum) has yellow or white flowers tinged with red, and green leaves edged in red.

USES: Ideal for small gardens where coarser, taller types would dominate, and under deciduous shrubs. Combine with hardy bulbs. Cut flowers last indoors in arrangements.

Lamium galeobdolon (syn. *Lamiastrum galeobdolon*)
Lamiaceae (Mint family)
SPOTTED DEAD NETTLE; YELLOW ARCHANGEL

PLANT TYPE: *Evergreen perennial*
ZONES: *4–9*
HABIT: *1'–2' tall; spreads at will*
CULTURE: *Partial to full shade; any well-drained soil*
BLOOM: *Early summer*

This creeper can be counted on to nicely cover a multitude of landscape sins in a very short time. It spreads on branching surface runners that develop rootlets at each node as they progress. Silvery-mottled evergreen leaves grow opposite each other on flexible square stems. They have a distinctive odor when crushed. Spotted dead nettle shines even more when the short, small, bright yellow flowers appear in the spring. With 2 hooded lips and brown markings, the flowers emerge in the axils of the leaves, which are in whorls around the upright stems.

CULTIVATION: A carefree and rampant spreader. Does not like extreme summer heat. Plant seedlings or rooted cuttings in spring or fall, spaced 12"–18" apart. Do not fertilize. Shear the plant back every year or two for control and to neaten the patch.

Propagate by division in spring or fall; root stem cuttings in summer.

RELATED PLANTS: 'Hermann's Pride' has smaller, dark green metallic leaves, mounds to 8", and is not invasive; 'Variegatum' has mostly silver leaves with green veins that sometimes revert to all green.

USES: Under dark green evergreens; in woodland settings and informal, shady gardens. Allow it to crawl over rotting stumps and other eyesores in undeveloped areas.

Liriope spicata
Liliaceae (Lily family)
CREEPING LILYTURF

PLANT TYPE: *Evergreen perennial*
ZONES: *5–10*
HABIT: *To 18" tall; spreads at will*
CULTURE: *Partial sun to full shade; moist, well-drained soil*
BLOOM: *Late summer*

Spreading by underground runners, the dark green mat of tough, straplike foliage, ¼" wide,

provides a coarse counterpoint to nearby turf grasses. Dark green leaves 18" long have tiny teeth along their edges and pointed tips. Mid season they are interspersed with tiny pale lavender or off-white flowers clustered along stems that barely clear the arching foliage. Black berries sometimes appear afterward. Foliage stays green until January or so, when winter damage in colder regions may cause the leaves to become ragged and brown-edged.

CULTIVATION: Durable and fast spreading. Plant in spring or fall. Space sprigs 4"–6" apart, containerized plants 12"–18" apart. Cut back to a couple of inches in late winter with shears or lawn mower. Tolerates drought, as well as salt spray in coastal plantings. Propagate by dividing rooted stems in spring. Few pest problems, possibly slugs.

RELATED PLANTS: 'Silver Dragon' is compact at 6"–8" tall and variegated with white stripes on the leaves, but is less robust. Lilyturf (*L. muscari*) has a clumping habit and slightly wider leaves than *L. spicata;* the flowers may be lavender or white. Not invasive, it's useful for

edging. Varieties of lilyturf are excellent substitutes for grass in Florida.

USES: A good grass substitute in shady areas where it's free to roam. Holds soil on slopes; covers hard-to-mow areas, where surface tree roots inhibit anything else from growing. Dark foliage sets off larger hardy bulb varieties, then covers their ripening foliage.

Lithodora diffusa (syns. *Lithospermum diffusum;* *L. prostratum*)

Boraginaceae (Borage family)

GROMWELL

PLANT TYPE: *Evergreen shrub*
ZONES: *6–7*
HABIT: *6"–12" tall; spreads to 12" wide*
CULTURE: *Full sun to partial shade; loose, acid, well-drained soil*
BLOOM: *Summer*

Prostrate, hairy, woody stems form broad mounds covered with masses of evergreen foliage. Their inch-long dull green leaves are narrow and slightly hairy. However, these leaves play second fiddle to the abundant bright blue tubular flowers, ½" long, that cluster gaily at the ends of the trailing stems until frost. A pest-free asset in the home landscape.

CULTIVATION: Resents having its roots disturbed, so transplant carefully. Plant in spring or fall in sandy soil with leaf mold added, if possible. Needs some watering in summer. Trim back leggy stems after flowering. Propagate from semi-ripe cuttings in July, or from seed in the fall.

RELATED PLANTS: 'Heavenly Blue' spreads to 18". 'Grace Ward' is also azure-blue.

USES: Charming in rock gardens and trailing over walls.

Mentha requienii

Lamiaceae (Mint family)

CORSICAN MINT; JEWEL MINT OF CORSICA

PLANT TYPE: *Semi-evergreen perennial*
ZONES: *7–9*
HABIT: *To 3" tall; spreads at will*
CULTURE: *Full sun to partial shade; moist, well-drained soil*
BLOOM: *Summer*

A dainty creeping mat of bright apple-green, this tiny wonder is semi-evergreen. It spreads vigorously by means of underground stems, or runners. Its masses of miniature ⅛" leaves, arrayed on square stems, are mosslike in appearance. They exude a scent of peppermint when crushed by foot traffic. Sparse pale purple flowers whorled loosely around the stems add a flush of summer color.

CULTIVATION: Plant rooted cuttings or nursery stock in spring or fall about 6" apart. Corsican mint spreads moderately fast but dies back over the winter in cold areas. Propagate from rooted runners. Replant if necessary every 3 or 4 years.

RELATED PLANTS: Various mint species have different foliage, scents, and culinary or medicinal uses: Pineapple mint (*M. suaveolens* 'Variegata') has variegated white-and-green leaves; peppermint (*M.* × *piperita*) has purplish-green leaves; eau-de-cologne mint (*M.* × *piperita* 'Citrata') has perfumed purple-tinged leaves; Bowles' mint (*M.* × *villosa* var. *alopecuroides*) has rounded leaves, purple-pink flowers, and a spearmint flavor.

USES: Not for culinary or medicinal use. Corsican mint is planted in large patches for effect; it's also appropriate along paths and in rock gardens. May be grown in pots.

Pachysandra terminalis 'Variegata'

Buxaceae (Box family)

SILVEREDGE PACHYSANDRA

PLANT TYPE: *Evergreen perennial*
ZONES: *4–8*
HABIT: *6"–12" tall; spreads indefinitely*
CULTURE: *Partial to full shade; moist, neutral to acid, well-drained soil*
BLOOM: *Spring*

The whorls of foliage on the upright stalks of this variegated version of a reliable landscape standby are green with silver or

cream-to-white mottling. Each leaf is somewhat glossy, spoon-shaped, and toothed toward its tip. Mildly musk-scented, the off-white, sometimes purplish-tinged flowers are inconspicuous, but loved by honeybees. Sometimes white berries appear in the fall. Winter sun may burn the foliage of plants sited under deciduous trees, and extreme summer heat and drought may cause some dieback. Otherwise this tough plant is virtually carefree.

CULTIVATION: Choose a shady area, as too much sun bleaches the foliage. Transplants easily and fills in by rooted underground stems. 'Variegata' is not quite as vigorous as its plain green cousin; it doesn't tolerate foot traffic, and it doesn't grow well in coastal areas. Plant in fall or early in spring, roughly 4 plants per square foot. Divide older plantings by lifting clumps of matted stems and trimming off rooted chunks to locate elsewhere. Shear or mow every few years to renew the planting. Propagate in

spring from stems rooted in either water or damp vermiculite.

RELATED PLANTS: Lower-growing 'Green Carpet' has improved deep green foliage. Semi-evergreen Allegheny spurge (*P. procumbens*) has duller gray-green, coarser, wider leaves and greenish-purplish flowers, and it spreads more slowly.

USES: Forms islands or patches as an alternative to lawn; a living mulch under trees and shrubs. Protects soil in naturalized areas and semi-woodland settings. Variegation brightens deep shade, adding texture and color to those areas where greens predominate. Obscures eyesores such as rotting stumps and ripening bulb foliage.

Pratia pedunculata (syns. *Laurentia fluviatilis; Isotoma fluviatilis*)
Campanulaceae (Bellflower family)
PRATIA
PLANT TYPE: *Perennial* ZONES: *9–10* HABIT: *To 1½' tall; creeps indefinitely* CULTURE: *Partial shade; moist, fertile soil* BLOOM: *Spring*

With its creeping stems, this prostrate spreader washes over the soil as a sea of green. Roundish, shiny, ½" dark green leaves with jagged teeth at their edges decorate the small, erect stems. Leaves are tipped with asymmetrical, solitary, star-shaped flowers in the spring. A lovely blue, they are 1½" long with upper lips of 2 lobes and lower lips of 3 lobes.

CULTIVATION: Full sun in cool climates. Plant in spring or fall,

spaced 6"–8" apart. Will not take foot traffic. Propagate in autumn by division or seed.

RELATED PLANTS: 'County Park' is ½" tall, vigorous, and evergreen. *P. angulata* is a creeping evergreen with star-shaped white flowers.

USES: For naturalized areas. Lovely with a solitary columbine or cineraria.

Sarcococca hookeriana var. *humilis*
Buxaceae (Box family)
SWEET BOX; CHRISTMAS BOX
PLANT TYPE: *Evergreen shrub* ZONES: *6–9* HABIT: *1½'–2' tall; spreads 8' or more* CULTURE: *Partial to full shade; rich, acid, humusy soil* BLOOM: *Mid winter to early spring*

A landscape treasure all year, this miniature spreading shrub has no downtime. Sweet box's upright woody stems are covered with narrow, pointed lustrous, dark green leaves that form matted clumps of evergreen foliage. Leaves are 1"–3" long and stay fresh-looking year-round. Tiny flowers cluster in the axils of the leaves in very early spring, their white petals and pink anthers fragrant with the scent of honey. These give way to round, fleshy, ⅜" black berries in summer and autumn. This plant is virtually pest free.

CULTIVATION: Choose a shaded site to avoid fading or browning foliage from strong sun. Plant nursery-grown stock or root divisions about 3' apart in early spring. Because they are slow-growing, mulch between the plants to discourage weeds and retain soil moisture while they knit together. No routine pruning is required. Propagate from semi-ripe cuttings in mid summer or from seed in autumn. Tolerates some pollution.

RELATED PLANTS: Var. *digyna* is similar to var. *humilis* but produces suckers. *S. confusa* has black fruit, tiny leaves. Fragrant sarcococca (*S. ruscifolia*) has similar leaves and red fruits, and grows to 6' in zones 8–9.

USES: On the West Coast and in the South, grows in deep shade. Good under wide overhanging roofs, awnings, large trees. Cut in winter for indoor display.

Tradescantia virginiana

Commelinaceae (Spiderwort family)

VIRGINIA SPIDERWORT; COMMON SPIDERWORT

PLANT TYPE: *Perennial*
ZONES: *5–10*
HABIT: *Grows 1'–3' tall; to 2' wide*
CULTURE: *Full sun to partial shade; any moist soil*
BLOOM: *Late spring to mid summer*

C overs a lot of ground with interesting vertical texture. Features dense clumps of erect,

fleshy stems covered with narrow, pointed, 12" green leaves. Its flowers, 1"–3" wide, have 3 open, flared petals nestled in greenish leaflike bracts at stem ends. The petals, usually deep blue or purple, last only a day but they flower successively until all buds are opened, so plants are long-blooming. By mid season, the sprawling foliage begins to look unkempt and benefits from cutting back.

CULTIVATION: Easy to grow. Plant in spring or fall. Withhold fertilizer to discourage excessive foliage growth. Cut foliage back hard in mid summer to stimulate new compact growth and repeat flowering when season grows cooler. Divide clumps every 3 or 4 years in order to control spreading. Divide in spring to propagate, or root stem cuttings in moist, sandy soil by snapping off stems at joints. Will self-sow and bloom in the second year.

RELATED PLANTS: In addition to the many cultivars to choose from in ranges of blue: 'Blue Stone' has lavender flowers; 'Innocence' has white; 'Iris Pritchard' has white tinged with violet; 'Osprey' has pure white with a blue center; 'Pauling' has mauve-pink; 'Purple Dome' has deep purple.

USES: Woodland settings, wild gardens, shade borders, and slopes.

HERBS

Herbs are among the oldest cultivated plants, prized for their medicinal and culinary importance, and also used as a dye. Recently, there has been an explosion in the popularity of culinary herbs—not just common ones like parsley, sage, rosemary, and thyme, but more exotic ones like lemon grass and anise hyssop. Cut herbs are expensive to buy, so it pays to grow your own—and you can harvest them fresh whenever you need them. A decorative pot of your favorite and most used culinary herbs can sit right outside the kitchen door—easy for picking, even in the rain.

Herbs encompass all types of plants—annuals, perennials, bulbs, even a few trees and shrubs. Before they season your cooking, culinary herbs are an attractive element in the perennial or mixed border, formal herb garden, and vegetable garden. Most culinary herbs are used for their leaves; many have edible flowers as well (parsley is one exception). Even if you don't relish eating the flowers or using them as garnish, they add to the herb's beauty and utility in the garden by attracting bees and butterflies. Many herbs are good companions for vegetables, deterring pests and/ or increasing the vigor of the plants;

others attract beneficial insects.

You could devote a garden completely to herbs, or introduce them here and there among your ornamentals. Try some curly parsley as a handsome edge to a border. Many of the Mediterranean herbs are especially suited for sunny, well-drained sites. Some gardeners like to tuck them between stones in a pathway. Or, as is done in Britain, plant them among flagstones in a patio—not just small, creeping herbs like thyme and oregano, but also larger plants like rosemary and borage. Allow enough flagstones between each herb so it looks as if the herbs

grew there on their own. If you have time and patience, you may even enjoy creating a traditional knot garden, whose intricate pattern is best viewed from above.

Agastache foeniculum (syn. *A. anethiodora*)
Lamiaceae (Mint family)
ANISE HYSSOP

PLANT TYPE: *Perennial*
ZONES: *5–9*
HABIT: *3'–4' tall*
CULTURE: *Full sun to light shade; any well-drained soil*
BLOOM: *Mid summer*

A North American prairie wildflower with an upright branching habit, anise hyssop has dense, deep-lilac-colored terminal flower spikes 5"–6" long. A close look at the spikes reveals small 2-lipped flowers. Like other members of the mint family, it has square stems and opposite leaves. It bears ovate leaves, 3"–4" long, with serrated edges. The entire plant has a distinctive licorice aroma, indicative of the flavor of both the flowers and the leaves. The plant attracts bees and butterflies.

CULTIVATION: Unlike most perennials, anise hyssop blooms the first year when started from seed. Plant outdoors as soon as all danger of frost is past, or sow seeds indoors at least 6 weeks before the last spring frost date. Transplant outside after danger of frost has passed, allowing at least 12"–15" between plants. In warm climates, sow the seed directly in the garden in autumn. As flowers fade, cut the spikes down to the nearest leafing branch—in several weeks you'll be rewarded with more flowers. Cut the plant down to the ground after a killing frost. It is late to come up in the spring, but don't despair; have patience (and be sure to mark where it is planted so you don't accidentally dig it up before it emerges). Anise hyssop readily self-seeds.

RELATED PLANTS: 'Tutti Frutti' has larger pinkish-lavender flowers. 'Firebird' has coppery-orange blooms.

USES: The flowers produce abundant nectar that yields a delicious light, fragrant honey. You can make a refreshing tea from the leaves and flowers. Anise hyssop is lovely grown behind lavender or paired with lemon balm or bee balm.

Allium schoenoprasum
Liliaceae
(Lily family)
CHIVES

PLANT TYPE: *Perennial*
ZONES: *3–9*
HABIT: *10"–18" tall*
CULTURE: *Full sun; slightly moist, well-drained soil*
BLOOM: *Mid spring*

Native to Asia, Europe, and North America, chives and their many relatives have been cultivated for millennia. They were

noted in Chinese herbals over 5,000 years ago for their ability to stimulate the appetite and to ease a cough. The hollow grasslike leaves grow in clumps. Chives are attractive in the garden not only for their foliage, but also for their flowers—lavender-pink pompon-like blooms comprising smaller florets. A perennial herb, this plant dies back after autumn frost in cold-winter areas, and regrows each spring.

CULTIVATION: Chives can be readily propagated in mid spring by dividing a clump. Simply dig up the clump and gently tear it into 2 or more sections, separating it from the leaves down through the soil and roots. Replant the smaller clumps, spacing them 12"–18" apart. You can also sow seeds outdoors in early spring as soon as the soil is workable.

RELATED PLANTS: Nodding onion (*A. cernuum*) is perennial in the Pacific Northwest and California. It looks like a loose-formed, nodding chive flower. It's appealing in the garden, and useful in the kitchen.

USES: The leaves are used for their mild oniony flavor in cook-

ing. Although the flowers appear delicate, they are also quite flavorful—oniony but not overpoweringly so. Chives are attractive at the edge of a border, and they also do quite well grown in pots. Their flowers make an interesting counterpoint to yellow or orange nasturtiums.

Allium tuberosum
Liliaceae
(Lily family)
GARLIC CHIVES; CHINESE CHIVES

PLANT TYPE: *Perennial*
ZONES: *4–9*
HABIT: *18"–30" tall*
CULTURE: *Full sun to partial shade; average soil*
BLOOM: *Mid summer to early fall*

Garlic chives are hardy perennial herbs with narrow, flattened gray-green leaves that grow about 12" tall. The leaves are grasslike in appearance, but solid enough to hold themselves upright, looking handsome all summer. The flower stalks rise above the leaves, 18"–30" in height, topped with a flat-headed cluster of sweet-smelling white, star-shaped flowers.

CULTIVATION: Plant from mid spring through summer, allowing 12" between plants. Garlic chives are self-seeding and can be aggressive. Divide and thin as necessary at any time. If the plant starts getting woody, trim the foliage to within an inch of the ground to rejuvenate the plant. Do not allow garlic chives to go to seed in a perennial garden, or you'll have seedlings coming up everywhere.

RELATED PLANTS: *Tulbaghia violacea* (society garlic) is gaining popularity in the garden. Hardy in zones 9–10, where the leaves are evergreen, it is grown as an annual in other areas. The fleshy gray-green basal leaves form broad clumps and smell strongly of onions or garlic when bruised. Small, star-shaped lilac flowers are borne in clusters of 8–20 in 2½" umbels atop a 12"–24" stalk. Society garlic flowers over a long period of time, from spring into summer. The sweet scent of the flowers belies their onion-garlic flavor.

USES: Although the leaves are familiar as an edible herb, the flowers too have a garlicky flavor—toss them in a salad or stir-fry. Garlic chives are attractive in a perennial border, providing a green background for low-growing plants like lamb's ears and pansies. Late to bloom, the white flowers show up best against a dark background, such as a trellis of climbing nasturtiums or the heart-shaped leaves of moonflowers.

Aloysia triphylla (syn. *Lippia citriodora*)
Verbenaceae (Vervain family)
LEMON VERBENA

PLANT TYPE: *Shrubby perennial*
ZONES: *8–11*
HABIT: *To 10' tall in mild climates, 3'–5' when grown as an annual*
CULTURE: *Full sun; evenly moist, well-drained soil*
BLOOM: *Early summer*

Native to South America, this tender, deciduous, shrubby perennial is grown as an annual in most parts of the U.S. Sweetly lemon-scented, the narrow, 3" pale green leaves grow in lancelike whorls; they are brittle and paper-thin, with a rough texture. In mild climates where it is grown year-round, it blooms with loose clusters of white or pale purple flowers. This is one of the most fragrant of plants for a garden—when touched, the leaves release an intense lemon perfume. In cold-winter areas, it can be potted up and brought indoors for winter.

CULTIVATION: Usually grown from rooted cuttings rather than from seed. Allow at least 24" between plants. Prune regularly to encourage a bushy habit. Easy to train into a standard form or to espalier. In cold-winter climates,

---

bring indoors to a cool, dry, well-lit place for the winter. Water sparingly, and allow plants to go dormant until early spring.

RELATED PLANTS: *Lippia dulcis* is used as a sweetener—it is 1,000 times sweeter than sucrose. *L. graveolens* (Mexican oregano) is used like oregano in Mexico and Central America.

USES: The leaves are used in fruit compotes, to flavor drinks, and to make teas; the essential oil is used in perfume and lotions. In mild climates, plant near the back of a border for strong vertical accent. The thin leaves rustle gently in the lightest breeze. Makes a good foil for any of the larger polygonums in the garden.

Anethum graveolens
Apiaceae (Parsley or carrot family)
DILL; DILLWEED; DILLSEED

PLANT TYPE: *Annual*
ZONES: *Not applicable*
HABIT: *To 3' or more*
CULTURE: *Full sun; prefers fairly good, well-drained soil*
BLOOM: *Mid summer*

Dill's name comes from an Old Norse word meaning "to lull," and oil from the seed is still used to soothe colicky babies and settle adult digestive upset. Originally native to Asia, dill has naturalized throughout most of temperate Europe and North America, growing along roadsides and in undeveloped areas. A single, hollow green stem branches to leafstalks that bear fine, feathery bluish-green leaves. Slightly domed umbels of yellow flowers, resembling miniature umbrellas, appear at the ends of the branches in mid summer. These are followed by the seeds (actually fruits), distinguished by their prominent ribs.

CULTIVATION: Dill will grow in poor soil as long as it's well-drained. In mild climates, grow it in sunny, open areas, but in more temperate areas, protect its willowy stems from the wind. If you plan on saving seeds, don't grow near fennel or cross-pollination will occur. Dill has delicate roots and does not transplant well; sow directly in the garden in late spring or early summer. Thin plants to 12"–15" apart. Planted on the north side of the garden, dill will not shade lower-growing plants.

RELATED PLANTS: 'Fernleaf,' an All-America winner, is a base-branching dwarf plant that grows only 18" tall and is well-suited for container culture. 'Dukat' is a Finnish strain with exceptional flavor and vigorous foliage.

USES: The ancient Egyptians used dill as a medicinal herb more than 5,000 years ago. Ancient Romans wove the yellow flowers into dual-purpose wreaths to grace their banquet halls—freshening the air with their spicy aroma while adding to the decor. Today dill is

grown as a culinary herb. Use leaves fresh or dried, in salads or with fish. The seeds give dill pickles their name and characteristic flavor. The flowers have a milder yet similar flavor to that of the leaves. Dill is handsome planted near the back of the garden, or against a brick wall where you can appreciate its tall, fernlike foliage.

Artemisia dracunculus var. *sativa*

Asteraceae (COMPOSITE FAMILY)

FRENCH TARRAGON; ESTRAGON

PLANT TYPE: *Perennial*
ZONES: *3–10*
HABIT: *18"–24"*
CULTURE: *Full sun to partial shade; well-drained soil*
BLOOM: *Not applicable*

Native to eastern Europe, French tarragon is a lovely, many-branched plant. As it grows, it forms a slowly spreading colony of upright stems with attractive narrow leaves. It very rarely flowers and is sterile, never setting seed.

CULTIVATION: Plant rooted cuttings in spring after all danger of frost is past, allowing 20" between plants. Pinch regularly for culinary use and to keep plants bushy and erect. Divide plants every second or third spring to maintain vigor and flavor. In cold-winter areas, mulch in late autumn with chopped leaves after the ground has frozen.

RELATED PLANTS: Russian tarragon (*A. dracunculus* ssp. *dracunculoides*) is often sold as French tarragon. Similar in look, it is much hardier—but tasteless. To be sure you are getting the right tarragon, rub the leaves: French tarragon has a unique peppery-anise smell.

USES: Prized for the distinctive flavor of its leaves, French tarragon is essential in French cooking. It's a good companion plant, enhancing the growth of most vegetables. Handsome in the garden when you pair it with other narrow-leaved herbs like summer and winter savory, or when contrasted with bold-leaved plants like nasturtium.

Borago officinalis

Boraginaceae (Borage family)

BORAGE; STARFLOWER

PLANT TYPE: *Annual*
ZONES: *Not applicable*
HABIT: *18"–36" tall*
CULTURE: *Full sun; prefers a light, poor, dry soil*
BLOOM: *Spring to fall, depending on the climate*

This lovely herb with its hairy, dark gray-green leaves, was once believed to have great powers, bringing joy and happiness wherever it grew. The ancient

Greeks and Romans believed that borage brought courage. Native to the Mediterranean regions, borage has long been cultivated in northern Europe. It was brought to America by the early settlers, and was first listed in an American seed catalog in 1806. Today, borage is grown both as a medicinal and culinary herb. Grayish prickly hairs cover virtually the entire plant. Large oval leaves with wavy edges grow alternately along hollow, somewhat succulent, branched stems. Star-shaped, brilliant blue 1" flowers, borne in clusters, attract bees.

CULTIVATION: Borage tolerates a range of soils, but prefers less fertile, dry soil. Direct-seed into the garden after all danger of frost is past. Once planted, the seeds germinate quickly. Roots are very delicate, making borage difficult to transplant. Allow at least 12" between plants, more in warmer climates. Borage will self-seed freely, so unless you harvest all the flow-

ers, you probably won't have to worry about planting this herb in subsequent years.

RELATED PLANTS: Rarely, a white- or pink-flowered variety is seen.

USES: The flower petals and young leaves are edible, with a mild cucumber-like flavor. However, even the small leaves may be a bit hairy for your taste. Traditionally, borage flowers are used to flavor wine drinks; candied, the flowers were popular sweets in the last century. Lift the flowers from the hairy sepals before using. Freeze them in ice cubes and add to refreshing summer drinks. Borage pairs well with nasturtiums: Not only are their colors complementary—sky blue and bright orange—but their flavors also go well together. An upward view of the plant best shows off the beauty of the drooping flowers, so plant at the top of a hill or on sloping ground where you can view it from below.

Calendula officinalis 'Apricot Sherbet'

Asteraceae (Composite family)

CALENDULA; POT MARIGOLD

PLANT TYPE: *Annual*
ZONES: *Not applicable*
HABIT: *12"–18" tall*
CULTURE: *Full sun; prefers rich loam*
BLOOM: *Late spring to early summer in cold-winter areas; winter to spring in mild-winter areas*

Christians called this plant marygold, or marybud, because it bloomed at the festivals celebrating the Virgin Mary. Native to Asia and southern Europe, it was brought to America by early settlers. The stem is slightly fuzzy, with soft 6" leaves. Yellow or orange 1½" flowers are

composed of concentric rows of ray florets surrounding smaller florets, which make up the center disk. For all their beauty, the flowers have no fragrance. Calendulas don't like very hot weather. In cold-winter regions, they put on a big show of color in late spring and early summer, and if the summer is not too hot, they may bloom intermittently and rebloom in autumn. 'Apricot Sherbet' is a lovely shade of warm apricot.

CULTIVATION: Direct-seed calendulas in the garden after all danger of frost is past. A second planting, made at the beginning of July, will insure a fall harvest. Thin plants to 12" apart. If you deadhead the plants religiously in spring and summer, they may give another burst of color as the weather turns cooler.

RELATED PLANTS: 'Apricot Bon Bon' is a fully double, warm apricot-colored variety that grows 12"–15" tall. 'Kablouna,' a recent introduction, has long-lasting, vibrant orange flowers on stems that can grow to 24" tall. 'Art Shades Mixed' grows to 24" with apricot, orange, and cream-colored blooms. 'Double Lemon

Coronet,' 12" tall, has large yellow blooms. 'Fiesta Gitana Mixed' is an early dwarf, double-flowered mix in a range of colors. 'Pacific Beauty Mixed' bears 3½" flowers on 18" stems in shades of apricot, orange, and yellow.

USES: The culinary use of calendula dates back to ancient Rome, when powdered petals were used as a substitute for expensive saffron. Dry the petals and keep them in a tightly sealed container in a cool dry place for use out of season. Calendulas are excellent cut flowers—they add a burst of sunlight in a border, and are equally happy in an informal cottage garden or a formal bed.

Chamaemelum nobile (syn. *Anthemis nobilis*)
Asteraceae (Composite family)
CHAMOMILE; ENGLISH CHAMOMILE
PLANT TYPE: *Perennial*   ZONES: 5–9   HABIT: *Creeping to 1" tall; flowers to 12" high*   CULTURE: *Full sun to partial shade; prefers moist, well-drained soil*   BLOOM: *Mid summer*

Chamomile has been cultivated for over 2,000 years as an ornamental ground cover. It is also known as "apple of the earth," for its apple-scented foliage and flowers, as well as its low-growing habit. Chamomile is a creeper, with fernlike leaves that can form a mat around the rooting spot of the plant stem. Small, daisy-like flowers are composed of white petals surrounding a conical yellow disc. With successive pickings, the flowers will grace the garden from mid summer until they are killed by the frost of autumn.

CULTIVATION: Although chamomile prefers rich soil, it will survive in poor soil, providing it is well-drained. Chamomile is easily grown from seed planted directly in the garden in spring, and will self-seed once established. In an established planting, you can divide the runners in early spring. Harvest the flowers when the petals begin to droop slightly. Lay the flowers on a sheet or a screen in the sun (with a cloth below to catch whatever falls through) so they can dry quickly.

RELATED PLANTS: *Matricaria recutita* (German chamomile) is an annual with finely divided leaves on 24"–30" stems. It grows in full sun in well-drained, ordinary garden soil. Herbal tea made from its flowers has a sweeter flavor than that of English chamomile.

USES: Long used by herbalists as a calmative for the stomach and nerves, chamomile has mild sedative properties. The dried flowers are used in their entirety to make tea. Chamomile is lovely planted between stepping stones in the garden, interplanted with pansies, or mixed with forget-me-nots.

Coriandrum sativum
Apiaceae (Parsley or carrot family)
CORIANDER; CILANTRO; CHINESE PARSLEY
PLANT TYPE: *Annual*   ZONES: *Not applicable*   HABIT: *To 2'*   CULTURE: *Full sun; prefers well-drained, fairly rich soil*   BLOOM: *Late spring to early summer*

Among the oldest of the culinary herbs and spices, coriander seeds were used by the Chinese as a flavoring for beverages, cakes, and candies more than 5,000 years ago. Technically speaking, this plant, in its different stages, is both a spice and an herb, as spices are plants generally harvested for their bark or seeds, while herbs are usually cultivated for their leaves. The look of this fast-growing plant changes as it grows. The first (lower) leaves are deeply lobed. When harvested at this stage, it is called cilantro or Chinese parsley. Soon, the upper leaves become narrow and fern-like. White to pale pink flowers

are borne in umbels like those of other members of the carrot family. Yellowish-brown coriander seeds, ¼" in diameter, form from uncut flowers.

CULTIVATION: Coriander tolerates a range of growing conditions, but grows best in rich soil. It is daylight sensitive, so if you are growing it for the seeds, sow before June 21 and it will quickly flower; sown after the 10th of July, it will stay in leaf longer before it blooms and sets seed. Sow the seeds directly in the garden, after danger of frost is past, about 1" deep; allow 12"–15" between plants. The delicate root system does not transplant well. Coriander grows and germinates quickly. It will generally flower within 9 weeks of sowing, so make successive plantings every 2–3 weeks. If allowed to go to seed, it will happily self-sow throughout the growing season, and some seeds may germinate the following year.

RELATED PLANTS: 'Slo Bolt' is more heat-resistant and will remain longer at the broadleaf stage before flowering than will the species.

USES: With a unique flavor reminiscent of sage and lemon peel, cilantro leaves are favored in Chinese, Thai, and Mexican cooking. The seeds are more earthy and cinnamony, and are used frequently in Asian and Indian cuisine. Coriander is lovely and airy planted near the front of a border—just realize that its beauty is fleeting. Grow next to flat-leaved parsley, bronze fennel, or chamomile for an interesting play of textures and hues.

Cymbopogon citratus
Poaceae (Grass family)
LEMON GRASS

PLANT TYPE: *Perennial*
ZONES: *9–11*
HABIT: *To 6' tall*
CULTURE: *Full sun to light shade; evenly moist, well-drained, slightly acid loam*
BLOOM: *Not applicable*

Native to the tropics of southern India and Ceylon, lemon grass is an attractive plant in the garden, gaining in popularity and availability in recent years. In cold-winter climates, it can be grown as a potted plant and overwintered indoors. It forms a clump of grassy, aromatic, lemon-scented leaves, which have a stiff midrib and sharp edges. In temperate gardens it rarely flowers.

CULTIVATION: Lemon grass is grown not from seed, but from divisions. Plant in the garden in spring, after all danger of frost is past, allowing 2'–3' between plants. In areas with no winter frost, this is an evergreen perennial. It thrives in hot weather, but keep it well-watered, especially in summer. To maintain soil moisture, apply a thick mulch in late spring. Fertilize with fish emulsion in spring and summer. Do not feed in winter.

RELATED PLANTS: None.

USES: The leafy bases of the mature stems, prized for their lemon flavor, are used in Asian cooking. In the garden, lemon grass is handsome set apart as a specimen plant or—with its height—used in the back of the border, providing a cooling background for hot-flowered perennials like monarda. A lovely pot plant in cold-winter areas.

Helianthus annuus
Asteraceae (Composite family)
SUNFLOWER

PLANT TYPE: *Annual*
ZONES: *Not applicable*
HABIT: *To 10' or more*
CULTURE: *Full sun; prefers well-drained, friable soil of almost any type*
BLOOM: *Summer*

With the size, shape, and brilliance of the sun, this native North American flower is impressive. In cultivation, flowers can measure 12" or more across. In the wild, the flower is smaller but still notable. The sunflower is the only major crop to originate in the lower 48 states, and it was introduced from America to Europe in the late 1500s. Russia has developed many modern culti-vars, and today it is the largest commercial producer of sunflower seeds. Broad heart-shaped leaves are rough and somewhat hairy. Large flowerheads consist of 20–25 showy yellow-orange ray flowers surrounding a yellow, brown, or purple-brown central disk.

CULTIVATION: Sunflowers grow quickly from seed. Plant seeds directly in the garden, 1" or more deep, 2 weeks after the last spring frost date. Allow 10"–15" between plants. The looser the soil, the deeper the roots will establish themselves. Keep well-watered; fertilize every 2 weeks with fish emulsion; side-dress with compost. The plants can get unwieldy in the garden, often toppling after heavy winds or rains. Staking will help only if the supports are deep enough in the ground. Protect tall varieties by planting in a sheltered location.

RELATED PLANTS: 'Sunspot' is a dwarf variety growing only 2' tall, yet bearing full-sized flowers—perfect for the front of a flower border. 'Prado Red' is a branching variety that grows to 4', bearing small, deep red flowers with a hint of yellow around a brown disk. 'Italian White' grows to 6', bear-ing 4" white blooms with choco-late centers surrounded by a thin band of yellow on pointed petals. 'Music Box' is a multi-branching Dutch variety that grows to 3' tall, with 4"–5" blooms in a range of bright colors—from yellow and deep gold to bicolors of bronze and mahogany—all with chocolate tufted disks. 'Sunrich Orange' is a single-stemmed variety, 3'–5' tall,

with deep golden petals and a pollenless disk that make it a great cut flower. 'Russian Mammoth' grows 8'–10' tall bearing bright yellow 10"–12" blooms, and the best edible seeds.

USES: Edible flat seeds that develop from the disk flowers are a delicacy to birds, animals, and people. Brown-bag the flower as it matures to keep birds away, or just enjoy the creatures that come to feed from this magnifi-cent plant. Sunflowers are a showy backdrop to a garden. They make an excellent screen to hide an ugly wall or fence, and are showstopping when paired with rudbeckias and crocosmias for a vivid display. Make a sun-flower house for a child: Plant sunflowers in a square, and 1–2 morning glories to climb up each flower stalk; loosely tie string from one "wall" of sunflowers to the other, so the morning glories create a sky-blue ceiling.

Heliotropium arborescens (syn. *H. peruvianum*)

Boraginaceae (Borage family)

HELIOTROPE; COMMON HELIOTROPE; CHERRY PIE

PLANT TYPE: *Perennial*
ZONES: *10–11*
HABIT: *2'–4' tall*
CULTURE: *Full sun; average to rich, well-drained soil*
BLOOM: *Summer to killing frost*

A must for a fragrant summer garden, heliotrope has a rich aroma—like violets with vanilla overtones. One whiff evokes warm summer evenings on the porch, sipping juleps. In mild climates, this gem grows to 4' tall with a somewhat shrubby

form. Many hybrids are smaller, 18"–24" tall. The leaves are slight-ly hairy with a darkish purple cast. Small, dark royal-purple flowers are held tightly in a group, form-ing round, massed clusters of bloom. For pure sensual delight, every garden should have some heliotrope. A heat-loving plant, it thrives in the dog days of summer.

CULTIVATION: Heliotrope is usu-ally grown as an annual. In the hot South and West, give it some after-noon shade. This plant prefers rich soil, but will grow in average gar-den soil. Start seeds indoors 10–12 weeks before the last spring frost date. Seeds germinate best in warmth, about 70°–75°F. Trans-plant into the garden several weeks after danger of frost is past.

RELATED PLANTS: 'Marine' grows to 18" tall with compact, large royal-purple blooms and deep green foliage; 'Mini Marine' grows only 8"–12" tall. A white variety is being cultivated at the Hunt-ington Botanic Gardens in San Marino, California.

USES: A powder made from the flowers is used to scent soap and dusting powder, and the essential oil is used for perfumes. This herb is gorgeous interplanted with dusty miller, whose gray foliage sets off the heliotrope blooms wonderfully. For a hotter combination, combine with marigolds.

Hyssopus officinalis
Lamiaceae (Mint family)
HYSSOP

PLANT TYPE: *Perennial*
ZONES: *3–9*
HABIT: *12"–24" tall*
CULTURE: *Partial shade; ordinary garden soil*
BLOOM: *Summer to first frost*

Native to Eurasia, hyssop was first brought to America by early settlers, who used it medicinally. It escaped from cultivation and now grows wild from Quebec to Montana, and as far south as North Carolina. The multi-stalked herb has square stems that round off as they mature and flower. Small, narrow leaves are pointed or lance-shaped. Blue (sometimes pink or white) flowers are borne in the leaf axils. Hyssop is used to flavor the liqueur Chartreuse.

CULTIVATION: This is one of the few herbs that thrive in partial shade. Good, rich soil will result in luxuriant growth, but flavor and aroma will be sacrificed. In early spring, sow seeds directly in the garden in light, well-drained soil. If necessary, transplant in early summer, allowing 12" between plants. To extend the period of bloom, cut the plant back as it flowers, so tender new leaves will be produced. Once established, hyssop will self-seed in the garden.

RELATED PLANTS: The blue form has 2-lipped flowers and narrow, pointed leaves; the pink-flowered form has branching stems that turn woody at the base in their second year; there are also purple- and white-flowered forms. 'Netherfield' bears gold variegated leaves and white flowers. *H. officinalis* ssp. *aristatus* (rock hyssop) is a dense, compact plant with blue-and-purple flowers.

USES: Hyssop is used more for its medicinal value than as a pungent culinary herb. It makes an effective small hedge in a formal herb garden, and is charming paired with white-flowered borage and tricolor sage. Use as a companion plant to deter cabbage butterflies and to increase yields of vining vegetables.

Laurus nobilis
Lauraceae (Laurel family)
SWEET BAY; BAY LAUREL

PLANT TYPE: *Tree*
ZONES: *8–11*
HABIT: *To 30' tall when grown in the ground, to 6' in pots*
CULTURE: *Full sun to partial shade; sandy, neutral soil*
BLOOM: *Early spring*

Native to the Mediterranean, sweet bay is a handsome, tender evergreen tree. The shiny, leathery, dark green leaves have long been used as a seasoning. Leaves are pointedly oval and have a pleasant fragrance when crushed. In early spring, small, inconspicuous greenish-yellow flowers appear in tight clusters. They are followed by shiny black fruits in autumn. In most areas, sweet bay is grown in pots and overwintered indoors.

CULTIVATION: Sweet bay is grown in the ground in frost-free areas or in containers in colder regions. It is difficult to grow from seed and slow to grow from cuttings, taking up to 6 months to root. Set out small plants in spring after all danger of frost is past, using little organic matter in the soil. Do not mulch, as this plant prefers soil on the dry side, but do provide adequate water in summer. Sweet bay responds well to pruning, so you can grow it in the largest pot you can carry, and then prune it to size.

RELATED PLANTS: None.

USES: In warm climates, sweet bay makes a handsome specimen

plant or cornerstone to a garden. In colder climates, the potted plant is attractive when trained in a topiary form or allowed to grow in a tree shape. Move it outdoors for summer, indoors for winter.

Lavandula angustifolia (syn. *L. officinalis*) 'Provence'
Lamiaceae (Mint family)
LAVENDER

PLANT TYPE: *Semi-evergreen shrub*
ZONES: *5–9*
HABIT: *To 3' tall*
CULTURE: *Full sun; light, dry, well-drained soil*
BLOOM: *Spring to early summer*

Its name is derived from the Latin *lavare,* meaning "to wash"; its fresh scent was used in ancient Greece and Rome in bathwater and soaps, and for perfuming sheets. Native to the Mediterranean mountains and coast, lavender is a shrubby plant with woody branches and closely spaced, blunt, narrow grayish-green leaves. Small, fragrant lavender flowers, grouped in whorls of 6–10, appear on the ends of spikes 2' long. The plant may be evergreen in mild climates, but discolors and freezes back in cold weather. 'Provence' is one of the most fragrant varieties, bearing violet flowers and becoming an impressive shrub, especially in warm climates.

CULTIVATION: Lavender is best grown from a cutting—young plants are available at most nurseries. Plant it in the garden after all danger of frost is past, allowing 12"–18" between plants. The first year, cut off any flowering stems as they appear, to encourage the plant to grow more foliage and become bushier. Lavender can be grown from seed, but not easily—it's slow to sprout, with a germination rate of only 25–40 percent. Sow seeds indoors in late fall. In cold northern areas, seeds may not germinate until the following spring. By summer, the seedlings can be transplanted. Lavender is marginally hardy in cold areas, so mulch the plants well in late autumn to protect them through the winter. If you have space, move the plants indoors for the winter and grow them on a sunny windowsill or under lights. Lavender often begins to look ratty after about 4 years—dig up and replace the plants.

RELATED PLANTS: 'Alba' bears white flowers; 'Hidcote' has dark purple blooms; 'Munstead' flowers are lavender-blue; 'Jean Davis' bears pink flowers. 'Lavender Lady,' a new introduction, blooms the first year from seed. French lavender (*L. stoechas, L. dentata*) has long, narrow grayish-green leaves and rich, dark purple flowers. Less hardy, it thrives in warm climates.

USES: The most popular use of lavender is for fragrance in perfumes, soaps, and toiletries, especially sachets. Bees are attracted to lavender; lavender honey is a gourmet's delight. The plant is ideal for a large rock garden or for a low fragrant hedge. Grow lavender with roses or sage.

Levisticum officinalis
Apiaceae (Parsley or carrot family)
LOVAGE

PLANT TYPE: *Perennial*
ZONES: *3–10*
HABIT: *4'–7' tall*
CULTURE: *Full sun to partial shade; moist, rich, well-drained soil*
BLOOM: *Early summer*

Lovage is a majestic herb native to the mountains of the Mediterranean region. It grows in a large clump and looks like an overgrown celery plant. The big fleshy roots produce lots of stems; hollow stalks bear handsome, thrice-compound, dark green leaves. In early summer, lovage bears broad umbels of yellowish-green flowers, followed by handsome seedheads. Plants die down to the ground each fall and then regrow, greening up early in spring.

CULTIVATION: Plant in early spring from divisions, or sow seeds in late summer as soon as they turn brown and are ripe.

HERBS

Allow at least 3'–4' between plants when growing ornamentally. For herbal use, a single lovage plant is plenty for a family of 4. To keep in bounds, deadhead major blooms before the plant goes to seed. Remove unattractive brown leaves as necessary.

RELATED PLANTS: Celery is a smaller cousin of this herb, but it's more difficult to grow. For celery flavor without the crunch of the stalk, grow lovage.

USES: Use the leaves, stems, seeds, and roots for a strong celery flavor. You can make herbal straws from the stems—traditional for Bloody Marys. Lovage's strong presence is attractive at the back of the border.

Mentha × *piperita*
Lamiaceae (Mint family)
PEPPERMINT

PLANT TYPE: *Perennial*
ZONES: *5–9*
HABIT: *1½'–2' tall*
CULTURE: *Partial shade; moist, rich, well-drained soil*
BLOOM: *Mid summer*

Although the exact origins of the mints are no longer known, references link them to Europe, the Mediterranean, the Near East, and Hindustan. Today, more than 25 species of mint, hundreds of cultivars, and countless garden hybrids are grown around the world. In North America, peppermint has naturalized and can be found growing wild in damp places from Nova Scotia to Minnesota and south to Utah, Tennessee, and Florida. Medicinally, peppermint has been used as a stomach palliative since the first century A.D. Like other

members of the mint family, peppermint is distinguished by its square stems, which often have a reddish hue. Black peppermint has dark green leaves often tinged purple on purplish-green stems. It bears lilac-pink flowers at the tips of long spikes.

CULTIVATION: Although peppermint prefers partial shade, it will grow in full sun. Like other mints it is aggressive, spreading by underground runners, and can be very difficult to keep within bounds. Try growing it in a container sunk in the ground, with at least 1" of the pot above soil level. Some gardeners prefer to surround a planting of mint with strips of metal sunk 18" into the ground. Peppermint will die out if grown in the same spot in the garden for several years. Often it is a self-solving problem—the mint will run off and start growing in a new area all by itself.

Peppermint is usually not grown from seed. To propagate from roots or runners, pull up a

stem along with some roots. Lay the stem in a furrow 4" deep in a shady location. Bend the top 6" so it sticks out above the soil. Cover the stem with soil and tamp down. Space furrows 3' apart. Young plants are available at nurseries, garden centers, and mail-order companies. When weather and soil warm up, plant 12"–18" apart. If peppermint starts crowding the garden, simply pull up stems, but be aware that the stem is usually attached to an underground runner, so regrowth will continue.

RELATED PLANTS: 'Citrata' (lemon mint, eau-de-cologne mint, bergamot mint) has smooth, broad, dark green leaves lightly edged with purple, and purple flowers at the tips of short spikes in mid summer. This is one of the least aggressive mints. *M.* × *gracilis* 'Variegata' (ginger mint) is a culinary herb with smooth, fruit-scented grayish-green leaves variegated with yellow. Its tendency to sprawl in the garden is offset in mid summer by the light purple flowers borne in whorls along the stems. Spearmint (*M. spicata*) is the most common mint, garnishing glasses of iced tea and lemonade throughout the summer. It grows to 3' tall with medium green, strongly toothed, stalkless leaves on green stems. More compact than peppermint, it bears off-white to lavender flowers in whorls on slender spikes at the ends of stems and branches in mid summer.

USES: Peppermint is cultivated for its essential oil. It is handsome in the herb garden or mixed in a perennial border. Pair it with cleome and anise hyssop.

Ocimum basilicum 'Italian Large Leaf'
Lamiaceae (Mint family)
BASIL

PLANT TYPE: *Annual*
ZONES: *Not applicable*
HABIT: *To 2' tall*
CULTURE: *Full sun; fairly rich, well-drained, soil*
BLOOM: *Mid summer*

One of the most popular culinary herbs, originally native to tropical Asia, basil is now widely cultivated throughout the world. It is grown for the 1"–2" shiny green leaves, which have a somewhat spicy flavor when fresh, sweetening as they dry. There are over 160 different species of basil, but only about a dozen varieties are commonly grown and widely available. Like other members of the mint family, basil has square stems. The common culinary basil, or sweet basil, is an erect annual that grows about 3' high with a single, many-branched, upright stalk bearing 2 leaves at each joint. Flowers are small and white or lavender, growing on a tubular spike that rises above the leaves. When the plant flowers, leaf production decreases. 'Italian Large Leaf,' with leaves up to 4" in length, is traditional for pesto.

CULTIVATION: Basil is easily grown from seed. In all but the warmest temperature zones, start seeds indoors about 4–6 weeks before the last frost date. In warm areas, sow seeds directly into the garden. Do not plant out until night temperatures are above 50°F. Space tall basils 12" apart, dwarf varieties at least 6" apart, and Italian basil plants 15" apart. Within 4–6 weeks of transplanting, you can begin to harvest leaves. Fertilize several times during the growing season. As temperatures drop in autumn, pot up compact basils and move indoors.

RELATED PLANTS: There are numerous green-leaved basils: 'Cinnamon' has shiny green leaves, dainty rose flower spikes, and intense cinnamon fragrance laced with sweet basil essence. 'Compact Green Gem' ('Minimum') is a dwarf, globe-shaped compact variety to 12"; it's both ornamental and edible, with flavorful small leaves, good in pots or as an annual hedge. Round-leaved 'Genovese' is full-flavored and aromatic, growing to 24" tall. Repellent to Japanese beetles, 'Citriodorum' (lemon basil) has slightly narrowed, pointy light green leaves, and a compact habit to 15" tall; the lemony flavor is ideal for tea and potpourri. 'Lettuce Leaf' has broad, heavily savoyed leaves up to 4" long with smooth edges and deeply crinkled centers; it's mildly spicy, and sweet flavored. 'Thai,' a recent introduction from Asia, has green leaves and purple flowers and stems, growing to 24"; its strong flavor is good in Southeast Asian cuisine. Small, bushlike 'Spicy Globe,' excellent for containers, grows 10" tall like a small topiary.

Purple-leaved varieties include 'Dark Opal,' a striking landscape plant, 24" tall with very aromatic medium-large, somewhat fringed dark purple leaves. Decorative, zesty-flavored 'Genovese Grande Violetto' has large leaves with violet spots; it grows to 24". 'Purple Basil' has deep purple stems and leaves, sometimes mottled with green, and lilac to pale lavender flowers. 'Purple Opal' has pink flowers and deep garnet-purple leaves with a sharp bite, too pungent for pesto but excellent for herbal vinegars. 'Purple Ruffles,' an All-America Selection, has large, deep purple fringed leaves and mild flavor; it's handsome as an ornamental.

USES: Basil is an excellent culinary companion for tomatoes, and because it repels whiteflies and gnats, it is often grown as a companion plant with tomatoes in the garden. The scent of the foliage is wonderful. Plant some basil near the edge of a path or by the kitchen door so it is readily available to pick and toss into any fresh dish you are preparing.

Origanum vulgare
Lamiaceae (Mint family)
WILD MARJORAM; OREGANO

PLANT TYPE: *Perennial*
ZONES: *7–10*
HABIT: *1'–3' tall*
CULTURE: *Full sun; prefers dry, well-drained, alkaline soil, not too rich*
BLOOM: *Summer*

The name is derived from the Greek words *oros,* meaning "mountain," and *ganos,* meaning "joy." Imagine the native Mediterranean hillsides with 30 wild species of marjoram in bloom with their purplish-red tufts of flowers—mountains of joy, indeed. Wild marjoram is native to southern Europe and has naturalized in North America from Ontario and Quebec as far south as North Carolina and west to California and Oregon. It grows wild along borders of cornfields and in well-drained, stony soil. While it is a perennial in mild climates, it is usually treated as an annual in colder areas. Creeping underground roots produce woody, hairy, erect, square-stemmed purplish-brown stalks with small dark green leaves. Small ¼" purplish-red flowers grow in 1" tufts atop stems and branchlets. The leaves have a minty fragrance.

CULTIVATION: Seeds are slow to germinate. Start indoors at least 6 weeks before the last spring frost date. Sow on fine soil and cover with milled sphagnum moss; keep lightly moist. When 2"–3" tall, transplant outdoors, allowing 12" between plants. Keep shaded and protected from wind until well-established. Easily grown from cuttings in spring.

RELATED PLANTS: Greek oregano (*O. vulgare* ssp. *hirtum*) is also a beautiful perennial that is grown as an annual in colder climates. Unlike the other oreganos, it prefers a rich, moist soil. In warm climates it can grow to 3' tall. Oval ½" gray-green leaves are slightly pungent; this is the common seasoning for pizza. Large clusters of pale purplish-pink flowers bloom through the summer months. Sweet marjoram (*O. majorana,* syn. *Majorana hortensis*), also native to the Mediterranean, grows 12"–15" tall. A tender perennial, it winter-kills easily and so is often grown as an annual. Oval, downy gray-green leaves are borne on delicate, slightly reddish woody stems. The flowers are tiny and white, seeming to come out of the green bracts. Sweet marjoram blooms in late summer. Its flavor is warm yet spicy.

USES: Marjoram is a widely prized culinary herb. It dries well for use in winter in colder climates. Low-growing varieties are lovely edging a border or an herb garden. Taller varieties are handsome interplanted with lamb's ears or artemisia.

Pelargonium crispum 'Variegatum'

Geraniaceae (Geranium family)

VARIEGATED LEMON-SCENTED GERANIUM

PLANT TYPE: *Perennial*
ZONES: *9–11*
HABIT: *To 3' tall*
CULTURE: *Full sun; evenly moist soil*
BLOOM: *Early summer*

Scented geraniums, native to the Cape of Good Hope, are grown in a range of bouquets and flavors, with rose geranium the most popular, followed by lemon-scented. Their popularity isn't nearly what it was in Victorian days, when over 150 varieties were described in catalogs. Tender perennials, they are grown as annuals in most of the country. Leaf form varies greatly, and texture may be smooth, velvety, or even sticky. The back of the leaf releases the scent. *P. crispum* is one of the finest lemon-scented geraniums, with a treelike shape and small, fluted, ruffled leaves on upright stems; it bears orchid-pink blooms. 'Variegatum' has creamy-yellow variegations on the leaves.

CULTIVATION: Scented geraniums are grown not from seed, but from rooted stem cuttings. Most varieties are available commercially; or you can easily take a stem cutting from a favorite plant in late summer, grow it indoors all winter, and then plant it outside in spring. They are well-suited to growing in containers. Plant in a pot at least 5" deep—double that is preferable—using a mixture of 1 part perlite or sharp sand, 1 part well-rotted compost or garden loam, and 1 part peat moss. Feed with fish emulsion every 2–3 weeks. Scented geraniums are frost-tender, so you can treat them as annuals and let them die in the garden, or bring them indoors before frost and overwinter in pots in a sunny location. Remove leaves as they yellow.

RELATED PLANTS: 'Prince Rupert,' with its strong lemon scent, will grow into a small shrub in a good growing season. Less vigorous, milder-scented 'Prince Rupert Variegated' has ruffled green leaves with creamy white. *P.* 'Lady Mary' (syn. *P.* × *limoneum*) has fan-shaped, toothed leaves, and bears magenta flowers. More than 50 different rose-scented geraniums are in cultivation. Most grow over 4' tall, blooming in June and July in wondrous hues of lavender and pink. *P. graveolens* is a large plant with lavender flowers and deeply cut gray-green leaves. 'Lady Plymouth' is slow-growing with deeply cut, light green aromatic leaves. 'Gray Lady Plymouth' is one of the best variegated plants; vigorous with deeply cut gray-green leaves bordered with white. 'Rober's Lemon Rose' is one of the sweetest rose-scented and -flavored geraniums, whose long, thick leaves resemble tomato leaves.

USES: Scented geraniums are well-suited for growing in containers, but can also be planted in the ground. In the garden, partner with roses. In a large container, such as a whiskey barrel, surround these geraniums with basil 'Spicy Globe,' or with lettuces.

Petroselinum crispum var. neapolitanum

Apiaceae (Parsley or carrot family)

ITALIAN PARSLEY; FLAT-LEAF PARSLEY

PLANT TYPE: *Biennial*
ZONES: *Not applicable*
HABIT: *To 1' tall*
CULTURE: *Full sun to partial shade; moderately rich, well-drained soil*
BLOOM: *Second year, in spring*

Native to Europe and the Mediterranean, Italian parsley is gaining in popularity in American kitchens. Usually grown as an annual, it forms a low rosette as wide as it is high. Dark green leaves, divided into flat leaflets, have a triangular outline. In mild climates, the foliage remains through the winter; in cold-winter areas it dies down with a hard frost. In the second year, leafy stalks rise 12" or more over the foliage, bearing small umbels of greenish flowers.

CULTIVATION: Place seeds in very warm water and soak overnight. Germination is slow, so start seeds indoors at least 8 weeks before the last spring frost date. Many nurseries carry small plants. Allow 12" between plants in the garden. If you harvest often, side-dress with compost and fertilize with fish emulsion several times during the growing season.

RELATED PLANTS: 'Gigante' has a sweeter, milder flavor. The species *P. crispum* (curly parsley) has curled and crisped leaves. 'Extra Curled Dwarf' is a smaller, more compact plant. Var. *tuberosum* (Hamburg, or turnip-rooted parsley) is grown for the thick, fleshy, edible root.

USES: Italian parsley, widely used as a garnish, is a versatile culinary herb. In the garden, it is a handsome edging plant. It attracts the larvae—green-and-yellow caterpillars—of the swallowtail butterfly, so grow enough parsley for you and for them.

Rosmarinus officinalis

Lamiaceae (Mint family)

ROSEMARY

PLANT TYPE: *Shrubby evergreen perennial*
ZONES: *Zones 8–10*
HABIT: *3'–6' tall*
CULTURE: *Full sun to partial shade; evenly moist, alkaline, well-drained soil*
BLOOM: *Mid to late spring*

Native to the rocky coasts of France and Spain (the name is derived from the Latin *ros marinus,* meaning "sea dew"), this is a tender perennial shrub grown as an annual in many areas of the U.S. Rosemary is characterized by its evergreen, needle-like leaves that give off a piney odor when brushed against or crushed. The leaf color varies from gray-green to dark green, and is usually lighter on the reverse side, depending on the variety. Pale blue flowers (occasionally white-rose, pale lavender, or dark blue) appear in mid to late spring, and sometimes again in summer.

CULTIVATION: Rosemary can be grown from seed, but is slow to germinate and may take 3 years from seed to flower. It is usually grown from 4"–6" cuttings taken from the tips of growing stems. Root stems in moistened sand or vermiculite. Once rooted, transplant to a small pot. Set plants out in the garden 2–4 weeks after the last spring frost, allowing 12"–18" between plants. Use an organic fertilizer when planting, and again each spring.

RELATED PLANTS: Upright varieties include white-flowered 'Alba,' which is quite hardy outdoors, especially if well-mulched. 'Arp' has light blue flowers and widely spaced, thick gray-green leaves with a resinous coating. Very fragrant, it is reliably hardy to −10°F.

'Blue Boy' has a pleasant, fresh aroma and lovely medium blue flowers with delicately narrow, short, medium green leaves clustered vigorously along twisting light green stems. 'Collingwood Ingram' ('Rex #4') has bright blue flowers on graceful, curving stems with tightly spaced, thick, glossy, deep green leaves and a fresh scent. 'Gorizia' has light blue flowers and long, broad leaves twice the size of most cultivars, a gingery-sweet aroma, and rigidly upright stems blushed with reddish-brown; flowers cluster along the stem. 'Hill Hardy' ('Madalene Hill'), hardy to −10°F., has light blue flowers, dark green foliage growing compactly on upright stems, and a soft, assertive aroma; it often blooms in late fall and spring, and can grow 4'–5' tall and wide. 'Nancy Howard' has white flowers and large leaves on an upright plant; hardy to about -10°F., it has a very pleasant aroma. 'Tuscan Blue' is strongly upright with bright blue-violet flowers, wide, stubby, rich green leaves clustered thickly along reddish stems, and a mild, fresh scent. 'Prostratus' (creeping rosemary, or trailing rosemary) has deep blue flowers, a creeping, twisting, arching growth habit, and a rich scent.

USES: Over the centuries, rosemary has been credited with restoring the memory, bringing good luck, fending off witches, and disinfecting the air. Today it is grown worldwide as a culinary herb. The flowers have a flavor similar to that of the leaves, but much less pungent. Plant rosemary near the edge of a garden, or in a pot near the kitchen door

where you can easily brush it as you walk by. Salt-tolerant, it is an excellent plant to include in seaside gardens. In warm climates it makes a very attractive low hedge. Rosemary is easily cultivated as a container plant and trained in topiary forms—commonly as a tree, rounded, or in circular wreath form.

Salvia elegans
Lamiaceae (Mint family)
PINEAPPLE SAGE

PLANT TYPE: *Perennial*
ZONES: *9–11*
HABIT: *To 5' tall as a perennial, to 3' tall as an annual*
CULTURE: *Full sun; prefers light, sandy, well-drained soil*
BLOOM: *Late summer to fall*

Pineapple sage is named for the fruity fragrance of its leaves. A tender perennial, it is grown in most of the country as an annual. Dark green, rough-textured, opposite leaves grow along the entire length of the square stems. Vibrant red 1" tubular flowers, borne on terminal spikes 1' or more above the foliage, appear late in the growing season; in coldest areas, the plant may not bloom before a killing frost. Hummingbirds and butterflies are attracted to the sweet nectar of the edible flowers.

CULTIVATION: Plant after danger of frost is past in spring, allowing 18"–24" between plants. Feed with an all-purpose organic fertilizer after planting. If grown as a perennial, cut back and fertilize every spring. The plant can also be divided in spring.

RELATED PLANTS: 'Frieda Dixon' bears salmon-colored flowers. *S. dorisiana* (fruit salad sage) is also a perennial that grows to 3'. It bears shocking-pink flowers with a sweet, mixed-fruit flavor.

USES: Both flowers and leaves are used in cooking, giving a sweet, fruity flavor with a hint of spice and mint. In the perennial border pineapple sage brings a vibrant display of color late in the season. Site it so the bright red flowers are highlighted with the late afternoon sun. Works well in the middle of the flower border with bee balm, which blooms earlier.

Salvia officinalis
Lamiaceae (Mint family)
SAGE
PLANT TYPE: *Semi-evergreen perennial* ZONES: *3–10* HABIT: *2'–3' tall* CULTURE: *Full sun to light shade; prefers light, sandy, well-drained soil* BLOOM: *Late spring to early summer*

Native to the northern Mediterranean area, this popular culinary herb is an attractive semi-evergreen plant with oblong gray-green leaves with a pebbled texture. Eye-catching blue-violet flowers with lipped corollas appear in whorls. The stems can become woody and gnarled as the plant gets older. Sage is drought-tolerant.

CULTIVATION: Sage needs soil that is evenly moist in summer, dry in winter. Start seeds in spring or fall, transplanting into the garden when the seedlings are 2"–3" tall. Set plants out early in the spring, spacing 12"–18" apart. In cold climates, lightly mulch in the fall with several inches of shredded leaves; fertilize with fish emulsion or kelp liquid fertilizer at half strength in early spring. Prune existing plants back by at least a third to keep the plants bushy and to remove any deadwood. Propagate by dividing the plant in the spring, or by layering stems in the fall.

RELATED PLANTS: 'Aurea' is a compact variety with variegated yellow leaves; it does not flower. The same is true for 'Tricolor,' whose lower leaves have white margins and whose upper leaves are tinged purple with pink margins. Unfortunately it is not reliably winter-hardy. Gentian sage (*S. patens*) has large, 1", vibrant blue flowers in mid to late summer, with an even milder flavor than culinary sage blooms.

USES: Flowers and leaves are edible. Sage is often used for flavor-

ing fish, pork, and other meats and is a classic ingredient in poultry stuffing and Manhattan clam chowder. Throw small pieces of pruned sagewood on the barbecue to add unique smoked flavor to fish, pork, or poultry. Include sage in a perennial border as a cooling contrast to hot-colored flowers like tithonia, or add it to a monochromatic gray garden.

Satureja hortensis
Lamiaceae (Mint family)
SUMMER SAVORY
PLANT TYPE: *Annual* ZONES: *Not applicable* HABIT: *12"–18" tall* CULTURE: *Full sun; dry, sandy soil, amended with plenty of organic matter* BLOOM: *Summer*

Native to the Mediterranean area, this culinary herb gets its common name because its flavor is at its peak in early summer. The slender woody stems have a tendency to sprawl, giving a bushy look. Dark green ½" leaves are narrow and blunt-tipped. In summer, the plant is covered with tiny pink flowers.

CULTIVATION: Small plants are readily available from nurseries. Plant in the garden after all dan-

ger of frost is past, allowing 6"–8" between plants. Or sow seeds directly in the garden after danger of frost is past. Be patient; seeds may take up to 4 weeks to germinate. Mulch with salt hay to keep weeds down and to keep the leaves and flowers clean for harvesting.

RELATED PLANTS: Winter savory (*S. montana*) is a good-looking, shrubby, evergreen perennial. Tiny pointed leaves appear stacked on all 4 sides of the stems, creating an interesting square pattern. Hardy to zone 5, it blooms in late summer.

USES: The leaves are traditionally used to flavor string beans. Summer savory's leaves and flowers are somewhat less piquant than those of winter savory. This diminutive plant is lovely at the edge of a border. Grow it in a large container paired with chives and catmint.

soil may be. Leaves are large and dark green, with a rough, hairy texture. They are easily mistaken for the first-year growth of foxglove—a deadly mistake if you are using the plant medicinally. Flowers are attractive in one-sided clusters of bell-shaped blooms.

CULTIVATION: Comfrey can be grown from seed, but more commonly young plants are purchased at garden centers, nurseries, or by mail order. Space plants 18"–24" apart. Grow comfrey where you want it—if you try to dig it up and transplant it, you are likely to leave small bits of the long taproot behind, and each of those will produce a plant. Many gardeners prefer to grow comfrey in a large pot placed in a larger pot without a drainage hole, but with several inches of gravel or sand to keep the inner pot from sitting in water. This prevents the root from growing down through the drainage hole and into the garden. Comfrey readily self-seeds.

RELATED PLANTS: *S. grandiflorum* bears creamy flowers. It is lower growing and makes a handsome ground cover. *S. asperum* has bright blue flowers.

USES: Comfrey is an essential element in a medicinal herb garden. Its bold foliage and delicate flowers make it a welcome addition to the perennial border. It is lovely paired with borage and Virginia bluebells.

Thymus vulgaris
Lamiaceae   **(Mint family)**
THYME; COMMON THYME
PLANT TYPE: *Evergreen perennial*   ZONES: *4–9*   HABIT: *To 15" tall*   CULTURE: *Full sun; prefers poor, well-drained, rocky, alkaline soil*   BLOOM: *Spring to summer, depending on variety*

Thyme was used as incense in ancient Greek temples; the Romans used it as a culinary herb and kept it in the garden for their bees. Native to southern Europe, it is widely cultivated throughout North America, where it has escaped into the wild and now grows in warm, sunny fields. An evergreen herb with stiff, woody stems and velvety white twigs, it has opposite, aromatic gray-green leaves ¼" long. Lavender-pink to white flowers are borne in small whorls along the upper parts of the stems.

CULTIVATION: Thyme can grow in a range of soils; the richer the soil, however, the less flavorful the leaves. Start thyme seeds outdoors in spring, in a semi-shaded, moist location. When the seedlings are several inches tall, transplant them to full sun. An alternative is to

Symphytum officinale
Boraginaceae (Borage family)
COMFREY
PLANT TYPE: *Perennial*   ZONES: *3–9*   HABIT: *3'–4' tall*   CULTURE: *Full sun; average soil*   BLOOM: *Mid spring through summer*

Comfrey was prized by the ancient Greeks and Romans for its medicinal properties. Used to heal wounds and mend fractured bones, it was introduced to North America by the first settlers and has naturalized in many areas. It is a stalwart plant with a prodigious taproot, measured at over 10' long, which not only anchors it well but also insures a supply of moisture and nutrients to the plant no matter how dry the top-

plant them in a sunny location, but cover the area with shade cloth or landscape fabric to shade it; remove shading when plants are several inches tall. You can also start seeds indoors 6–8 weeks before the last spring frost date. Transplant outdoors when the plants are 2"–3" tall, spacing them 10"–15" apart (18" for spreading varieties).

RELATED PLANTS: There are more than 60 varieties of thyme. Some of the best include *T. serpyllum* (wild thyme, also known as creeping thyme and mother-of-thyme), with creeping woody stems that grow to 12" long and root easily along their length, and narrow, oblong leaves that have a lemony scent. Rosy-pink to purplish flowers appear on erect branches in small heads from June to September; they have a lemony, milder flavor than cultivated thyme. Var. *albus* is a tiny plant with bright, lemon-scented green leaves, and white flowers in June.

Var. *argenteus* 'Silver Lemon' grows 6" tall with a shrubby form; its green leaves are variegated silver. Not reliably winter-hardy, it needs shelter from cold winters. *T. × citriodorus* 'Aureus' (golden lemon thyme), with gold-edged leaves blooms later with light purple flowers and is not winter-hardy. It bears golden leaves, thrives in drought, and blooms in mid to late summer with pale lavender flowers. Its scent and flavor are pungent, not lemony. *T. pseudolanuginosus* (woolly thyme), not edible, is handsome nonetheless, with low-growing gray foliage. In mild-winter areas it is evergreen; in colder climates new leaves appear every spring, with sparse pink flowers in early summer.

USES: With its low, creeping habit, thyme is especially lovely grown between stepping-stones in a pathway, where it may be occasionally bruised by a footstep, releasing its fragrant oils into the air. Grow it at the edge of a garden or border, or include it in a rock garden. Put some in a container near the kitchen door where you can readily get a snippet for cooking. Flowers as well as leaves are edible. Thyme is especially pretty paired with a low-growing dianthus.

Tropaeolum majus 'Peach Melba'
Tropaeolaceae (Nasturtium family)
NASTURTIUM
PLANT TYPE: *Annual* ZONES: *Not applicable* HABIT: *6"–12" tall* CULTURE: *Full sun; ordinary garden soil* BLOOM: *Late spring .o killing frost*

The garden nasturtium is the most commonly grown species in a large genus that includes over 50 species of annuals and perennials native to South America and prized for their brightly colored red, orange, or yellow flowers and rounded green leaves. New introductions have mahogany, cream-to-pink, and speckled flowers. Climbing varieties can reach 6'–10', trailing along the ground or climbing up a trellis. Most hybrids are more compact, spreading 12"–18". Nasturtiums are drought-tolerant, low-maintenance annuals. 'Peach Melba' has flower petals the color of a sliced white peach with raspberry markings at the throat.

CULTIVATION: Nasturtiums thrive in relatively cool weather and cannot tolerate Southern summer heat. In some areas, they will fade in July and August and revive as the days cool in early autumn. Although they prefer full sun, in warmer areas they do best in light

shade. Never fertilize; rich soil results in abundant leaves with few blooms. Nasturtiums are easy to grow from seed. They need cool soil to germinate, so seed directly in the garden 2 weeks before the last spring frost date. Cover with ½" of soil; water well. Seeds can also be sown indoors in individual peat pots. Transplant to the garden, allowing at least 12" between plants.

RELATED PLANTS: 'Strawberries and Cream' bears scrumptious, rich creamy-colored flowers with strawberry-colored blotches at the base of each petal. 'Empress of India' has brilliant vermilion-red flowers that contrast with its deep blue-green foliage. 'Fordhook Favorites Mixed' is a vigorous climber that grows to 6' tall and bears single flowers in a good range of colors. 'Semi-Tall Double Gleam' is a trailing variety, spreading 3', with large, fragrant, double and semi-double flowers. 'Whirly-bird' has dark green foliage and upward-facing, spurless, semi-double flowers of tangerine, salmon, bright gold, deep mahogany, bright scarlet, or cherry-rose.

USES: The peppery flavor of the leaves and flowers is a great addition to salads and sandwiches. Use flowers from several different varieties tossed with a mix of lettuces for an elegant, tasty salad. Nasturtiums are lovely planted in front of lavender, and they're great for hanging baskets. Climbing varieties are fun on a boldly painted trellis.

PERENNIALS

Perennials provide the backbone of a flower garden. As each new growing season comes around, they reappear to grow and bloom again, adding color and interesting foliage without the intense feeding and watering demanded by annuals. With careful planning, a perennial garden can span the seasons. Beginning in spring as a complement to the first burst of color from bulbs, perennials continue through the summer months and well into fall. Although each perennial may be in flower for only a few weeks, its shape, habit, and foliage colors will provide lasting interest in the garden.

the ultimate size and shape of the plant. Is it upright or mounded, tall or short? Are the leaves grasslike or rounded, bold or more delicate? Does the foliage hold up well through the season? Only after answering these questions should you begin to look at flower color and shape, and time of bloom.

Perennials adapt well to both formal and informal settings. Plant them in flower beds and borders and where shrubs provide the height or spine of a mixed planting. They assort well with annuals and bulbs to extend the season of color both in the ground and in containers. Many are excellent as cut flowers, and some dry well, too. Use perennials with foundation plantings or among shrubs, in rock gardens and herb gardens, as ground covers in sun or shade, to hold banks threatened with erosion, in meadows or in native-plant or wild gardens. Some are even suitable for planting among vegetables.

In general, plants listed as perennials are herbaceous; that is, they die down and remain dormant for some period of the year, usually as a result of high or low temperatures or a shortage of water. But a few plants commonly considered along with perennials are somewhat woody and retain their shape all year long.

There are perennials suitable for all soils and all climate zones. Some tolerate dry soil; others like damp or even boggy conditions. Many are woodlanders, preferring shady places with rich, moist soil, while others thrive in full sun and where soil is poor; some are good

in the shallow soil often associated with rock gardens, others where soil is deep. In this huge group of plants there are, of course, some that require a great deal of attention, but there are also many that require little maintenance. The bulk of them are forgiving of inexperienced or even neglectful gardeners and put on a colorful display in spite of less-than-perfect conditions. With a little care and planning, they become the jewels of the garden.

When designing with perennials, it is wise to consider their floral attributes last. For an interesting display over the long haul, consider

---

Achillea millefolium
'Summer Pastels Mix'

**Asteraceae
(Composite family)**

COMMON YARROW

PLANT TYPE: *Perennial*
ZONES: *3–10*
HABIT: *2–2½' tall; 1½'–2½' wide*
CULTURE: *Full sun; well-drained soil*
BLOOM: *Summer through early fall*

Natives of Europe and western Asia, the yarrows have been extensively hybridized and are often considered a mainstay of the summer border, especially where soil tends to be poor and dry. 'Summer Pastels Mix' stretches the color palette for this species beyond whites, yellows, and rosy-pinks to assorted shades of red, pink, lilac, and salmon.

CULTIVATION: Set out plants in spring or fall. Grown without additional fertilizer, the stems are usually sturdy enough to forgo staking. Deadhead regularly for extended bloom. Yarrows are drought-resistant when established. Divide every 2–3 years to maintain vigor. Propagate by division, or start seed in late spring.

RELATED PLANTS: Other yarrows include *A. ptarmica* 'The Pearl,' which has buttonlike heads of double white flowers; the everpopular *A.* 'Coronation Gold,' with gray fernlike foliage and bright yellow flowerheads on 3' stems; *A.* 'Moonshine,' with paler flowerheads and gray-green leaves.

USES: Excellent as a cut flower, both fresh and dried. Striking in the perennial or mixed border. A fine companion for blue or purple campanulas or salvias.

Aconitum carmichaelii var. *wilsonii*

Ranunculaceae (Buttercup family)

MONKSHOOD

PLANT TYPE: *Perennial*
ZONES: 2–9
HABIT: *3½'–6' tall; to 2' wide*
CULTURE: *Full sun to light shade; rich, highly organic, well-drained soil*
BLOOM: *Late summer to early fall*

Chinese *A. carmichaelii* thrusts its imposing erect panicles of helmet-shaped dark blue flowers well above the clumps of divided dark green leaves. Its taller variety *wilsonii* makes a bold statement with its amethyst-blue flowers. All species are poisonous and must be sited with care.

CULTIVATION: Avoid windy sites. Plant in fall for best results, although container-grown stock establishes readily in spring if kept moist. Mulch in summer to retain soil moisture; a protective winter mulch is also beneficial where snow cover is unreliable. After flowering, deadhead below the base of the inflorescence to encourage lateral shoots and a later flush of bloom. Stake as necessary. Divide in spring or fall to increase stock.

RELATED PLANTS: The most poisonous species, *A. napellus* (garden monkshood), blooms somewhat earlier with violet flowers on 3' stems. *A. Lycoctonum* ssp. *vulparia* has creamy-white flowers.

USES: This excellent plant adds vertical impact to lightly shaded perennial or mixed borders. A good cut flower, but wear gloves to avoid skin contact with the poisonous sap. Lovely in combination with Japanese anemones and early fall-blooming asters.

Alchemilla mollis

Rosaceae (Rose family)

LADY'S MANTLE

PLANT TYPE: *Perennial*
ZONES: 3–9
HABIT: *Loose, rounded clumps 1'–2' tall and across*
CULTURE: *Full sun to light shade; well-drained but moisture-retentive soil, amended with organic matter*
BLOOM: *Spring*

This popular plant has velvety scalloped or lobed leaves that glisten with captured drops of rain or dew; droplets appear silvery in shade, golden in sun. The loose sprays of tiny chartreuse flowers give a frothy effect.

CULTIVATION: You can successfully plant lady's mantle in either spring or fall. Protect from hot sun. Divide in early spring before blooming. Deadhead to avoid self-seeding and cut back almost to the ground when leaves become shabby; fresh new growth appears in a few weeks. Keep roots cool and moist with a summer mulch; water deeply during dry weather.

RELATED PLANTS: *A. vulgaris* is very similar and may be just a variation. *A. alpina* (mountain mantle, or alpine lady's mantle) grows only 8" or so tall with sil-ver-rimmed leaves.

USES: Excellent at the front of the border or as a ground cover in partially shaded locations. Both foliage and flowers are useful for flower arrangements. Combines well with spring bulbs.

Anchusa azurea
'Loddon Royalist'

Boraginaceae (Borage family)

ITALIAN ALKANET

PLANT TYPE: *Perennial*
ZONES: *3–9*
HABIT: *To 3' tall; about 2' wide*
CULTURE: *Full sun; deep soil, enriched with organic matter*
BLOOM: *Spring*

From the eastern Mediterranean and Caucasus regions, Italian alkanet is noted for its intense blue flowers, arranged along curved stems shaped like the tail of a scorpion. The plants, which may reach 5', are somewhat coarse, sometimes ungainly. 'Loddon Royalist' is more com-pact and bushy; it bears bright gentian-blue flowers.

CULTIVATION: Plant in spring. Mulch in summer and water deeply during dry times. Deadhead for neatness and to avoid self-seeding. Best in north-ern climates. Short-lived at best, the cultivars must be propagated vegetatively by division or more often from root cuttings.

RELATED PLANTS: Other cultivars include the compact 'Little John,' 18" tall, and 'Dropmore,' which makes untidy plants up to 4' tall.

USES: In the perennial or mixed border, it is best used as a back-ground plant or filler. Good for cutting. A beautiful foil for spring daffodils and narcissus.

Anemone × hybrida
'Honorine Jobert'

**Ranunculaceae
(Buttercup family)**

JAPANESE ANEMONE

PLANT TYPE: *Perennial*
ZONES: *5–9*
HABIT: *3'–4' tall; clumps about 2' wide*
CULTURE: *Partial shade; deep, highly organic, well-drained, moisture-retentive soil*
BLOOM: *Late summer to fall*

The Japanese anemones on the market today are mostly of hybrid origin. Once established, they are superb low-maintenance perennials, with large compound

leaves that are attractive long before any blooms appear. The single, semi-double, or double flowers rise well above the clumps of foliage on robust but slender stems that will stand up to most weather. The classic 'Honorine Jobert' has pure white flowers, 2"–3" across.

CULTIVATION: Plant in spring and mulch well for the summer; toler-ates sun in the North. Keep well-watered until established, and apply a protective winter mulch in cold regions. The taller cultivars may need staking in windy places. Protect from slug damage. In-crease by division.

RELATED PLANTS: Other readily available cultivars include the white semi-double 'Whirlwind'; 'Margarete,' a deep pink semi-double; and 'September Charm,' a mauve-pink single. Similar *A. hupehensis* and *A. tomentosa* (espe-cially the cultivar 'Robustissima') are often lumped under the com-mon name Japanese anemone.

USES: Indispensable in late summer and fall gardens, in mixed and perennial borders, and among shrubs. A fine cut flower. Try 'Honorine Jobert' with elegant *Cimicifuga simplex* 'White Pearl.'

Aquilegia chrysantha 'Silver Queen'

Ranunculaceae (Buttercup family)

GOLDEN COLUMBINE

PLANT TYPE: *Perennial*
ZONES: *3–9*
HABIT: *2½'–3½' tall*
CULTURE: *Sun or partial to dappled shade; average, well-drained soil*
BLOOM: *Spring*

From Mexico and New Mexico, *A. chrysantha* has dainty yellow, long-spurred, 3"–4" flowers that dance atop mounds of delicately divided compound leaves. It has been used in breeding to develop the popular "long-spurred" hybrids. 'Silver Queen' has white flowers.

CULTIVATION: Golden columbine is one of the best for dry climates; it tolerates drought well but tends to be short-lived. Adding organic matter to the soil helps retain moisture. Plant in spring or fall; mulch in summer. Renew plant-

ings as old plants become woody. Protect from leaf miner damage. Columbines hybridize and self-seed with abandon; deadhead to avoid this. Propagate the species from seed, the cultivars by division or from commercial seed.

RELATED PLANTS: *A. canadensis*, native to light, moist woodlands of the eastern United States, has short-spurred yellow-and-red flowers. *A. × hybrida* includes many popular strains, such as the compact Biedermeier strain and the bicolored McKana Giants.

USES: Elegant grouped in a mixed or perennial garden or in very light woodlands. The compact species and cultivars are suitable for rock gardens. Cut flowers last only 2 or 3 days.

Aruncus dioicus

Rosaceae (Rose family)

GOATSBEARD

PLANT TYPE: *Perennial*
ZONES: *3–8*
HABIT: *4'–6' tall; clumps 3'–5' wide*
CULTURE: *Sun to partial shade in the North, light to deeper shade in the South; organically rich, moisture-retentive soil*
BLOOM: *Early to mid summer*

This Northern Hemisphere plant makes imposing clumps of leafy, branching stems above which rise large astilbe-like plumes of white flowers that fade to soft cream. The sex of male and female plants is impossible to determine until flowering time; the males are showier.

CULTIVATION: Plant goatsbeard in spring or fall, providing sufficient space for them to develop shrub-like proportions. The soil must be kept damp; water copiously during hot dry weather, especially in

the South. Staking is seldom necessary, unless plants are growing in the shade. Deadhead shabby plumes after flowering.

RELATED PLANTS: The cultivar 'Kneiffii' is a more delicate plant, to 3' tall with deeply cut, slender foliage. In limited space *A. aethusifolius*, a dwarf to 1' tall, makes a good substitute for astilbe.

USES: Plant goatsbeard at the back of perennial or mixed borders, or along the spine of island beds. The foliage mass makes a solid background for less robust but showier flowers, such as gladiolus, later in the season. Assorts well with most shrubs.

Asclepias tuberosa 'Hello Yellow'

Asclepiadaceae (Milkweed family)

BUTTERFLY WEED

PLANT TYPE: *Perennial*
ZONES: *3–10*
HABIT: *1'–2' tall*
CULTURE: *Full sun; average to poor, very well-drained soil*
BLOOM: *Late spring in the South, summer elsewhere*

The stiff upright stems of our native butterfly weed are topped by clusters of brilliant orange flowers that are most attractive to butterflies, especially Monarchs, who extract the sweet nectar. Slender pods, 4" long, containing masses of silky seeds follow. 'Hello Yellow' blooms freely with sunny, bright yellow flowers.

CULTIVATION: Plant container-grown stock in spring or fall; the strong tap roots resent disturbance, so exercise care. Plants are slow to emerge in spring, but once established require little maintenance. Deadhead to encourage a second crop of bloom. Propagate by root cuttings; seed is difficult.

RELATED PLANTS: The Gay Butterflies strain blooms in pink, red, and yellow. Swamp milkweed (*A. incarnata*) is taller and carries large heads of dusty pink flowers. Useful for damp soils.

USES: Both 'Hello Yellow' and the species are valuable in hot, full-sun positions, especially where the soil tends to be poor. Butterfly weed is good for cutting (control bleeding of the milky sap by searing with a match), and the pods make attractive dried arrangements. Combine with ornamental grasses for a natural look.

Aster × *frikartii* 'Wonder of Staffa'

Asteraceae (Composite family)

FRIKART'S ASTER

PLANT TYPE: *Perennial*
ZONES: *5–10*
HABIT: *2'–3' tall; loose clumps to 2' across*
CULTURE: *Full sun to very light shade; average, well-drained soil*
BLOOM: *Throughout the summer into fall*

This hybrid of *A. amellus* and *A. thomsonii* is recognized as one of the best perennials for extended, reliable bloom and mildew-resistant leaves. The rather floppy but strong branched stems bear beautiful lavender-blue flowers to 2½" across. 'Wonder of Staffa' and 'Mönch' are almost indistinguishable.

CULTIVATION: Plant in spring or fall and apply a winter mulch in cold climates. Deadheading extends blooming time; stake if you must, but it's better to allow the plants to use their neighbors for support. Divide every few years in spring to maintain vigor and to propagate.

RELATED PLANTS: The New England aster (*A. novae-angliae*) and New York aster (*A. novi-belgii*) and their wide range of cultivars are

indispensable in fall gardens. They range in height from under 1½' to over 6'. Colors range from white through pinks and lavenders to deep cerise, crimson, and purples.

USES: Frikart's aster is ideal for sunny beds and borders and as a cut flower. Plant alongside sturdy neighbors such as blue oat grass.

Astilbe × *rosea* 'Peach Blossom'

Saxifragaceae (Saxifrage family)

ASTILBE

PLANT TYPE: *Perennial*
ZONES: *4–9*
HABIT: *3'–4' tall; leafy clumps to 2' across*
CULTURE: *Partial shade; deep, highly organic, well-drained soil*
BLOOM: *Early summer*

A hybrid cultivar of *A. chinensis* and *A. japonica*, 'Peach Blossom' is one of the oldest of the hybrid astilbes grown today. It bears robust, fluffy plumes of pale pink flowers on sturdy stems, well above excellent dark green divided-and-toothed foliage. Unlike other astilbes it is fragrant, with a unique grape scent.

CULTIVATION: Plant astilbes in spring or fall. Keep roots cool with a summer mulch, and water deeply in dry weather. Do not allow to dry out. Divide every 3 years or so in order to maintain vigor and increase stock. Fertilize in spring. Protect with a winter mulch in cold regions. These tough plants are seldom bothered by pests or diseases.

RELATED PLANTS: There are numerous named hybrid astilbe cultivars, most listed under *A. × arendsii.* They bloom in white ('Bridal Veil') through pink ('Cattleya') to crimson ('Red Sentinel') hues. *A. chinensis* and its hybrids and cultivars are low-growing.

USES: Valuable plants grouped in the mid border, as well as among shrubs in lightly shaded positions. The lower sorts make useful ground covers; some are suitable for rock gardens. Astilbes and hostas are classic companions in shaded gardens.

Baptisia australis
Fabaceae (Pea family)
WILD BLUE INDIGO

PLANT TYPE: *Perennial*
ZONES: *3–10*
HABIT: *To 4'–5' tall; mounds to 3' across*
CULTURE: *Full sun to light shade; deep-average, well-drained soil*
BLOOM: *Spring to early summer*

This native has attractive blue-green foliage, divided into rounded leaflets. The spikes of purplish-blue pealike flowers are followed by inflated seedpods that blacken with age.

CULTIVATION: Plant container-grown stock in spring or fall; baptisias resent undue disturbance. Staking may be necessary in shaded

sites; deadhead and shape bushes after flowering, unless saving for dried pods. Drought-tolerant. Mulch in cold-winter regions until established. Increase by division in spring, but only when necessary. Wild blue indigo is not easily grown from seed; scarify fresh seed for best results. Germination is slow and variable.

RELATED PLANTS: *B. alba* (white false indigo), variously listed as *B. lactea* and *B. leucantha,* has handsome creamy-white flowers on blackish stems.

USES: The long-lasting, attractive foliage and solid bushy shape of wild blue indigo makes it a valuable perennial for beds and borders beyond its blooming time. Excellent in wild and native plant gardens, as well as more formal positions. Although not in the first rank as fresh-cut flowers, the fruits are interesting in dried flower arrangements. An attractive foil for azaleas.

Boltonia asteroides 'Snowbank'
Asteraceae (Composite family)
WHITE BOLTONIA

PLANT TYPE: *Perennial*
ZONES: *4–9*
HABIT: *3'–4' tall; erect clumps to 2'–3' across*
CULTURE: *Full sun to very light shade; average, well-drained soil*
BLOOM: *Late summer*

Native to open areas in the eastern U.S., boltonias bear hundreds of white ¾" daisies on loosely branching stems. The species may reach 7' in height, but 'Snowbank' is more in scale for residential gardens. Long-blooming and readily available.

CULTIVATION: Both early spring and fall plantings are satisfactory. Staking is seldom necessary in full sun where soil is lean, but in windy or more shaded positions, light support may be required. Tolerant of dry conditions but not prolonged drought. Regular division every 2–3 years helps to maintain vigorous plants.

RELATED PLANTS: A pink-flowered cultivar, 'Pink Beauty,' is not as floriferous but has larger flowers. *Kalimeris mongolica* (syn. *Boltonia indica*) blooms all summer long with double white flowers.

USES: 'Snowbank' assorts well in the flower border and informal garden with rudbeckias and coreopsis, as well as ornamental grasses. Attractive among broad-leaved evergreens such as leucothoe, mahonia, and low rhododendrons.

Campanula lactiflora
Campanulaceae (Bellflower family)
MILKY BELLFLOWER

PLANT TYPE: *Perennial*
ZONES: *6–9*
HABIT: *3'–5' tall; upright clumps 2'–3' across*
CULTURE: *Full sun to light shade; average, well-drained soil*
BLOOM: *Late spring through summer*

From the Caucasus region, milky bellflower has tall leafy stems crowned with robust clusters of bluish-white to lavender to deeper blue bell-shaped flowers, each about 1" long.

CULTIVATION: Plant in spring or fall in soil amended with plenty of organic matter. Shade from intense sun in the South. Water during dry periods; stake as necessary. Deadhead to encourage a second flush of bloom and to avoid self-seeding. To increase stock, root cuttings of young shoots or divide in spring or fall.

RELATED PLANTS: 'Loddon Anna' has pale pink flowers. Great bellflower (*C. latifolia*) makes tall, imposing clumps with purplish-blue flowers. Peach-leaved bellflower (*C. persicifolia*) and clustered bellflower (*C. glomerata*) are lower-growing and have flowers in white and a wide range of blues. Several other bellflowers, *C. carpatica, C. poscharskyana,* and *C. portenschlagiana,* are suitable for rock gardens, walls, and the front of a border.

USES: Plant milky bellflower toward the back of perennial or mixed borders. Combine with soft yellow mulleins or yarrows.

Cimicifuga racemosa
Ranunculaceae (Buttercup family)
BLACK SNAKEROOT; BLACK COHOSH

PLANT TYPE: *Perennial*
ZONES: *3–9*
HABIT: *4'–8' tall; 2'–3' wide*
CULTURE: *Full sun to partial shade; acid, highly organic, moisture-retentive soil*
BLOOM: *Mid to late summer or early fall*

Native to the eastern U.S., black snakeroot makes bold clumps of dark green divided leaves, above which rise long, elegant wands of tiny, clean white

flowers. Side branches extend the blooming period. Even after the flowers have passed, the spikes remain attractive.

CULTIVATION: Both spring and fall plantings are satisfactory. Fertilize lightly each spring and apply a summer mulch to retain moisture and keep roots cool. Water deeply during dry weather. Staking is seldom necessary; deadhead as required. To propagate, divide in early spring, but avoid unnecessary root disturbance.

RELATED PLANTS: Kamchatka bugbane (*C. simplex*) and its cultivar 'White Pearl' ('The Pearl') are popular for fall display. Their spikes are more robust but lack the delicate charm of our native species.

USES: Group black snakeroot in lightly shaded woodland or native plant gardens; use as an effective backdrop for shorter plants in mixed beds and borders. Combine with garden phlox or tall daisies.

Coreopsis lanceolata
Asteraceae (Composite family)
LANCELEAF COREOPSIS

PLANT TYPE: *Perennial*
ZONES: *4–9*
HABIT: *1'–2' tall; low clumps 2' across*
CULTURE: *Full sun; any well-drained soil*
BLOOM: *Late spring through summer*

Lanceleaf coreopsis is native to the eastern part of the U.S. Its solitary, bright yellow daisy flowers may reach 2½" in diameter. The lance-shaped leaves are mostly basal.

CULTIVATION: Plant in spring or fall; lightly fertilize poor soil in

spring. Deadhead routinely to extend blooming time; remove flower stems to the base to avoid a "porcupine" effect. Stake if necessary. Plants are short-lived in the garden; divide in spring to increase or replace stock.

RELATED PLANTS: Several cultivars are superior to the species. 'Goldfink' grows 10"–12" and has orange-centered flowers; 'Sterntaler' has golden flowers with a brown ring, on 12"–15" stems. Clear golden 'Baby Sun' grows to about the same height. Tickseed (*C. grandiflora*) is closely related to *C. lanceolata,* and the cultivars may be listed under either species. Pink *C. rosea* and thread-leaf coreopsis (*C. verticillata*) both have finely divided foliage. 'Moonbeam' has pale lemon flowers.

USES: Lanceleaf coreopsis is valuable at the front of sun-baked beds and borders, and assorts well in native plant and wild gardens. The species is good for cutting.

Cosmos atrosanguineus
Asteraceae (Composite family)
BLACK COSMOS

PLANT TYPE: *Perennial*
ZONES: *8–10*
HABIT: *2'–2½' tall, over bushy clumps 1' wide*
CULTURE: *Full sun; well-drained, moisture-retentive soil*
BLOOM: *Summer*

This Mexican native, reminiscent of dahlias, has velvety maroon flowers with an almost black center on wiry stems. Were it not for the strong fragrance of chocolate, these flowers might seem sinister rather than just mysterious. The green pinnate leaves are smooth-textured and form substantial clumps.

CULTIVATION: Tricky to grow, black cosmos is best planted in spring. Mulch in summer; provide winter protection in all but the warmest zones, or lift and store the tubers. Deadhead routinely to extend blooming time. Light support is often an advantage. Propagate by dividing the tuberous roots, taking cuttings in summer, or starting from seed.

RELATED PLANTS: The popular annual cosmos (*C. bipinnatus*) grows 2'–4' tall, with fernlike foliage and single flowers 2"–4" across. Traditionally, the blooms are white or deep pink, but modern hybrids come in shades of lavender, pink, magenta, or white as well as some lovely bicolors.

USES: Rare in U.S. gardens, but an interesting foil for silver-leaved or white-flowering plants. Important in red gardens, and sometimes planted with dark-foliaged dahlias or cannas. A good cut flower.

Crambe cordifolia
Brassicaceae (Mustard family)
COLEWORT; GIANT KALE

PLANT TYPE: *Perennial*
ZONES: *6–9*
HABIT: *4'–7' tall, 3'–4' wide*
CULTURE: *Full sun; alkaline, well-drained soil*
BLOOM: *Late spring to summer*

Native to the Caucasus region. Colewort makes a wide, loose clump of lobed leaves 2 long, similar to those of kale. Above them, enchanting airy sprays of tiny white flowers are borne on tall, leafless stems.

CULTIVATION: Prepare soil deeply to accommodate the deep taproot, and add lime if acidic. Plant from containers in spring or fall, but take care to avoid excessive root disturbance. Apply a winter mulch in cold regions, especially on fall-planted material. Stake as necessary, particularly in exposed positions. Deadhead to the base of the spent flowers to avoid seeding. Seeds take 3 years to reach blooming size; root cuttings are easy.

RELATED PLANTS: Sea kale (*C. maritima*) is less dramatic, with beautiful blue-green cabbagy leaves. Heads of white cruciform flowers are borne on 3' stems.

USES: Colewort is an impressive plant to provide height at the back of a border or along the spine of island beds. Spectacular sited in front of hemlocks, yews, or other evergreens for contrast. The thick young stems of sea kale are blanched for culinary use.

Delphinium elatum hybrids

Ranunculaceae (Buttercup family)

DELPHINIUM

PLANT TYPE: *Perennial*
ZONES: *3–8*
HABIT: *3'–8' tall; upright clumps 3' wide*
CULTURE: *Full sun; rich, well-drained, highly organic soil*
BLOOM: *Late spring to summer*

With their stately, old-fashioned beauty, delphiniums are bastions of the cottage and cutting garden. Despite their airy, somewhat fragile appearance, they thrive in cold-winter areas and are intolerant of hot summers. The *D. elatum* hybrids include several strains and numerous named cultivars that bloom in white through all shades of blue and lavender, some with a contrasting "bee" or eye in the center.

CULTIVATION: Plant delphiniums in early spring or early fall.

Nourish these greedy feeders in spring with a general-purpose organic fertilizer. Apply a thick organic mulch in summer to maintain moisture and keep roots cool. Stake individually for best results. Deadhead to the base of the flower spike to encourage lateral branching and a second flush of bloom. In early fall, plant out seedlings from spring sowings and rooted cuttings. Where conditions are unfavorable, treat as an annual. Delphinium thrives in the Pacific Northwest and in Maine. Protect from slugs. Prone to pests and diseases—aphids, red spider mites, botrytis, and mildew.

RELATED PLANTS: 'Blue Bird,' 6' tall, has blue flowers with a white bee and dark green divided leaves. It is one of the Pacific hybrid strain. *D. grandiflorum*, 1'–2', and *D. tatsienense*, 1½'–2', both have intense blue flowers.

USES: Magnificent in beds, in borders, and for cutting.

Dianthus plumarius

Caryophyllaceae (Carnation family)

COTTAGE PINK; GRASS PINK

PLANT TYPE: *Perennial*
ZONES: *4–9*
HABIT: *1'–1½' tall, over clumps of grassy foliage 8"–12" across*
CULTURE: *Full sun; alkaline, organic, well-drained soil*
BLOOM: *Early summer onward*

Cottage pinks are found in the wild in eastern Europe, and are the parents of many of today's garden pinks. Their distinctive single, semi-double, or double flowers, in white and various shades of pink and red, sometimes bicolored, are often very fragrant. The foliage is blue-green.

CULTIVATION: Plant in spring or fall. A light spring topdressing of lime or marble chips maintains soil alkalinity and assures rapid surface runoff. Deadhead routinely, almost to the ground, as flowers are spent. Mulch in cold-winter regions to avoid heaving and desiccation. Propagate from terminal cuttings, preferably with a "heel," in early summer.

RELATED PLANTS: Popular cultivars include 'White Ladies,' with pure white double flowers and good fragrance; 'Essex Witch,' with fragrant semi-double flowers, pink with a darker eye; and 'Ian,' with double scarlet flowers rimmed in crimson. These are probably hybrids and may be listed as such.

USES: Excellent for the front of a border or as edgings, for rock or wall gardens, for fragrance or herb gardens. A romantic cut flower; the petals retain their fragrance in potpourri.

Dicentra eximia 'Snowdrift'

Fumariaceae (Fumitory family)

FRINGED BLEEDING HEART

PLANT TYPE: *Perennial*
ZONES: *3–9*
HABIT: *1'–1½' tall; mounded clumps 1½' across*
CULTURE: *Full sun to partial shade; highly organic, well-drained soil*
BLOOM: *Spring to summer*

This bleeding heart from the eastern U.S. is among the best perennials. Its light to medium green or blue-green ferny leaves remain attractive throughout the season. The dainty, heart-shaped flowers, in shades of pink or white, are borne along arching stems. 'Snowdrift' has small, long-lasting pure white flowers.

CULTIVATION: Plant in spring or fall; in the South, site in the shade. Mulch in summer to maintain soil moisture; water during dry periods. A winter mulch is beneficial in cold regions, especially for fall-planted material. Remove spent flower stems and shabby foliage to the base; another crop of flowers and leaves will appear shortly. Low maintenance; seldom bothered by pests or diseases. Propagate from fresh seed in late summer, or divide established plants in spring.

RELATED PLANTS: Several excellent cultivars and hybrids are available: 'Luxuriant' has blue-green foliage and deep rose-pink flowers; 'Stuart Boothman' has reddish-pink flowers. A similar western species, *D. formosa,* is involved in the parentage of many cultivars.

USES: Superb in light woodlands, in native and wild gardens, and at the front of shaded borders; useful to face down low shrubs, camouflaging their unsightly bare lower branches.

Dictamnus albus

Rutaceae (Rue family)

GAS PLANT

PLANT TYPE: *Perennial*
ZONES: *2–9*
HABIT: *2'–4' tall; erect bushes 2'–3' wide*
CULTURE: *Full sun to light shade; highly organic, moisture-retentive soil*
BLOOM: *Late spring to summer*

A long-lived, low-maintenance perennial from southern Europe and Asia, this plant slowly develops into large clumps of fragrant dark green pinnate leaves, above which rise erect spikes of clean white flowers. The seedpods that follow are star-shaped and

smell deliciously of citrus. Gas plant is poisonous if ingested.

CULTIVATION: Plant container-grown stock in spring; avoid field-grown material because gas plants resent disturbance. Two seasons or more are required before the plants become established, but they are well worth the wait. Grows best where summer nights are cool. Staking or spraying are seldom necessary. Water deeply during droughts, and mulch in summer. Deadhead unless the seeds are needed for propagation or as dried flowers. Sow seed as soon as it is ripe, and overwinter out of doors; germination will occur in spring but may be spotty.

RELATED PLANTS: 'Purpureus' has soft purplish-mauve flowers, accented with purple veins.

USES: A fine plant for perennial and mixed borders. The seedpods are very attractive in dried flower arrangements.

Dodecatheon meadia

Primulaceae
(Primrose family)

COMMON SHOOTING STAR

PLANT TYPE: *Perennial*
ZONES: *4–9*
HABIT: *Erect stems 1'–2' tall, over a basal rosette 1' wide*
CULTURE: *Partial to full shade; rich woodland soil*
BLOOM: *Late spring*

This native woodland plant makes rosettes of long, oblong leaves with a slick surface. Its white or pink flowers are arranged like the spokes of an umbrella atop strong pinkish stems. Each nodding, dartlike flower has backswept petals and a pointed purple cone of stamens.

CULTIVATION: Plant in early spring or fall. Keep well-watered until the foliage dies back in hot weather; mulch in summer. Be alert for slugs. This is the most readily cultivated species. Propagate from fresh seed, or divide in early spring or fall.

RELATED PLANTS: The western species *D. hendersonii* is similar but has more rounded leaves and produces tiny white bulblets at the base.

USES: Shooting stars are charming for native plant and light woodland gardens, as well as for rock gardens. Excellent accent plants for evening gardens; a nice contrast to Japanese primroses.

Echinacea purpurea 'White Swan'

Asteraceae
(Composite family)

PURPLE CONEFLOWER

PLANT TYPE: *Perennial*
ZONES: *3–9*
HABIT: *1½'–2' tall; mounded clump about 2' wide*
CULTURE: *Full sun; average, well-drained soil*
BLOOM: *Throughout the summer to fall*

Native to the central and eastern U.S., purple coneflowers bloom with purplish-pink flowerheads, 6" or so across, with drooping ray flowers ("petals") accented by a raised brown disk. The flowers are held above the mass of rather coarse, rough, dark green leaves. Slightly shorter than the species, 'White Swan' has white daisy flowers, 3"–4" across.

CULTIVATION: Plant in spring or fall. Purple coneflower is tolerant of heat, humidity, and dry conditions; additional water is seldom necessary. Staking is sometimes needed if soil is overly rich. Mulch in severe winter areas. Deadhead for neatness and to encourage further blooming; cut back hard after the first flush of bloom for a good fall crop. This plant is very attractive to butterflies; it's also prone to powdery mildew and Japanese beetles. Propagate the cultivars by division in spring, since seed will not come true to name.

RELATED PLANTS: Other cultivars of note include 'Bright Star,' which has rosy-pink flowers on stems to 3½' tall; 'Magnus' is similar, but its rays are more horizontal.

USES: Excellent in cutting gardens; in native plant, meadow, and wild gardens; and in beds and borders. Combines well with daylilies.

Erigeron × hybridus 'Rotes Meer'

Asteraceae
(Composite family)

HYBRID FLEABANE

PLANT TYPE: *Perennial*
ZONES: *5–7*
HABIT: *1'–2½' tall; clumps 2' across*
CULTURE: *Full sun; average to poor, well-drained soil*
BLOOM: *Late spring to fall*

The hybrid fleabanes bear abundant single, semi-double, or double 1"–2" daisies in the pink and lavender color range, on sturdy, well-foliaged stems. They rise from neat basal rosettes of leaves. Most have the native *E. speciosus* (Oregon fleabane) in their parentage. 'Rotes Meer' has semi-double pink flowers about 1½' tall.

CULTIVATION: Plant in spring or fall. Stake the taller ones with twiggy growth. Deadhead routinely; cut back hard in mid to late summer for a strong fall flush of bloom. Seldom bothered by pests and diseases. Provide noonday shade in hot regions. Propagate the cultivars by division in spring. Some cultivars can be grown from seed, but vegetative propagation ensures uniform results.

RELATED PLANTS: Other hybrid cultivars include 'Prosperity,' 1½' tall with large, clear mauve-blue flowers, and 'Rose Jewel,' 1½' tall with rosy-pink flowers. 'Double Beauty' has deep violet double flowers on 1½'–2' stems.

USES: Long-blooming as a cut flower, and in beds and borders. The shorter cultivars are suitable for rock gardens.

Filipendula rubra 'Venusta' ('Magnifica')

Rosaceae (Rose family)

QUEEN OF THE PRAIRIE

PLANT TYPE: *Perennial*
ZONES: *3–9*
HABIT: *6'–8' tall; 3'–4' across*
CULTURE: *Full sun to partial shade; organic, moisture-retentive soil*
BLOOM: *Summer*

Queen of the prairie, despite its common name, is native to the eastern part of the U.S. It makes an impressive clump of dark green compound leaves, jagged along the edges. Above this mass rise robust stems that terminate in huge plumes of peach-pink flowers resembling cotton candy. 'Venusta' is deeper pink.

CULTIVATION: Plant in spring, especially where winters are cold. Grows best where summers are not too hot and dry; soil must not dry out in summer. Water deeply if necessary, and mulch to retain moisture. Insulate shallow roots with evergreen boughs or salt hay in cold zones. Deadhead to the ground after flowering and cut back shabby foliage. Staking is seldom necessary. Propagate by division, preferably in spring.

RELATED PLANTS: White single- or double-flowered dropwort (*F. vulgaris*) is attractive for smaller gardens.

USES: 'Venusta' needs space to show its stuff. A superior accent plant in large borders or for massing beside ponds and lakes where the soil remains moist. An attractive companion for large ornamental grasses or evergreen shrubs.

Gaillardia × grandiflora 'Burgundy'

Asteraceae (Composite family)

HYBRID BLANKETFLOWER

PLANT TYPE: *Perennial*
ZONES: *3–10*
HABIT: *2'–3' tall; clumps 1½'–2' across*
CULTURE: *Full sun; average, well-drained soil*
BLOOM: *Early summer to fall*

This cross between *G. aristata* and *G. pulchella* has resulted in one of the longest-blooming and easiest perennials to grow. Regrettably, the plants are not long-lived, flowering themselves into an untimely decline. The deep red 3" flowers are carried on stems 2' tall or higher.

CULTIVATION: Plant in spring or fall. Blanketflowers tolerate drought well; mulch in summer to cut down on weeding. Deadhead routinely to extend flowering; cut back hard in late summer to encourage a strong fall crop. Taller cultivars may need staking. Propagate cultivars every 2 or 3 years, by division in spring or fall, or by cuttings in summer. Seed-grown plants are variable.

RELATED PLANTS: 'Goblin' grows 1' tall; its gray-green, lance-shaped basal leaves make a good foil for the 3"–4" bright red daisies, banded with yellow, that rise above. 'Golden Goblin' has all yellow flowers. Only 6"–8" tall, 'Baby Cole' has red flowers tipped with yellow.

USES: Valuable in wild or native plant gardens and meadows, as well as in flower beds and borders. A fine cut flower. Seedheads attract birds to the winter garden.

Gentiana asclepiadea

**Gentianaceae
(Gentian family)**

WILLOW-LEAVED GENTIAN

PLANT TYPE: *Perennial*
ZONES: *5–8*
HABIT: *1'–2' tall; clumps 1½'–2' across*
CULTURE: *Partial to full shade; deep, highly organic, neutral to acid soil that retains moisture but is not waterlogged*
BLOOM: *Summer to early fall*

Willow-leaved gentian can be found growing on the damp moors and hills of central Europe. It makes clumps of well-foliaged stems that arch gracefully. Usually arranged in pairs, each willow-shaped (ovate-lanceolate) leaf may reach 3" long. The vibrant, deep azure-blue trumpet-

shaped flowers arise in the axils of the upper leaves.

CULTIVATION: Plant in spring or fall. Fresh seed germinates best if given a cold period. Provide a winter mulch in cold areas; a summer mulch is beneficial to maintain a cool root zone. Divide only if necessary to build stock; gentians resent disturbance.

RELATED PLANTS: Our native *G. saponaria* blooms at the very end of the season with clear blue bottle-shaped flowers. Rough gentian (*G. scabra*) has clusters of bell-shaped sapphire-blue flowers in autumn.

USES: Willow-leaved gentian is a choice plant for cool shaded or partially shaded beds, borders, or woodland gardens. Pair with Japanese anemones.

Geranium 'Johnson's Blue'

**Geraniaceae
(Geranium family)**

HARDY GERANIUM

PLANT TYPE: *Perennial*
ZONES: *5–9*
HABIT: *1½'–2' tall; mounded clumps about 2' across*
CULTURE: *Full sun to partial shade; average, well-drained soil*
BLOOM: *Late spring to summer*

The cultivar 'Johnson's Blue' is a hybrid of *G. himalayense* and *G. pratense*. It often makes sprawling clumps of divided foliage, above which bloom masses of clear blue 1"–2" flowers. It seldom sets seed, and blooms over a long period.

CULTIVATION: Plant in spring; fall planting is successful in regions with mild winters. In the South, plant in the shade. Fertilize lightly

each spring and mulch well in summer to conserve moisture. Rust may be a problem, but otherwise pests and diseases are few. Cut back shabby foliage. Propagate by division in spring.

RELATED PLANTS: Several hardy geranium species are garden-worthy ornamentals. Among the best are *G. macrorrhizum* (bigroot geranium), a fine ground-cover

plant. It has pink flowers over shallowly lobed, divided leaves; these are strongly scented and provide good fall color. *G. himalayense,* 1½' tall, has violet to blue flowers; *G. pratense,* 3' tall, has purple flowers. Both have several cultivars. *G. sanguineum,* 1' tall, has pink flowers; its long-blooming variety *striatum* is deservedly popular.

USES: 'Johnson's Blue' is excellent in mixed or perennial borders; attractive with white Siberian iris or peonies.

Gunnera manicata

Gunneraceae (Gunnera family)

GIANT RHUBARB

PLANT TYPE: *Perennial*
ZONES: *7–10*
HABIT: *6'–8' tall; massive clumps about as wide*
CULTURE: *Full sun to partial shade, especially where sun is intense; deep, highly organic, moisture-retentive soil*
BLOOM: *Early summer*

This enormous plant from southern Brazil has rough brownish-gray-green leaves, each of which may reach 10' across; they are borne aloft on robust, hairy stems. The relatively inconspicuous greenish flowers, arranged in huge clublike clusters, nestle among the foliage.

CULTIVATION: Plant in spring, or fall in warm regions. These heavy feeders benefit from a spring dressing of fertilizer, and copious supplies of well-rotted manure or compost. Mulch in summer, protect the crowns in winter, and don't allow to dry out. Propagate by division or start from seed.

RELATED PLANTS: Although not related, for design purposes gunneras might be considered as "mega" ornamental rhubarbs.

USES: At their best massed along banks of streams, ponds, and lakes, where their enormous size and stately bearing is an asset. A strong foliage accent plant in partially shaded woodland gardens. Partner with astilbes, primulas, ligularias, and other moisture-loving plants.

Gypsophila paniculata 'Bristol Fairy'

Caryophyllaceae (Carnation family)

BABY'S BREATH

PLANT TYPE: *Perennial*
ZONES: *3–9*
HABIT: *To 3' tall; broad clumps 3'–4' across*
CULTURE: *Full sun; alkaline, very well drained soil*
BLOOM: *Summer*

Baby's breath is a Eurasian plant that is widely cultivated commercially and in residential gardens for fresh-cut or dried flowers. A myriad of small pure white or pink flowers bloom on brittle stems in a billowy, tangled mass. Its lance-shaped gray-green foliage contrasts well with other plants. The classic 'Bristol Fairy' has double white flowers.

CULTIVATION: Set out young plants in spring, or sow seed

directly. The deep fleshy roots resent disturbance but may be dug to make pencil-thick root cuttings. Spring dressings of lime chips are beneficial where soil tends to be acid. Stake early with grow-through supports, peony rings, or bamboo canes and twine; the top-heavy flower masses are particularly susceptible to weather damage. Deadhead to the ground for a second flush of bloom. Apply a winter mulch in cold areas.

RELATED PLANTS: Double white 'Snowflake,' 3' tall, blooms early and tolerates hot climates well. 'Pink Star,' 1½' tall, has double bright pink flowers. Creeping baby's breath (*G. repens*) and its pink cultivar 'Rosea' seldom top 1' tall.

USES: Baby's breath provides a light, airy feeling to perennial and mixed flower beds. Excellent for cutting.

Helleborus niger

Ranunculaceae (Buttercup family)

CHRISTMAS ROSE

PLANT TYPE: *Perennial*
ZONES: *3–9*
HABIT: *12"–15" tall; clumps 1' wide*
CULTURE: *Partial to full shade; deep, rich, well-drained soil, amended with organic matter*
BLOOM: *Late winter to early spring*

This native of southern Europe has a special charm all its own. The shyly nodding saucer-shaped flowers, 1–3 per stem and 2" or so in diameter, open pure white and become pink as they age. The basal evergreen leaves are divided into toothed leaflets and are handsome throughout the season. The entire plant is poisonous.

CULTIVATION: Plant in spring or early fall. Fertilize lightly in spring and apply a summer mulch of organic matter. Water deeply during dry weather. Remove shabby foliage if necessary. Protect in a cold frame or with a heavy mulch of dry leaves for earlier bloom in cold regions. Be alert for slugs. Divide in spring after blooming, or transplant self-sown seedlings.

RELATED PLANTS: Easier to grow, the later blooming Lenten rose (*H. orientalis*) has become popular. Its attractive evergreen foliage is about 2' tall. The white, pink, or maroon flowers are frequently speckled. Setterwort (*H. foetidus*), 1½–2' tall, bears clusters of greenish flowers and fingered evergreen leaves.

USES: Christmas rose is attractive in front of shrubs, along shaded pathways, and in woodland gardens. A good cut flower.

Hemerocallis 'Joan Senior'
Liliaceae (Lily family)
DAYLILY
PLANT TYPE: *Semi-evergreen perennial* ZONES: *3–9* HABIT: *2' tall; grassy clumps 2' wide* CULTURE: *Full sun; well-drained soil, amended with organic matter* BLOOM: *Summer*

Hybrid daylilies are possibly the most popular perennials in America today. They make tough clumps of grassy leaves; naked stems bear few to many trumpet-shaped flowers at their tips. Colors range from almost white through yellows, pinks, and lavenders to oranges, reds, and purples. Many flowers are frilled and ruffled. A mid-season daylily, 'Joan Senior' has nearly white flowers, 6" wide, flushed with green at the throat.

CULTIVATION: Plant in spring or fall. Mulch in summer; daylilies are tolerant of drought but bloom more freely if watered deeply during dry times. Deadhead daily. Diseases and pests, except for deer, are few. Divide when necessary, making sure that each division contains a fan of leaves.

RELATED PLANTS: Thousands of named hybrid daylilies are listed by the American Hemerocallis Society. Some are early flowering (ruffled yellow 'Mary Todd'), some mid-season (rosy 'Becky Lynn'), and others late (bright orange 'Tusitala'). Some are fragrant (clear yellow 'Hyperion'); some repeat bloom ('Stella d'Oro').

USES: Plant in beds or borders, among shrubs, to control erosion on exposed banks, and in containers. Attractive with grasses.

Heuchera 'Palace Purple'
Saxifragaceae (Saxifrage family)
CORAL BELLS
PLANT TYPE: *Perennial* ZONES: *4–9* HABIT: *2'–2½' tall, over rounded clumps 1½' across* CULTURE: *Full sun to partial shade; well-drained soil, amended with organic matter* BLOOM: *Late spring to summer*

The cultivar 'Palace Purple' has been variously ascribed to several species of coral bells, but is currently listed alone. Its wrinkled, beet-red to maroon, maple-shaped leaves vary in color from plant to plant and from site to site. Wiry stems bear sprays of tiny, delicate pink flowers that rise above the leaves, but 'Palace Purple' is primarily grown for its foliage.

CULTIVATION: Plant in spring, or fall in the South; in cold regions mulch well to avoid heaving, especially if fall-planted. Protect from intense sun. Mulch in summer and water if dry. Deadhead if grown for flowers, otherwise remove the flower stalks. Divide good selections in spring.

RELATED PLANTS: Most of the coral bells available are hybrids listed as *H. × brizoides.* Many are grown for their pink, red, or white flowers, and include pink 'Chatterbox,' red 'Mt. St. Helen's,' and 'White Cloud.' Cultivars selected for their striking foliage have recently entered the marketplace. These are mostly grown in shade. Examples are 'Chocolate Veil' and 'Ruby Veil.' *H. cylindrica* is quite unusual; it grows 2' tall with heart-shaped leaves and spikes of olive-green flowers.

USES: In beds and borders, combine with silvery lamb's ears or underplant with *Ajuga reptans* 'Burgundy Glow.' In shade, combine with ferns, barrenwort, lungwort, or hostas.

Hosta sieboldiana 'Frances Williams'

Liliaceae (Lily family)

PLANTAIN LILY; HOSTA

PLANT TYPE: *Perennial*
ZONES: *3–8*
HABIT: *2½'–3' tall; robust clumps 3'–4' across*
CULTURE: *Partial to full shade; well-drained, highly organic, moisture-retentive soil*
BLOOM: *Late summer*

This plantain lily is a Japanese native, with rounded or heart-shaped, 1'–1½' long, bluish or gray-green leaves. Its surface is ribbed and puckered, giving an interesting textural effect in a shady garden. The late summer

flowers are pale lavender, but are often hidden by the leaves. 'Frances Williams' is one of the showiest cultivars, with blue-green leaves edged unevenly with gold that can light up a dark corner.

CULTIVATION: Plant in spring or fall. A thick summer mulch helps to retain moisture but may be too attractive a hiding place for slugs; pine straw or finely chopped leaves are good mulches for hostas. Water deeply during prolonged drought. Cut back shabby leaves as necessary. Deter slugs and snails with superior hygiene. The other major pest is deer. Propagate by division.

RELATED PLANTS: Countless hosta species and cultivars are available, and are described by the American Hosta Society. Among the best is fragrant plantain lily (*H. plantaginea*), 2' tall, with glossy dark green leaves and white flowers.

USES: 'Frances Williams' makes a spectacular foliage accent plant in shady beds or among shrubs. Contrast with astilbes and ferns. Smaller hostas are suitable as edging plants or in rock gardens.

Hylotelephium spectabile (syn. *Sedum spectabile*) 'Indian Chief'

Crassulaceae (Stonecrop family)

SHOWY STONECROP

PLANT TYPE: *Perennial*
ZONES: *4–10*
HABIT: *1½'–2' tall, and about as wide*
CULTURE: *Full sun to light shade; sandy, free-draining soil*
BLOOM: *Late summer to fall*

Showy stonecrop is native to eastern Asia, but several cultivars attributed to this species may indeed be hybrids. It has numerous fleshy, upright stems, bearing opposite pairs of succulent light green leaves. Dense heads of flowers, green in the bud stage, change color as they open and are attractive to butterflies. 'Indian Chief' has deep pinkish-red flowers.

CULTIVATION: Plant showy stonecrop in spring or fall. Except in lean soil, staking may be necessary as the flowerheads become topheavy; pinching the plants at 6"–12" results in stockier plants with smaller, lighter flowerheads. Avoid fertilizer. Supplementary watering is necessary only during prolonged droughts in hot regions. Be alert for aphid damage.

Propagate by rooting cuttings in early summer, or divide established plants.

RELATED PLANTS: Other cultivars include white 'Stardust' and strong pink 'Brillant.' The popular hybrid 'Autumn Joy' has pink flowers, turning to copper and rusty-bronze, on 2' stems.

USES: 'Indian Chief' assorts well with ornamental grasses and fall asters in beds and borders, especially in lean soils. Suitable for containers.

Lavatera thuringiaca 'Barnsley'
Malvaceae (Mallow family)
TREE MALLOW
PLANT TYPE: *Perennial*   ZONES: *5–9*   HABIT: *5'–6' tall; 3'–4' across*   CULTURE: *Full sun to light shade, especially in hot regions; average, well-drained soil*   BLOOM: *Early summer through fall*

From central and southeastern Europe, tree mallow makes large rounded bushes of hairy gray-green foliage. The large pink flowers, similar to their close relatives, hollyhocks, are borne aloft on branched stems and are solitary or in clusters in the leaf axils. The white or blush-pink flowers of 'Barnsley' have a deep pink eye.

CULTIVATION: Plant in spring; mulch in summer and water deeply during dry weather. In cold regions protect with a winter mulch. Staking is not necessary; pests and diseases are not a problem. Propagate tree mallow from young shoots in summer, as seed may not come true.

RELATED PLANTS: *L. cachemiriana* is a little taller, with silky pink trumpet flowers arranged in branched clusters.

USES: 'Barnsley' and the species are valuable for adding height and their long-blooming season to perennial and mixed beds and borders. Not useful as fresh-cut flowers, but the fruits are interesting in dried flower arrangements.

Lobelia siphilitica
Campanulaceae (Bellflower family)
GREAT BLUE LOBELIA
PLANT TYPE: *Perennial*   ZONES: *4–8*   HABIT: *2'–3' tall, over clumps 1½'–2' across*   CULTURE: *Full sun to partial shade; constantly moist but not boggy, highly organic soil*   BLOOM: *Late summer*

This native of wet areas of the eastern U.S. makes strong clumps of foliage. Above rise erect, leafy stems topped with terminal spikes of 2-lipped, 1" blue flowers. There are white forms.

CULTIVATION: Plant in spring or fall, providing shade in hot areas. Lobelia often self-sows; since it is

a short-lived perennial, you may want to grow on any seedlings that develop. Sow fresh seed in fall and overwinter outdoors. Mulch in summer to retain moisture; water deeply during dry times. In cold climates, discourage heaving with a winter mulch. Deadhead to the base of the spike for further bloom; staking is seldom necessary. Divide in spring as necessary.

RELATED PLANTS: The native cardinal flower (*L. cardinalis*) has scarlet flowers; the two species sometimes grow together in the wild. There are several perennial hybrids and cultivars, with flowers in white and shades of pink, red, purple, and blue.

USES: Beautiful massed beside ponds, streams, and lakes, and in wet areas of wild or native plant gardens. Also useful in well-prepared perennial beds and borders. Combine with Japanese anemones, grasses and rushes, or sweet pepper bush.

Lupinus Russell hybrids
Fabaceae (Pea family)
RUSSELL LUPINE

PLANT TYPE: *Perennial*
ZONES: *4–7*
HABIT: *3'–4' tall; clumps 2' wide*
CULTURE: *Full sun to light shade; rich to average, well-drained, neutral to acid soil*
BLOOM: *Late spring to early summer*

This magnificent hybrid strain has several species in its heritage. The fingered foliage is handsome in its own right, but above the mass of leaves, strong erect flower spikes thrust upward. Pealike, often bicolored flowers crowd along the upper stem for 1½' or more. The color range includes cream, yellows, pinks, lavenders, purples, and reds.

CULTIVATION: Treated as annuals in warm climates; spring planting is best in the North. Sow seed in pots in late summer; hasten germination by scarification, nicking or filing the seed coat to facilitate the uptake of water. Cuttings from basal growth root readily. Avoid root disturbance. Deadhead to the base of the flower spike for later bloom. Stake tall sorts. Control slugs and be alert for aphids, which carry virus diseases. Lupines are short-lived; propagate frequently to replace spent plants.

RELATED PLANTS: The Dwarf Minarette and Gallery strains grow only 15"–18" tall. The tree lupine (*L. arboreus*), a California native, has spikes of lemon-yellow flowers on 6' plants.

USES: Lupines are attractive in flower beds with peonies and hybrid sages.

Lychnis chalcedonica
Caryophyllaceae (Carnation family)
MALTESE CROSS

PLANT TYPE: *Perennial*
ZONES: *3–9*
HABIT: *3'–4' tall; 1'–1½' wide*
CULTURE: *Full sun; moisture-retentive, well-drained soil*
BLOOM: *Summer*

The common name, Maltese cross, describes this plant's flower shape rather than its native eastern Russia. Another name, scarlet lightning, refers to the intense vermilion-red flowers. These are arranged in dense dome-shaped clusters atop sturdy hairy stems, clothed with clasping, somewhat coarse leaves.

CULTIVATION: Plant in spring or fall. Replace frequently with young divisions, made in spring or fall. Fertilize lightly in spring and mulch in summer. Water only during prolonged drought. Staking may be necessary. Camouflage the sometimes-shabby lower stems with shorter-growing companions.

RELATED PLANTS: Rose campion (*L. coronaria*) is popular for its mats of silvery furred leaves as well as its brilliant cerise flowers. The white cultivar 'Alba' is less strident. German catchfly (*L. vis-caria*) has clusters of strong purplish-pink flowers; it is suitable for the front of the border.

USES: Plant Maltese cross as an accent to enliven perennial and mixed borders. Combine with strong yellow daylilies for a hot color scheme, or tone down with silvery artemisia or white daisies.

Lysimachia clethroides
Primulaceae (Primrose family)
GOOSENECK LOOSESTRIFE

PLANT TYPE: *Perennial*
ZONES: *3–9*
HABIT: *2'–3' tall, over upright plants about 3' wide*
CULTURE: *Full sun to light shade; average, moisture-retentive soil*
BLOOM: *Mid to late summer*

Gooseneck loosestrife is native to China and Japan but makes itself quite at home in American gardens. Indeed, it is often invasive and may become troublesome. It has erect leafy stems topped with a shepherd's-crook inflorescence of starry white flowers.

CULTIVATION: Plant gooseneck loosestrife in spring or fall. Maintain soil moisture with a summer mulch; water regularly in dry weather. Staking is seldom necessary. Beware of this plant's invasive tendencies. Deadhead as soon as flowers are spent to avoid self-seeding. Propagate by division of established plants, or start from seed.

RELATED PLANTS: Circle flower, or yellow loosestrife (*L. punctata*), also tends to take over, especially in damp soils. It grows about 2' tall and has 1" bright yellow flowers all along its stems, providing a radiant punctuation in the perennial border or in a dry meadow. Golden creeping Jenny (*L. nummularia* 'Aurea') is a lovely foliage ground cover.

USES: Plant gooseneck loosestrife in open areas where there is plenty of room, especially if the soil is moist. Suitable for the flower border or among shrubs; do not allow it to take over. Makes an attractive cut flower.

Macleaya cordata (syn. Bocconia cordata)
Papaveraceae (Poppy family)
PLUME POPPY

PLANT TYPE: *Perennial*
ZONES: *3–9*
HABIT: *6'–8' tall; leafy clumps 3'–4' across*
CULTURE: *Full sun to light shade; average, well-drained soil*
BLOOM: *Summer*

This elegant, unpoppy-like plant is native to China and Japan. It is an aggressive spreader with deep, thong-like roots and lovely, lobed gray-green leaves that are silvery on their undersides. The tiny cream flowers have numerous prominent stamens but lack petals. On the upper part of the unbranched stems, the flowers are so numerous that they appear as fluffy plumes. All parts of the plant contain an orange sap that will stain both skin and clothes.

CULTIVATION: Plant in spring or fall. If growth is slow, fertilize lightly in spring, but this is only necessary with the poorest soils. Avoid rich soils, as growth will be soft and require staking. Deadhead right after blooming to avoid self-seeding. Propagate by division, by separating offsets, or by taking softwood cuttings in summer.

RELATED PLANTS: *M. microcarpa* is very similar but is even more aggressive. Its flowers are a rich bronzy color.

USES: A spectacular specimen plant at the back of the border or beside large bodies of water in landscape settings. Combine with ornamental grasses or shrubs. Spectacular paired with climbing hydrangea.

Monarda fistulosa 'Violet Queen'
Lamiaceae (Mint family)
WILD BERGAMOT

PLANT TYPE: *Perennial*
ZONES: *3–9*
HABIT: *2'–3' tall; spreading 1½'–3' across*
CULTURE: *Full sun to light shade; moisture-retentive, well-drained soil, amended with organic matter*
BLOOM: *Late summer*

Wild bergamot is native through much of the U.S. and has been used extensively (with *M. didyma*) in breeding some of the hybrid bee balms on the market. Its leaves, to 4" long, are hairy and fragrant of mint. The leafy stems bear tiers of white or lavender 2-lipped flowers, which are very attractive to bees, butterflies, and hummingbirds. 'Violet Queen' has deep purple flowers.

CULTIVATION: Plant wild bergamot in the spring or fall. Be alert for signs of powdery mildew on the foliage. Spray with a natural fungicide, if needed. Thin young shoots to improve air circulation. Water deeply during dry weather; stress caused by dry soil renders plants more susceptible to fungal diseases. Avoid overly rich or fertilized soil, which results in rank growth that will then need to be staked. Increase by division in spring or fall, or take late-spring cuttings. These plants tend to decline after a few years, and need regular renewal.

RELATED PLANTS: Native bee balm (*M. didyma*) is showier. 'Cambridge Scarlet' and 'Croftway Pink' are popular hybrid cultivars.

USES: For wildlife or native plant gardens, or perennial borders. A fine companion for white lilies and *Veronica spicata* 'Icicle.'

Myosotis scorpioides
Boraginaceae (Borage family)
FORGET-ME-NOT
PLANT TYPE: *Perennial*
ZONES: *3–8*
HABIT: *6"–10" tall, and about as wide*
CULTURE: *Partial to light shade; moist soil, amended with organic matter*
BLOOM: *Spring to early summer*

Forget-me-nots are widespread across Europe and Asia. Their sometimes-hairy branched stems may reach 15"–18" long, but are prostrate at the base and then become upright. The oblong leaves grow up to 2" long; the bright blue ¼" flowers, accented with a yellow eye, are arranged in a coiled cluster that resembles the tail of a scorpion, for which it is named.

CULTIVATION: Plant in spring or fall. In the North, it is acceptable to grow in full sun if the soil is kept constantly wet. Maintenance is low, except for weeding out extra self-seeded plants. Shear after bloom to avoid excess seeding and to encourage later bloom. Slugs may be troublesome. Propagate from seed, or divide in spring or fall.

RELATED PLANTS: *M. sylvatica* (woodland forget-me-not) is often treated as a biennial. Abundant clear blue flowers, also with a yellow eye, create a blue haze in mass plantings. Cultivars and strains with white, pink, and lavender flowers are available.

USES: Mass along stream banks, lakes, and ponds. Perfect to underplant assorted primroses, astilbes, rushes, and rodgersias.

Nepeta × *faassenii* 'Six Hills Giant'
Lamiaceae (Mint family)
CATMINT
PLANT TYPE: *Perennial*
ZONES: *3–10*
HABIT: *To 3' tall, above clumps 3' wide*
CULTURE: *Full sun; dryish, free-draining soil, on the lean side*
BLOOM: *Early to late summer*

Its nativity was in question, but 'Six Hills Giant' is now considered to be a taller, more robust selection of the sterile hybrid *N.* × *faassenii*. Billowy mounds of gray-green aromatic foliage are topped by a haze of bloom. The 2-lipped, ¾", dark purplish-blue flowers are borne along the upper 12" of arching stems.

CULTIVATION: Plant in spring or fall. Catmint may need gentle staking if grown in partial shade. Avoid rich or heavily fertilized soils. For repeat bloom, cut back by about half after flowering. Pests and diseases are few; cats enjoy rolling in catmint but are discouraged by inserting barberry twigs among the young stems in spring. Superior to the species in damp climates. Propagate by division, or take cuttings of young growth.

RELATED PLANTS: The species *N.* × *faassenii* grows 1'–2' tall, with soft gray crinkled leaves and lavender flowers. The cultivar 'Dropmore' has larger flowers; 'Snowflake' has white flowers.

USES: Useful along pathways and massed as an underplanting for roses such as 'Iceberg' and 'New Dawn.'

Oenothera macrocarpa (syn. *O. missouriensis*)

Onagraceae (Evening primrose family)

OZARK SUNDROPS

PLANT TYPE: *Perennial*
ZONES: *4–9*
HABIT: *6"–18" tall; sprawling clumps 1'–2' wide*
CULTURE: *Full sun; deep, organically rich, free-draining soil*
BLOOM: *Summer*

Ozark sundrops grow in the wild in the south-central part of the U.S. The stems spread widely along the ground, with the tips turning upward. The lance-shaped, dark green leaves are covered with soft hairs. In the early evening, solitary red flower buds burst into fragrant, delicate yellow 2"–3" cup-shaped flowers, which last through the following day. Attractive seedpods follow.

CULTIVATION: Plant in spring or fall. Keep watered during dry weather; a summer mulch is beneficial, especially in less-than-ideal hot regions, where light shade helps. Hot weather may temporarily reduce or halt blooming. Mulch in winter in cold zones. Deadhead routinely to extend flowering. Propagate by division in spring or after blooming, or root summer cuttings.

RELATED PLANTS: Day-blooming sundrops (*O. fruticosa*) is a taller plant, with more but smaller bright yellow flowers. 'Fireworks' has reddish 18" stems. Showy or white evening primrose (*O. speciosa*) and its pink cultivar 'Rosea' are attractive day-bloomers, but tend to be invasive.

USES: This is an excellent front-of-the-border plant; good for rock gardens. Partner with 'Crater Lake Blue' speedwell.

Paeonia lactiflora 'Festiva Maxima'

Paeoniaceae (Peony family)

GARDEN PEONY

PLANT TYPE: *Perennial*
ZONES: *2–8*
HABIT: *1½'–3½' tall; leafy clumps 2'–3' across*
CULTURE: *Full sun to light shade; deep, organically rich, well-drained soil*
BLOOM: *Late spring to early summer*

Although derived mostly from the northeast Asian species *P. lactiflora,* garden peonies have been extensively bred, incorporating characteristics from other species. The long-stemmed, divided leaves are dark green, and remain handsome long after flowering is over, providing a foil for later bloomers. The flowers, single, semi-double, or double, some 3"–4" across, are carried singly or in clusters atop sturdy stems; their color range includes whites, pinks, and reds. Many are delightfully fragrant. The American Peony

Society lists a huge number of cultivars currently available. Specialists list early, mid-season, and late-blooming cultivars. 'Festiva Maxima' is an early bloomer with fragrant, double white flowers, flecked with red.

CULTIVATION: Best planted in fall, with the crown not more than 1"–2" below the soil surface. Water deeply during dry times; apply a summer mulch and fertilize in spring. Support the plants with a peony hoop or by another method. Remove side shoots to obtain the largest flowers; very heavy flowers may need to be staked individually. Be alert for botrytis mold, which can attack the unopened buds; spray with a natural fungicide and destroy infected vegetation. Virus-carrying aphids may feed on the buds; their "honey-dew" attracts ants. In hot regions select early flowering cultivars. Garden peony grows best where winters are cold. Propagate by division in fall.

RELATED PLANTS: Tree peonies (*P. suffruticosa*), 3'–6' tall, are magnificent shrubs, grown in few American gardens. Their solitary flowers, in the white, pink, red, and yellow range, may exceed 6" across.

USES: Garden peonies are appropriate for perennial and mixed borders and as cut flowers. They assort well with other early summer bloomers such as *Gaura lindheimeri,* hybrid sages, and columbines.

Papaver orientale
Papaveraceae (Poppy family)
ORIENTAL POPPY

PLANT TYPE: *Perennial*
ZONES: *3–8*
HABIT: *1½–4' tall; coarse clumps 2'–3' across*
CULTURE: *Full sun; deep, highly organic, well drained soil*
BLOOM: *Late spring to early summer*

The Oriental poppy is native to southwestern Asia, but many of the cultivars on the market are probably hybrids with other species. Regardless of parentage, they all have hairy, rather coarse, divided foliage, which mostly dies down at the onset of hot weather. The solitary, lush bowl-shaped flowers, to 6" across, have a central cluster of striking black stamens surrounded

by crumpled-tissue-paper petals, often blotched with deep purple at the base. At one time, only single flowers in strident vermilion were available; today whites, delicate and stronger pinks, oranges, reds, and mahogany shades, lavenders and purples are offered, some double. Best in cool climates.

CULTIVATION: Plant in fall, before growth commences. Disturb minimally; divide after blooming every 3 to 5 years to maintain vigor. Fertilize lightly in spring and apply a summer mulch. Propagate by division in fall, or take root cuttings after blooming.

RELATED PLANTS: Cultivars include 'Warlord,' one of the best deep reds; 'Showgirl,' with ruffled pink flowers; 'Glowing Rose,' which blooms early with bright watermelon-pink blooms; and flame-red 'Bonfire.' *P. somniferum* (opium poppy), *P. nudicaule* (Iceland poppy), and Shirley poppies are best treated as annuals.

USES: Plant Oriental poppies as spring accents in mixed and perennial beds; plan to fill their space after they die down. If used as a cut flower, sear the base of the stem to prevent "bleeding" of the milky sap.

Penstemon barbatus 'Rose Elf'
Scrophulariaceae (Figwort family)
COMMON BEARD TONGUE

PLANT TYPE: *Perennial*
ZONES: *2–9*
HABIT: *To 1½' tall; clumps 1'–1½' across*
CULTURE: *Full sun; fertile, very well-drained soil*
BLOOM: *Early to mid summer*

Common beard tongue is found in the wild in southwestern parts of the U.S. It makes a tufted clump of grassy basal leaves; sturdy branching stems, to 3' tall, bear narrow panicles of 1" tubular scarlet flowers, each with a yellow-bearded lip. Shorter 'Rose Elf' has long-blooming rosy-pink flowers.

CULTIVATION: Plant in spring, or fall in mild climates. Penstemons are short-lived at best, so be prepared to renew plants every few years. Avoid organic mulches in summer as crown rot often results; surface moisture must run off readily. Protect with evergreen boughs or salt hay in cold-winter regions. Deadhead to the base of the flower stem. Propagate the cultivars by division in spring, or from cuttings in summer.

RELATED PLANTS: *P. digitalis* 'Husker Red' is an important recent introduction from the University of Nebraska. Light blush-pink or white flowers rise above beet-red basal foliage; it's extremely cold-hardy.

USES: 'Rose Elf' is appropriate for rock gardens or the front of perennial or mixed gardens. Combine it with fleabanes or dianthus for good effect.

Phlox divaricata

Polemoniaceae (Phlox family)

WILD SWEET WILLIAM; WILD BLUE PHLOX

PLANT TYPE: *Perennial*
ZONES: *4–9*
HABIT: *To 1' tall, over mats 12"–15" wide*
CULTURE: *Partial shade; well-drained, highly organic soil*
BLOOM: *Spring*

Wild sweet William is native to woodland areas of the eastern U.S. It makes slowly spreading mats of creeping stems clothed in 2" semi-evergreen leaves. The 1" pale lavender or mauve flowers cluster atop wiry stems.

CULTIVATION: Plant in spring or fall. Mulch in summer; shear back to the basal mat after blooming for neatness. Be alert for slugs; powdery mildew may be a nuisance. Propagate from cuttings taken from nonflowering shoots, or divide in spring or early in autumn.

RELATED PLANTS: 'Fuller's White' is a superior cultivar with pure white flowers. Var. *laphamii* is more sun-tolerant and has darker blue flowers. Meadow phlox (*P. maculata*) and garden phlox (*P. paniculata*) are standards for summer perennial borders; stems 4' or so tall bear large trusses of often fragrant flowers in whites, pinks and reds, lavenders, mauves, and purples.

USES: Wild sweet William is charming along woodland paths or at the front of shaded borders. A useful ground cover with spring-blooming narcissus, it also assorts well with other shade-loving perennials such as fringed bleeding hearts.

Platycodon grandiflorus 'Komachi'

Campanulaceae (Bellflower family)

BALLOONFLOWER

PLANT TYPE: *Perennial*
ZONES: *3–9*
HABIT: *To 2' tall, over clumps 1'–2' wide*
CULTURE: *Full sun to light shade; fertile, well-drained soil*
BLOOM: *Summer*

This species from eastern Asia adapts well to American gardens. Its erect stems, 2'–3' tall, branch above and are well-clothed with slightly grayish-green oval leaves, which turn yellow in fall. The balloon-shaped buds, solitary at the top of the stems, pop open into 5-lobed flowers, 2" wide, of deep-purple, pink, or white. 'Komachi' has clear blue flowers.

CULTIVATION: Plant in spring or fall, taking care not to disturb the fragile roots more than is necessary; pot-grown plants are recommended. Taller sorts may need staking, especially in warm

regions. Deadhead routinely. It is wise to mark where balloon-flowers are planted as they are slow to begin growth in spring. Pests and diseases are seldom a problem. This plant does not tolerate hot, humid climates well. Propagate by division in late spring, or start from seed in spring.

RELATED PLANTS: 'Albus' has pure white flowers on 2'–2½' stems; similar 'Shell Pink' has pale pink flowers. The early flowering 'Mariesii' (15") and 'Apoyama' (10"–12") have violet-blue flowers.

USES: Plant balloonflower in mixed and perennial borders; the shorter-growing sorts are suitable for rock gardens. This is a good cut flower; sear the base of the stem to prevent "bleeding."

Primula japonica

Primulaceae (Primrose family)

JAPANESE PRIMROSE

PLANT TYPE: *Perennial*
ZONES: *5–8*
HABIT: *1'–2' tall*
CULTURE: *Lightly dappled shade; moist, highly organic soil*
BLOOM: *Late spring*

From Japan, this primrose is one of the Candelabra types. Its ½"–1" flowers, in white, pinks, and reds to crimson, are borne on leafless stems, one 8- to 10-flowered tier above the other. The wrinkled, spatula-shaped leaves are all basal.

CULTIVATION: Plant in spring or fall; seed may be sown as soon as it is ripe. The soil must remain constantly moist; mulch in summer and water deeply in dry weather. Unless seed is required, deadhead to the ground after flowering. Be alert for slugs, which revel in the damp, shaded conditions that suit Japanese primroses. In cool-summer climates with wet soil, you can grow them in full sun. Build stock by dividing plants after blooming time.

RELATED PLANTS: There are a host of garden-worthy primroses, but many are for specialists. Readily available, easy to grow kinds include the solitary-flowering English primroses (*P. vulgaris*),

their hybrids and cultivars, and the polyanthus, now known as the Pruhonicensis hybrids, which have clusters of brightly colored flowers on each stem.

USES: Japanese primroses adapt well to waterside gardens where the soil remains damp, but also do well in beds and borders if soil conditions permit. Good companions include *Iris pseudacorus* and astilbes. Massed and allowed to naturalize among shrubs or in open shaded locations, they make a glorious sight.

Rehmannia elata
Gesneriaceae (African violet family)
REHMANNIA

PLANT TYPE: *Perennial*
ZONES: *8–10*
HABIT: *2'–3' tall, over clumps 2' wide*
CULTURE: *Full sun to full shade; fertile, free-draining soil*
BLOOM: *Spring through fall*

This perennial, often misidentified as *R. angulata,* is native to China. It blooms over a very long period with purplish-pink, tubular, 2-lipped flowers about 2"–3" in length; its yellowish throat is speckled with crimson. The coarsely toothed leaves, which may attain 10"–12" in length, are evergreen in mild climates. They form a basal rosette and elegantly clothe the lower portion of the plant.

CULTIVATION: Plant in spring or fall. Seed germinates readily. Maintain soil moisture with a summer mulch, but do not smother the crown. Water during dry weather. Deadhead to encourage further bloom. Rehmannia is susceptible to slugs and snails; use a

finely textured mulch like pine straw or cocoa hulls. Propagate by cuttings or root cuttings.

RELATED PLANTS: *R. glutinosa* is only 1' or so tall and spreads widely; its flowers are an unusual shade of buff-purple.

USES: A fine border plant in mild zones; elsewhere useful as a summer bedding plant or in containers for patio or conservatory. Long-lasting as a cut flower.

Rodgersia aesculifolia
Saxifragaceae (Saxifrage family)
FINGERLEAF RODGERSIA

PLANT TYPE: *Perennial*
ZONES: *5–8*
HABIT: *3'–5' tall, over bold clumps 3'–5' across*
CULTURE: *Sun to partial shade; moist, organically enriched soil*
BLOOM: *Late spring to summer*

Grown mostly for its foliage, this Chinese species has bold leaves (resembling those of the horse chestnut) on long, hairy stalks. Large flower panicles, 1'–2' long, are composed of clusters of small creamy-pink blooms. Although the flowers lack petals, the stamens and sepals are quite showy.

CULTIVATION: Plant in spring. Shelter plants from strong winds, which can damage the handsome foliage. Maintain soil moisture with a summer mulch and water deeply if necessary. Plants that dry out may exhibit leaf scorch. Remove spent flowers after bloom. Be sure to allow sufficient space for these plants to develop and show off their potential. Shade from intense sun. Propagate by division, or start from seed.

RELATED PLANTS: *R. pinnata* (featherleaf rodgersia) has bronzy leaves and panicles of rosy-pink flowers; 'Superba' grows 3'–4' tall and bears striking, divided, bronze-tinged emerald-green leaves, comprising 5–9 narrowly oval leaflets, and panicles of bright pink star-shaped flowers in summer; the superb *R. tabularis* (now correctly *Astilboides tabularis*) has shield-shaped leaves, 3' or so across, and large astilbe-like plumes of white flowers.

USES: Plant rodgersias beside water or in bog gardens for good effect. They are most attractive planted as accent foliage plants with irises, primroses, astilbes, and other lovers of damp soil.

Romneya coulteri
Papaveraceae (Poppy family)
MATILIJA POPPY

PLANT TYPE: *Perennial*
ZONES: *6–10*
HABIT: *3'–7' tall; 3'–4' across*
CULTURE: *Full sun; deep, gravelly, very well drained soil*
BLOOM: *Late spring to early summer*

This native of southern California has striking blue-green, deeply divided foliage. The somewhat fragrant, magnificent pure white poppy flowers, each 6" wide and accented with a central cluster of yellow stamens, are carried on branched blue-green stems. Matilija poppy is drought-tolerant, and invasive under good conditions.

CULTIVATION: Plant in spring or fall, preferably from pots. The deep roots are very brittle and resent disturbance. Cut back almost to ground level at the end of the season. In cold regions, apply a winter mulch of evergreen boughs or salt hay. Propagate from root cuttings in fall.

RELATED PLANTS: The cultivar 'White Cloud' is perhaps superior to the species. Var. *trichocalyx* is similar, but may be more hardy.

USES: A spectacular border plant, but care must be taken to corral the widespreading roots. Valuable to control erosion and in wide borders along roads or driveways. An attractive cut flower.

Rudbeckia fulgida var. *sullivantii* 'Goldsturm'
Asteraceae (Composite family)
ORANGE CONEFLOWER

PLANT TYPE: *Perennial*
ZONES: *3–9*
HABIT: *1½'–2' tall; clumps to 1½' across*
CULTURE: *Full sun; average, well-drained soil*
BLOOM: *Mid summer to fall*

Orange coneflowers are native to the mid-Atlantic and southeastern states as well as the Midwest. They tend to have rather coarse, hairy leaves, the basal ones on long stalks. Their strong, branching flower stems are upright and terminate in bright orange flowerheads, 1½"–3" across, each with a central dark brown cone. 'Goldsturm' may be the finest selection, with flowers to 4" across on uniform plants, 1½'–2' tall. Very long blooming and tough.

CULTIVATION: Plant in spring or fall. 'Goldsturm' prefers a moister soil than other coneflowers; mulch in summer, and water if necessary. Apply a light spring dressing of fertilizer in poor soils. Deadhead routinely to prolong flowering. Pests and diseases are few. Propagate only vegetatively to retain the desirable characteristics, preferably by division or from cuttings.

RELATED PLANTS: Shining cone-flower (*R. nitida*) has greenish cones; among its well-known cultivars is 'Herbstonne,' which may reach 6' tall. Sweet coneflower (*R. subtomentosa*), 4' tall, has velvety leaves; the soft yellow flowers have brown cones. Cutleaf coneflower (*R. laciniata*), 6'–7' tall, has deeply cut leaves; its yellow flowers have drooping ray flowers ("petals"). 'Hortensia' ('Golden Glow') is a fully double cultivar.

USES: 'Goldsturm' is widely grown massed with ornamental grasses and *Hylotelephium* 'Autumn Joy.' It also assorts well with other perennials in mixed borders, especially when hot color combinations are desired. Striking with *Crocosmia* 'Lucifer' or with blue cultivars of *Salvia farinacea;* or cool off with *Calamintha nepeta.* Useful in open meadow and wild gardens, and in the cutting garden.

Salvia × *sylvestris* 'Blue Hills'
Lamiaceae (Mint family)
HYBRID SAGE
PLANT TYPE: *Perennial* ZONES: *4–9* HABIT: *15"–18" tall; to 18" wide* CULTURE: *Full sun; fertile, well-drained soil* BLOOM: *Summer*

Hybrid sage is probably derived from several species, and its precise nomenclature is somewhat confused. 'Blue Hills' has erect branched stems that end in dense spikes of true-blue flowers. The rough leaves are gray-green and aromatic. It may be listed under *S. nemerosa.*

CULTIVATION: Plant in spring, or fall in the South. Additional water is seldom necessary for established plantings, but good drainage is essential. Mulch in cold-winter regions with evergreen boughs or salt hay. Deadhead to extend blooming; cut back in late summer for fall bloom. Stake as necessary, particularly in hot areas, where stems may be weak. Propagate by division, or by terminal cuttings of young growth.

RELATED PLANTS: Other cultivars include 'East Friesland,' which has deep purplish-blue or violet flowers, and similar but longer-blooming 'Lubeca.' Ungainly azure sage (*S. azurea*) has long spikes of brilliant clear blue flowers in fall; biennial *S. argentea* (woolly sage) is grown for its bold silver leaves. Several cultivars of *S. officinalis* (culinary sage) provide interesting

foliage effects in ornamental gardens. Many tender perennial sages are grown as annuals in the North: *S. leucantha* (Mexican bush sage), *S. patens* (gentian sage), and *S. guaranitica* (especially 'Argentine Skies') are readily available.

USES: 'Blue Hills' is useful in mixed and perennial borders throughout the summer. Attractive in the front to midsection with *Coreopsis verticillata* 'Moonbeam' or *Achillea* 'Taygetea.'

Saxifraga × *urbium*
Saxifragaceae (Saxifrage family)
LONDON PRIDE
PLANT TYPE: *Perennial* ZONES: *6–8* HABIT: *Flower stems 1'–1½' tall; basal clumps 1' across* CULTURE: *Partial to full shade; moist, well-drained soil* BLOOM: *Spring to early summer*

Sometimes known as *S. umbrosa*, London pride has smart dark green, rounded basal foliage, reddish on the undersides,

arranged in rosettes. The flowers arise on hairy pink stems, forming light, airy panicles of tiny delicate whitish or pale pink flowers above.

CULTIVATION: Plant London pride in spring or fall. Shallow-rooting; mulch in cold winters. Deadhead after flowering for neatness. Be alert for slugs, especially where soil is organically enriched. Propagate by division or from seed.

RELATED PLANTS: Strawberry begonia (*S. stolonifera*), neither a strawberry nor a begonia, is a useful ground-cover foliage plant for shade. Its flowers are similar to those of London pride, but the hairy foliage is veined in silver or gray; the undersides are also reddish.

USES: Plant London pride at the front of perennial or mixed borders, in rock gardens, and along pathways. Attractive with low spring-flowering bulbs, such as grape hyacinths, or with variegated lily turfs or lungworts.

Scabiosa caucasica
Dipsacaceae (Teasel family)
PINCUSHION FLOWER

PLANT TYPE: *Perennial*
ZONES: *3–8*
HABIT: *1½–2½' tall; 1'–2' across*
CULTURE: *Full sun to partial shade; alkaline, well-drained soil*
BLOOM: *Mid to late summer*

As its botanical name implies, pincushion flower is native to the Caucasus region. Its gray-green leaves are often lobed, the basal ones on long stalks. The flat heads of flowers may reach 3" across; the showy outer florets are in shades of blue, lavender, or white.

CULTIVATION: Plant in spring. Start from seed in spring or early summer. Fertilize lightly in spring, and top-dress with lime chips in acid soils. Do not allow soil to dry out in summer. Deadhead to the base of the flower stem to encourage further bloom. Staking is seldom attractive; instead, allow the long flower stems to flop onto sturdier plants. This perennial is slow-growing; it does best where summers are cool. Divide only when necessary to increase stock.

RELATED PLANTS: Worthwhile cultivars: 'Miss Willmott' is a good clean white; 'Fama' has large lavender flowers on 18" stems. Dove scabious (*S. columbaria*) has smaller flowers on 12"–18" stems; 'Butterfly Blue' and 'Pink Mist' are long-blooming.

USES: Pincushion flower makes a superb cut flower and is equally at home assorting with late-summer flowers or shrubs. Try it behind 'Crimson Pygmy' barberry.

Solidago 'Goldenmosa'
Asteraceae (Composite family)
GOLDENROD

PLANT TYPE: *Perennial*
ZONES: *3–9*
HABIT: *2½'–3' tall, over clumps about 2' across*
CULTURE: *Full sun to light shade; average, well-drained soil*
BLOOM: *Mid summer to fall*

Although goldenrods are native to North America, or perhaps because they are considered wildflowers, they have not attained the level of popularity as garden plants here that they have in Europe. Many hybrid cultivars are on the market today, all with substantial branched clusters of tiny flowerheads, each surrounded by a single row of yellow ray flowers. The rough foliage makes an attractive foil. Contrary to popular belief, goldenrod does not cause hayfever; however, it often grows in areas with ragweed, a highly allergenic plant. 'Goldenmosa' is a readily available cultivar.

CULTIVATION: Plant in spring or fall. Fertilize lightly in spring where soil is poor, and water during prolonged periods of dry weather. Deadhead to encourage further bloom. Staking should be necessary only for tall cultivars or where soil is overly rich. Thin young shoots in spring to improve air movement and discourage mildew; spray with a natural fungicide if necessary. In cold regions, protect new plantings with a winter mulch. Divide in spring or early fall; the cultivars must be propagated vegetatively.

RELATED PLANTS: Other fine cultivars include 'Peter Pan,' 2½' tall, which blooms late with canary-yellow flowers, and 'Cloth of Gold,' 1½' tall, with dense, deep yellow flowerheads. Recently introduced *S. spathulata* 'Golden Fleece' makes a fine ground-cover plant; late-blooming *S. rugosa* 'Fireworks' has long narrow fingers of brilliant yellow flowerheads.

USES: Excellent in sunny flower beds and borders; particularly handsome with the flat yellow heads of achillea, and with assorted asters. Attractive to bees and butterflies, goldenrod species are effective in wild and native plant gardens. A good cut flower.

Stachys byzantina
Lamiaceae (Mint family)
LAMB'S EARS

PLANT TYPE: *Perennial*
ZONES: *4–9*
HABIT: *1'–1½' tall, over mats about 1' across*
CULTURE: *Full sun; average to lean, well-drained soil*
BLOOM: *Late spring to summer*

From southwestern Asia, lamb's ears are prized for the low-growing mats of soft, furry gray leaves. These are oblong or rounded, densely covered with hairs. The leafy spikes of small purplish-pink to magenta flowers are of secondary importance; many authorities suggest removing them as they develop.

CULTIVATION: Plant in spring or early fall. Lamb's ears "melt out" in the humid summers of many southern climates, as well as where soil is overly rich and drainage is poor, or during wet summers; botrytis and other fungal infections may occur under these circumstances. Established clumps are short-lived and should be invigorated by routine division every few years in the spring.

RELATED PLANTS: 'Silver Carpet' is a nonflowering cultivar. 'Helene von Stein' (big ears) tolerates heat better; its fuzzy leaves may reach 4"–6" in length. *S. macrantha* (big betony) is grown for its spikes of purplish-pink flowers above a lush mound of green, toothed foliage.

USES: This is a cooling edging plant along the front of sunny beds and borders, and beside paths or walkways.

Stokesia laevis 'Blue Danube'
Asteraceae (Composite family)
STOKES' ASTER

PLANT TYPE: *Perennial*
ZONES: *5–9*
HABIT: *12"–15" tall, over clumps about 1½' across*
CULTURE: *Full sun to light shade; very well drained soil*
BLOOM: *Summer to early fall*

Native to the southeastern U.S., Stokes' aster is so showy, it is seldom recognized as a wildflower. Its lance-shaped, coarse narrow leaves are evergreen in the South, deciduous in colder regions. The large terminal flowerheads, to 3"–4" across, bloom in shades of lavender, blue, pink, or white and may reach 2' tall. The diminutive 'Blue Danube' blooms early with deep lavender-blue flowers.

CULTIVATION: Plant in spring, or in early fall in warm climates. Fertilize lightly in spring. Established plants tolerate drought well, but abhor wet feet. Protect with a winter mulch in cold areas. The stems naturally spread along the ground; staking is unnecessary. Deadhead to prolong blooming; cut back for a second flush. Propagate the cultivars by division or from root cuttings in spring; seed-grown plants are not true to name.

RELATED PLANTS: Other fine cultivars include 'Alba' and 'Silver Moon,' both of which have white flowers; 'Klaus Jelitto' has blue flowers until the frost, on 18" stems.

USES: Good toward the front of perennial or mixed beds and borders, and for cutting. Plant 'Blue Danube' in front of *Artemisia* 'Powis Castle' for a silvery effect.

Thalictrum delavayi

Ranunculaceae (Buttercup family)

MEADOW RUE

PLANT TYPE: *Perennial*
ZONES: *5–9*
HABIT: *4'–5' tall, over clumps 2'–3' across*
CULTURE: *Partial shade; moist, highly organic soil*
BLOOM: *Mid to late summer*

This meadow rue, from western China, is one of the best for warm climates. The ferny green leaves are divided and lobed, forming a mass of foliage below the slender flower stems. The airy panicles of lilac flowers are showy despite their lacking petals; purple petal-like sepals and short stamens produce a delicate, airy effect.

CULTIVATION: Plant in spring or early fall. Fertilize lightly in spring and apply a summer mulch to retain moisture. Water deeply in dry weather. Staking is usually necessary; deadhead spent flowers. Propagate by division in spring, or start from seed.

RELATED PLANTS: 'Hewitt's Double' is a superior cultivar with double lavender flowers in mid summer; 'Album' is white-flowered. Columbine meadow rue (*T. aquilegifolium*) blooms in late spring, with light purplish-pink flowers on 2'–3' stems; dusty meadow rue (*T. flavum* ssp. *glaucum*) has yellow flowers in summer above blue-green leaves.

USES: Meadow rues add vertical impact to perennial and mixed borders. They make fine cut flowers. Contrast purple-flowered species with vibrant orange lilies.

Thermopsis villosa (syn. *T. caroliniana*)

Fabaceae (Pea family)

CAROLINA LUPINE; CAROLINA THERMOPSIS

PLANT TYPE: *Perennial*
ZONES: *3–9*
HABIT: *3'–5' tall; clumps 2'–4' across*
CULTURE: *Full sun to partial shade; deep, highly organic soil*
BLOOM: *Spring to early summer*

Carolina lupine grows wild in the southeastern part of the U.S. Erect, unbranched stems, well-clothed with bluish or gray-green fingered leaves, silky beneath, carry spikes of canary-yellow pea flowers along their upper 6"–12".

CULTIVATION: Plant container-grown plants in spring or early fall; disturb the plants as little as possible when planting as the deep taproot resents disturbance. Drought-tolerant when established. Staking may be necessary in light shade. Deadhead after blooming; cut back foliage when it becomes shabby in hot weather. Seldom bothered by pests. Propagate by

sowing seed in pots in spring; germination is hastened by scarification—file or gently nick seed coats to facilitate the uptake of water.

RELATED PLANTS: Golden banner (*T. rhombifolia, T. montana*) blooms a little earlier, with flowers on branched stems.

USES: Plant Carolina lupine in flower beds and borders for vertical effect in early summer. Attractive with brilliant blue *Anchusa azurea* 'Loddon Royalist.'

Tiarella wherryi

Saxifragaceae (Saxifrage family)

WHERRY'S FOAMFLOWER

PLANT TYPE: *Perennial*
ZONES: *3–9*
HABIT: *12"–15" tall, over clumps 1'–1½' across*
CULTURE: *Partial shade; moist, highly organic soil*
BLOOM: *Early summer*

Wherry's foamflower, native to the southeastern U.S., grows in moist wooded areas. It forms clumps of dark green, toothed leaves to 3½" across, which are sharply lobed; they often display red fall color. Slender spikes of tiny white or pinkish flowers rise well above the foliage.

CULTIVATION: Plant in spring. Apply a summer mulch to retain moisture; water deeply during dry weather. Seldom bothered by pests and diseases. Increase by division or start from seed.

RELATED PLANTS: Better known is Allegheny foamflower (*T. cordifolia*), which is very similar, but spreads by slender rooting stems.

USES: Wherry's foamflower is a superior woodland plant where clump-forming plants are needed. Excellent in combination with ferns, hostas, and astilbes. Allegheny foamflower makes a good ground cover for shade.

Trachelium caeruleum
Campanulaceae (Bellflower family)
THROATWORT

PLANT TYPE: *Perennial*
ZONES: *8–10*
HABIT: *2'–3' tall; 1'–1½' across*
CULTURE: *Full sun to partial shade; sweet, moist, well-drained soil*
BLOOM: *Summer*

Native to southern Europe, throatwort is usually grown as an annual or biennial in cold regions. This is a good container plant. Its flat-topped, dense but lacy branching heads of lavender or pale blue flowers may reach 4"–6" across. The individual flowers are only ¼" long. The 3" oval leaves are pointed and sharply toothed.

CULTIVATION: Plant in spring, or in mild climates in fall. Pinch young plants for bushiness. Keep well-watered throughout the season, and mulch in summer. Deadhead routinely for long bloom. Fertilize regularly if in containers. Propagate from summer cuttings; or sow seed in early summer to bloom the following year, or in late winter or very early spring for display the same season.

RELATED PLANTS: 'Purple Umbrella' is a purple-flowered cultivar. 'White Veil' has white flowers.

USES: Excellent for containers, or in perennial or mixed borders. A good cut flower. Attractive with yellow Marguerites and other lemon daisies.

Verbena canadensis 'Homestead Purple'
Verbenaceae (Vervain family)
CLUMP VERBENA

PLANT TYPE: *Perennial*
ZONES: *6–9*
HABIT: *3"–4" tall; mats about 15" across*
CULTURE: *Full sun to light shade; average to poor soil*
BLOOM: *Late spring through fall*

Although listed as a cultivar of North American *V. canadensis*, 'Homestead Purple' may indeed be a natural hybrid. It was discovered in Georgia and named by Drs. Dirr and Armitage. Its brilliant purple ¾" flowers cluster on sprawling stems, and bloom almost all season long. The stems root along their length, forming a wide mat. The dark green hairy leaves contrast well with the eye-popping floral display.

CULTIVATION: Plant in spring or early fall. Drought-tolerant when established; water only during prolonged drought. Deadhead to encourage further bloom. Pests and diseases are seldom a problem. Propagate from cuttings, or sever and replant rooted stems.

RELATED PLANTS: The species *V. canadensis* lacks the vigor of 'Homestead Purple.' South

American *V. bonariensis* has small clusters of lilac flowers atop 4' stems. Hardy only in warm regions, it self-seeds with abandon and behaves as a perennial elsewhere. The tender garden verbenas (*V.* × *hybrida*) come in various colors and are treated mostly as annuals.

USES: 'Homestead Purple' is excellent as a ground cover in hot gardens, and is useful tumbling over walls or the sides of containers. Use purple-leaved foliage plants such as sweet potato 'Blackie' or purple heart as a foil. Use *V. bonariensis* as a "scrim," or see-through plant, with bolder plants behind.

Veronica austriaca ssp. *teucrium* 'Crater Lake Blue'

Scrophulariaceae (Figwort family)

SPEEDWELL

PLANT TYPE: *Perennial*
ZONES: *3–9*
HABIT: *12"–18" tall; 12"–15" wide*
CULTURE: *Full sun to light shade; average, well-drained soil*
BLOOM: *Late spring through summer*

Among the speedwells, which are native to northern temperate regions of the world, 'Crater Lake Blue' is one of the best. It has loose clusters of flowers ½" wide along the stems and at the apex. These are a brilliant gentian-blue and contrast well with the 1½" dark green, germander-like leaves.

CULTIVATION: Plant in spring or early fall. Water only during severe droughts. Deadhead routinely for extended bloom. Where soil is overly rich or moist, the plants may become floppy and require light staking. They are seldom bothered by pests or diseases. Propagate by division.

RELATED PLANTS: Woolly speedwell (*V. incana*) has silvery leaves. 'Barcarolle,' 15" tall, and 'Minuet,' 10"–15" tall, are pink-flowered cultivars. *V. spicata* 'Icicle,' 18"–24" tall, has erect, dense terminal spikes of pure white flowers; *V. longifolia* 'Foerster's Blue,' 18" tall, has long dense spikes of intense dark blue flowers. *V. gentianoides,* 10" tall, has ice-blue flowers in spring.

USES: 'Crater Lake Blue' is ideal in rock gardens and at the front of mixed or perennial borders. Try it with deep pink thrifts.

Yucca filamentosa 'Variegata'

Agavaceae (Agave family)

VARIEGATED ADAM'S NEEDLE

PLANT TYPE: *Perennial*
ZONES: *4–10*
HABIT: *4'–6' tall; clumps 2'–3' across*
CULTURE: *Full sun; average, well-drained soil*
BLOOM: *Mid to late summer*

This native evergreen rosette-former, from the southeastern U.S., provides an architectural

quality that is difficult to duplicate. The gray-green leaves, 1" wide, are tipped with spines and may reach 2½' long. Strong, curling threads edge each leaf. Magnificent large panicles of 2" creamy-white bell-shaped flowers are a summer bonus. The leaves of 'Variegata' are striped with cream.

CULTIVATION: Plant in spring or fall. Drought-tolerant when established. Propagate by severing small plants, called offsets, from the base, or by taking root cuttings. Seed will not come true to name.

RELATED PLANTS: Other cultivars include 'Bright Edge,' with cream margined leaves, and 'Golden Sword,' with yellow along its edges. *Y. glauca* (soapweed, or Great Plains yucca) has grayish leaves only ¼" across.

USES: *Y. filamentosa* is valuable as a bold foliage accent or specimen plant, in mixed beds and borders, to punctuate the ends of walkways and paths, or in containers. Mass as an evergreen hedge or barrier. A fine companion for daylilies, tall *Hylotelephium* species, and rudbeckias. The tough roots control soil erosion.

ROSES

Ever since the Greek poet Sappho declared the rose Queen of Flowers in the 6th century B.C., this most exciting of plants has been cherished for its beauty and perfume. Romans grew *Rosa bifera* (the Twice-Blooming Rose of Paestum) to embellish their banquets. In the Middle Ages, *Rosa alba semi-plena* (our White Rose of York), which had been dedicated to the classic goddess Venus, was rededicated to the Virgin Mary. And Napoléon's wife Joséphine set the standard in Imperial France by collecting every rose she could get her hands on for her gardens at the Château de Malmaison.

The Chinese have been growing roses for almost as long as their recorded history. 'Old Blush,' the first of the China and tea roses to reach Europe (around the turn of the 19th century), quite literally transformed rose growing. European roses, for the most part, bloomed only once a year in spring or early summer. But with the introduction of 'Old Blush' and other Asian roses, it became possible to breed roses that would bloom from spring until the killing frosts of winter. No other flowering shrub delivers as continuous a display of flower and scent through as extended a season as the rose.

Whether you are a connoisseur or a novice rose grower, the requirements of roses are few. They prefer a full day of sun but will grow and flower with only four to six hours' worth. They need regular watering and applications of fertilizer. They are also easygoing where soil is concerned; if it drains well and has adequate amounts of organic material, roses will be happy. Pruning, once learned, is a simple way to maintain the health and look of your plants throughout the year. Many roses have a natural resistance to disease, so seek these out and make your job easier.

Roses have traditionally been segregated from other plant groups in the garden, but many gardeners are rediscovering the rose as an integral garden contributor. There are even roses that can tolerate shady spots. So experiment. Add shrub roses to any border areas you may have. Try mixing herbs and perennials underneath and around your roses—the companion plants will cover the lower canes of the more spindly bushes, and also provide color and interest during the roses' off-season. Plant roses in groups of two or three for color impact in a particular spot. You'll be amazed with the results. If you have a small patio or balcony, try some of the smaller roses in pots; they'll be very content. Some roses are lovely trailing over hanging pots. The possibilities are virtually endless.

So many types of roses have been developed through the ages that their individual classifications might be a little confusing. The old roses known as gallica, damask, alba, and moss are, for the most part, once-blooming and were all developed and made popular before 1900. Bourbon, Portland, China, polyantha, rugosa, and Noisette roses are also old roses, but for the most part these classes repeat-bloom, often throughout the season. The other group of old roses, called species roses, were discovered growing wild and brought into cultivation because of their garden worthiness. Many of the old roses are excellent garden shrubs, blending into the landscape and providing interesting, disease-resistant foliage and unusual flower colors and forms.

English roses are modern hybrids that combine the grace and fragrance of the old roses with the power of modern repeat-bloomers. Modern hybrid teas and floribundas have not been included in this guide. A great deal has already been written about them, and in many cases the old roses have such superior disease-resistance and fragrance, and they make such outstanding garden shrubs, that there is just no comparison. Furthermore, the sheer number of old garden roses, plus their variety of form—from dainty single flowers to huge cabbage roses—just adds to their appeal.

Keep in mind that all of this nomenclature is used merely to help classify similarly growing roses into easily identifiable groups.

Of all roses, only the species can be raised true to form from seed; all other roses must be propagated by asexual methods. There is some disagreement among rose growers about whether it's better to grow "own-root" or "grafted" roses. Both are asexual systems of propagation; in both, small pieces of a mother plant are used to grow identical reproductions of the original. In own-root production, small stems of the mother plant are rooted, producing a plant in which all parts—roots, stems, and flowers—are from the original plant. Grafting is a system that takes even smaller pieces of the mother plant and combines them with a selected rootstock, producing a combination of separate rootstock and cultivar.

Grafting permits commercial growers to produce large numbers of the same cultivar much faster. In colder areas of the country, own-root plants might be a bit hardier because even if the tops should freeze and die, the protected roots are able to develop new canes from the roots.

Roses come in such a varied palette of color, shape, growth habit, disease-resistance, and fragrance that you'll definitely need to give yourself time to choose cultivars that will best suit *your* needs. Check out neighborhood gardens, shop the local garden centers, and visit public gardens to take note of the most happy and healthy plants grown in your area. Learn to pick cultivars from the classes that most interest you, give them tender loving care, and rest assured they will reward you handsomely.

There are roses for every garden and every gardener, so don't let unfamiliarity deter you from growing these fascinating plants. Roses will respond to simple, sound gardening practices by producing fragrant, colorful blossoms for your home and garden.

For convenience' sake and by tradition, hybrid roses are listed alphabetically by cultivar name. Species roses are grouped under the genus *Rosa*.

'Abraham Darby'

**Rosaceae
(Rose family)**

ROSE 'ABRAHAM DARBY'

PLANT TYPE: *English (shrub rose)*
ZONES: *5–9*
HABIT: *To 6' tall (10' trained as a climber);
to 6' wide*
CULTURE: *Full sun to partial shade; rich, well-drained soil*
BLOOM: *Continuous, spring to fall*

The exquisite shape of its fully open blossom plus its charming sweet perfume combine to make 'Abraham Darby' one of the most popular introductions in the English rose class since its unveiling in 1986. Large, globular yellow buds open to strongly scented blooms that can be as much as 5" across. The blossoms are a rich swirl of peachy-pink and apricot, with yellow and cream base tones. The shiny dark green foliage has strong natural resistance to disease.

CULTIVATION: Plant bareroot roses in spring once the danger of frost is over, or container-grown roses at any time. Prepare a 2' × 2' planting hole with plenty of compost/planting mix. Remove dead flowers to encourage rebloom. Fertilize on a regular schedule, and prune in spring. Like many yellow- and apricot-colored roses, 'Abraham Darby' will need winter protection in the coldest zones.

RELATED PLANTS: Other fragrant apricot-colored English roses include 'Cressida,' which will grow up to 6'; 'Tamora,' which grows up to around 3', with exceptionally fragrant flowers on the orange side of apricot; and 'Ambridge Rose,' also low-growing, with peachy-pink-apricot blooms.

USES: An excellent cut flower; cut when the buds are about half open. Train over a low wall or fence, or use 'Abraham Darby' espaliered on a trellis. Plant daylilies in bronze and yellow shades to cover up the lower, leafless stems of the rose. Try training a purple *Clematis × jackmanii* or pink 'Nelly Moser' clematis into a climbing 'Abraham Darby'; the contrast of colors is spectacular. This is one of those roses that can be grown as a medium to tall shrub or, if trained onto a support, can be used as a climbing rose to 8'–10'.

'Autumn Damask'

Rosaceae (Rose family)

ROSE 'AUTUMN DAMASK'

PLANT TYPE: *Damask (old garden rose)*
ZONES: *4–9*
HABIT: *To 5' tall*
CULTURE: *Full sun; rich, well-composted soil*
BLOOM: *Spring to early summer, with a scattering of bloom into fall*

Want to plant a little piece of history? This is truly one of the most ancient roses still growing in gardens today. One indica-tion of just how long this rose has been in cultivation is the various names it goes by: The Roman writer Virgil called it the Twice-Blooming Rose of Paestum; it is also known as *R. damascena semperflorens, R. damascena bifera,* Rose of Castile, and Quatre Saisons. Clusters of ruffled, double, clear pink, astonishingly perfumed flowers adorn the 5' shrub. The canes are covered with a multitude of needle-like prickles, and the gray-green foliage has good resistance to disease. 'Autumn Damask' can be a bit reluctant to rebloom in areas with short, cool summers, but in the warm South and Southwest, it will provide 3 or 4 flowering cycles a season.

CULTIVATION: A light pruning in early spring is recommended. Damask roses seem not to like hard pruning, so it is necessary to deadhead regularly to prevent dieback of the main canes.

RELATED PLANTS: 'Summer Damask' is identical, except it blooms only once, in early summer. The Portland roses are direct descendants; try 'Comte de Chambord,' also pink, and 'Rose du Roi,' which is low-growing with red flowers.

USES: This is a rose for those who simply must have an old rose but can't give up precious garden space to once-blooming shrubs. Plant in groups of 2 or 3 so the canes intertwine and spill out over a garden path, or plant as a hedge to frame a garden room. The silvery-gray foliage and lilac flowers of lavender contrast with the old-rose charms of this cultivar.

'Belle Poitevine'

Rosaceae (Rose family)

ROSE 'BELLE POITEVINE'

PLANT TYPE: *Hybrid rugosa (old garden rose)*
ZONES: *3–9*
HABIT: *To 6' tall*
CULTURE: *Full sun to partial shade; tolerates poor soil*
BLOOM: *Recurrent, spring to fall*

Exquisite perfume, repeat bloom, extreme cold-hardiness, and strong resistance to disease are hallmarks of the rugosa roses, which are native to northern China, Korea, and Japan, and are often found growing on coastal sand dunes. Most rugosas have flowers in pink, purple, white, or red. Rugosas grown in hot inland gardens will not quite reach the heights they do in cool and coastal gardens. 'Belle Poitevine,' introduced in 1894, has 4" semi-double, sweetly fragrant flowers, bright rosy-pink to pinky-purple. The foliage is dark green and nicely wrinkled, with attractive autumn tones in the fall, and the shrub produces a fine supply of dark red hips that extend the season of this rose into winter. Rugosas are very sturdy plants, tolerating harsh winter gales and coming back year after year to grace the fortunate garden with their flower and fragrance.

CULTIVATION: Rugosas planted as own-root cuttings will colonize a large area; if space is a problem, make sure to select grafted plants. Good, well-drained soil, sun, and regular applications of water and fertilizer are about all this hardy rose needs. It will even tolerate light shade and still bloom. Unlike most other rugosa roses, it can have a problem with rust.

RELATED PLANTS: Other garden-worthy rugosas: 'Roseraie de l'Haÿ' has red-purple flowers; 'Frau Dagmar Hartopp' has silvery-pink flowers; *R. rugosa alba* has single white flowers; *R. rugosa rubra* has single red blooms. All will survive the coldest winters, repeat bloom, and provide a generous crop of brightly colored hips.

USES: Rugosas are best planted en masse as low to tall hedges, or in garden areas that are difficult to tend, as these roses require little attention. Plant 'Belle Poitevine' with white-flowered veronicas and multi-colored lupines for a low-maintenance area.

'Blanc Double de Coubert'
Rosaceae (Rose family)
ROSE 'BLANC DOUBLE DE COUBERT'

PLANT TYPE: *Hybrid rugosa (old garden rose)*
ZONES: *3–9*
HABIT: *To 6' tall*
CULTURE: *Full sun to partial shade; well-drained soil*
BLOOM: *Continuous, spring to fall*

Though 'Blanc Double de Coubert' recently celebrated its 100th birthday, it is still one of the most popular rugosa roses. This group of roses is named for its rugose, or wrinkled, foliage. Bright green leaves provide a strong background for powerfully fragrant, barely double white flowers, which open from exquisite white buds throughout the growing season. All rugosa roses are covered with large, needle-like prickles. 'Blanc Double de Coubert' has good fall color yet rarely sets large red hips.

CULTIVATION: This shrub will tolerate partial shade and poor soil; it is another extremely hardy cultivar for planting in areas where it's difficult to protect less hardy roses.

RELATED PLANTS: Other rugosa hybrids worth growing: 'Schnez-werg,' with semi-double white flowers; 'F. J. Grootendorst,' with small, double crimson blooms; 'Rose à Parfum de l'Haÿ,' with intensely fragrant red flowers; 'Scabrosa,' with single-petaled cerise flowers.

USES: Rugosas make excellent hedges with their dense growth, rough, dark green foliage, and canes festooned with vicious prickles that will deter unwanted intrusions. Plant white-flowering roses where night lighting will cause the flowers to brighten up the dark corners of a garden setting. Clumps of rosy-pink echi-nacea and tall, spiky, dark blue delphiniums will create a garden picture when contrasted with the white flowers and green foliage of this cultivar.

'Cardinal de Richelieu'
Rosaceae (Rose family)
ROSE 'CARDINAL DE RICHELIEU'

PLANT TYPE: *Gallica (old garden rose)*
ZONES: *4–9*
HABIT: *To 4' tall*
CULTURE: *Full sun; rich, well-drained soil*
BLOOM: *Once-blooming, spring to early summer*

One of the most popular of the old garden roses, this gallica hybrid, introduced in 1840, is justly famous for the unusual shade of its velvety dark purple flowers. Richly scented, the flowers are presented in clusters. The hardy shrub is dense with almost no prickles, and the smooth, shiny, dark green foliage, sometimes edged with red, has good resistance to disease. Not everyone wants to give up precious garden space to once-blooming roses, but gallicas are extremely hardy and have good resistance to diseases and pests. These lovely, unde-manding plants will charm the socks off the most blasé gardener, so don't ignore this group.

CULTIVATION: Select grafted plants if space is a problem because gallica roses spread to quite large dimensions if allowed to run around on their own roots. The spring-flowering roses are best pruned in early summer, after they finish flowering, unlike repeat-blooming roses, which are pruned in early spring before the new growth starts.

RELATED PLANTS: Other gallica roses to try: 'Charles de Mills' has deep red and purple blooms; 'Belle de Crécy' has extremely fragrant flowers in a blend of pink, purple, and gray; 'Camaieux' has striped lavender-pink and purple blooms; and 'Tuscany' has deep rich, dark red flowers.

USES: Plant where the dark smoky-purple flowers can be shown off to their best advantage, trained over a white wall or planted with white flowers for contrast. To extend the bloom into the summer, try planting this unusual rose with white-flowered bleeding heart and apricot foxglove.

'Cécile Brunner, Climbing'
Rosaceae (Rose family)
ROSE 'CLIMBING CÉCILE BRUNNER'

PLANT TYPE: *Climbing polyantha (old garden rose)*
ZONES: *7–9*
HABIT: *To 20' tall; to 20' wide*
CULTURE: *Full sun; rich, well-drained soil*
BLOOM: *Spring and fall, intermittently in summer*

Our grandmother's Sweetheart Rose, the bush form of this charming rose was hybridized in France in 1881 and was originally named 'Mlle. Cécile Brunner.' Most English

speakers pronounce the name *SEE-sil,* as though it were a man's name, but it actually remembers the young daughter of a well-known French nursery family. This vigorous climbing sport appeared in a California nursery in 1894 and has maintained a place in the hearts of gardeners ever since. Elegant, classically pointed buds produce clusters of small, hybrid-tea-shaped, double silvery-pink flowers with a strong, sweet tea-rose fragrance that has a rich, spicy-peppery undertone. This climbing rose has long been in commerce, and some of the plants sold will not rebloom as well as others. To make sure your selection will rebloom, it's best to check to see if the clone repeats in the nursery before buying.

CULTIVATION: 'Cl. Cécile Brunner' will tolerate most soils and conditions and even some drought, but like most climbing roses, it is tender in the coldest zones. Where climbing roses are marginal, try planting on a protected south- or west-facing wall where the plant will benefit from the heat radiated at night by the structure. Climbing roses need space and support for the amazing amount of flowers they produce.

RELATED PLANTS: If there isn't room for the climber, plant the bush form of 'Cécile Brunner'; the flowers are identical and the robust bush will grow to over 3', flowering continuously.

USES: Cut flower clusters and put them in small crystal vases to decorate the dining table. This tall, energetic climber can be planted to grow up into trees or used to cover an unsightly building or garage. Plant lavender and hollyhock around the base of the rose to cover the lower canes.

'Comte de Chambord'
Rosaceae (Rose family)
ROSE 'COMTE DE CHAMBORD'

PLANT TYPE: *Portland (old garden rose)*
ZONES: *4–9*
HABIT: *To 3' tall; to 2' wide*
CULTURE: *Full sun; rich, well-drained soil*
BLOOM: *Continuous, spring to fall*

Not many of these marvelous Portland roses were ever introduced, but they were very influential in the development of other rose classes, contributing a deep crimson-red color, cold-hardiness, and repeat bloom to their modern progeny. 'Comte de Chambord' is a compact, low-growing shrub that produces full, flat, wonderfully fragrant, glowing pink flowers with a charming, quartered, old rose shape. Large gray-green, naturally disease-resistant foliage provides the perfect background for the flowers.

CULTIVATION: Deadhead this rose regularly to encourage repeat bloom. A good organic mulch applied 3"–4" deep around the plant will both prevent weeds and help conserve precious water.

RELATED PLANTS: Other Portland roses to plant: 'Blanc de Vibert' grows somewhat taller and has white flowers with strong fragrance; 'Portland Rose' is low-growing with red flowers; the tall 'Yolande d'Aragon' has fragrant, bright pink flowers.

USES: A good cutting rose. Plant 2 or 3 in a cluster to maximize flower production and fragrance. Plant as a hedge where the continuous bloom and strong fragrance will be most appreciated. Plant feathery gypsophila and tall bearded iris with 'Comte de Chambord' to create a cozy cottage-garden look.

'Crested Moss'
Rosaceae (Rose family)
ROSE 'CRESTED MOSS'

PLANT TYPE: *Moss (old garden rose)*
ZONES: *4–9*
HABIT: *To 6' tall; to 5' wide*
CULTURE: *Full sun; rich, well-drained soil*
BLOOM: *Once-flowering, spring to early summer*

Discovered in 1827, growing over a convent wall near Fribourg in western Switzerland, this rose is officially a centifolia; but as 'Crested Moss' it has mossy growth on the sepals and is here

grouped with the moss roses. Whether called *R. centifolia cristata,* Chapeau de Napoléon, or just Cristata, the fully double, richly fragrant, strong deep pink blooms are large and cabbage-like. The mossy growth has the unique fragrance of pine or balsam, which comes away pleasantly on your hand when touched. The vast, arching canes are blanketed with light green foliage.

CULTIVATION: Like all once-blooming roses, 'Crested Moss' is best pruned just after flowering in early summer. Centifolia and moss roses have good cold-hardiness, but because the canes are very densely clothed in prickles, it is recommended if not absolutely necessary to provide protection from disease, especially powdery mildew. Grow in full sun, allow for adequate air circulation, and keep foliage as dry as possible by avoiding overhead watering.

RELATED PLANTS: Other moss roses worth growing: 'Nuits de Young,' with fragrant, double, dark red-purple flowers; 'Common Moss,' with beautiful cabbage-shaped, nicely scented clear pink blooms. There are a few repeat-blooming moss roses.

Among the best are 'Alfred de Dalmas,' a low-growing pink cultivar with lightly perfumed blossoms, and the extremely aromatic 'Salet,' which has double, bright pink flowers.

USES: The taller-growing moss roses can be trained onto a tripod or pegged to keep them under control. To peg a rose, take the long, supple canes and bend them over, attaching them to the ground with wire pegs. This will encourage more flower production all along the horizontal canes. Extend the blooming season by interplanting with long-flowering perennials such as tall phlox and daylilies.

'Duplex'
Rosaceae
(Rose family)
ROSE 'DUPLEX';
WOLLEY-DOD'S ROSE

PLANT TYPE: *Species hybrid (old garden rose)*
ZONES: *4–9*
HABIT: *To 5' tall; to 4' wide*
CULTURE: *Full sun; rich, well-drained soil*
BLOOM: *Once-flowering, spring to early summer*

This lovely rose is a chance hybrid between *R. pomifera* (Apple Rose) and an unrecorded garden rose, which happened around the turn of the century in the garden of the Rev. Wolley-Dod in Cheshire, England. Similar in most respects to the species parent, it's a bit shorter and produces somewhat smaller, prickly scarlet-red hips. Semi-double, soft clear pink flowers open to expose bright yellow stamens. Downy gray-green foliage and prickly canes give a woodland look. You will sometimes find this rose sold as *R. villosa duplex* or *R. pomifera duplex.*

ROSES

CULTIVATION: 'Duplex' will tolerate poor soil and some shade, conditions that would cause many other roses to curl up their roots and die. If conditions are right and cultivation is at its best, this rose will sometimes flower intermittently throughout the year. Try a good, deep organic mulch, and feed and water on a regular schedule.

RELATED PLANTS: *R. pomifera* is very similar to 'Duplex' but grows a bit taller with apple-scented foliage. *R. glauca* has small, ornamental gray-to-purplish foliage with small, star-shaped pink flowers; flower arrangers grow it for the unique color of the foliage.

USES: The downy gray foliage and red hips are attractive and blend well with other shrubs in the garden. To extend the flowering season and for a charming woodland effect, plant 'Duplex' with the dazzling spikes of red- or white-flowering astilbe and the blue bell-shaped flowers of tall-growing campanulas.

'Félicité Parmentier'
Rosaceae (Rose family)
ROSE 'FÉLICITÉ PARMENTIER'

PLANT TYPE: *Alba (old garden rose)*
ZONES: *3–9*
HABIT: *To 4' tall; to 3' wide*
CULTURE: *Full sun to partial shade; rich, well-drained soil*
BLOOM: *Once-blooming, spring to early summer*

A true and greatly beloved gem introduced in 1834, 'Félicité Parmentier' still has a heady perfume that can romance even the most jaded gardener. Her flowers are of the most exquisite old-rose shape, opening from yellowish buds to shell-pink blooms that pale to white on the outer edges. The shrub is compact, somewhat shorter-growing than most other albas, with gray-green foliage that makes a perfect foil for the fully reflexed blossoms. The canes are veiled in prickles of varying design.

CULTIVATION: Prune right after the plant finishes flowering in early summer. Remove deadwood and shorten canes only slightly. Mulch well and make sure the shrub has an adequate supply of water during dry spells. Albas grow and prosper with less direct sun than many other roses.

RELATED PLANTS: *R. alba semiplena* (the White Rose of York), a very ancient rose, has white, semidouble, fragrant flowers. The gray-green shrub, growing to 6' or more, will tolerate less sun than many other roses. 'Chloris' (Rosée du Matin) is an almost thornless alba growing to 6'; the fragrant flowers are a soft clear pink.

USES: Albas make great freestanding flowering shrubs for the back of the border, or hedges to wall in a garden room. The lovely alba family can usually help tuck something pretty and hardy into a garden corner that's hard to fill. To extend the flowering season into summer, try planting 'Félicité Parmentier' with spiky foxglove and bleeding heart, or underplant it with low-growing, clove-scented dianthus.

'Frau Dagmar Hartopp'
Rosaceae (Rose family)
ROSE 'FRAU DAGMAR HARTOPP'

PLANT TYPE: *Hybrid rugosa (old garden rose)*
ZONES: *3–9*
HABIT: *To 3' tall; to 4' wide*
CULTURE: *Full sun to partial shade; well-drained soil*
BLOOM: *Continuous, spring to fall*

A Danish introduction from 1914, 'Frau Dagmar Hartopp' is variously listed as 'Fru Dagmar Hastrup' and 'Frau Dagmar Hastrup.' The plant is lower-growing and wider-spreading than some of the other rugosas. Crinkled, rich vivid green leaves enshroud the plant and provide a setting on which the single, fragrant silvery-pink flowers are displayed. The plant continues to flower even after it has set its large tomato-red hips, so it isn't even necessary to deadhead this superb shrub. The fact that she flowers throughout the season *and* throws hips for fall and winter color makes her one of the most desirable of the rugosa roses.

CULTIVATION: 'Frau Dagmar Hartopp' will tolerate conditions other roses would not; poor soil and some shade will not give this rose any problem. It is also remarkably resistant to disease.

RELATED PLANTS: Other rugosa roses worth trying: 'Delicata' has fragrant lilac-pink flowers and grows to 3' tall; 'Linda Campbell,' a new hybrid with scarlet-red flowers that are hardly ever out of bloom, grows to 5' tall.

USES: Plant in groups of 2 or 3 in areas where a low ground cover is needed. A good rose for growing in pots, it will spill out over the rim, wafting its rich, somewhat sweet perfume into the patio garden. Plant with herbs like opal-leaved basil and lemon thyme for a contrast of foliage and scents.

'Gertrude Jekyll'
Rosaceae (Rose family)
ROSE 'GERTRUDE JEKYLL'

PLANT TYPE: *English (shrub rose)*
ZONES: *5–9*
HABIT: *To 5' tall and 5' wide in cold-winter areas; to 12' tall and 8' wide in mild-winter areas*
CULTURE: *Full sun; rich, well-drained soil*
BLOOM: *Repeat-blooming, spring to fall*

This is one of the great English roses. Its hybridizer, David Austin, feels that 'Gertrude Jekyll' is one of his most fragrant introductions to date; in fact, there was some talk of using this cultivar to reestablish the rose perfume industry in England. It is a tall shrub, often growing to more than 10' in a single season! Blossoms have a distinctive old-rose charm with bright pink, double, intensely fragrant blooms. The canes are extremely thorny and the dark green foliage repels disease with ease.

CULTIVATION: 'Gertrude Jekyll' can be pruned hard in spring or left on its own to grow as tall as it wants. A rose with the vigor of this one requires the best cultivation: regular applications of fertilizer and water and a good, deep, rich organic compost to keep the roots moist and cool. The lengthy,

arching canes can be pegged by bending them over and tying them back onto themselves with garden tape. Called self-pegging, this gives the plant a billowy, heart-shaped appearance. Pegging like this will also increase the production of flowers.

RELATED PLANTS: Other English roses: the very winter-hardy 'Constance Spry,' once-blooming, grows to 10' or more with bright pink, double, sweetly aromatic flowers; 'Claire Rose' is tall-growing with blush-pink to white fragrant flowers; 'Kathryn Morley' is tall with lushly scented shell-pink flowers.

USES: Train 'Gertrude Jekyll' over a tall fence or place her in the back of the garden for height and color, but make sure that some canes fall to the front so that the flowers are about nose high, inviting all to breathe in her beguiling perfume. Hide the lower canes with tall spikes of delphinium and foxglove underplanted with white snow-in-summer.

'Graham Thomas'
Rosaceae (Rose family)
ROSE 'GRAHAM THOMAS'

PLANT TYPE: *English (shrub rose)*
ZONES: *4–9*
HABIT: *To 6' tall and 6' wide in cold-winter areas; 10'–12' tall and 8' wide in mild-winter areas*
CULTURE: *Full sun to partial shade; rich, well-drained soil*
BLOOM: *Repeat-blooming, spring to fall*

Its unique, deep buttery-yellow blossoms billowing out over the heads of other roses, and its rich tea-rose scent, make 'Graham Thomas' one of the most popular of English roses. Good yellow roses are few and far between; truly great yellow roses are downright rare. This is yet another tall-growing shrub rose that can take a gardener by surprise, so be fore-warned that it can reach monumental proportions in the right climate. The flowers are deeply cupped, the outer petals reflexing back to create a petticoat-like effect of fragrant, rich buttery-yellow petals. Yellow roses often fade quickly in the intense sun of summer, but 'Graham Thomas' holds on to its marvelous color better than almost any other yellow rose. The great shrub rose 'Iceberg' is one of the parents and has passed along its tolerance of partial shade to this rose.

CULTIVATION: Yellow roses are usually less winter-hardy than other colors, so be prepared to provide protection in cold-winter zones. Pruning can be as hard as the garden and gardener need. Try arching the long, bendable canes over on themselves and tying with garden tape. This will encourage every bud eye to break and produce clusters of flowers along the horizontally held canes. Provide winter protection in the coldest zones.

RELATED PLANTS: Other yellow-flowered English roses: 'Golden Celebration' has fragrant, cupped,

deeper golden-yellow flowers, and does not grow as tall; 'Symphony,' also good for growing in pots, is lower-growing, to around 4', and its flat, full flowers are pure yellow; 'The Pilgrim' is another tall grower, to 6', and the full, flat, sweet-scented flowers are pale yellow fading to almost white.

USES: 'Graham Thomas' will make a good climber, cascading over a wall or garden arch in warmer parts of the U.S.; in other areas, plant in groups of at least 3 plants for a magnificent display. Plant a deep blue clematis in this bush and let it climb and flower with the yellow roses.

'Great Maiden's Blush'

Rosaceae (Rose family)

ROSE 'GREAT MAIDEN'S BLUSH'

PLANT TYPE: *Alba (old garden rose)*
ZONES: *4–9*
HABIT: *To 6' tall; to 6' wide*
CULTURE: *Full sun to partial shade; rich, well-drained soil*
BLOOM: *Once-blooming, spring to early summer*

If the plethora of names this rose has acquired over the centuries is any indication, 'Great Maiden's Blush,' which has been grown since before 1550, has been a very popular rose indeed. La Seduisante (The Seductress), La Virginale, and probably the most famous, Cuisse de Nymphe Émue (Thigh of the Passionate Nymph), are but a few. Among the most ancient garden roses, albas are well-represented in Renaissance paintings. A superb shrub rose, the gray-green foliage is very free of disease. The informally shaped blush-pink flowers emit the most delicate and effervescent perfume, and the tall,

arching shrub displays its flowers along the canes in a most bewitching manner. Alba roses are rock-hardy, even in the coldest zones.

CULTIVATION: Most roses don't relish shade. Usually, when a rose is listed as shade-tolerant, it will grow and flower in less sun than other roses, but produce only 50 percent of the flowers it would have produced in full sun. 'Great Maiden's Blush' can be an exception to the rule if given lots of tender loving care.

RELATED PLANTS: Other alba roses: 'Maxima' (also known as Great Double White and The Jacobite Rose), grows up to 7' with fragrant white flowers shaped much like 'Great Maiden's Blush'; 'Maiden's Blush,' or 'Small Maiden's Blush,' has all the charm of its taller namesake, but on a smaller plant.

USES: Nothing could be more impressive than a long, tall hedge of 'Great Maiden's Blush,' creating a garden room or lining a driveway. Plant silver-foliaged artemisia, spiky-flowered navy-blue delphiniums, and red-striped parrot tulips around it to recreate a Flemish painting in your garden.

'Harison's Yellow'
Rosaceae (Rose family)
ROSE 'HARISON'S YELLOW'

PLANT TYPE: *Hybrid foetida (old garden rose)*
ZONES: *3–9*
HABIT: *To 7' tall; to 7' wide*
CULTURE: *Full sun; rich, well-drained soil*
BLOOM: *Once-blooming, spring to early summer*

This rose was discovered growing in New York City, in the garden of George Harison, a lawyer who gardened on Manhattan Island back when there was still open space for farms. He gave it to a local nurseryman who propagated it and introduced it into commerce in the 1830s. There is some controversy over whether or not this is the Yellow Rose of Texas. What is not disputed is that 'Harison's Yellow' is readily propagated by rooted suckers and was widely spread across the country by our pioneer mothers. It is one of the most commonly found old garden roses and a sure indicator that there was a pioneer homesite nearby. The sulphur-yellow flowers are double and cupped; the brown canes appear wrapped with needle-like prickles.

CULTIVATION: 'Harison's Yellow' is not particular as to soil and is extremely cold-hardy. With *Rosa*

foetida as one of its ancestors, it will be necessary to protect it from blackspot in areas where that disease is a problem. Otherwise, it is a completely undemanding rose.

RELATED PLANTS: *R. foetida persiana* (Persian Yellow Rose) grows to 5' and has double yellow flowers.

USES: A good rose for a restored country garden, 'Harison's Yellow' will grow with minimum care. To naturalize in the garden fringes, combine it with perennial centranthus or red valerian.

'Mme. Alfred Carrière'
Rosaceae (Rose family)
ROSE 'MME. ALFRED CARRIÈRE'

PLANT TYPE: *Climbing Noisette (old garden rose)*
ZONES: *7–10*
HABIT: *To 12' tall; to 12' wide*
CULTURE: *Full sun to partial shade; rich, well-drained soil*
BLOOM: *Continuous, spring to fall*

Noisette roses were developed in South Carolina at the very beginning of the 19th century by a local French rice planter, John Champney, who gave seeds and plants of his new rose to his friend and fellow countryman Philippe Noisette. Noisette sent some of the first plants to his brother in Europe, and these seedlings immediately won the hearts of rose lovers. Noisettes are usually quite tender, but 'Mme. Alfred Carriere,' which was introduced in 1879, is the exception as she will tolerate a bit more cold than most others of the class. This rose makes a somewhat open-growing climber with pale blush-white, globular, extremely fragrant flowers. The sparse foliage is shiny

light green, and the rambling, curved canes have only scattered prickles. Noisettes are extremely popular in the South and other warm zones of the U.S. They are among the most prolific bloomers and have a lovely perfume.

CULTIVATION: This cultivar is rather undemanding; it will tolerate partial sun and will grow and flower with abandon. Protection from powdery mildew may be necessary in areas where the disease is a problem.

RELATED PLANTS: Other Noisettes worth growing: 'Lamarque,' which has pure white flowers that sometimes have a hint of lemon tones, grows to a whopping 15'; 'Crépuscule,' with sunset-colored orange-apricot flowers, grows to 10'; and 'Gloire de Dijon,' with buff-yellow flowers tinted pink, also grows to 15'.

USES: Plant where this lovely rose can drape itself over a wall or clamber up through a tree so the arching canes display their pale flowers backlit against the blue of the sky. It can also be grown in a large container. The globular flowers are a bit loose but

hold well if cut as a half-open bud. Plant a dwarf pink spirea and blue veronica at the base of the climber to cover up the lower canes.

'Mme. Hardy'
Rosaceae (Rose family)
ROSE 'MME. HARDY'

PLANT TYPE: *Damask (old garden rose)*
ZONES: *4–9*
HABIT: *To 5' tall; to 5' wide*
CULTURE: *Full sun; rich, well-drained soil*
BLOOM: *Once-flowering, spring to early summer*

After all these years, 'Mme. Hardy' is still one of the most elegant white roses in existence. The flowers have a haughty, almost disdainful appearance, but are quite capable of melting the most world-weary rose lover's heart. Monsieur Hardy was the curator of the Luxembourg Gardens in Paris at the turn of the 19th century. He named his rose for his wife, Félicité, in 1832, and what a way to be remembered! This once-flowering rose combines characteristics of both damask and alba roses, or possibly resulted as a chance cross with a Portland rose. Flowers of the purest white imaginable open from flesh-pink buds that are

crowned with lovely, long ornamental sepals. The blossoms cloak the plant with an absolutely heavenly perfume. The cupped blooms reflex back to fully petaled, flat flowers with a distinctive green eye at the center. This sturdy shrub is overlaid with both prickles and medium green foliage.

CULTIVATION: Not a demanding rose, but if you give her the best care, 'Mme. Hardy' will repay you with bouquet after bouquet to grace the home and garden. Prune lightly after flowering in early summer, as damask roses resent cutting into the large older canes.

RELATED PLANTS: Other white old garden roses to grow: 'Leda,' which has white flowers dipped with crimson on the tips, grows to 6'; 'Mme. Zöetmans,' white with blush-pink at the center of the flowers, grows to 4'. If you can't make yourself plant a once-blooming rose, then try the English rose 'Fair Bianca,' whose white flowers almost reproduce the elegant blooms of 'Mme. Hardy' on a shrub that flowers continuously and grows to 3'.

USES: A great cut flower. As the centerpiece of a border garden, the perfect white blooms will really glow. Mix with pyramids of blue veronica and drifts of dianthus planted to cover the lower canes.

'New Dawn'
Rosaceae (Rose family)
ROSE 'NEW DAWN'

PLANT TYPE: *Large-flowered climber*
ZONES: *4–9*
HABIT: *To 10' tall; to 8' wide*
CULTURE: *Full sun; rich, well-drained soil*
BLOOM: *Continuous, spring to fall*

This rose had the honor of receiving the very first plant patent in the United States, which was issued in 1930. A superb hardy climber, 'New Dawn' is a sport of 'Dr. W. Van Fleet,' to which it is identical in every way except that 'New Dawn' reblooms throughout the season. Fat round buds open to semi-double, pale blush-pink, fragrant flowers that are borne on single stems or in clusters of 3–5. The foliage is a shiny dark green and the very long flowering canes are sheathed in large, wicked prickles. 'New Dawn' is still one of the most widely grown climbing roses, even after all these years; it is insect- and disease-resistant, and an ideal rose for those areas of the country where most climbers are either too tender or bloom only once.

CULTIVATION: Plant from bare root in the spring and train the long canes onto a support structure. This is a rather undemanding cultivar that will grow and flower for years with a minimum of care. Prune older canes back to the bud union and tie new growth in their place. This will encourage the plant to continue to grow and flower.

RELATED PLANTS: 'Dr. W. Van Fleet' is identical but doesn't rebloom. 'Nymphenburg,' with fragrant, semi-double salmon-pink flowers, repeats and grows to 10'; once-blooming, fragrant apricot 'Alchymist' grows to 12'.

USES: Train over walls or up into dead fruit trees, where the fragrant flowers will spill out over the garden. Underplant with blue drumstick-like flowers of echinops and lavender-pink-flowered Japanese anemone, which will contrast with the glossy leaves of 'New Dawn.'

'Old Blush'
Rosaceae (Rose family)
ROSE 'OLD BLUSH'

PLANT TYPE: *China (old garden rose)*
ZONES: *7–9*
HABIT: *3'–6' tall; to 4' wide*
CULTURE: *Full sun; rich, well-drained soil*
BLOOM: *Continuous, spring to fall*

Before being brought to Europe in the middle to latter part of the 18th century, 'Old Blush' had graced Chinese gardens for centuries. One of the parents of modern roses, this and other China roses were soon used in hybridizing with existing European roses, imparting the unique ability to bloom almost continuously throughout the season. 'Old Blush,' also known as Parsons' Pink China and Common Monthly Rose, is thought to be "The Last Rose of Summer" of poem and song. Fragrant, two-toned pink, semi-double flowers are produced in loose, open clusters. The shrub is twiggy and has an upright habit with dark green foliage and few prickles. All China roses root readily from cuttings, and you can find this lovely old cultivar growing around home-steads and cemeteries all over the mild South and West. China roses have another unique characteristic; their flowers grow darker in sunlight, unlike most roses, which fade under direct sun.

CULTIVATION: China roses are on the tender side, so in their upper ranges, plant them in protected areas. They are rather undemanding as to soil types or cultivation, surviving for decades in abandoned sites. Prune lightly, removing dead-wood and cutting back the flowering tips only to new buds.

RELATED PLANTS: 'Slater's Crimson China,' another very early introduction from Asia to Europe, is the direct parent of all repeat-blooming red roses. It grows much like 'Old Blush,' except the flowers are a deep, rich crimson.

USES: China roses do very well in pots; in the coldest areas, the pots can be brought into a cool garage or basement for the winter. 'Old Blush' makes a lovely, perpetually flowering, low-growing hedge. Plant it with pale blue scabiosa and deep purple heliotrope, where the scent of the heliotrope will fool garden visitors into thinking how fragrant your roses are!

Rosa banksiae banksiae
Rosaceae (Rose family)
WHITE LADY BANKS' ROSE

PLANT TYPE: *Species (old garden rose)*
ZONES: *7–9*
HABIT: *To 20' tall; to 20' wide*
CULTURE: *Full sun; rich, well-drained soil*
BLOOM: *One long flowering in early spring, occasional rebloom in fall*

Nothing could be more spectacular than clouds of White Lady Banks' Rose in full bloom; she flowers with such wanton abandon! Although classed with species roses, this double white form is actually a garden hybrid. The true wild form is thought to be *R. banksiae normalis,* which has single (5-petaled) white flowers. Discovered in southern China and brought to Europe in the early part of the 19th century, the various forms of *R. banksiae* are tender in cold damp climates; but given a warm wall or a sunny Southern garden, no other rose can blanket itself in blooms as recklessly as she does. This cultivar has small white, double pompon-shaped flowers that are produced in large sprays all over the mature plant; individual flowers are the size and shape of popcorn. The double forms are only slightly fragrant. The foliage is dark green and shiny, and the plants are evergreen and usually thornless. If you prefer a thornless form, select thornless plants from the nursery.

CULTIVATION: Flowers are produced only on mature canes, so do not prune this rose the way you prune other climbing roses. Thin out the older canes and cut out any unnecessary growth, but leave as much growth as possible to flower.

RELATED PLANTS: *R. banksiae lutea* is the double yellow variety. *R. b. normalis* has single white flowers that have the fragrance of violets. *R. × fortuniana* is thought to be a hybrid of *R. banksiae* and *R. laevigata* and has large, fragrant, double white flowers.

USES: Allow this rose to climb up over a garage roof or cover a pergola walk. Try planting several to cascade down a bank or hillside. A pink mandevilla vine trained up into White Lady Banks' Rose will extend the flowering season through summer.

Rosa eglanteria
Rosaceae (Rose family)
EGLANTINE ROSE; SWEETBRIAR
PLANT TYPE: *Species (old garden rose)* ZONES: *4–9* HABIT: *To 12' tall; to 8' wide* CULTURE: *Full sun to partial shade; rich, well-drained soil* BLOOM: *Once-flowering, spring to early summer*

The Eglantine Rose is one of the most cherished of English wildflowers. Popping out of hedgerows and peaking over cottage garden walls, it can be seen each spring flowering all over England. The 2" pink flowers are single (5 petaled) and have a delicious fragrance, but the real secret of this rose is that the foliage is fragrant. Walk around a garden and if you smell green pippin apples, there is sure to be an Eglantine planted somewhere nearby. The fragrance is strongest on warm, humid mornings. The plant can reach 12' or more with long, vaulting canes that are practically bursting with prickles.

CULTIVATION: You can allow this sentimental favorite to grow as large as it wants, but it's best to prune back the old growth in spring to encourage new tips, which emit the strongest scent. Otherwise, it's not too demanding. In fact, you will often find it naturalized in some parts of the country.

RELATED PLANTS: The Penzance hybrids, 'Lady Penzance,' with yellow-and-copper flowers, and 'Lord Penzance,' with rose-and-yellow flowers, have small, single blooms and aromatic foliage. 'Manning's Blush' has double pale pink blooms and strongly scented foliage.

USES: Plant a hedge of Eglantine along a property line or driveway; you'll love the fragrance, and the feeling of safety you'll have that no intruder would be so foolish as to attempt a crossing anywhere near it. Plant with combinations of lady's mantle (*Alchemilla mollis*) and species primula for a woodland look.

Rosa foetida bicolor
Rosaceae (Rose family)
AUSTRIAN COPPER ROSE
PLANT TYPE: *Species hybrid (old garden rose)* ZONES: *4–9* HABIT: *6'–8' tall* CULTURE: *Full sun (light shade in the hottest zones); any well-drained soil* BLOOM: *One long flowering, spring to early summer*

Grown before 1590, this radiantly colored rose is a survivor. Austrian Copper is one of the first roses to bloom in spring and is often found on old homesites and abandoned farmsteads throughout the country. Shining yellow buds open to single (5-petaled) flowers that are incandescent orange-scarlet and intense yellow on the underside of the petals. Yellow roses were once very uncommon; this one was introduced into Europe from Asia Minor in the 16th century. All modern yellow and orange roses trace their ancestry back to the species *R. foetida* (Austrian Yellow Rose). It is very susceptible to blackspot and has passed the problem on to its modern descendants. The Latin *foetida* comes down to us in English as fetid, or "stinking." For some, the fragrance is fruitlike, but to others, it does have a slightly unpleasant scent.

CULTIVATION: This is a hardy, undemanding rose that, once established, will survive with little care. If you have room for a wide-spreading rose, plant Austrian Copper as an own-root plant and it will cover an area of 25 square feet; or plant grafted plants where space is at a premium. In areas with high humidity and summer rains, this rose will need some protection from blackspot. Prune by removing dead canes from the clump and lightly cutting back live canes.

RELATED PLANTS: Austrian Yellow and *R. hemisphaerica* (Sulphur Rose) are both yellow spring-blooming roses with all the charms and problems of Austrian Copper.

USES: A great rose for those hard-to-get-at garden areas, this vigorous and hardy shrub will grow and flower for years with a minimum of care in mild-winter areas. Group it with clumps of charming *Tulipa clusiana* (lady tulip), where the early flowering rose and the red-and-white-striped blooms of the tulip will complement each other; or mix Austrian Copper Rose with spiky blue-flowered buddleias so the tall-growing plants will intertwine, creating lovely bouquets.

Rosa hugonis
Rosaceae (Rose family)
FATHER HUGO'S ROSE

PLANT TYPE: *Species (old garden rose)*
ZONES: *5–9*
HABIT: *To 8' tall; to 5' wide*
CULTURE: *Full sun; rich, well-drained soil*
BLOOM: *Once-blooming, spring to early summer*

This species rose was brought back from China at the beginning of the 20th century and can still be found in many gardens. Known as the Golden Rose of China, it is truly a spectacular sight in spring. Primrose-yellow 2½" flowers blanket the drooping branches; foliage is small and fern-like. Some plants are nearly thornless while others are densely barbed. The foliage creates a good autumn display when the leaves color up and the small hips turn dark red.

CULTIVATION: A good rose for poor soil and wild gardens, where it will do best when planted on its own roots. Many of the yellow species roses are subject to cane

dieback, so prune out infected canes right to the ground when dieback is first noticed.

RELATED PLANTS: *R. primula*, with small yellow flowers and aromatic foliage, grows to 6'. 'Canary Bird' has clear bright yellow flowers and grows to 7'.

USES: Plant Father Hugo's Rose along a wooded path where the yellow blooms will brighten the spring garden, and fall color and hips will extend the season well into winter. Mixed with feathery-flowered aruncus and woodland columbine, it creates an eye-popping picture in spring.

Rosa moschata
Rosaceae (Rose family)
MUSK ROSE

PLANT TYPE: *Species (old garden rose)*
ZONES: *5–9*
HABIT: *6'–10' tall; to 6' wide*
CULTURE: *Full to partial sun; rich, well-drained soil*
BLOOM: *Sporadically, spring to fall*

Grown in England since the reign of Henry VII, the Musk Rose conjures up images of woodland faeries romping through misty Arden Forest. This is one of the truly old roses to rebloom, another being 'Autumn Damask.' The Musk Rose is thought to be one of the parents, with 'Old Blush,' of the Noisettes. Over the years, there has been a diligent search for this rose as it was thought to be extinct, but recently several nurseries have begun to reintroduce it. The fragrance really sets it apart from other roses. Intense and musky, no other rose smells quite like the Musk Rose. Buds are produced in large sprays of single-petaled or double, small, strong-scented white flowers. The foliage is dark green and has good disease-resistance.

CULTIVATION: The Musk Rose will tolerate quite a lot of shade and poor soil, and still bloom.

RELATED PLANTS: 'The Garland' was one of Gertrude Jekyll's favorite climbing roses. It produces large clusters of small white to pink flowers on a strong plant climbing to 15'. 'Nastarana' can grow to quite large dimensions and has musk-scented white flowers with a pink tint.

USES: In warmer areas, plant with the dark burgundy flowers of chocolate cosmos—and yes, it really does smell like chocolate. In colder areas, plant the similarly colored knautia, with its deep red scabiosa-like flowers. Start your own fragrance garden along a wall, setting up Musk Rose as the back centerpiece, to be surrounded by leaf-scented geraniums and your choice of the many-shaded and very fragrant tall bearded irises. Add your favorite herbs, such as rosemary and lemon verbena, and your friends may just spend all their free time in your fragrance garden, taking it all in!

'Sally Holmes'
Rosaceae (Rose family)
ROSE 'SALLY HOLMES'

PLANT TYPE: *Shrub*
ZONES: *5–9*
HABIT: *To 8' tall; to 6' wide*
CULTURE: *Full sun to partial shade; rich, well-drained soil*
BLOOM: *Continuous, spring to fall*

Over the last few years, 'Sally Holmes' has been opening the eyes of American gardeners to the undiscovered charms of single-petaled roses. Gardeners tend to start by planting hybrid teas the size of dinner plates, with all the allure of an ersatz plastic posy, and think that's all roses are about. The 5-petaled roses can evoke the country charms of a cottage garden through their unsophisticated simplicity, or anchor a neomodernist design with the simple restraint of their basic flower construct. Depending on where you are gardening, 'Sally Holmes' can develop into a low-growing bush or a climbing shrub. 'Sally Holmes' produces clusters of apricot buds that open to single white, mildly fragrant flowers that take on lovely pink tones in cool weather. The dark green and glossy foliage is naturally resistant to disease. 'Sally Holmes' is not an old rose by any means, but she does have a unique charm that will surprise you if you have never planted single roses.

CULTIVATION: Prune lightly if growing this cultivar as a climber. The long, arching canes will need some support.

RELATED PLANTS: 'Bonica' will make a low climber to 6', and the double pink flowers are produced with abandon. 'Cocktail' is a tall grower to 8'; the single flowers

are brilliant red with yellow eyes. 'Ballerina' has single pink flowers with white eyes; it makes a shrub with arching canes to 6'.

USES: 'Sally Holmes' can be grown in a large pot on a patio garden, or in a large mound to cover up an unsightly garden building. Plant several to form a privacy hedge. Combine with tall, ferny-leaved annual cosmos and multicolored columbine for a woodland setting, or plant with ornamental grasses in a naturalistic garden.

'The Fairy'
Rosaceae (Rose family)
ROSE 'THE FAIRY'

PLANT TYPE: *Polyantha*
ZONES: *4–9*
HABIT: *To 3' tall; to 4' wide*
CULTURE: *Full sun to partial shade; rich, well-drained soil*
BLOOM: *Continuous, spring to fall*

Polyantha roses were developed in the mid-19th century by crossing a dwarf form of *Rosa multiflora* and China roses to produce low-growing, repeat-flowering bedding roses. Polyanthas were superseded in this century by the development of floribunda roses, which they helped to parent. Even though they are long out of fashion and difficult to find, there are a number of polyanthas worth planting. 'The Fairy' is one of those roses that just will not go away. You find it in gardens where the gardener doesn't plant roses! Growing wider than tall, 'The Fairy' will create a low mound of color. The double, pompon-shaped, small pink flowers are borne on long, flat sprays that arch out from the plant on the new growth. The flowers do not drop off the rose bush easily, so it is necessary to deadhead on a regular schedule to keep a tidy appearance.

CULTIVATION: A fairly tough rose, 'The Fairy' will tolerate some shade and still bloom. It can be somewhat prone to powdery mildew. Given adequate care, this is truly an undemanding rose.

RELATED PLANTS: 'Baby Faurax' will grow to 1' or so and has small, unusually colored flowers that come as close to blue as you can get in a rose. 'China Doll' is another polyantha with weeping growth; the small flowers, produced in large sprays, are pale pink with yellow.

USES: Plant 'The Fairy' where it can cascade over a wall or at the edge of a pond where the charming, delicate pink flowers will be reflected by the water. You can even grow it in a pot or hanging basket where the arching sprays of flowers will be shown to their best advantage. Try growing 'The Fairy' in a large pot with blue-flowered forget-me-nots and cool, coral-colored salvia for contrast.

'Variegata di Bologna'
Rosaceae (Rose family)
ROSE 'VARIEGATA DI BOLOGNA'

PLANT TYPE: *Bourbon (old garden rose)*
ZONES: *4–9*
HABIT: *6'–10' tall; to 5' wide*
CULTURE: *Full sun; rich, well-drained soil*
BLOOM: *Once-blooming, spring to early summer*

Bourbon roses reached the height of their popularity in the mid-19th century. Resulting from a cross of 'Autumn Damask' and 'Old Blush,' they were first discovered on the Île de Bourbon, now Réunion, in the Indian Ocean. Seeds were sent to Paris, and Bourbons achieved popularity due to their lovely perfumes and repeat bloom. The theatrically striped blooms of 'Variegata di Bologna' create a carnival-like atmosphere in the spring garden. This cultivar has the largest flowers and is the strongest growing of the striped Bourbon and hybrid perpetual roses. The double, cupped flowers are striped with crimson-purple on a blush-white background. A sweet fragrance spills out of the unusually marked blossoms. 'Variegata di Bologna' is reported to produce a few blooms after the first flush, but in fact it hardly ever does. The shrub some-

times sports to a purple flower that is thought to be the parental form.

CULTIVATION: All Bourbon roses need to have their older canes thinned out at pruning time to encourage the new growth that produces the best flowers. 'Variegata di Bologna' is prone to blackspot.

RELATED PLANTS: 'Vick's Caprice,' with soft pink flowers striped with white, is a low-growing plant that repeats well. 'Reine des Violettes,' with fragrant, rich, dark grape-purple blooms, is taller growing, to 6', and repeats well.

USES: 'Variegata di Bologna' will make a small climber to use at the back of the border; or plant this cultivar as a centerpiece just for the spectacular display of striped blooms in spring. Mix with clumps of tall foxglove and silvery-foliaged artemisia.

'York and Lancaster'
Rosaceae (Rose family)
ROSE 'YORK AND LANCASTER'

PLANT TYPE: *Damask (old garden rose)*
ZONES: *4–9*
HABIT: *To 5' tall; to 4' wide*
CULTURE: *Full sun; rich, well-drained soil*
BLOOM: *Once-blooming, spring to early summer*

This was the rose chosen by the Tudor kings to symbolize the union under their dynasty of the two factions of the Wars of the Roses. Ancient roses, damasks were probably brought back by knights returning from the Crusades. Damask roses possess a strong, unique fragrance; in fact, the fragrance is often described as "the old-rose scent." A typical damask rose, 'York and Lancaster' grows tall, producing long, curving, bristly canes with the usual downy gray-green damask foliage. The petals are blush-white or light pink; at times the flowers are all one color, and sometimes the colors are mixed in the same bloom, but they are never striped. Although the blooms are double, they have an informal look and open up to display the yellow stamens.

CULTIVATION: Given a good, deep rich soil and generous organic mulch, 'York and Lancaster' is quite capable of producing truly outstanding flowers. Prune in early summer after the shrub has finished flowering. Damask roses resent hard pruning, which often results in cane dieback. To prevent this, be sure to avoid cutting into the larger canes.

RELATED PLANTS: There has been some confusion in commerce between 'York and Lancaster,' which may be bicolored, and the striped gallica 'Rosa Mundi.' The gallica is vividly striped pale pink

on a crimson background, and it is much lower growing.

USES: Plant in the back of the border and peg to maximize flower production. Extend the flowering season of this once-blooming rose by planting it with repeat-blooming tall bearded iris, white-flowered Shasta daisies, and clumps of brightly flowered pennisetum.

SHRUBS

Shrubs are a staple of landscapes everywhere. Through the seasons, year after year, they stand ornamental duty in public places and on private property, so ubiquitous that they are often taken for granted. Consider residential yards, where evergreen shrubs planted around the foundation of a new home thrive happily over the years, virtually un-noticed, until they completely obscure the facade of the home. What a testimony to the dependability and self-reliance of shrubs!

The glory of shrubs is their potential beyond unimaginative foundation plantings. Selected with care—and planted strategically around yards and gardens for full ornamental effect—they are noticed and enjoyed, enhancing the beauty of the landscape and the value of the property.

Shrubs are usually defined as being shorter than 25' and having multiple woody stems. Like trees, they bear either deciduous leaves, which may have attractive fall color but drop off for winter, or needled or broad evergreen leaves, which remain through the winter. And like trees, they can be counted on to add winter interest with a variety of textured and colorful

barks, fruits and berries, and cones. Shrubs may bloom in spring, summer, or fall—often with the bonus of wonderful fragrance—and may be valued most for their unusual shapes, wonderful foliage, and ability to withstand shearing into hedges.

Shrubs become the infrastructure of the landscape. They provide variation in height and shape and are ideal for delineating property lines, punctuating doorways, decks, and walkways, screening utilities and other eyesores, blocking wind and harsh sun, attracting wildlife, and reducing lawn size. Planted individually, they create a focal point in the landscape. Include small shrubs in the flower

border to anchor the bed, convey a sense of permanence, and add winter interest.

Although many shrubs are forgiving of a certain amount of neglect, their beauty and durability are enhanced by routine mainte-nance. Many—evergreens in particu-lar—are shallow-rooted and need watering during dry periods in the summer. A 3" layer of organic mulch conditions the soil and helps it retain moisture. Attentive pruning of injured or diseased branches, suckers, and old wood keeps shrubs vigorous. Other pruning should be restricted to trimming the occasional branch that rubs against a wall or encroaches on nearby walks or wires. A shrub that is properly selected for its site never needs severe annual prun-ing to control its size.

Shrubs are available from local nurseries, garden centers, and mail-order sources. As with trees, the advantage to buying locally is that the plants are likely to be larger, with their roots already in soil (either in containers or balled-and-burlapped), offering greater flexibility in planting time. Mail-order sources offer more choice, but plants are usually small and arrive bare-rooted, needing immediate planting.

Berberis thunbergii 'Atropurpurea Nana' ('Crimson Pygmy')

Berberidaceae (Barberry family)

JAPANESE BARBERRY

PLANT TYPE: *Deciduous shrub*
ZONES: *4–8*
HABIT: *To 2' tall; 3'–4' wide*
CULTURE: *Full sun; dry soil*
BLOOM: *Spring*

An adaptable landscape staple, barberry is one of the first shrubs to show leaves in the

spring. Tiny yellow or whitish flowers dangle among the tufts of small deep reddish-purple leaves ranged along the densely branching stems that are also punctuated by small thorns. Bright red oval berries develop in the fall long after the leaves have turned deep orange, scarlet, or purple, and dropped.

CULTIVATION: Withstands urban conditions but resents wet soil; easily transplanted if containerized. Plant in spring or fall. Pruning is not necessary, but is tolerated. Propagate from softwood cuttings in June or July.

RELATED PLANTS: 'Rose Glow' has mottled red-silver leaves that mature to reddish-purple; 'Aurea' has gold new leaves that become green. The autumn foliage of 'Sparkle' is red, yellow, and orange. 'Kobold' is compact with green leaves. Other varieties of Japanese barberry have red foliage that turns gold in fall.

USES: Ideal for hedges, groupings, foundation planting, beds, and borders. The berries attract wildlife.

Buddleia davidii 'White Knight'
Loganiaceae (Logania family)
BUTTERFLY BUSH

PLANT TYPE: *Deciduous shrub*
ZONES: *5–9*
HABIT: *10'–15' tall; to 10' wide*
CULTURE: *Full sun; prefers fertile, well-drained soil*
BLOOM: *Summer*

The profuse, steady blooming and graceful profile of this reliable gem are easy to take for granted. Flowers appear in June at the tips of the new growth on its arching stems. Coveted by butterflies and other beneficial insects, blooms resemble miniature lilacs, their tiny white florets packed into slightly dropped, tubular clusters that have a light scent. Although the soft gray-green foliage does not turn color in fall, it does stay attractive and silvery long after first light frost.

CULTIVATION: Transplants easily and grows with gusto. Plant nursery-grown, containerized stock in spring. Pruning existing shrubs to

soil level in the spring fosters vigorous, dense new growth and limits height somewhat. Deadheading faded blossoms encourages abundant and constant flowering all summer. Propagate from softwood cuttings in June or July.

RELATED PLANTS: 'Black Knight' has dark purple flowers; 'Pink Pearl' has light violet-pink flowers. 'Nanho' series plants are more compact at 3'–5' and are ideal for smaller gardens. They have white, blue, or purple flowers with orange "eyes." *B.* 'Lochinch,' a hybrid, has silver foliage, stiffer stems, and paler lavender-blue flowers.

USES: In groups as informal hedges, as accents by doorways or drives. Integrates well into shrub or flower borders.

Buxus microphylla
Buxaceae (Box family)
LITTLELEAF BOXWOOD

PLANT TYPE: *Evergreen shrub*
ZONES: *5–9*
HABIT: *3'–4' tall; 1'–4' wide*
CULTURE: *Full sun to partial shade; prefers moist, slightly acid, well-drained soil*
BLOOM: *Spring (inconspicuous)*

Although littleleaf boxwood produces tiny, inconspicuous yellowish flowers in spring, they are inconsequential. This shrub is highly valued for its dense, glossy, fine-textured foliage. The evergreen leaves are small and smooth-edged, ½"–1" long, shiny dark green above and paler below, with tiny indents at their tips. The foliage has a distinctive pungent odor, which signals to animals tempted to chew on them that the branches are poisonous.

CULTIVATION: Boxwoods dislike heavy clay soil. Plant nursery-grown, balled-and-burlapped stock in the spring through early summer. Plant containerized plants through early fall. Stock should be at least 3 years old. A northern exposure or harsh summer sun may burn the foliage. Avoid crowding if planting in a row for a hedge. Boxwood's surface roots are very vulnerable to damage and need protective mulch. Roots compete vigorously for soil nutrition, so do not plant turf or other ground covers nearby. These are fairly heavy feeders; fertilize with slow-acting fertilizer every spring. No pruning is necessary except to remove damaged branches or to shear as hedges. Shelter from drying winds.

RELATED PLANTS: 'Compacta,' normally 12" tall, can be mowed to 4" every couple of years as a ground cover. Var. *japonica* (Japanese boxwood) grows to 6' with a relaxed habit. Var. *koreana* (Korean boxwood) is the hardiest and grows more slowly to only 2'; its foliage has a tendency to turn yellow or brown in winter. 'Winter green' is a cultivar of compact habit that stays green in winter.

USES: Hedges, foundation plantings, containers, topiary, edging.

Camellia japxonica

Theaceae (Tea family)

JAPANESE CAMELLIA; COMMON CAMELLIA

PLANT TYPE: *Evergreen shrub*
ZONES: *8–10*
HABIT: *10'–15' tall; 6'–10' wide*
CULTURE: *Partial shade; moist, acid, humusy soil*
BLOOM: *Fall to winter*

With their pyramidal habit, camellias introduce winter elegance into residential yards. At the ends of branches covered with glossy, leathery evergreen leaves 4" long, plump buds appear in late fall. The subsequent stunning waxy flowers, which bloom all winter, are 3"–5" wide. Single or double, they may be white, pink, rose, red, or bicolored.

CULTIVATION: Cold is a threat to these flowers, which turn brown and mushy if frozen. Site shrubs near protective walls. Plant nursery-grown containerized stock when camellias are most dormant. Plant them shallowly, and mulch well. Prune after flowering for shape, if desired. Propagate from seed planted immediately, or from

cuttings taken from the current year's growth in May through fall.

RELATED PLANTS: 'Adolphe Audusson' is an older, reliable, dark red-flowered cultivar that is cold-hardier than most. There are over 2,000 other *C. japonica* cultivars. *C. reticulata* is more like a tree, with huge, single pale pink flowers up to 9" across. Sasanqua camellias (*C. sasanqua*) have smaller foliage, bloom earlier, and are very easy to use in the landscape.

USES: Accent near dooryards; focal point in courtyards. Incorporate with hollies, azaleas, and ferns as foundation plantings or in beds. Containerize as standards or espalier.

Cornus stolonifera (syn. C. sericea)

Cornaceae (Dogwood family)

RED TWIG DOGWOOD; RED OSIER DOGWOOD

PLANT TYPE: *Deciduous shrub*
ZONES: *2–8*
HABIT: *7'–9' tall; spreads by underground stems to 10' or more*
CULTURE: *Sun to partial shade; any moist soil*
BLOOM: *Spring*

Enjoy a treat every season with this shrub. It greets spring with flat clusters of small off-white flowers nestled among new medium green foliage. Come summer, the blooms give way to clusters of white pealike berries, coveted by birds and other wildlife as fall approaches. The autumn finale features reddish foliage and a bonus of bright purplish-red stems. After the leaves drop, these wonderful stems redeem dreary winter landscapes until spring.

CULTIVATION: Easily transplanted because of their fibrous, shallow root systems. Plant nursery-grown, bare-root or balled-and-burlapped stock in spring or fall. Fast growing, the branches of these loose, multi-stemmed shrubs show the best twig color if they are pruned to the ground every spring or two to encourage new stem growth. Propagate from softwood cuttings in June or July. If branches are low to the ground, propagate by layering.

RELATED PLANTS: 'Nitida' (green twig dogwood) has green stems. 'Kelseyi' is a dwarf version of red twig, with sparse flowers and fruit; 'Silver and Gold' has variegated foliage with cream-and-yellow stems; 'Cardinal' stem color fades from deep red to pink to yellow-green as winter persists. 'Flaviramea' (yellow twig dogwood) has yellow stems.

USES: Site along stream banks and shrub borders; effective as hedges if pruned. Set in front of dark green conifers to showcase the red stems.

Daphne odora 'Aureomarginata

Thymelaeaceae (Mezereum family)

WINTER DAPHNE

PLANT TYPE: *Semi-evergreen shrub*
ZONES: *7–9*
HABIT: *To 4' tall; 4'–5' wide*
CULTURE: *Full sun to partial shade; any well-drained soil*
BLOOM: *Late winter*

The charm of this shrub is in its delicate, fragrant, long-lasting flowers. They bloom in 1" clusters of tiny florets at the ends of each branch. Rosy-purple buds open to reveal pale pink petals. 'Aureomarginata' has narrow yellow edges on the elongated oval dark green foliage, which is evergreen in the South. It is a bit hardier than regular winter daphne. All parts of the plant are poisonous.

CULTIVATION: Tolerates some shade and sandy soil. Withstands some drought during summer. Plant nursery-grown, containerized stock to reduce transplant difficulties. Set plants shallowly in the soil to assure good drainage. No need to prune unless branches are injured; they tend to be brittle and weak, and will benefit from winter protection. Shrubs tend to be short-lived and may suddenly die, despite regular, vigorous growth. Propagate from softwood cuttings in June or July.

RELATED PLANTS: In 'Variegata,' the yellow leaf edges are more pronounced, the flowers paler. *D. × burkwoodii:* 'Carol Mackie' grows to about 3' tall and wide, with fragrant pink flowers and cream-edged foliage, which persists through winter in many regions.

USES: Grow in containers. Makes a fine accent by the door or along a walkway, so passersby can stop to smell the flowers. Combine with evergreens and bulbs in foundation plantings or borders.

Deutzia gracilis 'Nikko'

Hydrangeaceae (Hydrangea family)

SLENDER DEUTZIA

PLANT TYPE: *Deciduous shrub*
ZONES: *4–8*
HABIT: *2'–4' tall; 3'–4' wide*
CULTURE: *Full sun to very light shade; any soil*
BLOOM: *Spring*

This dwarf version of deutzia forms a low, wide mound of flexible, graceful branches that drape onto the ground. They are decorated by profuse, 2"–4" long, upright clusters of single white flowers, 4 petals per flower, nestled among the deep green leaves. Foliage turns a rich maroon before it drops in the fall.

CULTIVATION: Easy to transplant. Plant nursery-grown, containerized stock in the spring. Because blooms appear on the previous year's wood, prune after flowering if needed. Warm spells in late fall may trigger flowering, so plants may suffer some winterkill that should be removed. Propagate easily with softwood cuttings taken at any time of year.

RELATED PLANTS: *D.* × *rosea* 'Carminea,' also a dwarf form, has pale to dark rose-colored flowers.

USES: Ground cover or edging plant; along walks, in the forefront of shrub beds, in rock gardens.

Euonymus alatus 'Compactus'
Celastraceae (Staff-tree family)
WINGED EUONYMUS

PLANT TYPE: *Deciduous shrub*
ZONES: *4–8*
HABIT: *To 10' tall, and as wide*
CULTURE: *Full sun to shade; any well-drained soil*
BLOOM: *Late spring (inconspicuous)*

A reliable landscape staple, this large shrub takes center stage at the end of the season, when most other shrubs have had their show time. As fall approaches, medium, flat green leaves take on a pinkish tinge. This deepens daily, culminating in a crescendo of brilliant scarlet by first frost. Then, as the leaves drop, they expose dense layers of horizontal squarish branches, some with distinctive corky growths, or "wings," along their edges that provide interest all winter.

CULTIVATION: Balled-and-burlapped or containerized stock, 1'–1½' tall, is easily transplanted in spring or fall. Shade does not necessarily affect fall color, but branching becomes less dense. The massed, fibrous roots tend to stay shallow in the soil, so mulching to maintain desired soil moisture is advisable. Winged euonymus accepts, but rarely needs, heavy pruning. Propagate from softwood cuttings in June or July.

RELATED PLANTS: *E. alatus,* the species, is taller than the variety 'Compactus' and less densely branching, showing many more corky growths on the stems. 'October Glory' is only 6'–8' tall; 'Rudy Haag' is even smaller, at 4'–5' tall and wide.

USES: Ideal for hedges, specimens, or shrub borders. Looks striking with a backdrop of evergreen trees in the fall.

Forsythia × *intermedia*
Oleaceae (Olive family)
BORDER FORSYTHIA

PLANT TYPE: *Deciduous shrub*
ZONES: *5–9*
HABIT: *8'–10' tall; 10'–12' wide*
CULTURE: *Full sun to partial shade; any soil*
BLOOM: *Spring*

Although it is not true that there would be no spring if there were no forsythia, this shrub is so ubiquitous in residential landscapes that it's possible to think so. Forsythia welcomes the new season with lemon to golden-yellow, trumpet-shaped, 1" flowers arrayed along billowy, irregularly arching, bare branches. As blooms fade, medium green, toothed, 3"–4" oval leaves appear for the summer. In fall these turn a purplish-brown and drop, revealing flower buds ready for the next spring.

CULTIVATION: Plant nursery-grown, balled-and-burlapped containerized stock in spring or fall. Propagate from softwood cuttings in June or July. If branches are low to the ground, you can propagate by layering. Prune just after flowering to control size. Renovate by cutting out thick, old stems every year or two.

RELATED PLANTS: 'Beatrix Farrand' is vigorous, growing to 7' tall and 7' wide, and densely flowered; 'Spectabilis' grows to 9' tall, spreading to 7'; 'Lynwood Gold' has a more upright habit to 7' tall. 'Nana,' a dwarf form, grows to only 5' and is slow to flower.

USES: Too unwieldy for a formal shrub border, this sprawler is best used as an accent plant, in a screen or hedgerow, or grouped on slopes to retain soil. It can be pruned as a hedge, but flowering is then limited as buds are cut away.

Fothergilla major
Hamamelidaceae
(Witch hazel family)
LARGE FOTHERGILLA

PLANT TYPE: *Deciduous shrub*
ZONES: *4–8*
HABIT: *6'–10' tall; 5'–10' wide*
CULTURE: *Full sun to partial shade; moist, loamy, acid, well-drained soil*
BLOOM: *Spring*

This thoroughly delightful, multi-stemmed, rounded shrub bursts with small white, upright, spiky flowers resembling stubby bottlebrushes before its leaves appear. Blooms are lightly fragrant. Then leaves of basic green are densely arrayed along its slightly crooked, upright stems until fall, when they color individually in many shades of orange, red, and yellow before dropping.

CULTIVATION: Because it is a bit tricky to transplant, plant balled-and-burlapped or containerized stock in spring. Slow-growing fothergilla takes a while to hit its blooming stride. Propagate from seed or by layering. Routine pruning is not needed. Virtually pest free.

RELATED PLANTS: 'Huntsman' has good fall color. Dwarf fothergilla (*F. gardenii*) has yellow to orange to scarlet fall color, and flower spikes over 1" long.

USES: Good in a shrub border, along foundations, in groups. Enhances woodland plantings. Underplant with spring bulbs or wildflowers. A good partner for witch hazels and azaleas.

Hydrangea quercifolia 'Snowflake'
Hydrangeaceae
(Hydrangea family)
OAKLEAF HYDRANGEA

PLANT TYPE: *Deciduous shrub*
ZONES: *5–9*
HABIT: *4'–6' tall; 4'–6' or more wide*
CULTURE: *Full sun to partial shade; moist, acid, well-drained soil*
BLOOM: *Summer*

A handsome presence in residential landscapes, this shrub makes a strong statement throughout the year. In spring, its trademark oak-type leaves, gray-green with suede undersides, appear at the tips of coarse, irregular, brittle branches covered with shaggy reddish-beige bark. With summer come splendid tubular flower clusters, 6"–12", composed of budlike fertile and petaled sterile florets.

White at first, these age over the season to cream tinged with pink. By fall, when the foliage turns reddish-purple and drops, the flowers persist, dried to a lovely beige.

CULTIVATION: Plant nursery-grown, containerized stock having at least 2 or 3 woody stems in spring. The shallow, fibrous roots make these shrubs easy to transplant, and they will gradually spread by means of root suckers. Mulch to assure essential soil moisture for roots. Prune just after flowering because next season's buds are formed on the current year's wood. Propagate from fresh seed, by layering branches that are low to the ground, or by dividing the parent plant.

RELATED PLANTS: 'Snow Queen' has denser, more upright flowers, and bronzy-red fall color; 'Pee Wee' stays compact at 3' tall.

USES: As specimens or part of a shrub border; naturalized in woodland situations. Combine with sourwood or Virginia sweetspire for a fall color medley. Underplant with minor bulbs to complement peeling bark on bare stems in early spring.

Ilex × meserveae 'Blue Princess'

Aquifoliaceae (Holly family)

MESERVE HOLLY

PLANT TYPE: *Evergreen shrub*
ZONES: *4–8*
HABIT: *12'–15' tall; to 10' wide*
CULTURE: *Full sun to partial shade; acid, well-drained soil*
BLOOM: *Spring (inconspicuous)*

Bred for cold-hardiness, this vigorous hybrid holly has a lot to offer residential landscapes, especially in areas that have real winters. The classic spiny holly leaves are a dark, glossy blue-green, slightly smaller than those of American holly. Densely arrayed along purplish stems, they are upstaged, however, by abundant red berries that encrust the branches most of the fall and winter.

CULTIVATION: Avoid siting these shrubs with a southern exposure as winter sun damages foliage. Nursery-grown, containerized stock is best planted in spring, but fall is also a good time. Because hollies have female and

male flowers on separate plants, be sure a male is in the area for optimum pollination. Routine pruning is not necessary, but shaping can be done during winter dormancy. December is a good time to cut some berried branches for the holidays. Leaves and berries are poisonous.

RELATED PLANTS: 'Blue Prince' is the cold-hardy consort of 'Blue Princess' and has a compact shape, handsome leaves and no berries, but generous supplies of pollen. 'Blue Girl' is also cold-hardy and reported to be faster growing. 'China Girl' has large red berries and greener, slightly curled leaves; handles hot summers well.

USES: Foundation plantings, hedges, shrub border along property lines. Good in containers.

Itea virginica

Grossulariaceae (Ribes family)

VIRGINIA SWEETSPIRE; VIRGINIA WILLOW

PLANT TYPE: *Deciduous shrub*
ZONES: *5–9*
HABIT: *3'–5' tall; usually wider than tall*
CULTURE: *Full sun to partial shade; prefers moist, fertile soil*
BLOOM: *Summer*

This multi-stemmed shrub is a highlight of every landscape it graces. Informally rangy, with dense branching near the tops of its slender, upright, flexible stems, it sports shiny, rich green, 4" leaves for summer. It then proceeds to cover itself in additional glory with upright 6" tassels of fragrant, small white flowers at the ends of its multitude of leafy twigs. As fall approaches, the leaves turn a gorgeous purplish,

almost fluorescent red and then drop, revealing reddish stems. These serve as a backdrop to lingering cylindrical clusters of brownish capsules, which dry and drop off before the foliage does.

CULTIVATION: Plant nursery-grown, 2'–4' containerized stock in spring or fall. Virginia sweetspire spreads by underground roots and gradually becomes wider than it is tall. Propagate from softwood cuttings taken in summer.

RELATED PLANTS: 'Henry's Garnet' offers 6" flowers, marvelous fall color, and tolerance of both heat and cold.

USES: Naturalizes in moist areas of the yard; makes a good informal hedge or shrub border along property boundaries, stream banks, and foundations; interesting as specimens.

Kalmia latifolia 'Olympic Fire'

Ericaceae (Heath family)

MOUNTAIN LAUREL

PLANT TYPE: *Evergreen shrub*
ZONES: *4–9*
HABIT: *7'–15' tall, and as wide*
CULTURE: *Full sun to full shade; moist, cool, acid, well-drained soil*
BLOOM: *Spring*

SHRUBS

These agreeable evergreen shrubs aim to please almost every season. Dense and rounded in youth, they grow leggier and more interestingly shaped as they age. New spring foliage is bronzy yellow-green, changing to glossy, rich green at maturity, then dark green—even purplish—in winter in the North. 'Olympic Fire' has large, dark red buds that open to ¾" rosy-pink flowers, blooming in dense clusters 4"–6" across at the ends of stems.

CULTIVATION: Fibrous roots make for easy transplanting. Plant containerized or balled-and-burlapped stock in spring or fall. Plant high in clay soil to facilitate drainage. Mulch to protect shallow roots, and deadhead spent flower clusters. Prune out older, gnarled stems to stimulate new stem growth. Mountain laurel will respond to severe pruning to renew entire shrub. Propagate in summer from softwood cuttings or by layering low-growing branches.

RELATED PLANTS: 'Ostbo Red' is similar, with bright red buds and soft deep pink opened flowers; 'Alba' has white flowers; 'Bravo' has deep pink buds and

flowers, and red-stemmed new shoots; 'Elf' is a compact dwarf with pink buds and white flowers; 'Pinwheel' flowers are maroon, with white scalloped edges; 'Snowdrift' has pure white flowers in compact mounds of dark foliage; 'Tinkerbell' is miniature at less than 2' tall, with pink flowers.

USES: Useful for both wild and formal situations. Mass for a dramatic focal point; naturalize in woodland settings. Combine with flowering dogwood, redbud, and spring bulbs.

Lagerstroemia indica 'Natchez'

Lythraceae (Loosestrife family)

CRAPE MYRTLE

PLANT TYPE: *Deciduous shrub*
ZONES: *7–9*
HABIT: *To 21' tall, and as wide*
CULTURE: *Full sun; moist, well-drained soil*
BLOOM: *Summer*

The welcome mat is out up North for this Southern delight, and for good reason. Among the charms of the multi-stemmed fast grower is its lovely stem color. After about 5 years, its gray coat begins to flake off in places, revealing wonderfully smooth, cinnamony dark brown and creamy blotches. Flowers form at the end of the current year's growth on the branches. With the trademark crinkly petals that resemble crepe paper, 'Natchez' has clusters of white flowers 6"–12" long and 4"–7½" wide that constantly renew themselves. The shrub blooms from late June almost until frost, then its glossy green leaves turn red and orange in autumn, and drop.

CULTIVATION: Plant containerized or balled-and-burlapped nursery stock in spring. Prune to remove injured branches. Crape myrtle will tolerate cutting to nearly ground level in the spring to encourage larger blooms and to control plant growth. It can be trained as a single- or multi-stemmed plant. This shrub likes hot weather and will grow in dry soil. Propagate from softwood cuttings in June or July. If branches are low to the ground, it's possible to propagate by layering.

RELATED PLANTS: 'Hopi' is spreading, semi-dwarf, hardy, and mildew-resistant, with pink flowers; 'Okmulgee' is only 3' tall, with abundant red flowers; 'Powhatan' has heavy foliage and purple flowers.

USES: Singly as a specimen; in rows as a screen, or in groves; to accent an entrance or shade a patio or pool area. Smaller types will grow in containers. Used as street trees in parts of the South.

Nandina domestica 'Compacta'

Berberidaceae (Barberry family)

NANDINA; HEAVENLY BAMBOO

PLANT TYPE: *Deciduous shrub*
ZONES: *6–9*
HABIT: *3'–4' tall; to 2' wide*
CULTURE: *Full sun to shade; moist, fertile to average soil*
BLOOM: *Summer*

The compact versions of nandina are a wonderful addition to the home landscape. Their unique tiers of fine, narrowly compound leaves gracefully soften the somewhat stiff posture of their bamboo-like, branchless stems. Young spring foliage is tinted pinkish-bronze, aging to a lustrous bluish-green. At stem tips, clusters of modest white flowers appear in sprays 12" long. They give way in fall to dramatic billows of bright red berries draped front and center on the shrub, well into the winter. Foliage turns reddish in autumn before dropping.

CULTIVATION: Nandinas are easily transplanted from containers in spring or fall. Once established, they spread slowly by means of suckers that spring up from the roots. They are very adaptable to soil and light extremes, even blooming confidently in shade. Some pruning is needed to shape these plants. Prune out old stems every year or two to renew the overall shrub. To make it appear denser, cut back some of the newer suckers by a third of their height every year. Propagate by semi-ripe cuttings taken in summer.

RELATED PLANTS: 'Nana' and 'Harbour Dwarf' are both dwarf versions. 'Alba' has white berries and lighter green foliage. Virus-free 'Firepower' has dense, deep red spring and fall foliage.

USES: Containers for dwarf forms; foundation planting, groves, and hedges for taller versions.

Nerium oleander 'Ruby Lace'

Apocynaceae (Dogbane family)

OLEANDER; ROSE BAY

PLANT TYPE: *Evergreen shrub*
ZONES: *8–10*
HABIT: *6'–8' tall, and as wide*
CULTURE: *Full sun to partial shade; prefers fertile, well-drained soil*
BLOOM: *Summer*

If it didn't already exist, folks in California, south Texas, and Florida would have to invent oleander—it is such a useful, forgiving landscape stalwart for their climate and soil conditions. 'Ruby Lace' is an upright, bushy, rounded shrub, clothed with narrow leaves in whorls around its greenish stems. Dark green year-round, the leaves set off its stunning rich red flowers 3" wide. Crinkle-edged with fringed lips, they are clustered on new growth at the stem tips. Their peak bloom is from early summer to mid fall, but they don't limit themselves to these months. All plant parts are poisonous; even deer avoid oleander.

CULTIVATION: Plant in spring or fall. Water well until established. The weedy growth style requires some pruning to domesticate this shrub in the yard. Prune in winter, cutting back older stems to ground level and pinching back others to control shrub height. Propagate in mid summer from softwood cuttings, fresh seed, or division.

RELATED PLANTS: 'Casablanca' has single white flowers; 'Compte Barthelemy,' double red; 'Hardy Pink,' single, salmon-colored; 'Isle of Capri,' single, light yellow; 'Petite Pink' (dwarf, 3'–4' tall), single, pale pink; 'Sister Agnes' (to 20'), single white.

USES: Ideal for coastal landscapes—as borders, screens, or hedges along foundations, driveways, property lines, and walks—because oleanders tolerate salt and wind. Group to screen salt spray along the shore. They take polluted conditions, hot desert settings, and marshy situations in stride. Good for containers.

Philadelphus coronarius

Hydrangeaceae
(Hydrangea family)

MOCK ORANGE;
SWEET MOCK ORANGE

PLANT TYPE: *Deciduous shrub*
ZONES: *4–8*
HABIT: *10'–12' tall; 10'–12' wide*
CULTURE: *Full sun to partial shade; moist, humusy, well-drained soil*
BLOOM: *Late spring*

Albeit a single-season stand-out, this old-time favorite takes full advantage of its time to shine. It has large, rounded, stiff upright stems that sag a bit with age. During the growing season, these stems are covered with basic green, 1½"–4" leaves that do not show fall color before dropping in the fall. In the springtime, when the creamy-white, orange-blossomy fragrant flowers that are the glory of this shrub appear, mock orange lights up the landscape. Flowers have 4 petals, but are sometimes double, and measure 1½" across. They bloom in groups of 5–7 at the tips of branches for a brief, magical time.

CULTIVATION: Easy to transplant, easy to grow, this shrub is tough and virtually carefree. Plant nursery-grown, containerized stock in the fall. Prune this vigorous grower in late spring after it flowers by cutting out its oldest, thickest stems at the soil level. When an older shrub gets bedraggled, renew it by cutting the entire shrub back to the ground. Propagate from softwood cuttings taken in June or July, or sow fresh seed.

RELATED PLANTS: 'Duplex' ('Nanus') is a small, compact form at 4' tall. 'Variegatus' has fragrant flowers; its leaves have creamy-white edges. New hybrids are not readily available in the trade and many lack the fragrance that is the delight of this shrub. *P.* × *cymosus* cultivars grow 6'–8' tall with an open habit; some are fragrant. *P.* × *lemoinei* cultivars grow 4'–8' tall, doing well to zone 5; 'Avalanche' is 4' tall with white flowers. *P.* × *virginalis* cultivars grow 5'–9' tall, and are hardy to zone 5. 'Miniature Snowflake,' 3' high, has fragrant double flowers.

USES: A nostalgic dooryard focal point for the brief time it is in bloom, but otherwise not an outstanding landscape asset. Blends unobtrusively into a shrub border or along the back property line.

Pieris japonica
'Mountain Fire'

Ericaceae (Heath family)

JAPANESE ANDROMEDA;
LILY-OF-THE-VALLEY BUSH

PLANT TYPE: *Evergreen shrub*
ZONES: *5–8*
HABIT: *9'–12' tall; 6'–8' wide*
CULTURE: *Partial shade; acid, humusy, well-drained soil*
BLOOM: *Spring*

For quiet, graceful, year-round elegance this handsome shrub has few peers. Its evergreen foliage presides over the seasons, with rosettes of narrow, finely toothed, lustrous leaves arrayed on angular woody stems. In spring the new foliage of 'Mountain Fire' is a glossy, vivid red. With the rich green of mature foliage, it backdrops the flower buds that it has carried all winter. These bloom for 3 or more weeks in spring as dramatic, waxy, urn-shaped, pendulous white clusters, 3"–5" long. Their delicate, light scent matches the delicacy of the flowers.

CULTIVATION: Choose a site sheltered from wind and direct sun (may be grown in zone 4 with winter protection). Plant balled-and-burlapped or containerized stock in spring or fall. Japanese andromeda needs regular moisture. A slow grower, it will not need regular pruning for size. If pruning to guide shape, prune after it has flowered, before the new buds for next spring form. Propagate from softwood cuttings or layered branches. In the Northeast it is plagued by lacebugs, often because of stress due to dry soil and too much sun.

RELATED PLANTS: 'Dorothy Wyckoff' and 'Flamingo' have pink flowers. 'Red Mill' grows to 9' and needs some sun; 'Temple Bells' is dwarf, with large white flowers in dense drifts; 'Variegata' foliage is rimmed with white; it has white flowers.

USES: Large shrubs as specimens in spacious yards, or massed in the shrub border with other broad-leaved evergreens such as rhododendron, azalea, mountain laurel, and holly. Accent plant by an entrance. Smaller types blend into mixed borders, shade gardens, and rock gardens.

Potentilla fruticosa 'Primrose Beauty'

Rosaceae (Rose family)

SHRUBBY CINQUEFOIL

PLANT TYPE: *Deciduous shrub*
ZONES: *2–7*
HABIT: *4'–5' tall; to 6' wide*
CULTURE: *Full sun to partial shade; prefers fertile, moist, well-drained soil*
BLOOM: *Summer*

This sturdy landscape standby provides buttercups all summer. It boasts a broadly rounded shape with many slender, erect stems, softened by the wealth of fine-textured foliage. Leaves are composed of 5–7 small, delicate leaflets, their gray-green spring color turning to a darker green for summer. Successive waves of 1" flowers resembling buttercups bloom faithfully on 'Primrose Beauty' branch tips throughout the summer until frost. A jaunty primrose-yellow with slightly darker centers, flowers age to a paler yellow. The foliage yellows prior to dropping in the autumn.

CULTIVATION: Not only does this shrub transplant easily, but it is virtually care-free thereafter. Its versatility recommends it for northern landscapes where winters take a toll on plants. Plant nursery-grown, containerized stock in spring or fall. Prune to renew by removing a third of the older stems in late winter every year or two. Shrubby cinquefoil can handle being cut to the ground every couple of years to maintain a dense, compact habit; it flowers on new wood. Propagate from softwood cuttings taken in summer, or by division in spring or fall.

RELATED PLANTS: A sampling of the numerous cultivars of potentilla: 'Abbottswood' grows to 3' tall with white flowers and bluish-green leaves; 'Beesii' grows to 2' with bright yellow flowers, silvery-green leaves; 'Boskoop Red' is semi-dwarf with early blooming, bright red flowers and bright green foliage; 'Coronation Triumph,' good for the Midwest, is 3'–4' tall, with bright yellow flowers; 'Daydawn' grows to 30" with peachy-pinkish-creamy flowers and medium green leaves; 'Tangerine' is 2'–4' tall with deep orange-red flowers, gray-green leaves.

USES: Mixed borders, low hedges, combined with other shrubs, in foundation plantings. Use dwarf types as woody ground cover on sunny banks and in rock gardens.

Rhododendron Exbury hybrid 'Hotspur'

Ericaceae (Health family)

HOTSPUR AZALEA

PLANT TYPE: *Deciduous shrub*
ZONES: *5–6*
HABIT: *8'–12' tall; nearly as wide*
CULTURE: *Partial shade; moist, acid, humusy, well-drained soil*
BLOOM: *Spring*

Its crowning glory—bountiful clusters of deep red-orange flowers—make 'Hotspur' a standout in the home landscape for nearly 2 weeks every spring. Comprising up to 30 flowers per cluster, these abundant blooms nearly overwhelm established shrubs. The medium green summer foliage is deciduous, dropping in the fall.

CULTIVATION: This azalea can't handle extreme heat; it does best in cooler northern regions. Plant shallowly to accommodate a tendency to surface root. Plant balled-and-burlapped or containerized young plants 1'–4' tall.

Deciduous azaleas propagate well from softwood cuttings taken early in the season. They grow quickly at first, slowing and spreading as they age. These shrubs are prone to powdery mildew.

RELATED PLANTS: Among the Exbury and Knap Hill hybrid azaleas are dozens of specimens boasting brilliantly colored blooms in yellow, cream, pink, orange, and red. Other deciduous azalea hybrid groups include the Ghent (Gandavense) crosses of European with American natives, such as orange-red 'Coccineum Speciosum' and yellow 'Daviesii,' both late bloomers. Late-blooming Mollis hybrids, such as 'Koenigin Emma' and 'Koster's Yellow,' are orangish-yellow and slightly less hardy.

USES: Specimens as focal points, grouped along property lines, incorporated into flower borders, in naturalized settings.

Rhododendron 'Loder's White'

Ericaceae (Heath family)

RHODODENDRON

PLANT TYPE: *Evergreen shrub*
ZONES: *7–8*
HABIT: *To 20' or more tall; to 15' wide*
CULTURE: *Partial shade; moist, acid, well-drained soil*
BLOOM: *Spring*

Sporting the classic, large, narrow, 8"–12" dark green leaves that are the pride of rhododendrons, this cultivar's evergreen foliage provides a wonderful backdrop for its marvelous flowers. Their big, conical clusters of wide, funnel-shaped blooms are mauve-

pink in bud, fading to pure white when fully opened. When they decorate the ends of branches every spring, it is an event to be celebrated.

CULTIVATION: Plant nursery-grown, balled-and-burlapped or containerized stock in spring or fall. Deadhead spent blossoms on smaller shrubs, where they are within easy reach, to stimulate new growth and improve their appearance. Prune, if desired, to keep shrubs dense. Do renewal pruning in winter when shrub is dormant. Propagate from soft-wood cuttings or layering.

RELATED PLANTS: 'County of York' is more widely available; it has huge white flower clusters, tolerates sun, and is hardier. 'Catawbiense Album,' extremely hardy, has white flowers from lavender buds.

USES: Singly as specimens; grouped for accents or screens; naturalized in woodland settings.

Spiraea prunifolia (syn. *S. prunifolia* var. *plena*)

Rosaceae (Rose family)

BRIDAL WREATH

PLANT TYPE: *Deciduous shrub*
ZONES: *5–9*
HABIT: *To 6' tall; to 6' wide*
CULTURE: *Full sun; rich, moist loam*
BLOOM: *Spring*

With white flowers trailing down its branches in spring, this lovely shrub is an eye-catcher in the garden. The leaves tend to turn scarlet-orange in autumn, giving the plant interest long after the flowers are gone. It grows up to 6' tall with slender, upright branches and shiny, dark green leaves. The double flowers are long-lasting.

CULTIVATION: Plant nursery-grown spirea in spring or fall. Propagate from softwood cuttings in June or July. If the branches are low enough to the ground, you can propagate by layering them in summer.

RELATED PLANTS: *S. thunbergii* is the earliest spirea to bloom, growing to 5' tall with slender, arching branches and small, pure white flowers. *S. × vanhouttei,* the showiest and most commonly

cultivated spirea, grows 6'–8' with gracefully arching branches. *S. veitchii* grows up to 12' with spreading, arching branches covered with flat clusters of creamy-white flowers in early summer.

USES: Long-lasting spirea blossoms make good cut flowers, often finding their way from the garden into bridal bouquets and wedding decorations. Include several spireas at the back of the border for sequential bloom in spring, or create a flowering screen. Plant blue-flowered spring bulbs such as grape hyacinths or squill around the base of the shrub.

Syringa patula 'Miss Kim'
Oleaceae (Olive family)
MANCHURIAN LILAC; KOREAN LILAC
PLANT TYPE: *Deciduous shrub* ZONES: 3–8 HABIT: *4–8' tall; 3'–5' wide* CULTURE: *Full sun; average to alkaline soil* BLOOM: *Early summer*

The ideal lilac for those who want their lilacs and a year-round landscape asset, too, this sturdy, dense shrub, while upright in habit, is rounded and full. Its dark green leaves are 2"–5" long. Mildew-resistant, they maintain a good appearance all season. They set off the dense, tubular clusters of tiny florets 3" long, which appear at the ends of branches of last year's wood. Either singly or in pairs, the purple buds open to clear blue about 2 weeks after common lilacs. In fall, the leaves turn to purple before dropping.

CULTIVATION: Allow plenty of space around this lilac when planting to assure enough room for good air circulation when it's mature. Plant nursery-grown, balled-and-burlapped or containerized stock in spring or fall. Be patient; plants may not bloom for the first year or two but are worth the wait. To keep 'Miss Kim' attractive, deadhead after flowering. Compact and slow to become overgrown, these shrubs will eventually grow shaggy. Prune them back to soil level in early spring to renew them. Unlike other lilacs, this plant is difficult to propagate from softwood cuttings.

RELATED PLANTS: Manchurian lilac is often confused with Meyer lilac (*S. meyeri, S. palibiniana*) or littleleaf lilac (*S. microphylla*). They share a smaller, neater, broader shape, and smaller leaves. The multitude of hybrids and clones (possibly up to 2,000) of common lilac (*S. vulgaris*) generally bloom earlier in a wide variety of shades of white, blue, lavender, and pink; growing to 20', they have lusher fragrance and coarser, leggier habits.

USES: Group as hedges, screens, or windbreaks. Softens the corners of buildings. Excellent cut flowers for indoor arrangements.

Taxus baccata 'Repandens'
Taxaceae (Yew family)
SPREADING ENGLISH YEW
PLANT TYPE: *Evergreen shrub* ZONES: 5–9 HABIT: *To 2' high; to 6' wide* CULTURE: *Full sun to partial shade; any well-drained soil* BLOOM: *Spring (inconspicuous)*

The spreading English yew is the hardiest of the English yews. This little gem combines all the dependable yew virtues in a compact, versatile package. Its horizontal branches droop slightly to form a pleasing shape. The flattish needles are a handsome deep green borne on overlapping branches. This shrub looks lovely any time of year. Yews are dioecious—both male and female flower, but only the female bears the berries. The fleshy fruit is red with a poisonous seed inside. Leaves are poisonous as well, to both people and animals.

CULTIVATION: Yews are available in nurseries and from mail-order sources. Plant balled-and-

burlapped shrubs in spring or fall; bare-root plants need to be planted in spring as soon as they arrive. Yews thrive in indirect light, so you can tuck in these gems along a northern or eastern exposure. Protect from wind and reflected summer heat and light, which can burn the needles. The plants rarely need pruning; prune in winter to remove deadwood or to train to a shape.

RELATED PLANTS: The species *T. baccata,* best known as English yew, is often used as a hedge. It requires frequent pruning as it can grow to 40' tall with a 30' spread. 'Repandens Aurea' grows only 18" high and 6' wide. It has short, overlapping branches crowded with yellow-edged leaves. 'Aurea' (golden English yew) has striking golden needles that turn green in their second year. With continued pruning, you can maintain the lighter color. 'Fastigiata Robusta' is an erect form with ascending, closely packed branches. The narrow, dark green needles grow all around the branches; this tree grows to 30' tall with a 5' spread. *Taxus × media* 'Hicksii' is a good, slow-growing yew with a columnar form. A tough plant, it will grow to 20' tall and 6' wide.

USES: Yew is one of the most suitable shrubs for planting near a typical American home. Its size will not overtake surrounding structures, making it a preferred plant for low-maintenance foun-

dation planting—you don't have to prune it to keep it in bounds. It is a favorite plant for creating a somewhat undulating evergreen ground cover that can set off larger plantings.

Viburnum opulus 'Compactum'

Caprifoliaceae (Honeysuckle family)

EUROPEAN CRANBERRY BUSH; SNOWBALL VIBURNUM

PLANT TYPE: *Deciduous shrub*
ZONES: *3–8*
HABIT: *4'–6' tall; 5'–7' wide*
CULTURE: *Full sun to partial shade; prefers moist soil, either acid or alkaline*
BLOOM: *Spring*

This lovely shrub confers grace and beauty on the most humble setting. Its upright, multistemmed, arching branches round its profile. They are decorated with 3–5 lobed, glossy dark green leaves with slightly hairy undersides, resembling maple leaves. 'Compactum' boasts particularly abundant flowers and fruit. First

3"–5" flat white flower clusters composed of tight, tiny, budlike fertile flowers ringed by flat-petaled sterile ones drape it in spring. Then they give way in late summer to drooping clusters of bright red berries that dry to raisin-like fruits coveted by birds. Then the foliage, tinged purplish-red or yellow, drops.

CULTIVATION: Sturdy and self-reliant, this shrub tolerates city conditions but dislikes hot dry weather. It transplants as balled-and-burlapped stock very easily in spring or fall. Prune to keep shrubs dense; renew aged shrubs in winter. Propagate from softwood cuttings.

RELATED PLANTS: 'Nanum' is dwarf at 18"–24", bearing no flowers or fruit; 'Roseum' ('Sterile') has white, snowball-shaped, 2½" flower clusters and no berries; hard-to-find 'Xanthocarpa' has yellow berries and yellow fall foliage. American cranberry bush (*V. trilobum*) is hardy to zone 2. Cultivars are normally 8'–10' tall, with red or yellow berries.

USES: The smaller 'Compactum' is particularly useful in modest-size residential landscapes. Plant in rows for an informal hedge along drives or property lines. Mass several as a focal point, or mix with other shrubs in borders. Plant in front of conifers to showcase the white flowers and fall berries.

TREES

Imagine a spacious residential yard richly landscaped with curving walkways, handsome walls, and beds and borders of colorful and interesting perennials, shrubs, annuals, and bulbs— but no trees. Imagine, no trees! Sometimes it requires this exercise of the imagination to overcome our tendency to take trees for granted. Only then are we reminded of the significant role they play in our yards.

Aesthetically, trees provide an architectural transition from the inert buildings on a property to the living landscape they inhabit. The vertical presence of trees forms a framework—establishing scale and creating a balance for the overall design. They define borders, soften edges, and link the ground with the sky by roofing it with their canopies. Practically, trees planted in protective rows moderate the indoor climate of nearby buildings by blocking hot sun in the summer and cold winds in the winter.

Trees also extend their protection to the world of plants, screening them from wind and rain. They further create and define microclimates by transposing light, filtering and blocking it to create various kinds of shade. They contribute numerous orna-mental assets to the landscape, such as colorful flowers and foliage, fruits, seeds, and textured bark, over all the seasons of the year. Trees also provide habitat—shelter and food—critical to the survival of backyard wildlife.

Trees are commonly distin-guished from shrubs by their single stems and their height—usually over 25' tall; they are conveniently defined by the nature of their foliage as either evergreen or deciduous. Leaves of evergreen trees stay green throughout the winter. Some, such as pines and spruces, have needle-shaped leaves; others, such as southern magno-lias, have broad leaves. Deciduous trees drop their leaves in the fall and go dormant over the winter months.

Choosing a suitable tree for your property is an exercise in possibilities. Because there are so many kinds to choose from, it is important to narrow down your choices by having a clear idea of a tree's purpose and location in your yard.

What do you want the tree for? Is it to be a specimen—a sin-gle gorgeous plant that holds cen-ter stage in the yard to show off its beauty? Perhaps it is for shade over a porch or patio. Formal rows of stately evergreens screen out noise and neighbors, whereas informal groves of trees create and define woodland settings to relieve harsh sunny landscapes. Small flowering trees enhance a garden area or punctuate a large lawn. Other trees provide fruit and cones as well as beauty. Many kinds of trees are suitable for growing in large containers for many years.

Most trees want lots of sun, space to grow, and decent soil. However, some are better than others at handling wet, poor, or acid soil. Trees listed as small are typically under 45' tall, medium ones are 45'–60', and tall ones are over 60' tall at maturity. Consider nearby walls, overhead wires, driveways, and the height of your house—then choose a tree whose mature size will be compatible with these elements of the landscape.

Purchase trees from local nurseries and garden centers or by mail. The advantage of buying locally is that the plants are usual-ly larger and likely to have their roots in soil, either wrapped in burlap or in containers, which gives you more flexibility in planting time over the growing season. The advantage of buying by mail is that you have a much wider choice. However, these mail-order trees are typically quite small, and because they arrive bare-root, they are best planted as soon as they arrive in the spring or early fall.

Acer palmatum
Aceraceae (Maple family)
JAPANESE MAPLE

PLANT TYPE: *Deciduous tree*
ZONES: *5–8*
HABIT: *To 20' tall; to 20' wide*
CULTURE: *Full sun to partial shade; moist, average soil*
BLOOM: *Spring*

Graceful Japanese maples are highly prized for their abundance of delicate leaves. With 5–7 lobes, some leaves are extremely narrow and finely toothed, creating a lacy effect that softens the landscape. In addition to the familiar green leaves, some varieties have deep red, yellow, or even variegated leaves. Many have foliage that turns deep purple in autumn before it falls to the ground.

CULTIVATION: The best time to plant nursery-grown Japanese maples is in the spring, although fall is also suitable. Choose containerized trees 15"–6' tall. Plant in a sheltered location in light

shade to enhance red leaf color. Propagate by sowing ripe seeds, budding, or grafting onto species understock.

RELATED PLANTS: 'Bloodgood' has red leaves throughout the season. 'Aureum' has rounded greenish-gold spring and fall foliage. 'Atropurpureum' has season-long red leaves and is extremely hardy. The threadleaf types (*A. palmatum* Dissectum group) have very finely cut foliage.

USES: Excellent for shade, as screens, or as specimens. Red-leaved types stand out dramatically against a backdrop of evergreens. Weeping types integrate easily into garden beds and borders. Ideal for containers.

Amelanchier canadensis
Rosaceae (Rose family)
SERVICEBERRY; SHADBLOW

PLANT TYPE: *Deciduous tree*
ZONES: *3–7*
HABIT: *To 20' tall; to 10' wide; multi-stemmed*
CULTURE: *Sun to partial shade; moist, slightly acid, well-drained soil*
BLOOM: *Spring*

A landscape gem, serviceberry has something for every season. It welcomes spring with lovely, upright 2"–3" spikes of numerous white flowers before its leaves emerge. These give way to drooping clusters of sweet, edible purplish-black berries in early summer. Then in fall the leaves turn golden or orange before they drop in October.

CULTIVATION: Serviceberry is tolerant of shade. It transplants easily because of its fibrous, shallow root system. Plant nursery-grown stock in spring or fall. It's commonly

grown from seed, but since it spreads by suckers from the crown, it can be divided. Low-growing branches can be layered in early spring or fall.

RELATED PLANTS: Downy serviceberry (*A. arborea*) is often confused with serviceberry. Though more vigorous, it is used almost interchangeably in the nursery trade. 'Robin Hill' does better in cooler areas.

USES: Ideal for naturalized areas, by streams and ponds, as an understory planting, along property borders. Berries attract songbirds and small mammals.

Arbutus menziesii
Ericaceae (Heath family)
MADRONE; PACIFIC MADRONE

PLANT TYPE: *Evergreen tree*
ZONES: *7–9*
HABIT: *50'–75' tall; almost as wide*
CULTURE: *Full to partial sun; average to poor, slightly acid, well-drained soil*
BLOOM: *Late spring*

This statuesque tree lends drama to any landscape. It boasts broad, glossy evergreen leaves up to 6" long. The conspicuous clusters of small whitish, bell-shaped flowers that appear at the ends of the twigs in May give way to fleshy, colorful orangish-red fruits later in the season. As the vivid tan-and-maroon bark ages, it flakes away, exposing tender, bright green bark later in the summer.

CULTIVATION: Madrone prefers poor dry soils; water sparingly. Although it prefers Pacific coastal climates, it is vulnerable to drying winds. Best sown from seed on site, because it is somewhat difficult to transplant. Plant nursery-grown seedlings, which grow fast, when they are at least 6" tall. Difficult to grow outside its native California region.

RELATED PLANTS: Strawberry tree (*A. unedo*), an 8'–20' evergreen shrubby tree that flowers and fruits simultaneously in fall, is adaptable to California climate and soil extremes. Drought- and wind-resistant, it is suitable for lawns or raised beds. 'Elfin King,' a dwarf version with contorted stems, flowers and fruits almost continuously; it is ideal for containers.

USES: Showcase this handsome tree as a specimen in a large residential yard. Conspicuous fruits attract songbirds and other wildlife.

Calocedrus decurrens (syn. *Libocedrus decurrens*)
Cupressaceae (Cypress family)
CALIFORNIA INCENSE CEDAR

PLANT TYPE: *Evergreen tree*
ZONES: *5–8*
HABIT: *30'–100' tall; 8'–10' wide*
CULTURE: *Full sun to partial shade; moist, fertile, well-drained soil*
BLOOM: *Spring (inconspicuous)*

A stately sentinel for the spacious residential landscape, this conifer boasts aromatic, glossy evergreen foliage resembling the fan-shaped scaly leaves of arborvitae. It also features reddish-brown bark and small cones. Typically it is narrowly columnar, branching to the base of its stem.

CULTIVATION: This cedar is most at home in its native West. It thrives in good soil and moist air, but needs some shelter from strong winds. Plant nursery-grown stock in spring or early fall. Propagate from seed. California incense cedar can be grafted onto Western arborvitae (*Thuja plicata*).

RELATED PLANTS: 'Aureovariegata' has yellow foliage, variably patterned. 'Compacta' is smaller, and densely branched.

USES: Lends formal elegance to spacious landscapes as a specimen; appropriate for screens.

Carpinus caroliniana
Betulaceae (Birch family)
AMERICAN HORNBEAM

PLANT TYPE: *Deciduous tree*
ZONES: *3–9*
HABIT: *To 30' tall, and as wide; multi- or single-stemmed*
CULTURE: *Partial sun to shade; moist, fertile, well-drained soil*
BLOOM: *Spring*

An excellent tree for a small yard, especially one with shade. Slow-growing and -spreading, with slightly drooping branch tips, hornbeam offers interesting, muscular-looking blue-gray bark and medium green leaves through the season. Its late spring catkins, or flowers, give way to clusters of winged nuts. The leaves turn a bright orange-red in the autumn before dropping.

CULTIVATION: Will tolerate damp soil, but not very dry soil. Grows naturally in some shade as an understory plant, but can handle sun. A bit tricky to transplant. Plant nursery-grown stock 5'–6' tall, containerized or balled-and-burlapped, in the spring. Start from seed in the fall.

RELATED PLANTS: Taller European hornbeam (*C. betulus*) takes shearing and pruning well and has yellow fall color. Japanese hornbeam (*C. japonica*) has a distinctive flat top and a fan shape. American hop hornbeam (*Ostrya virginiana*) is often confused with hornbeam, but it has rough leaves and coarse, peeling bark.

USES: Specimen, street, or patio tree. Lovely at the edge of a bog garden.

Catalpa bignonioides
Bignoniaceae (Bignonia family)
COMMON CATALPA; INDIAN BEAN
PLANT TYPE: *Deciduous tree*   ZONES: *5–9*   HABIT: *30'–40' tall, and as wide*   CULTURE: *Full sun; moist, fertile, well-drained soil*   BLOOM: *Summer*

Once it passes its awkward adolescence and branches freely, this tree dominates the landscape. Dramatic white pyramidal clusters of trumpet-like flowers, with frilled edges and yellow and purple markings, are the hallmark of the catalpa. Rising above the dramatic green or yellowish, broad oval leaves, they yield long bean pods that often persist after the leaves fall in autumn.

CULTIVATION: Catalpa loves hot summers. Extremely resistant to urban pollution, it is fast-growing, tough, and durable. Therefore, it should be forgiven its tendency to drip spent petals, seedpods, and large leaves. Accepts pruning to more shrubby dimensions. Susceptible to wind damage. Plant nursery-grown, containerized

stock in spring or fall. Cultivars are best propagated by softwood cuttings in summer.

RELATED PLANTS: 'Aurea' has yellow foliage; 'Nana' is dwarf. Western catalpa (*C. speciosa*) is the cold-hardier species. Young foliage of the smaller *C. × erubescens* 'Purpurea' is purple, then greens as it ages.

USES: A showy specimen in a spacious setting; otherwise use with restraint.

Cedrus deodara
Pinaceae (Pine family)
DEODAR CEDAR
PLANT TYPE: *Evergreen tree*   ZONES: *7–8*   HABIT: *40'–80' tall; 30'–40' wide*   CULTURE: *Full sun to partial shade; dryish, slightly acid, well-drained soil*   BLOOM: *Early autumn (inconspicuous)*

This handsome conifer has dramatic, angular, dark green pyramidal architecture. It bears male and female cones in late summer on branches from which spurs bearing tufted clusters of up to 30 stiff grayish-green, bluish, or silvery needles grow. These branches are wide-spreading, with

tips that droop when young, then stiffen with age.

CULTIVATION: Deodars are most commonly used in the West or Southwest. They dislike transplanting, so choose containerized stock from the nursery. The best planting time is fall; next best is spring. Once established, they are dependably drought-resistant. To retard their spread and make them denser, prune back new spring growth on side branches about halfway. Propagate from seeds or rooted cuttings collected in October.

RELATED PLANTS: The cultivar 'Aurea' has golden needles; 'Kashmir' is very hardy; 'Fastigiata' is columnar, with more upright branches; the branches of 'Pendula' droop toward the ground, then turn up, and will grow flat on the ground or wall. 'Shalimar' is among the hardiest, and has blue-green needles.

USES: Showcase as single specimens. Slow growers, they do well in containers.

TREES

Cercis canadensis
Fabaceae
(Pea family)
REDBUD

PLANT TYPE: *Deciduous tree*
ZONES: *4–9*
HABIT: *20'–30' tall; 25'–35' wide*
CULTURE: *Full sun to partial shade; moist, fertile, well-drained soil*
BLOOM: *Spring*

Flowers sprout from the branches before the leaves on this charming small tree. It commonly has a trunk that is divided near its base, making it look like a shrub. Deep reddish-purple buds become pink-to-purple pealike flowers lasting 2 or 3 weeks. Distinctive dried brown pods, 2"–3" long, form later in the summer and persist among the striking, heart-shaped yellow fall foliage until well after it drops in October.

CULTIVATION: This tree is adaptable to either acid or alkaline soils, and tolerant of wetness and dryness. Since redbuds are a bit difficult to transplant, choose a

small size. Plant nursery-grown, balled-and-burlapped stock in the spring or fall. Prune occasionally after blooming, to eliminate multiple weak branches near the base, and to shape. Propagate from softwood cuttings in June or July. Varieties are grafted onto the species. This tree can be grown from ripe or properly stored year-old dry seed.

RELATED PLANTS: 'Alba' has pure white flowers; 'Forest Pansy' has purple foliage and is a bit less drought-tolerant; 'Wither's Pink Charm' has pale pink flowers with no purplish tinge; 'Royal White' has large white flowers and best cold-hardiness. Western redbud (*C. occidentalis*) is more multi-stemmed and shrublike, and is very drought-tolerant.

USES: Singly as a specimen, or in groups; integrates well into shrub borders or naturalized areas. Combine with white flowering dogwood. Smallness suits single-story homes.

Chionanthus retusus
Oleaceae
(Olive family)
CHINESE FRINGE TREE

PLANT TYPE: *Deciduous tree*
ZONES: *5–8*
HABIT: *15'–25' tall; to 20' wide*
CULTURE: *Full to partial sun; moist, acid, well-drained, fertile soil*
BLOOM: *Late spring*

This tree for all seasons features fluffy, upright spikes of pure white, star-shaped, fragrant flowers 4" long. Appearing at the ends of the current year's growth on branches of both male and female plants, they are set off by shiny, oval, leathery green leaves

late in the spring, when almost everything else has bloomed. On female plants, flowers give way to hanging, grapelike clusters of blue berries that ripen in the fall about the time the foliage turns yellow. Combined with the highly attractive ridged or peeling gray-brown bark, these features make Chinese fringe tree a landscape treasure.

CULTIVATION: Grows slowly. Tolerates the heat of the South, and air pollution. Chinese fringe tree may be rounded and shrubby or it may have a distinct trunk. Pruning maintains an appropriate scale for a mixed or shrub border. A companion fringe tree nearby promotes best fruiting. Plant nursery-grown, balled-and-burlapped stock in the spring. Difficult to propagate.

RELATED PLANTS: White fringe tree (*C. virginicus*) is shrubby with an open, spreading silhouette, and larger leaves. Dwarf fringe tree (*C. pygmaeus*) grows to only 3'–4'.

USES: Plant either singly or in groups for dramatic effect. Suitable for stream banks and shrub borders.

Davidia involucrata
Nyssaceae (Tupelo family)
DOVE TREE; HANDKERCHIEF TREE

PLANT TYPE: *Deciduous tree*
ZONES: *6–8*
HABIT: *40'–60' tall; to 35' wide*
CULTURE: *Light shade; moist, humusy, well-drained soil*
BLOOM: *Late spring*

The novelty "flowers" are this tree's attraction. While the actual flowers are insignificant 1" globes, it is the white bracts surrounding them that are special. Usually one long and one short, they droop gracefully from the twigs like handkerchiefs or the wings of doves (hence its name), waving in a breeze for nearly 2 weeks. The medium green summer foliage browns and drops rapidly after a hard freeze, leaving handsome orange-brown scaly bark for winter interest.

CULTIVATION: These broad, pyramidal, linden-like trees take full sun only if their roots are kept moist. They appreciate a site sheltered from wind. Plant nursery-grown, balled-and-burlapped stock up to 3' tall in spring or fall. Plan to prune away multiple stems in the second year to train as a tree. Dove tree may take up to 10 years before starting to bloom. Propagate from ripe seed in the autumn or from semi-ripe cuttings in spring.

RELATED PLANTS: *D. involucrata* var. *vilmoriniana* is a bit hardier.

USES: Showcase as a specimen tree.

Elaeagnus angustifolia
Elaeagnaceae (Oleaster family)
RUSSIAN OLIVE; WILD OLIVE

PLANT TYPE: *Deciduous tree*
ZONES: *2–7*
HABIT: *12'–20' tall, and as wide*
CULTURE: *Full sun; light to average soil*
BLOOM: *Late spring*

Notable for its narrow gray-green foliage and silvery, sometimes thorny spreading branches, this tree turns heads in the landscape. Its inconspicuous, fragrant yellow flowers, nestled where the narrow leaves join the branches, become small orangish-yellow olive-like berries with silvery scales in late summer. Its crooked trunk and shedding bark are revealed after leaves drop in autumn.

CULTIVATION: Transplants easily. Salt-tolerant, Russian olive is adapted to seashore and highway sites. It does not like heat and humidity in the South, preferring drier climates. Plant container-grown nursery stock, 1'–4' tall, in spring or fall. Propagation from seed in fall is preferred.

RELATED PLANTS: Silverberry (*E. commutata*) is smaller, with silvery-yellow flowers and fruit. Evergreen *E. philippinensis* is 8'–15', open and upright, with red fruit.

USES: Versatile for use as hedges, screens, and windbreaks along highways or in coastal landscapes. Use as an accent in a shrub or mixed border; naturalize to prevent soil erosion. Berries attract and support some songbirds and game birds.

Franklinia alatamaha (syn. Gordonia alatamaha)
Theaceae (Tea family)
FRANKLIN TREE

PLANT TYPE: *Deciduous tree*
ZONES: *5–8*
HABIT: *10'–20' tall, and as wide; multi-stemmed*
CULTURE: *Full sun to light shade; moist, humusy, acid, well-drained soil*
BLOOM: *Late summer*

Resembling camellias, franklinia's large, single white flowers, centered with a mass of yellow stamens, are about 3" across. Its upright, open branches bear glossy, oblong, dark green leaves that turn deep orange-red in fall, and drop in early winter. Woody seed capsules remain until January, providing winter interest.

CULTIVATION: This tree's sparse, fibrous root system makes transplanting difficult. Plant nursery-grown, balled-and-burlapped or containerized stock in early spring. Root softwood cuttings in spring, hardwood cuttings in late fall. Sow moist, ripe seed immediately.

RELATED PLANTS: Loblolly bay (*Gordonia lasianthus*) resembles franklinia, with evergreen leaves and white flowers. Blooms May to October in the South.

USES: Showcase as a specimen tree. Use as a shrub farther north.

Halesia monticola
Styracaceae (Storax family)
MOUNTAIN SILVERBELL

PLANT TYPE: *Deciduous tree*
ZONES: *6–9*
HABIT: *To 50' tall; to 35' wide*
CULTURE: *Full sun to partial shade; moist, somewhat acid, well-drained soil*
BLOOM: *Late spring*

Lovely, pendant, bell-like white flowers 1"–2" long crown this small upright tree in glory. They appear in clusters of 2 or 3 on the undersides of the twiggy branches before leaves emerge, then toward autumn, give way to interesting 4-winged fruits that remain after the foliage turns a striking yellow and falls.

CULTIVATION: Plant nursery-grown, containerized plants 2'–4'

tall in spring or fall. Propagate from softwood cuttings in early summer or from seed in fall. Varieties are either grafted or budded on the same species.

RELATED PLANTS: 'Rosea' has pale pink flowers. Carolina silverbell (*H. tetraptera, H. carolina*) is virtually identical to *H. monticola*, only smaller.

USES: Specimen or accent. Striking when naturalized along stream banks or integrated into a mixed or shrub border.

Jacaranda mimosifolia
Bignoniaceae (Bignonia family)
JACARANDA

PLANT TYPE: *Deciduous tree*
ZONES: *9–10*
HABIT: *25'–50' tall; 15'–30' wide*
CULTURE: *Full sun; prefers sandy, lightly moist soil*
BLOOM: *Spring*

Exotic is the word for this tropical beauty. The funnel-shaped blue to violet flowers, 2" long, appear in 8" clusters before the leaves in spring or summer. They are followed by feathery compound leaves made of 16 or more pairs of leaflets, each sub-

divided into another leaflet pair, that drop in late winter. The seed capsules are rounded and flat.

CULTIVATION: Jacarandas can withstand some chill once they are mature. Young plants may rebound from a freeze as multi-stemmed shrubs. This tree is tolerant of most soil conditions; avoid overwatering. Stake single-stem plants to train a sturdy trunk. Prune side branches for treelike shape. Propagate from seed in the spring, or from semi-ripe cuttings in June or July.

RELATED PLANTS: 'Alba' has white flowers, longer bloom time, denser foliage. *J. acutifolia*, often confused in the trade with *J. mimosifolia*, is smaller and has less ferny foliage.

USES: An ornamental specimen in tropical countries worldwide. Use along a patio, in terraced landscapes, or isolated on a hillside or other spacious landscape. Will grow in containers.

Koelreuteria paniculata

Sapindaceae
(Soapberry family)

GOLDENRAIN TREE

PLANT TYPE: *Deciduous tree*
ZONES: *5–9*
HABIT: *30'–35' tall; 20'–40' wide*
CULTURE: *Full sun; ordinary garden soil*
BLOOM: *Summer*

Aptly named, this tough little tree shines with large, spiky, pyramidal clusters of showy yellow flowers generously sprinkled on the ends of the branches of its broad, open-leaf canopy. Its light green leaves are narrow leaflets with toothed edges that turn yellow in autumn before dropping. The yellow-greenish fruits mature in late summer into inflated, lantern-like pinkish-beige pods that persist into winter.

CULTIVATION: Goldenrain tree can handle drought, alkaline soil, wind, and air pollutants. For best results, plant nursery-grown stock 2'–6' tall. Water young plants until they are established. Control tendency to random branching by pruning for shape. Propagate from root cuttings in late winter, or from ripe or properly stored year-old seed in autumn.

RELATED PLANTS: 'Fastigiata' is columnar, narrow, more upright, and less commonly available. Chinese flame tree (*K. bipinnata*) is larger but less hardy; pods are pink to reddish.

USES: Shade tree for patios, decks, and pools. Ornamental in small yards and near one-story homes. Sometimes seen lining streets and driveways.

Liquidambar styraciflua 'Burgundy'

Hamamelidaceae
(Witch hazel family)

SWEET GUM

PLANT TYPE: *Deciduous tree*
ZONES: *5–9*
HABIT: *60'–75' tall; 40'–50' wide*
CULTURE: *Full sun; ordinary soil*
BLOOM: *Spring*

Although it does have inconspicuous flowers, sweet gum is known best for its trademark sticky, spiky, hard 1" balls that follow bloom and remain into winter. It also boasts glossy, dark green leaves, 6" wide with pointed lobes, that turn a handsome red, purple, or bright orange before they drop in the fall. 'Burgundy' holds its deep purple fall leaves into winter. Spreading as it ages, the bark develops ridges, and the branches sport corky wings for an interesting winter view.

CULTIVATION: Tolerates heat and drought. Encourage deep roots by periodic soaking. Prune only to remove super-low branching. Difficult to transplant, so in fall use nursery-grown, balled-and-burlapped or containerized stock 2' tall. Propagate from seed, or by layering or grafting named varieties.

RELATED PLANTS: 'Rotundiloba' features round-lobed leaves, does not set fruit. 'Palo Alto' has bright orange fall foliage. *L. formosana* is used more on the Pacific coast.

USES: Ornamental street tree; a good shade-tree specimen for large yards.

Oxydendrum arboreum

Ericaceae (Heath family)

SOURWOOD

PLANT TYPE: *Deciduous tree*
ZONES: *4–9*
HABIT: *25'–30' tall; 15'–20' wide*
CULTURE: *Full sun to part shade; humusy, moist, acid, well-drained soil*
BLOOM: *Summer*

A headliner for the home landscape, this tree puts on a great show. First to appear are drooping spikes holding lacy clusters of small, fragrant, bell-shaped white flowers that contrast with glossy green summer foliage. Then, dramatic elongated sprays holding beige seed capsules drape the leaf canopy, setting off the brilliant red or purplish fall foliage.

CULTIVATION: This is a slow grower, shrubby for the first decade or so; the best specimens branch near the base. Plant nursery-grown, containerized stock in early spring or fall. Choose young plants so that their deep, coarse lateral roots can adjust easily to transplanting. Mulching is especially important to prevent competition from turf-grass. Propagate from softwood cuttings, which root readily in summer. Sow ripe or properly stored year-old seed in autumn.

RELATED PLANTS: None.

USES: Showcase as a specimen. Plant at property edges to highlight boundaries, brighten corners. Combines well with oakleaf hydrangea. A favorite of honey bees, sourwood yields wonderful honey.

Parkinsonia florida (syns. *Cercidium floridum; C. torreyanum*)
Fabaceae (Pea family)
BLUE PALO VERDE

PLANT TYPE: *Deciduous tree*
ZONES: *8–9*
HABIT: *To 30' tall, and as wide*
CULTURE: *Full sun; dry, normal to poor soil*
BLOOM: *Spring*

Billowy clusters of yellow flowers 2"–4" long nearly obscure the bluish-green branches in spring, and may repeat later in the

season. The small leaves, made up of 1–3 pairs of leaflets, fall early on, revealing the intricate pattern of spines, branchlets, and flat yellow-brown summer seedpods that is the lovely architecture of this tree. Adapted to desert life in Arizona, southern California, and New Mexico, it features smooth blue-green bark.

CULTIVATION: Fast-growing and tough. Will survive droughty areas because it is leafless most of the year and loses very little moisture through transpiration. However, it prospers and becomes denser under cultivation with deep but infrequent watering and fertilizer. Let larger limbs remain twiggy to shade the bark. Sunscald makes it vulnerable to borers.

RELATED PLANTS: Little palo verde (*P. microphyllum*) has yellowish-green bark and leaves, and is even more drought-tolerant; Sonoran palo verde (*P. praecox, P. plurifoliolatum*) has a greenish trunk and an especially attractive open form, but is less cold-hardy.

USES: As specimens or in groves; lovely in desert or oasis settings. Attracts birds.

Picea breweriana
Pinaceae (Pine family)
BREWER'S SPRUCE

PLANT TYPE: *Evergreen tree*
ZONES: *5–9*
HABIT: *To 120' tall; to 50' wide*
CULTURE: *Full sun; very moist, well-drained soil*
BLOOM: *Spring (inconspicuous)*

Their large, elegant, pyramidal shape gives these slow-growing spruces a formal appearance. They stand as sentinels in their native California and Oregon mountains, with horizontal swooping branches sporting pendulous branchlets 7'–8' long. Among the glossy, dark green stubby needles nestle purplish 3" cones. A commanding sight, these trees are relatively rare in residential landscapes.

CULTIVATION: Generally, even large spruces transplant well, due to their shallow, fibrous root system. Plant nursery-grown, balled-and-burlapped stock in spring or fall. Most spruces can handle some clay, but not heat, drought, or air pollution; Brewer's spruce is even more tender, needing more moisture and cooler temperatures. In fact, they are rarely happy outside their native California and Oregon mountains, at an altitude of about 7,000'.

RELATED PLANTS: Norway spruce (*P. abies*) is among the most hardy and wind-resistant of all spruces. Its many low-growing and dwarf varieties are staples of residential yards. 'Nidiformis' is a compact 3' tall; 'Pendula' grows to only 2', spreading 5' or more. Serbian spruce (*P. omorika*) is considered the best ornamental spruce for Eastern yards.

USES: Specimens (rare in cultivation in the U.S.).

Pinus parviflora
Pinaceae (Pine family)
JAPANESE WHITE PINE
PLANT TYPE: *Evergreen tree* ZONES: *4–7* HABIT: *25'–50' tall, and as wide* CULTURE: *Full sun; average, well-drained soil* BLOOM: *Spring (inconspicuous)*

This pine is recommended for its handsome, wide-spreading profile and bluish-green, finely textured, 5-needled foliage tufted along its branches. Punctuated with abundant cones, the pyramidal, dense architecture spreads with age, becoming increasingly picturesque as it matures. Japanese white pine is adaptable, and well tolerates clay soils, salt, exposure, and assorted urban insults.

CULTIVATION: Plant nursery-grown, balled-and-burlapped or containerized stock in fall or very early spring. Keep roots moist, and follow up with regular watering the first year. Taproots make transplanting of established older pines difficult. To encourage density and slow growth, pinch about half of each candle (the new growth at branch tips) in late spring. Propagate by seed.

RELATED PLANTS: 'Adcock's Dwarf' is slow-growing, more rounded, and dense; 'Glauca' has silvery-blue needles; 'Brevifolia' is narrower with sparser branching and stiffer, bristlier needles.

USES: Singly as specimens, or grouped in groves in larger yards. Plant along property boundaries or on berms as screens.

Prunus Sato-zakura group (syn. *P. serrulata*) 'Kwanzan'
Rosaceae (Rose family)
JAPANESE FLOWERING CHERRY
PLANT TYPE: *Deciduous tree* ZONES: *5–6* HABIT: *20'–35' tall; to 25' wide; vase-shaped* CULTURE: *Full sun to partial shade; moist, ordinary soil* BLOOM: *Spring*

There are more than 120 named varieties of ornamental cherry that are now collectively labeled Sato-zakura group. Know the stunning 'Kwanzan' cherry by its double pink flowers, in clusters of 3–5, that bloom along its stems before foliage appears. The narrow leaves are reddish-tinged in spring, becoming glossy dark green as they mature. They turn bronzy-red before dropping in the fall. 'Kwanzan' is among the hardiest of the flowering cherries. So glorious is

its spring show that it can be forgiven its tendency toward a short life and vulnerability to disease.

CULTIVATION: Plant nursery-grown container stock in fall. Water especially well the first year. Prune crossed or injured branches as needed. Softwood cuttings root easily, though most cherries are grafted onto closely related species.

RELATED PLANTS: 'Amanogawa' is narrow, with fragrant pink, semi-double flowers; 'Mt. Fuji' has early blooming, fragrant white, semi-double flowers; 'Shiro-fugen' grows vigorously, with pink buds opening to white, then pinkish flowers.

USES: Singly or grouped, as specimens or for shade; accents for a patio, formal walk, or oriental garden.

Quercus coccinea
Fagaceae (Beech family)
SCARLET OAK
PLANT TYPE: *Deciduous tree* ZONES: *4–9* HABIT: *70'–75' tall; 40'–50' wide* CULTURE: *Full sun; dry, sandy, slightly acid, infertile soil* BLOOM: *Spring (inconspicuous)*

Sharing the stately, handsome profile of its oak relatives, scarlet oaks are treasures. Their classic oak-type, pointy-lobed leaves are lustrous dark green with whitish undersides. The leaves emerge in May, followed quickly by drooping male flowers. Eventually, ½"–1" acorns form. The stunning, brilliant scarlet fall foliage is the hallmark of this tree. Add to its virtues resistance to heat, drought, and salt. It is the official tree of Washington, D.C.

CULTIVATION: Scarlets are not as readily available in nurseries and garden centers as they should be. Their deep taproot makes transplanting tricky. Plant nursery-grown, balled-and-burlapped stock in spring. Allow 3 years for these trees to become established. Propagate by grafting.

RELATED PLANTS: Developed in England, 'Splendens' is an improved form that has a rounded leaf canopy with excellent fall color.

USES: A specimen for spacious properties; a shade tree to line streets and drives. Acorns from these oaks are favorites of songbirds, game birds, small mammals, and deer.

Rhus typhina 'Laciniata'
Anacardiaceae
(Cashew family)
STAGHORN SUMAC

PLANT TYPE: *Deciduous tree*
ZONES: *3–8*
HABIT: *15'–25' tall; 15'–25' or more wide; multi-stemmed*
CULTURE: *Full sun; poor, dry, well-drained soil*
BLOOM: *Summer*

The coarse, leggy winter silhouette of 'Lacinata' is softened in other seasons by its fine-textured, ferny foliage. The deeply divided leaves are initially bright green, turning to a medium green, then to yellow and shades of orange and scarlet in the fall. Its small, pyramidal yellow flower clusters give way to berries in stubby, dense, spiking bright red bunches that become darker red as fall approaches. Pest free.

CULTIVATION: Plant nursery-grown, balled-and-burlapped stock any time of year. Once established, the shallow, spreading roots sucker to develop new stems, building plant colonies. Tolerates most urban conditions, although its brittle stems are vulnerable to wind, snow, and ice damage. Responds to severe pruning back to soil level in winter with vigorous new spring growth.

RELATED PLANTS: 'Dissecta' has more deeply divided, finer textured leaves. *R. glabra* (smooth or scarlet sumac) is similar, with smooth twigs and leaves.

USES: Not really a garden plant— better for naturalizing. At home along roadsides and at the back of residential properties. Good for holding soil on banks. Plant in clumps. Berries coveted by songbirds, small mammals, and deer.

Sophora japonica 'Regent'
Fabaceae (Pea family)
JAPANESE PAGODA TREE

PLANT TYPE: *Deciduous tree*
ZONES: *4–8*
HABIT: *50'–75' tall; to 50' wide*
CULTURE: *Full sun; well-drained soil*
BLOOM: *Late summer*

Sophoras are valued for their scented, profuse, creamy flowers and glossy blue-green foliage. They have a reputation for delaying initial bloom as long as 25 years, but 'Regent' blooms within its first decade. Blooms drop off in a rain of petals before they actually fade; then green, segmented, 8" seedpods develop. They persist into winter, long after the foliage has dropped. Sophoras are the latest of the large ornamental trees to flower in the North.

CULTIVATION: Plant young nursery-grown, containerized stock in spring or fall. Withstands heat and drought; hot summers, especially warm nights, may encourage flowering at a younger age. Easily grown from seed.

RELATED PLANTS: 'Pendula' has drooping branches but rarely flowers; 'Princeton Upright' is similar to 'Regent' but features more compact, upright branching.

USES: Good as specimens in residential lawns.

Stewartia pseudocamellia
Theaceae (Tea family)
JAPANESE STEWARTIA
PLANT TYPE: *Deciduous tree* ZONES: *5–8* HABIT: *20'–40' tall; to 25' wide; pyramidal-oval shape* CULTURE: *Full sun, but needs afternoon shade in hotter regions; moist, acid soil* BLOOM: *Summer*

A wonderful landscape prize featuring round white, 2½" flowers in July. With their 5 petals surrounding yellow stamens, they resemble camellias. Handsome 2"–3½" elongated leaves show a youthful purplish tinge in spring, turning to rich green in summer. In autumn they turn yellow, red, or even purplish before they drop. For a finale, the interesting blotchy tan, creamy, cinnamon peeling bark provides winter interest. Virtually problem free.

CULTIVATION: Japanese stewartia is difficult to transplant, so plant containerized or balled-and-burlapped nursery stock that is 4'–5' tall or less in the spring. Little pruning is necessary. This tree appreciates protection from wind, and having its roots in

shade if possible. Propagate from softwood cuttings in summer; sow seed in autumn.

RELATED PLANTS: Korean stewartia (*S. pteropetiolata* var. *koreana*) is very similar with slightly larger, flattened flowers. Mountain camellia (*S. ovata*) is shrubbier, but not as showy.

USES: As specimens to showcase multi-season beauty; as a lovely accent near the front door. Their small size is in scale for patios and courtyard gardens or as anchors for garden beds and borders.

Ulmus americana 'American Liberty'
Ulmaceae (Elm family)
AMERICAN LIBERTY ELM
PLANT TYPE: *Deciduous tree* ZONES: *2–9* HABIT: *60'–80' tall, and as wide* CULTURE: *Full sun; rich, moist soil* BLOOM: *Spring*

Nostalgia for the elm-lined streets of the Northeast and Midwest fueled the 20-year research effort to find an elm resistant to the Dutch elm disease (DED) that destroyed most American elms after World War II. The result, the American Liberty elm,

retains the trademark upright, vase-shaped, wide-canopied profile of its species, although its branches spread more widely as it ages. Its tiny greenish flowers are inconspicuous. Its dark green, 3"–6", saw-toothed leaves turn yellow in the fall before dropping.

CULTIVATION: These fast-growing trees transplant easily. They accept a variety of soil conditions and pH, even tolerating salt, wetness, and urban conditions. Plant in spring or fall. Prune in fall. These trees are propagated from cuttings to assure that resistance to DED is retained. Like most elms, however, they suffer from a host of pest problems.

RELATED PLANTS: *U. parvifolia* (Chinese or lacebark elm) is tough, fast-growing, and resistant to DED. So is 'Pioneer,' a cross between smooth-leaved and Scotch elm. Some DED-resistant hybrids of European and Asiatic elms have also been developed, such as 'Sapporo Autumn Gold,' 'Homestead,' and 'Urban.' There are 6 different cultivars within the Liberty series.

USES: Stately street trees; towering shade trees for spacious front yards.

VEGETABLES

Millions of backyard gardeners grow at least a few of their favorite vegetables each year; in fact, some folks can't imagine a summer without fresh-picked peas or ripe home-grown tomatoes. Yet despite their popularity, vegetables frequently get short shrift in the overall garden design, stuck off in a utilitarian bed all by themselves and planted in pencil-thin rows that resemble single-crop farm fields in miniature. In recent years, however, gardeners have begun both to rediscover our rich vegetable heritage and to appreciate these edible plants for their beauty as well as their flavor.

Many types of vegetables have at least one quality that makes them desirable as ornamental plants in the garden. For some, it is their brightly colored fruits or blossoms; for others, their attractive foliage or growing habit. And certain varieties of plants, such as eggplant or amaranth, lend interest to the garden all summer long.

Gardeners in temperate zones grow almost all their vegetables as annual crops, either harvesting the plants whole as they mature (like carrots or beets) or picking them continuously and letting them produce until either mid-summer heat or killing frosts and reduced daylight put an end to their season. Try thinking of vegetables not as food crops, but as "edible annuals," and you'll begin to notice new places in which to grow them. Suddenly, it might make sense to plant a few hot-pepper seedlings in the sunny bed next to the daylilies, or to grow the beautiful strap-leaved 'Lacinato' kale as a dark accent in a bed or border. The possibilities are endless.

Generally speaking, vegetables prefer growing in full sun for at least six hours a day, and in average-to-good soil with plenty of organic matter. Healthy vegetables take up a lot of nutrients from the soil (especially in a three-season, intensive garden planting), so it's important to "complete the cycle" by composting your crop, yard, and kitchen wastes and returning them to the soil, along with other natural materials.

In recent years gardeners have debated the relative merits of modern hybrids versus more traditional, or "heirloom," vegetables. The definition of an heirloom vegetable is a fairly loose one. It generally refers to open-pollinated varieties (ones that reproduce true to type from seed) that are more than 50 years old, though often much older. In more specific terms, heirlooms tend to be varieties that have been preserved by devoted gardeners, usually outside the commercial seed trade. However, many seed companies have begun to sell, and even specialize in, heirloom vegetables, and a whole new generation of gardeners has rediscovered the variety and excellence of these plants. Especially notable modern hybrids are designated AAS, having been chosen as All-America Selections during seed trials in a particular year.

In the end, though, the choice is not really between modern hybrids and more traditional varieties. The only true measure of a successful variety is how it performs in *your* garden. With thousands of excellent varieties being offered every year, and new ones being developed all the time, vegetable gardeners should feel twice blessed. Every year in the garden should be a time to enjoy the company of old friends and to meet interesting new ones.

Allium ampeloprasum var. *porrum* (syn. *A. porrum*) 'Bleu de Solaise'

Liliaceae (Lily family)

LEEK

PLANT TYPE: *Bulb*
ZONES: *Not applicable*
HABIT: *2'–3' tall*
CULTURE: *Full sun to partial shade; fertile, well-drained soil*
HARVEST: *Summer through early spring (if overwintered)*

Historians tell us that the Roman emperor Nero ate leeks regularly to clear his voice before singing recitals; in fact, his fellow Romans nicknamed him Porrophagus, or "leek eater." Leeks are one of the hardiest vegetables, developing a sweeter flavor after the first frosts of fall and holding their quality even after freezing and thawing. In most zones, leeks will winter over in the garden under mulch protection; in the coldest regions, they can be grown in or transplanted to a cold frame or poly tunnel for winter and early spring harvest. 'Bleu de Solaise' ('Blue Solaize') is a French heirloom variety with blue-green leaves that turn violet in cold weather.

CULTIVATION: Sow leek seeds in flats 2–3 months before the last spring frost date, planting them about ¼" deep and ¼" apart. When the seedlings are 3" tall, replant them 1"–2" apart or in individual small cells. At around 10 weeks of age, begin hardening off plants; meanwhile, prepare a bed in the garden, adding in compost or aged manure. After a week's time, transplant leeks to the garden, 4"–6" apart in raised beds or in rows spaced 1'–2' apart. Set plants into a narrow planting hole about 6" deep, filling the hole in loosely with soil until only 2" or so of leaves shows above the ground.

As the leeks grow taller during the season, hill up soil or apply mulch around the plants; this helps the leeks to grow taller and blanches more of their lower stems. To harvest, loosen soil around leeks with a hand fork and pull them up as needed.

RELATED PLANTS: 'St. Victor' is a newly selected variety of the classic 'Bleu de Solaise.' Other excellent leeks include 'American Flag' ('Giant Musselburgh'), 'Giant Caretan,' and 'Lyon' ('Prizetaker'). For late summer or early fall harvest, try 'Kilima,' 'King Richard,' 'Otina,' 'Pancho,' or 'Varna' (for bunching).

USES IN THE LANDSCAPE: Plant leeks in beds or rows, or in deep, oblong containers where they provide fall and winter interest. The leaves of leeks are fountain-shaped and their growing habit contrasts well with kale, another extremely hardy vegetable. Overwintered in the garden, leeks will look attractive in early spring next to daffodils and other spring-flowering bulbs.

Allium cepa, Cepa group, 'Ailsa Craig Exhibition'

Liliaceae (Lily family)

ONION

PLANT TYPE: *Bulb*
ZONES: *Not applicable*
HABIT: *12"–18" tall*
CULTURE: *Full sun; fertile, well-drained soil*
HARVEST: *Summer through fall*

Homegrown onions, like other vegetables, offer a variety and a quality otherwise unavailable to cooks. Best of all, they are rather easy to grow and yield abundantly while taking up fairly little space. 'Ailsa Craig Exhibition' has large round bulbs with straw-yellow skin and moderately pungent flesh—what most of us refer to as "Spanish onions."

Before selecting a particular variety to grow, check to see whether it is a long- or short-day type. Long-day onions are recommended for regions above latitude 38° north, where summer daylight exceeds 15–16 hours. Short-day onions are more appropriate for areas below the 38th parallel, where maximum summer daylight is 11–12 hours. Some onion varieties are billed as "intermediate" and set bulbs successfully in either the North or the South.

CULTIVATION: Onions started from seed tend to be less prone to disease and of a higher quality than onions grown from sets. (Plant onion seed the same year you purchase it, since it germinates poorly after longer storage.) Start seeds indoors in flats in late winter or early spring, about 4–6 weeks before you plan to transplant outside. Sow seeds ¼" deep and about ¼" apart in narrow rows. Start fertilizing when plants are 2" tall and keep leaves cut back to 4"–5" in height. Harden off plants for 5–7 days before transplanting into the garden. Water the flats thoroughly, and gently separate seedlings, planting them 4" apart in rows spaced 12"–18" apart. Onions can also be direct-seeded in the garden and thinned to stand 4" apart. Keep plants well-watered and mulched. Weed carefully by hand, since onions have shallow root systems.

Harvest onions when most of the tops have begun to wither and flop over. Pull up bulbs and let them cure in a dry location out of full sun for a couple of days before bringing them inside to complete drying on racks. When the tops are completely dry, clip them back and store onions in mesh bags in a cool dry location.

RELATED PLANTS: 'Red Torpedo' ('Italian Red Bottle') forms bulbs 6"–8" long; the flavor is spicy and good for fresh use, but it's not a good storage type. It can be grown in the North, but is recommended for Southern gardeners. 'White Portugal' ('Silverskin') is a good heirloom variety with medium-size flattened bulbs; the flesh is fine-grained, mild, and sweet. A short-day type, it grows in the North as well.

Shallots (*A. cepa*, Aggregatum group), an excellent crop for the home garden, are closely related to bulb onions. Try 'Golden Gourmet,' a Dutch yellow variety, or 'Gray Shallots,' esteemed in France as the most flavorful type.

Hardy perennial onions for greens include Welsh, or bunching onions (*A. fistulosum*), and the Egyptian, or topset onion (*A. cepa*, Proliferum group). Both types are extremely hardy and grow well in the bed or border.

USES IN THE LANDSCAPE: Neither bulb onions nor shallots have much value as landscape plants. Grow Welsh or Egyptian onions in the bed or border.

Allium sativum var. *ophioscorodon* 'Spanish Roja'
Liliaceae (Lily family)
GARLIC

PLANT TYPE: *Bulb*
ZONES: *Not applicable*
HABIT: *To 2' tall*
CULTURE: *Full sun to partial shade; fertile, well-drained soil*
HARVEST: *Summer (from fall planting)*

Garlic's role in many cuisines is so important that it's amazing more gardeners don't grow their own. The tightly wrapped white heads of long-storing garlic found in the supermarket are fine for cooking, of course, but there are hundreds of other varieties now available to backyard gardeners, ones that exhibit a whole spectrum of colors, sizes, and tastes.

The two basic types of garlic are hardnecks (var. *ophioscorodon*) and softnecks (var. *sativum*). Hardnecks, also called rocamboles, send up a stiff flower stalk, or

scape, and produce underground bulbs that typically have one concentric ring of large cloves. Softnecks generally don't send up a flower stalk, and they produce a head with overlapping layers of smaller cloves. In general, softnecks store longer than hardnecks, while hardnecks are hardier and perform better in regions that have cold winters. 'Spanish Roja' is an heirloom hardneck, with 6–13 brownish cloves per head.

CULTIVATION: Plant garlic in the fall, at the same time you would put in other hardy bulbs such as tulips, about 4–6 weeks before the ground freezes for the winter. Softneck varieties can also be spring-planted, but the bulbs harvested later in the same growing season will be smaller. Garlic grows best in a well-worked soil that contains lots of organic matter. Planting large cloves will result in larger bulbs at harvest-time. Plant individual cloves, scar side down, about 2" deep and 4"–6" apart in rows or beds. Apply a heavy layer of mulch after planting to prevent frost-heaving of the soil over the winter.

When plants appear in the spring, water them like other green vegetables and fertilize.

Hardneck garlics send up a coiled flower stalk in late spring or early summer. When the stalk begins to uncoil and straighten up, cut it off to encourage bulb growth. Harvest bulbs in mid to late summer, when over 50 percent of the leaves have yellowed and become dry and the necks are getting soft; bulbs left too long in the ground will sprout. Fork up garlic bulbs and bring them to a dry, airy location to cure before storing. It often takes a few years for garlic to acclimate itself fully to a particular garden or region. Fortunately, it's easy to save and replant the best cloves every year, thus improving your own strain.

RELATED PLANTS: Other popular hardnecks include 'Carpathian' and 'German Red.' 'Inchelium Red' is a softneck garlic that has very large bulbs with 12–19 cloves in layers; it stands summer heat well and tastes great. Another good softneck is 'Silverskin,' an excellent keeper. The popular, mild-tasting bulb known as elephant garlic (*A. ampeloprasum* var. *porrum,* or *A. porrum*) is, botanically speaking, a kind of bulbing leek. Each head has only a few large cloves. This variety is recommended for mild-winter regions, where hardnecks don't grow well. Plant cloves about 4"–6" deep in fall, and remove the flower stalk the following spring.

USES IN THE LANDSCAPE: Garlic seldom produces flowers; its slender leaves make a much less showy plant than other relatives such as chives or leeks. One of the traditional uses of garlic in the landscape is to control pests as a companion plant for roses and other

perennials. Experiment with different combinations, but be forewarned that garlic often prefers growing on its own.

Apium graveolens var. _dulce_ 'Golden Plume'

Apiaceae (Parsley or carrot family)

CELERY

PLANT TYPE: *Biennial grown as an annual*
ZONES: *Not applicable*
HABIT: *To 18"–30" tall*
CULTURE: *Full sun to partial shade; fertile, well-drained, moisture-retentive, neutral to slightly alkaline soil*
HARVEST: *Late summer to early winter*

More backyard gardeners should try growing celery. It's no more demanding or harder to grow than cole crops, and the taste of the homegrown item is far superior to the watery, insipid bunches at the supermarket. What's more, celery plants come in a variety of forms, from the familiar kind with the crisp, enlarged stalks (petioles) to varieties of "cutting celery," grown for their leaves, and celeriac (*A. graveolens* var. *rapaceum*), a versatile, turnip-rooted

vegetable with a mild celery flavor. 'Golden Plume,' as its name suggests, has pale yellow stalks.

CULTIVATION: Start celery in flats about 10–12 weeks before transplanting to the garden, sowing the fine seeds thinly and tamping the soil down lightly. Like carrot seed, celery germinates slowly, requiring about 2–3 weeks. When seedlings have 2 true leaves, plant them up to individual cells or small pots. Harden off plants outdoors by cutting back on water; do not set plants where temperatures fall below 55°F. Transplant seedlings in the garden after all danger of frost is past, setting them out 6"–8" apart in rows spaced 2'–3' apart.

Water and fertilize plants regularly during the growing season. Apply an organic mulch to keep the soil cool and conserve moisture. Celery is shallow-rooted, so weed plants carefully and by hand. In the early fall, hill up soil around the plants to a level just below the top leaves. This will help blanch green varieties and will also protect the plants from light frosts.

RELATED PLANTS: The widely available 'Golden Self-Blanching' is an older variety similar to 'Golden Plume.' 'Utah 52–70' is a good, tall green celery; another good variety of the Utah type is 'Ventura,' with its crisp stalks and well-developed heart. For cold-climate growers, 'Giant Red' is an excellent choice; the stalks are 10"–13" tall, light green tinged with burgundy-purple, and extremely hardy; if the plants are hilled up, they will blanch to a pretty shell-pink. The taste is strong but good.

Gardeners interested in growing the no-fuss cutting or leaf celery should try 'Zwolsche Krul' or 'French Dinant.' 'Prague Model' is one of the best varieties of celeriac, or celery root. It has a long growing season but requires less attention than regular celery. Other improved varieties of celeriac include 'Brilliant' and 'Dolvi.'

USES IN THE LANDSCAPE: Celery's medium-tall stalks and bright green leaves make a nice edging for a bed or border. They mix well with both fine-leaved foliage plants like ferns (both plants prefer moist growing conditions) and bright annual flowers like snapdragons. Pink- and red-stalked varieties provide a colorful variation. If wintered over, celery can be harvested for its delicious seeds, which have many culinary uses.

Asparagus officinalis 'Jersey Knight Improved'
Liliaceae (Lily family)
ASPARAGUS
PLANT TYPE: *Perennial* ZONES: *2–7* HABIT: *4'–5' tall* CULTURE: *Sun to partial shade; rich, neutral soil* HARVEST: *Spring*

A sparagus has delighted the palates of diners since ancient times, and today it remains one of the true pleasures of the home garden season. Once it is well-established, preferably in a spot of its own next to the annual vegetable garden, an asparagus bed will keep producing tender, delicious spears every spring for up to 20 years or even longer. 'Jersey Knight Improved' is the new "supermale" asparagus developed at Rutgers University,

and it is much more productive, disease-resistant, and long-lived than most older strains.

CULTIVATION: The quickest way to grow asparagus is to buy year-old roots, called "crowns." Select a location for a semi-permanent bed and dig a trench 12"–15" deep, spacing beds 4' apart. In the bottom of the trench, form mounds of soil 6"–10" high and wide, mixed with compost or dried manure; space mounds 18" apart. Drape asparagus roots over the mounds, setting the tops of the crowns 3"–5" below the top of the trench. Start filling in the trench with soil, covering crowns 1" deep at first. As shoots emerge, add soil until the bed is level.

Keep the bed well-weeded and watered. Don't plan on harvesting any shoots during the first year. In the second year you can snap off a few stalks for use; begin regular harvesting in the spring of the third year. To maintain an asparagus planting, cut off the "ferns" after they die back in fall, and top-dress the bed with aged manure.

RELATED PLANTS: 'Mary Washington' is still the most widely

grown strain of asparagus among home gardeners. 'Jersey King' is another supermale in the Rutgers series, one that is widely adapted and productive. Developed in California, 'UC 157' is recommended for regions that have mild winters. Given patience, asparagus is not hard to raise from seed: Two good heirloom varieties for which seed is still available are the French 'Argenteuil Early' and the American 'Conover's Colossal.'

USES IN THE LANDSCAPE: The tall and feathery asparagus "ferns" make an attractive border in summer and early fall, and serve as an ideal backdrop for plants like cosmos and phlox. The lacy ferns are also useful in floral arrangements.

Beta vulgaris, Cicla group, 'Rainbow Chard'
Chenopodiaceae (Goosefoot family)
SWISS CHARD
PLANT TYPE: *Biennial grown as an annual* ZONES: *Not applicable* HABIT: *To 2' tall* CULTURE: *Full sun to partial shade; average garden soil* HARVEST: *Summer through early winter*

S wiss chard, a close relative of the garden beet, is grown strictly for its tall leaves with their fleshy central stalks. Harvesting just the outer leaves of the plant ensures continuous production, but even if you cut all the stalks back to 2" above the ground, you can expect to get a second crop of smaller leaves. 'Rainbow Chard' is one of the most beautiful and interesting varieties, with midribs ranging in color from orange and yellow to pink and crimson-red. A few years ago, 'Rainbow Chard' was dropped from the seed trade, but it is still maintained by the Seed Savers Exchange and is again available to home gardeners in the U.S.

CULTIVATION: Sow seed outdoors in early to late spring, ½" deep and 2" apart in rows spaced 18"–24" apart. Thin young plants to 8"–12" apart. For a late-season crop, sow from late summer through mid fall. In mild-winter climates, Swiss chard can over-winter in the garden with mulch protection. In colder regions, it makes a good winter crop for the cold frame or greenhouse.

RELATED PLANTS: Many fine varieties are available, including 'Rhubarb' ('Ruby'), a popular ornamental plant with brilliant purple-red leaves and midribs. 'Argentata' is a vigorous Italian heirloom that grows 2'–3' tall. Other good varieties are 'Fordhook Giant,' 'Lucullus,' and a European strain known as 'Perpetual Spinach,' which is extremely hardy and has an extended harvest season.

USES IN THE LANDSCAPE: Most varieties are ornamental and fit in an ornamental bed or border as well as they do in the vegetable garden. Plant 'Rainbow Chard'

where the leaves can catch the early morning and late afternoon light.

Beta vulgaris, Crassa group, 'Chioggia'

Chenopodiaceae (Goosefoot family)

BEET

PLANT TYPE: *Biennial grown as an annual*
ZONES: *Not applicable*
HABIT: *Tops 12"–15" tall; roots 1"–2½" in diameter*
CULTURE: *Full sun to partial shade; loose, loamy, slightly acid soil*
HARVEST: *Summer through fall*

Different varieties of beets are grown either for their sweet roots or for their showy and flavorful green or red tops. Beets are also important in some parts of the world in the production of refined sugar or as livestock feed (the truly mammoth-rooted, white-fleshed beets of this type are called mangel-wurzels). 'Chioggia' is a fast-growing and beautiful Italian heirloom that has concentric rings of white and salmon-pink flesh; the flavor of the roots is mild and sweet.

CULTIVATION: Beet "seeds" are actually seed clusters; presoak them overnight before planting. Prepare the bed before planting by working in plenty of compost or dried manure, plus some bone-meal for good root development.

Sow seeds ½" deep and 1"–2" apart in rows spaced 18"–24" apart. Thin plants to 3" apart in the row or bed before roots develop. Providing consistent moisture will help roots remain tender and free of "zoning," or woodiness.

RELATED PLANTS: 'Burpee's Golden' is nonbleeding but has poorer germination than other beets (sow seed more heavily). Other excellent varieties include 'Early Wonder' and 'MacGregor's Favorite' (for greens); 'Detroit Dark Red' (for canning); 'Cylindra' (also known as 'Formanova,' this variety is cylindrical, making it good for slicing); and 'Lutz Green Leaf' (for winter storage).

USES IN THE LANDSCAPE: Showy greens make a lovely edging.

Brassica juncea 'Red Giant'

Brassicaceae (Mustard family)

MUSTARD GREENS

PLANT TYPE: *Annual*
ZONES: *Not applicable*
HABIT: *16"–18" tall*
CULTURE: *Full sun to partial shade; average to rich garden soil*
HARVEST: *Spring through fall*

Mustard greens come from eastern Asia, where they have been cultivated for the past 2,500 years. Their flavor ranges from mild to hot and peppery, and many varieties are quite ornamental with leaves that may be savoyed (crinkled) and colored either bright green or reddish-purple. 'Red Giant' is a popular mustard from Japan; it is slow-bolting and has a nice mild taste. Mustards stand well through the first light frosts of the fall, so plant in mid to late summer as well as in the spring.

CULTIVATION: Direct-seed mustard either in spring or summer, sowing seeds thinly, ¼"–½" deep, in rows spaced 18" apart. Thin the young plants to 6"–8" apart in the row or bed. Harvest the side leaves of the plants first. For salad use, mustard leaves are best when picked at 4"–6" long; use the larger, more pungent leaves for cooking. Mustard greens are also delicious as part of a cut-and-come-again mesclun, or mixed salad planting.

RELATED PLANTS: 'Osaka Purple' is an extremely pretty variety from Japan with 12"–14" plants that have purple-red veining. 'Green Wave' (AAS 1957) is a popular American mustard with frilly, hot-tasting, dark green leaves. Other mild-tasting Oriental greens that resemble and are grown like mustard include mizuna (kyona), komatsuna (mustard spinach), and tatsoi. All three of these plants belong to the species *Brassica rapa* and are closely related to heading forms like napa and Chinese cabbage.

USES IN THE LANDSCAPE: Mustard, especially 'Red Giant,' 'Osaka Purple,' or 'Green Wave,'

is very attractive when mixed with other leafy plants (mizuna, red cos lettuce, parsley) or with flowers like chrysanthemums.

***Brassica oleracea,* Acephala group, 'Red Russian'**

Brassicaceae (Mustard family)

KALE

PLANT TYPE: *Biennial grown as an annual*
ZONES: *Not applicable*
HABIT: *To 2'–3' tall*
CULTURE: *Full sun to partial shade; average to fertile soil*
HARVEST: *Summer through early winter*

Kale is one of the oldest cultivated forms of the European wild cabbage, and this leafy, non-heading vegetable is still highly prized for its taste, nutritional value, hardiness, and ornamental use in the garden. The flavor of kale, like that of many cold-hardy vegetables (Brussels sprouts, leeks, parsnips), actually improves after a frost, making this plant especially important in cold-climate gardens after other green vegetables have given up the ghost. 'Red Russian'

is an outstanding and popular heirloom whose oak-leaved plants are blue-green with reddish-purple veins; in cold weather the leaves completely turn reddish-purple and are highly ornamental.

CULTIVATION: Kale grows best as a fall crop, since it prefers cool weather. Plant seeds about 3 months before the first fall frost date, sowing ¼" deep and 1" apart in rows spaced 24"–30" apart. Thin the young plants to 12"–15" apart in the row, or start seeds indoors in flats and transplant seedlings 12"–15" apart. Harvest individual leaves of plants, taking the larger, lower leaves first. Kale tastes sweeter after a frost; provide some mulch protection to extend the harvest season into the winter. In zones 7–10, kale can winter over in the garden with mulch protection.

RELATED PLANTS: Another beautiful variety is 'Lacinato,' an Italian heirloom with very dark-colored, straplike, blistered leaves—one of the most ornamental vegetable plants around. Of course, there are also the brightly colored "flowering kales," which have colorful centers and frilly-leaved heads. Various hybrids are available, including 'Nagoya Mix' (red, white, and rose centers with greenish-purple outer leaves) and 'Chidora Red.' Collards, very closely related to kale, are tolerant of heat as well as cold. Good varieties include 'Champion' (with compact plants), 'Georgia,' and 'Green Glaze.'

USES IN THE LANDSCAPE: Kale is a versatile, hardy ornamental plant that is especially valued in the fall after other more tender plants have succumbed to early frosts. The midribs and veins of 'Red Russian' leaves turn an attractive rose color in cool weather. 'Lacinato,' with its dark blistered leaves, is the best accent in beds, alongside white or brightly colored flowers like dahlias or phlox. Flowering kale hybrids make excellent formal edgings and grow well in fall containers or window boxes.

Brassica oleracea, Botrytis group, 'Green Comet'

Brassicaceae (Mustard family)

BROCCOLI

PLANT TYPE: *Annual*
ZONES: *Not applicable*
HABIT: *12"–16" tall*
CULTURE: *Full sun to partial shade; fertile soil*
HARVEST: *Summer through fall*

The familiar type of broccoli that we see in the market—the kind with the large single head—derives from the European wild cabbage (*Brassica oleracea*), the same plant that is the parent of cabbage, kale, and cauliflower. An older type of broccoli, the Italian or "sprouting" kind, produces many smaller shoots instead of one single head. 'Green

Comet' is one of the many fine F_1 hybrid broccolis now available to home gardeners; it was named an All-America Selection in 1969.

CULTIVATION: Broccoli likes growing in cool weather, but needs fairly warm soil (70°–75°F.) to germinate, so it's best to start this vegetable indoors in flats 6 weeks before the last spring frost date and transplant to the garden. Fall crops can be sown directly in the garden in mid to late summer. Sow seeds ¼"–½" deep in flats; once seedlings have grown 4–5 leaves, replant them to 3"–4" soil blocks or peat pots. Harden off seedlings and transplant to the garden, spacing them 12"–18" apart in rows spaced 24"–30" apart. Give growing plants abundant moisture and side-dress with compost or aged manure. To discourage insect pests, cover crop with a floating row cover or spray plants with Bt, a biological control. Harvest when heads have reached ⅔ their mature size, before the tiny yellow flowers begin to appear; plants will send out smaller side shoots after the main head has been harvested.

RELATED PLANTS: Other hybrid varieties include 'Premium Crop' and 'Super Dome.' Old openpollinated varieties like 'Calabrese' and 'De Cicco' are also good for the home gardener. 'Romanesco' forms beautiful, whorled chartreuse heads and makes an excellent fall crop.

USES IN THE LANDSCAPE: Broccoli is seldom grown as an ornamental plant, although 'Romanesco' produces stunning flowerheads.

Brassica oleracea, Botrytis group, 'Snow Crown'

Brassicaceae (Mustard family)

CAULIFLOWER

PLANT TYPE: *Biennial grown as an annual*
ZONES: *Not applicable*
HABIT: *Short, thick stem; head 7"–8" in diameter*
CULTURE: *Full sun to partial shade; fertile, well-drained, neutral soil*
HARVEST: *Summer and fall*

Botanically, there is little if any difference between broccoli and cauliflower; they belong to the same group within the same species. The main distinction is the shape and color of the flowerhead (cauliflower is usually rounded and blanched white, while broccoli has a more prominent green stalk), as well as the fact that the cauliflower plant, once the head is cut, does not produce additional side shoots. 'Snow Crown' is a fast-growing F_1 hybrid (50–55 days) that has mediumlarge domed heads weighing about 2 pounds; it's a good variety for summer or fall harvest.

CULTIVATION: Cauliflower heads develop their ideal round shape when grown quickly—in cool or mild weather, in a humus-rich soil, and with consistent moisture.

Start cauliflower seed in flats and transplant up to individual pots. Harden off seedlings and plant out in the garden 4–6 weeks after sowing; space plants 18" apart in rows spaced 24"–30" apart. Mulching around plants helps to conserve soil moisture. Protect against insect damage by applying Bt or using a floating row cover. Many disease and insect problems can be avoided by growing cauliflower (and other cole crops) in a 4- to 5-year rotation with noncruciferous crops.

Some cauliflowers are billed as "self-blanching," but to ensure an attractive white head, one that does not become yellow or "ricey," it helps to blanch the heads. As soon as the small white heads become visible, gather the outer leaves of the plant up over them and bind them loosely with twine or a rubber band. Check the developing heads periodically and harvest while the white "curd" of the head is still tight and white.

RELATED PLANTS: 'Early Snowball' is a popular variety that has 5"–6" white heads. 'Veitch's Autumn Giant' is an old variety that is a good fall crop, with 3' plants and 8"–10" heads. 'Violet Queen' is an attractive purple-headed hybrid that doesn't need tying or blanching; the older 'Purple Cape' is hardy to zone 6 with winter protection.

USES IN THE LANDSCAPE: Cauliflower is not widely grown outside the annual vegetable garden; the plant's leaves are often rather plain, but purple-headed varieties (which do not require blanching) can be attractive as an accent in a bed planting.

Brassica oleracea,
Capitata group,
'Early Jersey Wakefield'

Brassicaceae (Mustard family)

CABBAGE

PLANT TYPE: *Biennial grown as an annual*
ZONES: *Not applicable*
HABIT: *10"–15" tall*
CULTURE: *Full sun to partial shade; fertile, slightly acid soil*
HARVEST: *Summer through fall*

Cabbage tends to have fewer fans in America than in parts of Europe or Asia, perhaps because few things are as unappealing as its smell and taste when overcooked. On the other hand, there's nothing that compares to the sweet, juicy taste of a homegrown head of cabbage. And America does have a cabbage tradition. The fine variety known as 'Early Jersey Wakefield' is one of our country's most distinguished and time-tested garden heirlooms, hailing from Jersey City, New Jersey, in the 1840s. Its small, cone-shaped heads are ideal for the backyard garden, producing early and requiring little space.

CULTIVATION: Start seeds for early and mid-season varieties in flats, 4–6 weeks before transplanting to the garden; pot on seedlings to individual cells or soil blocks. Harden off seedlings and transplant 15"–18" apart in rows spaced 24"–30" apart. Fertilize with compost or dried manure and mulch to conserve soil moisture and discourage head-splitting. Control insects with Bt or by using a floating row cover.

For fall crops, transplant seedlings to the garden in mid to late summer. Fall-harvested cabbages keep well when wrapped in newspaper and stored in a cool, humid location.

RELATED PLANTS: Other excellent varieties include the hybrid 'Stonehead' (AAS 1969) and 'Brunswick,' a widely adapted heirloom. Good red cabbages include 'Lasso' and the hybrid 'Ruby Perfection.' Savoy cabbages (good for coleslaw) include 'Julius' and the large, attractive hybrid 'Savoy Ace.'

USES IN THE LANDSCAPE: Cabbage plants, with their interesting leaf colors and head shapes, are useful in beds or mixed vegetable/flower plantings. Savoy cabbage varieties are particularly ornamental. Ranging in color from yellow-green through deep red-purple, the large heads make especially good foils for brightly colored flowers such as marigolds, zinnias, and lavatera.

Brassica oleracea,
Gemmifera group, 'Rubine'

Brassicaceae (Mustard family)

BRUSSELS SPROUTS

PLANT TYPE: *Biennial grown as an annual*
ZONES: *Not applicable*
HABIT: *To 3' tall*
CULTURE: *Full sun to partial shade; fertile, slightly acid soil*
HARVEST: *Fall through winter*

Like other cold-hardy crops, Brussels sprouts taste sweeter and better after the first frosts of the season. The tall, sturdy plants are among the last vegetables to survive into late fall or early winter. In warmer-winter climates, sprouts can often be overwintered with mulch protection. 'Rubine,' with its vivid reddish-purple stem and leaves, is the most ornamental Brussels sprout available.

CULTIVATION: Brussels sprouts require a long growing season (85–125 days). Start seed in flats in early spring, transplanting to the garden 4–6 weeks later, or direct-seed in the outdoor garden about 4 months before the first fall frost date. Cover seed thinly with ¼"–½" of soil; thin or transplant seedlings to stand 18" apart in the row. When setting out transplants, mix compost or dried manure with bonemeal and add to the planting hole. Control insects with Bt or by using a floating row cover.

Once sprouts start to form along the stem, pinch off the plant's growing tip to encourage good sprout development. Sprouts mature from the bottom of the plant up. Harvest when they reach 1"–2" in size by breaking off the leaf below the sprout and then snapping off the sprout.

RELATED PLANTS: Good varieties of the more familiar green Brussels sprouts include the old standard 'Long Island Improved' and the hybrid 'Jade Cross' (AAS 1959).

USES IN THE LANDSCAPE: In colder zones, it's not uncommon to see Brussels sprouts covered with early snow, looking like miniature palm trees tricked out for Christmas.

Capsicum annuum 'Islander'
Solanaceae
(Nightshade family)
PEPPER

PLANT TYPE: *Annual*
ZONES: *Not applicable*
HABIT: *2'–3' tall*
CULTURE: *Full sun; average to rich, well-drained garden soil*
HARVEST: *Summer to first frost*

Peppers are native to tropical America, where their wild relatives grow as large and shrubby perennials, often with small, brightly colored, incredibly hot or pungent fruits. Most cultivated varieties of peppers belong to the species *C. annuum,* including the sweet bells, as well as cherry, jalapeño, paprika, and cayenne or chili peppers. Less widely grown, except in the southern U.S., is *C. frutescens,* which is the pepper used in the preparation of Tabasco sauce. 'Islander' is a hybrid sweet bell pepper with pale yellow flesh and an attractive light lavender skin that eventually ripens to dark red.

CULTIVATION: Start pepper seeds in flats or plugs about 6–8 weeks before the last spring frost date, sowing seeds ¼" deep and 4" apart. Provide gentle bottom heating until plants emerge. Transplant seedlings into 3" pots when they are 2" tall and have their first true leaves. Harden off plants after the last spring frost date, and transplant to the garden when the weather is warm and settled. Transplant seedlings 12"–18" apart in rows spaced 2'–3' apart. Place a paper collar around the stems of plants to discourage cutworms. In areas with cool spring weather, cover plants with cloches or a slitted row cover to provide additional heat and/or use a black paper mulch around plants.

RELATED PLANTS: Other good bell peppers include the early hybrid 'Ace' and old home-garden favorites like 'Bull Nose' and 'California Wonder.' Nonbell sweet peppers include 'Cherry Sweet,' 'Aconcagua,' and the excellent heirloom 'Nardello.'

Hot peppers well-suited to home gardens include the popular

'Hungarian Yellow Wax Hot,' 'Senorita' (a mild hybrid jalapeño), 'Early Jalapeño,' and the classic 'Long Red Cayenne.' Other good hot peppers belong to other species and, although less well known in the U.S., are worth trying. These include 'Arledge Hot' (a *C. frutescens* Tabasco-type pepper) and 'Habañero' (*C. chinense,* the hot Scotch bonnet pepper grown in the West Indies). Varieties like 'Aji Amarillo' and 'Aji Colorado' belong to *C. baccatum,* a South American species of sprawling, shrubby plants that bear small, pungent fruits; recommended for gardeners in zones 8–10.

USES IN THE LANDSCAPE: Many pepper varieties have showy fruits, but the most ornamental are the compact, bushy types bearing small fruits that exhibit a wide color range, from dark purple through crimson, often with different-colored fruits borne at the same time. Good examples are 'Purple Sparkler,' 'Bolivian Rainbow,' 'Christmas,' 'Pretty in Purple,' and variegated-leaved 'Trifetti.' These and many other varieties are suitable low-growing bedding plants. Peppers are also handsome grown in containers. When frost threatens, small varieties can be potted up and wintered over indoors.

Cichorium endivia 'Gros Bouclée'

Asteraceae (Composite family)

ENDIVE; ESCAROLE

PLANT TYPE: *Annual*
ZONES: *Not applicable*
HABIT: *Heads to 12"–18"*
CULTURE: *Full sun to partial shade; average garden soil*
HARVEST: *Spring through fall*

Endive and escarole are leafy plants, valued as highly as lettuce in some parts of Europe. A species of chicory, endive is often sold in markets under that name, though it should not be confused with witloof ("white leaf") chicory, whose roots are forced by growers in winter to produce the pale fusiform heads we call Belgian endive. Escarole is a term used mainly in America to refer to the broader-leaved varieties of endive. 'Gros Bouclée' is an old French variety with long, curled leaves and a very tight heart. The more finely cut-leaved, curly varieties of endive are sometimes called by their French name, *frisée*.

CULTIVATION: If you can grow good lettuce in your garden, you can grow endive. Sow seeds outside in early spring, planting ⅛" deep and about 1" apart in rows spaced 18"–24" apart. You can also start seeds indoors in flats and transplant seedlings in the garden 3–4 weeks later. Endive and escarole also make a good fall crop. Sow seeds from mid summer to early fall, depending on your climate, and harvest heads before the first killing frost.

Many varieties of endive and escarole have tight heads that blanch their inner hearts all by themselves. For looser-headed varieties, it's a good idea to slip a large rubber band around the plant's outer leaves about 7–10 days before you plan to harvest the head. This makes the inner leaves less bitter-tasting.

RELATED PLANTS: In addition to 'Gros Bouclée,' other good escaroles include 'Sinco,' 'Broad-Leaved Batavian,' and 'Green Curled Ruffec.' 'Très Fine Maraichere' (or 'Frisée') refers to a small class of French endives as well as to a specific variety. The 6" heads have frilly, mild-tasting leaves. There are several good selections available, including 'Rhodos' and 'Coquette.' More upright endives include 'Traviata,' 'Neos,' and 'Salad King,' the last of which requires tying to blanch its large 22"–24" heart.

USES IN THE LANDSCAPE: The leafy heads of endive and escarole are most useful as low edging plants for formal beds and borders.

Cichorium intybus 'Rossa di Treviso'

Asteraceae (Composite family)

RADICCHIO

PLANT TYPE: *Perennial grown as an annual*
ZONES: *Not applicable*
HABIT: *10"–12" tall*
CULTURE: *Full sun to partial shade; slightly acid, average garden soil*
HARVEST: *Fall through winter*

Radicchio burst onto the American scene several years ago as a chic designer-salad ingredient. For most people, a little of it goes a long way since the taste is bitter though very pleasant in combination with other greens.

Italians refer to all heading forms of chicory as radicchio, but in America we tend to think of the leafy types that, when cut back, produce the baseball-size heads that have become so familiar at the market. The variety 'Rossa di Treviso' does not form a tight, rounded head like other radicchios, but instead has slender, elongated leaves that resemble a head of Belgian endive or romaine lettuce. The leaves remain green until after the first few frosts of fall, when they turn an attractive burgundy variegated with white veins.

CULTIVATION: Radicchio prefers cool weather. Direct-seed outdoors beginning 4–6 weeks before the last spring frost date, sowing seeds ¼" deep and thinning young plants to stand 8"–10" apart in the row or bed. In zones 8–10, plant radicchio in the fall for a late winter or early spring harvest; protect plants with a light mulch of straw or leaves.

For spring-seeded crops of heading types, cut back plants around Labor Day, leaving about 1" or so of the stem. The plants will sprout the familiar round heads, which are ready for harvest about 4–6 weeks after cutting

back. To make the flavor of the radicchio milder and less bitter, spread mulch around the heads to blanch them. Some radicchio varieties are self-heading and do not need to be cut back to form heads.

RELATED PLANTS: Other fine varieties include 'Castelfranco' and 'Giulio,' which don't need to be cut back to form heads, and 'Rossa di Verona,' a classic type that is somewhat hardier than 'Rossa di Treviso.'

USES IN THE LANDSCAPE: The red-and-white marbled leaves of radicchio make a handsome edging on paths and borders.

Cucumis sativus 'Lemon'
Cucurbitaceae (Gourd family)
CUCUMBER

PLANT TYPE: *Annual*
ZONES: *Not applicable*
HABIT: *Vine to 6' or more*
CULTURE: *Full sun; average, well-drained garden soil*
HARVEST: *Summer to first frost*

Closely related to melons, the cucumber ranks as one of the most popular home-garden vegetables for pickling as well as slicing. In some regions of the world, cucumbers are quartered and given to children as a special treat—every bit as refreshing as an ice-cream cone, and a whole lot healthier. 'Lemon' (also known as 'Crystal Apple') is an easy-to-grow heirloom variety that has become popular again in recent years as a home-garden variety. The 2"–3" round pale yellow fruits can be eaten either peeled or unpeeled.

CULTIVATION: Plant cucumber seed outdoors after the soil has

warmed to 70°F. or higher. Sow seeds ½" deep and about 2" apart in rows spaced 5'–6' apart. Thin plants to 8" apart in the row. You can also plant 8–10 seeds in circular hills or mounds spaced 5'–6' apart. To save space, grow the vines up a sturdy, large-gauge wire trellis or other support, allowing 1'–2' between plants.

Fertilize with compost or dried manure at planting time and side-dress plants again while the vines are still upright and before they begin to "run." Give plants plenty of water when they are young, and also after the blossom stage when they are beginning to set fruit.

RELATED PLANTS: Good slicing cucumbers include 'Marketmore 80,' 'Spacemaster 80,' and 'Suyo Long' (a 10"–18" Chinese "burpless" cuke). For pickling, try 'Northern Pickling' or 'Vert de Massy.' Mid East or Beit Alpha cucumbers are crisp, excellent for salads; varieties include 'Aria,' 'Sweet Crunch,' and 'Sweet Alphee.'

USES IN THE LANDSCAPE: All vining cucumbers make good ground-cover plants, although growing the vines vertically on a fence or trellis is much more ornamental and showcases the fruits and flowers to better effect. Small-fruited and yellow varieties like 'Lemon' and 'Boothby's Blonde' are particularly good candidates for trellising, as are long-fruited cucumbers like 'Suyo Long.'

Cucurbita maxima 'Red Kuri'

Cucurbitaceae (Gourd family)

SQUASH

PLANT TYPE: *Annual*
ZONES: *Not applicable*
HABIT: *6'–9' bristly trailing vines*
CULTURE: *Full sun; fertile, well-drained soil*
HARVEST: *Late summer to first frost*

Along with maize (corn) and beans, American Indians consider squash to be one of the "three sisters" of their agriculture. The crops complement each other not only in the field but nutritionally as well, together providing most of the vitamins and amino acids necessary to maintain a healthy diet.

Not everyone has room in their garden for winter squash. Unlike most summer squash (*C. pepo*), which grow on bushy plants, long-season winter varieties tend to have sprawling vines. Several good bush or semibush types are available, however, so it shouldn't be hard to find one that fits your space requirements. 'Red Kuri' (also known as 'Orange Hokkaido') is an excellent Japanese squash that bears 2–3 fruits per plant, weighing 4–7 pounds each. The fruits are very attractive, teardrop-shaped and with a bright scarlet skin.

CULTIVATION: Plant seeds outside after the last spring frost date,

sowing them ½"–1" deep and 6" apart in rows spaced 6'–8' apart. Thin young plants to 18" apart in the row. You can also plant squash in circular hills set 5'–6' apart in the row; plant 6–8 seeds per hill and later thin to the best 3 plants. Once hot weather sets in, mulch around the base of plants to conserve soil moisture; water regularly during hot, dry weather. Harvest winter squash before the first fall frost, when the fruit begins to look dull and the skin becomes too hard to puncture easily with a fingernail. Cure outside if possible for a few days before storing.

RELATED PLANTS: Most of the familiar winter squash varieties belong to the species *C. maxima*, with the main exceptions being 'Acorn,' 'Delicata,' and many pumpkins (*C. pepo*). In fact, gardeners concerned with space should consider growing 'Acorn' or 'Delicata,' both of which have bush or semi-bush plants. Other distinguished *C. maxima* varieties include 'Baby Blue Hubbard'

(semi-bush, 4–6 pounds), 'Buttercup' (vine and bush varieties, 3–5 pounds), and 'Queensland Blue' (vining, 8–15 pounds). For fall decorations and centerpieces, grow the lovely 'Turk's Turban' or the true French pumpkin called 'Rouge Vif d'Etampes.' The popular tan-fruited 'Butternut' (vine and bush varieties, 3–5 pounds) belongs to *C. moschata*.

USES IN THE LANDSCAPE: The long, sprawling vines of 'Red Kuri' and other winter squash varieties make a good ground cover; one of the best places to grow them is on the mound of an old compost heap in a sunny location. You can also train the vines to grow as a screen on a sturdy trellis or fence. As fruits develop, provide additional support by tying a sling underneath them to the vertical support.

Cucurbita pepo 'Ronde de Nice'

Cucurbitaceae (Gourd family)

ZUCCHINI

PLANT TYPE: *Annual*
ZONES: *Not applicable*
HABIT: *To 3'–4' tall*
CULTURE: *Full sun; fertile soil*
HARVEST: *Summer to first frost*

Prolific and easy to grow, the main problem with zucchini and other kinds of summer squash is having too much of a good thing. If kept well-picked, plants just keep producing. One strategy for using up the bounty is to pick summer squash very young. Not only does this keep you ahead of the harvest and avoid baseball bat zucchini, but the flavor of baby squash is exquisite, and the fruits can be used whole in many dishes. 'Ronde de Nice' is a round French zucchini best picked when 1" in size, although 4" fruits are also lovely for stuffing. The fruits are flavorful and delicate but bruise easily, making them impractical for shippers but terrific for backyard gardeners.

CULTIVATION: Sow squash seeds in the garden after the last spring frost date. Plant ½"–1" deep and 6" apart in rows spaced 4' apart. Thin young plants to 1' apart in the row. You can also plant 6–8 seeds in circular hills set 4' apart in the row; thin to the best 3 plants in every hill. Once the weather turns hot, mulch around plants to conserve soil moisture.

RELATED PLANTS: All the popular types of summer squash belong to the species *C. pepo*. Other good zucchinis include the classics 'Cocozelle' and 'Black Zucchini,' as well as the lovely yellow hybrid 'Gold Rush.' Perhaps the most traditional summer squashes are 'Early Yellow Summer Crookneck' and 'Early Prolific Straightneck' (AAS 1938). Scallop, or pattypan, squashes are also fun to grow and include both oldies like 'Benning's Green Tint' and more recent F$_1$ hybrids like 'Sunburst.'

USES IN THE LANDSCAPE: Bush zucchini plants are the most ornamental of the summer squashes, making good individual specimens in a bed next to brightly colored flowers such as geraniums or showy marigolds. They grow well in a large round container like a half whiskey barrel.

Cynara scolymus 'Green Globe'

Asteraceae (Composite family)

GLOBE ARTICHOKE

PLANT TYPE: *Perennial*
ZONES: *8–10*
HABIT: *3'–6' tall*
CULTURE: *Full sun; rich, well-drained soil*
HARVEST: *Late spring through fall*

Native to the Mediterranean region, the artichoke is a large, vigorous plant with serrated, sometimes prickly leaves. The globe- or cone-shaped flower buds are harvested for eating before they begin to open. Artichokes can be treated as short-lived perennials only in a mild-winter climate such as that found in coastal California, but they can also be grown successfully as long-season annuals or biennials in the colder regions. 'Green Globe' is the longtime standard

variety, producing 3"–4" chokes with attractive, thick green bracts.

CULTIVATION: Plant crowns 6"–8" deep and 6' apart in rows spaced 8' apart. Apply mulch to maintain even soil moisture and, at the end of the season, to protect the crowns from freezing.

In zones 5–7, start artichoke seeds indoors about 12 weeks before the last spring frost date. After 6 weeks, move plants to a cold frame or unheated greenhouse. Select the best seedlings and transplant to the garden, spacing plants 2' apart. If you can winter over plants indoors or under a heavy mulch, replant them 6' apart the following season. Harvest artichokes either when the buds are very young or when they have fully formed, but before the scales, or bracts, begin to open.

RELATED PLANTS: 'Green Globe Improved' produces largely spineless plants. The new variety 'Imperial Star' (150 days from seed) has a sweet, mild flavor and buds that resist premature opening. 'Violetto' (110–150 days) forms small, elongated purple chokes; it's an attractive variety, even for northern gardeners.

USES IN THE LANDSCAPE: Artichokes make striking specimen plants at the back of a bed; their silvery-green leaves are useful in a night garden and act as a foil for either white or brightly colored flowers. Any artichokes left to open on the plants will produce beautiful, thistle-like flowers, which can be dried and used in floral arrangements.

Daucus carota ssp. *sativus* 'Artist'

Apiaceae (Parsley or carrot family)

CARROT

PLANT TYPE: *Biennial grown as an annual*
ZONES: *Not applicable*
HABIT: *Tops to 15"–20"; roots to 7"–8"*
CULTURE: *Full sun to partial shade; light or well-worked soil*
HARVEST: *Summer (early spring if overwintered)*

The familiar garden carrot belongs to the same species as that equally familiar wildflower known as Queen Anne's lace, which has edible white roots. The French seed house of Vilmorin did extensive breeding work with carrots in the late 19th century, which resulted in many of the popular types we still grow today, including 'Chantenay' and 'Nantes.' 'Artist' is one of the many F$_1$ hybrid crosses between 'Nantes' and 'Imperator' and has a good sweet flavor. 'Artist' is also available as pelleted seed, which is seed coated with clay to make spacing and thinning easier.

CULTIVATION: Dig the planting bed deeply before sowing carrot seed, removing any stones or pebbles, loosening the soil, and breaking up any clods of earth. Carrots do well when they're grown in raised beds, especially in gardens with heavy soil.

Presoak carrot seeds overnight and mix with soil or wood ashes to separate seeds before planting. Sow seeds thinly and cover with ¼"–½" of soil. Carrot seed germinates slowly, and the young plants will not be visible for 2 weeks or more; keep the bed well-watered during this time. After plants appear, thin the seedlings to 1" apart in the row. Later on, thin plants to 3" apart, using the thinnings as baby carrots.

For fall harvest or overwintering, sow carrot seed in mid to late summer. Carrots will survive light frosts, but mulch the bed thickly before the first heavy freeze. Pull back the mulch to harvest carrots from the garden throughout the winter and early the following spring.

RELATED PLANTS: Other good hybrids include 'Bolero,' a 6"–7" Nantes type, and 'Flyaway,' which has good resistance to carrot fly. Many fine heirloom carrots are still around as well, including the American native 'Danvers Half Long' and 'Scarlet Nantes.' Gardeners with heavy or shallow soils should try growing 'Royal Chantenay,' 'Oxheart' ('Guerande'), or the 1"–2" round 'Rondo' ('Paris Market').

USES IN THE LANDSCAPE: Use carrots for edging beds or borders, where the medium-tall, dark green feathery tops make a nice counterpoint to signet marigolds, blazing star (*Liatris spicata*), lavatera, chives (regular or garlic), and other plants that have slender or lacy leaves.

Eruca sativa

Brassicaceae (Mustard family)

ARUGULA; ROCKET-SALAD; ROQUETTE

PLANT TYPE: *Annual*
ZONES: *Not applicable*
HABIT: *To 6" tall*
CULTURE: *Full sun to partial shade; average to rich, neutral soil*
HARVEST: *Spring through fall*

The sharp, peppery taste of arugula has won the hearts of salad fans in recent years. This Mediterranean plant is extremely easy to grow and it loves cool weather, making it an excellent spring and fall crop almost anywhere, and a good contender for growing in the winter cold frame or greenhouse.

CULTIVATION: In spring through late summer, sow seeds approximately 1" apart in rows or prepared beds spaced 3" apart; rake the seeds in lightly. For a continuous harvest, sow new seeds every 3–4 weeks during the season. The peppery, lobed leaves are tastiest when picked at 6" long or smaller. Harvest by cutting individual leaves to ensure a second crop. Arugula will bolt quickly in hot weather, at which time its taste becomes much sharper. In most zones, arugula seeded in the fall will winter over in the garden or cold frame.

RELATED PLANTS: *E. sativa selvatica,* the so-called "Italian rustic" arugula, is shorter and has more deeply lobed leaves than common arugula. It is also much slower to bolt, making it a good choice for gardeners in warmer regions. One newly introduced variety is 'Sylvetta.'

USES IN THE LANDSCAPE: Sprinkle arugula seed in a rock garden or border for a quick crop before you replace it with annual bedding plants.

Lactuca sativa 'Lollo Rossa'

Asteraceae (Composite family)

LETTUCE

PLANT TYPE: *Annual*
ZONES: *Not applicable*
HABIT: *6"–8" rosette of leaves*
CULTURE: *Full sun to partial shade; moisture-retentive, average to rich soil*
HARVEST: *Spring through fall*

America's "lettuce literacy" has really taken off in recent years, and the number of outstanding varieties available has increased as well. With color and flavor characteristics suited to every palate and every season, there's no reason not to try multiple kinds of lettuce in the home garden. The basic types of lettuce include looseleaf (or cutting) varieties, which have a nonheading rosette of leaves. 'Lollo Rossa' is a beautiful example of this type, with deeply frilled leaves that are green near the heart and crimson red at the tips. Other forms include crisphead, Bibb (also

known as butterhead or Boston lettuce), and cos (or romaine).

CULTIVATION: Start seeds in small soil blocks or cell packs 3–4 weeks before they'll go into the garden. Fertilize every 2 weeks with half-

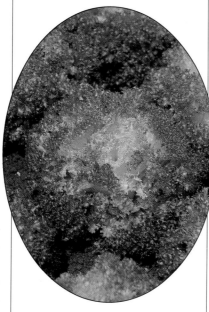

strength liquid fertilizer. Harden off plants by reducing water and temperatures for 2–3 days before transplanting to the garden. Seedlings can be transplanted as soon as the garden soil is dry enough to work in the spring. Plant seedlings 8"–12" apart in rows spaced 12"–18" apart. Lettuce can also be direct-seeded; sow seeds thinly, about 1" apart, and cover lightly with soil. Keep the seedbed watered and thin young plants to 8"–12" apart in the row.

Some varieties of lettuce can tolerate more heat and cold than others; read catalog descriptions carefully, and grow a range of varieties in succession that are appropriate to your garden's growing conditions. One way to reduce

heat stress in summer lettuce is to plant seedlings in partial shade or in the shade of taller crops such as pole beans.

RELATED PLANTS: Looseleaf lettuces include popular heirlooms like 'Black-Seeded Simpson,' 'Deertongue' ('Matchless'), and 'Oakleaf,' as well as more recent introductions like 'Red Sails' (AAS 1985). There are many fine examples of Bibbs, including 'Kagraner Sommer,' 'Merveille de Quatre Saisons' ('Four Seasons'), and 'Sucrine' ('Little Gem'). Crispheads include the original 'Iceberg' (introduced in 1894) and 'Red Grenoble.' Cos or romaine varieties include 'Paris White Cos,' 'Rouge d'Hiver,' and 'Rubens Red.'

USES IN THE LANDSCAPE: Plant lettuce wherever there's some space in the garden throughout the growing season; varieties with frilly or brightly colored leaves even work well in the ornamental bed or border.

Lycopersicon esculentum (syn. *L. lycopersicum*) 'Super Marmande'

Solanaceae (Nightshade family)

TOMATO

PLANT TYPE: *Annual*
ZONES: *Not applicable*
HABIT: *To 4' tall*
CULTURE: *Full sun; average to fertile soil*
HARVEST: *Summer to first frost*

For most backyard growers, a real homegrown tomato is the payoff for all the work that goes into planting, weeding, watering, and otherwise tending to the garden. So much is made of the taste of vine-ripened tomatoes because nothing on the market matches it. Even locally grown, in-season tomatoes often seem disappointing once you've found your own favorite varieties to grow. And no hydroponic or greenhouse tomato ever matches up.

If you have the space, it's best to grow 1–2 plants of several different tomato types: cherry or currant tomatoes for salads; plum tomatoes for paste or drying; beefsteaks for slicing and all-purpose use. 'Super Marmande' is a selection from the classic French slicer 'Marmande.' The scarlet-red fruits are 6–8 ounces, slightly flattened, with ribbed shoulders. The flesh is firm and the flavor excellent. Recommended for growers in northern and moderate zones.

CULTIVATION: Start seeds in flats or cell packs, 6–8 weeks before the last spring frost date. Plant seeds ¼"–½" deep and sow thinly. Provide gentle bottom heating until plants germinate. Once seedlings have 2–3 true leaves, transplant into individual 3"–4" pots or cells. Set plants slightly deeper than they were growing before to encourage healthy root development.

Harden off seedlings for several days after all danger of frost is past, and transplant to the garden when the weather is warm and settled. For seedlings of determinate and semi-determinate varieties (those that stop growing at a certain height), plant 1'–2' apart in the row or bed; for indeterminate varieties (those whose vines keep growing throughout the season), plant 2'–3' apart. Place paper collars around the stems of plants to discourage cutworms. Indeterminate tomatoes should be given

some support, whether that involves tying them to a wooden stake with soft cloths as the vines grow, growing them on a trellis, or simply making cages out of heavy-gauge wire. Determinate tomatoes don't need staking or caging, but they do benefit from having soil hilled up around them when they reach 1'–2' in height.

RELATED PLANTS: Many fine heirloom tomatoes are available to home gardeners, including 'Brandywine' (pink slicer, 78 days), 'Striped German' (bicolored slicer, 78 days), 'Cuostralee' (red slicer, 82 days), and 'Costoluto Genovese' (red stuffing tomato, 80 days, recommended for hot climates). Other good choices include the determinate hybrid 'Celebrity' (AAS 1984, 72 days) and, for short-season growers, 'Stupice' (small red fruits, 52 days). For sauce tomatoes try 'Giant Oxheart' (pink, 87 days) and 'Amish Paste' (red, 80–85 days). Stuffing tomatoes with hollow cavities include 'Dad's Mug' (red, 85–95 days) and 'Zapotec Pleated' (pink, 80–85 days).

Among cherry tomatoes, the large red 'Gardener's Delight' (65 days) stands out, as does the yellow determinate 'Golden Nugget'

(56 days). Even smaller than cherry tomatoes is the flavorful, bite-size "currant tomato," which comes in red and golden colors and is ideal for salad use, but requires frequent picking.

USES IN THE LANDSCAPE: Trained on a trellis, tomatoes make a strong vertical statement in the garden. Grow white, yellow, purple, or orange-fruited varieties for color interest.

Phaseolus vulgaris 'Marbel'
Fabaceae (Pea family)
FILET BEAN; FRENCH BEAN; HARICOT VERT

PLANT TYPE: *Annual*
ZONES: *Not applicable*
HABIT: *12"–18" tall*
CULTURE: *Full sun; average, well-drained, slightly acid soil*
HARVEST: *Summer through first frost*

The common garden bean comes in hundreds of interesting varieties. Some gardeners appreciate the easy culture and compact size of bush types; others swear by the productivity and flavor of their favorite pole bean. Recently the long, slender pods of filet beans have become popular with both chefs and home gardeners. In fact, skinny French varieties like 'Marbel' are ideal for backyard growing: the compact bushes require frequent picking (every 2–3 days in hot weather), and the beans need to be used as soon as possible after harvest. For a commercial grower, these traits are a pain in the neck. But for cooks and gardeners looking for the freshest and highest-quality string beans, the filet type represents the top of the line.

CULTIVATION: Beans need warm soil (65°–80°F.) to germinate and grow well. Plant seeds after the last spring frost date, wetting them lightly and coating them with a bacterial inoculant powder. Sow seeds for bush bean varieties 1" deep and about 4" apart in rows or beds spaced 2'–3' apart. For a continuous crop, sow bean seeds every 2–3 weeks throughout the season.

Filet beans need to be picked very young, when the pods are long and very thin, about ⅛"–¼" in diameter. Older pods are tough and stringy. Keeping plants picked also encourages production of new beans. Especially during hot weather, check plants every few days and pick beans as needed. Never harvest or work around beans when there is dew or rain on them; it's easy to transfer disease from plant to plant when they're wet.

RELATED PLANTS: There are many other named varieties of bush filet beans, including fairly new stringless ones, such as 'Maxibel,' 'Decibel,' and 'Tavera.' These don't have to be picked quite as frequently as the classic older varieties, such as 'Fin de Bagnols' and 'Triomphe de Farcy.'

USES IN THE LANDSCAPE: 'Marbel' filet beans, as well as similar varieties, have lovely, slender green pods heavily streaked with purple (a color that disappears in cooking). In the vegetable garden, a wide-row planting of beans gains visual interest when interplanted with 'Dark Opal' basil, fronted by lower-growing, brightly colored annuals such as portulaca or 'Alaska' nasturtiums, and backed by slightly taller cutting flowers like globe amaranth, strawflowers, or love-in-a-mist.

Pisum sativum 'Knight'
Fabaceae (Pea family)
GARDEN PEA

PLANT TYPE: *Annual*
ZONES: *Not applicable*
HABIT: *Vine to 2'*
CULTURE: *Full sun to partial shade; slightly acid, average garden soil*
HARVEST: *Early summer through fall*

Peas are one of the first pleasures of the annual garden, growing well in the cold weather of early spring and maturing before the dog days of summer set in. Although peas have been cultivated in Europe since the Stone Age, early examples were almost certainly harvested as starchy dried peas—nutritious and long-storing, but scarcely as exciting as the fresh, sweet shelling peas we know today. Much breeding work has gone into peas, producing the wide spectrum of varieties available to modern gardeners. Different strains grow on dwarf, semi-dwarf, and tall vines. There are varieties designed for early harvest, and later types that yield a main crop suitable for fresh use, canning, and freezing.

When we think of peas, we usually picture the full-podded garden or English pea that must be shelled. However, it's also worth planting the two types of edible-podded peas (*P. sativum* var. *macrocarpon*): snap peas, which have fully formed seeds and firm, fleshy pods; and snow peas, which have slender pods and tiny, almost undeveloped seeds. 'Knight' is an American variety named in honor of Thomas A. Knight, who began hybridizing peas in 1787. It is an early pea (56–62 days) with dwarf 2' vines that do not require staking. Pods are 3½"–4" long, filled with medium-size peas.

CULTIVATION: Plant peas outside as soon as the soil can be worked in the spring. Moisten seeds before planting, and mix with a bacterial inoculant powder. To support semi-dwarf or tall climbing varieties, set up a trellis, wire support, or pea fence down the center of each double row before planting. Plant peas 1" deep and 3"–4" apart in double rows spaced 6"–8" apart, allowing 3'–4' of space on either side of the double row. In warm climates, spread an organic mulch around the plants to keep soil temperatures cool. Keep the soil evenly moist.

RELATED PLANTS: Other excellent shelling peas for fresh use include 'Alderman' (70–75 days, vines 5'–6' tall), 'Lincoln' (65–70 days, 18"–30" dwarf vines), and 'Thomas Laxton' (55–65 days, 30"–36" semi-dwarf vines). The most widely grown snap pea is 'Sugar Snap' (AAS 1979), which has vines 4'–6' tall. Snow peas include 'Oregon Sugar Pod' (60–70 days, 24"–30" dwarf vines).

USES IN THE LANDSCAPE: Grow the taller climbing varieties of peas on trellises or other supports as a screen or backdrop for tall spring or early summer flowers. Some older varieties known as field peas (*P. sativum* var. *arvense*) are great for dried use and also boast ornamental flowers or pods. 'Blue-Pod Capucijners' has bicolored flowers (lavender and magenta-rose) and bluish-purple pods on 4'–5' vines.

Raphanus sativus
'D'Avignon'

**Brassicaceae
(Mustard family)**

RADISH

PLANT TYPE: *Annual*
ZONES: *Not applicable*
HABIT: *Tops to 6" tall; 3"–4" roots*
CULTURE: *Full sun; average to fertile, well-worked soil*
HARVEST: *Spring through fall*

Radishes often provide the first fresh harvest from the annual vegetable garden, growing and maturing fast in the cool weather of spring. They require little space, interplant well with most other crops, and generally can fill in anywhere, at any time throughout the growing season. The

familiar round red radish of salad bar fame is only one form of this versatile vegetable, which comes in a rainbow of colors and a wide range of types. Some are even suitable for long-term winter storage, making the radish just as valuable at the end of the season as it is at the beginning. 'D'Avignon,' a slender radish about 3"–4" long, is very pretty with its scarlet skin and creamy white tip. This traditional variety is a somewhat more refined version of the popular 'French Breakfast' radish.

CULTIVATION: To ensure a continuous harvest, make small plantings of radish seed every week or two from early spring through early fall, except during the hot mid-summer season. Sow seeds ½" deep and about ½" apart in a bed or wide-row band. When the young plants' leaves begin to clump together, thin plants to 2"–3" apart in the row or bed. Water frequently as needed to ensure fast growth of roots. After mid summer, plant seeds for the large, long-season Oriental radishes about 2" apart in rows spaced 18" apart. Make sure the soil in the row or raised bed is loose and

deeply worked; these big fall radishes require the same culture as carrots.

RELATED PLANTS: In addition to 'D'Avignon,' other good carrot-shaped radishes include 'China Rose' and 'White Icicle.' Red round radishes include 'Cherry Belle,' 'Crimson Giant,' and 'Red Pak.' Round radishes also come in different colors, including 'Burpee White' and the ornamental 'Plum Purple.'

For fall-storage varieties, try growing the pretty 'Violet de Gournay' or the heirloom 'Round Black Spanish,' which has pure white flesh and rough black skin. Daikon radishes (Longipinnatus group) include the mild-tasting 'Tokinashi' ('All Seasons'), which has 12"–15" roots that can weigh 1–2 pounds. Another radish seldom grown today is the aerial radish (Caudatum group), which comes from India and is commonly known as rat-tail radish. This plant's long purple seedpods can be picked when young and tender and added whole to salads, or stir-fried.

USES IN THE LANDSCAPE: Radish greens are attractive in the garden. If not pulled, radishes will send up stalks with lovely white or pink flowers.

Rheum × *cultorum* (syn.
R. rhabarbarum) 'Victoria'

**Polygonaceae
(Buckwheat family)**

RHUBARB

PLANT TYPE: *Perennial*
ZONES: *4–9*
HABIT: *3'–4' tall*
CULTURE: *Full sun; fertile, well-drained, slightly acid soil*
HARVEST: *Spring through early summer*

Rhubarb has been valued as a medicinal plant since ancient times. Not until early 19th-century England did it gain acceptance as an edible, and soon it became the quintessential cottage-garden plant. Rhubarb is hardy, easy to grow, long-lived, vigorous, and productive, with each plant yielding 2–6 pounds of stalks each year. The reddish-green stalks, or petioles, while too sour to eat raw, are perfect for pies and jams that benefit from a fruit high in acidity. In fact, rhubarb's other common name is "pie plant." 'Victoria' traces its ancestry to the Myatts, early rhubarb growers in 19th-century England. Its broad crimson stalks are thick, tender, and very tart.

CULTIVATION: Plant roots or crowns. With patience, rhubarb can also be started from seed, but it may not come true to type. Choose a permanent location, since established plants will remain productive for 20 years or longer. Dig planting holes about 1' deep and 2' in diameter, and work in plenty of compost or dried manure. Place roots so they sit 2"–3" below the surface of the soil. Cover with soil and gently tamp down with the back of a spade. Water well.

During the first season of growth, side-dress plants with compost or dried manure, water during dry periods, and mulch to conserve soil moisture and keep down weeds. Do not harvest any stalks during the first year, and cut off any flower stalks the plants may produce. Spread an organic mulch around plants in the fall. Begin harvesting stalks in the spring of the second growing sea-

son. Side-dress plants with compost or dried manure every year in the summer or early fall, after they have stopped producing stalks.

To divide older plants, dig up the crowns early in the spring. Cut off several root sections with a clean, sharp knife and then replant the old crown. Some gardeners complain that their rhubarb stalks are more green than red. While redness varies somewhat by variety, plants grown in full sunlight tend to have redder stalks. In all but aesthetics, green stalks are every bit as tasty and useful as the red ones.

RELATED PLANTS: Common strains include 'MacDonald,' 'Valentine,' 'Canada Red,' and 'Cherry Red.' 'Glaskin's Perpetual,' a green-stalked variety not widely grown in the U.S., is good-tasting and low in oxalic acid; it establishes itself quickly from seed.

USES IN THE LANDSCAPE: Rhubarb grows well in beds and borders. It is most often sited close to the annual vegetable garden or near patches of other edible perennials such as asparagus. An ideal place would be the site of an old compost heap or near a livestock

barn—someplace convenient to an abundant source of dried manure or other rich organic matter. The large, palmate leaves form a handsome backdrop for bright annual flowers like snapdragons and zinnias. Combine rhubarb with other foliage plants like coleus, tricolor amaranth, or purple basil for interesting leaf contrasts. (Except for the fleshy leaf stalks, all parts of the rhubarb plant—including the leaves—are toxic and should not be consumed.)

Solanum melongena **var.** ***esculentum*** **'Violette di Firenze'**

Solanaceae (Nightshade family)

EGGPLANT

PLANT TYPE: *Annual*
ZONES: *Not applicable*
HABIT: *To 3' tall*
CULTURE: *Full sun; warm soil*
HARVEST: *Summer to first frost*

Today we enjoy eggplant for its culinary uses as well as its ornamental fruit and flowers. In fact, there's a famous Middle Eastern eggplant dish whose name, in English, means "the imam fainted." Sometimes the taste of a homegrown eggplant can be just that good. 'Violette di Firenze' is one of the beautiful Italian bicolored eggplants, which also include 'Rosa Bianca.' These bicolors do best in warmer growing zones.

CULTIVATION: Eggplant loves hot weather, so gardeners in cool or short-season areas need to choose varieties that will ripen under those conditions. Start seeds in flats about 8 weeks before the last spring frost date. After seedlings have grown 3 true leaves, transfer plants to individual cells or small peat containers, potting on to a larger size later as the plants grow larger. Harden off seedlings and transplant to the garden about 2–3 weeks after all danger of frost is past, and when the weather is warm and settled. Set out plants 18"–24" apart in rows spaced 3' apart.

Eggplant will generally not set fruit when night temperatures fall below 70°F. Especially in cooler growing zones, provide additional heat by mulching around plants with black paper, which will also help suppress weeds. Cover plants with a floating row cover after transplanting to keep out flea beetles.

RELATED PLANTS: Dark purple eggplants include heirloom 'Black Beauty' and the hybrid 'Dusky,' which ripens reliably even in the North. 'Morden Midget' is a good nonhybrid variety for short-season areas. More unusual varieties include the skinny 10" 'Pintong Long' from Taiwan, the hardy and productive 'Thai Green,' and *S. integrifolium* 'Turkish Orange,' which bears bite-size orange fruits.

USES IN THE LANDSCAPE: Until the early 1900s, most American gardeners considered eggplant,

when they grew it at all, an ornamental plant. Many varieties still have their use in an ornamental bed, with their lavender or white flowers and pretty foliage and fruits.

Spinacia oleracea 'Bloomsdale Long Standing'

Chenopodiaceae (Goosefoot family)

SPINACH

PLANT TYPE: *Annual*
ZONES: *Not applicable*
HABIT: *6"–10" tall*
CULTURE: *Full sun to partial shade; fertile, slightly acid soil*
HARVEST: *Spring through fall*

Spinach grows best in cool weather, though several recently developed varieties have good resistance to premature bolting. Still, in regions of the country where summer weather gets hot, it's best to plant spinach early in the spring, and then again in late summer for a fall crop. 'Bloomsdale Long Standing' is a classic home-garden variety, with tender, dark green leaves that are heavily savoyed (crinkled). In moderate-winter climates, it is hardy enough to sow in the fall for harvest the following spring.

CULTIVATION: Spinach seed germinates in soil temperatures as low as 35°F., so begin planting outdoors as soon as the ground can be worked in the spring. If your soil is acidic, add lime in fall to prepare the bed for spring planting. Plant seeds ½" deep and 1" apart in rows spaced 12"–18" apart. Thin young plants to 4"–6" apart. As the weather heats up, mulch around plants to conserve moisture and keep the soil cool; this helps prevent premature bolting. Keep

plants well-watered, and side-dress with compost or dried manure.

RELATED PLANTS: Heirloom spinaches include 'King of Denmark,' 'Norfolk,' and smooth-leaved 'Viroflay.' 'Indian Summer,' 'Tyee,' and smooth-leaved 'Space' are excellent F₁ hybrids. For mid-summer crops, plant a heat-loving spinach substitute. Good choices include New Zealand spinach (*Tetragonia tetragonioides*), Malabar climbing spinach (*Basella alba*), and orach, or mountain spinach (*Atriplex hortensis*).

USES IN THE LANDSCAPE: The low rosettes of spinach leaves make a lovely informal edging for beds. The most ornamental varieties are those with heavily savoyed leaves, like 'Bloomsdale.'

Valerianella locusta 'A Grosse Graine'

Valerianaceae (Valerian family)

MÂCHE

PLANT TYPE: *Annual*
ZONES: *Not applicable*
HABIT: *To 18" tall*
CULTURE: *Full sun to partial shade; average to rich soil*
HARVEST: *Spring through fall*

Mâche is a delightful little plant that goes by a whole

host of other names, including corn salad and lamb's lettuce. It grows best in cool weather and is hardy enough to overwinter under mulch protection in warmer zones, and to grow well in winter cold frames or greenhouses farther north. Recently rediscovered as a gourmet salad ingredient, mâche has a mild, slightly nutty flavor; its spoon-shaped leaves hold salad dressing and mix well with other greens. 'A Grosse Graine' (French for "big-seeded") is an heirloom mâche that is still one of the most popular varieties.

CULTIVATION: Plant mâche in early spring for an early crop, and again in late summer to early fall for a late fall or overwintered crop. Sow seeds thickly in beds or in wide rows spaced 18" apart. Plants germinate slowly but grow quickly once they emerge. To harvest, pick individual leaves or wait to harvest the whole rosette of leaves. Mâche is slow to bolt, and the leaves remain tasty even after it does.

RELATED PLANTS: Other fine old mâche varieties include 'Verte de Cambrai' and 'Verte d'Etampes.' 'Coquille de Louviers' is pretty and exceptionally cold-hardy. 'Vit' is a fast-growing variety that overwinters well.

USES IN THE LANDSCAPE: Mâche's small rosettes of leaves make a charming low edging in cool weather. Well-suited to container culture, it is also one of the best crops for growing in a cold frame in winter.

Zea mays 'Golden Bantam'
Poaceae (Grass family)
SWEET CORN

PLANT TYPE: *Annual*
ZONES: *Not applicable*
HABIT: *To 5'–7' tall*
CULTURE: *Full sun; fertile soil*
HARVEST: *Summer to first frost*

Long before European settlement, indigenous peoples from South America to southern Canada were growing many varieties of corn. There is even evidence that some Native American peoples segregated different varieties and crossed them to produce uniform hybrids. Today's modern hybrids of sweet corn are sweeter and in most respects better than the older open-pollinated strains. Yet fine heirlooms such as 'Golden Bantam' still define for many people the rich-but-not-sugary-sweet taste of real homegrown sweet corn.

CULTIVATION: Plant seeds 1" deep and 3"–4" apart in rows spaced 30" apart. To ensure good cross-pollination, plant in blocks or hills. Thin plants to stand 1' apart in the row. Side-dress with fertilizer once during the season, and water during dry spells. Weed carefully around the stalks since corn has shallow roots. Hill up soil around cornstalks to prevent wind blowdown.

Sweet corn cross-pollinates very easily, so it's best to grow only one variety at a time. Do not grow sweet corn near varieties of

ornamental corn or popcorn. Harvest all varieties of sweet corn for fresh eating when kernels are in the tender "milk" stage.

RELATED PLANTS: 'Earlivee' is an excellent and early F_1 yellow hybrid. New hybrids come along all the time; some of the best include 'Sugar Buns' (yellow), 'Double Gem' (bicolor), and 'Silver Queen' (white). Heirloom corns are good if picked young. Open-pollinated varieties include 'Ashworth' (yellow), 'Black Mexican' or 'Black Aztec' (white ears, turning blue-black when older), 'Country Gentleman' (white), and 'Stowell's Evergreen' (white).

USES IN THE LANDSCAPE: Many varieties have impressively tall stalks and sometimes attractive leaves and silks, striped or ringed with reddish-purple markings. Corn interplants well with 'Mammoth Russian' or other tall sunflowers, as well as with pole beans. In the fall, dried cornstalks and the mature ears of colorful varieties like 'Black Mexican' or 'Bloody Butcher' have ornamental uses at Halloween and Thanksgiving.

VINES

Graceful vines add a different dimension to the garden: verticality. Suitable to any landscape, from small terrace to large property, vines make efficient use of space. Taking up little area on the ground, they can soar 50 to 80 feet or more—with a little support.

Vines are varied—they can be deciduous, evergreen, tender annual, hardy perennial, woody, flowering, and/or foliage plants. And vines are versatile—they can soften stark architectural edges, hide an unsightly fence, provide a living screen growing on a trellis, or add interesting form. They fit into small spaces or blanket a huge area, and most vines make efficient ground covers. Splendid accent plants, they turn a nondescript post into a focal point, and offer a rainbow palette of flowers and leaves, making it easy to find a vine to complement existing plants in the garden. Some flowering vines are fragrant; be sure to site them where you can appreciate their sweet aroma.

Many vines grow beautifully in containers. Train them upward on supports, or let them trail down from window boxes or hanging baskets. Evergreen species, especially, make excellent privacy screens when grown on trellises. On a pergola or over an arbor, vines will provide summer shade much more quickly than a tree.

Vines can be trained into a variety of shapes—wisteria into a tree form, and others, such as grape, into espalier. There are fast- and slow-growing vines to meet your needs. Some of the fast-growers, however, can quickly get out of hand; pruners will keep them in line. Many vines thrive even with severe pruning.

Vines climb in one of several ways. Clinging vines, such as English ivy, support themselves by aerial rootlets, which easily attach to any rough surface. Other clinging vines, such as Boston ivy and Virginia creeper, use holdfasts, or disklike suction cups, to climb and hold on to smooth or rough surfaces. Vines with twining stems or tendrils need support. Non-clinging vines, including honeysuckle, twine up a support either clockwise or counterclockwise. Try to start a twining vine by wrapping it gently around the support; if it falls off within half an hour, you wound it the wrong way. Wound correctly, it will merrily carry on skyward. Most species in the same genus twine in the same direction, but curiously, Chinese and Japanese wisterias do not. Some plants that are called vines have no real means of support—bougainvillea, for example, needs to be tied to a trellis. On its own, it will sprawl.

Ampelopsis brevipedunculata
Vitaceae (Grape family)
PORCELAIN BERRY

PLANT TYPE: *Perennial*
ZONES: *5–8*
HABIT: *To 20'*
CULTURE: *Full sun to partial shade; any soil*
BLOOM: *Summer (inconspicuous)*

Native to northeastern Asia, this vigorous woody vine is often mistaken for a wild grape, with its 3-lobed leaves and twining tendrils. In fall, the foliage turns a lovely scarlet. The flowers are inconspicuous; grow it for the unusual berries. Borne in clusters in late summer and early fall, the berry-like fruits start out yellowish-green and mature to different hues of blue with a unique crackled effect that resembles fine porcelain. Eventually, the fruits blacken.

Be forewarned—this vine has naturalized in many areas and is considered an invasive weed by some. Once in your garden, it's difficult to get rid of.

CULTIVATION: Easily grown from softwood cuttings taken in the spring, or from hardwood cuttings taken in late summer, porcelain

berry can be cultivated almost any-where. To grow an exceptional vine, site this plant in well-drained, humusy soil. Place it where you can get close enough to appreciate the charming fruit. Prune in early spring to thin and shape the vine. Head it back to keep it within bounds.

RELATED PLANTS: The cultivar 'Elegans,' with lovely variegated leaves, is much better behaved, and highly recommended.

USES: Porcelain berry can easily cover a barn, given support. Train it up the posts of a porch, where you can keep a watchful eye on it. The vine is often cut in fall, the clusters of fruits used in flower arrangements.

Antigonon leptopus

Polygonaceae
(Buckwheat family)

CORAL VINE

PLANT TYPE: *Perennial*
ZONES: *8–10*
HABIT: *20'–40'*
CULTURE: *Full sun; poor, very well drained soil*
BLOOM: *Mid summer to fall*

This lovely vine of many names—*rosa de montaña*, mountain rose, corallita, queen's wreath, Confederate vine—is native to Mexico, and widely grown in the hot South, Southwest, and California. A deciduous flowering vine, it climbs by tendrils located at the ends of the flowering branches. Coral vine has a graceful habit—the branches cascade and curl back on themselves, making it appear to be covered in bloom. Long trailing sprays of deep rose, pink, or (rarely) white flowers last as long as the weather stays warm. Attractive leaves have a distinctive, folded-heart shape, and a bright spring-green color. The thick tuberous roots are winter-hardy, and will quickly send up new stems in the spring. Minor frost may cause some dieback, but as long as the roots do not freeze, the vine will rejuvenate.

CULTIVATION: Coral vine thrives in locations that could bake other plants. Secure the young vine to a strong support to promote vertical growth—an arbor works well, or the wall of a house. This low-maintenance plant thrives with little attention and is pest- and disease-resistant. Do not fertilize unless you want a profusion of leaves and few flowers. Coral vine is drought-tolerant, but appreci-ates regular deep watering in sum-mer. During periods of prolonged drought, it may die back to the ground. Thin and shape by prun-ing in fall. After the flowers fade, you can cut the vine back to the base. Mulch the roots well if the temperature threatens to go below 25°F.

RELATED PLANTS: Silver lace vine (*Polygonum aubertii*) is also a member of the buckwheat family. The billowy white flowers of this hardy vine (zones 5–10) last from mid summer until fall. Like coral vine, it thrives in conditions that thwart many other vines, and is virtually pest-free. It stands up to strong winds and is a good city plant, tolerant of pollution.

USES: Coral vine's blooms are long-lasting as cut flowers. Trained on a fence, it creates an effective screen during the growing season. Grown along the ground, it is a tough ground cover, rapidly cover-ing bare areas. Lovely with blue passionflower intertwining with its deep pink flowers.

Beaumontia grandiflora

Apocynaceae
(Dogbane family)

HERALD'S TRUMPET;
EASTER LILY VINE

PLANT TYPE: *Evergreen woody perennial*
ZONE: *10*
HABIT: *15'–30'; twining, arching form*
CULTURE: *Full sun; rich, well-drained soil amended with plenty of organic matter*
BLOOM: *Spring and summer*

This tender vine is a real show-stopper when it blooms with fragrant lily-like trumpets. The 5" white flowers, borne in clusters at the ends of the branches, are lightly tipped in pink, with green veins at the throat. The large, glossy 6"–9" leaves are handsome by themselves, giving a tropical look to this Himalayan native. Give the roots and vine plenty of room to spread out. Herald's trumpet thrives in heat and high humidity, languishes in cold and dry climates.

CULTIVATION: The vine is heavy and needs sturdy support from the time it is young. In early spring, before flowering, water well and fertilize; you will be rewarded with magnificent blooms and lux-uriant foliage. Prune in fall, thin-ning out oldest branches to reduce overall mass and encourage pro-duction of lateral flowering shoots. Herald's trumpet flowers on old wood, so leave ample 3-year-old wood to bear the next year's flowers.

RELATED PLANTS: Other vining members of the dogbane family include Chilean jasmine (*Mande-villa laxa*) and *M. splendens* 'Alice du Pont.' Semi-tropical vines, they are lovely grown in pots, trained on a small trellis or tripod sup-port. More modest in growth habit, they can be brought indoors in cold climates for winter.

USES: Herald's trumpet provides a perfect accent in a grand garden, sited where it will command a lot of attention. It makes a good screen, easily covering a fence or twining up a column. Planted with wisteria, it will follow in sequence of bloom.

Bougainvillea 'Texas Dawn'
Nyctaginaceae (Four-o'clock family)
BOUGAINVILLEA

PLANT TYPE: *Semi-evergreen woody perennial*
ZONES: *9–10*
HABIT: *To 30' or more*
CULTURE: *Full sun; well-drained garden soil*
BLOOM: *Almost year-round*

Native to Brazil, bougainvillea is one of the showiest of the flowering vines. A large, heavy, twining vine with robust, thorned stems, it requires sturdy support. The brightly colored parts of the plant are not the flowers, but are made up of 3 showy bracts (spe-cialized leaves) that surround very small white flowers. Bract colors are vivid—hot pink, magenta, crimson, bronze, yellow, orange, and white of varying hues. The heart-shaped leaves add interest when the bracts fade. 'Texas Dawn' bears magnificent large sprays of purplish-pink bracts.

CULTIVATION: Plant in spring, in a location where the roots can spread and be warmed by the heat of the sun reflecting from a wall, building, or patio. Bougainvillea is fussy about having its roots dis-turbed, so be very gentle when planting. Carefully cut the bot-tom of the container away and set the plant in the hole. Then cut the container vertically in 3 or more places, peeling away the sides; fill the hole with soil. Water deeply until it sets out new growth. Fasten the vine well to its support. Tie individual branches to keep them from whipping in the wind and shredding their leaves.

Overly rich soil promotes lux-uriant foliage at the expense of flower and bract formation. To encourage flowering, cut back to minimal watering. An evenly bal-anced organic fertilizer is optional in spring. Heavy pruning keeps a bougainvillea within bounds. It can be cut back completely in spring and fall, and will grow back and bloom the following season. Keep suckers pruned back and long branches removed to maintain shape and keep overall plant vol-ume and weight down. Beware of thorns—they are extremely sharp.

RELATED PLANTS: The species that are generally cultivated are *B. glabra,* with long-lasting flowers and less vigorous habit, and *B. spectabilis,* which is showier and more tolerant of cool tempera-tures. Other choice cultivars include 'Barbara Karst,' whose bracts are bright red when grown in full sun, bluish-crimson in partial shade. 'California Gold' ('Sunset') has pale yellow bracts, and blooms when quite young. 'Mrs. Butt' ('Crimson Lake') is an old-fashioned bougainvillea with crimson bracts. 'San Diego Red' ('San Diego,' 'Scarlett O'Hara') bears deep red bracts and is quite hardy. 'Tahitian Dawn' has gold bracts that mature to rosy-purple.

USES: Bougainvillea is common in California and Southern landscapes. It creates a living wall when trained to grow up one side of a wall and cascade over the top, or up and over a pergola. Bougainvillea's hot colors are cooled when planted near blue ceanothus.

Campis × tagliabuana 'Madame Galen'
Bignoniaceae (Bignonia family)
TRUMPET CREEPER

PLANT TYPE: *Woody perennial*
ZONES: *4–8*
HABIT: *25'–30'*
CULTURE: *Full sun; rich, well-drained soil*
BLOOM: *Mid summer*

This somewhat restrained trumpet creeper is a hybrid of *C. radicans* and *C. grandiflora.* Not as aggressive as either of its parents, it climbs by aerial rootlets, attaching its stems to any rough surface, and needs strong support. In mid summer it is in its glory, in full bloom with loose terminal clusters of 6–12 gorgeous, 3", trumpet-shaped salmon-red flowers that attract hummingbirds to the garden.

CULTIVATION: Support young vines until the clinging rootlets form.

The rootlets do not hold tightly to a surface. Heavy winds can separate branches from their support unless well secured. Cut out suckers to keep vines from becoming too invasive. Prune to reduce the overall volume of the branches; pinch back growing tips to encourage strong growth at the base of branches. Provide ample water throughout the growing season.

RELATED PLANTS: Trumpet vine (*C. radicans*) is a vigorous native American that can grow to 40'. Lovely 3" orange blooms marked with red open in mid July; seed capsules 5" long persist through the winter. Hardy in zones 4–8, the vine dies to the ground in areas with freezing winters, and regrows in spring. 'Flava' is a yellow-flowered variety.

Chinese trumpet creeper (*C. grandiflora*), hardy in zones 7–8, is more restrained, suitable for smaller gardens. Its large scarlet blooms are magnificent in mid summer.

USES: Trumpet creeper is best covering large stone walls, trained up the trunk of a sizable tree, or filling in against a large fence. Trained from an early age, and kept pruned, it will grow into a beautiful hedge and can be the focal point of the garden.

Clematis 'Henryi'
Ranunculaceae (Buttercup family)
CLEMATIS

PLANT TYPE: *Perennial*
ZONES: *4–8*
HABIT: *12'–15' in warmer climates; to 10' in colder areas*
CULTURE: *Full sun; rich, moist, slightly alkaline, well-drained, well-worked soil*
BLOOM: *Summer*

Clematis, regal in form and flower, is often called the Queen of Climbers. These well-mannered vines with twisting, slender stems are equally majestic in daytime and in early evening. Jackman clematis (*C. × jackmanii*) with its lovely purple blooms, was the first large-flowered hybrid developed, and is still a favorite. 'Henryi,' a white flowered cultivar of the Jackman clematis, bears abundant white flowers, 4"–6" in diameter, from July to October. 'Henryi' will die to the ground in cold-winter areas, regrowing each spring.

CULTIVATION: Clematis are particular, thriving when the vine is in full sun and the roots are cool and shaded. Dig a deep hole, at least twice as deep as the roots. Amend the soil with plenty of organic matter, adjusting the pH to about 7.0—add lime to neutralize acid soil, or bone meal to neutralize very alkaline soil. Put half the amended soil back in the hole. Secure the support before

you plant the vine. Plant the crown 2"–3" deep and cover with soil. Mulch well with organic material. Gently tie the fragile stems to the support. Fertilize once with a balanced fertilizer during the growing season. Water regularly. Clematis are shallow-rooted and don't appreciate root competition from nearby plants.

After flowering, cut back the current season's wood on those clematis that bloom in early summer to fall. Or prune in spring, when the buds swell. Cut back the plant to 6"–12" and you will get bushy new growth, with maximum new wood for the new flowers. Clematis that bloom in mid spring will flower on 1-year-old wood. Prune these varieties lightly after they flower; remove seedheads and thin lightly.

RELATED PLANTS: There are evergreen and deciduous species of this twining vine. With over 100 named cultivars, flowers come in a variety of sizes, shapes, and colors, from large open saucers to dainty bells, in hues of cerise, pink, mauve, purple, lavender, blue, yellow, and white. 'Ville de Lyon' has 5", velvety carmine flowers on 10'–12' vines. 'Nelly

Moser' is a classic, with pale pink petals and a central stripe of deep pink; the huge 7"–9" flowers bloom profusely in May and June and often repeat in September. The tender, luscious *C. florida* 'Alba Plena' makes a bold statement in gardens of the South and West, with its fully double white center. Grow it as an annual in the North, or provide protection indoors during winter. Sweet autumn clematis (*C. terniflora*) which can grow to 15' or more, is prized for its fragrant 1"–1½" flowers that grace the vine from late summer to fall.

USES: Clematis can handsomely cover a split-rail fence, arbor, or trellis—lovely with pink or red climbing roses. The flowers are surprisingly long-lasting when cut. The seedpods that follow the flowers are highly ornamental, both on the vines and in dried flower arrangements.

Euonymus fortunei 'Silver Queen'

Celastraceae (Staff-tree family)

WINTERCREEPER; AMERICAN BITTERSWEET

PLANT TYPE: *Evergreen woody perennial*
ZONES: *4–8*
HABIT: *Slowly, to 10'*
CULTURE: *Full sun to partial shade; any soil*
BLOOM: *Spring (inconspicuous)*

This attractive trailing vine is extremely adaptable, thriving in both the cold Midwest and the hot, arid Southwest. Its rootlike holdfasts enable it to climb on any rough surface. Handsome, fine-textured, glossy-green foliage covers the spreading stems. This plant has two forms. As a juvenile, the slender clinging stems have small

leaves. An established plant may throw out some mature branches, bushy in form, bearing inconspicuous flowers and bright red fruit, and larger, leathery leaves. 'Silver Queen' is regal with white-edged leaves.

CULTIVATION: Allow 1'–2' between plants. Mulch well to discourage weeds. (Once established, the dense leaf cover will keep weeds from germinating.) Prune in spring only to direct its growth or keep within desired bounds. Prune out mature branches as soon as they appear, to maintain an even look. Cuttings taken from mature branches will result in shrublike plants. In the coldest regions, protect from sunburn in winter caused by reflected snow glare.

RELATED PLANTS: A number of choice cultivars are available. Easily trained 'Coloratus' provides fall and winter interest, with green leaves that turn reddish-purple in autumn. A slow-growing trailer, 'Gracilis' has green leaves variegated with cream that turn pink as the weather gets cold. 'Minimus,' also known as baby wintercreeper, has ½" leaves, making it a good, fine-textured cover for a low wall; slower-growing 'Kewensis' has even tinier leaves. The mounding, shrubby, large-leaved 'Vegetus,' handsome in autumn with its orange fruit, grows 4' tall and can easily cover an area 15'–20' wide.

USES: Compared to most vines, wintercreeper is restrained in its growth, so it is well-suited to a low-maintenance garden. It clings without support to brick, concrete, or wood. Equally good as a ground cover, or trained up a low wall or against the foundation of a house. This vine roots easily along the stem in any moist, well-drained soil, making it an ideal choice for growing on slopes to control erosion.

Hedera helix 'Gold Child'

Araliaceae (Aralia family)

ENGLISH IVY

PLANT TYPE: *Evergreen perennial*
ZONES: *7–10*
HABIT: *To 10'*
CULTURE: *Full sun to partial shade; prefers moist, well-drained, neutral to slightly alkaline soil*
BLOOM: *Rarely*

English ivy is a tough vine with glossy 2"–4" leathery green leaves with lighter green veins. Never let it grow where you don't want it—it climbs by tenacious aerial roots, and when you pull off an established patch of ivy you may rip the paint off a building or pull off pieces of brick and mortar. Ivies have two forms, juvenile and mature. The juvenile form, with its vining habit, is most commonly seen. Unpruned, as ivy ages it forms mature, upright branches with larger, more rounded leaves. Clusters of small white, starry flowers appear,

followed by greenish to blackish berries. 'Gold Child' is an outstanding variegated ivy, with leaves edged in gold and varying hues of green in center.

CULTIVATION: In hot dry climates and snowy-winter areas, grow in partial shade to protect the leaves. To grow ivy as a ground cover, allow 12"–18" between plants. To promote rooting and quick growth, add organic matter to the soil; water in the morning to keep the soil evenly moist. Prune regularly to keep it within bounds and in the juvenile form. Cuttings from mature ivy stems will result in upright, shrublike plants. When grown as a ground cover, mow ivy in early spring to encourage new growth. Within a couple of weeks, new leaves will appear to replace those removed.

RELATED PLANTS: There are more than 100 cultivars of English ivy, each unique: 'Aureo-variegata' is yellow variegated; 'Baltica,' with white veins, is somewhat drought-tolerant and hardy to zone 3; '238th Street,' discovered in New York City, has heart-shaped leaves and is hardy to zone 5/6; 'Gold Heart' with yellow markings at the

center of the leaves, is hardy in zones 8–10.

USES: English ivy is prized as a shade-tolerant ground cover, yet it will happily grow vertically when given support for the aerial roots. Whether grown as a formal ground cover, planted on a hillside for erosion control, trained on a fence to resemble an evergreen hedge, or allowed to climb its way up the walls of an edifice, the rootlets hold the ivy well in place. Ivy can also be trained to grow on topiary forms, formal or whimsical.

Humulus lupulus

Cannabaceae (Hemp family)

HOP; COMMON HOP; EUROPEAN HOP; BINE

PLANT TYPE: *Perennial often grown as an annual*
ZONES: *8–10*
HABIT: *20' or more*
CULTURE: *Full sun; moist, rich, well-drained soil*
BLOOM: *Early to mid summer*

Hops are tender, fast-growing perennial vines that are grown as annuals in most areas. They climb by tendrils, easily growing 20' or more in a single season. Hops are dioecious—male and female flowers are borne on separate plants. Both male and female vines are attractive, with large, fuzzy, 3-lobed light green leaves.

CULTIVATION: Hops will tolerate partial shade, wind, and drought. For a head start on the growing season, sow seeds in fall for spring vines; seeds will not germinate once the weather warms. In cold-weather areas, set plants in the garden after danger of frost has passed. Where the vine is hardy, prune it back to the base of the plant each spring, removing half of the new shoots. Hand-train the vine on a lattice or other support in the direction you want it to go, and it will continue to climb by itself.

RELATED PLANTS: 'Aureus' has attractive yellow-green leaves. Japanese hop (*H. japonicus*) is an annual grown for its ornamental value; more vigorous, it can reach to 35' in a growing season. The large handsome leaves, 6"–8" across, have 5–7 deeply cut lobes. 'Variegatus' has lovely green-and-white variegated leaves.

USES: The vine can cover a trellis, arbor, fence, or porch, making a quick-growing, seasonal screen. Versatile in the home kitchen, the pinecone-like flowers from female plants are used in brewing beer, adding the somewhat bitter flavor; also, new spring shoots can be cut 6"–8" long and cooked like asparagus.

Hydrangea petiolaris (syn. *H. anomala* ssp. *petiolaris*)

Hydrangeaceae (Hydrangea family)

CLIMBING HYDRANGEA

PLANT TYPE: *Woody perennial*
ZONES: *5–9*
HABIT: *To 50' or more*
CULTURE: *Full sun to partial shade; prefers moist, deep, well-drained, fertile loam*
BLOOM: *Late spring*

Climbing hydrangea is not for those who are faint of heart. Almost bigger than life, it needs to be grown where its size is in scale with its surroundings. It is slow to get going, but after several years it becomes a vigorous climber. The aerial rootlets anchor it well, but it can topple unless its support is firmly in the ground. In spring, the vine leafs out with attractive, finely toothed, heart-shaped leaves. Late in spring, the vine is resplendent with 6"–8", lacy white-cap flower clusters, held away from the foliage on long stems. In autumn, the leaves drop to reveal handsome shedding red bark that adds interest to the winter garden.

CULTIVATION: Before planting, amend the soil with plenty of organic matter. Grow it against an

---

indestructible surface, as the rootlets can destroy old masonry and wood structures. Prune as needed to thin and keep in shape. If flower production decreases, do a severe rejuvenescent pruning in winter or early spring.

RELATED PLANTS: Big-leaf or garden hydrangea (*H. macrophylla, H. hortensia, H. opuloides*) is a handsome deciduous shrub with a rounded habit that grows 4'–8' tall. Flowers are pink, white, or blue in large clusters. In acid soil, the flowers will be blue or purple; in alkaline soil, pink to red.

USES: Especially handsome climbing up a large established tree or tall pillar. Without support, it is still impressive as a rambling vine.

Ipomoea alba (syn. *Calonyction aculeatum*)

Convolvulaceae (Morning glory family)

MOONFLOWER

PLANT TYPE: *Perennial usually grown as an annual*
ZONES: *9–10*
HABIT: *10'–15' or more*
CULTURE: *Full sun; well-drained garden soil*
BLOOM: *Mid summer to frost*

This vigorous, night-blooming, tropical American vine has soft green, heart-shaped leaves attractive even before it flowers. Depending on weather, it begins blooming in mid summer or later. One by one, flowers open; in a week or two, the vine is covered with fragrant, iridescent white flowers. Every evening, satiny white blooms are a sight to behold, 5"–6" across once they unfurl, then closing in the morning when the first rays of the sun shine on them. Although each

bloom lasts but a single night, new buds are always forming to keep vines blooming for several months.

CULTIVATION: Moonflower thrives in hot weather. Start seeds indoors in peat pots, or direct-seed in the garden when soil temperature is over 70°F. Scarify the seeds by scoring or nicking with a knife, then soak overnight in tepid water. Plant seeds ½" deep in the garden, 8"–15" apart. Seeds may be slow to germinate. Provide strong support—trellis, fence, post, or arbor. In full bloom, the vine can be very heavy. Feed every couple of weeks.

RELATED PLANTS: Blue moon-flower (*I. indica, I. acuminata, I. learii*), also called dawnflower, grows to 35' tall. It has deep violet 4" flowers with white throat and lighter blue highlights. Cypress vine (*I. quamoclit, Quamoclit pennata*), with delicate, finely cut foliage and 1½" bright red, funnel-shaped flowers, is an annual vine that grows to 20'. Blooms open widely at sundown and in early morning, closing when sun is directly on them.

USES: Plant with its day-blooming cousin, the morning glory, for

bloom day and night. Well-spaced on supports outside a south-facing window, the vine makes a living screen to shade a hot sunny room in summer. Grow where you can enjoy the marvelous flowers at night; place a chair or bench near the vine so you can watch it open, and look for the night pollinators that are lured by its sweet fragrance.

Ipomoea purpurea
Convolvulaceae (Morning glory family)
MORNING GLORY

PLANT TYPE: *Perennial grown as an annual*
ZONE: *10*
HABIT: *To 10' or more*
CULTURE: *Full sun; rich, well-drained soil*
BLOOM: *Summer to frost*

Morning glory is one of our best-loved vines. Large heart-shaped leaves are lovely even before the bloom of funnel-shaped flowers to 5" across. Each flower lasts a single day, opening in the early morning, closing by noon. Flowers may be a solid color—white, pink, crimson, purple, blue—or bicolor; rarely are double flowers seen.

CULTIVATION: Drought-tolerant, morning glories will grow in

most any garden soil. Soak seeds overnight in tepid water; sow outdoors, ½" deep, after all danger of frost is past. Get a head start by sowing indoors 4 weeks early in individual peat pots. Outdoors, allow 12" between plants. Provide support for the vines to twine around—strings attached to the eaves, trellises, stakes, a gazebo—almost anything less than 1" in diameter. Feed every 2–3 weeks with fish emulsion.

RELATED PLANTS: Cultivars include 'Giant Cornell,' carnelian-red with a white edge; large white 'Alba'; and wine-red, white-throated 'Darling.' There are over 500 species of *Ipomoea* and related plants. *I. tricolor* includes some favorite hybrids: classic sky-blue 'Heavenly Blue'; light blue 'Summer Skies'; rosy-lavender 'Wedding Bells'; and striped blue-and-white 'Flying Saucers.'

USES: Morning glories grown on a trellis provide a lovely summer screen. It's easy to make a "sunflower house" for a child: Plant three "walls" of sunflowers with 'Heavenly Blue' morning glories twining up them; then train the morning glories across strings strung from the tops of the sunflowers, creating a sky-blue roof.

Lonicera × heckrottii
Caprifoliaceae (Honeysuckle family)
EVERBLOOMING HONEY-SUCKLE; GOLDFLAME HONEYSUCKLE

PLANT TYPE: *Semi-evergreen perennial*
ZONES: *5–9*
HABIT: *To 12'*
CULTURE: *Full sun to partial shade*
BLOOM: *Late spring to frost*

Everblooming honeysuckle is a twining, semi-evergreen vine with showy, fragrant flowers that attract hummingbirds in summer. The flowers, borne in terminal clusters, cover the vine in May and continue as new growth is produced, until frost kills it back. Blooms are rich yellow inside, scarlet-purple outside; after a day or so, the outside turns pink. Even the stems are an attractive pink. Green leaves have glaucous undersides. This is considered one of the choicest of all honeysuckles for its restrained growth.

CULTIVATION: Cut back the stems after they bloom to maintain shape. You can train everblooming honeysuckle in a tight mound by judicious pruning.

RELATED PLANTS: There are over 150 species of honeysuckle, though only a few are readily available and desirable in cultivation. Sweet-scented Japanese honeysuckle (*L. japonica*), considered a weed by many, will grow in inhospitable places that other plants scorn, rooting wherever it touches the ground. Several cultivars are not as rampant as the species. 'Purpurea' (purple honeysuckle) has reddish-tinged flowers and purple-fringed leaves. 'Halliana' (Hall's honeysuckle) has white flowers and green leaves. Tender 'Gold Net' is distinctive for yellow variegated leaves. Trumpet or coral honeysuckle (*L. semper-virens*) is native to the Northeast and can grow to 50'. It has a lovely open form, producing alluring, 2", coral-to-red trumpet-like flowers in summer, followed by scarlet fruit in autumn. 'Sulphurea' has lovely yellow flowers; 'Superba' bears vivid scarlet blooms.

USES: Makes an attractive screen when trained on a trellis or fence. Plant it where you can appreciate its fragrance and color. Near an entryway or garage—where you pass it frequently—would be a good location.

Parthenocissus tricuspidata 'Veitchii'
Vitaceae (Grape family)
VEITCH'S CREEPER; VEITCH'S BOSTON IVY
PLANT TYPE: *Perennial*   ZONES: *4–10*   HABIT: *To 40'*   CULTURE: *Partial shade; prefers fertile, evenly moist soil*   BLOOM: *Summer (inconspicuous)*

This cultivar of Boston ivy is a highly adaptable deciduous vine that climbs by means of flat adhesive disks at the ends of branching tendrils. It is the juvenile form of the species, with smaller (1") leaves that are tinged purple. Leaves may be simple, with 3 pointed lobes, or compound, with 3 leaflets. The greenish flowers are inconspicuous, but you'll be aware the plant is in bloom by the hum of honeybees that flock to its flowers. In fall, the leaves give a colorful show in red and gold before dropping off. One of the charms of this vine, as of Boston ivy, is its habit—as it climbs, the leaves overlap one another, forming a handsome water-shedding screen.

CULTIVATION: Veitch's creeper is easy to grow in sun or shade, but it prefers partial shade and will tolerate almost any soil type. Be sure to provide ample water throughout the growing season. To cover a wall, plant the vines close to the support, allowing 2'–3' between vines. Encourage branching when the vines are young by cutting back the stems. Initially, you will have to guide the branches up the support. Prune the vine, once established, in early spring to keep within bounds and to guide the growth.

RELATED PLANTS: Boston ivy (*P. tricuspidata*) is sometimes confused with English ivy, but Boston ivy is obvious in autumn, when its leaves turn brilliant scarlet and yellow before dropping off. The

mesh of branches and the persistent blue berries give the vine winter interest. New spring leaves are purplish, maturing to large (up to 8") green, 3-lobed leaves on long stems that stand out from the branches, gracefully fluttering in the breeze. Virginia creeper (*P. quinquefolia*), often confused with poison ivy (*Toxicodendron radicans*), is easily identified by its 5 leaflets, 2"–6" long, with coarsely toothed margins. New leaves in early spring are tinged purple, then mature to deep green before turning bright scarlet in autumn.

USES: Spectacular climbing up the side of a building, Veitch's creeper is best suited to stucco, stone, or brick, as it can grow between wooden shingles and wreck wooden edifices.

Passiflora caerulea

**Passifloraceae
(Passionflower family)**

**PASSIONFLOWER;
BLUE PASSIONFLOWER**

PLANT TYPE: *Perennial*
ZONES: *7–10*
HABIT: *To 15'*
CULTURE: *Full sun; most well-drained garden soils*
BLOOM: *Summer*

Spanish priests in the tropical New World named these vines, seeing in parts of the flowers symbols of the Passion of Christ—the crown of thorns, the hammer and nails. One of the hardiest passionflowers, this is a woody climber, attaching itself to supports with corkscrew-like tendrils. The flowers are very showy—wide-open white petals with blue filaments (looking like the "crown"). In full bloom, the flowers are breathtaking, almost covering the vine. Egg-shaped

yellow fruit follows the flowers. Often, both fruit and flowers are on the vine at the same time.

CULTIVATION: Grow in a sheltered location. Provide a strong trellis, fence, or good-size shrub for the vine to climb. Suckers may appear at the base of the mother plant; prune them off or the vine will become unruly. Stems may die back to the ground each winter, but roots are hardy, sending up new shoots in late spring. Some varieties are self-pollinating; maypop (*P. incarnata*) plants need cross-pollination.

RELATED PLANTS: 'Constance Elliott' has fragrant, pure white blooms. *P.* 'Incense' is pollen-sterile and cannot be used as a pollinator; enjoy it for magnificent violet flowers. Most other varieties are semi-tropical vines. *P.* × *alatocaerulea* is a fragrant hybrid with white-and-pink flowers and contrasting purple, blue, and white filaments. *P. manicata* is a fast-growing, vigorous vine with a profusion of bright red flowers with a blue crown. *P. racemosa*, the best red-flowered variety, has deeply lobed leaves.

There are numerous varieties with edible fruit: *P. edulis* (purple

granadilla) has smallish white-and-purple flowers, and egg-sized purple fruit. *P. laurifolia* (yellow granadilla or water-lemon) has white flowers with red and purple spots; it bears yellow fruit. *P. ligularis* (sweet granadilla) also has yellow fruit. *P. quadrangularis* (giant granadilla) is a commercial variety with large, fragrant white flowers marked with red and purple, and large yellowish-green fruits that grow to 9" long. *P. incarnata*, known as maypop, is a southeastern American native, with white, pink, and purple flowers, and egg-sized yellow fruit.

USES: Most passionflowers are grown for their exceptional blooms. They are attractive container plants with a tripod, stake, or cage for support. Where hardy, they are excellent grown up the side of a wall, or overhanging a large window. Some varieties produce edible fruit as well. Semitropical varieties bear fruit 1–2 years after planting—perhaps 15 pounds of fruit a year—in summer to late autumn.

Polygonum aubertii

**Polygonaceae
(Buckwheat family)**

**SILVER LACE VINE;
FLEECEFLOWER**

PLANT TYPE: *Semi-evergreen perennial*
ZONES: *5–10*
HABIT: *To 15'–30'*
CULTURE: *Full sun; most ordinary soils*
BLOOM: *Late summer to fall*

This twisting vine climbs quickly with wiry, intertwining stems. Small greenish-white flowers billow along the tops of the branches in 6"–8" panicles, making a beautiful end-of-season show when so much else in the garden has passed its prime. In areas with cold winters, it is deciduous; in milder climates, evergreen. New leaves are glossy pale green, tipped red in spring. Foliage is distinctively arrow-shaped with wavy edges. A great vine for urban areas, it is drought- and pollution-tolerant.

CULTIVATION: In regions with hot summers, plant in partial shade. During the summer, water deeply once a month. Tie the branches to a support to train young plants. Pinch growing tips to make a bushier vine. Prune in fall, and plant will regrow the following spring. If you prune in mid spring to control shape and form, flowering will be delayed.

RELATED PLANTS: *P. baldschuanicum* (Bukhara vine) is more restrained in its growth, to only 20'. It bears heart-shaped leaves and the blooms turn pink as they age.

USES: Silver lace vine quickly hides a fence or covers an arbor. It is tough, so put it in locations that would challenge other vines —in a windy or very sunny and dry place. For best effect, let it cascade over a fence or wall.

Trachelospermum jasminoides
Apocynaceae
(Dogbane family)

STAR JASMINE;
CONFEDERATE JASMINE

PLANT TYPE: *Evergreen perennial*
ZONES: *8–10*
HABIT: *To 20'*
CULTURE: *Full sun to shade; prefers moist, well-drained soil of any type*
BLOOM: *Spring to mid summer*

Native to China, star jasmine is one of the most widely grown vines in the United States. Its popularity in the South is evidenced by its other name, Confederate jasmine. This weakly twining vine is a great addition to any landscape, attractive year-round with sweetly fragrant flowers and handsome, oval, dark green foliage. The 2"–3" star-shaped flowers have slightly twisted petals at the end of short tubes. Their fragrance perfumes the air from early May until mid summer, attracting bees and butterflies. A versatile vine, star jasmine trails or climbs, grown in the ground or in a pot.

CULTIVATION: Choose a plant with long branches to train as an upright vine. In the early stages, tie branches to a sturdy support. Prune as necessary to keep in shape, pruning mature vines annually to encourage new flowering branches while removing older woody branches. Fertilize in early spring and again in late summer for healthy growth and good foliage color. Keep well-watered through the spring and summer; do not let this plant dry out.

RELATED PLANTS: 'Variegatum' has lovely green-and-white leaves. It is hardier than the species. Yellow star jasmine (*T. asiaticum*), hardy to zone 7, is a good choice for slightly colder climates. Light yellow flowers are delightfully fragrant from April through June, with wavy petals held erect above deeper, dull green leaves.

USES: Supple branches give rise to the different looks this vine can take—a sprawling ground cover spreading 4'–5', an elegant frame for an entryway, or a living screen grown on a fence. It grows happily up a trellis in a narrow space; in a pot, it can look like a cascading small shrub.

Tropaeolum peregrinum
Tropaeolaceae
(Nasturtium family)

CANARY CREEPER;
CANARY BIRD FLOWER

PLANT TYPE: *Annual*
ZONES: *Not applicable*
HABIT: *To 10'*
CULTURE: *Partial shade; rich, well-drained soil*
BLOOM: *Summer*

Canary creeper's uniquely fringed yellow flowers, produced in abundance throughout the summer, resemble small canaries. The leaves are handsome—pale green and rounded, with 5 deeply cut lobes. Provide support so it can make a handsome show, whether grown in a container or allowed to climb a wall or cover a fence. The flower is edible, with a spicy peppery flavor and slightly bitter aftertaste.

CULTIVATION: This plant grows easily from seed and germinates best in cool soil. Direct-seed 2 weeks before the last frost date in spring, allowing at least 12" between plants. Cover with ½" of soil, and water well. To start indoors, sow seeds in soil blocks or peat pellets so the root system is not disturbed. Keep the vine well-watered throughout the growing season, and provide support.

RELATED PLANTS: *T. majus* (garden nasturtium) comes in a handsome vining or trailing form, with colorful, edible flowers of red, yellow, orange, burgundy, or peach, and rounded green leaves that also have a spicy, peppery flavor.

USES: Canary creeper makes a beautiful, colorful annual screen, climbing a trellis or a fence. Not too vigorous, it can decorate a wall of the house or scale a brick chimney. Pair it with blue clock vine for an outstanding color combination.

Wisteria sinensis 'Alba'
Fabaceae (Pea family)
WHITE CHINESE WISTERIA

PLANT TYPE: *Woody perennial*
ZONES: *5–9*
HABIT: *To 40' or more*
CULTURE: *Full sun; moist, well-drained, humusy loam*
BLOOM: *Spring*

Wisterias are the most popular of all vines. With their dripping racemes of fragrant, pea-like flowers and large, sinuously twining stems, they stand out in any landscape. Unlike Japanese wisteria, whose flowers open from top to bottom, all the flowers in the 6"–12" racemes of Chinese wisteria open at once, just before the leaves emerge. Delicate looking, large, compound leaves are composed of 7–13 small (2"–3"), oval, light green leaflets. Their bright color provides a contrast with that of other vines, giving a fresh look even in mid summer. Blooms are followed by velvety, beanlike pods. 'Alba' has pure white, fragrant flowers.

CULTIVATION: Wisteria needs plenty of water when flowering. Leaves may appear yellowish when grown in alkaline soil—give

an iron supplement to green them up. Fertilize with superphosphate in early spring to promote bloom before buds break. Wisteria takes several seasons before it blooms, building up a storehouse of food before expending energy to produce flowers. Once the plant has begun flowering, prune to keep it in shape. To encourage bloom and cut down on vegetative growth, prune after it finishes blooming or in winter. Cut back long branches to 3–5 buds. Creative pruning can give a unique form to the plant, weaving it through a split-rail fence, or making a self-supporting tree.

RELATED PLANTS: *W. sinensis* 'Purpurea' bears the popular violet blooms. 'Plena' is a double-flowered variety. Japanese wisteria (*W. floribunda*) has flower clusters that range 8"–48" in length in shades of white, pink, and violet, in more than 40 recognized varieties. 'Alba' bears white flowers in 18"–24" racemes. 'Issai' has blue-violet flowers in 12" clusters. 'Violacea-Plena' is lovely with double purple flowers. 'Rosea' bears fragrant pink blooms. 'Macrobotrys' is magnificent with purple-blue flowers on racemes 3' long. 'Longissima,' as its name implies, has the longest flower clusters, up to 4'. *Wisteria × formosa* is a hybrid of the Japanese and Chinese wisteria. Its fragrant blooms open simultaneously.

USES: Elegant in a woodland, twining up a tree, but the wisteria will eventually strangle the support tree. Traditionally, wisteria is planted on a sturdy arbor or pergola; it's especially lovely reflected in a pond or pool.

PLANT HARDINESS ZONE MAP

The map at the right shows the approximate range of minimum temperatures for each of the 10 major plant hardiness zones in the United States as well as neighboring Canada and Mexico. Zone 1 represents the lowest minimum temperature (below −50°F.); in zone 11, the opposite extreme found in the southernmost regions and in Hawaii, the minimum temperature is a balmy 40°F.

Find your own geographical area on the map and use the color key in the lower right-hand corner to determine your plant hardiness zone and the approximate range of minimum temperatures. By using this information in combination with other local climate data concerning sun, snow, rain, and wind, you can choose the correct plants for your garden with a high degree of certainty. Your local Cooperative Extension service can provide additional information about plants that are best suited to your zone.

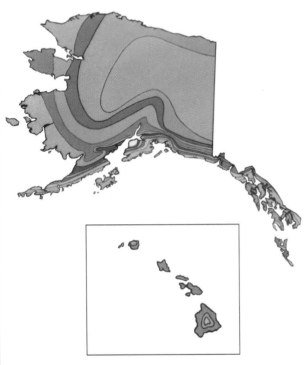

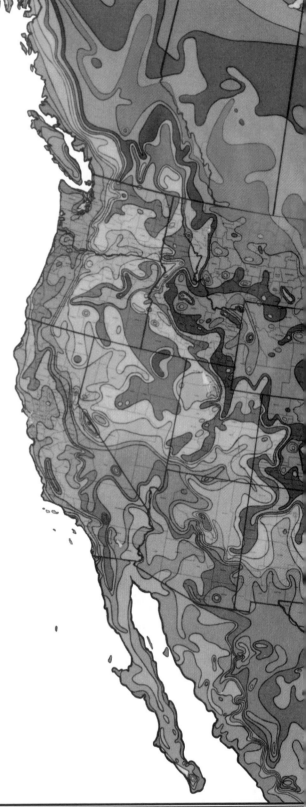

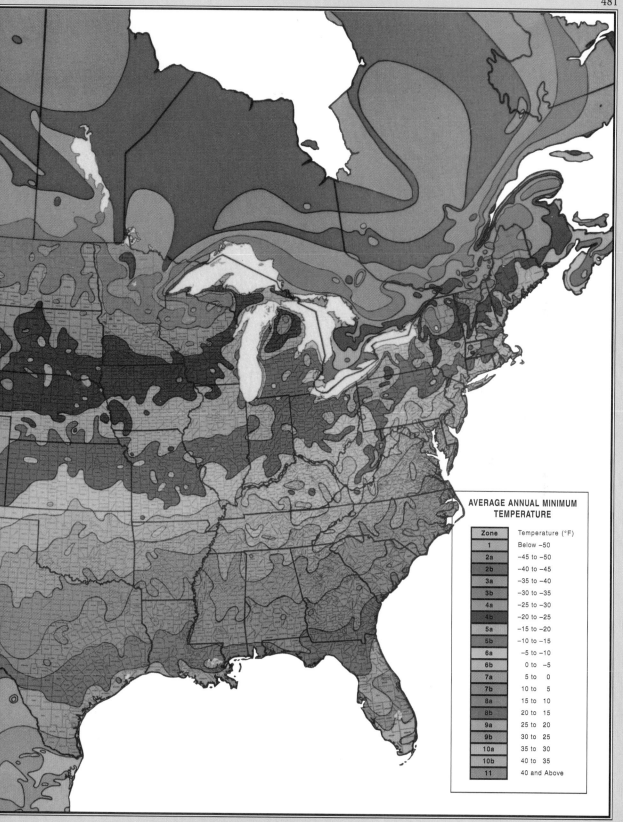

AVERAGE ANNUAL MINIMUM TEMPERATURE

Zone	Temperature (°F)
1	Below −50
2a	−45 to −50
2b	−40 to −45
3a	−35 to −40
3b	−30 to −35
4a	−25 to −30
4b	−20 to −25
5a	−15 to −20
5b	−10 to −15
6a	−5 to −10
6b	0 to −5
7a	5 to 0
7b	10 to 5
8a	15 to 10
8b	20 to 15
9a	25 to 20
9b	30 to 25
10a	35 to 30
10b	40 to 35
11	40 and Above

INDEX

PHOTO CREDITS